ASPEN PUBLISHERS

MW00654890

Construction Law Han

Second Edition

by Richard K. Allen and Stanley A. Martin

Changes continue to sweep through the construction industry: new technologies are reconfiguring how the design and construction industry functions, new project proposal systems are creating better and less expensive execution of projects for public and private owners, and demand for improved public infrastructure has driven innovation in new financing and delivery techniques for privately financed infrastructure projects. Contractors, designers, and owners have become more sophisticated, and an army of skilled consultants now serves the industry.

The *Construction Law Handbook* has been a stalwart reference source for the industry. It is designed to address the current state of the business of construction and construction law, and is written by a variety of distinguished construction professionals, including architects, engineers, accountants, lawyers, and consultants. All of these outstanding professionals have written their chapters in "plain English," so the important information in their chapters can be understood by the entire industry.

Highlights of the 2010 Cumulative Supplement

*   A new section and subsections discussing the ConsensusDOCS 310 Green Building Addendum.

*   A case study on the *Takota Corporation* case and its applicability to terminations.

*   Increased coverage federal contracting and the effect the Stimulus Act has had on it.

*   A new subsection on the Registry of Disaster Response Contractors.

Wolters Kluwer

Law & Business

- In international arbitration, interconnectivity now exists between arbitration and litigation, as seen by The European Court of Justice's decision in the *West Tankers* case.

The Table of Cases, Table of Statutes and Regulations and Index have been updated to reflect all the changes to the text.

10/10

ASPEN PUBLISHERS

CONSTRUCTION LAW HANDBOOK

Second Edition

RICHARD K. ALLEN
STANLEY A. MARTIN

2010 Cumulative Supplement

This supplement supersedes all previous supplements.

Wolters Kluwer
Law & Business

AUSTIN   BOSTON   CHICAGO   NEW YORK   THE NETHERLANDS

This publication is designed to provide accurate and authoritative information in regard to the subject matter covered. It is sold with the understanding that the publisher is not engaged in rendering legal, accounting, or other professional services. If legal advice or other professional assistance is required, the services of a competent professional person should be sought.

> —From a *Declaration of Principles* jointly adopted
> by a Committee of the American Bar Association
> and a Committee of Publishers and Associations

© 2011 Aspen Publishers. All Rights Reserved.

Printed in the United States of America

1 2 3 4 5 6 7 8 9 0

Library of Congress Cataloging-in-Publication Data
   Construction law handbook/Richard K. Allen, Stanley A. Martin, editors.-2d ed.
      p. cm.
   Includes index.
   ISBN 978-0-7355-7446-5 (set)—ISBN 978-0-7355-7815-9 (vol. 1); ISBN 978-0-7355-7816-6 (vol. 2); ISBN 978-0-7355-9289-6 (supplement)
     1. Construction industry—Law and legislation—United States.
2. Construction contracts—United States.

About Wolters Kluwer Law & Business

Wolters Kluwer Law & Business is a leading provider of research information and workflow solutions in key specialty areas. The strengths of the individual brands of Aspen Publishers, CCH, Kluwer Law International and Loislaw are aligned within Wolters Kluwer Law & Business to provide comprehensive, in-depth solutions and expert-authored content for the legal, professional and education markets.

CCH was founded in 1913 and has served more than four generations of business professionals and their clients. The CCH products in the Wolters Kluwer Law & Business group are highly regarded electronic and print resources for legal, securities, antitrust and trade regulation, government contracting, banking, pensions, payroll, employment and labor, and healthcare reimbursement and compliance professionals.

Aspen Publishers is a leading information provider for attorneys, business professionals and law students. Written by preeminent authorities, Aspen products offer analytical and practical information in a range of specialty practice areas from securities law and intellectual property to mergers and acquisitions and pension/benefits. Aspen's trusted legal education resources provide professors and students with high-quality, up-to-date and effective resources for successful instruction and study in all areas of the law.

Kluwer Law International supplies the global business community with comprehensive English-language international legal information. Legal practitioners, corporate counsel and business executives around the world rely on the Kluwer Law International journals, loose-leafs, books and electronic products for authoritative information in many areas of international legal practice.

Loislaw is a premier provider of digitized legal content to small law firm practitioners of various specializations. Loislaw provides attorneys with the ability to quickly and efficiently find the necessary legal information they need, when and where they need it, by facilitating access to primary law as well as state-specific law, records, forms and treatises.

Wolters Kluwer Law & Business, a unit of Wolters Kluwer, is headquartered in New York and Riverwoods, Illinois. Wolters Kluwer is a leading multinational publisher and information services company.

ASPEN PUBLISHERS SUBSCRIPTION NOTICE

This Aspen Publishers product is updated on a periodic basis with supplements to reflect important changes in the subject matter. If you purchased this product directly from Aspen Publishers, we have already recorded your subscription for the update service.

If, however, you purchased this product from a bookstore and wish to receive future updates and revised or related volumes billed separately with a 30-day examination review, please contact our Customer Service Department at 1-800-234-1660 or send your name, company name (if applicable), address, and the title of the product to:

ASPEN PUBLISHERS
7201 McKinney Circle
Frederick, MD 21704

Important Aspen Publishers Contact Information

- To order any Aspen Publishers title, go to *www.aspenpublishers.com* or call 1-800-638-8437.
- To reinstate your manual update service, call 1-800-638-8437.
- To contact Customer Care, e-mail *customer.care@aspenpublishers.com,* call 1-800-234-1660, fax 1-800-901-9075, or mail correspondence to Order Department, Aspen Publishers, PO Box 990, Frederick, MD 21705.
- To review your account history or pay an invoice online, visit *www.aspenpublishers.com/payinvoices.*

CONTENTS

Sections listed below appear only in the supplement and not in the main volumes.

About the Supplement Editors

About the Contributors

Chapter 3   **Industry Workforce Shortages**

Chapter 5   **The Use of Technology for Project Collaboration and Building Information Modeling**

   § 5.01   New Technologies in Construction

   § 5.02   Building Information Modeling
- [A] What is Building Information Modeling?
- [B] How is BIM Used?
  - [1] Single Data Entry; Multiple Use
  - [2] Design Efficiency
  - [3] Consistent Design Bases
  - [4] 3D Modeling and Conflict Resolution
  - [5] Conflict Identification and Resolution
  - [6] Take-offs and Estimating
  - [7] Shop and Fabrication Drawing
  - [8] Visualization of Alternative Solutions and Options
  - [9] Energy Optimization
  - [10] Constructability Reviews and 4D Simulations
  - [11] Reduced Fabrication Costs and Errors
  - [12] Facilities Management
    - [a] Functional Simulations
  - [13] Code Compliance Checking
  - [14] BIMstorm™—Worldwide Real-Time Collaboration

   § 5.03   Issues in BIM Implementation
- [A] Technical Issues—BIM Guidelines and Standards
  - [1] NBIMS, Version 1.0
  - [2] Owner Mandated Standards
  - [3] Interoperability
- [B] Commercial Issues
  - [1] Absence of Standard BIM Contract Documents
  - [2] Contractor's Guide to BIM
  - [3] ConsensusDocs BIM Addendum
- [C] Legal Issues
  - [1] Standard of Care
  - [2] Design Delegation and Professional Responsibility
  - [3] Intellectual Property

              [4]   Insurability
              [5]   Data Translation
              [6]   Data Adequacy
              [7]   Privity, Third Party Reliance, and the Economic Loss Doctrine
              [8]   *Spearin* Implied Warranties

§ 5.04   Use of Building Information Modeling for Your Project?
        [A] How Will the Model(s) be Used?
        [B] Who Will Own and/or License the Model(s)?
              [1]   Owner Owns Modeling Information
              [2]   Designer Owns Modeling Information
              [3]   All Parties Own Whatever They Create
              [4]   What Is the Model's Contractual Status?
              [5]   How Will Modeling Requirements Be Specified?
              [6]   How Will the Model Be Administered?

§ 5.05   BIM as a Collaborative Framework—Integrated Project Delivery
        [A] The Need for Integrated Project Delivery
        [B] The Development of Integrated Project Delivery
        [C] Five Major Structural Elements of Integrated Project Delivery
              [1]   Early Involvement of Key Participants
              [2]   Shared Risk/Reward Based on Project Outcome
              [3]   Joint Project Control
              [4]   Reduced Liability Exposure
              [5]   Jointly Developed/Validated Targets
              [6]   Subcontractors, Consultants, and Joining Agreements
        [D] Four Minor Elements of Integrated Project Delivery
        [E] Brief Comparison of Integrated Project Delivery Agreements
        [F] The Implications of Integrated Project Delivery

§ 5.06   Conclusion

Chapter 8 Design Build

§ 8.08   Private Sector Design-Build Contract Document Forms
        [A] American Institute of Architects Design-Build Contract Documents (available at www.aia.org)
              [2]   A142™—2004 Standard Form of Agreement Between Design-Builder and Contractor

                [a]   A441™—2008 Standard Form of Agreement Between Contractor and Subcontractor for a Design-Build Project

          [4]   B143™—2004 Standard Form of Agreement Between Design-Builder and Architect

                [a]   C441™—2008, Standard Form of Agreement Between Architect and Consultant for a Design-Build Project

      [B]   ConsensusDOCS/Associated General Contractors of America Design-Build Contract Documents (available at www.agc.org or www.consensusdocs.org)

         [11] AIA/AGC Recommended Guidelines for Procurement of Design-Build Projects in the Public Sector: AGC 480

                [a]   Certificates of Substantial and Final Completion for Design-Build Work: ConsensusDOCS 481 and 482

Chapter 8A   **Construction Management**

Chapter 10   **Project Finance**

   § 10.02   Basic Structure of Project Finance Transaction

      [B]   Sources of Financing

         [3]   Third Party Support

           [d]   Government Agencies

               [i]   Tax Credits

                   [a]   Production Tax Credits

                   [b]   Investment Tax Credits

               [ii]   Cash Grants

               [iii] Tax Credit Bonds

                   [a]   Clean Renewable Energy Bonds

                   [b]   Qualified Energy Conservation Bonds

               [iv] Loan Guarantees

Chapter 11   **Environmental Issues**

Chapter 12   **Green Design and Construction: Risk Management in a Sustainable World**

Chapter 13   **Climate Change: A View from the Stratosphere**

   § 13.06A   Current Mitigation Efforts

      [A]   EU-ETS

      [B]   Asia

      [C]   North America

[D]   Obama, the American Clean Energy &
      Security Act, and the Construction
      Industry

Chapter 14   AIA Contract Documents

§ 14.05   Integrated Project Delivery and Construction
           Management
           [A]   Integrated Project Delivery
                 [1]   IPD Guide
                 [2]   A295 documents (sometimes referred to as the
                       transitional documents)
                 [3]   SPE Documents
                 [4]   Multi-Party Agreement
           [B]   Construction Management

Chapter 15   Overview of ConsensusDOCS Form Contracts

§ 15.16   ConsensusDOCS 752 Standard Subcontract for Work
           on a Federal Construction Project

§ 15.17   725 Standard Subsubcontract Agreement

§ 15.18   ConsensusDOCS 235 Cost of the Work Agreement

§ 15.19   ConsensusDOCS Procedures and Revision Cycle

§ 15.20   ConsensusDOCS 310 Green Building Addendum
           [A]   Overview of the ConsensusDOCS 310
                 Green Building Addendum
           [B]   Current Practice for Green Contracts Is
                 Not Best Practice
           [C]   Elected Green Status—Defining a
                 Green Building
           [D]   Neutral Rating System
           [E]   Green Building Facilitator
           [F]   Risk Allocation
           [G]   Outlook

Chapter 16   Sales Contracts/Uniform Commercial Code

**Chapter 19   Construction Wrap-Ups: Owner and Contractor
                Controlled Insurance Programs**

Chapter 20   Design Professional Insurance Issues

Chapter 22   Differing Site Conditions

Chapter 24   Obtaining Adequate Compensation for Delay

**Chapter 25   Subcontractor's Rights and Remedies for the
                Owner's Defaults in Payment**

Chapter 26   Exceptions to No-Damages-For-Delay Clauses

CONTENTS

Chapter 28   Terminations

§ 28.03   Termintation for Default
[B]   Grounds for Default Termination
[4]   Material Breach Justifying Default
[a]   Case Study: *Takota Corporation*

Chapter 29   Construction Failures

Chapter 30   Compensatory Damages

Chapter 31   Consequential and Punitive Damages

Chapter 32   Liquidated Damages

Chapter 33   Recovery of Interest and Attorneys' Fees

Chapter 34   Performance Bonds

Chapter 36   Indemnity of the Contract Surety

Chapter 37   New and Unique Aspects of Federal Contracting

§ 37.01   Introduction
[A]   The Stimulus Act
[B]   The New E-Verify Rules
[C]   Labor Rules

§ 37.02   Procurement Regulations
[H]   Socioeconomic Rules
[5]   Registry of Disaster Response Contractors

Chapter 39   When and How to File a Federal Contract Claim

Chapter 39A   Transportation Investment as Part of Economic Recovery—Is This a New Day for U.S. Infrastructure?

§ 39A.01   Executive Summary

§ 39A.02   The Context for Stimulus Funding—Economic Situation

§ 39A.03   The Need for Greater Investment

§ 39A.04   The Economic Recovery and Reinvestment Act of 2009

§ 39A.05   Significance of Including Transportation in ARRA

§ 39A.06   Details of ARRA's Transportation Components

§ 39A.07   Tracking the Impacts on the Economy and Transportation Construction Industry

§ 39A.08   Early Progress in Delivery of Benefits

§ 39A.09   Implications for Future Policies and Programs, and Commitments to Transportation Investment

§ 39A.10   Conclusion

Chapter 41   **Contracting for International Construction Works**

Chapter 42   **The Foreign Corrupt Practices Act and Multinational Anti-Bribery Initiatives**

§ 42.03   Beyond the FCPA: Multinational Anti-Corruption Initiatives
[G]   Other International Anti-Corruption Initiatives
[1]   Executive Order 13116
[2]   Jakarta, Indonesia
[3]   Lesotho Highland Water Project
[H]   U.S. Implementing Legislation

Chapter 43   **International Dispute Resolution**

Chapter 44   **Claims Avoidance and Dispute Management**

Chapter 46   **Arbitration of Construction Disputes and Enforceability of Awards**

Table of Cases to Main Volumes

Table of Cases

Table of Statutes and Regulations

Table of Authorities

Index

ABOUT THE SUPPLEMENT EDITORS

Stanley A. Martin is partner in the Boston office of the national law firm of Holland & Knight LLP. His practice focuses on construction and public contract law. Mr. Martin received a degree in architecture from the Massachusetts Institute of Technology and a J.D. degree from Boston College Law School. He is an author of several manuals, articles, and text chapters on construction law issues, and is one of the co-authors of *Project Delivery Systems for Construction* (published by the Associated General Contractors of America). Mr. Martin has taught construction law courses at M.I.T. and Northeastern University, and has lectured extensively on industry topics. He has served on the Corporate Advisory Council of the Boston Society of Architects, and as a board member of the Associated General Contractors of Massachusetts. Mr. Martin is also a former board member and Secretary of the Boston Architectural College.

Richard K. Allen is a registered professional civil engineer and construction law attorney who has 28 years of combined design and construction law practice experience. He is Stantec's Senior Vice President and responsible for its East Coast operations. Prior to joining Stantec, Mr. Allen was the CEO and President of Dufresne Henry, Inc., which was acquired by Stantec in April 2006. Mr. Allen is active in numerous professional engineering and legal associations, and has published more than two dozen articles relating to design and construction issues. Mr. Allen has extensive experience in water resources design and construction administration on projects throughout the Pacific Northwest and New England. He served for 17 years as an attorney at the Boston law firm Gadsby Hannah, LLP, becoming a partner and later chairman of the design and construction law practice there. Since 2004, Mr. Allen has been named in *Boston Magazine* as one of Massachusetts' "Super Lawyers." He was also listed in *International Who's Who of Construction Lawyers* in 2005. Mr. Allen is a registered professional engineer in the states of Florida, New York, Maine, Massachusetts, New Hampshire, Vermont, and Washington.

ABOUT THE CONTRIBUTORS

Kymberli Aguilar has experience handling all aspects of general civil litigation matters, with a particular emphasis on multi-party construction disputes. Her practice also includes various transactional matters such as, advising clients regarding the planning of construction projects and planning and negotiating construction and design professional agreements. She has been integrally involved with matters concerning delay and impact claims, design deficiency claims, payment dispute claims, cost overrun claims and construction defect claims. Kymberli's practice includes the representation of owners, designers, contractors, and public entities with respect to commercial and residential projects.

Andrew Argyris is an associate in the Construction and Government Contracts Group at Howrey LLP. His practice focuses on advising clients in resolving complex construction and government contracts disputes. Mr. Argyris received his B.A. from Amherst College. He received his J.D. from Sandra Day O'Connor College of Law, Arizona State University.

Gregory S. Arnold, LL.M, is a Senior Bond Claims Representative II with The Hanover Insurance Group, Inc., Home Office, Worcester, Massachusetts, where he responds to contract surety, commercial surety and fidelity claims, plus assists with product development and training.

Mr. Arnold was a Non-Commissioned Officer, serving as a Military Courts-Martial Reporter in the United State Marine Corps, with duty stations in Japan and the Philippines. He then graduated from Union College and University with a Bachelor of Science in Political Science, *cum laude* and with Departmental Honors. He received a Juris Doctorate from Western State University College of Law and an LL.M (Insurance Law) from The University of Connecticut School of Law.

Mr. Arnold started his surety claims career as Bond Claims Trainee and then Bond Claims Manager for the West, with Great American Insurance Company in Orange, California, and then Bond Claims Manager for the Mid-West, at Great American's Home Office in Cincinnati, Ohio. He then accepted a position as Bond Claims Superintendent/Assistant Secretary with Highlands Insurance Company at its Home Office in Houston, Texas, with his last position there being Assistant Vice President of Claims. Mr. Arnold then formed Claims Management Associates, Inc. in Houston, Texas, primarily providing surety claim run-off services for Highlands, plus performing desk relief and run-off assistance to other, smaller sureties and those in transition. After a brief period working for Mid-State Surety Corporation/Guarantee Company of North America USA, he accepted his current position in the Bond Claims Department at Hanover.

His recent contributions to international insurance scholarship include his law journal publications, *The Doubtful Impact of an Optional Federal Charter on the Reinsurance Collateral Debate*, 43 Tort Trial & Ins. Prac. L.J. 79 (2008), American Bar Association, and *Recent Developments in the Financial Products and Services Industry*, 43 The International Lawyer (2008), American Bar Association. His domestic surety and insurance scholarship include a writing contribution to the *CGL/Builder's Risk Monograph*, 2004, Tort Trial & Insurance Practice Section, American Bar Association. His papers and panel participations include: "The Surety's Good Faith Investigation," CMA Group, Inc., National Claims Conference, Chicago, IL, April 1989; "The Good, Bad and Ugly: Lawyers, Consultants and Company People Traveling Down The Same Road Together," panel presentation, National Bond Claims Conference, Pinehurst, NC, Oct. 1994; "Treatment of Pay-When-Paid Clauses Under Federal Law on Bonded Projects in Virginia," Surety Association of South Texas, San Antonio, May 17, 2000; and *Issues and Practical Considerations for the Surety in Using Subcontractor Ratification Agreements*, 17th Annual Northeast Surety and Fidelity Claims Conference, Atlantic City, NJ, Sept. 2006.

Mr. Arnold has been a guest lecturer on surety law topics at Roger Williams University and is licensed and certified as an insurance and surety claims adjuster in several states.

Laura Bourgeois is an associate in the Construction Group at Howrey LLP. She advises on commercial and construction matters for various construction, engineering and infrastructure projects both private and Government contracts. Ms. Bourgeois received her Bachelor of Architecture from the University of Louisiana and practiced architecture with Page Southerland Page until attending law school. She received her Juris Doctor degree from The George Washington University Law School.

Terrence L. Brennan is a partner in the New Orleans office of Deutsch, Kerrigan & Stiles, LLP. His practice includes all areas of construction law. He actively represents owners, architects, engineers, surveyors, contractors, suppliers and building construction sureties. Mr. Brennan has been the Department Head of the firm's Construction Section since 1990. Mr. Brennan graduated with a degree in architecture from Kansas State University in 1976 and his J.D. degree from University of Kansas in 1979. He has assisted in teaching courses concerning the legal aspects of professional practice for the College of Architecture and Design at Tulane University. From 1990 to 2000 he also taught "Construction Industry Law" at Loyola University of the South. Mr. Brennan has extensive experience in construction industry insurance issues and alternative dispute resolution methods and procedures.

Terrence L. Brookie is a member of the law firm of Frost Brown Todd LLC in its Indianapolis, Indiana office. He concentrates his practice in the areas of construction law, surety law, and business litigation. Mr. Brookie is a frequent speaker for construction and commercial groups, and has lectured and written numerous articles for several industry groups and professional organizations in the construction industry. He is a member of the American Bar Association's Forum on the Construction Industry (Governing Committee), TIPS Fidelity/Surety Law Committee, and Construction Litigation Committee. Terry is a Fellow of the American College of Construction Lawyers (Board of Governors), and selected by his peers for inclusion in *The Best Lawyers in America,* 2005–2010. Mr. Brookie received a B.A. from Denison University and his J.D. from the Indiana University School of Law.

Donald Brown is an associate in Alston & Bird's Construction and Government Contracts Group. Donald received his J.D. in 2007, with honors, from the University of North Carolina at Chapel Hill School of Law, where he was an article and comments editor for the *North Carolina Journal of International Law and Commercial Regulation.* Donald also attended the University of North Carolina at Chapel Hill for undergraduate studies, and in 2002 received a Bachelor of Science in Business Administration from the Kenan-Flagler Business School. Donald's practice is diverse, representing owners, contractors, and architects, with a specific focus on EPC Contracts for major energy facilities.

Stephen Buryk is an Economics and Russian Studies major at Lehigh University in Pennsylvania. He is a research associate at Eco-Securities, focusing on novel emissions reductions technologies in the emerging voluntary carbon market.

Stephen D. Butler is the former General Counsel of Parsons Brinckerhoff, Inc. and remains PB's Counsel for Major Projects, providing advice and counsel on large projects and claims. Prior to joining PB, Mr. Butler led Bechtel Corporation's litigation department as Manager of Litigation before becoming its Managing Counsel for complex cases and claims such as the Central Artery Tunnel Project in Boston. Steve is also a Fellow in the American College of Construction Lawyers and a Director of the American Arbitration Association.

Joe F. Canterbury, Jr. is a partner in the Dallas, Texas law firm of Canterbury, Elder, Gooch, Surratt, Shapiro & Stein, P.C. His practice is centered in the construction industry. Mr. Canterbury has argued construction and employment law cases before state and federal courts, including the Supreme Court of the United States. Mr. Canterbury is the author of *Texas Construction Law Manual* (1st and 2nd editions, Shepards/McGraw-Hill) and co-author with Rob Shapiro of the 3rd edition (Thomson-West, 2005). He is a Member of the American Arbitration Association National Construction Dispute Resolution Committee and a Member of the Board of Directors and Executive Committee of the AAA. He is also the Past President of the American College of

Construction Lawyers; a Founding Member and Past Chairman of the Construction Law Sections of the Dallas and Texas Bar Associations; and author of various articles on construction law and ADR.

Jimmy A. Castex, Jr. is a partner in the New Orleans office of Deutsch, Kerrigan & Stiles, LLP. He maintains a diverse litigation practice, but primarily focuses construction law. Mr. Castex represents many owners, architects, engineers, and contractors. After service to his country in the United States Army (1986–1989) and the United States Army Reserve (1990–1993), Mr. Castex received his J.D. from Loyola University School of Law in New Orleans, Louisiana in 1996.

Matt Coglianese heads up the environmental and green construction practice at Peckar & Abramson, a national firm. He practices in the areas of litigation and environmental law, emphasizing CERCLA, RCRA, wetlands and Clean Water Act issues, brownfields redevelopment, toxic torts, and state and local environmental matters. Mr. Coglianese has substantial experience in construction matters, including green building and sustainable development, and has participated in environmental litigation at the federal, state and local levels. His practice also includes environmental and corporate counseling, permitting and corporate due diligence. He served as Assistant Regional Counsel with the United States EPA in Atlanta, Georgia, where he handled enforcement of federal water and air pollution laws. As senior attorney with a major Los Angeles-based petroleum company, he was responsible for managing numerous Superfund and state hazardous waste sites throughout the country. He also was in charge of client counseling regarding legal responsibilities and remedy selection, as well as overseeing litigation and outside counsel. Mr. Coglianese is the author and co-author of numerous articles on environmental law including: *Wetlands Guidance Remains Cloudy*, Southeast Florida Real Estate, July 2007; *Green Development, Here to Stay*, America Bar Association Environmental Litigation Committee Newsletter, Fall 2007; *The Toxic Mold Threat to Commercial Property*, The Real Estate Finance Journal, Spring 2003; *Easing the Red Tape on Cleanups*, Area Development Online, December 2004; *Mold Mania*, Builder Magazine, Summer 2003; *Brownfields Come of Age in South Florida*, Florida Environments, 1996 and *The Self-Critical Analysis Privilege*, The Florida Bar Environmental and Land Use Law Section Bulletin, 1995. He also lectures frequently on environmental topics. Mr. Coglianese's lectures include: Sustainable and Conservation Based Development (moderator) Florida Chamber of Commerce, Summer School, 2008; Green Construction Part II—Liability Risks with Green Building Construction, Dade County Bar Association's Construction Law Committee; Advanced Strategies for Structuring Engineering, and Closing Brownfield Transactions, Annual Growth Management & Environmental Permitting Conference (panelist); Florida Environmental Network, Inc., 2005; Toxic Tort Law Update, The Florida Bar's Environmental and Land Use Law Section, Summer 2003; Brownfields, Florida Chamber of

Commerce's Environmental Permitting Summer School, 1997–2007; Annual Environmental and Land Use Update, The Florida Bar, 1995 and 1996 and Brownfields, What Are They & Why Do They Matter? The Florida Bar, 1996. Mr. Coglianese received his B.A., *cum laude*, from the University of Rhode Island in 1976, his Ph.D. in Biology in 1981 from Texas A&M University and his J.D. in 1984 from the University of Miami School of Law. He is admitted to practice law in Florida and California.

Jared Cohane is a litigation attorney with Pepe & Hazard LLP in Hartford, Connecticut. He represents general contractors, construction managers, subcontractors and sureties in a wide variety of construction-related disputes in state and federal courts, arbitration and mediation. Mr. Cohane has experience litigating claims arising out of the construction of power plants—both domestically and abroad—before federal courts and in arbitration. He also counsels clients during the course of construction projects, so as to achieve optimal resolutions of claims as they arise and to avoid litigation. He has authored and co-authored various articles on construction-related litigation issues, including the emerging law on electronic discovery. Mr. Cohane is a graduate of Oberlin College and received his J.D., *with honors*, from the University of Connecticut School of Law. He is admitted to the practice of law in the states of Connecticut and Massachusetts, the United States Court of Claims and various federal district courts.

Dan Crowley is an international disputes consultant with Project Advisors International LLC who brings his unique 30 years of industry experience extending from mason, general contractor, construction manager and project executive to his services. Mr. Crowley provides his clients with computerized delay and schedule analyses, disruption, inefficiency and quantum analyses, surety investigations and industry project controls peer reviews. Mr. Crowley is also a member of various domestic project development ventures where he provides project controls, overview and risk management consulting services for both commercial and residential developments. Mr. Crowley has been recognized and accepted as an expert witness before numerous domestic courts and boards and international tribunals.

Tobias J. Cushing is an associate at Saxe Doernberger & Vita P.C. Mr. Cushing represents corporations in insurance coverage disputes involving commercial general liability, commercial property, directors & officers and professional liability insurance. In particular, he has handled cases involving environmental liability, construction defects and health-care provider reimbursement disputes. Mr. Cushing also consults with a number of clients to improve their existing insurance programs and has represented them in renewal negotiations with insurance carriers. He has also argued various motions, tried cases and represented clients in a number of settlement negotiations and commercial transactions.

Mr. Cushing received his J.D. from Quinnipiac University School of Law and an LL.M. in Insurance Law from University of Connecticut School of Law.

John Denniston, now a retired partner, was a member of Covington's Government Contracts practice group. His practice focused on contract claims and appeals, bid protests, Federal Supply Schedule contracts, contract cost accounting and pricing issues, contract fraud investigations, suspension and debarment proceedings, patent and technical data rights, classified contract security arrangements, and private supply and construction contracts. Mr. Denniston was extensively involved in the preparation, negotiation and litigation of large, complex claims for equitable price adjustments. Currently, Mr. Denniston is working in a non-legal capacity on pro bono projects for organizations that are involved in addressing science and public policy issues, environmental issues and issues relating to developing countries. He also has been involved in fundraising for these organizations. Mr. Denniston also has served as an arbitrator in resolving private contractual disputes.

Daniel J. Donohue is a shareholder in the Tysons Corner, Virginia office of the law firm of Akerman Senterfitt Wickwire Gavin, where his practice concentrates on Government Contracts and Construction law. Dan is active in the Associated General Contractors of America and is past Chair of AGC's Federal Acquisition Regulation Committee. He is a member of the adjunct faculty of George Mason University Law School, where he teaches Appellate Writing and Legal Drafting. Dan is a 1975 graduate of the College of the Holy Cross in Worcester, Mass. and received his J.D. from the Catholic University of America, Washington, D.C. Dan is admitted to practice law in Virginia, Maryland, the District of Columbia and New York.

Mortimer L. Downey, III serves as a Senior Advisor to Parsons Brinckerhoff, providing advisory and management consulting services to the firm and to its client base, including public and private owners, developers, financers and builders of infrastructure projects worldwide. Mr. Downey previously served as Chairman of PB Consult and as a Principal Consultant. Recently, Mr. Downey served on the Transportation Policy Committee for the Obama Presidential campaign, and during the presidential transition was appointed as leader of the Department of Transportation Agency Review Team.

Mr. Downey held the position of U.S. deputy secretary of transportation for eight years, the longest serving individual in that post. As the Department's chief operating officer, Mr. Downey developed the agency's highly regarded strategic and performance plans and had program responsibilities for operations, regulation and investments in land, sea, air and space transportation. He also served on the President's Management Council, as Chairman of the National Science and Technology's Committee on Technology, as a member of the Trade Promotion Coordinating Council and as a member of the Board of Directors of the National

Railroad Passenger Corporation (Amtrak). In a prior Administration he had served as an Assistant Secretary of the Department.

Previously, Mr. Downey was for 12 years the executive director and chief financial officer of the New York Metropolitan Transportation Authority (MTA), the nation's largest independent public authority, directing its capital programs totaling over $20 billion, including development of new public and private financing techniques, and had responsibility for oversight of capital project designs, budgets, schedules and performance. He has also worked at the U.S. House of Representatives Committee on the Budget, and at the Port Authority of New York and New Jersey.

Mr. Downey has received numerous professional awards, including election to the National Academy of Public Administration, where he has served as Chairman of the Board of Directors. He has been honored with the Frank Turner Lifetime Achievement award from the Transportation Research Board, the American Society of Public Administration's Truitt Award for transportation management, the W. Graham Claytor Award for contributions to intercity passenger rail, lifetime achievement awards from the American Public Transportation Association and the Council of University Transportation Centers, the Leadership Award from the Intelligent Transportation Society of America and the National Member of the Year Award from the Women's Transportation Seminar.

He is a member of the Board of Directors of the Eno Transportation Foundation and has served on the National Academy of Science's Committee on Science & Technology Countermeasures to Terrorism. He was a member of the Office of Management and Budget's Performance Measurement Advisory Council, served on a DOT special panel to report on safety impacts of Mexican truck operations in the United States, and recently joined the Industry Leaders Council of the American Society of Civil Engineers.

A 1958 graduate of Yale University with a B.A. in Political Science, Mr. Downey earned his masters degree in Public Administration from New York University, completed the Advanced Management Program at the Harvard Business School and served as an officer in the United States Coast Guard Reserve.

Dennis C. Ehlers is a Partner in McManus Schor Asmar & Darden LLP's Government Contracts Practice Group. He represents government contractors of all sizes and in all industries in bid protests, disputes, and claims before state and federal boards of contract appeals, the Government Accountability Office, Court of Federal Claims, and United States Court of Appeals for the Federal Circuit. He also represents large and small commercial contractors in the construction and other fields with contract issues/disputes/litigation. He assists his government and commercial contractor clients in all phases of their dealings with the Government and private owners. He has also been involved in litigating mold cases. Prior to joining the firm, Mr. Ehlers practiced law for eight years with the United States Air Force Judge Advocate General's Corps (JAG), serving stateside and overseas as a base-level contracts attorney and practicing in several other areas of the law, including government ethics, tort claims, and medical malpractice, healthcare, federal employment, administrative, and criminal law. He presently continues his military service as an Air Force Reserve trial attorney (in the rank of Major) assigned to the JAG's Commercial Litigation Division (Government Contracts) which defends the Air Force against bid protests and contract claims in the Court of Federal Claims. Mr. Ehlers is licensed in the District of Columbia, Tennessee, and Georgia and is a member of the Boards of Contract Appeals Bar Association and Federal Bar Association. Mr. Ehlers received his J.D. degree (cum laude) from the University of Georgia (UGA) School of Law, a Master of Business Administration degree from UGA's graduate business school, the Terry College of Business, and a B.A. degree (cum laude) in Biology from Southern College.

Eric D. Foerg is an associate in the law firm of Frost Brown Todd LLC in its Indianapolis, Indiana office. Mr. Foerg concentrates his practice in construction and surety litigation. Prior to attending law school, he was a National Labor Relations Board Field Examiner in Portland, Oregon. He graduated *cum laude* from Butler University with High Honors in Finance. During law school at the University of Michigan, he was an Extern for Chief Judge Robert L. Miller, Jr., Northern District of Indiana, and also participated in the Sidley—IIEL WTO Moot Court Competition—where his team received Best Written Submission, Runner-Up. He is a member of the American Bar Association's Forum on the Construction Industry, Indiana State Bar Association's Construction & Surety Division, Defense Research Institute, Defense Trial Counsel of Indiana, Indianapolis Bar Association, Indiana Construction Association (Leadership Development Committee), Surety Association of Indiana, and an Associate Member of the Indianapolis American Inn of Court.

Joseph T. Getz is a partner with the law firm of Less, Getz & Lipman. His practice areas include construction, fidelity and surety. He is a member of the Memphis, Tennessee, Mississippi and American Bar Associations; American Bar Association Forum Committee on Construction, Fidelity and Surety Law Committee; Construction Financial Management Association; Associated Builders & Contractors; and Tennessee Association of Construction Counsel. Mr. Getz has been awarded the designation of Mid South Super Lawyer in the areas of construction and surety law. Mr. Getz is a frequent lecturer on construction, surety and fidelity law topics. He has numerous publications including *Pyramids and Privity, a Discussion of the Miller Act*, for the Defense Research Institute and *Advanced Construction Law in Tennessee* for the National Business Institute. He is also coauthor of *Handling Fidelity & Surety Claims*, Wiley

Publications, and West Publication's *Building and Construction Agreements*, Aspen Publications, *Construction Law Handbook*. Mr. Getz received his B.B.A. degree from the University of Mississippi and his J.D. degree from Memphis State University.

Suzanne Harness is both a licensed architect and a construction attorney with more than thirty years of experience in the design and construction industry. As Managing Director and Counsel at the American Institute of Architects, Suzanne is responsible for the content of AIA Contract Documents. With her staff and the AIA Documents Committee, she works actively in the creation and revision of the AIA's standard form contracts. Ms. Harness was first licensed as an architect and practiced architecture in Washington, DC firms for several years before joining a commercial real estate development company as a project manager. Later she managed the design and construction of federal projects for the General Services Administration, including the modernization of the Department of Justice and the design of the District of Columbia federal courthouse annex. She received her J.D. from the George Washington University Law School and practiced in the Washington, DC office of Seyfarth Shaw LLP representing architects, owners, and contractors in litigation and contractual matters until joining the AIA in September 2002. Ms. Harness is a member of the bar in Virginia and the District of Columbia and serves on the steering committee of Division 2 of the ABA Forum on the Construction Industry. She received a B.S. cum laude and M.Arch in Architecture from The Catholic University of America and is a life member of Tau Beta Pi, the national engineering honor society.

Kyle E. Hart is a partner in the law firm of Fabyanske, Westra & Hart in Minneapolis, Minnesota, where he limits his practice to the construction industry. Mr. Hart represents owners, sureties, contractors, and subcontractors.

James Heath is Head of US Origination for EcoSecurities, based in their New York office. Mr. Heath has extensive experience in the areas of carbon finance, emissions trading and renewable energy, with an emphasis on sourcing carbon offset projects both in North America and internationally under the Clean Development Mechanism (CDM) of the Kyoto Protocol. He joined EcoSecurities in 2005, and managed many of the first projects developed and registered under the CDM. Prior to joining EcoSecurities, Mr. Heath worked with the Tropical Ecology, Assessment and Monitoring (TEAM) Initiative at Conservation International in project management and scientific development capacities. He holds a Master's degree in Environmental Change and Management from Oxford University and a Bachelor's degree in BioEnvironmental Sciences from Texas A&M University.

Andy Howard is an associate in Alston & Bird's Construction and Government Contracts Group. As part of his government contracts practice, Andy represents clients in the negotiation of government contracts, and in pre-and post-award bid protests, suspension and debarment proceedings, and in civil and criminal investigations. On the construction side Andy represents owners and contractors in transactional and litigation matters including mediations, arbitrations and trials. Andy earned his J.D., *cum laude*, in 2002 from the Walter F. George School of Law at Mercer University and received a B.A. in political science in 1998 from Furman University. Andy is a contributing author of *The Construction Contracts Book: How to Find Common Ground in Negotiating Design and Construction Contract Clauses* published by the American Bar Association in 2004, and is a member of the American Bar Association's Construction Industry Forum, where he serves on the Division 2 Steering Committee.

Gerard W. Ittig, an attorney in Washington, D.C., specializes in construction contract claims and disputes throughout the United States and internationally. His experience includes heavy construction projects (dams, roads, bridges), power and petrochemical plants, marine and industrial installations, and commercial buildings. Using his litigation experience, Mr. Ittig has authored numerous articles on contract issues and has written manuals on project management for use in the United States, the Middle East, and Europe. Mr. Ittig also holds a Bachelor of Science degree in Electrical Engineering.

Geoffrey T. Keating has been counsel to contractors, engineers, public and private owners, and sureties for over 35 years. His work has encompassed all phases of construction contracts with particular emphasis on public works and international infrastructure. Representative projects include military installations, air bases, ports, dams, subway tunnels and stations, bridges, and power plants. Overseas work includes civil works projects in Egypt, Saudi Arabia, Brazil, Russia, Italy, Iraq, Mexico and U.S. Embassy, and USAID projects. Mr. Keating has litigated many complex construction disputes before the U.S. Courts and Boards of Contract Appeals, state courts, and arbitration tribunals. He also has serves as a construction arbitrator. Active on construction law committees of the American Bar Association, Public Contract Law Section, Mr. Keating has chaired committees on Construction Claims, and Architect-Engineer Services. He was on the faculty of the Stanford University, Construction Executive Program. He has presented seminars addressing international contracts in Uganda, the Peoples Republic of China, Saudi Arabia, Dubai and at the United Nations. In 2006–2007 he consulted on matters relating to new public procurement regulations for the new Iraqi Government and the government of Vietnam. Mr. Keating also is a member of the District of Columbia and Maryland Bars; of the American College of Construction Lawyers; the West Group Construction Advisory Board; the faculty of the International Law Institute; and the American Bar Association, Forum Committee on Construction. He also is listed in Chambers & Partners, Leading Lawyers in Construction, Who's

Who in International Construction and D.C. Super Lawyers. He is Of Counsel to McManus, Schor, Asmar & Darden LLP, Washington, D.C.

Stephen P. Kelly is Of Counsel in the Construction and Design Section of Stoel Rives LLP.

Stephanie Kirby, PE is a principal in the VOSK Group. Ms. Kirby has been involved in the design and construction of transportation projects from highways to ferry terminals since stepping in to the transportation arena 19 years ago. She was the Construction Manager for Sound Transit for the construction of the Pine Street Stub tunnel and the retrofit of the Downtown Seattle Transit Tunnel for Light Rail. Prior to becoming the deputy construction manager she was the design manager for both the Stub Tunnel and the Retrofit of the Downtown Seattle Tunnel. Prior to coming to Sound Transit, she worked for the Washington State Ferries as a Design Supervisor, overseeing the design of the Clinton Ferry Dock Expansion and the Edmonds Overhead Ferry terminal projects.

Pavan I. Khoobchandani is an associate in the Tysons Corner, Virginia office of Akerman Senterfitt LLP and is a member of its Construction and Government Contracts Groups. His construction practice includes the representation of public and private owners and developers in contract review and drafting, as well as in delay and defect litigation relating to public, commercial, and multi-family projects. He is a graduate of Boston University and received his J.D. in 2003 from the Georgetown University Law Center.

Sam Krevor is a Project Manager with EcoSecurities in New York City. He did his Ph.D. at Columbia University focusing on the development of a carbon sequestration technology.

Michael I. Less is a partner with the law firm of Less, Getz & Lipman. His practice areas include construction and surety. Mr. Less is a member of the Memphis, Tennessee and American Bar Associations; American Bar Association Forum Committee on Construction; and Tennessee Association of Construction Counsel. Mr. Less has been awarded the designation of Mid South Super Lawyer in the areas of construction and surety law. He has numerous publications, including *Place Your Bets—and Your Insurance—on a Casino Construction Project* for the American Bar Association; *Casino Construction—The New Mecca or Money Pit* for the Construction Financial Management Association; *Laws of Payment Bonds* for the American Bar Association; and *Improving the Odds for a Well Managed Project: Practical Tips in Casino Construction*, The Gaming Lawyer, Summer 2000. Mr. Less is a past President of the Tennessee Association of Construction Counsel. Mr. Less received his B.A. degree from the University of Missouri and his J.D. degree from the University of Memphis.

Joseph A. McManus, Jr. is a partner in the Washington, D.C. law firm of McManus, Schor, Asmar & Darden LLP where he concentrates his practice on all phases of construction and government contract law. Mr. McManus formerly served as Law Clerk to Chief Justice Solibakke of the Armed Services Board of Contract Appeals while on active duty with the U.S. Air Force, JAG Corps; was in private practice in Atlanta, Georgia; and served as General Counsel to the Clark Construction Group (CEI). Mr. McManus is a past President of the American College of Construction Lawyers. He frequently served as arbitrator on local, national, and international cases and has appeared as an expert witness in cases involving construction documents, more specifically AIA documents. He has published extensively in the legal arena. Mr. McManus is a member of the District of Columbia, New York, North Carolina and Georgia bars. He received his B.A. in 1969 from College of the Holy Cross and his J.D. in 1972 from Duke University Law School.

John T. W. Mercer is the co-founder and Chairman of Mercer Thompson LLC, an energy boutique law firm founded in June, 2009 and specializing in all aspects of project development and finance for electric utilities and independent power producers, including in the areas of renewable and clean power technology. Until his resignation in June, 2009, he was partner in the international law firm of Troutman Sanders LLP, where he was the firm-wide head of the Project Development and Finance Practice Group. Over the past 15 years, Mr. Mercer and his team have assisted clients in developing and/or acquiring more than 160 projects in over 40 countries on six continents and in raising more than $40 billion of non-recourse/limited recourse project and acquisition financing. He received his J.D. from the University of Michigan Law School in 1977 and his A.B. from the University of Michigan in 1973.

Jeff Morales is a senior vice president of Parsons Brinckerhoff. He has a strong public sector background with a focus on transportation policy and management. His national leadership was underscored by being appointed as a member of the Transition Team for President-Elect Barack Obama, responsible for developing a roadmap for the incoming Administration, including key policy recommendations and preparation of the Transportation Secretary-designate. An expert in strategic planning and program implementation, Jeff is nationally recognized for developing innovative policies and practices that have resulted in improved productivity and customer service across the agencies he has served, and for introducing new approaches and programs to promote environmental awareness and sustainability.

Prior to joining PB, Jeff was Director of the California Department of Transportation (Caltrans), where he managed a $10 billion program and more than 23,000 employees working to build, maintain and operate the largest state transportation system in the U.S. He also served as executive vice president of the Chicago Transit Authority (CTA), where he spearheaded major reforms to improve service and increase ridership at the nation's second-largest transit agency. Prior to his tenure at the CTA, he was a senior staff member with former Vice President Al Gore's National Performance Review, the task force designed to reinvent the federal government. In 1996–1997, Jeff was Issues Director of the White

House Commission on Aviation Safety and Security. He also held senior positions at the U.S. Department of Transportation and on the staff of the U.S. Senate.

Amanda K. Morken is an associate in the Washington, D.C. office of McManus, Schor, Asmar & Darden LLP. She focuses her practice in the Litigation and Special Project Groups and is involved in all aspects of construction litigation before courts and national and international arbitration panels. Ms. Morken received her J.D. from Hamline University School of Law and is admitted to practice before the Supreme Court of the State of Minnesota, the United States District Court for the District of Minnesota, the United States Court of Appeals for the Eighth Circuit and the District of Columbia Court of Appeals.

James F. Nagle is a nationally known expert in government contracts and construction law. He received his Bachelor's degree from Georgetown University School of Foreign Service; his J.D. from Rutgers; and his LL.M. and S.J.D. in government contracts from the National Law Center, George Washington University. He is one of only an estimated three people who have ever received this distinction. Mr. Nagle has written six books on federal contracting, Nash, Cibinic and Nagle, *Administration of Government Contracts*, 4th ed. (George Washington University Press 2006); Whelan and Nagle, *Cases and Materials on Federal Government Contracts*, 3rd ed. (Foundation Press 2007), the leading law school textbook on the subject; *Federal Procurement Regulations: Policy, Practice and Procedures* (American Bar Association Press [ABA], 1987); *How to Review a Federal Contract and Research Federal Contract Law*, Second Edition (ABA Press, 2000); *Federal Construction Contracting* (Wiley Law Publications, 1992); *The History of Government Contracting*, Second Edition (George Washington University Press, 1999). He has also co-authored and co-edited *Washington Building Contracts and Construction Law* (Butterworth (now Aspen) Publishers, 1994). Besides being a contributing author to eight other books, his over 80 articles, on subjects as diverse as protests, changes, terminations, claims, and the Federal Acquisition Regulation, have appeared in such publications as the *Public Contract Law Journal*, *Military Law Review*, *NCMA Journal*, and *Contract Management*.

Victor C. Oblas, PE began his career as an engineer with Kramer Chin Mayo (KCM) in Seattle in the early 1970s. He spent 14 years with KCM doing planning studies, design and construction management. Following work in the Consulting arena, Vic spent 12 years with the Municipality of Metropolitan Seattle serving in increasingly responsible positions, including Director of Technical Services responsible for Metro's entire Transit and Water Capital Program. Vic has extensive experience in construction management for complex public projects including the Downtown Seattle Transit bus tunnel construction and its recent conversion to accommodate light rail. He served as Construction Manager representing the Public Facilities District for Safeco field.

Leslie O'Neal Coble serves as associate general counsel for Brasfield & Gorrie, LLC, a commercial general contractor based in Birmingham, AL. Prior to joining Brasfield & Gorrie in 2007, Leslie was a shareholder at Greenberg Traurig, P.A. in Orlando in the construction practice group.

A graduate of the University of Florida and of the University of Florida College of Law, Leslie has practiced in the area of construction law for 30 years. She has been active in many professional organizations, including the ABA Forum on Construction, where she served on the Governing Committee and as Chair. She is a Fellow of the American College of Construction Lawyers, where she served on the Board of Directors and is also a Fellow of the ABA Foundation. She is a member of the American Board of Trial Advocates. Leslie is board certified in the area of Construction Law by the Florida Bar.

Leslie has spoken to many industry and construction law organizations, including the American Institute of Constructors, the ABA Litigation Section, the ABA Forum on Construction, the ABA Fidelity & Surety Law Committee. She has published numerous articles and book chapters and is a co-author of *Construction Damages and Remedies* (ABA Press 2003).

Alan Pemberton heads Covington's Government Contracts practice group. His practice includes government contracts, construction litigation, and other complex civil litigation and ADR. Mr. Pemberton has practiced in the government contracts area since 1982, and his practice includes bid protest and other procurement litigation before GAO, agency boards of contract appeals, the federal courts and ADR tribunals. He advises contractors and grantees about the full range of government proposal, performance, compliance, regulatory, transactional and legislative issues. Mr. Pemberton also serves as Vice Chair of the firm's public service committee, and has for many years been active in prisoners' rights and other civil rights matters. Mr. Pemberton is an Adjunct Professor of Law at Georgetown University Law Center (constitutional law), Vice President of the Indigent Civil Litigation Fund, Inc., a Fellow at the American Bar Foundation, and a Member of the Committee on Pro Se Litigation, U.S. District Court for the District of Columbia.

Louis R. Pepe is a litigation attorney with Pepe & Hazard who focuses his practice on construction contract cases, business torts and commercial contract disputes. He represents his clients in state and federal courts as well as in arbitration, mediation and other ADR proceedings. Mr. Pepe received a B.Mgt.E. degree and an M.S. in Management from Rensselaer Polytechnic Institute, and a J.D., *with distinction*, from Cornell Law School. He is admitted to the practice of law in Connecticut and before the United States Supreme Court and numerous federal district courts and courts of appeal. He has taught in seminars presented by the Connecticut Bar Association on trial practice and has presented seminars in business and construction litigation throughout the country. Mr. Pepe has also taught a course on arbitration at the University of Connecticut Law School. Mr. Pepe is a former president of the Connecticut Bar Association (2005–2006), a Fellow in the American College of Trial Lawyers and in the American College of Construction Lawyers, and an Associate of the American Board of Trial Advocates. He is listed in *Who's Who in America*, *Who's Who in American Law*, *The International Who's Who of Construction Lawyers*, and *Best Lawyers in America*.

Perkins Coie's National Construction Group's practice is focused on design, construction and procurement issues for public and private clients. It includes the full spectrum of services from transactions, through advice, to dispute resolution. The group has been involved in a wide variety of high profile projects including Safeco Field, Benaroya Hall, Colorado River Casino and Resort, Everett Events Center, Chicago Lakefront Millennium Park, Museum of Flight, University of Alaska, Fairbanks Museum of the North, Immunex Headquarters, Lincoln Square, Soldier Field Stadium Renovation, Starbucks Office Building, Hoover Dam Visitors' Center, Four Seasons Hotel, Bellevue City Hall, Anchorage Dena'ina Civic and Convention Center Sound Transit Light Rail, Nintendo Headquarters, and many other public and private projects in the United States and Asia. Contributors to the Exceptions to No-Damages-For-Delay-Clauses include Richard Prentke, Frederick Rivera, Graehm Wallace, Andrew Greene and Melissa Robertson (Seattle); Jodi Feuerhelm, P. Derek Petersen and Aaron Welling (Phoenix); Michael Kreger and Kyan Olanna (Anchorage); Scott Greene and Jan Feldman (Chicago); Jeffrey Cowman and Zachary Lange (Denver); and Richard Boardman and Christine Salmi (Boise).

Brian Perlberg is Executive Director and Senior Counsel for the new industry-endorsed ConsensusDOCS, the ground-breaking effort of consensus contracts which are transforming the construction industry. He speaks throughout the country on the ConsensusDOCS, and has written several articles on the subject. Mr. Perlberg also serves as AGC's Senior Counsel for Construction law. He is AGC's primary attorney for all contract and construction law matters, including AGC's participation in the Engineers Joint Contract Documents Committee (EJCDC), and commenting upon the American Institute of Architects (AIA) documents. In addition, Mr. Perlberg serves on the American Bar Association (ABA) Forum on the Construction Industry Steering Committee for Contract Documents.

Jennifer Plitsch is special counsel in Covington's Government Contracts practice group where her practice includes a wide range of contracting issues for large and small businesses in both defense and civilian contracting. Ms. Plitsch's practice involves advising clients on contract proposal, performance, and compliance questions as well as transactional and legislative issues. Her practice also includes bid protest and contract claims and appeals litigation before GAO, agency boards and the federal courts. She has particular expertise in advising clients on Federal Supply Schedule contracts, including the complex pricing requirements imposed on pharmaceutical products under the VA FSS. Ms. Plitsch is active in pro bono work and in 2001 received the Charles F.C. Ruff Pro Bono Lawyer of the Year award.

Guy A. Randles is a partner in the Construction and Design Section of Stoel Rives LLP and a member of the Washington and Oregon bars.

Tracy Alan Saxe is a skilled commercial litigator with more than 25 years of experience in insurance coverage issues. Since 1990, he has focused his practice on insurance coverage litigation on behalf of policyholders, handling cases involving coverage for comprehensive general liability, directors & officers, professional liability, builder's risk, subguard, first party property damage, additional insured and business interruption claims. Mr. Saxe has handled cases involving coverage for construction defects, completed operations, product liability, property damage and bodily injury related to mold and asbestos, bodily injury related to construction, "sick building" syndrome, environmental claims, business interruption, employment disputes, patent infringement, contempt, RICO, unfair practices, breach of fiduciary duty, bad faith and professional malpractice. Mr. Saxe is well versed in issues relating to late notice, allocation, subrogation, contribution, indemnification and the duty to defend. Mr. Saxe has been an Adjunct Professor of Law at Quinnipiac University School of Law where he has taught courses in Insurance Law. He is also a frequent lecturer nationally on insurance coverage topics. Mr. Saxe received his J.D. from Georgetown University Law Center and B.S. in Policy Studies from Syracuse University. He is a member of the Connecticut, District of Columbia, New York, Pennsylvania, and Washington State Bar. He has successfully tried numerous jury and court trials in state and federal courts, has handled cases before the federal, state trial and appellate courts in Connecticut, New York, Pennsylvania, Virginia, Maryland, Massachusetts, California, Washington State, Texas, Florida, Delaware, Indiana and Michigan, and has successfully mediated and arbitrated many disputes.

Laurence Schor is a partner in the Washington, D.C. law firm of McManus Schor Asmar & Darden, LLP, where he concentrates his practice on all phases of construction and government contract law. He is the former managing partner of the Washington, D.C. office of Smith, Somerville & Case, LLC, and has served as the Assistant General Counsel for NASA Support in the office of the General Counsel, U.S. Army Corps of Engineers, and as an attorney at the Marshall Space Flight Center for NASA. He has authored articles, book chapters and course manuals on government contracts and construction topics and lectures regularly for professional groups on issues arising in these areas. He is an active Arbitrator and Mediator. Mr. Schor is admitted to practice in the District of Columbia Court of Appeals, the Maryland Court of Appeals, the Supreme Court of Texas, the United States Court of Federal Claims, the

United States District Court for the District of Columbia, the United States District Court for the District of Maryland, the United States Courts of Appeal for the Federal, the District of Columbia, and the Fourth and Eleventh Circuits. He holds a Bachelor's degree in Business Administration from Southern Methodist University, a J.D. from the University of Texas, Austin, School of Law, and a Master of Laws degree from George Washington University, with an emphasis in Government Procurement.

Bruce H. Schoumacher is a shareholder and co-chair of the Construction Law Group of Querrey & Harrow, Ltd. in Chicago. He received his B.S. degree from Northwestern University and MBA and JD degrees from the University of Chicago. He practices in the area of construction claims, litigation, arbitration, mediation and contracts. He is the author, co-author or contributing author of several books, including *Engineers and the Law, Construction Law, Successful Business Plans for Architects, Construction Law Handbook* (1st ed.), and *Construction Business Handbook*. He has written numerous articles on construction law and regularly speaks at construction law seminars. He is a Fellow of the American College of Construction Lawyers, an officer of the Society of Illinois Construction Attorneys, a member of the Special Committee on Construction Law of the Illinois State Bar Association, and an officer and director of the Chicago Building Congress.

John Spangler is Chair of Alston & Bird's Construction and Government Contracts Group and has over 25 years of experience handling construction-related transactions and disputes. He is past Chair of the Atlanta Bar Association's Construction Law Section and is a former member of the Governing Committee of the American Bar Association's Forum on the Construction Industry. Mr. Spangler received his J.D. in 1980 from Washington University School of Law in St. Louis, Missouri and his A.B. in economics in 1977 from the University of Illinois. He is named in *Chambers USA Guide to America's Leading Business Lawyers 2003–2007* as one of the country's leading construction attorneys, is one of Georgia's Top 100 Super Lawyers, and is named in *The Best Lawyers in America* and *Who's Who Legal—Georgia*.

April R. Walkup is a shareholder and chair of the Employment and Labor Group at Querrey & Harrow, Ltd. in Chicago. She earned her B.A. from Purdue University and her J.D. from The John Marshall Law School. She is a member of Chicago Bar Association, the Illinois State Bar Association, Defense Research Institute, for and contract drafting and interpretation. As chair of Querrey & Harrow's Employment Practice Group, she regularly works with contractors advising them on employee-related issues.

Barbara G. Werther is a partner in the Construction Group at Howrey LLP. She focuses on construction litigation. Prior to joining the firm, she was a partner at Thelen LLP and a senior partner with Arent Fox and also with a government contract and construction litigation boutique firm in the Washington area. For more than 30 years, Ms. Werther has represented contractors in disputes regarding substantial claims for delays, acceleration, inefficiencies, default terminations, and construction catastrophes, both locally and nationally. She has also represented both sureties and contractors in performance and payment bond disputes. In the past ten years, she has litigated or settled six large contractor claims against the General Services Administration. Ms. Werther has lectured extensively on the subjects of scheduling, delays, inefficiencies, changes and differing site conditions, terminations for default, and the impact of environmental statutes on contractors to various clients and trade associations. She was a speaker and panel moderator at the Annual Construction Superconference from 1991 to 2006 on such topics as "Construction Collapses," "Who Wants to be a Construction Millionaire?," "Default Terminations: The Weakest Link," and "Contractors are from Mars and Owners are from Venus." She was a speaker on Litigation Risk Assessments at the 2004 Annual TIPS conference, and a speaker on "How to Try a Construction Case to a Jury" at the ABA Construction Forum in 2006. She was an editor of the *Public Contract Law Journal* and is a member of the Public Contract and Litigation sections of the American Bar Association. She has co-authored a chapter on "Terminations" for the *Construction Law Handbook*. She is hosting the fourth Annual Women In Construction Conference in Washington, DC in 2009, featuring the most well-respected women in construction as panelists, and continues to host the conference annually. In addition, Ms. Werther has lectured on the topic of *Design Build Projects* to CREW and trains young attorneys for the National Institute for Trial Advocacy. Ms. Werther has also been recognized as one of the leading construction attorneys in the United States in the 2007 editions of the *Best Lawyers in America*, the *Chambers USA Guide to America's Leading Business Lawyers*, and *2006–2009 Washington DC Area's Best Lawyers*. She received her J.D. from The George Washington University and is admitted to practice in Virginia and the District of Columbia.

John D. Willet is a Partner with the law firm of Less, Getz and Lipman, PLC in Memphis, Tennessee, where his practice includes construction, surety, corporate, business litigation, and insurance. Mr. Willet has been a frequent lecturer and has written several articles on construction issues. Mr. Willet received his B.S. degree from the University of Southern Mississippi and his J.D. degree form the University of Memphis, where he was a member of the Law Review and a founding member and editor of the Tennessee Journal of Practice and Procedure. Mr. Willet is a member of the Memphis, Tennessee and American Bar Associations. Mr. Willet serves on the Steering Committee for Division Four of the American Bar Association Forum on the Construction Industry as well as the Forum's Technology Committee. Mr. Willet is a member of the Tennessee Association of Construction Counsel, and is the Chair of its Technology Committee. Mr. Willet is a member of the Associated Builders and Contractors of Tennessee and the

Associated General Contractors of Tennessee. Mr. Willet also serves on the Board of Directors of the Cooper-Young Development Commission.

Jason B. Yost is an attorney at Mercer Thompson LLC, an energy boutique law firm founded in June, 2009 and specializing in all aspects of project development and finance for electric utilities and independent power producers, including in the areas of renewable and clean power technology. Prior to joining Mercer Thompson, he was a partner in the Project Development and Finance Practice Group of the international law firm of Troutman Sanders LLP. He received his B.S. from the University of Florida, his J.D. from the Georgia State University College of Law (*cum laude*) and his M.B.A from the J. Mack Robinson College of Business at Georgia State University.

Craig Coulter is a senior consultant with Stantec's Climate Change Services practice. Mr. Coulter's expertise spans greenhouse gas management, including developing greenhouse gas inventories and disclosure reports; reducing emission baselines; verification of greenhouse gas inventories and carbon offsets; regulatory assessment, and providing strategic guidance in carbon markets and sustainability efforts. His industry experience includes the oil and gas sector, manufacturing, transportation, and retail. Mr. Coulter also regularly teaches GHG management and related ISO based training courses. Mr. Coulter joined Stantec in 2007 and has a B.A. from The Colorado College.

CHAPTER 3

INDUSTRY WORKFORCE SHORTAGES

Leslie O'Neal Coble

§ 3.01   IS THERE A LABOR SHORTAGE? IF SO, WHAT CAUSED IT?

Page 43, add to end of section:

Since August 2008, the forecast for construction labor has changed drastically. The combination of the credit freeze, recession, and collapse of the real estate market have caused the loss of nearly one million construction jobs in the last year. According to the U.S. Bureau of Labor Statistics ("BLA"), construction had the highest industry unemployment rate—17.4%—over 12 months. The overall unemployment rate was 9.7%.

BLA reported that construction job losses totaled 79,000 in June and 992,000 over 12 months. These losses cut across all sectors of the construction market—residential building, nonresidential specialty trades and heavy and civil engineering.

Despite the "stimulus" legislation passed earlier this year, it appears that the construction market may not begin recovery until 2010. Even then, it is unlikely that construction levels will reach those seen in 2000–2006 for quite some time, if ever.

These economic conditions make it unlikely that construction wages will increase. It is also unlikely that construction companies will invest in employee training, since there may be no jobs for the newly trained workers.

Unfortunately, these economic conditions will likely decrease the number of people choosing construction as a career. When the construction market rebounds in a few years, the shortage of skilled workers will pose a challenge for the construction industry.

CHAPTER 5

THE USE OF TECHNOLOGY FOR PROJECT COLLABORATION AND BUILDING INFORMATION MODELING

Howard W. Ashcraft & Kymberli Aguilar

Page 85, replace entire chapter with the following:

§ 5.01   New Technologies in Construction

§ 5.02   Building Information Modeling
    [A]   What is Building Information Modeling?
    [B]   How is BIM Used?
        [1]   Single Data Entry; Multiple Use
        [2]   Design Efficiency
        [3]   Consistent Design Bases
        [4]   3D Modeling and Conflict Resolution
        [5]   Conflict Identification and Resolution
        [6]   Take-offs and Estimating
        [7]   Shop and Fabrication Drawing
        [8]   Visualization of Alternative Solutions and Options
        [9]   Energy Optimization
        [10]   Constructability Reviews and 4D Simulations
        [11]   Reduced Fabrication Costs and Errors
        [12]   Facilities Management
            [a]   Functional Simulations
        [13]   Code Compliance Checking
        [14]   BIMstorm™—Worldwide Real-Time Collaboration

§ 5.03   Issues in BIM Implementation
    [A]   Technical Issues—BIM Guidelines and Standards
        [1]   NBIMS, Version 1.0
        [2]   Owner Mandated Standards
        [3]   Interoperability
    [B]   Commercial Issues
        [1]   Absence of Standard BIM Contract Documents
        [2]   Contractor's Guide to BIM

            [3]   ConsensusDocs BIM Addendum
      [C] Legal Issues
            [1]   Standard of Care
            [2]   Design Delegation and Professional
                   Responsibility
            [3]   Intellectual Property
            [4]   Insurability
            [5]   Data Translation
            [6]   Data Adequacy
            [7]   Privity, Third Party Reliance, and the Economic
                   Loss Doctrine
            [8]   *Spearin* Implied Warranties

§ 5.04   Use of Building Information Modeling for Your Project?
      [A] How Will the Model(s) be Used?
      [B] Who Will Own and/or License the Model(s)?
            [1]   Owner Owns Modeling Information
            [2]   Designer Owns Modeling Information
            [3]   All Parties Own Whatever They Create
            [4]   What Is the Model's Contractual Status?
            [5]   How Will Modeling Requirements Be Specified?
            [6]   How Will the Model Be Administered?

§ 5.05   BIM as a Collaborative Framework—Integrated Project
       Delivery
      [A] The Need for Integrated Project Delivery
      [B] The Development of Integrated Project Delivery
      [C] Five Major Structural Elements of Integrated Project
           Delivery
            [1]   Early Involvement of Key Participants
            [2]   Shared Risk/Reward Based on Project Outcome
            [3]   Joint Project Control
            [4]   Reduced Liability Exposure
            [5]   Jointly Developed/Validated Targets
            [6]   Subcontractors, Consultants, and Joining
                   Agreements
      [D] Four Minor Elements of Integrated Project Delivery
      [E] Brief Comparison of Integrated Project Delivery
           Agreements
      [F] The Implications of Integrated Project Delivery

§ 5.06   Conclusion

§ 5.01   NEW TECHNOLOGIES IN CONSTRUCTION

Firms and organizations in the construction industry are addressing issues such as efficiency, productivity and quality in the built environment by using new technologies and rethinking traditional project delivery frameworks. Currently, the use of Building Information Modeling ("BIM") and the maturation of project websites are enabling efficient information exchange and aligning the construction industry with the expectations of a leaner, greener and more sustainable society.

In the recent years, there has been a marked increase in the use of BIM within the construction community. BIM has been widely adopted by designers, contractors, specialty contractors and fabricators and many public[1] and private owners[2] are requiring BIM. Studies by Stanford University's Center for Integrated Facility Engineering report that BIM use has risen significantly and that the BIM use would continue to increase in the near future.[3] Between 2006 and 2007, the number of licensed seats of Autodesk's flagship BIM product, Revit, doubled from 100,000 to 200,000.[4] Recent 2009 statistics support such growth in the use of BIM. The 2009 McGraw Hill study reports that half of the construction industry is using BIM or BIM-related tools, which is up 75% from 2007.[5] The majority of BIM users, owners, contractors and architects alike, see the value in BIM and recognize that the full potential of its benefits has yet to be realized.[6] In support of this explosive growth, standards are now emerging for BIM[7] and related issues, such as

---

[1] For example, the General Services Administration, the United States Army Corps of Engineers, and the United States Coast Guard all have BIM requirements.

[2] During the last six months, the author has been involved in developing project documents for six hospitals and several major tenant improvement projects. All of these projects are being implemented in BIM.

[3] Gilligan and Kunz, *VDC Use in 2007: Significant Value, Dramatic Growth, and Apparent Business Opportunity*, Center for Integrated Facility Engineering, Report TR171 (2007).

[4] Autodesk press releases in 2006 and 2007 reported 100,000 Revit seats sold through June 8, 2006 and over 200,000 seats sold through May 4, 2007.

[5] The Business Value of BIM, McGraw Hill SmartMarket Report (2009) p. 5. Additionally, the report indicates that 42% of the users are at an expert or advance level (three times the amount reported in 2007); half of contractors report using BIM or BIM-related tools (four times more than the level reported in 2007).

[6] The Business Value of BIM, McGraw Hill SmartMarket Report (2009) p. 9. Interestingly, engineers see the least value in BIM, with 12% seeing no meaningful value and three in five engineers reporting that they are just scratching the surface when it comes to considering the value of BIM. This likely reflects the struggle engineers have finding sufficient BIM content or software that works for their purposes.

[7] Most notably, the National Building Information Science's National Building Information Modeling Standard V. 1.0, http://www.facilityinformationcouncil.org/bim/publications.php.

electronic data licensing and file transfer.[8] BIM is not tomorrow's vision; it is today's reality.

While the acceptance and usage of BIM within the building community has certainly increased, industry-wide challenges remain. The two most significant challenges are: (1) implementation of BIM on a technical level; and (2) legal concerns (including, but not limited to appropriate commercial models, risk allocation and the ownership of modeling information).

Project websites and BIM work naturally together. Project websites support collaboration at a process level. They regularize and document project communications and serve as a joint resource and archive. Properly maintained project websites allow the project participants access to the most updated information, including changes to the federated set of models that comprise the totality of digital information about the facility. As the project progresses, the website will also house all schedules, change orders, back-up documentation and requests for information from the individual parties. With project information available in a one paperless location, the parties are certain to reduce inefficiencies have consistently plagued the construction industry. BIM extends this collaboration by providing a framework for concept interaction. This leads to a common basis of understanding with regard to what is being created and how realizing the vision will be accomplished.

Building Information Modeling does not require a collaborative project delivery process, but when used with Integrated Project Delivery it capitalizes on the power of Building Information Modeling as a collaborative framework as well as the cost and quality advantages of single entry, multiple use. Integrated Project Delivery incorporates certain common features of early involvement of key contributors, open communication, team decision making, and a sharing of risk and reward based on project success, an environment that was made for the collaboration and sharing of data.

On the whole, new technologies in the construction industry are exciting and are providing substantial opportunities for the future. For example, as the use of BIM and other technologies have become more refined, the opportunity to evaluate building performance and receive immediate feedback on design alternatives early in the design process has increased. Accordingly, BIM is being used for a variety of sustainable

---

[8] *See, e.g.,* American Institute of Architects standard documents C-106, *Digital Data Licensing*, E-201 *Digital Data Protocol*, and the Associated General Contractor's Document 200.2, *Electronic Communications Protocol Addendum.*

design activities, including but not limited to, design optimization, visualization, day-lighting, and energy analysis.[9]

§ 5.02 BUILDING INFORMATION MODELING

[A] What is Building Information Modeling?

The National Institute of Building Science ("NIBS")[10] defines Building Information Modeling as follows:

> *A Building Information Model, or BIM, utilizes cutting edge digital technology to establish a computable representation of all the physical and functional characteristics of a facility and its related project/life-cycle information, and is intended to be a repository of information for the facility owner/operator to use and maintain throughout the life-cycle of a facility.*[11]

Although the definition references a singular Building Information Model, in current practice, the design is built from a set of interrelated models that can exchange information between their differing software platforms. It is this federated set of models that comprise the totality of digital information about the facility and, for the purpose of this definition, are the Building Information Model.

The definition is also interesting for what it omits. The definition does not mention three dimensional modeling although this is one of the most visible and immediately understood aspects of BIM. This omission is explained in the phrase ". . . a computable representation of all the physical . . . characteristics of a facility . . . ." The computable representation is a simulation of all physical characteristic such that three dimensional views become just one logical manifestation of the model. In BIM, three dimensional design is an inherent feature, not an enhancement. Moreover, because it is "computable", the information in the BIM can be extracted, manipulated, and analyzed digitally. This greatly increases the utility of the BIM information.

The descriptor ". . . all the physical and functional characteristics. . . . expands BIM beyond earlier three dimensional design tools. In BIM, the building is not just a three dimensional picture. Instead, it is a

---

[9] For additional information regarding the role BIM can play in sustainable design, see *Building Information Modeling for Sustainable Design—Autodesk, Revit, White Paper*; and Using BIM for Greener Designs—Revit Building Information Modeling and Erin Rae Hoffer, *Sustainable Design Made Easy with BIM*, [acronym] 2007, pp. 5.and Salman Azhar, PhD, BIM for Sustainable Design: Results of an Industry Survey, JBIM, Spring 2010, pp. 27–28.

[10] National Institute of Building Science is responsible for the National Building Information Modeling Standard (NBIMS).

[11] www.nibs.org/newsstory1.html.

digital simulation of the facility that can be viewed, tested, designed, constructed and deconstructed digitally. This promotes iterative design optimization and the ability to "rehearse" construction before ever moving labor, material, and equipment into the field.

The information maintained in a BIM also differs from the level and type of information maintained by traditional design tools. The difference between BIM and traditional design approaches is most striking when changes are made to the design. For example, in a traditional CAD package, the designer draws lines to illustrate the location of walls, windows, doors, or similar structures. In effect, the computer is an efficient pencil. In a BIM design, however, the designer selects a pre-programmed wall object embedded with information about all of its relevant characteristics, not just its shape. If a window is needed, a window component is dropped onto a wall component that knows how to integrate the window into the wall and which can communicate with other components that may need to change (perhaps because of thermal differences) to accommodate the new window. Design by arranging components is sometimes referred to as designing with Legos because the design is built from a toolbox of existing elements.[12]

Because the BIM is a "computable representation" every manifestation of the BIM is automatically current. For example, sections or elevations are just different manifestations of the BIM information. If you make a change in plan view (and, therefore to the underlying BIM data), the elevation and section views that are built from the same BIM data will automatically reflect the changes. Without any further intervention, schedules, tables and other related data reflect the updated information. This also increases design efficiency and makes it virtually impossible for drawings to be internally inconsistent.

In addition, the BIM contains data concerning the object attributes that can be extracted to as schedules, tables, bills of materials or other data that can be printed, evaluated, or sent to other programs for analysis. Because the information is based on the central model, and reflects the current design, the potential for error is reduced.

The definition continues by including, as information in the BIM, ". . . and its related life-cycle information. . . ." This indicates that the BIM contains the functional information necessary to evaluating the operational facility and optimizing its performance for efficiency, sustainability or other criteria.

Finally, the definition states that the BIM is to be a "repository" of data for facility management. The BIM is meant to be a living document that owners can use to manage their facilities as well as build them. BIM's potential for facility management is perhaps its most important role, but it is a role that is just beginning to be explored.

---

[12] BIM systems also allow the designers to customize existing elements, or create new elements, that can then be incorporated into the design.

[B]   How is BIM Used?

[1]   Single Data Entry; Multiple Use

Traditional construction practices require the same information to be used multiple times by multiple organizations. Identical information is entered into different programs that provide specific solutions, such as structural analysis, code compliance, material quantities or cost estimates. Every repetition is an opportunity for inconsistency and error. Moreover, even if information is digitally translated from one program to another, translation can alter or corrupt the data. And versioning can be a nightmare, even with compatible programs. Drawing backgrounds are a recurring example of this problem. The architect's consultants need to upload and maintain the basic design backgrounds they receive from the architect. These backgrounds, however, will change as the design develops and each party must take considerable care to ensure that they are working with the latest versions of the basic documents. The contractors and vendors must take the information provided by the designers, often in paper form, and enter it into their systems. As the design develops, changes in one party's documents must be transferred back to the others. Errors begin to creep into the documents because updates are incompletely or incorrectly entered, and work can be wasted because parties are working from outdated information, Figure 1, below, shows an example of structural design information in the Revit structural design model and in ETABS, a structural analysis program.

By consolidating information into a unified data source, the likelihood of data entry, translation, or versioning errors is greatly decreased.

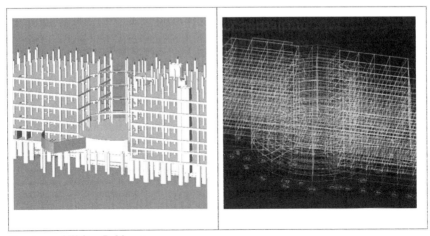

Courtesy of Walter P. Moore.

FIGURE 1: STRUCTURE DESIGN IN REVIT AND ETABS

[2] Design Efficiency

Although the greatest efficiencies are obtained when BIM is used collaboratively (with a collaborative or integrated project delivery), BIM design can aid a traditional design process. BIM software can reduce the cost of preparing 2D drawings in a conventional project, especially when designs are changing rapidly.[13] For example, in Revit®, any change in plan view automatically updates any section affected by the change. In another modeling system, Tekla Structures, changes in dimension or geometry automatically update details and related features. Moreover, using data rich elements instead of drawn objects, accelerates creation of contract drawings.

[3] Consistent Design Bases

BIM modeling ensures that all parties working from the model share the same base. Under current practice, not all participants may be operating directly from the model. However, if the participants are using software that is compatible with the model, the base information can be moved, imported, or exported from the model. Moreover, periodic imports into 3D visualization software, such as Autodesk's NavisWorks Manage quickly exposes inconsistencies.

[4] 3D Modeling and Conflict Resolution

The BIM model can render the design in three dimensions and does not require separate software to explore the model visually. This allows better exploration of space, visualization of light studies, and improved communication and understanding of design concepts within the team and with project stakeholders.

[5] Conflict Identification and Resolution

On complex projects, conflict identification and resolution is an extraordinarily expensive and difficult task. In many instances, designers do not have the time or budget to fully explore and resolve conflict issues. In other instances, full coordination cannot be accomplished during the design phase because the contractor will later design key systems, such as HVAC or life safety equipment that is not reflected in the design drawings. Even in a complete design-bid-build project, construction details and layouts may require information regarding the actual equipment that will be installed.

---

[13] In discussion with the author, design firms with significant BIM experience have reported 50% reduction in time to produce drawings as compared to conventional 2D CAD drawing.

This information deficit is typically addressed by warning the contractor that the design is "diagrammatic" and that coordination will be required. Traditionally, the contractor coordinates physical drawings of different systems by overlaying them on light tables to determine if the various systems can actually be constructed in the allowed space. Alternatively, drawings for each discipline are merged and printed as color-coded composite drawings. Conflicts that are identified are brought to the designer's attention through the request for information process, where solutions can be developed and clarifications issued. But light table resolution is inherently a two dimensional process applied to a three dimensional problem. It is notoriously difficult and fraught with error. For these reasons, conflicts are a primary source of contractor claims.

Building Information Modeling greatly reduces conflict issues by integrating all the key systems into the model. Design BIM systems can detect internal conflicts and model viewing systems, such as Navis-Works®, can detect and highlight conflicts between the models and other information imported into the viewer. See Figure 2 for a example of clash detection within the BIM system. The solution can then be checked to ensure that it resolves the problem and to determine if it creates other, unintended, consequences.[14] In a complex project, the savings derived from coordination can completely offset the model's cost.

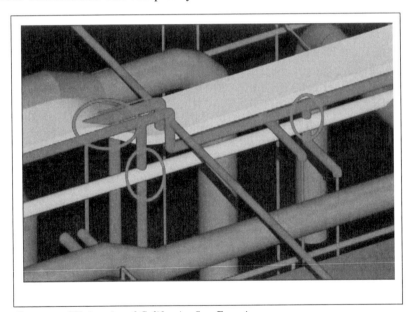

Courtesy of University of California, San Francisco.

**FIGURE 2: CLASH DETECTION IN NAVISWORKS
MANAGE**

---

[14] NavisWorks® was used to model LucasFilm's Digital Arts Center and identified several significant conflicts before construction commenced and was used to check field construction, again identifying mislocated elements and penetrations.

[6]   Take-offs and Estimating

The model contains information, or can link to information, necessary to generate bills of materials, size and area estimates, productivity, materials cost, and related estimating information. It avoids the processing material take-offs manually thus reducing error and misunderstanding. Moreover, the linked cost information evolves in step with the design changes. The estimating advantages are so significant that some contractors create models on 2D designed projects just to use the model's estimating capabilities.

[7]   Shop and Fabrication Drawing

In some instances, the models can provide construction details and fabrication information. This reduces costs by reducing the detailing effort and increases fabrication accuracy. In addition, because conflicts are resolved through the model, there is greater confidence that prefabricated material will fit when delivered. This allows more construction work to be performed offsite in optimal factory conditions. Subcontractors in the steel and MEP trades, regularly use models to fabricate their products.

[8]   Visualization of Alternative Solutions and Options

Because it is inherently a 3D process, models are excellent methods for evaluating alternative approaches. Moreover, the ability to evaluate how changes affect key attributes, such as energy use, enhances the model's usefulness as a thinking tool. However, the software interface can interfere with the creative process. In a study of one system, users noted that it was not "sketchy," and therefore impeded the initial creative process.[15] This may lead to using freeform design tools initially with the results being loaded into the BIM system for refinement.[16]

[9]   Energy Optimization

Building Information Modeling systems, such as Autodesk's® Revit®, can provide information for energy analysis. They can be used to evaluate lighting design and options, are in conjunction with their material take-off capabilities, and can generate documentation necessary for LEED™ certification.[17] By linking a BIM with tools like Autodesk® Green Building Studio® or Integrated Environmental Solutions®' Virtual

---

[15] L. Khemlani, *Autodesk Revit: Implementation in Practice*, Arcwiz (2004).

[16] Supporting graphic creativity is already being addressed by the primary software houses. For example, Autodesk's Architectural Desktop® and Google's Sketch Up®.

[17] Building Information Modeling for Sustainable Design, Autodesk® 2005.

Environment[18] which is a web-based energy analysis service, architects and designers can perform whole building analysis, optimize energy efficiency, and work toward carbon neutrality earlier in the design process. For example, designers can predict factors such as the amount of light that can be brought into a particular space for alternative skylight configurations, VOC content, reflectivity, the seasonal impact on energy use and the design variation impact on the need for cooling and artificial lighting throughout the day and throughout the year.[19,20] Public and private owners and designers are more cognizant than ever about the need for, and benefits of, sustainable design and creating buildings that minimize negative impacts. This is highlighted by the increase in number of people attending the USGBC's Greenbuild convention, the number of people pursuing LEED™ accreditation, and the number of projects being registered for LEED™ certification.[21]

[10]   Constructability Reviews and 4D Simulations

Using the model, the contractor can visualize the entire structure, gaining a greater understanding of the challenges involved in its construction. By integrating 4D capabilities, the contractor can also simulate the construction process, which significantly increases the contractor's ability to evaluate and optimize the construction sequence. The interaction between scheduling software and the model can also be used to evaluate the effect of construction delays and errors.

[11]   Reduced Fabrication Costs and Errors

The ability to use information in the model to directly create fabrication drawings avoids a problematic and difficult step in the construction process. In a traditional work flow, the fabricators must

---

[18] Additional examples of building performance software available are: Autodesk® Ecotect™, Hevacomp™, Energy Plus™, Delight™, Radiance™, HEED™, Homer™, Virtual DOE™, Bently HEVACOMP™, and Climate Consultant™.

[19] Erin Rae Hoffer, *Sustainable Design Made Easy With BIM*, [acronym], at 5.

[20] For example, simulations for the GSA's Herbert C. Hoover Building in Washington D.C., helped redesign an infill structure within the building's courtyard. The solution included the effects of a green roof and skylight, showing where daylight and cooling or heating needs would change. For the nearby White House Visitor Center and Law Library, BIM modeling allowed the project team to keep ceiling as high as possible, introduce maximum daylight and integrate new supply-air distribution, all enhancing the indoor environmental quality. The model also helped to determine the needed life-safety egress and to reduce the project's impact on historic facilities.

[21] Erin Rae Hoffer, *Sustainable Design Made Easy With BIM*, [acronym], at 6 (a design professional article states, "The new vision on the part of the building owners is that operating costs are long term. [ ] The awareness that we have a mandate to be responsible to employees is more visible.").

review the plans and specifications, prepare fabrication drawings, compare them to other fabrication and design drawings, have them reviewed by the design team, and eventually release the drawings for fabrication. Errors can occur at any stage. By using the data in the model, dimensional errors, conflicts, and integration errors can be avoided or significantly reduced. In addition, the model can be updated with as-built information allowing accurate fabrication of custom components, such as building facades.

[12] Facilities Management

If the model is properly maintained during construction, it becomes a tool that can be used by the owner to manage and operate the structure or facility. Modifications and upgrades can be evaluated for cost effectiveness. Data contained in the model can be used for managing remodeling, additions and maintenance. For example, BIM space components can be supplemented to track information such as room numbers, area calculations, and occupant censuses. Equipment objects can record information such as a manufacturer, warranty information, room location, equipment specifications, reference URLs, just to name a few.

Extending the benefits of BIM downstream to improve management and operations phases of a facility's lifecycle is crucial to today's building environment. Unlike the design and construction phases, the information needs of facility managers continues for the lifecycle of the facility.[22] Although it has not yet become commonplace to use BIM information downstream by facility managers, the importance of BIM's potential cost savings in the area of facility management cannot be ignored.[23]

Public and private owners are starting to issue standards and guidelines that mandate delivery of digital handover data. To be the most useful, however, the BIM data must be channeled into a variety of facility software management systems.[24] Although there are several versions of facility management software emerging that can leverage BIM data, an

---

[22] The Spring 2010 Journal of Building Information Modeling indicates that 85% of the lifecycle cost of a facility occurs after construction is completed. David A. Jordani, *BIM and FM: The Portal to Lifecycle Facility Management*, JBIM, Spring 2010, p. 13.

[23] In fact, the NIST Interoperability Study indicated that two-thirds of the $15.8 billion lost are due to inadequate interoperability that occurs during the operation and maintenance phases. David A. Jordani, *BIM and FM: The Portal to Lifecycle Facility Management*, JBIM, Spring 2010, p. 13.

[24] The following systems are regularly used in facility management: Computerized Maintenance Management Systems (CMMS), Computer Aided Facility Management (CAFM), Integrated Workplace Management Systems (IWMS), Building Control Systems, and Enterprise Resource Planning Systems (ERP) for asset management and accounting.

increasing number of vendors are working to support CObie[25] format. CObie has been described as, "an open standard for capture and delivery of digital data as it is created during design, construction, and commissioning for use in operations."[26] It provides a vehicle for commercial BIM authoring software to provide data used by the variety of facility management downstream software systems. Although BIM for facilities management is still in its infancy, capturing and efficiently using digital information about a facility, its assets and systems is valuable to all parties involved in a project; contractors and designers can extend their services by responding to the need and owners can receive a return on their BIM investment for the life of the facility.

[a] Functional Simulations

The 3D and conflict checking mechanisms can be used to simulate and evaluate emergency response and evacuation. For example, Navis-Works® was used at the Letterman Digital Arts Center to assure that fire response vehicles could navigate the parking structures.

[13] Code Compliance Checking

BIM and integrated design review can greatly streamline the code review process. Finland and Singapore have developed design review software and in the United States, the International Code Council ("ICC") is working to automated code compliance and simplify code compliance checking against the ICC International Codes (I-Codes) and federal, state, and locally adopted versions of the I-Codes (SMARTcodes).[27] In addition to expediting code review and permitting, SMARTcodes will allow designers and others to secure information on their building regulatory questions from the software without having to contact building regulators. Moreover, code officials may print the results or view the building design in 3D, with non-complaint elements highlighted and accompanying explanations of the violation.

Such code compliance technology capitalizes on the concept of interoperability, the transparent flow of data and other information between users. Using model checking software, designers will be able to check a building design for compliance anytime during the course of design by running SMARTcodes against the BIM. The ability to regularly

---

[25] For further information regarding the uses of CObie, see the Whole Building Design Guide at www.wdbg.org/resources/cobie.php.

[26] David A. Jordani, *BIM and FM: The Portal to Lifecycle Facility Management*, JBIM, Spring 2010, p. 15.

[27] For more information visit www.smartcodes.org. Additionally, ICC is currently allowing the public to view a SMARTcodes demonstration at http://www2.iccsafe.org/io/smartcodes/demo.cfm.

run and access code compliance information will create efficiency through elimination of costly project delays and potential re-bidding. Additionally, by automating and sharing data, regulatory authorities/building departments can reduce the time they take to review plans and increase code compliance, allowing staff resources to be shifted to the field perform enhanced building inspections. Most importantly, the use of code compliance technology will likely lead to a significantly higher probability plans and specifications being readily accepted and approved when submitted to regulatory authorities for approval.

[14] BIMstorm™—Worldwide Real-Time Collaboration

In the past few years, BIM technology has been used in very innovative and exciting ways—to create what has been termed a BIMStorm™. BIMStorm™ revolutionized real-time BIM collaboration on the Internet and have mobilized people from around the world. In January 2008, a cross-section of building industry professionals used the Internet to meet virtually in Los Angeles for BIMStorm™ LAX, where they designed—in real time—over 60 Los Angeles city blocks encompassing over 50 million square feet in just 24 hours.[28] The event demonstrated how new technology processes and collaboration can improve design. Numerous users were able to access data and work on multiple projects in real-time, making massive scale collaboration possible. The projects were shared and visible to all participants via open standards based exchanges and a model server, which allowed the participants to change how normal transactions would happen and minimize coordination driven communication.[29] Users logged in through the Internet to view and interact with data. The data then became authoritative source data. Both teams and individuals would design portions of 420 projects. As design teams on the West Cost closed for the night, engineer and design teams from Hawaii, Asia, and Europe would pick up the projects in real time and would go from there. Building code checking using International Code Council happened simultaneously. Although projects progressed with varying levels of detail, they were all in ICF format.[30] Since the first BIMStorm™ LAX, there have been numerous BIMStorm organized to demonstrate new design processes. Some of these were virtual and others happened at a conference, like BIMStorm™ AEC EcoBuild in Washington, D.C., in

---

[28] Kimon Onuma, FAIA, *Integration Today Using Open Standards: BIMstorm™, Rotterdam to Los Angeles and Beyond*, JBIM, Spring 2008, p. 16.

[29] Kimon Onuma, FAIA, *Integration Today Using Open Standards: BIMstorm™, Rotterdam to Los Angeles and Beyond*, JBIM, Spring 2008, p. 17.

[30] Kimon Onuma, FAIA, *Integration Today Using Open Standards: BIMstorm™, Rotterdam to Los Angeles and Beyond*, JBIM, Spring 2008, p. 16–17.

December 2008.[31] The next BIMStorm™ that is currently being planned is BIMStorm™ Haiti.[32] The possibility for changing the culture of architecture and design throughout the world using the BIMStorm™ collaborative process is enormous and very real.

§ 5.03   ISSUES IN BIM IMPLEMENTATION

Despite BIM's many advantages, its adoption continues to face significant implementation barriers.

[A]   Technical Issues—BIM Guidelines and Standards

Several associations have published literature in an effort to bring the industry together and to memorialize a standard and/or clear guidelines describing information related to BIM.

[1]   NBIMS, Version 1.0

Exchanging information accurately and efficiently between different project participants is essential to the project's success. Unambiguous, machine-interpretable exchanges of BIM information offer amazing benefits to the building industry, but they require several types of broadly adopted standards to really be effective. In December 2007, the National Building Information Modeling Standard[33] (NBIMS) Version 1—Part 1: *Overview, Principles, and Methodologies*, was published as an attempt to begin to memorialize shared data, rules, definitions, metadata, and model views to support a well understood and uniform framework for BIM deployment. The NBIMS Prologue states that a goal of NIBS is to, "[d]evelop an open and shared National Building Information Model Standard that will reduce the overhead and risk to stakeholders requiring BIM implementation to improve mission and business execution."[34]

---

[31] Statistics from BIMStorms in 2008: 14 BIMStorms, 3,000 participants, 14 countries, 2,458 sites, 3,964 buildings, 493,914 rooms and 45,140,077 square meters of space. http://www.bimstorm.com.

[32] http://sites.google.com/site/planhaiti/.

[33] NIBS is now run through buildingSMART alliance. In 2007, the Board of Directors of the National Institute of Building Sciences (NIBS) established the "buildingSMART alliance" The buildingSMART alliance is a council of NIBS and builds on former NIBS programs such as the former North American Chapter of the International Alliance for Interoperability—IAI-NA which is now buildingSMART International.

[34] National Building Information Modeling Standard V. 1.0, Part 1: Overview, Principles, and Methodologies, p. 27.

[2]   Owner Mandated Standards

As the use of BIM has increased throughout the industry, owners have begun to develop their own BIM standards and guidelines that must be implemented during the project. As of Spring 2010, at least the following entities have established their individual BIM standards: The U.S. General Services Administration (GSA); the U.S. Army Corps of Engineers (UACE); United States Coast Guard; Department of Veterans Affairs; Division of State Facilities, Department of Administration for the State of Wisconsin; Texas Facilities Commission for the State of Texas; Indiana University; Triton College, Los Angeles County Community College District; and San Diego Community College District.

Although each of the standards and guidelines vary to a certain degree, each usually contain high-level categories related to:

• An Introduction (including objectives)

• BIM Roles and Responsibilities

• BIM Project Requirements

• Modeling Requirements

• BIM Application and Analysis Requirements

• BIM Process and Implementation

• Glossary/Abbreviations/Resources

These published guidelines have answered a need to define the process and establish requirements, procedures and protocols for the utilization of BIM in various stages of projects. They develop an open and shared standard for BIM, define BIM modeling and analysis requirements, facilitate a collaborative environment between all parties, use BIM as an information and communication tool, assist to execute coordinated project documents through parametric modeling and enable the long term viability and usage of the BIM database through facilities management software.

In April 2010, the Department of Veterans Affairs published The VA BIM Guide v. 1.0. The Guide lays out its "building information lifecycle vision" including the goal of converting to the use of BIM and the IPD methodologies to deliver higher value and maximizing the lifecycle building performance. To accomplish this, the VA has mandated that Industry Foundation Classes-compliant BIM authoring tools be used for all major construction and renovation projects beginning in 2009. The Guide discusses the implementation of BIM, beginning with the type of project delivery (design-bid-build, design build or integrated design process). It addresses the use of open standards and BIM management plans (design and construction) outlining the design/construction strategy and for using BIM technology. BIM Responsibilities include BIM managers from all major design/technical disciplines/trades and construction the side. The Guide provides for model sharing and specifics BIM requirements mandated by the parties (including the minimum requirements for special coordination and clash detection). Finally, it discusses the approved software for VA projects, modeling requirements and drawing requirements for paper printing. The VA BIM Guide is very recent and thorough example of an entity's commitment to both embrace and standardize enhanced construction processes and technology.

[3]   Interoperability

Interoperability is a significant technical obstacle. Current practice uses a variety of software tools and building information modeling packages to achieve the total design, analysis, detailing and fabrication needs of a project. Although much of the information is can be freely exchanged, there are limitations, especially when information must be iteratively imported and exported between applications ("round tripping"). These are discussed in more detail later in this chapter. In addition, the utility of modeled information may depend greatly on the foresight of the initial planners. For example, if design information is to be directly used for cost analysis or fabrication, it must be organized as the contractor or fabricator would use the information, even if this differs from the standards traditionally used for design documents.

[B]   Commercial Issues

[1]   Absence of Standard BIM Contract Documents

Although some BIM standards have emerged, lack of standard contract documents continues to hinder development of BIM. Standard contract documents perform four key functions. First, they validate a business model by providing a recommended framework for practice. As noted above, a consensus business model for BIM is progressing but is not complete and/or widely adopted. Second, standard documents establish a consensus allocation of risks and an integrated relationship between the risks assumed, compensation, dispute resolution, and insurance. Custom agreements, unless crafted by seasoned practitioners, are often unbalanced and overlook key issues. Third, standard documents reduce the effort involved in documenting the roles and responsibilities on a project. Designers want to design structures, not structure contracts. Finally, crafting custom documents increases the transaction costs, and thus reduces the profitability of every transaction. Unfortunately, the traditional standard contract documents provide little guidance to the BIM practitioner.

For example, regarding electronic information transfer, the AIA contract language consists of the following:

> 1.3.2.4 Prior to the Architect providing to the Owner any Instruments of Service in electronic form or the Owner providing to the Architect any electronic data for incorporation into the Instruments of Service, the Owner and the Architect shall by separate written agreement set forth the specific conditions governing the format of such Instruments of Service or electronic data, including any special limitations or licenses not otherwise provided in this Agreement.[35]

In 2007, the AIA introduced the "separate written agreements" envisioned by the 1997 documents, the Digital Data Licensing Agreement[36] and the Digital Data Protocol Exhibit.[37] These are a radical departure from the traditional "closeted" approach to design information and allow information to be freely used for appropriate purposes.[38] As such, these documents are helpful additions to the existing document sets, but they do not attempt to address BIM's implications. And AIA Document A201-1997, *General Conditions of the Contract for Construction*, does not discuss electronic documents, except to state that electronic documents provided by the architect are "instruments of service."[39]

[2] Contractor's Guide to BIM

The Associated General Contractors of America have also published the second edition of "Contractor's Guide to BIM". It is a reference that was prepared by contractors to provide guidance regarding not only the terminology surrounding BIM, but also to provide them with a better understanding of what it means to use BIM on a project (including clarification of responsibilities and risk allocation) and ultimately, the benefits that BIM can provide. The guide acknowledges that BIM is a tool that enables the construction industry to more efficiently operate in new and expeditious ways and generally introduce the subject of BIM with industry wide concepts. It can is also seen as a "how-to" outline for getting started.

---

[35] AIA Document B141-1997, § 1.3.2.4.

[36] AIA Document C106-2007.

[37] AIA Document E201-1997.

[38] In contrast, the documents published by the Engineers Joint Contract Documents Committee (EJCDC) take a very conservative approach toward electronic information. They disallow any reliance on the electronic information and place the risk of errors and discrepancies on the receiving party. This approach may be appropriate to the transfer of CAD files, but is totally inconsistent with a collaborative (BIM) approach. *See* EJCDC C-700, § 3.06.

[39] AIA Document A201-1997, § 1.6.1.

[3]   ConsensusDocs BIM Addendum

At the time of this writing, ConsensusDocs has circulated draft copies of a contract addendum to address BIM use. It attempts to provide both a framework and a process for using BIM, and should be available, when issued, at www.consensusdocs.org.

[C]   Legal Issues

Although the distance is narrowing, there still remains a gap between BIM as an emerging technology and the legal and commercial structures that support—and sometimes undermine—its use. The following are a brief summary of several of the current legal issues affecting BIM.

[1]   Standard of Care

BIM can affect the standard of care in several ways. At the most basic level, is it below the standard of care *not* to use BIM if using BIM can readily solve design issues that resist solution when attacked with traditional tools? Clash detection of complex structures is an obvious example.

Historically, designs were developed to a nearly complete level with details omitted to be completed by the contractor from the final, but "diagrammatic" design. In part, this practice was justified because the designer did not know which specific systems would be chosen by the contractor. In other cases, the final layouts were deemed part of the contractor's means and methods and, therefore, not the designer's concern. Because the design was not complete when issued, coordination was often overlooked. More often than one would like, this resulted in designs that could not be coordinated by the contractor or, if it could eventually be coordinated, had a layout that was inefficient and expensive. Many delay and impact claims are born from this coordination problem.

These coordination problems can almost be eliminated if BIM is used. BIM allows the designer, the contractor and the subcontractors to dimensionally check their respective work and assure that physical conflicts do not occur. Clash reports can be automatically run in the BIM software, or multiple models can be imported into a common viewer, such as Autodesk/NavisWorks JetStream.[40] Physical conflict issues can be eliminated during the design phase and confirmed with electronic

---

[40] In theory, clash detection can be done using light table overlays. However, they rarely identify all potential clashes. The author has recently learned of a hospital design with fully coordinated 2D drawings that when converted into a BIM model were found to contain over 100 significant clashes. Not surprisingly, sophisticated owners of complex facilities are routinely requiring full clash detection in BIM.

submittals. Given the expense and disruption caused by clashes discovered during construction, and the ease with which this problem is solved, does the standard of care *require* that the designer use tools that eliminate this costly problem? In the author's opinion, traditionally coordinated 2D drawings are no longer sufficient for complex structures, particularly those with significant mechanical, electrical and plumbing systems.[41]

Building Information Modeling also permits rapid comparison of alternatives with iterative improvements in cost, energy utilization and sustainability. Moreover, sustainability goals require the use of BIM and collaborative project methodologies. Where sustainability is a goal—and it is in many projects today—can traditional approaches be justified?

There are also standard of care issues arising from *how* BIM is implemented. Although it is convenient to discuss *the* model used for a project, in practice, project design is an amalgamation of interlocking models created by different project participants. These federated models must be able to exchange information accurately—which requires forethought and discussion between participants. In addition, the designer needs to determine the model's granularity, i.e., the detail to which information is depicted as this affects the interface between the designer's and the implementer's responsibilities. Similarly, the designer needs to determine what information will reside in the model and what information will reside in specifications or 2D CAD drawings.

[2] Design Delegation and Professional Responsibility

Our tri-partite division between design, construction and ownership places the architect and engineer as master of the design with responsibility to safeguard the public against unsafe structures. To achieve this public policy, the appropriate design professional must sign and seal the construction documents to signify responsibility for the design. Moreover, the statutes and regulations require the designer to be "in responsible charge." California Business and Professions code sections 6703 and 5535.1 are typical examples of this statutory requirement.

> *The phrase "responsible charge of work" means the independent control and direction, by the use of initiative, skill, and independent judgment, of the investigation or design of professional engineering work or the direct engineering control of such projects.*
> *The phrase does not refer to the concept of financial liability.*[42]

---

[41] The author represented the owner of a university laboratory where a partially diagrammatic design was used for the MEP systems. When the systems were modeled, many conflicts were found supporting the contractor's argument that it had to "redesign" the systems, not merely coordinate them.

[42] Cal. Bus. & Prof. Code § 6703. There are companion statutes for surveyors (B&P § 8703) and geologists. (B&P § 7806).

The phrase "responsible control" means that amount of control over the content of technical submissions during their preparation that is ordinarily exercised by architects applying the required professional standard of care.[43]

The concept of responsible charge requires that work be performed by the licensed professional, or under his or her supervision. But in a BIM world, there is a gray intersection between work performed by the design professional, work performed by the software, and work performed by unlicensed professionals.

First, the technology can perform certain design work historically performed by design professionals. Structural design and detailing software, for example, is capable of modifying the connection details in response to design changes, such as the length of a beam. This occurs without input from the design professional and in response to an algorithm that the design professional did not develop and may not even understand.

Second, the ability to exchange data between models, and to collaborate through the models, creates the possible—and perhaps desirable—result that design details created by subcontractors and vendors will be incorporated into the model and the final construction documents.[44]

These issues are not entirely new. For years, engineers have relied on analysis programs using programming code the engineers have never seen and might not be able to understand.[45] Similarly, some portion of design has always existed in the coordination drawings, shop drawings and submittals issued by the contractor and its sub-contractors. But with BIM, what were ancillary or supporting documents are now part of the model, and possibly the contract documents themselves. The gap between statutory requirements and good professional practice is widening. Statutory definitions of responsible charge are out of step with the emerging practice and must be modified to support design collaboration while preserving public safety and confidence.

The converse of professional responsibility is whether activities by the software are the unlicensed practice of architecture or engineering. A recent case decided in a different context highlights the licensing issue. In

---

[43] Cal. Bus. & Prof. Code § 5535.1.

[44] This recently occurred in a Northern California hospital where the final mechanical drawings were prepared by the mechanical subcontractor, but stamped by the mechanical engineer (who had worked collaboratively with the subcontractor and could be said to be in responsible charge).

[45] In the early days of the author's litigation practice, engineers would occasionally be required to produce the programming code used to analyze an engineering problem and explain to a confused court and jury, how the program was constructed and why it was reliable, before introducing the results. This requirement has largely evaporated as analysis software has become commonplace.

Frankfort Digital Services v. Kistler,[46] an individual used bankruptcy software to prepare his Chapter 7 bankruptcy. The software, which was not designed by a lawyer, was an "expert system" that provided advice about filing options and "knew the law" as respects various jurisdictions. A series of adversary proceedings were initiated against the software provider, and using California law, the Ninth Circuit held:

> Frankfort's system touted its offering of legal advice and projected an aura of expertise concerning bankruptcy petitions; and, in that context, it offered personalized—albeit automated—counsel. *Cf. Landlords Prof'l Servs.*, 215 Cal. App. 3d at 1609. We find that because this was the conduct of a non-attorney, it constituted the unauthorized practice of law.[47]

Design and detailing software also "knows" about the construction regulations, such as building codes. Moreover, they contain the specialized knowledge of engineering principles that is beyond the ken of laymen. From a legal perspective, there is little difference between Frankfort's bankruptcy software and advanced BIM tools.

There is a difference in use, however. In most instances, BIM design software is used by licensed professionals, rather than a lay individual, as in *Frankfort*. But if the design changes are not under the responsible charge of a licensed professional, this distinction is diminished.

[3] Intellectual Property

The fluid nature of the "model" concept creates new intellectual property issues: what is the design, where is the design, and who owns it? As noted previously, current design practice uses a set of interlocking models with a primary model controlling basic geometry that is enhanced by subsidiary design and fabrication models. These models can be supported, or interact with, external analysis models, cost models and scheduling software. In a very real sense, the design is the dynamic whole of these parts.

But if this is true, who owns this dynamic design? The theoretical answer delves deeply into intellectual property concepts of joint efforts, derivative works, and work for hire. The practical answer lies in well drafted contract documents that pre-determine who will own specific parts of the model and which parts will be licensed for use.[48]

The locus of the design also creates issues. Because the design may physically reside on multiple servers in multiple locations, and parts or all

---

[46] 477 F.3d 1117 (9th Cir. 2007).

[47] 477 F.3d 1117, 1126 (9th Cir. 2007).

[48] Design professionals are often concerned that their additions to a BIM software's library of components will be "adopted" by others who have access to a project model. This is the high tech equivalent of copying a firm's standard details. Although

of the design may exist outside the project jurisdiction, the ability to protect intellectual property may be decided under foreign law. And as discussed below, insuring a dispersed design may also test the limits of coverage.

[4] Insurability

BIM raises property and liability insurance issues. The property insurance issues relate to who has rights in the model(s) (and hence has an insurable interest), and where the model(s) exist. This is clearly an area where the insurance industry needs to respond and the author understands that several carriers are issuing electronic "valuable papers" coverage to complement existing professional liability policies.

The liability issues are simpler. Professional liability policies are clearly broad enough to cover a designer's use of BIM. BIM is part of current professional practice and should not be treated differently than designing with CAD.

The two professional liability insurance provisions most likely to create coverage disputes are joint venture exclusions and means and methods exclusions. The joint venture exclusion could conceivably be applied to claims arising from projects performed under multi-party collaborative contracts if the contracts are poorly drafted. Means and methods exclusions, applicable to some policies, could apply if the design required, or implied, a specific, but incorrect, method. In addition, if the design professional is providing software development or web hosting for the project, care should be taken to assure that these services are not outside the professional liability definition of the policy.[49]

Contractors engaged in BIM projects should have contractor's professional liability coverage because their design contributions could conflict with the design exclusion in their commercial general liability policies. Moreover, the contractor's CGL policy will not cover purely economic losses (such as would arise from loss of modeling information), thus it is important that if the general contractor hosts and maintains the model, there be first party coverage for the loss of modeling information that includes economic losses, or that the contractor have a professional style policy broad enough to cover this loss.

---

reprehensible, and you can craft contract language to prohibit it, there is no practical way to quell this "borrowing", because enforcing the firm's copyright would require constant vigilance and expensive legal action.

[49] The author has reviewed enhancements to standard professional liability policies that are designed to expand coverage to include IT tasks related to BIM, such as management and hosting of the project model(s). However, these enhancements are not standard and interested design professionals should discuss these issues with their professional liability broker.

[5]   Data Translation

The ability to use information for multiple purposes (data repurposing) is a primary benefit of BIM. Data that supports architectural design can be used for structural engineering, cost analysis, sustainable practices, fabrication, and more. Because the industry currently relies on a set of interconnected BIM products and analysis tools, it is vital that information be accurately transferred from one program to another, and in many cases, be accurately returned to the originating program after it has been enhanced elsewhere (round-tripping). This goal is interoperability.

For some purposes, interoperability has been effectively achieved. Geometric information can generally be exported and imported from one program to another without difficulty. However, the additional data describing attributes of design elements may, or may not, successfully transport or round-trip between programs. Part of the problem may arise because translation conduits have not yet been written. But at a more fundamental level, if two programs have dissimilar features only the common features will be translated. Thus, some information may not survive translation.

Interoperability is a major issue. An oft cited National Institute of Standards and Technology study estimates that the annual cost of inadequate interoperability in the United States is $15.6 billion,[50] and a recent McGraw Hill study reports that project participants estimate that lack of adequate interoperability adds 3.1% to total project cost.[51] Moreover, the BIM experts surveyed for this report are most concerned with interoperability.

BIM has emerged as a critical catalyst in the effort to create interoperability within the building community. However, with all disciplines envisioning a place for BIM, the need for interoperability is heightened as firms invest deeper in its uses. As firms become experts in BIM, they begin to face the limits of its use.[52]

Interoperability is also seen as a critical factor in transitioning to Integrated Project Delivery. Interoperability will become more of an issue as we continue to push for the use of new technology, whether it be BIM or any other technology that gets us closer to an integrated project delivery system. The goal is to be able to develop within the project [build] team an attitude that improves the process by having teams that are fully integrated and cooperative with each other. One needs to be able to take advantage of technology that allows the free flow of information

---

[50] Gallaher, O'Connor, Dettbarnm Jr., & Gilday, *Cost Analysis of Inadequate Interoperability in the U.S. Capital Facilities Industry*, NIST 2004, pp. 6-1, 6-3.

[51] *Interoperability in the Construction Industry*, McGraw Hill SmartMarket Report (2007) p. 11. Interestingly, architects and engineers estimated a higher impact than contractors.

[52] *Id.*

from the submittal stage to the operations and maintenance phase. Interoperability is a challenge to achieving that.[53]

Although interoperability remains a significant issue, significant progress has been made and standards are continuing to develop. In the United States, the National Institute of Building Science, as mentioned above, has undertaken the most extensive attempt to define BIM. NIBS released the first version of the NBIMS for comment on March 13, 2007 and issued Version 1.0 on December 18, 2007.[54] Its purpose is described as:

> The NBIMS will provide the diverse capital facilities industry with a vision of how to support and facilitate communications throughout the facility lifecycle, from project inception through design and construction, even past demolition for improved operations, maintenance, facility management, and long-term sustainability.
>
> The document was assembled by over thirty subject matter experts from across the capital facilities industry. It provides both a snapshot of where this burgeoning capability exists today as well as identifies work still needing to be accomplished. This first part of Version 1.0, which is now out for review, will be followed by Part 2 at the end of the year. Part 2 will contain items to be standardized across the industry using the NIBS congressionally authorized consensus process.
>
> The NBIMS has six goals: 1) Seek industry wide agreement, 2) Develop an open and shared standard, 3) Facilitate discovery and requirements for sharing information throughout the facility lifecycle, 4) Develop and distribute knowledge that helps share information that is machine readable, 5) Define a minimum BIM, and 6) Provide for information assurance for BIM throughout the facility lifecycle. As an initiative under the Building SMART® Alliance, it is garnering support from the widest spectrum of associations, agencies, organizations, vendors, and individual practitioners ever assembled.

On a global level, the buildingSMART International[55] (bSI) (formally International Alliance for Interoperability (IAI)) facilitates interoperability by defining Industry Foundation Classes[56] as a uniform basis for collaborative information use and exchange. buildingSMART International has more than 400 members in 24 countries and is the leading

---

[53] Ricardo Aparicio, Manager General Electric, President, Construction Users Roundtable.

[54] Version 1.0 of the standard is available at: http://www.facilityinformation council.org/bim/publications.php.

[55] www.buildingmart.com.

[56] IFCs are an object oriented, open source, data format for specifying elements in a BIM. A BIM that utilizes IFCs should create data files that can be read and manipulated by other IFC compatible software. The primary BIM vendors, such as Autodesk, Graphisoft, and Bentley (as well as others) support the IFC standards.

interoperability organization.[57] In North America, the IAI functions as a council of the National Institute of Building Sciences.[58]

Developing universal standards is complicated and the goal of complete interoperability through International finance Corporation ("IFC") remains elusive. Progress continues to be made and supported by green standards. Most software packages can support basic IFC functionality and improvement will continue. Although IFC is not, in the short term, a robust solution to interoperability.

Other solutions are being developed to facilitate interoperability. In addition to supporting IAI standards, Autodesk's Revit BIM systems are available in discipline optimized versions that use a common engine that permit tight integration between the related models. Other software producers also have links between their programs and related products.

Miscommunication and misunderstanding can lead to loss and liability. To reduce potential liability, digital data transfer agreements replete with liability waivers and caveats regarding use have become common.[59] At their extreme, these documents prohibited reliance on the electronic documents and require that the receiving party compare the digital information against hard copy documentation. But prohibiting reliance undermines the single advantage of digital information, its ability

---

[57] Many of the primary BIM platforms support the IFC standards. For example, Bentley Architecture (www.bentley.com), ArchiCad (www.graphisoft.com) and Revit (www.autodesk.com) are fully or partly IFC compliant.

[58] www.iai-na.org.

[59] EJCDC Doc. C700 contains a defensive digital transfer document. It states:

§ 3.06 Electronic Data

A. Unless otherwise stated in the Supplementary Conditions, copies of data furnished by Owner or Engineer to Contractor or Contractor to Owner or Engineer that may be relied upon are limited to the printed copies (also known as hard copies). Files in electronic media format of text, data, graphics, or other types are furnished only for the convenience of the receiving party. Any conclusion or information obtained or derived from such electronic files will be at the user's sole risk. If there is a discrepancy between the electronic files and the hard copies, the hard copies govern.

B. Because data stored in electronic media format can deteriorate or be modified inadvertently or otherwise without authorization of the data's creator, the party receiving electronic files agrees that it will perform acceptance tests or procedures within 60 days, after which the receiving party shall be deemed to have accepted the data thus transferred. Any errors detected within the 60-day acceptance period will be corrected by the transferring party.

C. When transferring documents in electronic media format, the transferring party makes no representations as to long term compatibility, usability, or readability of documents resulting from the use of software application packages, operating systems, or computer hardware differing from those used by the data's creator.

to be efficiently exchanged and repurposed. Thus, current practice is evolving to allow relying on transferred data for specifically identified uses.

In 2007, the American Institute of Architects created a digital transfer document that does not have any substantive caveats.[60] The recipient has the right to use the information for the specific project in one of four ways:

- Store and view;

- Reproduce and distribute;

- Integrate (incorporate additional digital data without modifying data received); and

- Modify as required to fulfill obligations of the Project.[61]

But, provided the recipient uses the information for the project and in accordance with the rights granted, it can rely on the accuracy of the information. This modern approach requires that both parties understand the needs of the other and any limits on effective interoperability.

[6]   Data Adequacy

Even if data is transferred accurately, issues can be caused by differing needs of transmitter and recipient. Tolerances are a significant issue. For example, the tolerances necessary for analyzing a steel frame structure (structural engineer's interest) are different from those required to construct the steel frame (fabricator/erector's interest), which are different from those required for the curtain wall system (manufacturer's interest). Data currency requirements, (whether information is up-to-date) also differ between project participants. Just as with data translation, it is important for persons transmitting and receiving data to understand and agree on acceptable tolerances and currency.

[7]   Privity, Third Party Reliance, and the Economic Loss Doctrine

Design professionals have long sought to distance themselves from economic disputes between the contractor and the owner. Where the contractor asserts direct claims, designers have argued that they are not liable because they aren't in privity with the contractor and that the

---

[60] AIA Document E201 (2007). The document does contain a warranty that the transmitting party is the owner of the data or has the right to transmit the data to the recipient (§ 2.1).

[61] AIA Document E201 (2007) Project Protocol Table, § 3.2.

damages sought are not recoverable due to the economic loss doctrine. These arguments have been partially successful, although the scope and exceptions to the economic loss doctrine varies between jurisdictions.[62]

But if information is provided for another's reliance, privity is not necessary to recover economic damages. The essentials of a negligent misrepresentation claim are set forth in Restatement of Torts Second section 552 as follows:

> (1) One who, in the course of his business, profession or employment, or in any other transaction in which he has a pecuniary interest, supplies false information for the guidance of others in their business transactions, is subject to liability for pecuniary loss caused to them by their justifiable reliance upon the information, if he fails to exercise reasonable care or competence in obtaining or communicating the information.
>
> (2) Except as stated in Subsection (3), the liability stated in Subsection (1) is limited to loss suffered:
>
> (a) by the person or one of a limited group of persons for whose benefit and guidance he intends to supply the information or knows that the recipient intends to supply it; and
> (b) through reliance upon it in a transaction that he intends the information to influence or knows that the recipient so intends or in a substantially similar transaction.
>
> (3) The liability of one who is under a public duty to give the information extends to loss suffered by any of the class of persons for whose benefit the duty is created, in any of the transactions in which it is intended to protect them.[63]

From the prior discussion of data transfer and interoperability, it should be plainly understood that an acknowledged data recipient can state a claim under § 552 and that privity and the economic loss doctrine will have little sway.

Although these defenses are diminished, risk is not necessarily increased. The ability to share model information between designer and contractor leads to better quality documents and the avoidance of physical clashes.[64] Thus, designers increase their exposure by providing information, but by reducing the probability and severity of project failure, can effectively reduce their risk.

---

[62] For an excellent summary of the economic loss doctrine in construction cases, *see*, Andrus, Gessford & Joyce, *The Economic Loss Doctrine in Construction Cases: Are the Odds for Design Professionals Better in Vegas?*, J ACCL, Winter 2008, p. 53.

[63] Restatement of Torts 2d, § 552.

[64] During private discussions with a major supplier of electronic plan management services, the author was told that the service provider has seen a significant reduction in addenda if building information modeling is used. This is an indication that BIM produced plans are more consistent and complete.

[8] *Spearin* Implied Warranties

The *Spearin* Doctrine, introduced by the Supreme Court in 1918, allocated defected design risk by implying an owner's warranty that plans are complete and accurate. The *Spearin* court found that "the one who provides the plans and specification for a construction project warrants that those plans and specifications are free from defect."[65] Although initially a defensive doctrine, *Spearin* has evolved into an offensive weapon that permits contractors to recover whenever plans have errors or omissions,[66] which is almost certain to occur in any real project.

In principle, *Spearin* does not affect design professionals because the implied warranty is solely from owner to contractor. In practice, however, it overshadows much of construction litigation because, in any delay and impact claim, it encourages the contractor to allege design deficiencies that will trigger the absolute *Spearin* warranty. Caught between the contractor and the designer, many owners believe they must cross-claim against the design professional to protect against inconsistent verdicts and less scrupulous owners view the design professional as a funding source for resolving the contractor's claim.

The *Spearin* doctrine does not apply to performance specifications because the owner has not dictated how the work will be performed.[67] Thus, the characterization as "design" or "performance" specifications determines the existence of the implied warranty—and often the result.[68] Specifications containing performance and prescriptive elements (hybrid specifications), results have had differing outcomes because it is deter- mining the essential character of specifications is difficult.

> . . . [T]he distinction between design specifications and performance specifications not always clear, and many specifications are hybrids. The general consensus of authority in the conventional design-bid- build context is that, where the owner designates particular compo- nents, dimensions, material types or qualities, or other details, the owner impolitely warrants those details. [cit. omit] On the other hand, where the specifications simply set forth the performance characteristics of the end product and leave to the contractor how to achieve those results, no implied warranty is said to arise. [cit. omit]

---

[65] United States v. Spearin, 248 U.S. 132 (1918).

[66] *See, e.g.*, Hercules Inc. v. United States, 24 F.3d 188, 197 (Fed. Cir. 1994).

[67] Stuyvesant v. United States, 834 F.2d 1576, 1582 (Fed. Cir. 1987); White v. Edsall Constr.Co. Inc., 296 F.3d 1081, 1085. (Fed. Cir. 2002).

[68] For a criticism of the design/performance litmus test, *see, The Spearin Doctrine: The False Dichotomy Between Design and Performance Specifications*, 25 Pub. Con. L.J. 47 (1995).

As one commentator has summarized, "liability follows from design responsibility. [citations omitted][69]

If the project design incorporates material information provided by the contractor, there will be no implied warranty.[70] For example, in *Austin v. United States*, the contractor agreed to design, manufacture, test, and deliver an innovative digital data recording system.[71] The contract contained detailed specifications as to the method of constructing the system, but the contractor determined that the contract would be impossible to perform using those specifications.[72] It modified the design, but was still unable to successfully execute the contract.[73] The court denied the contractor the defense of impossibility, finding that because the contractor had integrated his own design into that of the original contract, he warranted his ability to successfully perform those substituted specifications.[74]

In a fully modeled project, particularly in a collaborative project where subcontractor and vendor information is incorporated into the design, it appears that courts would turn to cases of hybrid specifications to determine whether to imply a warranty. This will be a factual inquiry, but the deeper a contractor's involvement in the design, the less likely a warranty will be implied.

The contractor's ability to discover defects (the patent deficiency exception to Spearin) is also increased with collaborative BIM. As noted recently:

> First, wholesale implementation of BIM methodology contemplates, if not demands, full participation by the contractor in reviewing the design model early-on in the design process. In such event, the contractor may lose the benefit of the owner's implied warranty by application of the patent defect exception to the Spearin Doctrine which requirement patent errors be recognized. To point out the obvious, BIM participation by the contractor may and could well lead to timely (preconstruction) discovery and correction of certain design errors so as to abrogate any subsequent necessity to invoke the Spearin doctrine. Nevertheless, it is a certainty that certain design errors in certain circumstances will not be detected. In such instances, the right of the contractor who participates in BIM to invoke the Spearin Doctrine involves an analysis of whether an error otherwise latent should be considered patent. In that regard, it is not

---

[69] Hamersmith & Lozowicki, *Can the Spearin Doctrine Survive in a Design-Build World: Who Bears Responsibility for Hybrid Specifications*, J. ACCL Winter 2008, 123, 129.

[70] Austin Co. v. United States, 314 F.2d 518, 520 (Ct. Cl. 1963).

[71] *Id.* at 519.

[72] *Id.*

[73] *Id.*

[74] *Id.* at 520.

unreasonable to project that the invocation of the Spearin Doctrine by a contractor and BIM participant in such a situation will be set quite high.[75]

Thus, the contractor's involvement in design, which may defeat the designer's economic loss and privity defenses, may also diminish the contractor's implied warranty claims.[76]

§ 5.04   USE OF BUILDING INFORMATION MODELING FOR YOUR PROJECT?

Implementing BIM within a design or construction organization requires commitment to developing new workflows and competencies. Implementing BIM on a project requires planning and consideration of the following issues. Attorneys assisting their clients should assure that these issues are considered at the project's inception.

[A]   How Will the Model(s) be Used?

The level of information in the model(s) and the protocols for their use and management will depend upon how the model(s) will be used. Thus, the participants should outline the planned uses to allow all parties to understand how they should create and manage their data. Possible uses to consider are:

- Solely for design;
- For coordination and clash detection;
- For estimating material quantities;
- For continuous cost estimating in support of target value design;
- For structural, wind or other analyses;
- For energy use, light studies, sustainability, or other optimizations;
- For construction simulation (construction rehearsal);
- For creation of shop or fabrication drawings;
- For review of submittals;
- For support of LEED submittals;
- For code compliance checking;

---

[75] O'Brien, T., *Building Information Modeling, Sailing on Uncharted Waters*, Conference Paper, ABA Forum on the Construction Industry, October 2007, p. 30, 31.

[76] *Id.*, O'Brien also agrees that the contractor's participation in design undermines the *Spearin* implied warranty, at least with respect to aspect of the design where the contractor contributed.

- For agency review; and

- For facility management.

[B]   Who Will Own and/or License the Model(s)?

In most instances, it does not matter who owns the model as long as all parties have sufficient licensed rights to use the model(s) for project purposes. However, it is important that the issue be settled because ownership of jointly created works can be troublesome. There are three primary options, all of which are workable provided the details are correctly handled in the contract documents.

[1]   Owner Owns Modeling Information

This option will be preferred by many institutional and public owners because they typically own information created for them, such as contract documents. Under this option, all of the project participants must be licensed to use the modeling information for project purposes. Design professionals, at least, will also want the right to display their designs for promotional or educational purposes and may want the right to reuse elements created for the project.

The "owner owns" approach also raises the issue of what information in the model should be transferred to the owner. BIM software contains a modest amount of predefined elements that can be aggregated into a design. But designers will extend this palette by developing their own standard library of elements and will develop custom elements for use with a specific design. These elements are portable and reusable, much like architectural detail libraries. Even if the owner obtains title to the design model, designers should reserve ownership of their standard library elements so they can reuse their standard elements on later projects. In addition, designers should be indemnified against liability arising from later modifications and reuse of the model(s).

[2]   Designer Owns Modeling Information

This option is consistent with traditional AIA contract documents that define designs as the architect's instruments of service, and for that reason, may be preferred by some. The owner, the contractor, and others who need to use the information would be licensed to use the information by appropriate language in the designer's agreement. The owner's license needs to include the ability to use the modeling information for operation and maintenance, including revisions to the project. Because the owner's license will include limited reuse, the designer should be indemnified against liability arising from subsequent modifications and reuse.

[3]   All Parties Own Whatever They Create

Although this approach sounds simple, it requires cross-licensing between all parties and, thus, provisions in all of the principal contracts. Other than this additional complication, it is similar to the designer owning the modeling information.

Finally, the project insurance program should assure that the modeling information, whichever party owns it, is insured for the respective interests of the parties.

[4]   What Is the Model's Contractual Status?

This question raises practical and legal issues.

First, what is the scope of the contractually significant model? As noted previously, projects are built from a series of interrelated models rather than a single, global model. Beyond the primary design model, there may be mechanical design models, structural design models, structural fabrication models, mechanical fabrication models, analysis models and possibly others. Is associated cost and schedule information part of the model? Before contractual status is conferred, the parties should determine what is, and isn't, contained in the contractual model.[77]

Second, under current practice portions of the design will not be modeled. Standard details, for example, are often provided as two dimensional drawings because they have not been converted to modeled forms. Information that must be more precise than supported in the model will also be provided as traditional CAD drawings. Similarly, topographical, civil and landscaping information may be conventionally drawn. Finally, specifications will likely exist outside of the building information model(s). Thus, the complete design will be an amalgam of modeled and unmodeled information.

When building information models first appeared, they were denied contractual status. The hardcopy drawings printed from the model, together with the additional traditional prints, were the only contract documents. But flattening the model into printed sheets sacrifices the three-dimensional information and the additional information associated with the model and its elements. To avoid this result, more current practice considers the model *one of* the contract documents.[78]

---

[77] It should be noted that this distinction is less important in fully integrated projects because liability is waived or limited between the parties and compensation is determined by project, rather than individual performance. Although not unimportant, in an integrated project the model becomes a means to achieving project goals rather than a yardstick for judging individual responsibility.

[78] The American Institute of Steel Contractors, a pioneer in supporting modeling, has always maintained that the model should be a relied on contract document. *See, e.g.,* Appendix "A" to the AISC Manual of Steel Practice.

But if the model is only one of the contract documents, inconsistencies may arise between two dimensional and modeled information. The order of precedence depends upon project specifics, but in general, because the model is fully coordinated and dimensionally accurate, it should be the primary dimensional control.

[5]   How Will Modeling Requirements Be Specified?

As anyone who has reviewed a comprehensive CAD standard can attest, it is possible to specify drawing standards to a very fine degree. In theory, it should be possible to similarly create a prescriptive BIM standard. In practice, however, this is difficult to accomplish.

Unlike current CAD projects, modeled projects use a variety of different, interacting, BIM software. Although the project documents may specify the primary BIM products, the subsidiary applications may not be determined until after contracts have been signed. Moreover, the depth to which a project is modeled and the scope of the model(s) use can vary from project to project. In addition, a participant's experience with modeling varies and many owners (and specification writers) are neither fully aware of the possible options, nor capable of defining what they need. At present, modeling requirements are rarely as detailed as a companion CAD standard, but they are being developed and refined with much greater specificity.

Instead of a detailed standard, either a performance or hybrid specification can be used. Performance specifications state the goal of BIM use without specifying how it will be accomplished. For example, the specification could state, among other things, that the model will be used for costing as well as design, will be provided to specialty contractors as a basis for their fabrication or shop drawings, and will be used to review and approve shop drawings and submittals. By defining the use, contracting parties are told who will be relying on information and for what purpose and can accordingly adjust their expectations and practices. But a performance specification will not provide the detail necessary to assure fluid and reliable communication or provide the drawing standards that the project team will need. Thus, if a performance approach is used, it should be supplemented by a post-contract BIM workshop where the parties meet to develop standards and protocols for their specific products, on that specific project, in order to meet the project goals. There are several workshop guides that can be used as references. For instance, see the BIM Project Execution Planning Guide, published by the Penn State Computer Integrated Construction Research Program (http://www.engr.psu.edu/ae/cic/BIMEx/).

A hybrid approach may also be used. In a hybrid specification, detail is provided regarding the types of allowable software, requirements for interoperability, depth of modeling and similar details, but the participants must augment these standards and protocols after the project has commenced. This hybrid approach is currently being used by the United States Army Corps of Engineers[79] and others.[80]

[6] How Will the Model Be Administered?

Model administration is comprised of three primary tasks that may, or may not, be performed by a single entity. First, the model needs to be hosted securely and reliably. This is an information technology task. Second, the model needs to be kept current with appropriate versioning and audit trails. Rights to access specific project areas need to be granted, audited and enforced. This is an administrative task. Finally, the authority to substantively change modeling information needs to be vested in the entity competent and professionally responsible for the content. This is a professional task.

The first two tasks can be assigned to any party. Models can, and are, hosted by the prime designer, the contractor, the owner, and by third-party consultants retained by the owner. This is a task that should be undertaken by the entity best capable of providing a secure and stable system. The administrative task can, again, be provided by the party most capable. A knowledgeable construction or program manager might be a logical choice because they routinely manage and facilitate information flow.

The professional task, however, must remain with the professionals responsible for specific aspects of the design. The structural system, for example, cannot be modified without the concurrence of the structural engineer. The building layout and base geometry cannot be modified without the concurrence of the architect. Thus, the BIM protocols should specify who will handle the hosting and administrative chores, but must define who has authority and responsibility for substantive content.

§ 5.05   BIM AS A COLLABORATIVE FRAMEWORK— INTEGRATED PROJECT DELIVERY

Building Information Modeling does not require a collaborative process. Designers can use the existing software to prepare traditional

---

[79] Although not publicly available as this paper was being written, in January of 2008, the Corps released its hybrid BIM specification "Attachment F" for use by its Project Representatives. As an example of a hybrid provision, the publicly released drafts require use of USACE approved software, open standards and IFC compliance, and modeling of anything normally shown at ¼ inch scale. In addition to the prescribed standards, the specification states that the model should be sufficient for costing (a performance standard) and require the design-builder to submit a plan that includes for development of the digital model more detailed protocols after contract award.

[80] On March 13, 2008, AGC announced that it was issuing its Building Information Modeling Addendums to be used with the ConsensusDocs standard form agreement. Previously, AGC had issued its *Contractor's Guide to Building Information Modeling* to assist contractor's in understanding and implementing BIM.

plans and specifications without providing the digital model to the contractor, its sub-contractors and suppliers, or even to the owner, itself. Contractors can create models for estimating, fabricating or construction simulation without ever sharing the information. But doing so wastes the power of Building Information Modeling as a collaborative framework and discards the cost and quality advantages of single entry, multiple use. Moreover, an insular approach ignores current best practices favoring integrated project delivery with Building Information Modeling at its core.

[A] The Need for Integrated Project Delivery

The construction industry has long been plagued by fragmented and fractious project delivery processes. Competitive low bid procurement, guaranteed maximum price and similar contract structures have fostered an individualistic, zero-sum approach to construction. These processes, in conjunction with other influences, have resulted in declining labor productivity. According to research by Dr. Paul Teicholz at the Stanford University Department of Civil & Environmental Engineering, construction labor productivity has declined by approximately 20% between 1964 and 2004, whereas industrial productivity has increased approximately 200% during the same period.[81] Estimates of waste in construction are similarly alarming. The Construction Industry Institute estimates that 57% of all construction activity does not add value.[82] An earlier study concluded that 30% of project costs were wasted because of mismanagement caused by the division between design and construction.[83] Owners are understandably concerned and the Construction Users Roundtable (CURT), a leading construction owner organization, has concluded that wholesale industry change is necessary to achieve successful projects.[84]

After analyzing the causes of declining productivity, CURT issued a policy report mandating integrated project delivery methodologies.[85] The report proposed four elements of a new policy framework.

> **Owner Leadership:** Owners, as the integrating influence in the building process, must engage in and demand that collaborative teams openly share information and use appropriate technology. CURT should establish policy and procedures to implement change in the AEC industry and encourage other building owner organizations to join the effort.

---

[81] Teicholz, P. as reported in AEC/Bytes Viewpoint No. 4, April 14, 2004 and elsewhere.

[82] CII (2004).

[83] C. Ibbs, et al., *Determining the Impact of Various Construction Contract Types and Clauses on Project Performance*, CII (1986).

[84] *Optimizing the Construction Process: An Implementation Strategy*, WP-1003, Page 4, The Construction Users Roundtable, July 2006.

[85] *Collaboration, Integrated Information and the Project Lifecycle in Building Design, Construction and Operation*, WP-1202, The Construction Users Roundtable, August 2004.

Integrated Project Structure: The building process cannot be optimized without full collaboration among all members of the design/build/own project. CURT and other owner organizations should establish policies that support such collaboration.

Open Information Sharing: Project collaboration must be characterized by open, timely, and reliable information sharing. CURT should advocate the establishment of procedures and protocols to achieve this end.

Virtual Building Models: Effectively designed and deployed information technology will support full collaboration and information sharing and will lead to more effective design/build/manage process. CURT should endorse establishing technology-based lifecycles that optimize the creation, interaction, and transport of digital information throughout the building process.

CURT's vision of an integrated project built around virtual building information models was sharpened in a later report on implementing the optimized building process.

Technology/Building Information Modeling

Desire for re-use of project information beyond the building design created by architects and engineers will drive market adoption of building information models. Standards will be established for how building information models are developed with regard to content and modeling methods to produce information supporting downstream BIM automation services that are aligned with the owner's business objectives. Ultimately, for BIM to succeed, owners must acknowledge that all risk comes from them and ultimately returns to them.

Owners must set the tone for the project by requiring their design and construction teams to use the latest technologies. Including these requirements in requests for proposals is one simple step that owners can start using. Further, the owner should use the technology as well.

Owners should support industry initiatives to create standards where they are needed. Owners should also increase their awareness of the technology tools their consultants and contractors are using on their projects. Owners must recognize that the choice of technology solutions will affect their projects, not just during the development phase, but also after the project is completed and operating.[86]

Information Sharing

An essential element woven throughout the vision of transformation to an optimized model is the ability for all parties to communicate freely. Current practices of silence for fear of liability must be eliminated and a new process where decisions are made at the highest and most appropriate level of competency must be established to leverage team knowledge. . . . This issue most certainly is the

---

[86] *Optimizing the Construction Process*, supra, at 14.

greatest obstacle to transformation and the realization of the optimized project. Owners must demand this openness and transparency
from the team entity of which they are a part.[87]

CURT's message is quite clear. Projects should capitalize on the
competencies of all project participants and must promote open communication using the best technologies available. Building Information
Models should be at the core of the process. Although the CURT reports
called for change, they did not explain how to create the radical
transformation required.

[B]   The Development of Integrated Project Delivery

In June of 2007, the American Institute of Architects California
Counsel in partnership with McGraw Hill issued *Integrated Project
Delivery: A Working Definition*.[88] This document set forth the fundamental assumptions and framework for a fully integrated project. These
include early involvement by all key participants, compensation and risk
tied to project, not individual success, open communication between all
participants and collaborative decision making. The *Working Definition*
directly responded to CURT's call to action. The concepts in the *Working
Definition* were further developed by a joint American institute of
Architects and AIACC task force and published on November 5, 2007 in
Integrated Project Delivery: A Guide.[89] As defined in the *Guide*:

> Integrated Project Delivery (IPD) is a project delivery approach that
> integrates people, systems, business structures and practices into a
> process that collaboratively harnesses the talents and insights of all
> participants to optimize project results, increase value to the owner,
> reduce waste, and maximize efficiency through all phases of design,
> fabrication, and construction.

The *Guide* provides the fundamental principals to IPD, a road map
for its implementation and the outline for alternative legal and business
models supporting IPD. Both the *Working Definition* and the *Guide*
recognized that the technology of BIM was intertwined with the process
of IPD. A Note on Building Information Modeling:

> It is understood that integrated project delivery and building infor
> mation modeling (BIM) are different concepts—the first is a process
> and the second a tool. Certainly integrated projects are done without
> BIM and BIM is used in non-integrated processes. However, the full
> potential benefits of both IPD and BIM are achieved only when they

---

[87] *Id.*

[88] http://www.ipd-ca.net.

[89] http://www.aia.org/ipdg.

are used together. Thus, the IPD phase descriptions included here assume the use of BIM.[90]

Similarly, although the *Working Definition* did not foreclose having an integrated, but unmodeled project, the committee concluded:

> Although it is possible to achieve Integrated Project Delivery without Building Information Modeling, it is the opinion and recommendation of this study that Building Information Modeling is essential to efficiently achieve the collaboration required for Integrated Project Delivery.[91]

In its discussion of IPD implementation, the *Guide* explicitly recognizes that IPD will be executed through BIM and that BIM provides a framework for collaboration.

> Building Information Modeling (BIM), a digital, three-dimensional model linked to a database of project information, is one of the most powerful tools supporting IPD. Because BIM can combine, among other things, the design, fabrication information, erection instructions, and project management logistics in one database, it provides a platform for collaboration throughout the project's design and construction. Additionally, because the model and database can exist for the life of a building, the owner may use BIM to manage the facility well beyond completion of construction for such purposes as space planning, furnishing, monitoring long term energy performance, maintenance, and remodeling.[92]

Others, particularly the Lean Construction Institute,[93] have promoted collaborative approaches to design and construction delivery. LCI prepared the first multi-party integrated form contract used in the United States and which formed the basis for the ConsensusDocs Series 300 integrated agreement.[94] LCI also supports the use of BIM. In May of 2008, the AIA introduced two document sets for integrated project delivery, one set assumes delivering a project using a Single Purpose Entity,[95] and the other follows a more traditional owner-architect[96]/owner-contractor[97] approach. And in April 2009, the AIA released the a

---

[90] *Integrated Project Delivery: A Guide*, explanatory note at page 20, AIA/AIACC 2007.

[91] *Integrated Project Delivery: A Working Definition*, AIACC 2007, p.1.

[92] *Integrated Project Delivery: A Guide*, § 4.1, AIA/AIACC 2007.

[93] http://www.leanconstruction.org.

[94] The collaborative documents are the 300 series ConsensusDocs and are available at www.consensusdocs.com.

[95] Standard Form Single Purpose Entity Agreement for Integrated Project Delivery C195 (2008).

[96] Standard Form of Agreement Between Owner and Architect for Integrated Project Delivery B195 (2008).

[97] Standard Form of Agreement Between Owner and Contractor for Integrated Project Delivery A195 (2008).

standard form multi-party agreement for IPD through which the owner, architect, contractor and potentially other key project participants execute a single agreement for the design, construction and commission of the project.[98] (A brief comparison can be found in section 5.5 below.) The evolution of BIM and the development of integrated project delivery through sound IPD contracts will result in an increasing number of fully modeled, fully integrated projects.

[C]   Five Major Structural Elements of Integrated Project Delivery

A full IPD project has five major structural elements:

- Early involvement of key participants;
- Shared risk and reward based on project outcome;
- Joint project control;
- Reduced liability exposure; and
- Jointly developed and validated targets.

The sections below discuss the importance of each element and how it affects IPD behaviors. The influence diagram in Figure 3, summarizes the discussion by linking elements to behaviors.

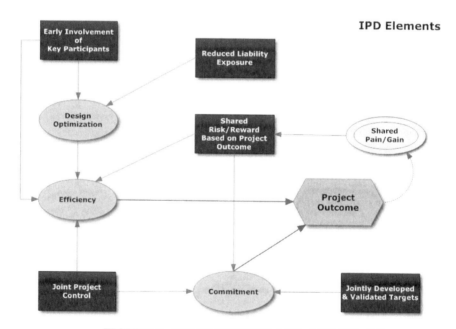

FIGURE 3: IPD ELEMENTS AND OUTCOMES

---

[98] Standard Form Multi-Party Agreement for Integrated Project Delivery C191 (2009).

[1]   Early Involvement of Key Participants

Early involvement of key participants—defined as those who have the greatest influence on project success—is the most important IPD element. A project participant deeply influences project success if it can impart knowledge that improves the effectiveness or constructability of design or if its interactions with other organizations enhances project productivity. Identification of key participants is specific to a given project, but—in addition to the owner, designer, and builder—key participants generally include the mechanical, electrical, and plumbing designers and contractors because their knowledge strongly affects design and these parties must cooperate closely for the project to proceed smoothly. Depending upon the project, steel erectors, framers, curtain wall contractors, major equipment vendors, and others may similarly be key participants. The key participants' diverse viewpoints improve project performance in many ways. Studies of creativity in commercial contexts note that teams with diverse backgrounds are more creative.

> . . . [O]ne common way managers kill creativity is by assembling homogeneous teams. The lure to do so is great. Homogeneous teams often reach "solutions" more quickly and with less friction along the way. These teams often report high morale, too. But homogeneous teams do little to enhance expertise and creative thinking. Everyone comes to the table with a similar mind-set. They leave with the same.[99]

The broad experience of the diverse team also benefits target value design. Designers provided with information concerning effectiveness and constructability of alternative concepts, can more accurately choose systems and layouts that efficiently achieve the project goals. Moreover, the key specialty contractors can provide pricing information that is current and accurate, leading to better price control and fewer surprises. Finally, when parties are engaged in developing the project design, they develop a commitment to the overall project, not just to their individual component.

The timing of key participant involvement is also important. Key participants should become engaged when their participation will benefit the project. This is almost always earlier than traditional design and construction practice, and the reference to "early" is meant to highlight this change in practice. It does not imply that all key participants commence simultaneously, and in most projects, the core team will be augmented by additional key participants as the project progresses. Restated, the rule is that key participants should become involved at the appropriate time, which is when their contributions will significantly affect project outcome.

---

[99] T. Amabile, *How to Kill Creativity*, Harvard Bus. Rev., Sept.–Oct. 1998.

[2]   Shared Risk/Reward Based on Project Outcome

IPD agreements tie compensation to achievement of project objectives. Although formulations vary, all or part of the participants' profit is placed at risk and profit may be augmented if project performance is met or exceeded. Individual profit is not a function of the amount of work performed, or of individual productivity, but is proportionate to overall project success. Tying profit to project performance discourages selfish actions. Because of the compensation structure, selfishness is self-defeating. Shared risk/reward also increases project commitment. The parties perceive that they are rowing the same boat. Thus, a party benefits by providing suggestions or assistance to other parties. Parties become interested in how they can optimize the whole project, not just a single system or element.

Shared risk/reward also serves to align the parties to the project objective. If compensation is based on achieving that objective, it behooves each party to understand precisely what the objective is and how it is best achieved.

Reward structure requires careful consideration. In her study of creativity, Professor Teresa Amabile concluded that monetary incentives are not a principle driver for highly creative teams,[100] although an absence of reward or recognition was often correlated with low creativity.[101] A recent study of six completed IPD projects uncovered pointed disagreement concerning the necessity of rewards programs.[102] Some participants believed they were absolutely essential, others thought that they were unnecessary.

This disagreement may reflect the difference between corporate and individual viewpoints. A firm considering IPD must assess the risk of engaging in the project. Expressed preference studies show that people are willing to accept a higher risk if they believe the activity is beneficial.[103] The possibility of superior profitability also lowers psychological barriers to entry.[104] Managers considering whether to commit their organizations to IPD will consider its potential benefits to their organization. Shared reward not only makes risk more tolerable, it provides a

---

[100] T. Amabile, *Managing for Creativity*, Harvard Bus. School 9-396-271, February 1996.

[101] *Id.*

[102] *Integrated Project Delivery: Case Studies*, Joint Report of the American Institute of Architects California Council and the American Institute of Architects, 2010.

[103] P. Slovic, *Perception of Risk*, Science, Vol. 236 (1987).

[104] A major barrier is the concept of *anticipated regret*. When a person recommends or undertakes a task that it could have avoided or ignored, the person runs the risk of embarrassment or otherwise regretting a decision he or she did not have to make. Anticipated regret amplifies risk perception. Nordgren, et al., *Unpacking Perceived Control in Risk Perception: The Mediating Role of Anticipated Regret*, J. Behavioral Decision Making 20:533-544 (2007). The opportunity for superior performance can help overcome this barrier to implementing IPD.

basis for rationally preferring IPD projects. Thus, a workshop of design and construction managers concluded:

Shared Risk/Reward Pool

The Group felt that structuring participant's compensation to be raised or lowered according to performance against predetermined targets is the most important and effective driver—it provides a monetary reason to collaborate.[105]

In contrast, once an organization has committed to an IPD project, its employees are motivated by a combination of intrinsic as well as extrinsic rewards. Participants in IPD projects have commented that the positive, non-antagonistic focus of IPD is, itself, a significant reward. Thus, the supposed disagreement may simply reflect the viewpoint differences of persons considering IPD compared to those already engaged in a collaborative project.

Shared risk and reward should extend to all key IPD participants, not just the owner, contractor and designer. Key participants are those who have a significant effect on project outcome, particularly if project outcome is tied to their successfully working with others. These subcontractor and consultant key participants can be brought into the IPD agreement by flow-through provisions in their respective agreements with the contractor and designer, or can be included in the IPD agreement by "joining agreement" amendments.

[3]   Joint Project Control

Joint project control requires real communication between the parties. To achieve consensus, the parties must clearly explain the issues from their perspectives and listen to the perspectives of others. The increased understanding provides a clearer and jointly held understanding of the issues. Miscommunication, although certainly possible, is less likely.

Joint project control also reinforces the communal nature of the undertaking. It is not "their project." It is "our project." In addition, joint project control balances the interests of the parties and provides a check against favoring the interests of one party over the other. It also reflects a fundamental fairness. In IPD, parties are accepting risk based on project outcome and should certainly have a voice in decisions that affect those risks.

Joint project control also affects the perception of risk, as well as risk itself. Risk perception research indicates that perils a party cannot

---

[105] *Experiences in Collaboration: On the Path to IPD*, AIA National/AIA California Council, p. 9, 2009.

control are feared more than those they can.[106] As noted below, fear chills creativity, and results in defensive behavior. It also results in excessive risk hedges through explicit or implicit contingencies. Thus, joint management serves to reduce defensive behavior and avoids unnecessary contingency expense.

In an IPD project, joint project control is effected through a project management team comprised of at least the owner, contractor, and designer. The project management team is authorized to manage the project to achieve the jointly agreed objectives. Thus, each member of the project management team must have the authority to bind its respective entity and each party must be able to rely on the agreements of the others. Senior management "second-guessing" of project level decisions is toxic, undermining trust and reducing parties' willingness to place project objectives ahead of their short-term interests.

Joint project control is a significant paradigm shift for many owners. Traditionally, the owner's project representative functioned as the owner's "eyes and ears," but did not actively participate in the development of design or construction solutions. Instead, the contractor or designer proposed options and solutions that were approved or disapproved by the owner's senior management after being communicated by the project representative.

The IPD owner, in contrast, is actively involved in the development and analysis of options and solutions. This level of owner involvement and control is, in fact, one of the major advantages of IPD for owners. In no other project delivery method does the owner have such a strong role in fashioning the project to meet its needs. But this strength implies responsibility to commit sufficient capable resources authorized to make reliable decisions. This change in practice can be particularly difficult for owners that have traditionally vested their project representatives with little authority.

Although all current IPD agreements have some form of joint project control, the detailed decision process and ultimate authority of the participants varies significantly. Variation is inevitable given the needs of specific projects and participants. But joint project control is designed to provide parties at risk with some control over the risks they have undertaken and to increase parties' commitment to the project as a whole. Thus, skewing control in favor of one party or the other may undermine the behaviors IPD seeks to create.

One approach that attempts to balance project control is shown in the flow chart (Figure 4) below. In this approach, unanimous decisions at the project management team level are binding and unappealable. If the project management team is unable to reach a decision, a senior management team decides the issue by majority vote. This is also binding and unappealable, unless the owner decides to override the decision by

---

[106] P. Slovic, *Perception of Risk,* Science, V. 236 (1987).

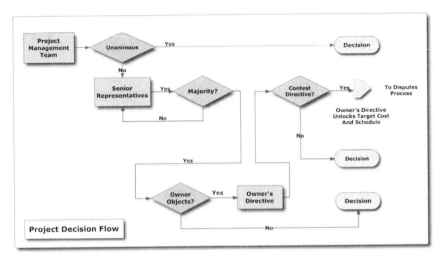

FIGURE 4: PROJECT DECISION FLOW

issuing an owner's directive. If the designer or contractor challenges an owner's directive, it is resolved through the contract's dispute process and may result in an adjustment to project cost and schedule. Thus, all parties have a voice in decisions and authority is fairly evenly distributed with the owner having slightly more authority through the owner's directive. The owner's authority is balanced, however, by the ability to appeal unilateral owner decisions through the dispute process.

[4] Reduced Liability Exposure

The primary reasons for limiting liability are to increase communication,[107] foster creativity, and reduce excessive contingencies.

Information sharing and collaboration support all three components of creativity. Take expertise. The more often people exchange ideas and data by working together, the more knowledge they will have. The same dynamic can be said for creative thinking. In fact, one way to enhance the creative thinking of employees is to expose them to various approaches to problem solving. With the exception of

---

[107] The liability concern, and its potential harm, was neatly summarized in the commentary *Intelligent Building Models and Downstream Use*, Comments of the Technology in Architectural Practice Advisory Group submitted for the 2007 revisions to AIA Documents B141 and A201, AIA 2005.

We fear there will be a tendency, driven by valid concerns about liability and insurability, to prevent such use of the architect's design data. We believe this is the wrong answer and would jeopardize the future of architectural practice as we know it. . . . Obstacles to a free flow of data among the project participants should be overcome so that the architecture firm can deliver the full value of its work to the client and be rewarded commensurately.

> *hardened misanthropes, information sharing and collaboration*
> *heighten peoples' enjoyment of work and thus their intrinsic motiva-*
> *tion.*[108]

Unfortunately, freely exchanging information can lead to greater liability. For example, many states[109] permit actions for negligent misrepresentation under the guidelines of section 552 of the Restatement of Torts, Second.[110] Under that standard, a person providing errant information is liable for the damage caused to anyone whose reliance was intended. This has lead to bottling up information to limit liability expansion, although this diminishes creativity and performance. Liability waivers support creativity by removing this concern.

In addition, liability waivers serve to generally reduce fear of failure. In a creative project, there must always be a safety net below people who make suggestions. A climate of fear is not conducive to creativity and undermines intrinsic motivation.[111]

Liability exposure also directly raises project costs through increased contingency allocations. A rational negotiator assesses the risks his or her organization faces, attempts to quantify the risk, and includes an allowance in the project cost. This rational action is repeated by each participating organization with the result that the summed risk allowances exceed the actual contingency required for the project. Moreover, the division of project contingency into many smaller allocations impairs effective contingency management.

Liability concerns also create hidden costs caused by defensive design and reluctance to consider using new materials and techniques. Old practices may be costly and inefficient, but they are comfortable and appear safe.

---

[108] T. Amabile, *How to Kill Creativity,* Harvard Bus. Rev., Sep.–Oct. 1998.

[109] *See, e.g.,* Bily v. Arthur Young & Co., 3 Cal. 4th 370 (Cal. 1992).

[110] § 552. Information Negligently Supplied for the Guidance of Others

(1) One who, in the course of his business, profession or employment, or in any other transaction in which he has a pecuniary interest, supplies false information for the guidance of others in their business transactions, is subject to liability for pecuniary loss caused to them by their justifiable reliance upon the information, if he fails to exercise reasonable care or competence in obtaining or communicating the information;

(2) Except as stated in Subsection (3), the liability stated in Subsection (1) is limited to loss suffered;

(a) by the person or one of a limited group of persons for whose benefit and guidance he intends to supply the information or knows that the recipient intends to supply it; and

(b) through reliance upon it in a transaction that he intends the information to influence or knows that the recipient so intends or in a substantially similar transaction.

(3) The liability of one who is under a public duty to give the information extends to loss suffered by any of the class of persons for whose benefit the duty is created, in any of the transactions in which it is intended to protect them.

[111] T. Amabile, *How to Kill Creativity,* Harvard Bus. Rev., Sep.–Oct. 1998.

Liability waivers also reduce litigation costs, and can be justified on this ground alone, but as noted above, the primary reason for liability waivers is to increase communication, creativity, and to limit unnecessary contingencies.

[5]   Jointly Developed/Validated Targets

Jointly developed targets are the parties' first collaborative act. They document the parties' agreement regarding objectives and confirm that they are achievable. In addition, the targets serve as metrics for compensation adjustment and as goals for target value design. Because they are jointly developed, each party owns the objectives and is committed to their achievement.

Jointly developed and validated targets are the mission statement of the IPD project.

[6]   Subcontractors, Consultants, and Joining Agreements

Contractors and Architects rarely perform their full contractual scope of work, delegating much of their scope to subcontractors and consultants. Architects may retain less than half of the total design fee and some contractors retain no self-performed work, at all. If IPD seeks to energize the people actually doing the work, it must clearly engage subcontractors and consultants. Moreover, if IPD is to provide the owner with a sufficient buffer against cost overruns, the subcontractors and consultants—or at least the key participants—must also share in the risk/reward structure.[112]

Because IPD is a collaborative, trust-based delivery method, the consultants and subcontractors chosen must embrace IPD and must be able to work cooperatively with the other parties. Thus, in most IPD structures, the subcontractors and consultants are jointly chosen by the owner, designer, contractor team, or the team has interview and veto rights over the designer's and contractor's preferred consultant and subcontractor choices.[113]

There are two primary methods for incorporating the key consultants and subcontractors: subagreements and joining agreements.

In the subagreement approach, the key IPD elements are flowed through the prime agreement (designer or contractor) into the subagreement (consultant or subcontractor). This includes key risk and reward terms as well as any liability limitations and waivers. The at-risk

---

[112] As a general rule, at least half of the anticipated construction cost should be within the risk/reward structure, and preferably more.

[113] Another option is to have each new project participant interviewed by the entire team that precedes it. Although this may work on smaller projects, it becomes increasingly cumbersome as the number of project participants increases.

compensation of the subcontractor or consultant is a portion of the at-risk compensation of its respective prime. In almost all instances, the business structure of the subagreements mirrors the business structure of the IPD agreement, except that the subcontractors and consultants are less involved and have no or limited voting rights at the project management level.

In a joining agreement approach, the key subcontractors and consultants execute an agreement that amends the IPD agreement to add them as a party. The risk/reward provisions are amended with each added key subcontractor or consultant to reflect the amount of compensation the added party has placed at risk. If all parties are added to a single agreement, the IPD agreement must distinguish between types of parties when determining issues, such as joint project control.

[D]   Four Minor Elements of Integrated Project Delivery

Virtually all IPD projects use the following elements which are adapted to the specific project: (1) collaborative decision making; (2) collocation; (3) building information modeling; and (4) design and construction management techniques.

Collaborative decision making focuses on the actual design and construction of the project. The IPD project should be organized to capitalize on all team member insights while providing context. Collaborative decisions lead to a deeper understanding of the problems and their solutions. When contractors and subcontractors are engaged in analyzing design issues, they can visualize, and help resolve, construction issues before they actually occur. This leads to a better understanding of design intent and few questions during the execution phase. Additionally, if parties participate in developing concepts and solutions they will be committed to the solution and more willing to see it though.

Collocation is the act of placing multiple entities within a single location. At some time during the project, it will be critical for all or portions of the team to be working together in the same location. Physical proximity[114] increases the quality and quantity of interactions. It also builds relationships and trust—both highly necessary in an IPD project. On larger projects, collocation may be a semi permanent state with all key team members at a single structure or location. On smaller projects, collocation may be used judiciously to accelerate progress at critical junctures. But even on the smallest projects, some collocation will be beneficial as creative development is best done in the same physical location.

---

[114] Virtual collocation is becoming increasingly possible, but even the best systems, such as Cisco's Telepresence or HP's Halo, are still not equivalent to physical presence.

BIM, as explained further above, provides a common platform to exchange detailed concepts of how a building will be designed, constructed, and operated. It allows optimization through iterative simulation that can reduce cost, and improve productivity and sustainability. BIM also increases team efficiency by reducing data re-entry and error through repurposing information. BIM can act as a common library and facilitate with facility management. The Lean Construction Institute[115] provides tools to maximize value and minimize waste and is leading the way in reforming management of production design, engineering, and construction for capital facilities.

Sound design and construction management techniques are critical tools for implementing IPD principles. They provide guidance regarding how to effectively communicate and collaborate. At project conception, the project team should determine how the project will be managed and should implement clear and effective rules for communication and collaboration.

[E]   Brief Comparison of Integrated Project Delivery Agreements

Below is a chart that summarizes the comparison of the three form integrated project delivery agreements available: AIA C191 (three-party agreement), AIA C195 (LLC formation, agreement governing the LLC, and three separate agreements, and CONSENSUS DOCS 300 (three-party agreement). The chart focuses on the key features of the agreement and compares how: (1) project decisions are made; (2) how and when target costs are set; (3) how compensation and incentives are structured; (3) how changes in the work and contingency are addressed; (4) risk allocation, including insurance, indemnity, and limitation of liability; (5) transparency and access to project documents and records; and (6) dispute resolution procedures.

---

[115] http//www.leanconstruction.org.

IPD CONCEPT	AIA C191 FAMILY (Three-Party Agreement)	AIA C195 FAMILY (LLC formation + agreement governing LLC + Three separate agreements)	CONSENSUS DOCS 300 (Three-Party Agreement)
Decision Making	The Project Management Team ("PMT") is responsible for the day to day management of the project and executes the decisions of the Project Executive Team ("PET"). Decisions must be unanimous and are binding unless reviewed by the PET, which also must act unanimously. The PMT does not have authority to make decisions that impact Target Cost or Contract Time. If the PMT is unable to reach consensus, any member may refer the matter to the PET for resolution. The PET has the sole authority to approve issues that result in a change to the Target Cost or the Contract Time. There is an option for an "Owner's Directive," which is similar to the Hanson Bridgett model. There is some tension and confusion between the roles and authority of	Decisions for the LLC are made by a "Governance Board" consisting of an odd number (5 or more). Owner has majority with 1 more representative than the non-owner members. Chair person is one of the Owner's representatives. Member has sole discretion to replace its representative at anytime and without approval of the Governance Board. Authorizations, approvals, or other actions require the unanimous vote of the Board unless specifically designated in the Agreement to be decided by majority vote.	The Project Management Group ("PMG") has ultimate decision making authority. The PMG includes a representative from the Owner, the Designer, and the Constructor. It can also include other critical project participants by invitation, but with limited voting rights (e.g., items that directly concern that participant's work) and they are subject to removal. The decision making process encourages consensus among PMG members but, if a consensus is not reached, the Owner decides, unless the decision implicates life, health, property and public welfare <u>and</u> is required to be made by a licensed design professional, in which case the Designer decides. The PMG receives most of its input from, and meets regularly with, the Collaborative Project Delivery Team ("CPD"),

IPD CONCEPT	AIA C191 FAMILY (Three-Party Agreement)	AIA C195 FAMILY (LLC formation + agreement governing LLC + Three separate agreements)	CONSENSUS DOCS 300 (Three-Party Agreement)
	the PMT and PET. The document says that PMT decisions are binding, unless the PET acts, which can create some uncertainty concerning PMT decisions. Adjustments to the Target Cost are through Modification, which includes Owner's Directives and Change Orders.		which includes the Owner, Designer, and Constructor, plus other design consultants and Subcontractors involved in the preconstruction phase that sign Joining Agreements.
Target Cost	The Target Cost is set before the conclusion of the Criteria Design Phase. Contractor and Architect develop the Target Criteria Proposal and if the Owner approves the Target Criteria Proposal, a Target Criteria Amendment is executed establishing the Target Cost, the Project Definition, the Project Goals, and the Project Schedule. If Owner rejects, the agreement is terminated and the owner pays the other parties the amount due and owning under the contract documents without reference	The Target Cost is set before the conclusion of the Criteria Design Phase. Construction Manager ("CM") develops the Target Cost in consultation with Owner and Architect. After the CM and Architect reach a consensus, they present the Target Cost to the Owner and the Owner evaluates and either approves or disapproves. If Target Cost is approved, it may only be adjusted under limited circumstances through Change Order. If Owner rejects, then Architect, CM and Owner revise	Project Target Cost Estimate ("PTCE") is based on 100% Construction Documents and is binding after approval by the Project Management Group ("PMG"). The PTCE includes all design and construction costs including contingencies. Before PTCE is set, the Constructor provides ongoing cost modeling for all phases: preliminary, schematic, design development, and construction documents. If the proposed PTCE exceeds the Project Budget: (1) Owner can either

IPD CONCEPT	AIA C191 FAMILY (Three-Party Agreement)	AIA C195 FAMILY (LLC formation + agreement governing LLC + Three separate agreements)	CONSENSUS DOCS 300 (Three-Party Agreement)
	to a specific provision. However, § 4.2.3 allows a GMP on the cost of preparing a Target Criteria Proposal.	scope, schedule, value engineer, etc., to see if they can reach a consensus on Target Cost. If consensus not reached, new LLC is dissolved and the governing agreement is terminated.	increase the Project Budget or terminate the agreement; (2) PMG can authorize re-bidding or renego-tiating; (3) PMG may direct the CPD to provide value engi-neering and redesign to bring the PTCE in line with the Project Budget. The above process is similar to traditional preconstruction services and the PTCE is not set until design is complete.
Compensation	Profit is earned through: (1) "Goal Achievement Compensation," regardless of whether the Target Cost is exceeded; and (2) realized "Incentive Compensation" if actual costs are below the Target Cost at the end of construction. If the Target Cost is exceeded, the Owner will either continue to pay all Costs of the Work, which includes Architect's and Contractor's salaried employees; **OR** the Owner has a check the box option to not reimburse the C and A for any further	The A/CM and other Non-Owner Members of the LLC are reimbursed for direct costs and a percentage of indirect costs incurred during design and construc-tion of the project. Profit is earned through: (1) "Goal Achievement" set in the Target Cost; and (2) realized "Incentive Compensation" if actual costs are below the Target Cost at the end of construction. Non-Owner Members forfeit the Goal Achievement if they fail to achieve a project	Designer's and Constructor's base compensation takes a traditional approach. **Designer:** Compensation for basic services is either based on actual costs or Fee. Fee is subject to adjustments for changes in design services caused by project delays provided Designer is not at fault. Fee may also be adjusted for Ad-ditional Services mutually agreed to by the PMG. **Constructor:** Compensation is broken down by Preconstruction and

IPD CONCEPT	AIA C191 FAMILY (Three-Party Agreement)	AIA C195 FAMILY (LLC formation + agreement governing LLC + Three separate agreements)	CONSENSUS DOCS 300 (Three-Party Agreement)
	Labor Costs but only continue to pay for material, equipment and subcontractor costs. (§ 4.2 and § 4.2.4). 100% of the Architect's and Contractor's Fee is at risk. (§ 4.4.1) As noted above, the Owner still has the obligation to make all Goal Achievement Compensation payments that were earned regardless of whether or not the Target Cost has been exceeded. **Note:** Project Schedule is not directly tied into compensation. It may be part of the Goal Achievement Compensation but the agreement does not really discuss what happens if the Project Schedule is exceeded.	goal, regardless of fault. Incentives are forfeited if Actual Costs exceed Target Cost regardless of fault. If the Target Cost is exceeded, Architect, CM and other non-Owner members will continue to perform their respective work without further compensation for direct or indirect costs. Therefore, the Target Cost essentially sets a guaranteed maximum price that the Owner will pay for design and construction of the project. The Owner also has the right to reject any recovery plans presented by the Architect and CM.	Construction services. Fee for Preconstruction may be based on stipulated sum, actual cost, or other basis. Compensation for the Construction is Cost of the Work plus Fee. Fee may be stipulated sum or other basis. Fee may be adjusted for change orders and delays not caused by Constructor. If the actual cost of the project is less than the PTCE, the parties share in savings on a percentage or other basis mutually agreed upon. If the PTCE is exceeded, either the Owner bears the entire cost or the extra cost is shared by the Parties based on mutually agreed percentages or another basis. If the losses are shared, the Parties will agree whether the Designer's and Constructor's Fees are, or are not, at risk, and, if so, whether the total amount of each Fee is, or is not, the limit of liability.

IPD CONCEPT	AIA C191 FAMILY (Three-Party Agreement)	AIA C195 FAMILY (LLC formation + agreement governing LLC + Three separate agreements)	CONSENSUS DOCS 300 (Three-Party Agreement)
Changes & Contingency	The Target Cost Breakdown is to identify all costs, fees and contingency amounts. The parties are to develop a risk matrix that identifies principle risks for planning, designing and constructing the project. The risk matrix will be used to establish the Target Cost contingencies. Target Cost may be only be amended for specific reasons: (1) Quantity variations where unit prices are used; (2) Cost variations from specified allowances; (3) Owner initiated changes in the Project Definition; (4) Owner initiated changes to the Project Schedule; (5) material defects in Owner supplied services and information; and (6) Force Majeure. **Note:** There is not a definition for what constitutes a Project delay, and does not appear to be any relief for schedule delays unless it is an Owner initiated change in the Project Schedule.	Target Cost includes a contingency for uncertainty in the scope of Work, risk, potential indemnity costs, market conditions, and other factors. Does not discuss how contingency is used. Target Cost cannot be adjusted except: (1) Owner-initiated changes in the "Project Definition" or Project Schedule; (2) Force Majeure events; (3) Reduction in Target Cost because project goal is not achieved and, Goal Achievement compensation is not awarded; or (4) other reasons upon unanimous, agreement of the Members.	Change Orders appear to only apply to the Constructor and follow a somewhat traditional process but are limited to the following conditions: (1) material change in scope of Work; (2) changes required by regulatory agencies; (3) differing site conditions; (4) a compensable delay; or (5) claims for which the Owner is found liable. Constructor can use contingency to cover costs that are not recovered through the change order process. Contractor can request, and Owner can order, a Change Order for changes in the Work, timing, or sequencing that impact the PTCE or the Contract Time. Change orders are resolved through negotiations between Owner and Constructor. The PMG performs a "root cause assessment" on a monthly basis to determine if Change Orders granted should result in an

IPD CONCEPT	AIA C191 FAMILY (Three-Party Agreement)	AIA C195 FAMILY (LLC formation + agreement governing LLC + Three separate agreements)	CONSENSUS DOCS 300 (Three-Party Agreement)
			adjustment to the PTCE. The PMG's decision on whether to increase the PTCE directly impacts whether the participants receive an incentive reward or potentially share in a loss.
Risk Allocation	**Insurance:** Has default normal insurance provisions with an assumption that it will be replaced by an OCIP, if available. (Similar to Hanson Bridgett model) **Indemnity:** Mutual comparative indemnity for personal injury and property damage. **Liability Waiver**: Complete waiver subject to 7 exceptions: (1) Willful Misconduct; (2) Express Warranty; (3) Owner's Payment; (4) Express Indemnification; (5) Failure to Procure Insurance; (6) Damages arising from liens, etc; and (7) Damages covered by insurance.	**Insurance:** Includes LLC controlled insurance program. **Indemnity:** Members are protected by the LLC and are indemnified by the LLC for claims arising from their acts or omissions, except for; (1) willful misconduct; and (2) obligations arising under the Member's separate agreements with the LLC. The LLC provides indemnity to the Architect and CM under separate agreement for damages, losses and claims not covered by the CCIP except for the Architect's and CM's willful misconduct. **Limited Liability:** Separate A/C/O Agreements are to include clauses	**Insurance:** Parties provide traditional construction project insurance coverage—Builder's Risk, E & O, CGL, workers comp and auto. Agreement did not include waiver of subrogation language for Constructor's and Designer's insurance. There is a waiver of subrogation between Owner and Constructor for damages covered under the property insurance, except as to proceeds of the policy. **Indemnity:** The Owner, Architect, and Constructor have separate indemnity obligations to each other for damages arising from bodily injury and property damage on a comparative fault basis: Meaning, the party is only responsible to the extent its act

IPD CONCEPT	AIA C191 FAMILY (Three-Party Agreement)	AIA C195 FAMILY (LLC formation + agreement governing LLC + Three separate agreements)	CONSENSUS DOCS 300 (Three-Party Agreement)
	Note: Although there is a waiver of consequential Damages, the agreement allows for liquidated damages.	waiving all claims between Members other than claims and losses arising from a Member's willful misconduct or insured risks. Owner's Agreement limits LLC's and Architect's/CM's liability to (1) amount of Incentive Compensation Layer; and (2) sums recovered from insurance required by governing agreement and separate A/C Agreements. However, under the compensation sections of the Architect and CM agreements, the Architect and CM have the ultimate risk for exceeding the Target Cost because they must continue to perform their respective work and service without further compensation for direct or indirect costs.	or omission caused the damage and will be reimbursed for defense costs paid in excess of indemnitee's percentage of liability. **Limited Liability:** Project Risk Allocation has two options—(1) "Safe Harbor Decisions" or (2) "Traditional Risk Allocation." Regardless of the option selected, there is a mutual waiver of consequential damages. Under the Safe Harbor, the Parties waive liability against each other for acts, omissions, mistakes, or errors in judgment arising from joint decisions made in good faith by the PMG, unless the party is in willful default of an obligation under the Agreement. Under the Traditional Risk Allocation, each Party remains fully liable for its own negligence and breaches of contract

IPD CONCEPT	AIA C191 FAMILY (Three-Party Agreement)	AIA C195 FAMILY (LLC formation + agreement governing LLC + Three separate agreements)	CONSENSUS DOCS 300 (Three-Party Agreement)
			and warranty but there is an option to cap Designer's and Constructor's liability to a specified amount for uninsurable risk.
Document & Record Access	Parties must maintain books and records for 3 years after final payment. Owner has the right to audit upon reasonable notice, except for previously agreed rates, unit prices and lump sum amounts.	The LLC must maintain accounting records. Any Member or its representatives may inspect the LLC's accounting records, the Agreement, and the LLC's Certificate of Formation, for any purpose reasonably related to the Member's Interest in the LLC. The LLC has the right to audit Members' accounts to verify direct and indirect costs per A/CM separate agreements. The Owner has right to audit LLC's accounts per Owner's separate agreement.	There is a high degree of transparency between the Owner, Designer and Constructor. The PMG has access to all costs models, accounting records and documents used in formulating the PTCE. Designer and Constructor must keep full and detailed accounts with respect to all costs for their respective portions of the project, which is subject to Owner's audit. Owner's accountants will substantiate Constructor's final costs within 15 days of delivery to the PMG and before issuance of a final certificate for payment.

IPD CONCEPT	AIA C191 FAMILY (Three-Party Agreement)	AIA C195 FAMILY (LLC formation + agreement governing LLC + Three separate agreements)	CONSENSUS DOCS 300 (Three-Party Agreement)
Dispute Resolution	After the PMT and PET levels, PET may refer a dispute to the Dispute Resolution Committee, which consists of senior representatives and a Project Neutral. The Project Neutral will endeavor to mediate the dispute within 15 days. If the matter is not resolved, and depending upon the check box option chosen, the matter will either be (1) Arbitrated by the Project Neutral; (2) Arbitrated by the AAA; or (3) A party specified "other."	Members attempt to reach a mutual consensus on all disputes within 15 days notice of dispute. If consensus is reached, CM distributes all recorded resolutions to the appropriate parties. If Members fail to reach consensus, disputes are then presented to Governance Board who has 30 days from notice to reach a consensus. If a consensus is not reached, the matter is referred to arbitration through a "Dispute Resolution Committee," which includes one chief executive of each Member and a "Neutral" arbitrator, who is the chair. If mutual resolution is not achieved within 60 days, the Neutral decides the matter. The Neutral's decision is final and binding.	Disputes not resolved through the dispute resolution proceedings are resolved either by binding arbitration or litigation, whichever option is selected by the Parties. Initial dispute resolution is through direct discussion between the Parties and, if the dispute is not resolved within 5 business days, the matter is referred to the PMG. If not resolved by PMG, the parties can opt for non-binding "mitigation" measures: (1) project neutral; or (2) dispute review board. If mitigation measures are not selected, the Parties must mediate the dispute. Findings through "mitigation" measures may be introduced as evidence at a subsequent adjudication. Unresolved disputes will be submitted to binding arbitration or litigation.

[F]   The Implications of Integrated Project Delivery

Although IPD projects all share certain common features, early involvement of key contributors, open communication, team decision making, and a sharing of risk and reward based on project success, the legal structures supporting IPD can vary widely. AIA/AIACC's Guide recognizes three primary variants: relational agreements, single purpose entities and alliance/alliance like agreements and even within these categorizations, there are individual variations and hybrids. An accurate assessment of legal implications requires examination of the specific approach used.

One of the first implications of IPD is an increase in process cost. Most of the IPD approaches require intensive team formation and process design phases. In IPD, the parties are creating a virtual organization for project execution and it takes time and effort to determine how the individual participants will fit into and interact in this project team. This initial process design phase is also a period where the parties begin to build the bonds of trust they will need during the project. The increased process cost will be recaptured through greater project efficiency—provided the project is of sufficient size.[116]

The second implication is a shift from fault based liability allocation to allocation based on project outcome. In most IPD scenarios, project outcome risks (budget, schedule & quality) are allocated through compensation incentives. If a project overruns its targets, the non-owner parties' profits are reduced or eliminated. If the project exceeds expectations, the non-owner parties' profits increase. This project risk sharing supplants traditional intramural liability assessments and is reflected by liability waivers or limitations among the project participants. Because litigation between owner, contractor and designer are the most common and costly forms of construction litigation, the reduction of these intramural claims greatly reduces the parties' risk.

Because IPD is collaborative at its core, the economic loss doctrine, third party reliance and privity issues defenses discussed previously are largely ineffective. Similarly, the *Spearin* warranties are diminished or eliminated. But because risk and liability have been allocated by contract, the importance of these concepts is diminished. Liability to third parties is not significantly altered in an integrated project and the parties rely on project or individual insurance to protect against this risk.

A third implication is a change in work and cash flow. In an IPD project, the most intensity design period (detailed design using the AIA/AIACC parlance) occurs earlier in the project. This, along with the

---

[116] If the participants have prior collaborative experience, especially if with each other, then the process costs are greatly reduced. The author is aware of integrated projects as small as $10 million, but the teams had prior experience with each other and IPD, and were already committed to the process.

process design effort, will shift the timing of design costs, even though the total design cost will not necessarily increase. In addition, because work is assigned on a "best person" basis, some of the work done by designers in the traditional construction documents phase will be supplanted by detailed design performed by contractors and vendors. Designers should recognize that they are selling creativity, not just hours and will need to adjust their internal business models to reflect this reallocation.[117]

Finally, many of the legal issues discussed in regard to BIM also apply to IPD, but more intensely. For example, the design delegation/ professional responsibility issue is heightened by the deeper collaboration between the parties. Who owns the design and similar intellectual property issues are also amplified by IPD. But, the fluid nature of IPD should not justify poor delineation of responsibilities—although that may occur if the parties plunge into IPD without clarifying individual roles. Blurring of roles affects insurance coverage if work bridges between entities. Eventually, we may see omnibus insurance products designed for IPD, but presently, care must be taken to assure that the parties are adequately covered using a portfolio of existing products.

IPD, and to a lesser degree BIM itself, can create new exposures for all project participants. But these new exposures are created in an environment that is "self healing." Because risk and reward are jointly shared, the parties are stimulated to solve problems rather than assign blame. Moreover, by involving key contributors at an early stage, many more potential problems will be discovered and resolved long before they occur. Thus, the probability of failure and the magnitude of its conse-quence diminish even if the avenues for claims are expanded. And to a great degree, the expanded claims potential is reduced or eliminated by the internal liability waivers contained in the IPD agreement.[118]

§ 5.06   CONCLUSION

BIM is being used to solve some of the construction industries most pressing and important issues. The development and standardized use of BIM addresses issues of efficiency (both in the end product and throughout the design and construction of the project), productivity, quality, and sustainability in ways that only a scant few years ago, people

---

[117] If you evaluate a designer's services from a value perspective, it is apparent that designers undercharge for the truly valuable and creative effort that occurs during the early phases of a project and then "make up" for the shortfall by selling many units of clerical work during the construction documents and sometime construction administration phases. If the latter phases are reduced, design professionals will need to increase their "creative process" compensation.

[118] These conclusions are less applicable to "hybrid" IPD agreements. For example, if liability is not waived, but only limited, the parties still have an incentive to assign blame. This can undermine joint problem solving. Thus, by being more "contractually conser-vative" the parties may actually increase their potential risk.

could only have dreamed possible. Using BIM to solve increasingly complex problems will naturally lead to its use in collaborative settings and will likely lead to project delivery methods aligned with collaboration, like IPD. Although the full use and potential of BIM and IPD have not been realized, they have already opened a world of possibilities for innovation and creativity in the built environment.

CHAPTER 8

DESIGN BUILD

Daniel J. Donohue
Pavan I. Khoobchandani

§ 8.07 CONTRACTUAL ARRANGEMENTS COMMON IN DESIGN-BUILD—TEAM BUILDING

Page 225, replace the URL in note 8 with:

http://www.schiffhardin.com/design-build/designer-led.html (last visited July 13, 2009).

§ 8.08 PRIVATE SECTOR DESIGN-BUILD CONTRACT DOCUMENT FORMS

[A] American Institute of Architects Design-Build Contract Documents (available at www.aia.org)

[2] A142™—2004 Standard Form of Agreement Between Design-Builder and Contractor

Page 227, add new subparagraph [a] before subparagraph [3]:

[a] *A441™—2008 Standard Form of Agreement Between Contractor and Subcontractor for a Design-Build Project*

The A441-2008 is a new fixed-price agreement that establishes the contractual relationship between the contractor and subcontractor in a design-build project. It incorporates the terms and conditions of the A142-2004 and provides for the services of a subcontractor on a design-build project. Previously, there was no form agreement to flow down to a subcontractor the essential provisions of the design-build family of documents.

[4] B143™—2004 Standard Form of Agreement Between Design-Builder and Architect

Page 228, add new subparagraph [a] before subparagraph [5]:

[a] C441™—2008, Standard Form of Agreement Between Architect and Consultant for a Design-Build Project

The C441 is a new agreement that establishes the contractual relationship between the architect and a consultant providing services to the architect on a design-build project. It incorporates by reference a preexisting prime agreement between the design-builder and architect and flows down to the consultant the essential provisions of the design-build family of documents.

[B] ConsensusDOCS/Associated General Contractors of America Design-Build Contract Documents (available at www.agc.org or www.consensusdocs.org)

[11] AIA/AGC Recommended Guidelines for Procurement of Design-Build Projects in the Public Sector: AGC 480

Page 231, add new subparagraph [a] before subparagraph [12]:

[a] Certificates of Substantial and Final Completion for Design-Build Work: ConsensusDOCS 481 and 482

ConsensusDOCS 481 and 482 are used to establish substantial and final completion of design-build work.

§ 8.09 DESIGN-BUILD IN THE PUBLIC SECTOR

[A] State Statutes Allowing Design-Build for Public Projects

Page 234, replace the URL in note 10 with:

http://www.marshall-group.com/april2007.pdf (last visited July 13, 2009)

Page 236, replace the last two paragraphs of subsection with:

Information regarding state statutes and legislation regarding the design-build project delivery method is available at http://www.dbia.org/advocacy/state/ (last visited on July 13, 2009).

§ 8.11   BENEFITS OF DESIGN-BUILD—ARE THEY BEING REALIZED?

[B]   Information About Risk Allocation in Public Design-Build Contracts and Whether Potential Benefits Are Realized

Page 247, replace the URL in note 16 with:

http://www.ncppp.org/resources/papers/battellereport.pdf   (last   visited July 13, 2009).

CHAPTER 8A

CONSTRUCTION MANAGEMENT

Bruce H. Schoumacher
April R. Walkup[*]

§ 8A.04   CONSTRUCTION MANAGER LICENSING

Page 257, add to note 50:

; Tarsitano v. Bd. of Educ., 385 Ill. App. 3d 868, 324 Ill. Dec. 573, 896 N.E.2d 359 (1st Dist. 2008) (where Illinois appellate court held that legislature intended that contracts for goods and services which are economically procurable from only one source and those for utility services are to be exempt from the competitive bidding provision of the School Code).

§ 8A.08   CONSTRUCTION MANAGEMENT LIABILITY

[A]   Bodily Injury

[1]   Contractual Duties

Page 265, add to note 111:

; Reno v. Concrete Coring, Inc., 2005 Ohio 3062, 2004 Ohio App. LEXIS 2856 (2005) (where Ohio appellate court held that when an employee of a subcontractor is injured while performing work for his or her employer that is inherently dangerous, the owner and/or general contractor owes no duty of care to that employee).

Page 265, add to note 112:

; Williams v. Martin Marietta Alumina, Inc., 817 F.2d 1030 (3d Cir. 1987) (where United States Third Circuit Appellate Court held that, "as applied to an employee of an independent contractor, section 343 is referred to as the 'safe workplace' doctrine," under which one who contracts with an

[*] The authors acknowledge the assistance of Alicia Garcia and Emily Widmer in preparing this supplement.

independent contractor has a duty to provide a safe workplace for the employees of the independent contractor.").

[D] Design Defects

Page 267, add to note 126:

; Presnell Constr. Managers, Inc. v. EH Constr., LLC, 134 S.W.3d 575 (Ky. 2004) (construction manager had a duty independent of its contractual duties to not supply false information to contractor, and thus, contractor's complaint stated a cause of action against manager for negligent misrepresentation, even though there was no privity of contract between manager and contractor, where complaint alleged that manager supplied faulty information and guidance to contractor that resulted in economic loss).

Page 267, add to note 127:

; Henriquez v. Parsippany Constr. Co., Inc., 62 A.D.3d 749, 879 N.Y.S.2d 512 (N.Y. 2009) (a builder or contractor is justified in relying upon the plans and specifications which he or she has contracted to follow unless they are so apparently defective that an ordinary builder of ordinary prudence would be put upon notice that the work was dangerous and likely to cause injury).

Page 267, add to note 128:

; Hunt Constr. Group, Inc. v. U.S., 281 F.3d 1369 (C.A. Fed. 2002) (government contractor has a duty to seek clarification of a patent ambiguity in contract, but when ambiguity is latent, court will construe the ambiguous term against the government as drafter of the contract, provided that the contractor's interpretation is reasonable and the contractor relied on that interpretation when preparing its bid).

[F] Delayed Site Access

Page 269, add to note 138:

; Trocom Constr. Corp. v. City of New York, 51 A.D.3d 533, 859 N.Y.S.2d 41 (N.Y. App. Div. 2008) (damages are recoverable for delays caused by a contractee's bad faith or willful, malicious, or grossly negligent conduct, as are damages for uncontemplated delays, irrespective of contract clause prohibiting damages for delay).

[G]   Construction Contract Administration

[3]   Support Services

Page 270, add to note 152:

; L.K. Comstock & Co., Inc. v. Morse/UBM Joint Venture,153 Ill. App. 3d 475, 505 N.E.2d 1253 (Ill. App. 1st Dist. 1987) (delay damage waiver provision of contract between owner and contractor precluded contractor from recovering delay damages from owner's construction manager in view of extensive responsibilities given to the construction manager by the contract, notwithstanding other provision of contract requiring any contractor who caused loss to another to defend and save harmless the construction manager in any suit, provision that contractor would not be required to indemnify construction manager for claims arising out of the construction manager's own negligence, and provision that time would be extended if delays occurred as a result of acts or omissions of the construction manager).

CHAPTER **10**

PROJECT FINANCE

Stephen Butler
John T. W. Mercer
Jason B. Yost

§ 10.02   BASIC STRUCTURE OF PROJECT FINANCE
           TRANSACTION

[B]   Sources of Financing

    [3]   Third Party Support

    [c]   *Bilateral Agencies*

    [ii]   Development Assistance

Page 304, add new subsections after § 10.02[B][3][c][ii]:

    [d]   *Government Agencies*

On February 17, 2009, President Obama signed into law the American Recovery and Reinvestment Act of 2009 (H.R. 1) (the ARRA). Among other things, the ARRA put into place new, and greatly expanded a number of already existing, federal incentives and policies in an effort to encourage renewable and energy efficiency programs as well as support for other infrastructure development. Of the $789 billion included in the bill, project developers are able to take advantage of a number of enhanced incentives, including (i) tax credits, (ii) cash grants, (iii) tax credit bonds, and (iv) loan guarantees.[58.1]

    [i]   Tax Credits   The ARRA extended and enhanced the previously existing production tax credits and investment tax credits.

[58.1] This discussion relates only to a small percentage of the government programs and incentives that were included in the ARRA. Developers of projects may be able to benefit from a number of additional programs and incentives that are beyond the scope of this discussion.

[a] Production Tax Credits

The federal renewable electricity production tax credit (PTC) is a per-kilowatt-hour tax credit (ranging from 1.0¢/kWh to 2.1¢/kWh (as such amounts have been adjusted for inflation for the 2008 tax year)) for electricity generated by qualified energy resources and sold during the taxable year. Originally enacted in 1992, the PTC has been renewed and expanded numerous times.[58.2] The ARRA revised the previously available credit by: (1) extending the in-service deadline for most eligible technologies; and (2) allowing facilities that qualify for the PTC to opt instead to take the federal business energy investment credit (ITC) or an equivalent cash grant from the U.S. Department of Treasury.[58.3] The duration of the credit is generally 10 years after the date the facility is placed in service, but there are limited exceptions.

[b] Investment Tax Credits

The federal business energy investment tax credit (ITC) is a second tax credit that is available for equipment used in solar energy property, wind, geothermal, biomass and marine energy projects. As opposed to the PTC, the ITC is taken entirely in the year that a project is placed into service. The amount of the possible credit ranges from 10% of expenditures for geothermal, microturbines and CHP to 30% of expenditures for solar, fuel cells and small wind projects.

[ii] Cash Grants In lieu of taking PTC and/or ITC for new installations, the ARRA also allows for eligible developers to accept cash grants from the U.S. Treasury Department. Grants are available to eligible property (including solar energy property, fuel cells, small wind turbines, microturbines, geothermal heat pumps, and combined heat and power (CHP) systems and certain other qualified facilities) placed in service in 2009 or 2010, or placed in service by the specified credit termination date (which varies, depending on the type of technology) if construction began in 2009 or 2010. Grant amounts range from 10% of the basis of the property for geothermal heat pumps, microturbines and CHP to 30% of the basis property for solar, fuel cells, small wind turbines, and certain other qualified facilities. Only tax-paying entities are eligible for this grant. Federal, state and local government bodies, nonprofits, qualified energy tax credit bond lenders, and cooperative electric companies are not eligible to receive this grant. In addition, partners or pass-through entities for the entities described above are also not eligible to receive this grant.[58.4]

[58.2] Database of State Incentives for Renewables and Efficiency (www.dsireusa.org).
[58.3] *Id.*
[58.4] *Id.*

[iii]   Tax Credit Bonds   In addition to the tax credits and grants discussed above, the allowable bond volume for certain tax credit bonds that were previously available have been expanded. These include Clean Renewable Energy Bonds (CREBs) and Qualified Energy Conservation Bonds (QECBs). The advantage of both of these types of bonds is that they are issued—theoretically—with a 0% interest rate. The borrower pays back only the principal of the bond, and the bondholder receives federal tax credits in lieu of the traditional bond interest. The tax credit may be taken quarterly to offset the tax liability of the bondholder, subject to certain limits.[58.5]

[a]   Clean Renewable Energy Bonds

Under the ARRA, an additional $1.6 billion was allocated for "new" CREBs (those authorized under the Energy Improvement and Extension Act of 2008 (Div. A, Sec. 107) and the ARRA, collectively) for a total new CREB allocation of $2.4 billion. CREBs may be used by certain entities—primarily in the public sector—electric cooperatives, government entities (states, cities, counties, territories, Indian tribal governments or any political subdivision thereof), and by certain lenders—to finance facilities that generate electricity from the following resources: wind; closed-loop biomass; open-loop biomass; geothermal; small irrigation; hydropower; landfill gas; marine renewable; and trash combustion facilities. Public power providers, governmental bodies, and electric cooperatives are each reserved an equal share (33.3%) of the new CREBs allocation under the ARRA (approximately $2.4 billion).[58.6]

[b]   Qualified Energy Conservation Bonds

In addition to expanding prior limits on CREBs, the ARRA also expanded the allowable bond volume for QEBCs to $3.2 billion. QECBs may be used by state, local and tribal governments to finance certain types of energy projects. QECBs are qualified tax credit bonds, and in this respect are similar to new CREBs. In contrast to CREBs, however, QECBs are not subject to a U.S. Department of Treasury application and approval process. Bond volume is instead allocated to each state based on the state's percentage of the U.S. population as of July 1, 2008. The definition of "qualified energy conservation projects" for which QECBs are available is fairly broad and contains elements relating to energy efficiency capital expenditures in public buildings; renewable energy production; various research and development applications; mass commuting facilities that reduce energy consumption; several types of energy

---

[58.5] *Id.*
[58.6] *Id.*

related demonstration projects; and public energy efficiency education campaigns, as well as renewable energy facilities that are eligible for CREBs.[58.7]

[iv] Loan Guarantees Title XVII of the federal Energy Policy Act of 2005 authorized the U.S. Department of Energy (DOE) to issue loan guarantees for projects that "avoid, reduce or sequester air pollutants or anthropogenic emissions of greenhouse gases; and employ new or significantly improved technologies as compared to commercial technologies in service in the United States at the time the guarantee is issued." The DOE loan guarantee program is intended by Congress and DOE to offer loan guarantees for energy efficiency, renewable energy and advanced transmission and distribution projects in three major categories: (a) manufacturing projects, (b) stand-alone projects, and (c) large-scale integration projects that may combine multiple eligible renewable energy, energy efficiency and transmission technologies in accordance with a staged development scheme. As of August, 2009, no loan guarantees had actually been issued under the program.

The ARRA extended the authority of the DOE to issue loan guarantees and appropriated $6 billion to pay the cost of credit subsidies—expected to permit the issuance of approximately $60 billion of additional loan guarantees. Under the ARRA provisions, the DOE may enter into guarantees until September 30, 2011. In addition, a new section defining eligible technologies for new loan guarantees was added. For the new projects authorized by the ARRA, eligible projects include renewable energy projects that generate electricity or thermal energy and facilities that manufacture related components, electric power transmission systems, and innovative biofuels projects.

Guidelines for utilizing many of these incentives are still being developed by the government agencies that will oversee their disbursement/implementation. As with any government provided funding, there are, and are expected to be, a number of requirements that must be met before a developer is able to utilize these incentives. These requirements range from requiring recipients to register in the Central Contractor Registration (CCR) database; to requiring that the developers use American iron, steel, and manufactured goods in certain construction, alteration, maintenance, or repair projects; to requiring the payment of Davis-Bacon Act (40 U.S.C. § 31) wage rates to certain laborers. Each developer interested in utilizing any of these incentives will need to closely examine the requirements for obtaining and utilizing such incentives in determining to what extent they may be able to positively affect project economics.

[58.7] *Id.*

CHAPTER **11**

ENVIRONMENTAL ISSUES
Matthew P. Coglianese

§ 11.03   THE ENVIRONMENTAL REGULATORY
           FRAMEWORK APPLICABLE TO
           CONSTRUCTION PROJECTS

[A]   **Federal Legislation**

   [1]   **The Clean Water Act (CWA)**

   [a]   *Stormwater*

   [i]   **Overview**

Page 329, add to end of subsection:

While EPA and the states have ratcheted up enforcement of
stormwater regulations, the most significant regulatory development for
the construction industry occurred at the end of 2009. On December 1,
2009, EPA published its final rule for "*Effluent Limitations Guidelines and
Standards for the Construction and Development Point Source Category*"
(40 CFR Part 450). Among other things, the rule sets effluent limitation
guidelines for turbidity from stormwater runoff for all permitted construction and development (C&D) sites. The rule has been several years in the
making. Penalties for violating these new federal requirements—called
Construction and Development Effluent Limitations Guidelines (C&D
ELG)—can reach $37,500 per day per violation.

While not as stringent as the proposed rule, EPA has imposed new
nationwide monitoring requirements and enforceable numeric limits on
the amount of sediment that can run off any construction site that impacts
10 or more acres of land at any one time. The rule also specifies the types
of erosion and sediment controls that contractors must use (i.e. best
management practices or "BMPs") requiring the control of stormwater
runoff on all construction sites that disturb one or more acre of land. The
new rule took effect in February 2010 and will be phased in over
approximately four years. EPA did not address post-construction issues in
the construction and development ELG. Rather, EPA has initiated a
separate rulemaking to develop post-construction ELGs by November
2012.

The final rule and its preamble are lengthy, but basically the rule is comprised of numeric and non-numeric ELGs. Essentially, the ELG establish minimum control technologies that must be incorporated into every construction stormwater permit issued by EPA and states authorized to administer the NPDES permit program. Specific requirements include:

For all construction stormwater permits—Mandatory Best Management Practices (BMPs) using the best practicable control technology currently available relating to *Erosion and Sediment Controls* (40 CFR § 450.21(a)), *Soil Stabilization BMPs* (40 CFR § 450.21(b)), *Dewatering BMPs* (40 CFR § 450.21(c)), *Pollution Prevention Measures* (40 CFR § 450.21(d)), and *Prohibited Discharges* (40 CFR § 450.21(e)): these include the following set out in the Rule:

(a) Erosion and Sediment Controls. Design, install and maintain effective erosion controls and sediment controls to minimize the discharge of pollutants. At a minimum, such controls must be designed, installed and maintained to:
   (1) Control stormwater volume and velocity within the site to minimize soil erosion;
   (2) Control stormwater discharges, including both peak flowrates and total stormwater volume, to minimize erosion at outlets and to minimize downstream channel and streambank erosion;
   (3) Minimize the amount of soil exposed during construction activity;
   (4) Minimize the disturbance of steep slopes;
   (5) Minimize sediment discharges from the site. The design, installation and maintenance of erosion and sediment controls must address factors such as the amount, frequency, intensity and duration of precipitation, the nature of resulting stormwater runoff, and soil characteristics, including the range of soil particle sizes expected to be present on the site;
   (6) Provide and maintain natural buffers around surface waters, direct stormwater to vegetated areas to increase sediment removal and maximize stormwater infiltration, unless infeasible; and
   (7) Minimize soil compaction and, unless infeasible, preserve topsoil.
(b) Soil Stabilization. Stabilization of disturbed areas must, at a minimum, be initiated immediately whenever any clearing, grading, excavating or other earth disturbing activities have permanently ceased on any portion of the site, or temporarily ceased on any portion of the site and will not resume for a period exceeding 14 calendar days. Stabilization must be completed within a period of time determined by the permitting authority. In arid, semiarid, and drought-stricken areas where initiating vegetative stabilization

measures immediately is infeasible, alternative stabilization measures must be employed as specified by the permitting authority.

(c) Dewatering. Discharges from dewatering activities, including discharges from dewatering of trenches and excavations, are prohibited unless managed by appropriate controls.

(d) Pollution Prevention Measures. Design, install, implement, and maintain effective pollution prevention measures to minimize the discharge of pollutants. At a minimum, such measures must be designed, installed, implemented and maintained to:

(1) Minimize the discharge of pollutants from equipment and vehicle washing, wheel wash water, and other wash waters. Wash waters must be treated in a sediment basin or alternative control that provides equivalent or better treatment prior to discharge;

(2) Minimize the exposure of building materials, building products, construction wastes, trash, landscape materials, fertilizers, pesticides, herbicides, detergents, sanitary waste and other materials present on the site to precipitation and to stormwater; and

(3) Minimize the discharge of pollutants from spills and leaks and implement chemical spill and leak prevention and response procedures.

(e) Prohibited Discharges. The following discharges are prohibited:

(1) Wastewater from washout of concrete, unless managed by an appropriate control;

(2) Wastewater from washout and cleanout of stucco, paint, form release oils, curing compounds and other construction materials;

(3) Fuels, oils, or other pollutants used in vehicle and equipment operation and maintenance; and

(4) Soaps or solvents used in vehicle and equipment washing.

(f) Surface Outlets. When discharging from basins and impoundments, utilize outlet structures that withdraw water from the surface, unless infeasible.

For all construction sites that disturb 20 or more acres of land at one time (whether contiguous or not), the average turbidity for any discharge for any day may not exceed a numeric effluent limit of 280 NTU (turbidity measurement units)—the deadline for complying with this numeric limit will be about August 2011 (40 CFR § 450.22(a)). The 280 NTU effluent limit is expanded to include all construction sites that disturb 10 or more acres of land at one time (whether contiguous or not) in about January 2014. The turbidity effluent limit is limited to the 2-year, 24-hour storm event. As most states implement the federal stormwater rules, they will be responsible for establishing implementing the new regulations and standards.

EPA will include the new ELG provisions in a new five-year Construction General Permit (CGP) to be reissued no later than July 2011. As mentioned above, most states issue their own construction general permits, and the new ELG requirements must be incorporated into any new general permits issued after the effective date of the regulation (60 days after publication in the Federal Register). The requirements also apply to individual permits issued by states or EPA. (EPA currently issues permits for construction activities in four states, the District of Columbia and in certain U.S. territories and tribal areas.)

The new rule will require new responsibilities on new construction activities covered by the rule. On all projects where the numeric limit applies, the rule requires contractors to collect numerous stormwater runoff samples from all discharge points during every rain event and calculate the NTU level(s). The data is then averaged. If that average reading exceeds the "daily maximum limit of 280 NTU's," the site will be in violation of the new ELG.

The new ELG requirements will not directly apply to construction site "operators" until the requirements are incorporated into an individual or general NPDES stormwater permit that applies to their project(s), as described above. That is, the construction stormwater permit language is what will become the legally enforceable requirement that construction site "operators" must meet or face potential fines and penalties. Therefore, the implementation date of the new requirements will vary from state to state, depending on when states reissue their permits and whether projects are covered by individual or general permits.

EPA expects compliance with the new regulation to reduce the amount of sediment and other pollutants discharged from construction and development sites by approximately 4 billion pounds per year. EPA puts the annual cost of the rule at about $959 million, once fully implemented. Therefore, with increased regulatory scrutiny of construction projects and the new ELG rule, it is imperative that in the pre-planning stages of a project, the designated responsible party should fully identify and understand the applicable NPDES program and Rule requirements. For the EPA CGP, the "operator" of the construction site is responsible for obtaining a stormwater permit. There can be a single site operator, or multiple operators. That depends on the relationship between the owner, architect, general contractor, or any other team members, who may have contractual responsibility or similar duties. What is important is that from a regulator's perspective there is overlap on the definition of "operator." That is, the regulator may be able to seek penalties from both the owner and contractor, and, perhaps, others, for not obtaining a permit or for violation of permit conditions. So, it is important for the project team to communicate on the stormwater issue upfront and designate responsibility for obtaining the stormwater permit, including addressing all the permitting protocol such as producing a stormwater pollution prevention plan and daily compliance with the plan during the construction process.

Overall, the "operators" at a construction site, even if they did not obtain the permit, will be responsible for compliance and implementation of the conditions of the permit.

[ii]   Who Is Responsible for Obtaining the Required Stormwater Permit for a Construction Project?

Page 330, add to end of subsection:

Stormwater pollution remains a hot topic, and penalties for failure to comply are prevalent.[26.1] Construction firms must be particularly careful as stormwater pollution has become commonplace. [26.2]

[26.1] *Facilities Throughout the Southeast Ordered to Comply with Clean Water Act and Pay Penalties Totaling More Than $92,000, available at* http://yosemite.epa.gov/opa/ admpress.nsf/ab2d81eb088f4a7e85257359003f5339/e3fb9dd117b7b279852575d200545d 19!OpenDocument (last visited June 16, 2008). ("Six entities were cited for alleged stormwater-related violations of the CWA. Polluted storm water runoff is a leading cause of impairment to the nearly 40 percent of surveyed U.S. water bodies which do not meet water quality standards. Over land or via storm sewer systems, polluted runoff is discharged, often untreated, directly into local water bodies. The settlements and associated penalties include Gwinnett Convention and Visitors Bureau, for violations at the Gwinnett Braves Stadium in Lawrenceville, Ga. (civil penalty of $9000) Port of Pensacola, Fl., for violations at the port itself (civil penalty of $19,000) Boone County Board of Education, for violations at the Long Branch High School in Union, Ky. (civil penalty of $7,000) Drees Company, Inc., for violations at its Harmony subdivision in Union, Ky. (civil penalty of $15,000)

Fowler Reese, LLC, for violations at its Hickory Valley subdivision in Independence, Ky. (civil penalty of $3,500)

Orleans Home Builders, for violations at its Weldon Ridge-Arbor development in Cary, N.C. (civil penalty of $4,000)")

[26.2] *Construction Firm Faces Fine for Clean Water Violations in Worcester Development, available at* http://yosemite.epa.gov/opa/admpress.nsf/ab2d81eb088f4a7e8525 7359003f5339/1b11122a6f621ccf852575cb00732380!OpenDocument (last visited June 16, 2009). (A construction company building a 79-acre residential subdivision of townhouses in Worcester, Mass., faces up to $157,000 in penalties of for alleged violations of the federal Clean Water Act. Bailin & Associates, Inc. of Worcester has been constructing the subdivision since 2003. Because the company is disturbing more than one acre of land, they are required to apply for a water discharge permit—either an individual NPDES permit or a NPDES General Permit for Storm Water Discharges from Construction Activities. Though construction began in 2003, Bailin failed to apply for a NPDES permit until April of 2008. Additionally, Bailin failed to install and maintain adequate Best Management Practices (BMPs) at the site such as sedimentation control barriers, stockpile containment, and surface and slope stabilization. Lastly, Bailin violated the Clean Water Act by allegedly discharging stormwater from the construction site without a permit.)

[b]   Dredge and Fill/Wetlands

Page 334, add to note 39:

An important change made at the end of 2008 was that the EPA issued a final rule reverting back to the EPA's 1999 definition of a "discharge of dredged material." http://www.epa.gov/owow/wetlands/pdf/Tulloch_Conforming_Rule.pdf (last visited June 17 2009). The purpose of this rulemaking was to conform the regulatory text of the rule to match a court order that was issued in 2001. *Id.* at 3, column 3. (This rule conforms the language in the Code of Federal Regulations with the legal state of the regulations defining "discharge of dredged material" following the D.C. district court's decision invalidating the 2001 amendment to the regulations made by the *Tulloch II* rule. The effect of the district court's 2007 *NAHB* order was to reinstate the 1999 rule text. *Id.* It appears that determination whether a particular redeposit of dredged material in waters of the United States requires a section 404 permit will be done on a case-by-case basis, as long as it is consistent with the provided definition. *Id.* Another result of this rulemaking is that the definition of "incidental fallback" is deleted from the regulation, as is the language indicating that the agencies "regard" the use of mechanized earthmoving equipment as a regulable discharge. *Id.* The previous "grandfather provision," which provides exemptions from 404 permitting, however has been excluded from this final rulemaking. *Id.* at 4, column 1. Aside from some minor tweaks, the EPA has offered that this rule merely conforms with the regulations' definition of "discharge of dredged material" to reflect the judicial decision in the *NAHB* case and associated January 30, 2007, order. *Id.* at 4, column 2. For an excellent summary of this area of the law, see *Final Conforming Rule Fact Sheet available at* http://www.epa.gov/owow/wetlands/dredgedmat/ (last visited on June 17, 2009).

One nuance in this area of law is the split authority of the EPA and the Corps of Engineers to issue permits for the discharge of certain materials into bodies of water. When Congress created the Clean Water Act in 1972 it was established that ". . . § 404(a) of the CWA grants the Corps the power to "issue permits . . . for the discharge of . . . fill material.'" But the EPA also has authority to issue permits for the discharge of pollutants. Section 402 of the Act grants the EPA authority to "issue a permit for the discharge of any pollutant '[e]xcept as provided in' § 404."

The issue of what constituted a "fill material" and hence who had authority to issue certain permits was recently addressed by the United States Supreme Court in *Coeur Alaska, Inc. v. Southeast Alaska Conservation Council*, 2009 WL 1738643 (U.S. 2009). The Court found that "[t]he Corps and the EPA have together defined 'fill material' to mean any 'material [that] has the effect of . . . [c]hanging the bottom elevation' of water. The agencies have further defined the 'discharge of fill material' to include 'placement of . . . slurry, or tailings or similar mining-related materials.'" The Court then held that the slurry at issue was indeed a "fill material" as the definition given by the agencies was reasonable. Additionally, the Court concluded that the Corps, and not the EPA, had the power to regulate this material. Finally, the Court found that the EPA's ". . . performance standards do not apply to discharges of fill material." *Id.* at 11. After this case, industry participants should be mindful of the proper permit authority based on the pollutant at issue.

[c] What Is a Wetland?

Page 337, add to end of subsection:

After issuing initial guidance in June of 2007, the U.S. Environmental Protection Agency (EPA) and the U.S. Army Corps of Engineers (Corps) followed up in December 2008 and issued joint guidance on the terms and procedures used to determine the extent of federal control over water and wetlands.[72.1] This guidance intended to clarify the meaning of "waters of the United States," establishing the boundaries of jurisdictional waters, which became hotly contested and questioned after the U.S. Supreme Court's 2006 decision, *Rapanos v. United States*.[72.2] The split court in *Rapanos* defined and set recognizable limits on federal control over wet areas. In this regard, the Supreme Court considered whether the federal government could exercise jurisdiction over certain wetlands and tributaries under Section 404 of the Clean Water Act. The Justices issued five separate opinions in *Rapanos* (one plurality opinion, two concurring opinions, and two dissenting opinions), with no single opinion commanding a majority of the Court. Justice Scalia explained that waters protected by the Act are those that are "relatively permanent, standing or continuously flowing bodies of water" connected to traditional rivers or streams that can carry navigation, as well as wetlands with "continuous surface connection to such water bodies."[72.3] Justice Kennedy, in his concurring opinion, provided a different jurisdictional test, as he explained that the Act protects waters or wetlands that "possess a 'significant nexus' to waters that are or were navigable in fact or that could reasonably be so made."[72.4] In dissent, and joined by three other justices, Justice Stevens

---

[72.1] *Federal Agencies Issue New "Dredge and Fill" Permit Guidance Pertaining to Construction in U.S. Waters, Wetlands,* Jan. 21, 2009, *available at* http://newsletters.agc.org/environment/2009/01/21/federal-agencies-issue-new-dredge-and-fill-permit-guidance-pertaining-to-construction-in-us-waters-wetlands/ (last visited on July 7, 2009).

[72.2] 547 U.S. 715 (2006).

[72.3] Rapanos v. United States, 547 U.S. 715, 739 (2006).

[72.4] *Id.* at 759.

said lower courts could apply either the Scalia or Kennedy approach.[72.5] The challenge for lower courts after this decision has been whether to apply the legal tests provided by Justice Scalia or Justice Kennedy. As the aforementioned joint guidance suggests, it appears that EPA and the U.S. Corps of Engineers will continue to apply either test leaving lower courts the continuing challenge to choose an application of either test, based on governing law in the respective federal circuits.[72.6]

The challenges facing the lower courts seemed to have come to a head in late 2008. However on December 1, the United States Supreme Court declined to reconsider its definition of "waters of the United States," as it denied certiorari from an Eleventh Circuit case, *McWane Inc. v. United States*.[72.7] Despite public pressure from various interest groups,[72.8] the Supreme Court made its denial without offering any further insight into this matter."[72.9] It should be noted that in the Eleventh Circuit, the Kennedy standard is the controlling test and the sole method of determining CWA jurisdiction in that circuit.[72.10] However, this underscores the problem facing the public, as the standards vary depending on the district where the land is located.

In addition to its *"Rapanos Guidance,"* the EPA has issued a litany of correspondence, on its website, to clarify some key issues pertaining to the definition of a wetland.[72.11] The EPA pledges that it and the Corps

---

[72.5] *Federal Agencies Issue New "Dredge and Fill" Permit Guidance Pertaining to Construction in U.S. Waters, Wetlands supra.*

[72.6] *Id.*

[72.7] 505 F.3d 1208 (11th Cir. 2007).

[72.8] *Id.* (Associated General Contractors of America (AGC) submitted a brief in support of the government's petition for writ of certiorari, asking the Supreme Court to clarify its decision on federal regulation of wetlands in *McWane*, and arguing that "the Corps and EPA need clear and administrable rules defining the scope of the CWA's coverage").

[72.9] *Id.*

[72.10] *Id.*

[72.11] *See* EPA "One Sheet" *available at* http://www.epa.gov/owow/wetlands/pdf/CWA_Jurisdiction_Following_Rapanos120208.pdf (last visited July 7, 2009).

Summary of Key Points

The agencies will assert jurisdiction over the following waters:

—Traditional navigable waters
—Wetlands adjacent to traditional navigable waters
—Non-navigable tributaries of traditional navigable waters that are relatively permanent where the tributaries typically flow year-round or have continuous flow at least seasonally (e.g., typically three months)
—Wetlands that directly abut such tributaries

The agencies will decide jurisdiction over the following waters based on a fact-specific analysis to determine whether they have a significant nexus with a traditional navigable water:

—Non-navigable tributaries that are not relatively permanent

". . . will continually assess and review the application of this guidance to ensure nationwide consistency, reliability, and predictability in our administration of the statute."[72.12] Despite the various literature to help clarify its position, the 2008 *Rapanos* guidance is the most official interpretation and should be adhered to by industry participants. This guidance has the goal to "ensure that jurisdictional determinations and other relevant agency actions being conducted under the Section 404 program are consistent with the *Rapanos* decision."[72.13]

As a result, regulators will rely on this guidance when deciding whether construction activities impacting wetlands, tributaries and other waters require federal authorization.[72.14] The 2008 guidance has only made a few changes but following the aforementioned case, these changes are significant.[72.15] Notably, in the 2008 *Rapanos* guidance, the agencies

---

—Wetlands adjacent to non-navigable tributaries that are not relatively permanent
—Wetlands adjacent to but that do not directly abut a relatively permanent non-navigable tributary

The agencies generally will not assert jurisdiction over the following features:

—Swales or erosional features (e.g., gullies, small washes characterized by low volume, infrequent, or short duration flow)
—Ditches (including roadside ditches) excavated wholly in and draining only uplands and that do not carry a relatively permanent flow of water

The agencies will apply the significant nexus standard as follows:

—A significant nexus analysis will assess the flow characteristics and functions of the tributary itself and the functions performed by all wetlands adjacent to the tributary to determine if they significantly affect the chemical, physical and biological integrity of downstream traditional navigable waters
—Significant nexus includes consideration of hydrologic and ecologic factors

[72.12] *Id.* at 4. For a summary of all issues in this area, see the following website: http://www.epa.gov/owow/wetlands/guidance/CWAwaters.html.

[72.13] *Federal Agencies Issue New "Dredge and Fill" Permit Guidance Pertaining to Construction in U.S. Waters, Wetlands, supra* note 72.1.

[72.14] *Id.*

[72.15] *Id.*

What's in the New Guidance?

The 2008 *Rapanos* guidance generally builds upon the 2007 version, without substantial modifications. The revised 2008 guidance makes only three (3) noteworthy changes to the 2007 version (despite the fact that the agencies received 66,047 public comments on the draft). First, wetlands and waterways are subject to the CWA regime only if they have a relationship, or, in Judge Kennedy's words, a "significant nexus," to what the agencies call "traditional navigable waters" or TNW. The revised guidance clarifies that TNWs are broader than Rivers and Harbors Act Section 10 waters (33 U.S.C. § 403), and also include (1) waters deemed to be navigable-in-fact by the courts, (2) waters currently being used for—or that have historically been used for—commercial navigation or recreation, (3) waters that are "susceptible to being used in the future for commercial navigation . . . [or] recreation" when evidence of such use is more than "insubstantial or speculative." *See* 2008 *Rapanos* guidance page 5, footnote 20. AGC's comments on the 2007 guidance urged EPA and the Corps to better explain the concept of TNW. However, the agencies ultimately took a very expansive view of TNW (finding that commercial *recreation* is good enough!), and the 2008 guidance directly conflicts with AGC's position that TNWs should be limited to the Rivers and Harbors Act waters.

Second, the revised guidance attempts to clarify what the Supreme Court meant when it required wetlands and waterways to be "adjacent" to federally-controlled waters to receive their own federal protection. Adjacent is defined in the Corps regulations at 33 C.F.R. § 328.3(c) and means "neighboring, bordering, or contiguous." The 2008 guidance interprets this to mean that wetlands are adjacent to traditionally navigable waters when there is a hydrologic connection, even if the connection is intermittent (a continuous surface connection is not required!); when the wetlands are separated from jurisdictional waters by formations such as man-made dikes or natural river berms; or when the wetlands' proximity to jurisdictional waters is reasonably close, based on an ecological interconnection. AGC is concerned that this new language will, in effect, unlawfully expand the regulatory definition of adjacent as it is applied in the field.

And finally, the 2008 guidance attempts to clarify the term "tributary flow," another issue the Supreme Court introduced in the *Rapanos* decision. The revised guidance modifies the process for assessing flow in tributaries (for purposes of determining whether a tributary is relatively permanent), indicating that where the downstream limit is not representative of the stream reach as a whole, "the flow regime that best characterizes the entire tributary" should be used. The 2007 version of the interagency guidance stated that the flow characteristics of a particular stream reach should be evaluated at the farthest downstream limit of the reach (i.e., the point the tributary enters a higher order stream). AGC commented that assessing flow at the downstream point is not the most appropriate approach to characterizing the entire stream.

Significant Nexus

The 2008 guidance is consistent with the 2007 version in specifying that a "significant nexus" analysis will assess the flow characteristics and functions of the tributaries and the functions of the wetlands adjacent to the tributary to determine if they significantly affect the chemical, physical and biological integrity of downstream traditional navigable waters. A significant nexus determination includes consideration of hydrologic and ecologic factors. AGC argued that there needs to be actual data showing impacts to integrity of traditional navigable waters to establish a significant nexus, but the agencies chose not to modify the earlier guidance.

In addition, the 2008 guidance maintains the interagency procedure for reviewing and approving significant nexus-related jurisdictional determinations (JDs). A memorandum dated January 28, 2008, provides for a shorter, more efficient coordination process (than what was established by the 2007 *Rapanos* guidance) wherein the Corps districts act without EPA oversight. Specifically, when the Corps asserts CWA jurisdiction following a significant nexus finding, it notifies the appropriate EPA regional office. The EPA region then has 15 days to decide whether to make the final jurisdictional determination as a "special case," using a separate process in place since 1989. If EPA does not respond, the Corps will finalize the JD. AGC had expressed concern that the interagency coordination process outlined in the 2007 guidance was causing delays and recommended that coordination with EPA be ended altogether.

Processing Delays

In its comments on the 2007 version of the interagency guidance, AGC expressed concern regarding delays in finalizing official JDs (i.e., "approved JDs") and implications of those delays for permitting decisions and timing of associated construction projects. AGC pointed out the processing delays caused by data-intensive approved jurisdictional continue to maintain their position that regulatory jurisdiction exists over a water body under the Clean Water Act, if either the plurality test or the Kennedy "significant nexus" test is met.[72.16]

In November 2008, the EPA through its issuance of a final rule revised the definition of "navigable waters of the United States," as the term applies to the SPCC rule. This final rule was intended to change the definition to comply with a recent court decision.[72.17] This final rule

---

determinations called for by Regulatory Guidance Letter (RGL) 07-01, which was issued as part of the 2007 *Rapanos* guidance. (RGL 07-01 required all CWA Section 404 applicants to obtain an "approved JD" for each water body impacted by a project, regardless of whether jurisdiction was contested.) In response, the Corps issued RGL 08-02, clarifying that project proponents may request a preliminary JD based on an "effective presumption of jurisdiction over all of the wetlands and other water bodies at the site," essentially allowing a project proponent to concede jurisdiction. RGL 08-02 is currently in effect and replaces RGL 07-01.

[72.16] *Id. U.S. Senate Committee to Consider Wetlands Jurisdiction Expansion Bill,* May 1, 2009, *available at* http://newsletters.agc.org/environment/2009/05/01/us-senate-committee-to-consider-wetlands-jurisdiction-expansion-bill/ (last visited on July 9, 2009). A bill (S. 787) is currently being processed in the Senate that would expand federal jurisdiction over waters and wetlands under the Clean Water Act. The legislation would greatly expand the federal role beyond protecting wetlands and waters having an understandable "significant nexus" to navigable waters and regulate everywhere that rainwater happens to flow. Some industry experts think this bill could give the government such expansive regulatory tools so as to govern small waterways such as roadside ditches. The legislation would give the U.S. Army Corps of Engineers and the U.S. Environmental Protection Agency jurisdiction over all wet areas—however remote or intermittent—and over all activities (e.g., construction) affecting those waters. The federal permitting process would increase the cost of maintaining and delay necessary improvement of public and private infrastructure.

Senate EPW Committee Approves Expansion of Clean Water Act Jurisdiction, available at http://newsletters.agc.org/environment/2009/06/19/senate-epw-committee-approves-expansion-of-clean-water-act-jurisdiction/ (last visited on July 9, 2009). On Thursday, June 18, 2009, the Senate Environment and Public Works Committee passed S. 787, the Clean Water Restoration Act. The legislation was offered as an amendment sponsored by Chairwoman Barbara Boxer (D-Calif.), Senator Max Baucus (D-Mont.), and Senator Amy Klobuchar (D-Minn.). Republican committee members criticized the bill as a substantial expansion of federal jurisdiction over water by removing the term "navigable" waterways. Ranking Member Senator James Inhofe (R-Okla.) and Senator John Barasso (R-Wyo.) offered multiple unsuccessful amendments to address "negative impacts" on rural and agricultural communities. The bill has been placed on "hold" by some Republicans.

[72.17] *Navigable Waters' Definition Revised for Purposes of EPA's Oil Spill Program,* Feb. 3 2009, *available at* http://newsletters.agc.org/environment/2009/02/03/%e2%80%98navigable-waters%e2%80%99-definition-revised-for-purposes-of-epa%e2%80%99s-oil-spill-program/ (last visited on July 7, 2009).

Effective at the time of publication, EPA restored its original 1973 definition of "navigable waters" as follows:

    1.   All navigable waters of the United States, as defined in judicial decisions before passage of the 1972 Amendments to the CWA and tributaries of such waters,

    2.   Interstate waters,

reverted to the definition used in the 1973 amendments. The 1973 definition replaces the much broader definition that EPA had adopted in its July 2002 revisions of the SPCC program.[72.18] This broad definition was challenged in court by the petroleum industry and vacated in March 2008 by the U.S. Court of Appeals for the D.C. Circuit.[72.19]

Since the *Rapanos* decision, there have been about a dozen decisions that addressed the "significant nexus" standard. In a variety of factual circumstances, the clearest inference is that the Army Corps of Engineers should be consulted on wetland issues prior to undertaking activities that might disturb a wetland.

[2]   Oil Spill Prevention

Page 342, add to end of subsection:

In 2008, the EPA finalized amendments that affect the requirements under the Spill Prevention, Control, and Countermeasure (SPCC) rule. The new amendments also affect proposed revised compliance deadlines and according to some industry commentators, these amendments will "streamline the requirements."[94.1] According to the AGC, "A construction site with aboveground storage capacity of more than 1,320 gallons of oil (counting tanks only 55 gallons or greater) is subject to EPA's SPCC rule if a spill could reasonably be expected to discharge oil to U.S. navigable waters or adjoining shorelines."[94.2] Under the amendments, EPA made exemptions for hot-mix asphalt and hot-mix asphalt containers from SPCC requirements. This exemption allows construction site operators

---

3. Intrastate lakes, rivers, and streams that are utilized by interstate travelers for recreation or other purposes, and
4. Intrastate lakes, rivers, and streams from which fish or shellfish are taken and sold in interstate commerce.

[72.18] *Id.* ("The 2002 SPCC amendments stretched the definition of 'navigable waters' almost beyond recognition—defining it as 'waters of the United States' including all waters subject to the ebb and flow of tides; prairie potholes; mudflats; impoundments of waters; and waste treatment systems, including treatment ponds or lagoons designed to meet the requirements of the CWA, etc.").

[72.19] *See* American Petroleum Institute (API) v. Johnson, 541 F. Supp. 2d 165, 173 (D.D.C. 2008) (According to the plaintiffs, EPA failed to consider the recent U.S. Supreme Court decisions that curb EPA's regulatory reach under the CWA. The Court basically agreed and stated that EPA failed to provide a reasonable explanation as to why such a far-reaching re-definition of navigable waters was needed.).

[94.1] *EPA Finalizes Oil Spill Rule, Proposes to Extend Compliance Deadlines in Streamlining Effort,* Feb. 3, 2009, *available at* http://newsletters.agc.org/environment/2009/02/03/epa-finalizes-oil-spill-rule-proposes-to-extend-compliance-deadlines-in-streamlining-effort/ (last visited July 7, 2009).

[94.2] *Id.*

more flexibility as they can "exclude silos of hot-mix asphalt from the total oil storage capacity calculation for any given job site."[94.3]

The AGC is adamant that certain provisions will benefit contractors: ". . . the rule provides an SPCC Plan template that certain low-risk construction sites and other 'qualified facilities' may use for self-certification, [it] allows construction site owners and operators to use alternative spill control measures to meet certain rule requirements (i.e. facility diagram, security measures, and integrity testing) without obtaining prior approval from a Professional Engineer (PE), [it] amends the general secondary treatment requirement, among other things."[94.4]

Additionally, the EPA proposed to extend the deadlines by which facilities must have completed and implemented SPCC plans to allow covered facilities the opportunity to incorporate the new revised plan requirements into their plans[94.5] by November 10, 2010.[94.6] There have been several amendments and changes to this compliance date so it is difficult to forecast whether this is a hard deadline, or it will be subsequently amended.[94.7]

In November 2009, EPA published revisions to the December 2008 amendments detailed in the 2009 Supplement to this Chapter. The effective date of the rule amendments was January 14, 2010, with the compliance date November 10, 2010. Most of the 2008 amendments were finalized without any changes. The November 2009 revisions made several technical corrections to the December 2008 provisions. These corrections do not change rule requirements applicable to the construction industry. However, now that the rule is final and the compliance date is a hard deadline, a facility that starts operation after November 10, 2010 must prepare and implement a SPCC plan before beginning operations. (New oil production facilities have an additional six months after start of operations to prepare the SPCC plan).

[4] Hazardous Substances—Superfund (CERCLA) Liability and Brownfields

Page 348, insert footnote referent 108.1 after "lead paint" in first sentence of second full paragraph and add note 108.1:

[108.1] The U.S. Environmental Protection Agency's (EPA) new "Renovation, Repair, and Painting" program requires contractors who

---

[94.3] *Id.* ("The EPA will, however, continue to regulate asphalt cement (AC), asphalt emulsions, and cutbacks (which are not hot-mix asphalt), but the notice clarifies the flexibility contained in the current SPCC rule regarding these asphalt materials.").

[94.4] *Id.*

[94.5] *Id.*

[94.6] http://www.epa.gov/emergencies/content/spcc/index.htm.

[94.7] http://www.epa.gov/emergencies/content/spcc/index.htm.

work on certain projects to be certified and to follow specific lead-safe work practices by April 2010. *EPA Finalizes New Rule for Lead-Based Paint Renovation, Repair, and Painting,* AGC's Environmental Observer, Issue No. 3-08 April/May 2008, *available at* http://newsmanager. commpartners.com/agcenv/issues/2008-05-30/5.html (last visited on July 18, 2009).

The rule requires contractors to be certified and to follow specific best-care practices when conducting renovation, repair or painting projects in residences built before 1978, where a pregnant woman or a child under six years old lives (73 Fed. Reg. 21,693 (Apr. 22, 2008)). The same requirements will apply to residential, public or commercial buildings that are regularly occupied by a child under six years old. To qualify as a "child-occupied building," the same child would have to visit the building on at least two different days in a week, for at least three hours per visit, for a total of at least 60 hours per year.

More specifically, the rule requires that by April 2010:

- Workers performing renovations and dust sampling must be *properly trained*;

- Renovators, dust sampling technicians and firms performing these renovations must be *certified*;

- Lead-safe work practices must be *followed* during renovations; and

- Providers of renovation and dust sampling technician training must be *accredited.*

See also, Prepare Now to Meet EPA's Training and Certification Requirements for Lead-Based Paint Work, May 14, 2009, *available at* http:// newsletters.agc.org/environment/2009/05/14/prepare-now-to-meet-epas-training-and-certification-requirements-for-lead-based-paint-work/ (last visited June 18, 2009) (pre-1978 housing and child-occupied facilities are the focus of this law and anyone working on these types of projects must now obtain certification. The EPA has stated that the rule will affect paid renovators including: renovation contractors, maintenance workers in multi-family housing and painters and other specialty trades). The agency recently announced that it has begun to review and accredit training providers to conduct the courses that will allow affected contractors to become certified, per the new mandates. EPA expects training opportunities to begin in summer 2009. *Id.* Until that time, the EPA recommends that anyone performing renovation, repair and painting projects that disturb lead-based paint in pre-1978 homes, child care facilities and schools follow lead-safe work practices. *Id.* For example, all contractors should: contain the work area, minimize dust and clean up thoroughly. *See also* http://epa.gov/lead/pubs/renovation.htm (last visited July 7, 2009). As of December 2008, the rule will require that contractors performing renovation, repair and painting projects that disturb lead-based paint provide to owners and occupants of child care facilities and to parents and guardians of children under age six that attend child care facilities built prior to 1978 the lead hazard information pamphlet Renovate Right: Important Lead Hazard Information for Families, Child Care Providers, and Schools; a copy of the brochure is available at http://epa.gov/lead/pubs/renovaterightbrochure.pdf.

[a] Who Is Responsible for Meeting CERCLA Requirements?

Page 349, add to end of subsection:

The Supreme Court in *Burlington Northern & Santa Fe Railway Company, et al. v. United States Environmental Protection Agency, et al.* redefined how someone could be considered an "arranger" and therefore liable under CERCLA.[111.1] The lower court in this case found that the defendant could still be held liable under a "'broader' category of arranger liability" if the "disposal of hazardous wastes [was] a foreseeable byproduct of, but not the purpose of, the transaction giving rise to" arranger liability. However the Supreme Court narrowed this definition. The Court found that an entity may qualify as an "arranger" of the

---

[111.1] *Burlington Northern & Santa Fe Railway Co. v. United States Environmental Protection Agency*, 129 S. Ct. 1870 (U.S. 2009) (CERCLA liability under the arranger provision would attach for environmental contamination if an entity were to enter into a transaction for the sole purpose of discarding a used and no longer useful hazardous substance).

The court articulated the following as its syllabus:

"In 1960, Brown & Bryant, Inc. (B & B), an agricultural chemical distributor, began operating on a parcel of land located in Arvin, California. B & B later expanded onto an adjacent parcel owned by petitioners Burlington Northern and Santa Fe Railway Company and Union Pacific Railroad Company (Railroads). As part of its business, B & B purchased and stored various hazardous chemicals, including the pesticide D-D, which it bought from petitioner Shell Oil Company (Shell). Over time, many of these chemicals spilled during transfers and deliveries, and as a result of equipment failures.

Investigations of B & B by the California Department of Toxic Substances Control and the federal Environmental Protection Agency (Governments) revealed significant soil and ground water contamination and in 1989, the Governments exercised their CERCLA authority to clean up the Arvin site, spending over $8 million by 1998. Seeking to recover their costs, the Governments initiated legal action against Shell and the Railroads. The District Court ruled in favor of the Governments, finding that both the Railroads and Shell were potentially responsible parties under CERCLA-the Railroads because they owned part of the facility and Shell because it had 'arranged for disposal . . . of hazardous substances,' 42 U.S.C. § 9607(a)(3), through D-D's sale and delivery. The District Court apportioned liability, holding the Railroads liable for 9% of the Governments' total response costs, and Shell liable for 6%. On appeal, the Ninth Circuit agreed that Shell could be held liable as an arranger under § 9607(a)(3) and affirmed the District Court's decision in that respect. Although the Court of Appeals agreed that the harm in this case was theoretically capable of apportionment, it found the facts present in the record insufficient to support apportionment, and therefore held Shell and the Railroads jointly and severally liable for the Governments' response costs."

disposal of hazardous substances, for purpose of liability provision of CERCLA, when it takes intentional steps to dispose of a hazardous substance. In this regard, the Court held that an entity could not be held liable as an "arranger" merely for selling a new and useful product if the purchaser of that product later, and unbeknownst to the seller, disposed of the product in a way that led to contamination.[111.2] The Court held that "[b]ecause CERCLA does not specifically define what it means to 'arrang[e] for' disposal of a hazardous substance, the phrase should be given its ordinary meaning. In common parlance, 'arrange' implies action directed to a specific purpose."[111.3]

The second significant issue addressed by the Court was with regard to apportionment of liability and whether Potentially Responsible Parties (PRPs) were to be held jointly and severally liable under CERCLA.[111.4]

[111.2] *Id.* (The Court held manufacturer of agricultural chemicals that sold those chemicals to agricultural chemical storage and distribution facility was not liable as an "arranger" of the disposal of the chemicals, under CERCLA, for soil and water contamination at facility site; although manufacturer was aware that minor, accidental spills occurred during the transfer of chemicals from the common carrier to the facility's storage tanks after the product had come under the facility's stewardship, the manufacturer did not intend or arrange for such spills, as it took numerous steps to encourage its distributors, including facility, to reduce the likelihood of spills, providing them with detailed safety manuals, requiring them to maintain adequate storage facilities, and providing discounts for those that took safety precautions.).

[111.3] *Id.* at 1873.

[111.4] The Court articulated the following:

The seminal opinion on the subject of apportionment in CERCLA actions was written in 1983 by Chief Judge Carl Rubin of the United States District Court for the Southern District of Ohio. *United States v. Chem-Dyne Corp.*, 572 F. Supp. 802. After reviewing CERCLA's history, Chief Judge Rubin concluded that although the Act imposed a "strict liability standard," *id.,* at 805, it did not mandate "joint and several" liability in every case. *See id.,* at 807. Rather, Congress intended the scope of liability to "be determined from traditional and evolving principles of common law[.]" *Id.,* at 808. The *Chem-Dyne* approach has been fully embraced by the Courts of Appeals. *See, e.g., In re Bell Petroleum Services, Inc.,* 3 F.3d 889, 901–902 (C.A. 5 1993); United States v. Alcan Aluminum Corp., 964 F.2d 252, 268 (C.A.3 1992); O'Neil v. Picillo, 883 F.2d 176, 178 (C.A. 1 1989); United States v. Monsanto Co., 858 F.2d 160, 171–173 (C.A.4 1988). Following *Chem-Dyne,* the courts of appeals have acknowledged that "[t]he universal starting point for divisibility of harm analyses in CERCLA cases" is § 433A of the Restatement (Second) of Torts. United States v. Hercules, Inc., 247 F.3d 706, 717 (C.A. 8 2001); Chem-Nuclear Systems, Inc. v. Bush, 292 F.3d 254, 259 (C.A.D.C. 2002); United States v. R.W. Meyer, Inc., 889 F.2d 1497, 1507 (C.A. 6 1989). Under the Restatement, "when two or more persons acting independently caus[e] a distinct or single harm for which there is a reasonable basis for division according to the contribution of each, each is subject to liability only for the portion of the total harm that he has himself caused. Restatement (Second) of Torts, §§ 433A, 881 (1976); Prosser, Law of Torts, pp. 313-314 (4th ed. 1971). . . . But where two or more persons cause a single and indivisible harm, each is subject to liability for the entire harm. Restatement (Second) of Torts, § 875; Prosser, at 315-316." *Chem-Dyne Corp.,* 572 F. Supp., at 810.

The Court upheld the principle that apportionment would apply when a court has a reasonable basis for calculating liability.[111.5]

[5] Air Pollution—The Clean Air Act (CAA)

[a] *Diesel Engines—Particulate Matter*

Page 352, add after the second full paragraph:

The California Air Resources Board (CARB) has long been at the forefront of environmental initiatives. Recently, this organization sought approval from the EPA regarding the state's newly proposed standards for off-road diesel engine emissions. The effect of these standards would force California based construction companies to replace most heavy construction equipment, because the older equipment could not feasibly comply with the new standards.[118.1] According to one commentator, the EPA must review and approve California's standards before the state can legally enforce them, citing a Clean Air Act process called "granting a waiver of federal preemption." In this regard, if the EPA grants the state's waiver request, other states would be free to adopt California's new requirements, which apply to all off-road diesel fleets currently in use.[118.2] The cost of such regulation has been estimated to be billions of dollars.[118.3] It appears that this rule is still in the comment phase.[118.4]

The EPA believes that reducing emissions from diesel engines is one of the most important current challenges regarding air quality in the United States.[118.5] To address this issue, the EPA established the National Clean Diesel Campaign (NCDC) which includes regulatory programs to

---

In other words, apportionment is proper when "there is a reasonable basis for determining the contribution of each cause to a single harm." Restatement (Second) of Torts § 433A(1)(b), p. 434 (1963–1964).

[111.5] "Because the District Court's ultimate allocation of liability is supported by the evidence and comports with the apportionment principles outlined above, we reverse the Court of Appeals' conclusion that the Railroads are subject to joint and several liability for all response costs arising out of the contamination of the Arvin facility." *Id.* at 1883.

[118.1] *AGC Urges EPA To Deny California's Request to Enforce Costly, Unsafe Rule Requiring Replacement of Most Heavy Construction Equipment*, Jan. 7, 2009, *available at* http://newsletters.agc.org/environment/2009/01/07/agc-urges-epa-to-deny-californias-request-to-enforce-costly-unsafe-rule-requiring-replacement-of-most-heavy-construction-equipment/ (last visited July 7, 2009).

[118.2] *Id.*

[118.3] *Id.* The AGC website states that "industry estimates that the cost of compliance will reach roughly $13 billion in California alone, and even the state has put the cost at $3.4 billion. If other states across the nation adopt (or 'opt-in') to California's requirements, the cost to industry will be practically immeasurable."

[118.4] *See* docket, http://www.regulations.gov/fdmspublic/component/main?main=DocketDetail&d=EPA-HQ-OAR-2008-0691 (last visited July 7, 2009).

[118.5] http://www.epa.gov/cleandiesel/.

address in-use diesel engines by promoting a variety of cost-effective emission reduction strategies.[118.6] The EPA has articulated that these strategies include switching to cleaner fuels; retrofitting, repairing, repowering, and replacing equipment and reducing idling.[118.7] To effectuate some of these strategies, the EPA will use funding authorized under the Diesel Emissions Reduction Program the Energy Policy Act of 2005 (DERA).[118.8] Pursuant to DERA's funding authority, the Economic Recovery Act passed in 2009 includes $300 million to clean up diesel engines nationwide.[118.9] Potential recipients of stimulus funding had to apply to the EPA to request an award.[118.10] The potential recipient would have to propose in its application a "retrofit" project that would

---

[118.6] *Id.*

[118.7] *Id.*

[118.8] http://www.epa.gov/diesel/grantfund.htm. Funding sources are authorized by the National Clean Diesel Emissions Reduction Program which was created under Title VII, Subtitle G (sections 791 to 797) of the Energy Policy Act of 2005, Public Law 109-58, signed August 8, 2005 (EPAct). The National Clean Diesel Emissions Reduction Program is sometimes referred to as "DERA."

[118.9] *Stimulus Bill Offers Millions in Diesel Retrofit Funds*, Feb. 26 2009, *available at* http://newsletters.agc.org/environment/2009/02/26/stimulus-bill-offers-millions-in-diesel-retrofit-funds/ (last visited June 17 2009) (this funding "could result in grants of more than $1 million for AGC Chapters to distribute to member companies. The grant funding has increased six-fold from fiscal year 2008 and is designed to help construction companies and other diesel users reduce emissions from their fleets.").

[118.10] *ENVIRONMENTAL PROTECTION AGENCY RECOVERY ACT PROGRAM PLAN: DERA Program*, May 15, 2009, *available at* http://www.epa.gov/recovery/plans/dera.pdf. (last visited July 7, 2009).

Recipients will demonstrate in their applications how the proposed project:

—Preserves and/or creates jobs and promotes economic recovery;

—Maximizes job creation and economic benefit;

—Assists those most impacted by the current economic conditions;

—Provides investments needed to increase economic efficiency by spurring technological advances in science and health;

—Invests in transportation, environmental protection and other activities that will provide long-term economic benefits;

—Will be commenced as quickly as possible consistent with prudent management;

—Tracks, measures, and reports on the recipient's progress towards achieving the Recovery Act priorities.

Timeline of Major Milestones:

State Clean Diesel Grant Program

State Program *Notice of Intent to Apply* sent out: February 26, 2009 State Program Grant Work Plans and grant documents due to EPA: March 20, 2009 State Program Grants awarded: By April 17, 2009 State Grant Project Period: April, 2009–September 30, 2010 Wrap-up and Close-out: October 1, 2010–December 31, 2010

National Clean Diesel Funding Assistance Program

RFA posted: March 19, 2009 RFA closed: April 28, 2009 Award: June, 2009 Project Period: June, 2009–September, 2010 Wrap-up and Close-out: October 1, 2010–December 31, 2010

Smart Way Clean Diesel Finance Program

significantly reduce diesel emissions in its region and explain how it would use the federal monies to help its members implement diesel emission reduction strategies.[118.11] Eligible recipients include regional, local, state, port and tribal entities and certain nonprofit organizations (transportation-related).[118.12] Recipients will report the number of engines by sector and number of technologies applied for their grant projects. EPA will calculate lifetime emissions reductions benefits by pollutant (Particulate Matter [PM], Oxides of Nitrogen [NOx], Hydrocarbons [HC], Carbon Monoxide [CO] and Carbon Dioxide [CO2] -equivalents) based on the reported information.[118.13]

The EPA stated that "[t]he objective of the program is to reduce diesel emissions while using American Recovery and Reinvestment Act (Recovery Act) funding to maximize job preservation and/or creation and economic recovery through a variety of diesel emission reduction strategies."[118.14] The EPA also contemplated the magnitude of the problem related to diesel pollutants. "More than 11 million diesel engines in operation today do not meet EPA's new clean diesel standards, yet these engines have an average lifetime of 20 to 30 years."[118.15] Furthermore, the EPA added that its new initiatives had a direct correlation on human health. "Public health benefits are immediate when emissions control strategies are applied to older diesel engines. Diesel retrofit technologies reduce pollution from the existing diesel engine fleet by up to 90% for particulate matter (PM), up to 50% for nitrogen oxides (NOx), and up to 90% for volatile organic compounds. New on-highway heavy-duty vehicles are up to sixty times cleaner than those manufactured prior to 1990 . . . Recovery Act funding is likely to lead to reductions of hundreds of thousands of tons of pollution resulting in billions of dollars in health benefits"[118.16]

The program report also provides that: "[t]he DERA Program is positioned to provide information on clean diesel projects funded through

---

RFA posted: March 19, 2009 RFA closed: April 28, 2009 Award: June, 2009 Project Period: June, 2009–September, 2011 Wrap-up and Close-out: October 1, 2010–December 31, 2011

Emerging Technologies Clean Diesel Program

5 RFA posted: March 19, 2009 RFA closed: May 5, 2009 Award: June, 2009 Project Period: June, 2009–September, 2010 Wrap-up and Close-out: October 1, 2010–December 31, 2010

[118.11] *Id.*

[118.12] *Id.*

[118.13] *ENVIRONMENTAL PROTECTION AGENCY RECOVERY ACT PROGRAM PLAN: DERA Program*, May 15, 2009, *available at* http://www.epa.gov/recovery/plans/dera.pdf, at pg 9 (last visited June 17 2009).

[118.14] *ENVIRONMENTAL PROTECTION AGENCY RECOVERY ACT PROGRAM PLAN: DERA Program*, May 15, 2009, *available at* http://www.epa.gov/recovery/plans/dera.pdf (last visited June 17 2009).

[118.15] *Id.* at 2.

[118.16] *Id.* at 3.

the Recovery Act."[118.17] ". . . To report on interim progress, grantees are required to report, on a quarterly basis, progress on activities such as number of contracts awarded, number of engines retrofitted or replaced by sector (e.g. school buses, rail, or ports), the technology used for the retrofit and amount of EPA funds expended."[118.18] "Progress on these activities will ultimately lead to the installation of diesel engine retrofit technology which will then result in reduced emissions from diesel engines as well as job creation/retention. EPA grant recipients will report on the number of jobs created and/or retained, by full-time equivalencies, according to the latest OMB guidance provided for such reporting. EPA will track the implementation of these projects in the NCDC Database and on the recovery.gov website."[118.19]

The EPA also claims that it will be "using a combination of quarterly reporting from grantees and on-site and off-site monitoring by EPA Project Officers and auditors to evaluate the progress of each Recovery Act DERA grant. The DERA project officers will interact with grant recipients on a regular basis monitoring the progress of grants and resolving programmatic issues that arise."[118.20]

"The grant money must be used to carry out 'clean diesel' projects during the June 2009 to September 30, 2010 timeframe. Under the current grant announcement, EPA's funding will pay up to a certain percentage of the cost to purchase/install diesel emission reduction solutions on 'diesels' including medium and heavy-duty trucks and off-road construction equipment-100% for verified retrofit technologies (emission filters/ catalysts), idle reduction technologies and certified or verified engine upgrades (kits only); 75% for engine repowers (newer engine); and 25% for all vehicle or equipment replacements. EPA grants cannot fund the cost of emission reductions currently mandated under federal, state or local law."[118.21] "EPA will hold another grant competition in August 2009 (EPA fiscal year 2009 appropriations), although it will be for much less money—around $60M. There will be another opportunity to apply for funding in 2010."[118.22]

[118.17] *Id.* at 8.

[118.18] *Id.* at 7.

[118.19] *Id.*

[118.20] *Id.* at 10.

[118.21] *AGC Chapters Ask EPA for $30 Million to Clean Up Diesel Engines Nationwide,* May 14, 2009, *available at* http://newsletters.agc.org/environment/2009/05/14/agc-chapters-ask-epa-for-30-million-to-clean-up-diesel-engines-nationwide/ (last visited on June 18, 2009).

[118.22] *Id. See Miami-Dade County receives $2M to reduce diesel emissions,* South Florida Business Journal, June 29, 2009 *available at* http://southflorida.bizjournals.com/southflorida/stories/2009/06/29/daily14.html?ed=2009-06-30&ana=e_du_pub (last visited on July 7, 2009) ("Miami-Dade County's Office of Economic Development Coordination has received $2 million from the Environmental Protection Agency to repower approximately 300 agricultural irrigation pumps. Repower refers to the removal of an existing

[7]   **Polychlorinated Biphenyl (PCB) Waste Requirements and Risks**

Page 357, add to end of subsection:

Recently, EPA has taken an interest in the consequences of removing caulk that contains PCBs. EPA has learned that caulk containing PCBs was used in many buildings, including schools, in the 1950s–1970s. On September 25, 2009, EPA announced new guidelines for school administrators and building managers about how to manage PCBs in caulk and suggested tools to minimize possible exposure to the PCBs. Such "best practices" include:[141.1]

- Improving ventilation (open windows use of fans)
- Frequent cleaning to reduce dust and residue inside buildings
- Use a wet or damp cloth or mop to clean surfaces
- Use wet vacuums
- Do not sweep with dirty brooms or dusters
- Wash children's hands with soap and water, particularly before eating
- Wash children's toys frequently
- Wash hands with soap and water after cleaning, before eating and drinking.

EPA also recommends testing if there is concern and taking a PCB including (e.g. old transformers, fluorescent light bulbs, etc.). These "best practices" are particularly imperative when conducting remodeling and repairs.

---

engine and its replacement with a newer or cleaner engine that meets a more stringent set of engine emissions standards, according to an EPA spokesperson.").

[141.1] *See* EPA's website "PCBs in Caulk in Older Buildings," http://www.epa.gov.pcbsincaulk/ (last visited on June 17, 2010).

CHAPTER **12**

GREEN DESIGN AND CONSTRUCTION: RISK MANAGEMENT IN A SUSTAINABLE WORLD

Leah A. Rochwarg
Emily Donovan

§ 12.01   INTRODUCTION

Page 381, add before first full paragraph:

In the United States, buildings alone account for 39% of total energy use, 12% of total water consumption, 68% of total electricity consumption and 38% of the carbon dioxide emissions.[01]

According to the U.S. Green Building Council, building green will aid climate protection efforts by, among other things, reducing greenhouse gas emissions. With the Senate poised to take up comprehensive climate and energy legislation in 2010, the U.S. Green Building Council is urging legislators to pass a comprehensive bill that it maintains will move the United States away from dependence on fossil fuels and toward a clean energy future.[02] Moreover, the U.S. Green Building Council contends that the very same building sector which accounts for nearly 40% of our country's carbon footprint has the potential to serve as a low-cost, high-return investment strategy, a resource that remains largely untapped. It further contends that, not only will green building programs reduce energy consumption and greenhouse gas emissions through the retrofit of old, inefficient homes and buildings, they will create jobs and save consumers money.

Some suggest that we have seen little in the way of green building litigation, at least in part, because of a down economy. Despite the prevalence of green building initiatives in the public and private sectors, as of this writing there have been few well-publicized claims involving green building projects and even fewer green building litigations. Nevertheless, there are many who believe that a wave of green building

---

[01] Why Build Green?, www.epa.gov/greenbuilding/pubs/whybuild.htm.
[02] USGBC Urges Senate to Pass Comprehensive Climate and Energy Policy, www.usgbc.org/DisplayPage.aspx?CMSPageID=2124.

litigation (or "LEEDigation" as many prefer to refer to it) is inevitable. Regardless of whether you think green building will lead to more construction disputes, it is always prudent to advise clients of the unique risks attendant to individual construction projects, whether LEED certification is a goal or not. As with all construction projects, standard forms are inadequate and require modifications to properly manage and allocate risk unique to the individual project at hand. Consultation with knowledgeable legal and insurance professionals is strongly encouraged.

One of the first green building litigations in the United States was *Shaw Development v. Southern Builders*. In *Shaw Development v. Southern Builders*, the developer sued the contractor alleging that its failure to complete the project on time and to achieve the contractually-required LEED Silver rating resulted in the project losing a tax credit worth $635,000 on a $7.5 million project. Although the case settled, leaving us without any truly valuable insight as to how the courts or juries might treat such claims, Shaw provides an important lesson. This anecdotal lawsuit makes clear the importance of a transactional attorney's role in the any given project. Another green building claim involved a challenge to the U.S. Green Building Council's award of LEED Silver Certification on a new high school construction project known as Northland Pines. In Northland Pines, non-parties to the design and construction process challenged the award of LEED Gold Certification to Northland Pines High School in Eagle River, Wisconsin. The challenge, made over a year after the school was certified by the USGBC, was brought by seven people, including two professional engineers, who challenged the project's LEED certification alleging non-compliance with two prerequisites. In response to the challenge, the USGBC hired two professional consultants both of whom concluded that the Gold certification was proper.

Page 381, in third sentence of first full paragraph, replace "present" with "presents."

§ 12.03   ASSESSING AND MANAGING THE RISKS AND REWARDS OF BUILDING GREEN

[F]   Reference Standards vs. Contractual and Legal Requirements

Page 385, add to end of subsection:

In 2009, the International Code Council launched the development of a new International Green Construction Code (IGCC) initiative, subtitled "Safe and Sustainable: By the Book," committed to developing a model code focused on new and existing commercial buildings addressing green building design and performance. According to the ICC, the IGCC will work as an overlay to the ICC Family of Codes. The IGCC is written in mandatory language that provides a new regulatory framework. According to the ICC's website, the IGCC was designed with local, state and federal law in mind and will provide performance and prescriptive solutions, account for local conditions, work in tandem with leading Green rating systems.[5.1] The ICC is scheduled to issue Public Version 2.0 of the IGCC on November 3, 2010. Pending issuance of the IGCC in 2010, the ICC notes that Public Version drafts of the IGCC are available as adoptable language or as resource tools in the development or revision of green regulations at all jurisdictional levels, and are designed to integrate with existing I-Codes to create a new regulatory baseline for green construction.

[G]   LEED Certified vs. LEED Certifiable

Page 385, delete title and replace with:

[G]   LEED Certified vs. LEED Certifiable and Certification Challenges

Page 386, add to end of subsection:

The Green Building Certification Institute (GBCI), established in 2008 to administer project certifications and professional credentials and certificates within the framework of the U.S. Green Building Council's LEED Green Building Rating Systems™. In early 2009, GBCI assumed responsibility for administering the LEED certification program. According to its website, more than 17,000 commercial projects await certification as of June 2010.[5.2]

GBCI developed a LEED Certification Policy Manual dated April 2009 which includes a Certification Challenge Policy at Section 9. Left unchecked, the Certification Challenge Policy may represent the most significant legal risk for LEED certified projects since the inception of the LEED rating system in 1998. Among other things, the Certification Challenge Policy provides that GBCI may revoke previously granted LEED certification or take other action regarding LEED certification such as determine to reduce points or category of LEED certification previously granted, if GBCI determines that credits/prerequisites for LEED certification were granted based on erroneous determinations or inaccurately or falsely submitted documentation. The Policy encourages persons concerned with possible inaccurately granted LEED certification to contact the GBCI. There is no requirement that such person have any vested or other identifiable interest in the project. In addition, GBCI expressly reserves the right to institute an investigation and review of

---

[5.1] www.iccsafe.org.
[5.2] www.gbci.org.

such possible errors or inaccuracy or veracity of documentation even in the absence of a third-party complaint. As currently drafted, there is no limitation as to which LEED points may be challenged. Nor is there a statute of limitations for bringing a challenge to LEED certification.

[H]   Green Building Contracts

Page 386, replace first full paragraph with:

In the past two years alone, there have been countless articles, blogs, webinars, and seminars focusing on the legal and insurance issues attendant to green building projects. These sources are rife with valuable information and are often the most current source of up-to-date information about legal and insurance issues. Attorneys, owners, architects, contractors, insurers, and other industry professionals have contributed their perspectives and insights regarding issues attendant to green building projects, some unique to green building projects and others present on both traditional and green building projects.

In an effort to respond to and address the issues on green building projects, at least two industry organizations have made significant strides toward developing comprehensive, standard form, contract documents for use in conjunction with green building projects. These forms are updated periodically but cannot serve as a substitute for reasoned evaluation of the legal and insurance risks attendant to a given project.

ConsensusDOCS, endorsed by 23 leading construction industry organizations, has issued the *310 Green Building Addendum* which it promotes as the First Best-Practice Addendum for Use on Green Building Projects. The Green Building Addendum provides a comprehensive approach to identifying the roles and responsibilities for contractors, designers, owners, project managers and others involved in the construction project. The Green Building Addendum was developed by members of the ConsensusDOCS group to help advise the owner, establish parties' expectations, and avoid delays and other legal disruptions in the construction of buildings seeking to achieve green certification or other sustainable goals. According to the ConsensusDOCS Guidebook regarding Use of ConsensusDOCS Green Building Addendum, the Green Building Addendum is intended to modify, accompany and complement pre-existing or contemporaneously prepared design and construction agreements on projects where green building elements, goals, or, more formally, third-party rating recognition is sought. The ConsensusDOCS Guidebook regarding Use of ConsensusDOCS Green Building Addendum is available for download at www.ConsensusDOCS.org.

Page 386, replace third sentence of second full paragraph with:

As with all form agreements both the *ConsensusDOCS 310 Green Building Addendum* and the *AIA Document B214-2004, Standard Form of Architect's Services: LEED® Certification* should be modified to reflect the parties' intent based on a proper evaluation and assessment of the business, legal, and insurance issues specific to the construction project.

[I] Insurance Considerations and Coverage Issues in Building Green

Page 386, insert new footnote referent 5.3 to end of subsection title and add note 5.3:

[5.3] A complete discussion of all insurance issues exceeds the scope of this chapter. The author suggests that in evaluating appropriate types and limits of insurance for green building projects it is essential to consult a qualified insurance professional.

[1] Upgrade Coverage for Green Building

Page 386, replace text of subsection with:

Several insurance companies now offer green insurance to the U.S. commercial and residential marketplace. According to the Insurance Information Institute, as of December 2009, 22 companies offer 39 products and services specifically designed for new green buildings, and green building upgrades for existing buildings, either following a loss or in the course of normal renovations. As with the green building industry itself, the availability of insurance products and services continue to evolve.

As insurance companies develop a greater understanding of green building design and construction insurance issues, it is likely they will continue to update their offerings to better meet the needs and demands of the marketplace. As evidence of their improved understanding of green building and insurance issues, insurers have begun to allow certified buildings covered by green insurance to be repaired or rebuilt to the next highest certification level in the event of a loss. In pricing and evaluating available alternatives, it is important to clarify how the insurance policy defines "certification" and which green building rating system applies. The failure to read and understand the fine print may result in coverage gaps.

Newly available products include extending coverage for vegetated roofs on certified green buildings to vegetated swales, walls and other vegetation that reduces heat island effect. In 2010, at least one major insurer expanded its coverage of property owners' energy efficiency and other environmental upgrades. Perhaps in response to recent litigation between a project owner and its contractor seeking damages for lost tax credits, one insurance company has announced a product not previously available in the marketplace which protects policyholders who have received a tax incentive, a financial grant, loan or a similar benefit that helped them pay for energy efficiency improvements to their property. According to the company, if the policyholder suffers a loss or damage affecting those improvements and the institution that provided the incentive demands a refund, the coverage would take care of that repayment.[5.4] These new insurance products are significantly broader that previously available products.

According to at least one insurance consultant familiar with green building and insurance, additional property insurance issues which should be considered in evaluating the adequacy of existing insurance include: valuation; recertification costs; building laws and ordinances; recycling during rebuilding; and business income.[5.5] Many of these issues may be addressed through the procurement of green endorsements that have recently been developed by the Insurance Services Office (ISO) and by individual insurance companies.

§ 12.04   LEGAL ISSUES RELATING TO GREEN BUILDING

[C]   Potential for Disappointment

[1]   Potential Legal Theories

[d]   Negligence

[i]   Negligence in General

Page 396, replace third sentence of first full paragraph with:

The plaintiff must establish that the defendant owed the plaintiff a duty of care, that the defendant breached that duty, and that the breach caused the plaintiff harm.

[5.4] *Allianz Affiliate Fireman's Fund Introduces New Green Insurance Endorsements*, Ins. Bus. Rev., 24 June 2010.

[5.5] David R. Ackerman, *The Albert Advisor—Education Practice*, CPCU, ARM, AU, June 2010.

CHAPTER **13**

CLIMATE CHANGE: A VIEW FROM THE STRATOSPHERE

James S. Heath
Samuel C. Krevor
Stephen A. Buryk
Craig Coulter

Page 424, add new section 13.06A before § 13.07:

§ 13.06A   CURRENT MITIGATION EFFORTS

[A]   EU-ETS

The EU-ETS commenced operations in early 2005, regulating over 10,000 facilities which account for roughly 40% of Europe's GHG emissions. The period from 2005–2007 was a trial period (Phase I) which allowed the system to establish a market to trade EUAs, and to prepare to integrate the use of CERs and ERUs from the CDM and JI programs. Credit prices hit a high of €30 per tonne of CO_2 in April of 2006, but declined to less than €.10 by September of 2007 when it was learned that facilities had received too many allowances. This was a result of using estimates rather than verified facility GHG inventories completed prior to the start of the program. Despite the market volatility, over allocation of allowances, difficulties in getting trading systems up and running, and generally not being the focus of the trial, Phase I did achieve some modest GHG reductions, and set the stage for Phase II (Commitment Period) of the system.[19]

Phase II of the EU-ETS (2008–2012) brought some changes to the system. The number of allowances issued was reduced, penalties for non-compliance were increased from €40 a tonne to €100, and other industries, such as aviation, were brought into the system. EU-ETS Phase II will extend until 2012, when the Kyoto Protocol expires. A Phase III is scheduled from 2013–2020, which seeks 21% reductions in GHGs compared to 2005 levels. However, the agreement will likely be significantly impacted by negotiations on a post-Kyoto Treaty.

---

[19] Stauffer, Nancy, "Carbon emissions trading in Europe: Lessons to be learned" (http://web.mit.edu/mitei/research/spotlights/europe-carbon.html), Massachusetts Institute of Technology Energy Initiative.

[B] Asia

Reception and implementation of the Kyoto Protocol in Asia has been mixed at best. While Japan was viewed as having excellent opportunities to reach its Kyoto mandated reductions, they continue to see their emission levels rise. The Chinese government has stated climate change is a critical issue, but they are resisting any mandatory GHG limits in a post-Kyoto agreement despite large increases in emissions. Australia, like the United States, refused to ratify the Kyoto Protocol, but recently with a change in governing parties, the current government ratified the Kyoto Protocol and is in the process of setting up a carbon reduction scheme, scheduled to now start in 2011. India, like China, does not have any required reduction targets under the Kyoto Protocol, and maintains that the responsibility for reductions lies mainly with developed countries. However, India has been actively involved in CDM project development, with 398 out of 1455 projects worldwide as of March 2009 having originated in India, second only to China's 453.

[C] North America

Any hope of reviving the ratification of the Kyoto Protocol in the U.S. was dashed with the election of the Bush Administration in 2000. However, in 2007 the State of Massachusetts successfully argued before the Supreme Court that the United States Environmental Protection Agency was authorized to regulate GHGs if they are found to endanger public health or welfare. Despite the obligations laid out in Massachusetts vs. EPA and subsequent lawsuits, under the Bush administration no such determination was made. (*See* Sidebar: Obama, the American Clean Energy & Security bill, and Impacts on the Construction Industry.)

In Canada, the Kyoto Protocol was ratified in 2002, but the election of a conservative minority government led to a promise to develop a Canadian specific mechanism to reduce GHG emissions. This promise was articulated in the "Turning the Corner" framework released in April of 2007, but to date the system has been revised several times, is not close to implementation, and Ottawa appears to be looking for signals from the U.S. before moving forward.

Despite the lack of mitigation efforts at the federal level in the U.S. and Canada, several regional, provincial, and state initiatives have developed that are either in operation or are about to start their compliance phases. Due to pressure from critics of the oil sands industry, in 2007 the province of Alberta started the Specified Gas Emitters Regulation, requiring heavy industry to reduce GHG emissions intensity by 12% from an averaged baseline established between 2003–05.

On January 1, 2009, 10 Northeast and Mid-Atlantic states in the U.S. started compliance implementation of the Regional Greenhouse Gas Initiative (RGGI), which caps GHG emissions from the power (utility) sector and requires a 10% reduction of emissions by 2018. California passed climate change legislation in 2006, with implementation starting in 2009 and 2010, and has reached out to other states and provinces to form the Western Climate Initiative, which seeks to establish a regional compliance market for GHG emissions. Similar regional initiatives have also started in the Midwest and the South, and British Columbia, Ontario, Manitoba, and other Canadian provinces have either joined these regional initiatives or established their own GHG reductions policies and goals.

[D]   Obama, the American Clean Energy & Security Act, and the Construction Industry

The Obama administration platform included taking swift action on climate change, and developments have moved quickly. In April of 2009, the EPA issued the endangerment finding required by the Massachusetts vs. EPA case, finding that GHGs do in fact endanger public welfare. Also in April 2009, EPA issued a new rule requiring facilities with 25,000 metric tons of GHG emissions or more to report those emissions to the EPA on an annual basis.

In Congress, the House of Representatives narrowly passed the American Clean Energy & Security Act (ACES), which in addition to providing for a cap and trade emissions market, have significant provisions for improved buildings efficiency. Most significantly for the construction industry, the bill mandates a "national energy efficiency building code" for residential and commercial buildings, and 30% reductions in energy use for residential buildings by 2014, and 2015 for commercial buildings.

While the bill must still pass the Senate, the combination of GHG limits, energy use, and building mandates makes the ACES one of the most significant pieces of legislation for the construction and buildings industry in a generation.

CHAPTER 14

AIA CONTRACT DOCUMENTS

Suzanne H. Harness

___

§ 14.03   THE 2007 OWNER-ARCHITECT AGREEMENT FORMS

Page 435, add to list in second paragraph:

B202–2009 Programming

Page 436, add after second full paragraph:

Since 2007, the AIA has introduced two additional A201 Family Owner-Architect agreements that are based on B101–2007. They are B108™–2009, Standard Form of Agreement Between Owner and Architect for a Federally Funded or Federally Insured Project, and B106™–2010, Standard Form of Agreement Between Owner and Architect for Pro Bono Services.

B108–2009 is a standard form of agreement between owner and architect for building design and construction contract administration that is intended for use on federally funded or federally insured projects. B108–2009 was developed with the assistance of several federal agencies and contains terms and conditions that are unique to federally funded or federally insured projects. B108 is an update of B181–1994 but is based on B101 and incorporates the 2007 revisions.

B106–2010 is a new standard form of agreement between owner and architect for building design, construction contract administration, or other professional services provided on a pro bono basis. The architect's pro bono services are professional services for which the architect receives no financial compensation other than compensation for reimbursable expenses. A table format is provided which the parties use to designate the scope of the architect's pro bono services and the maximum number of hours to be provided by the architect for each designated pro bono service.

§ 14.04   2007 OWNER-CONTRACTOR AGREEMENT FORMS

[C]   AIA Document A201

Page 462, add to end of second full paragraph (Digital Information):

In late 2008, the AIA introduced E202™–2008, Building Information Modeling Protocol Exhibit, to provide the contractual structure needed to manage the use of Building Information Modeling (BIM). E202–2008 is not a stand-alone agreement, but is an exhibit to attach to any agreement for design services or construction on a project where the project team will use BIM. Parties executing E202 agree to incorporate it into any other agreement for services or construction on the project, thus ensuring consistency in BIM protocols and procedures across the project.

[2]   Article-by-Article-Description of A201–2007

[a]   *Article 1: General Provisions*

Page 469, add to end of subsection:

In 2010, with the support and feedback of industry stakeholders, the AIA revised the long-standing AIA A310™–1970, Bid Bond, and AIA A312™–1984, Performance Bond and Payment Bond.

The A310™–2010, Bid Bond, is a simple, one-page form that establishes the maximum penal amount that may be due to the owner if the selected bidder fails to execute the contract or fails to provide any required performance and payment bonds. In addition to generally updated language, A310–2010 adds language allowing the owner and contractor to extend the period of acceptance of the contractor's bid for up to 60 days without obtaining the surety's consent. A310–2010 also can be used by subcontractors when a bid bond is required by the contractor.

The A312™–2010, Performance Bond and Payment Bond, is one form that incorporates two bonds: one covering the contractor's perfor-mance, and the other covering the contractor's obligations to pay subcontractors and others for material and labor. In addition, A312–2010 obligates the surety to act responsively to the owner's requests for discussions aimed at anticipating or preventing a contractor's default.

As with A310, the language of A312–2010 has been updated. Some other changes made to the A312 Performance Bond include the addition of language clarifying that the owner's failure to comply with the notice requirements of Section 3.1 does not release the surety from its obliga-tions under the bond except to the extent the surety demonstrates actual prejudice. The A312–2010 Performance Bond also shortens the notice period for surety default under the bond from 15 days to 7 days. Further, the limit of the surety's obligation to the amount of the bond does not apply if the surety elects to undertake and complete the contract itself.

Changes made to the A312 Payment Bond include an increase in the period of time in which the surety must answer a Claimant's Claim from 45 days to 60 days, and added language stating that a failure of the surety to answer or make payment in the time period specified is not a waiver of the surety's and contractor's defenses to the Claim, but may entitle the Claimant to attorneys' fees.

Page 479, add new section after § 14.04:

§ 14.05   INTEGRATED PROJECT DELIVERY AND CONSTRUCTION MANAGEMENT

After the revisions to the design/bid-negotiate/build A201 family of documents in 2007, the AIA turned its attention to two other delivery methods, Integrated Project Delivery and Construction Management.

[A]   Integrated Project Delivery

[1]   IPD Guide

In 2007 the AIA introduced Integrated Project Delivery (IPD), a new method for delivering a construction project that integrates people, systems, and practices from the beginning of the design phase. This delivery method, which is intended to increase efficiency and reduce waste, was initially described in Integrated Project Delivery: A Guide (IPD Guide), a manual that is free for download at *www.aia.org/ipdg*. Written by a collaboration of the AIA's Documents Committee and AIA California Council, the IPD Guide sets forth several IPD principles and provides a roadmap, by project phase, for achieving those principles. The AIA took additional steps to lead the design and construction industry toward this more efficient and collaborative working environment through the 2008 release of new standard form contract documents.

[2]   A295 documents (sometimes referred to as the transitional documents)

The A295 documents consist of B195™–2008, an owner-architect agreement, and A195™–2008, a guaranteed maximum price (GMP) owner-contractor agreement, both of which incorporate A295™–2008, General Conditions of the Agreement for Integrated Project Delivery. The A295 documents provide a smooth transition from traditional delivery methods because they are based on a commonly used delivery model whereby the general contractor provides pre-construction services, such as cost estimating and constructability reviews, working in tandem with the architect during the design phase. The A295 General Conditions document departs from tradition, however, because instead of setting forth the duties of the owner, architect and contractor in separate silos, it creates a collaborative working environment by integrating the duties of each participant with the activities of the other two, and describes them sequentially for each of the IPD phases, from conceptualization through construction.

[3]   SPE Documents

The SPE documents, by contrast, are not based on a traditional delivery model, but represent an entirely new way to deliver a project. To achieve a closer alignment of interests, the AIA developed C195™–2008, Standard Form Single Purpose Entity Agreement for Integrated Project Delivery. Using C195, the owner, architect, construction manager, and perhaps other key project participants, each become members of a single purpose entity, the SPE, whose purpose is to furnish the skilled services necessary to design and construct the project. The SPE is a limited liability company, a business entity readily recognizable and available in all jurisdictions, that provides the benefit of limited liability to its members. The owner-member provides funding for the project under C196™–2008, the agreement between the SPE and the project owner. The architect, construction manager and other non-owner members provide services to the SPE using C197™–2008, an agreement between the SPE and any non-owner SPE member. The SPE itself does not perform professional services, but furnishes those services through contracts with its own members or with other licensed professionals. Under C197, the non-owner members are reimbursed for the costs they incur in providing services. They may earn profit through the achievement of project goals (goal achievement compensation), and a shared savings provision (incentive compensation). If one member earns profit, all members earn profit. For that reason, members are motivated to help each other achieve goals and monitor costs. This highly collaborative process has the potential to result in a high quality project for the owner, and substantial monetary and intangible rewards for the other members.

In 2010, the AIA completed the SPE set of documents with the publication of SPE-consultant and SPE-contractor agreements. These agreements are for use between the SPE and non-member consultants and contractors. Both agreements have been developed to further the collaborative principles of integrated project delivery in the SPE model.

C198™–2010, Standard Form of Agreement Between Single Purpose Entity and Consultant for Integrated Project Delivery, is coordinated for use with C195. The specific services the consultant is required to perform are set forth within the document as well as the Integrated Scope of Services Matrix, which is part of the C195 Target Cost Amendment.

In addition to traditional compensation for services, C198 allows the consultant to receive additional profit through incentive compensation and goal achievement compensation.

C199™–2010, Standard Form of Agreement between Single Purpose Entity and Contractor for Integrated Project Delivery, is also coordinated for use with C195. C199–2010 is intended to be a flexible document. C199 can be used for a contractor that only provides construction services, or it can also be used for a contractor that will provide both pre-construction and construction services. C199 is not intended for use in competitive bidding and relies upon an agreed-to contract sum, which can be either a stipulated sum (fixed price) or cost of the work plus a fee, with a guaranteed maximum price. In addition to compensation for the contract sum, C199 allows the contractor to receive additional profit through incentive compensation and goal achievement compensation.

[4] Multi-Party Agreement

AIA Document C191™–2009, Standard Form Multi-Party Agreement for Integrated Project Delivery, provides a third type of agreement model on the IPD spectrum. C191 establishes the basic legal framework for a multi-party agreement for integrated project delivery. C191 integrates the owner, architect, contractor, and perhaps other key project participants, under one agreement from the outset of the project. The parties are required to communicate, share information, and make decisions in a collective manner; establish project goals and compensation criteria based on the success of the project; collectively manage and allocate risk; and use BIM and other technologies to effectively manage the project.

C191 reflects a significant departure from traditional delivery models in that C191 aligns the success of the individual parties with project success. At the same time, C191 maintains the familiar roles and responsibilities of each of the parties. Accordingly, C191 takes the IPD collaborative process further than the Transitional documents but not as far as the SPE documents.

[B] Construction Management

In 2009 the AIA updated and revised the documents in the Construction Manager as Adviser family and the Construction Manager as Constructor family.

The Construction Manager as Adviser (CMa) documents are based on a delivery model in which the Construction Manager provides independent construction management services purely as an adviser to the owner. Those services begin in the design phase and continue through completion of the project. Under the Construction Manager as Adviser delivery model, the construction manager does not assume direct responsibility for construction of the project. Construction of the project is accomplished through the owner's contract or contracts with a general contractor or multiple prime trade contractors.

The Construction Manager as Constructor (CMc) family is based on a delivery model in which the construction manager provides preconstruction services in an advisory capacity and ultimately takes on the role of a construction contractor, including subcontracting and purchasing materials for incorporation into the project. The construction manager's compensation is divided between preconstruction phase services and construction phase services. For the preconstruction phase, the construction manager's compensation may be based on a lump sum, hourly basis, or some other formula. During the construction phase, the construction manager's compensation is based on the cost of the work plus a fee and may or may not be capped at a guarantee maximum price.

The following CMa and CMc documents were revised and renumbered in 2009. The document title references below include the old document numbers.

A132™–2009 (formerly A101™CMa–1992), Standard Form of Agreement Between Owner and Contractor, Construction Manager as Adviser Edition

A232™–2009 (formerly A201™CMa–1992), General Conditions of the Contract for Construction, Construction Manager as Adviser Edition

A533™–2009 (formerly A511™CMa–1993), Guide for Supplementary Conditions, Construction Manager as Adviser Edition

B132™–2009 (formerly B141™CMa–1992), Standard Form of Agreement Between Owner and Architect, Construction Manager as Adviser Edition

C132™–2009 (formerly B801™CMa–1992), Standard Form of Agreement Between Owner and Construction Manager as Adviser

G732™–2009 (formerly G702™CMa–1992), Application and Certificate for Payment, Construction Manager as Adviser Edition

G736™–2009 (formerly G722™CMa–1992), Project Application and Project Certificate for Payment, Construction Manager as Adviser Edition

G737™–2009 (formerly G723™CMa–1992), Summary of Contractors' Applications for Payment, Construction Manager as Adviser Edition

A133™–2009 (formerly A121™CMc–2003) Standard Form of Agreement Between Owner and Construction Manager as Constructor where the basis of payment is the Cost of the Work Plus a Fee with a Guaranteed Maximum Price

A134™–2009 (formerly A131™CMc–2003) Standard Form of Agreement Between Owner and Construction Manager as Constructor where the basis of payment is the Cost of the Work Plus a Fee without a Guarantee Maximum Price

These documents were revised to conform to the updates made in the 2007 A201 family of documents, including the dispute resolution check box; selection of an Initial Decision Maker in A132–2009, A133–2009 and A134–2009; and establishment of digital data protocols, with E201–2007 and E202–2008 referenced in the agreements.

In the Construction Manager as Adviser family, the payment application process and payment application forms were revised to better accommodate the difference between projects where the owner contracts with a general contractor and projects where the owner contracts with multiple prime contractors for construction of the work. In the case where the owner contracts with one general contractor, the construction manager reviews the contractor's periodic payment applications (G732–2009) and supporting materials and, upon certification, forwards each payment application and the supporting materials to the architect for review and certification. In the case of multiple prime contractors, the construction manager reviews the individual periodic payment applications (G732–2009) and supporting materials from each of the trade contractors. The construction manager uses data from the individual periodic payment applications to prepare a project application and certificate for payment (G736–2009) and a summary of the contractors' applications (G737–2009), and forwards those summary documents to the architect for review and certification for payment. The architect is only required to review and certify the project application and certificate for payment, not each individual contractor application for payment.

CHAPTER 15

OVERVIEW OF CONSENSUSDOCS FORM CONTRACTS

Brian Perlberg

Page 501, add new sections after § 15.15:

§ 15.16   CONSENSUSDOCS 752 STANDARD SUBCONTRACT FOR WORK ON A FEDERAL CONSTRUCTION PROJECT

The ConsensusDOCS Federal Subcontract builds off of the risk allocation principles found in the ConsensusDOCS 750 Standard Subcontract while tailoring requirements and practices of federal construction projects. This is the first standard subcontract that is tailored to address new federal acquisition regulations (FAR) that are now in effect, including new ethics compliance as well as suspension and debarment sanctions. Significantly, ConsensusDOCS comprehensively addresses mandatory FAR flow down provisions, including the Buy America Act, Davis-Bacon, and Anti-Kickback clauses through a sample exhibit that is included as a guidance document.[28]

The costs and consequences of suspension or debarment are severe and should be addressed in contract documents for federal work. The 752 Federal Subcontract flows down mandatory disclosure obligations of "credible evidence" of a violation of the civil False Claims Act or federal criminal laws related to its government contracts.[29] This requirement applies to all existing contracts and retroactively to those contracts on which the contractor has received final payment within three years prior to December 12, 2008.[30] There are also new business ethics and compliance requirements that apply to any subcontract or purchase order exceeding $5 million and a performance period of 120 days or more to complete. Provisions in section 12.7 flow requirements to subcontractors that include:

---

[28] *See* http://www.consensusdocs.org/downloads/752%20Guidebook%2006112009. pdf. Note that a modifiable sample exhibit is included in the ConsensusDOCS paid software.

[29] *See* section 12.8.2 "Proposals and Representations . . . the Subcontractor shall be bound to these requirements to the same extent as the Contractor."

[30] *See* http://www.consensusdocs.org/downloads/CO_0506_2009_75%20Legal.pdf.

- Adopting a written code of business ethics and conduct and make a copy of its code "available" to each employee working on the Covered Contract;[31]

- Exercising "due diligence" to prevent and detect criminal conduct; and

- Promoting an organizational culture that "encourages" ethical conduct and compliance with the law.

ConsensusDOCS 752 also affirmatively provides standards in regard to immigration status verification by requiring use of E-Verify to determine the employment eligibility verification of subcontractors and lower tiered subsubcontractors/vendors. These procedures meet proposed FAR requirements. The dispute resolution procedures in Article 11 are tailored for federal work so as not to prejudice the subcontractor but allow the contractor to fulfill its obligations to exhaust all dispute resolution procedures. The differing site conditions provisions also conform to government practices.[32] In addition, the remedies for termination for convenience and termination for cause are consistent with federal government policies and practices.

Below is the ConsensusDOCS sample FAR Mandatory Clause Exhibit pursuant to section 12.14. This sample should be revised to conform to the prime contract and any changes made to the FAR.

FEDERAL ACQUISITION REGULATION CLAUSES

The Subcontractor, by signing this Agreement, agrees to abide by the provisions of the Federal Acquisition Regulation, which are applicable to this Agreement in accordance with the Prime Contract. Particular attention is directed to the requirements of the following provisions.

FAR 52.203-6	Restrictions on Subcontractors Sales to the Government (Sept. 2006)
FAR 52.203-7	Anti-Kickback Procedures (July 1995)
FAR 52.203-12	Limitation on Payments to Influence Certain Federal Transactions (Sept. 2007)
FAR 52.203-13	Contractor Code of Business Ethics and Conduct (Dec. 2008)
FAR 52.203-14	Display of Hotline Poster(s) (Dec. 2007)
FAR 52.204-2	Security Requirements (Aug. 1996)
FAR 52.204-9	Personal Identity Verification of Contractor Personnel (Sept. 2007)

---

[31] For guidance on developing a Code of Business and Ethics Compliance see AGC, *"Federal Government Contractor Ethics and Compliance Programs, Toolkit and Guidance,"* 2009.

[32] *See* ConsensusDOCS 752 at section 3.3.

FAR 52.209-6   Protecting the Government's Interest When
                  Subcontracting with Contractors Debarred,
                  Suspended or Proposed for Debarment
FAR 52.212-5   Contract Terms and Conditions Required to
                  Implement Statutes or Executive
                  Orders-Commercial Items (Dec. 2008)
FAR 52.215-2   Audit and Records—Negotiation (June 1999)
FAR 52.215-12   Subcontractor Cost or Pricing Data (Oct. 1997)
FAR 52.215-13   Subcontractor Cost or Pricing Data—Modifications
                  (Oct. 1997)
FAR 52.219-8   Utilization of Small Business Concerns (May
                  2004)
FAR 52.219-9   Small Business Subcontracting Plan (Oct. 2001)
                  (ALT II)
FAR 52.219-22   Small Disadvantaged Business Status (Oct. 1999)
FAR 52.222-4   Contract Work Hours and Safety Standards Act—
                  Overtime Compensation (July 2005)
FAR 52.222-6   Davis-Bacon Act (July 2005)
FAR 52.222-7   Withholding of Funds (Feb. 1988)
FAR 52.222-8   Payrolls and Basic Records (Feb. 1988)
FAR 52.222-9   Apprentices and Trainees (July 2005)
FAR 52.222-10   Compliance with Copeland Act Requirements
                  (Feb. 1988)
FAR 52.222-11   Subcontracts (Labor Standards) (July 2005)
FAR 52.222-12   Contract Termination—Debarment (Feb. 1988)
FAR 52.222-13   Compliance with Davis-Bacon and Related Act
                  Regulations (Feb. 1988)
FAR 52.222-14   Disputes Concerning Labor Standards (Feb. 1988)
FAR 52.222-15   Certification of Eligibility (Feb. 1988)
FAR 52.222-21   Prohibition of Segregated Facilities (Feb. 1999)
FAR 52.222-26   Equal Opportunity (Mar. 2007)
FAR 52.222-27   Affirmative Action Compliance Requirements for
                  Construction (Feb. 1999)
FAR 52.222-35   Equal Opportunity for Special Disabled Veterans,
                  Veterans of the Vietnam Era, and Other Eligible
                  Veterans (Sept. 2006)
FAR 52.222-36   Affirmative Action for Workers with Disabilities
                  (June 1998)
FAR 52.222-37   Employment Reports on Special Disabled Veterans,
                  Veterans of the Vietnam Era, and Other Eligible
                  Veterans (Sept. 2006)
FAR 52.222-50   Combating Trafficking in Persons (Aug. 2007)
FAR 52.222-54   Employment Eligibility Verification (Jan. 2009)
FAR 52.223-14   Toxic Chemical Release Reporting (Aug. 2003)

FAR 52.225-13   Restrictions on Certain Foreign Purchases (Feb. 2006)
FAR 52.227-1   Authorization and Consent (Dec. 2007)
FAR 52.227-2   Notice and Assistance Regarding Patent and Copyright Infringement (Dec. 2007)
FAR 52.228-5   Insurance—Work on a Government Installation (Jan. 1997)

§ 15.17   725 STANDARD SUBSUBCONTRACT AGREEMENT

ConsensusDOCS 725 is a seven-page standard contract that provides the essential terms and conditions for a subsubcontract work agreement in an abbreviated fashion. Specialty contractors are performing a larger portion of construction work. This is in part due to the level of specific expertise that is required to perform increasingly complex construction work. Not only general contractors, but also subcontractors, are subcontracting portions of work to increase efficiency. Consequently, ConsensusDOCS created the first standard subsubcontract agreement. The agreement was written with the intent of a specialty subcontractor performing a specific task or portion of the work.

Because the scope of subsubcontract is intended for a discrete task, the ConsensusDOCS drafters made a decision not to incorporate the prime agreement by reference. Among other reasons, the drafters recognized that current practice may make it difficult for subsubcontractors to actually receive a copy of the prime contract. A general incorporation of terms and conditions might lead parties to unknowingly agree terms that might not be relevant to the scope of work at hand. Therefore, it is important that the essential provisions that need to be flowed down are specified by the parties. Also, the agreement provides references to separate exhibits which the parties will need to create in order to address important legal and insurance requirements. Detailed insurance provisions are included in the "long form" ConsensusDOCS agreements. This approach was taken, in part, to help the parties decide which provisions should apply for the specific scope of the work contracted between the parties. A sample insurance exhibit will be available in the near future.

Although this is the shortest agreement in length in the ConsensusDOCS catalog, the agreement does contain some of the innovative provisions found in the long form agreements. For instance, the reduction of retainage upon completion of a percentage of work is provided for in section 9.3. A provision granting access to owner project financing, was not included because it was not deemed appropriate this far down the contractual chain.

§ 15.18 CONSENSUSDOCS 235 COST OF THE WORK AGREEMENT

The terms and conditions of the ConsensusDOCS 235 agreement are consistent with the ConsensusDOCS 205 Standard Short Form Owner-Contractor Agreement, but provide for the contractor to receive payment for the cost of the work with a fixed-fee as opposed to a lump sum. Article 9 provides detailed provisions specifying items included in cost of the work, including such costs as labor, insurance premiums and rental equipment. Note that such provisions may be helpful for inclusion in lump-sum contracts in regard to addressing the cost of changes in the work. The contractor is also required to keep detailed financial records, which are accessible to the owner under this agreement.

§ 15.19 CONSENSUSDOCS PROCEDURES AND REVISION CYCLE

ConsensusDOCS has established formal procedures that are intended to further transparency in the drafting process.[33] Significantly, the procedures provide mechanisms to "ensure that it [ConsensusDOCS] represents diverse interests in the construction industry." Stakeholders in the design and construction industry are solicited to provide input which are then actively considered in the drafting process.[34] Moreover, any individual may provide comments through the ConsensusDOCS website.[35] In order to expand upon the input received from design professional associations in the original release, the ConsensusDOCS drafters have been more heavily relying upon individual design professionals and attorneys that primarily represent design professionals.

The procedures give the ConsensusDOCS drafters the title of the Contract Content Advisory Council, and create a standard five-year revision cycle.[36] The Content Council may propose revisions early, and is currently undertaking an expansive review of the ConsensusDOCS agreements with an anticipated release date in 2010. This review will enable ConsensusDOCS to proactively respond to the changing landscape of construction contracts, as well as make additional improvements based upon industry feedback. Despite the current slowdown in the design and construction industry, it appears that ConsensusDOCS continues to gain overall market share through increased familiarity and positive project usage.

---

[33] http://www.consensusdocs.org/downloads/ConDocsPR030209.doc.

[34] http://www.consensusdocs.org/about_procedures.html at section 4.5.

[35] http://www.consensusdocs.org/feedback/contact.htm.

[36] http://www.consensusdocs.org/about_procedures.html at section 4.1.

§ 15.20   CONSENSUSDOCS 310 GREEN BUILDING ADDENDUM

Brian Perlberg, Esq. and Geoffrey Washington, Esq.[37]

One of the most dramatic trends in the design and construction industry is the adoption of green buildings. According to a McGraw-Hill study, markets for green commercial and institutional buildings in the United States are projected to increase from $3 billion in 2005 to $96-140 billion by 2013. In 2007 alone, owners registered almost 1 billion square feet of new construction. An estimated 10 to 12% of non-residential construction started in 2008 were green projects. Favorable government support, coupled with increasing energy price volatility and affordable green technology, will continue to fuel the demand for greener construction and building operation. In 2008, 31 states passed green building policies compared with 13 states in 2005. For instance, the City of Baltimore recently enacted legislation which incorporates certain performance standards for "green building" into the building code for certain new construction projects. In an industry that is sometimes reluctant to change, green building appears to have reached a tipping point.

However, despite a critical need, construction contracts and risk management have simply not kept pace. Indeed, many form construction documents fail to account for these dramatic changes, often leaving basic issues regarding terminology, process, and risk unaddressed. Accordingly, several commentators predict increased litigation and frustration among project owners seeking to build green. In November 10, 2009, ConsensusDOCS published the ConsensusDOCS 310 Green Building Addendum (the "Green Addendum"), which is the first standard construction contract document that comprehensively addresses green building construction, and is a tool to proactively manage the risks and processes involved in building green.

Choosing between building green or a traditionally-built project is, from an owner's perspective, a business decision. Estimates project a typical green building to have increased construction costs of 6% over standard building costs. State and local governments have attempted to mitigate this impact by extending an array of tax incentive programs to offset the tax impact on "green" projects which achieve and conform to certain performance criteria. By reducing the tax burden by as much as 70 to 80%, these credits can make the difference for owners deciding whether green projects are worth their increased costs. Though some studies show that there is a 10-fold payback on the increased costs, initial

[37] Geoffrey W. Washington is a senior associate with Adelberg, Rudow, Dorf & Hendler, LLC, a Mid-Atlantic Regional firm, who concentrates his practice in complex business and construction litigation. For more information, call 410-539-5195 or visit www.AdelbergRudow.com.

results from some projects are starting to raise doubts whether certified green buildings are actually performing as projected.

The U.S. Green Building Council (USGBC) has released v3, its third version of its rating system, named Leadership in Energy and Environmental Design (LEED®). V3 attempts to address performance accountability by mandating biannual recertification of building perfor-mance.[38] Accountability for performance is a good thing for all parties, but a serious side effect is that a new type of uncertainty is thrown into the mix. Tax credit incentives, which potentially were an essential part of financing, presumably would be subject to potential biannual decertifica-tion. Consequently, buildings failing to meet projected outcomes often lead to something that is all too common in the construction industry—claims and litigation.

One of the first green building cases in the country occurred in Maryland and could preface the start of increased litigation associated with green buildings. This case, *Shaw Development v. Southern Builders*, highlights that traditional form contracts inadequately address green building construction from both process and risk management perspec-tives. A developer built a condominium project which encountered certain project delays. The contractor, complaining about a lack of payment, instituted a mechanics lien suit. The delays caused the loss of certain tax credits for the project, which were issued on an annual "use it or lose it basis." Subsequently, the passing of the calendar year resulted in the loss of the tax credits as the delays pushed the project past its completion date. The owner, therefore, filed a counterclaim against the contractor for millions in losses for failure to receive the tax credit.

This scenario highlights how pitfalls can occur when contract negotiations and documents fail to incorporate intervening changes in business practices. It is, therefore, important to understand that building green encompasses new business practices and procedures. This changed reality should be addressed before the contract is signed and work commenced. In other words, update your contractual and business practices upfront so that building green will benefit your bottom line, and the environment.

[A]   Overview of the ConsensusDOCS 310 Green Building Addendum

In addition to other new tools that can help practitioners adapt to new greener building practices,[39] the ConsensusDOCS Green Building

---

[38] *See*   http://www.duanemorris.com/articles/static/gentilcore_constructiontoday_sept09.pdf for an excellent discussion about LEED v3 by Ed Gentilcore.

[39] *See* AGC's *"A Contractor's Guide to Green Building Construction"* at www.agc.org/bookstore.

Addendum was written to advance best practices to manage the processes and team approach needed to successfully design and construct green buildings. The document addresses:

- **Terminology and General Principles:** defines key terms and principles so that everyone is on the same page
- **Green Status:** clarifies the owner's desired project goals
- **Green Measures:** establishes the required physical and procedural measures
- **Green Building Facilitator:** coordinates various participants' roles and responsibilities to achieve Green Measures and Green Status. Addresses *who* will be in charge of document collection and submission, and if necessary resubmission
- **Implementation:** describes how the parties incorporate and refine green measures into the plans and specifications, and resolve potential differences
- **Risk Allocation:** clarifies legal responsibilities.

The Green Addendum, a 10-page contract document which should be appended to each project participant's contract agreement, clarifies roles, responsibilities and procedures to maximize the successful delivery of green building objectives. In addition to coordinating with the ConsensusDOCS family of contract documents, the Addendum works well with AIA and other standard documents, as well as "original" agreements.

[B] Current Practice for Green Contracts Is Not Best Practice

When beginning the process of drafting a new standard document, the drafting working group first researched field-tested contract examples that worked well. Unfortunately, the contract examples were far from best practice. Current practices tend to dictate a final performance result without defining appropriate responsibilities for conducting the work. One example cursorily dictated to build a LEED silver-rated building. Consequently, much of the Green Addendum focuses on identifying the roles, responsibilities, and processes to identify and close potential gaps. Team collaboration is particularly important for success due to the highly interactive nature of highly performing building systems, as well using newer materials that carry less field testing. Fortunately, the Consensus-DOCS coalition was able to draw upon a diverse coalition of design professional, owner, contractor, and surety stakeholders with practical experience in the design and construction of green buildings.

[C]   Elected Green Status—Defining a Green Building

What constitutes green building is a fundamental question but not universally answered the same throughout the industry. USGBC has done an excellent job of creating a system which is widely-recognized as standard for rating buildings as green. However, some owners seek green building performance, but are not willing to spend the time and expense involved with an official certification. There are also other rating systems in the marketplace such as Green Globes or Energy Star that are now available. Some owners wish to focus on certain building performance aspects such as energy efficiency in selecting their green objectives.

The ConsensusDOCS 310 requires the owner to declare project goals as an elected green status, and the specific green measures which will achieve this elected goal. The measures are required to be outlined in a central report, which also clarifies which requirements are physical or procedural green measures. Physical Green Measures, such as an HVAC system performing at a certain energy rating, would constitute a physical green measure. Procedural Green Measures, such as recycling construction debris or using materials originating within a certain radius of the project site, is not something that would be apparent in the end project and would be considered a procedural green measure. The Procedural Green Measures must "specifically identify the Project Participant(s) that is to implement, perform and satisfy each . . ." measure.[40]

[D]   Neutral Rating System

The ConsensusDOCS 310 is well-suited for owners who desire LEED certification and contemplates the document submissions, qualifications and qualification requirements entailed with successfully fulfilling this as an elected green status. However, the drafters wanted the document to be flexible for other purposes as well and therefore did not tie the document to LEED standards alone.[41] This seems prescient now that LEED standards have changed and will continue to evolve, as well as jurisdictional building code requirements. Moreover, some owners will use this document to achieve green building performance without seeking formal certification. The Green Addendum is equally appropriate for either use.

[E]   Green Building Facilitator

The most significant concept was creating a Green Building Facilitator (GBF) to serve as the central contact to facilitate and coordinate the

---

[40] ConsensusDOCS 310 S § 6.5.

[41] Note that Green Globes and EPA Energy Star buildings are other possible certification or ratings sought in the green building marketplace.

successful achievement of the project's green goals. Currently, these functions are often haphazardly lumped onto existing project participant's responsibilities. The role of the GBF was created to give this essential project participant more thoughtful and coordinated responsibilities, as well as cooperation from other project participants. This role should be fulfilled by someone with the requisite skill and experience, and should come with appropriate compensation. The Green Building Addendum assumes that additional compensation will be specified in the underlying contract with the party serving as the GBF. This is referenced as a Governing Contract, and compensation expectations are also explained in the companion guidance document to the Green Addendum.[42]

A design professional, contractor, construction manager, or even a third-party consultant can be designated to serve as the GBF. It is anticipated that the additional work scope requirements will be included in the underlying Governing Contract with the design professional, design-builder, and contractor or construction manager. It is possible that an outside consultant could serve in this capacity as well, and this role might grow as a cottage industry; however, it is currently more likely that a project party will serve in this role. The ConsensusDOCS drafters plan to draft a separate Owner-GBF standard agreement in the near future.

The Addendum takes into consideration the increased coordination needed in the design and construction phases. To assist the GBF in performing its duties and obligations, there are numerous coordination, cooperation, and documentation requirements placed upon the appropriate project participants throughout the design and construction process. Project participants assisting in achieving green building measures, including specialty contractors, subcontractors, material suppliers, or other consultants, communicate and coordinate their efforts. Detailed resolution procedures are included in the Green Addendum to help address objections to selected green measures, and the GBF is placed in a counseling role to the owner on alternatives to address objections.

[F] Risk Allocation

Article 8's risk allocation section provides a straightforward approach. The Green Addendum is designed around the principle that the party in the best position to control and mitigate a risk is assigned that risk. The GBF is assigned liability for direct damages if an elected green status is not achieved. If for instance, LEED certification is not achieved, the GBF will be responsible to promptly correct the document submission in an appeal process. However, if rejection is due to the defective work of another project participant, that project participant is still directly (and solely) responsible under their Governing Contract. This harkens back to

---

[42] http://consensusdocs.org/wp-content/uploads/2010/04/310-Guidebook-April-2010.pdf

defining the fundamental roles of the project participants and retaining the design professional's core role of being responsible for design and the contractor to be in charge of the means and methods of building. Once the defective work is corrected, the GBF is responsible for the correction of the document submissions in an appeals process or a resubmission.

Significantly, the document clarifies that the failure to attain the Elected Green Status or intended benefits to the environment are consequential damages. Consequential damages related to a green building are described as an "Owner's loss of income or profit or inability to realize potential reductions in operating, maintenance or other related costs, tax or other similar benefits or credits, marketing opportunities and other similar opportunities or benefits."[43] So, for instance, failure to achieve a tax credit based on a level of LEED certification, which was the subject of the Shaw case described above, is a consequential damage. Liability exposure for a consequential damage is explicitly determined by the applicable Governing Contract. The ConsensusDOCS family of standard agreements specifically identifies such risks for the parties to communicate and negotiate.[44] Other standard industry documents typically have a consequential damages waiver. However, this provision is often the focus of significant negotiation, further highlighting the need to ensure the parties coordinate their contracting practices to reflect new green goals.

[G]   Outlook

The penetration of green building design and construction has taken hold in the United States. Well-designed, high-performing buildings may become synonymous with green buildings. Accordingly, building green requires updated standard documents to reflect new business practices, such as the ConsensusDOCS 310 Green Building Addendum. Now is the best time to proactively address these issues to avoid going from green to red (claims and litigation).

You can obtain a free excerpted sample and guidebook document at www.consensusdocs.org.

---

[43] ConsensusDOCS 310 § 8.2.
[44] See for instance ConsensusDOCS 200 § 6.6.

CHAPTER 16

SALES CONTRACTS / UNIFORM COMMERCIAL CODE

Terrence L. Brookie
Eric D. Foerg

§ 16.01   INTRODUCTION

[B]   Article 2 of the Uniform Commercial Code

Page 505, add after sixth sentence third full paragraph:

As of the time of this writing, Kansas, Nevada, and Oklahoma are the only three states to have introduced bills proposing to adopt the 2003 amendments to Article 2 (and Article 2A), but no state has officially enacted the 2003 amendments. To a limited degree, in 2005 Oklahoma embraced similar language by amending (effective January 1, 2006) Sections 2-105(1), 2-106(1), and 2A-103(1)(h) of its Commercial Code to exclude information from the definition of "goods" and to clarify that a license of information is not a contract for sale under Article 2. 12A Okl. St. §§ 2-105(1); 2-106(1); and 2A-103(1)(h). Oklahoma HB 3104, introduced on February 1, 2010, proposes amendments to forty-nine sections of Article 2 and four sections of Article 2A. Without formally introducing a bill, Texas also considered a scaled-back, compromise version of the 2003 Amendments, which addressed many of the concerns raised by industry groups as to the 2003 Amendments. The Texas House Committee on Business and Industry, in the 80th and 81st Legislatures, studied and held hearings regarding the 2003 Amendments. Submitted evidence and testimony eventually led to a modified version of the 2003 Amendments, which excluded many of the 2003 Amendments and revised others. The modified version has yet to be introduced, let alone adopted.

§ 16.02   BASIC PRINCIPLES APPLICABLE TO SALES CONTRACTS AND THEIR NEGOTIATION

[B]   The Applicability of the UCC

Page 507, replace text of note 4 with:

Bailey v. Skipperliner Indus., 278 F. Supp. 2d 945, 964 (N.D. Ind. 2003);

Page 508, replace text of note 8 with:

"Complications arise when the transaction involves both goods and services." TK Power v. Textron, Inc., 433 F. Supp. 2d 1058, 1061 (N.D. Cal. 2006). "The issue of mixed or hybrid goods often arises in the context of transactions involving software." TK Power, 433 F. Supp. 2d at 1061–62.

Page 508, replace text of note 9 with:

Fab-Tech, Inc. v. E.I. Du Pont de Nemours & Co., 311 Fed. Appx. 443 (2d Cir. 2009) (affirming breach of contract claims being barred by the UCC's four year statute of limitations).

Page 508, replace second and third sentences (and subsequent quote) in third full paragraph with:

Courts may adopt a blended approach, applying non-UCC law to the non-goods portions of the contract in certain circumstances involving a mix of goods and non-goods.[15] Such bifurcated treatment is based on three factors:

1. Whether the non-goods aspect of the transaction is clearly distinct and easily separable from the goods aspect.
2. Whether the alleged performance or non-performance pertains solely to the non-goods aspect of the transaction.
3. Whether it makes sense to apply the UCC to the non-goods aspect of the transaction and whether applying non-UCC law accords with the parties' intent.[16]

Page 508, replace text of note 15 with:

TK Power, 433 F. Supp. 2d at 1063.

Page 508, replace text of note 16 with:

TK Power, 433 F. Supp. 2d at 1064.

Page 509, replace text of note 20 with:

Linden v. Cascade Stone Co., Inc., 699 N.W.3d 189, 191 (Wis. 2005).

§ 16.06   TERMS OF THE CONTRACT

[A]   Introduction

Page 526, add to end of second full paragraph:

Thirty-seven states have adopted Revised Article 1 as of March 1, 2010. Twenty-six of those states have adopted the uniform definition of good faith, which requires all parties (not just merchants) to act honestly and to observe reasonable commercial standards of fair dealing. Effective July 1, 2010, Indiana is the 27th state to follow the uniform definition.

§ 16.08   PERFORMANCE OF SALES CONTRACTS

[B]   Passing of Title

Page 530, replace text of note 99 with:

First Nat'l Bank of Elkhart County v. Smoker, 286 N.E.2d 203 (Ind. Ct. App. 1972), *reh'g denied*, 287 N.E.3d 788 (Ind. Ct. App. 1972).

CHAPTER **19**

CONSTRUCTION WRAP-UPS: OWNER AND CONTRACTOR CONTROLLED INSURANCE PROGRAMS

Tracy Alan Saxe
Tobias J. Cushing

---

§ 19.03   WRAP-UP COVERAGE CONSIDERATIONS

[B]   Who Is an Insured

Page 644, add to end of second full paragraph:

Not clearly defining who is an insured and for what activity can cause disputes. *See, e.g.*, *American Protection Ins. Co. v. Acadia Ins. Co.*, 814 A.2d 989 (2003).

[C]   Deductibles and Self Insured Retentions

Page 645, add footnote referent 7.1 to end of the third full paragraph and add note 7.1:

[7.1] Mohegan Tribal Gaming Auth. v. Kohn Pedersen Fox Assocs., 36 Conn L. Rptr. 249 (2003).

[D]   Adequacy of Limits

[3]   Excess Wrap-Up Endorsements

Page 646, add new paragraph after block quote beginning "This insurance does not apply to any Wrap-Up that You are. . . .":

Because many Wrap-Ups provide completed operations coverage for a limited period of time, e.g., three years, corporate carriers have been starting to issue wrap exclusions with completed operations excess provisions:

This policy does not apply to any work performed by or on behalf of you under any Owner Controlled Insurance Program (O.C.I.P.) or Contractor Controlled Insurance Program (C.C.I.P.), otherwise referred to as Wrap Up Program, that you enter into except as respects excess coverage for the "Products-Completed Operations Hazard" for "your work."

[F]   Notice and Voluntary Payments

Page 650, insert brackets around number 2.

[2]   Voluntary Payments

Page 651, add to the end of carryover paragraph:

Similarly, the insurer needs to be involved in all settlements of litigation regarding the Wrap-Up. *See, e.g., Motiva Enterprises v. St. Paul Fire and Marina Ins. Co.*, 445 F.3d 381 (5th Cir. 2006).

CHAPTER **20**

DESIGN PROFESSIONAL INSURANCE ISSUES

Jimmy A. Castex, Jr.
Terrence L. Brennan

§ 20.02   SCOPE OF COVERAGE

Page 683, in note 9, change Schorr Bros. cite to:

182 A.D.2d 664, 582 N.Y.S.2d 258 (N.Y. App. Div. 2d Dept 1992).

Page 683, note 10, replace Volume Servs., Inc. cite to:

Volume Servs., Inc. v. C.F. Murphy, 656 S.W.2d 785 (Mo. App. 1983).

Page 685, in note 20, replace "1989" with:

1969

§ 20.03   TYPES OF COVERAGE

Page 688, note 36, replace "So..2d" with:

So. 2d

§ 20.04   START AND END OF COVERAGE

Page 695, replace cite in note 97 with:

400 N.E.2d 1256, 1261 (Mass. 1980).

CHAPTER **22**

DIFFERING SITE CONDITIONS
John Spangler
Andy Howard
Donald Brown

§ 22.01   INTRODUCTION

Page 731, in first sentence of second full paragraph, delete:

Today

§ 22.02   NATURE OF AVAILABLE REMEDIES

Page 732, replace text of note 2 with:

See, e.g., S. Comfort Builders, Inc. v. U.S., 67 Fed. Cl. 124, 133 (2005).

Page 732, in first sentence of first full paragraph, delete:

more recently

Page 733, add to note 8:

, *rev'd on other grounds,* 26 F.3d 141 (Fed. Cir. 1994) (table).

§ 22.03   CONTRACT CLAUSES

Page 734, note 11, add before Noralyn O. Harlow:

Stanley P. Sklar, *Drafting and Negotiating Construction Contracts,* 567 PLI/Real 31, 55 (2009) (discussing the process in the AIA A201);

Page 734, add to note 12:

(emphasis added)

Page 735, in first sentence of first full paragraph, replace "contract" with:

contrast

§ 22.05 NOTICE OF A CHANGED CONDITION

Page 737, replace text of note 14 with:

Ace Constructors, Inc. v. U.S., 70 Fed. Cl. 253, 273 (2006) (citing John Cibinic and Ralph Nash, *Administration of Government Contracts* 533 (3d ed. 1995); Seaboard Lumber Co. v. United States, 45 Fed. Cl. 404, 407 (1999); and Shepherd v. United States, 125 Ct. Cl. 724, 113 F. Supp. 648 (1953)).

Page 737, replace text of note 15 with:

George Sollitt Constr. Co. v. U.S., 64 Fed. Cl. 229, 291 (2005) (citing Schnip Bldg. Co. v. U.S., 227 Ct. Cl. 148, 645 F.2d 950, 959 (1981)).

§ 22.06 PROVING A CATEGORY I DIFFERING SITE CONDITION CLAIM

Page 739, replace text of note 22 with:

Wunderlich v. State, 423 P.2d 545 (Cal. 1967); Trafalgar House Constr., 73 Fed. Cl. at 703.

Page 739, replace second full paragraph with:

When ruling on a changed conditions claim, the courts frequently consider whether soil reports (which frequently accompany the bid documents) are actually a part of the contract. This precise issue was addressed by the court in *Millgard Corp. v. McKee/Mays.*[25] There, the court reasoned that if the soil report was not part of the contract documents, it could not be used to show that the site conditions actually encountered were "at variance with the conditions indicated by the Contract Documents."[26] Consequently, a disclaimer clause found in the contract, which expressly stated that the soil report was not a part of the contract documents, significantly impaired the contractor's claim. The contractor could only challenge the enforceability of the disclaimer

---

[25] 49 F.3d 1070 (5th Cir. 1995).
[26] *Id.* at 1072.

clause. This court noted a split of authority on this issue[27] and, in ruling that the soil reports were not a part of the contract documents, held:

§ 22.08   SITE INSPECTION AND DISCLAIMER CLAUSES

Page 742, replace first full paragraph with:

A contractor cannot disregard its site inspection obligations. As stated in *D.F.K. Enterprises, Inc. v. U.S.*,[34] a site inspection clause requires the contractor to make a pre-bid site investigation, the adequacy of which is measured against the standard of what a "reasonable, intelligent contractor, experienced in the particular field of work, would discover."[35] Applying this standard, the contractor is imputed to have that knowledge which a reasonably prudent contractor would have acquired from conducting a proper site inspection.[35.1] For example, in *Ryco Constr., Inc. v. U.S.*,[35.2] the contractor sought recovery, in part, for delays on its project which resulted from the discovery of an endangered frog species. In denying liability for the delays, the government pointed to a site inspection clause in the contract and the contractor's failure to conduct any inspection. Considering the clause, the court applied the reasonableness standard as follows:

While the site inspection clause may have applied had this dispute been about soil conditions or the quality of access to a remote site, the court does not believe that plaintiff could be expected not only to see frogs in a stream near the construction site, but also to know that certain of those frogs were an endangered species whose presence could lead to a lengthy delay in the completion of the project.[35.3]

Page 742, add footnote referent 37.1 after third sentence in third full paragraph and add note 37.1:

[37.1]*See, e.g.*, Whyte v. Am. Bd. of Physical Medicine and Rehabilitation, 393 F. Supp. 2d 880, 888 (D. Minn. 2005) ("Although Minnesota law recognizes the validity of exculpatory clauses, such clauses are generally disfavored. Thus, courts strictly construe exculpatory clauses against the party who benefits from the clause.").

---

[27] *Id.* (citing City of Columbia, Mo. v. Paul N. Howard Co., 707 F.2d 338 (8th Cir. 1983); Fattore Co. v. Metro. Sewerage Comm'n, 454 F.2d 537 (7th Cir. 1971)).

[34] 45 Fed. Cl. 280 (1999).

[35] *Id.* at 289–90 (citing Liles Constr. Co. v. United States, 197 Ct. Cl. 164, 185, 455 F.2d 527, 538 (1972); North Slope Technical Ltd., Inc. v. United States, 14 Cl. Ct. 242, 253 (1988)).

[35.1] *In re* Biggers Constr. Co., 81-1 B.C.A. (CCH) ¶ 14,848 (1980).

[35.2] 55 Fed. Cl. 184 (2002).

[35.3] *Id.* at 193, n.4.

§ 22.09   DAMAGES

Page 744, replace text of note 44 with:

Sauer Inc. v. Danzig, 224 F.3d 1340, 1349 (Fed. Cir. 2000) (quoting Elec. & Missile Facilities, Inc. v. U.S., 189 Ct. Cl. 237, 416 F.2d 1345, 1361 (1969)).

CHAPTER **24**

OBTAINING ADEQUATE COMPENSATION FOR DELAY

John B. Denniston
Alan A. Pemberton
Jennifer L. Plitsch[*]

§ 24.02   CAUSES OF COMPENSABLE DELAY

[A]   Changes

Page 811, note 13, replace Atlas Contractors Inc. citation with:

Atlas Contractors, Inc., ASBCA No. 34,545, 88-1 B.C.A. (CCH) ¶ 20,225 (1987)

Page 812, note 16, replace Robert McMullan & Sons, Inc. citation with:

Robert McMullan & Sons, Inc., ASBCA No. 19,023, 76-1 B.C.A. (CCH) ¶ 11,728 (1976), *overruled on other grounds by* England v. Sherman R. Smoot Corp., 388 F.3d 844 (Fed. Cir. 2004).

[C]   Defective Plans and Specifications

Page 814, add to note 32:

; American Ordnance LLC, ASBCA No. 54718, 10-1 B.C.A. (CCH) ¶ 34,386 (2010) (holding that "all delay due to defective or erroneous Government specifications are [sic] *per se* unreasonable and hence compensable") (citing Essex Electro Eng'rs v. Danzig, 224 F.3d 1283, 1289 (Fed. Cir. 2000)).

---

[*] The authors gratefully acknowledge the assistance of Scott A. Freling, Esq. and Christine Minarich, Esq. in the preparation of this supplement to this chapter.

141

[D] Other Causes of Delay

Page 818, add to note 50:

    See also Wayne Knorr, Inc. v. Dept. of Transp., 2009 WL 1324068, at *16 (Pa. Commw. Ct. May 14, 2009) (explaining that delay damages are only allowable for the "unreasonable portion of a government-caused delay") (citing Mega Constr. Co., Inc. v. United States, 29 Fed. Cl. 396, 425 (1993)).

§ 24.03 DEVELOPING A CLAIM

Page 819, note 53, add before Manuel Bros, Inc. citation:

Cumberland Cas. & Sur. Co. v. United States, 2008 WL 4725449 (Fed. Cl. July 3, 2008) (explaining "a contractor cannot recover where the delays are concurrent or intertwined and the contractor has not met its burden of separating its delays from those chargeable to the Government") (citing Essex Electro Eng'rs v. Danzig, 224 F.3d 1283, 1292 (Fed. Cir. 2000));

Page 820, add to end of section:

    Finally, contractors must be sure to explicitly reserve their right to recover costs that arise from delay whenever the parties enter into a formal contract modification to resolve an individual change order. In *Bell BCI v. United States*, despite "evidence of excusable delay from changed work" that was "so overwhelming that a reasonable person could not reach a contrary result," the U.S. Court of Appeals for the Federal Circuit relied on contract modification language to deny the contractor's delay and cumulative impact claims.[55.1] The contract language at issue provided that an increase in the total contract amount was "full and equitable adjustment" for the remaining direct and indirect costs of the change, including all delays resulting from the change.[55.2] The contract further provided that the contractor released the Government from "any and all liability under the Contract for further equitable adjustment attributable" to the change.[55.3] The court determined that this language was "unambiguous" and released the Government from "any and all liability" for cumulative impact and delay claims attributable to the modification.[55.4] This decision highlights the need for contractors to explicitly reserve their right to recover costs associated with delay in each contract modification, regardless of whether such impacts are known or foreseeable at the time.

[55.1] 570 F.3d 1337, 1342 (2009).
[55.2] 570 F.3d at 1339.
[55.3] 570 F.3d at 1339.
[55.4] 570 F.3d at 1341–42.

This is particularly important for government contractors because, in many cases, it may require taking an exception to the standard release language set forth in the Federal Acquisition Regulation.

§ 24.04   COMMON COMPENSABLE DELAY EXPENSES

Page 820, add to end of note 59:

See also Tecom Inc. v. United States, 86 Fed. Cl. 437, 455–56 (2009) (explaining and affirming *Servidone*'s discussion that the total cost method is disfavored, but sometimes permissible).

[A]   Idle Personnel and Equipment

Page 822, note 67, replace Cyrus Contracting, Inc. citation with:

Cyrus Contracting, Inc., IBCA No. 3233, 98-2 B.C.A. (CCH) ¶ 30,063 (1998)

[B]   Losses of Efficiency

Page 822, note 68, delete Capital Elec. Co. citation.

[C]   Additional Overhead

Page 823, add to note 74:

See also Commonwealth v. AMEC Civil, LLC, 677 S.E.2d 633, 650 (Va. App. 2009) (failing to award delay damages for overhead costs when the contractor's expert simply "relied wholly upon the unstated (and thus unproven) assumption that the [contractor] could not have recouped its home office overhead from other revenue-producing work").

Page 828, add to note 97:

; Packard Constr. Corp., ASBCA No. 55,383, 09-2 B.C.A. (CCH) ¶ 34,234 (2009) (finding that while the contractor was not entitled to compensation for days it was able to perform "significant and substantial" amounts of work, it was entitled to compensation for unabsorbed overhead for days it was "effectively on 'stand-by'").

Page 828, add to note 100:

For a general discussion regarding when a contractor may recover delay damages on behalf of its subcontractor, see Harper/Nielsen-Dillingham, Builders, Inc. v. United States, 81 Fed. Cl. 667, 674–77 (2008) (explaining the *Severin* doctrine).

[D]   Escalation Effects

Page 829, note 101, replace W.G. Yates & Sons Constr. Co. cite with:

W.G. Yates & Sons Constr. Co., ASBCA No. 49398, 01-2 B.C.A. (CCH) ¶ 31428 (2001)

CHAPTER 25

SUBCONTRACTOR'S RIGHTS AND REMEDIES FOR THE OWNER'S DEFAULTS IN PAYMENT

Gerard W. Ittig, Esq.

§ 25.02   THE EFFECT OF CONTRACT CLAUSES ON SUBCONTRACTOR REMEDIES

[D]   Incorporation By Reference

Page 838, add to end of first full paragraph:

For example, in *Dobson Bros. Constr. v. Ratliff, Inc.*, 2008 U.S. Dist. LEXIS 97283 (D. Neb. Nov. 6, 2008), the owner's contract required the general contractor to include an arbitration provision in its subcontracts. Although a separate arbitration clause was not contained in the subcontract, the general incorporation language achieved that result.

§ 25.04   THE EFFECTS OF THE CAUSE OF NON-PAYMENT

[A]   Trust Fund Statutes

Page 843, add after second full paragraph:

A difficulty can arise in tracing funds paid by the owner. *See, e.g., Shafer Redi-Mix, Inc. v. Craft*, _____ F. Supp. _____, 2009 U.S. Dist. LEXIS 21144 (W.D. Mich. Mar. 17, 2008).

§ 25.05   LIQUIDATING AGREEMENTS

[D]   Wording of the Liquidating Agreement

Page 846, add to end of subsection:

There are limitations on a subcontractor's ability to force the general contractor to pass claims through to the owner. In *State of Missouri f/u/b*

MWE Services, Inc. v. Sircal-Kozeny-Wagner, JV, 2009 U.S. Dist. LEXIS 13644 (W.D. Mo. Feb. 23, 2009), the general contractor made a determination that the subcontractor's claims were not sufficiently justified and refused to present them to the owner. The subcontractor accordingly sued the contractor for the claims, which were admittedly owner-caused, on a theory of a violation of good faith and fair dealing. Because the subcontractor was not able to present "substantial evidence of bad faith" regarding the general contractor's refusal to sponsor the claims, the lawsuit was dismissed.

CHAPTER 26

EXCEPTION TO NO-DAMAGES-FOR-DELAY CLAUSES

Perkins Coie LLP National Construction Group

§ 26.02   STATE-BY-STATE SURVEY

[C]   Arizona

[1]   Summary

Page 852, replace first paragraph of subsection with:

In Arizona, most public contracts must include a provision requiring negotiation for the recovery of owner-caused delay damages where the delay is unreasonable and outside the parties' contemplation. Although there are no cases on point, in cases where the statutory provision applies a blanket no-damages-for-delay clause should be unenforceable.

[D]   Arkansas

[3]   Construction and Enforcement of the Clause

Page 854, add to note 20:

See also Little Rock Wastewater Util. v. Larry Moyer Trucking, Inc., 321 Ark. 303, 311, 902 S.W.2d 760 (1995) ("Courts give only a restrained approval to 'no damage' clauses because of their harsh effect. While such clauses are not void as against public policy and will be enforced so long as the basic requirements for a valid contract are met, the courts accord such clauses a strict construction.").

[E]   California

[2]   Applicable Statutes

Page 856, add footnote referent 30.1 to end of first sentence in second (carryover) paragraph and add note 30.1:

[30.1] *Id.* at 49–50.

[3]   Construction and Enforcement of the Clause

Page 857, add footnote referent 34.1 after "(including unpublished decisions)" in first sentence of second full paragraph and add note 34.1:

[34.1] Rule 8.1115 of the California Rules of Court prohibits the parties or the court from citing or relying upon unpublished California court opinions in any court action.

[F]   Colorado

[3]   Construction and Enforcement of the Clause

Page 859, replace third and fourth sentences of second full paragraph with:

Tricon's suit for breach of express and implied covenants alleged that Lafarge failed to properly schedule and sequence the project, which led to "significant obstacles and costly delays" that amounted to interference with Tricon's performance of the subcontract.[41] The court found that Lafarge's failure to properly schedule and coordinate Tricon's activities constituted "active interference" with Tricon's performance.[42]

[S]   Louisiana

[1]   Summary

Page 877, replace subsection text with:

No-damages-for-delay clauses are enforceable in Louisiana, with certain exceptions.[120] The Louisiana Supreme Court and federal district court applying Louisiana law have recognized that no-damages-for-delay clauses may be invalid where the party seeking to invoke them has acted

---

[120] [Reserved]

in bad faith or with "gross fault."[121] Louisiana statutes also bar "no-damages-for-delay" clauses in public contracts if the delay was caused in whole or in part by the contracting public entity.[121.1]

[2] Applicable Statutes

Page 877, in first sentence of subsection, delete:

No Louisiana statute is directly applicable, but

Page 877, add to end of subsection:

This statutory provision limits the enforcement of "no-damage-for-delay" clauses in private contracts.[122.1] Likewise, no-damages-for-delay clauses are no longer valid and enforceable for public contracts under Louisiana Revised Statute § 38:2216(H), which provides as follows:

> Any provision contained in a public contract which purports to waive, release, or extinguish any rights of a contractor to recover cost of damages, or obtain equitable adjustment, for delays in performing such contract, if such delay is caused in whole, or in part, by acts or omissions within the control of the contracting public entity or persons acting on behalf thereof, is against public policy and is void or unenforceable.

[4] Exceptions to Enforcement

Page 878, replace text of subsection with:

Louisiana courts have not expressly recognized any exception to no-damages-for-delay clauses. However, the *Pellerin* and *Freeman* cases indicate that a Louisiana court likely would find such clauses unenforceable in private contracts where there is evidence of bad faith or intentional delay. Moreover, Louisiana statutes now invalidate "no-damages-for-delay" clauses in public contracts where the contracting public entity has caused the delay in whole or in part.

---

[121] Freeman v. Dep't of Highways, 253 La. 105, 127–30, 217 So. 2d 166 (1968) (upholding clause); Pellerin Constr., Inc. v. Witco Corp., 169 F. Supp. 2d 568, 584–85 (E.D. La. 2001) (no-damage-for-delay clause in private contract enforceable absent evidence of "intentional or gross fault"); *see also* James S. Holliday, Jr. & H. Bruce Shreves, La. Prac. Constr. Law § 8:10 (2009) ("'[n]o damages for delay' clause[s] are valid and enforceable in Louisiana").

[121.1] *See* La. Rev. Stat. Ann. § 38:2216 (2003) (public policy prohibits clauses barring delay damages where delay is caused by the contracting public entity).

[122.1] *Pellerin Constr., Inc.*, 169 F. Supp. 2d at 584–85.

[BB]   Nebraska

[3]   Construction and Enforcement of the Clause

Page 888, add to end of subsection:

In *Weitz Co., LLC v. Alberici Constructors, Inc.*, the subcontractor brought a claim against the general contractor, alleging that the general contractor failed to act in several instances which delayed the subcontractor's work and caused damages to the subcontractor. The general contractor relied on a "no damage for delay" provision contained in the prime contract with the owner, which was incorporated by reference in the subcontract, to argue that the subcontractor's claim was barred and should be dismissed. The no damages for delay provision in the prime contract provided that the owner would not be liable to the contractor or any subcontractor or supplier for damages arising out of or resulting from delays caused by or within the control of the contractor, or delays beyond the control of both the owner and contractor. The court interpreted this provision to mean that, in reference to the subcontractor's claim, the general contractor would not be liable for delay damages arising out of claims for which the owner and/or another subcontractor may be liable if the delay was within the subcontractor's control or beyond both the general contractor's and subcontractor's control, but the general contractor could be liable for damages caused by delay that was beyond the subcontractor's control and within the general contractor's control. The court ultimately denied the general contractor's Rule 12(b)(6) motion to dismiss, concluding that, because the subcontractor's complaint alleged that the delay was caused by the general contractor, the no damages for delay provision did not bar the subcontractor's claim.[168.1]

[EE]   New Jersey

[2]   Applicable Statutes

Page 891, add to note 174:

; N.J.S.A. 18A:18A-41.

[FF]   New Mexico

[1]   Summary

Page 893, in first sentence, add after "case law":

directly

[168.1] 2009 WL 115980, at *2-3 (D. Neb. 2009).

[2]   Applicable Statutes

Page 893, replace text of subsection with:

No New Mexico statute is directly applicable.[179.1]

[GG]   New York

[1]   Summary

Page 893, replace text of subsection with:

No-damages-for-delay provisions generally are enforced in New York subject to certain judicial exceptions.

[3]   Construction and Enforcement of the Clause

Page 894, note 181, add before Peter Scalamandre citation:

Worth Constr. Co., Inc. v. TRC Engineers, Inc., 55 A.D.3d 388, 865 N.Y.S.2d 95 (2008);

[HH]   North Carolina

[1]   Summary

Page 894, in second sentence of first paragraph, add after "These provisions":

are generally enforceable

Page 894, add footnote referent 182.1 after second sentence of first paragraph and add note 182.1:

[182.1] *See* APAC-Carolina, Inc. v. Greensboro-High Point Airport Auth., 110 N.C. App. 664, 431 S.E.2d 508 (1993).

[179.1] While not directly on point, N.M. Stat. Ann. § 13-1-170 (1997) allows state agencies and other public entities to issue regulations requiring "uniform clauses" in public contracts on a variety of subjects, including "adjustments in prices" and "permissible excuses for delay or nonperformance." No case law addresses whether this statutory section would permit a state agency to adopt uniform "no-damages-for-delay" clauses.

[KK] Oklahoma

[1] Summary

Page 899, replace text of subsection with:

Although no reported Oklahoma court case has addressed the enforceability of no-damages-for-delay clauses, one unreported case,[193.1] along with secondary authorities suggest that Oklahoma may recognize such clauses,[194] with exceptions.[195]

[3] Construction and Enforcement of the Clause

Page 899, replace first sentence of first paragraph with:

No reported Oklahoma case directly addresses the enforceability of no-damages-for-delay clauses.

Page 899, add to note 196:

; U.S. *ex rel.* M.L. Young Constr. Corp., 2005 WL 2396597 at *5.

Page 899, add to end of third full paragraph:

In an unreported decision, the federal district court for the Western District of Oklahoma refused to enforce a "no-damages-for-delay" clause as a matter of law, holding that issues of fact precluded summary judgment: "To the extent that this circuit recognizes an exception to delay damages clauses where a party has engaged in inequitable conduct, the record before the court shows that there is a factual dispute concerning this issue."

[4] Exceptions to Enforcement

Page 900, add to note 201:

See also U.S. *ex rel.* M.L. Young Constr. Corp., 2005 WL 2396597 at *5 (recognizing "inequitable conduct" exception).

[193.1] U.S. *ex rel.* M.L. Young Constr. Corp. v. The Austin Co., NO. CIV-04-0078-T, 2005 WL 2396597, *5 (W.D. Okla. Sept. 28, 2005) (refusing to grant summary judgment enforcing "no-damages-for-delay" clause based on evidence of inequitable conduct).

[LL]   Oregon

[1]   Summary

Page 900, replace text of subsection with:

In Oregeon, no-damages-for-delay provisions in public works contracts are deemed against public policy and are void and unenforceable. With respect to private contracts, however, it is uncertain whether Oregon courts will enforce no-damages-for-delay provisions.

[2]   Applicable Statutes

Page 900, replace text of subsection with:

In 2005, the Oregon Legislature enacted law which provides that any clause in a public improvement contract that "purports to waive, release or extinguish the rights of a contractor to damages or an equitable adjustment arising out of unreasonable delay in performing the contract, if the delay is caused by acts or omissions of the contracting agent or persons acting therefor," will be deemed against public policy and considered void and unenforceable.[201.1]

[3]   Construction and Enforcement of the Clause

Page 900, replace text of subsection with:

There[202] are no[203] reported Oregon[204] cases applying[205] the state statute that renders no-damages-for-delay provisions in public works contracts unenforceable.[206] On the other hand, *Northeast Clackamas County Electric Co-Operative v. Continental Casualty Co.*[207] involved application of a no damage clause contained in a private contract for the construction of power transmission lines. Because the case was based on diversity jurisdiction, the Ninth Circuit Court of Appeals looked to Oregon state law when determining whether to apply the no damage provision. The contractor had bid to construct power transmission lines over mountainous terrain. The Co-Op, which had accepted the contractor's bid, agreed to clear the right-of-way by its own operations and left

---

[201.1] 26 Or. Rev. Stat. Ann. § 279C.315 (2009).
[202] [Reserved]
[203] [Reserved]
[204] [Reserved]
[205] [Reserved]
[206] [Reserved]
[207] 221 F.2d 329 (9th Cir. 1955).

the contractor to construct the lines. When construction was about one-third complete the contractor requested a 30-day extension based on the Co-Op's delay in delivering poles and clearing the right-of-way. The extension was granted. A month later the contractor requested a second extension based on the same delays by the Co-Op and damage to the power lines caused by a windstorm. The Co-Op refused to grant the extension or pay the contractor unless it agreed to repair the storm damage at its own expense. The contractor refused, and the Co-Op terminated its contract.

The district court found that the delay in construction of the power line and the damage resulting from the windstorm were due exclusively to the Co-Op's failure to properly clear the right-of-way. There was no provision in the contract requiring the contractor to repair at its own expense storm damage caused by the Co-Op's failure to properly perform its duties. The Co-Op attempted to rely upon the no damage provision in the contract to assert that the contractor's only available remedy was an extension of time. The Ninth Circuit rejected the Co-Op's argument, concluding that, because the Co-Op had wrongfully insisted that the contractor pay for the storm damage at its own expense before the Co-Op would grant the contractor an extension, the Co-Op had unjustifiedly repudiated the no damage contract provision and the Co-Op's subsequent wrongful termination of the entire contract made enforcement of the no damage provision "impossible in fact and inapplicable in law."[207.1] Thus, the Ninth Circuit held that the no-damage provision did not apply to bar the contractor's claim and that the contractor could recover on a quantum meruit basis.[207.2]

In light of the foregoing, the validity of no-damages-for-delay clauses in private contracts is uncertain under Oregon law.

[MM]   Pennsylvania

[1]   Summary

Page 902, replace text of subsection with:

No-damages-for-delay provisions generally are enforced but are disfavored and strictly construed. Such provisions will not be enforced if enforcement is deemed inequitable due to the owner's interference.

[207.1] *Id.* at 335.
[207.2] *Id.*

[3]   Construction and Enforcement of the Clause

Page 902, note 209, replace "468" with "477–78".

[4]   Exceptions to Enforcement

Page 903, note 10, add after "see also":

James Corp. v. N. Alleghany Sch. Dist., 938 A.2d 474, 484 (Pa. Commw. Ct. 2007);

[RR]   Texas

[1]   Summary

Page 907, note 231, replace "Hubble" with "Hubbell".

Page 907, add to note 231:

See also West v. Triple B Servs., LLP, 264 S.W.3d 440, 449 n. 9 (Tex. Civ. App.—Houston [14th Dist.] 2008) (distinguishing *R.F. Ball Constr. Co.*).

[UU]   Virginia

[1]   Summary

Page 910, add footnote referent 250.1 to end of first sentence in first paragraph and add note 250.1:

[250.1] *See* Blake Constr. Co., Inc./Poole & Kent v. Upper Occoquah Sewage Auth., 266 Va. 564, 571, 587 S.E.2d 711 (2003).

[2]   Applicable Statutes

Page 910, in first sentence of first paragraph, replace "VCA § 2.2-4335" with:

VCA § 2.2-4335(A)

[VV] Washington

[3] Construction and Enforcement of the Clause

Page 912, note 254, add after "843,":

845

[4] Exceptions to Enforcement

Page 913, note 258, add after "179":

n.6

[YY] Wyoming

[3] Construction and Enforcement of the Clause

Page 916, replace first paragraph of subsection with:

In *Westates Construction Co. v. City of Cheyenne*,[268] the contractor contracted with the City to enlarge a water reservoir. The federal government, which retained broad supervisory authority over the project, suspended the contractor's work. As a result of the suspension of work, the contractor requested a change order that would compensate it for the anticipated delays and extra work created by the suspension. The contractor, however, failed to submit the required data in support of its request for a change order. Three years later, the contractor resubmitted its request for a change order, along with its supporting data, seeking additional compensation for the delay and extra work performed.

Page 916, add to end of subsection:

Several years later, in *City of Gillette v. Hladky Construction, Inc.*,[271] the court was faced with deciding whether the following contract provision amounted to a no-damages-for-delay provision that precluded the contractor's claim for delay damages:

> If the Contractor is delayed at any time in the commencement or progress of the Work by an act or neglect of the Owner or Architect, or of an employee of either . . . or by changes ordered in the Work . . . or other causes beyond the Contractor's control, . . .

---

[268] 775 P.2d 502 (Wyo. 1989).
[271] 196 P.3d 184 (2008).

then the Contract Time shall be extended by Change Order for such reasonable time as the Architect may determine.[272]

The City relied on this provision to argue that the contractor's exclusive remedy was an extension of time, not monetary damages. The contractor responded that the parties' contract did allow for recovery of money damages for delay, citing a provision in the contract that provided that the above-quoted contract provision would not preclude recovery of damages for delay by either party under other provisions of the contract documents. The contractor also relied upon another contract provision, which stated that the rights and remedies available under the contract documents "shall be in addition to and not a limitation of duties, obligations, rights and remedies otherwise imposed or available by law."[273]

The Supreme Court of Wyoming agreed with the contractor, holding that, because delay damages are generally available under common law, that remedies provided in a contract are generally not exclusive, and the contract provision relied upon by the City did not contain express language limiting the contractor's remedies or state that the contractor's remedy provided therein was exclusive, the contract provision at issue did not apply to bar the contractor's claim for delay damages. Citing a leading commentator on construction law, the court also noted that a "typical" no-damages-for-delay clause expressly states that a time extension is the contractor's "sole and exclusive" remedy for delay. Because the contract provision at issue did not contain express, limiting language to this effect, the court concluded that it was not a no-damages-for-delay clause.[274]

[4]   Exception to Enforcement

Page 917, replace text of subsection with:

The holding in *City of Gillette* suggest that, unless a no damage provision clearly and unequivocally states that an extension of time, or some other non-monetary remedy, is a contractor's "sole and exclusive" remedy for delay, the contract provision will not be enforced or interpreted to prelude a contractor's claim for delay damages.

---

[272] *Id.* at 199.

[273] *Id.* at 199–200.

[274] *Id.* at 200–201.

CHAPTER 28

TERMINATIONS

Barbara G. Werther[1]
Daniel K. Crowley[2]
Laura P. Bourgeois
Andrew M. Argyris[3]

---

§ 28.03   TERMINATIONS FOR DEFAULT

[A]   Background

Page 1004, add to end of the second full paragraph:

Likewise, a surety's entitlement to contract funds after taking over for a defaulted contractor may be diminished by the government's right to liquidated damages.[50.1]

[B]   Grounds for Default Termination

[2]   Failure to Make Progress

Page 1008, add footnote referent 70.1 to the end of the second sentence of the carryover paragraph and add note 70.1:

[70.1] *But see* McDonnell Douglas Corp. v. United States, 567 F.3d 1340 (Fed. Cir. 2009) (applying the *Lisbon* standard where the contract as modified lacks a set completion date) discussed in detail in § 28.03[B][2][a].

Page 1008, add after first full paragraph:

Kostmayer Construction, LLC is another case that emphasized the government's burden to show the contractor will not perform under the

---

[1] Ms. Werther is a Partner in the Construction Group at Howrey LLP.

[2] Mr. Crowley is with Project Advisors International, an international construction consulting firm.

[3] Ms. Bourgeois and Mr. Argyris are Associates in the Construction Group at Howrey LLP.

[50.1] U.S. Surety Co. v. U.S., 83 Fed. Cl. 306 (2008) (establishing that the government held a superior right to liquidated damages against the contractor prior to a takeover by the surety).

Lisbon standard.[72.1] In this case, Kostmayer entered into a contract with the USACE to provide hurricane protection and enlarge an existing levee in Louisiana. After slow progress by Kostmayer, the contracting officer issued a cure letter demanding immediate corrective measures and threatening to terminate Kostmayer for default if it did not perform certain tasks by the government's new deadlines. Kostmayer substantially satisfied the criteria in the cure notice; nevertheless, the contracting officer terminated the contract for "failure to make adequate progress as to endanger the timely completion of the contract."

Applying the *Lisbon* standard, the Board found the government "unreasonably underestimated Kostmayer's ability to timely complete the work." The default termination was improper for three main reasons. First, the decision to terminate was based in large part on the comparison of time elapsed on the project with percentage complete of the pay items. The Board found this analysis was unreasonable and flawed because, among other things, the contracting officer failed to give sufficient weight to the government's own estimates of degrees of completion. Second, the Board found that the government failed to adequately assess Kostmayer's commitment of additional resources; which, with seven months left on the contract, pointed to a likelihood that Kostmayer could fully perform. Third, the Board found fault with the government's decision to terminate because Kostmayer's actions in response to the cure letter gave the government adequate assurances of timely completion. Accordingly, the contracting officer had no reasonable basis to believe Kostmayer could not perform and the termination was not proper.

[a]   Case Study: McDonnell Douglas

Page 1013, replace first sentence of first paragraph with:

The *McDonnell Douglas* litigation, spanning 18 years and concerning a $4.8 billion contract to develop the A-12 stealth aircraft for the Navy, highlights the difficulty courts have with default terminations for failure to make progress.

Page 1014, add footnote referent 91.1 after first sentence of third (carryover) paragraph and add note 91.1:

[91.1] McDonnell Douglas Corp. v. United States, 76 Fed. Cl. 385 (2007).

[72.1] ASBCA No. 55053, 08-2 B.C.A. ¶ 33,869 (2008).

Page 1015, replace last sentence of carryover paragraph with:

In 2009, 18 years after the initial McDonnell Douglas suit was filed, the Federal Circuit affirmed the Court of Federal Claims noting that "the overall evidence of record supports a conclusion that the government was justified in terminating the contract for default."[91.2] In doing so, the court emphasized that the *Lisbon* standard is the law, but its application may vary depending on the facts.

The court began its analysis by acknowledging the difficult task it assigned the lower court when instructing it to determine "the performance required by the contract and *the contract completion date*" prior to deciding whether the default termination was reasonable.[91.3] When the government issued modification P00046, it did not modify other essential delivery dates. Application of the dates advocated by the government would result in an overlap of time that made no logical sense. As such, the court determined that at the time of termination, the contract no longer had a completion date. A strict construction of the *Lisbon* analysis to the facts would be difficult, as *Lisbon* did not address a situation where the contract had no fixed completion date. In the case of *McDonnell Douglas*, without a fixed completion date, there can be no comparison between the entire contract effort and the remaining time.

The court introduced other factors to consider when determining "whether the contracting officer had a reasonable belief that there was no reasonable likelihood of timely completion."[91.4] Emphasizing that the application of *Lisbon* is a case-by-case analysis, the court suggested looking at factors such as the contractor's failure to meet progress milestones, its problems with subcontractors and suppliers, its financial situation, and its performance history. Applying the facts, the court noted McDonnell Douglas's missed milestones, delayed deliveries, repeated insistence on restructuring the contract, potential bankruptcy, and "cost cutting efforts" that affected performance. The totality of the circumstances led the court to agree that the contracting officer acted reasonably in concluding that McDonnell Douglas would not be able to timely perform the remaining work.[91.5] Accordingly, the Federal Circuit affirmed the decision upholding the default termination.

[91.2] McDonnell Douglas Corp. v. United States, 567 F.3d 1340 (Fed. Cir. 2009).
[91.3] *Id.* (quoting *McDonnell Douglas*, 323 F.3d at 1018) (emphasis in original).
[91.4] *Id.* at 1350–51.
[91.5] *Id.* at 1351–53.

[3]   Abandonment or Anticipatory Repudiation

Page 1015, add to note 95:

; George Jerry Malone, PSBCA No. 6129, 08-02 B.C.A. ¶ 33958 (2008) (finding default termination was justified when mailman refused to deliver to a customer's mailbox along a route extension, thereby abandoning the contract).

[4]   Material Breach Justifying Default

Page 1022, add new subsection to end of subsection after [4]:

[a]   Case Study: Takota Corporation

In *Takota*, the Court of Federal Claims upheld a default termination where the contractor failed to follow contract specifications.[122.1] The Navy contracted with Takota Corp. to extend boat ramps and dredge a marina at the Marine Corps Air Station in Cherry Point, North Carolina. The Contracting Officer terminated Takota for default for failing to follow contract specifications. Takota then sought to convert its default termination to a termination for convenience. The court held that the contracting officer was justified in terminating the contract for default because Takota failed to shore the seawall before it began dewatering. The court asserted that that the contract "unambiguously required Takota to provide shoring or bracing in advance of dewatering." Additionally, the court held that Takota further breached the contract when it failed to shore the seawalls upon observing instability during dewatering, a clear violation of the contract's requirements to shore and brace the seawalls. The court asserted that Takota's delay argument was moot because Takota's termination was for reasons not related to the delay. Furthermore, Takota's failure to submit the required shoring and sheeting plan was not a peripheral, as Takota maintained, because it went to the "heart of the project" and caused a complete failure of the contract's purpose. Thus, the court held that Takota materially breached the contract and the contracting officer was justified in terminating the contract for default.

[122.1] Takota Corp. v. U.S., 90 Fed. Cl. 11, 17 (2009).

[D] Wrongful Default Terminations

[1] Defective Notice to Cure

[a] *Termination Without Proper Notice*

Page 1033, add to note 139:

; DCX-CHOL Enterprises, Inc., ASBCA No. 54707, 08-2 B.C.A. ¶ 33,889 (the Board was unpersuaded by a supply contractor's argument that the default termination was improper without advanced notice where the contractor failed to make timely delivery of goods).

[b] *Termination for Reasons Other Than Those Set Forth in Cure Notice*

Page 1038, add to note 163:

; *see also Takota Corp.,* 90 Fed. Cl. at 17 ("[T]ermination based on breach is a valid ground for termination even though the Navy did not rely on this justification when it issued the default termination").

[2] Waiver

Page 1039, add to note 170:

; *see Takota Corp.,* 90 Fed. Cl. at 22 (holding that contractor "failed to prove waiver because contractor did not continue performance after the completion date in reliance of the government's failure to terminate" and, thus, did not meet the two-part test for waiver).

Page 1040, add to note 171:

; *see also Labat-Anderson, Inc.*, ASBCA No. 54904, 08-1 B.C.A. ¶ 33761 (when the contractor missed the completion date and instead of terminating the contract, the government encouraged the contractor to continue performance, the Board found that the government waived its right to terminate and owed the contractor for performance of the work.).

Page 1043, add to note 188:

; *but see* DCX-CHOL Enterprises, Inc., ASBCA No. 54707, 08-2 B.C.A. ¶ 33,889 (rejecting contractor's waiver argument where the time periods between the missed delivery dates and the government's termination, between three and six months, were not unreasonable).

[E]   Other Defenses to Default Termination

[3]   Changes

[a]   *Change Orders and Constructive Changes*

Page 1065, add to note 297:

; *but see* LB&B Assocs. Inc. v. United States, 91 Fed. Cl. 142 (2010) (refusing to allow a contractor's "constructive change" defense when, after the contractor failed to fulfill its contractual obligations, the government forced the contractor to hire subcontractors in lieu of a default termination, which the government was entitled to do pursuant to the terms of the contract).

[G]   The Effect of a Wrongful Termination

Page 1089, note 427, replace remainder of note text beginning with "This regulation . . . to the government" with:

It is unclear if a contractor can take advantage of conversion to a termination for convenience with respect to wrongful default terminations of its subcontractors. *See* U.S. ex rel. Quality Trust, Inc. v. Cajun Contractors, Inc., 486 F. Supp. 2d 1255 (D. Kan. 2007) (when a general contractor terminates a subcontractor for default on a government project, the subcontractor does not get the benefit of the FAR provision converting an invalid default termination to a termination for convenience despite a flow-down clause in the subcontract); *but see* Morrison-Knudsen Corp. v. Fireman's Fund Ins. Co., 175 F.3d 1221, 1230 (10th Cir. 1999) (treating a contractor's improper default termination of a subcontractor as a termination for convenience where the subcontract flowed down all applicable FAR provisions and provided that a wrongful termination for default would be treated as a termination for convenience).

Page 1089, insert the following paragraph after the first paragraph:

Prejudgment interest may also be recoverable where a termination for convenience arises from a wrongful termination for default. *See Morrison Knudsen Corp. v. Ground Improvement Techniques, Inc.*, 532 F.3d 1063 (10th Cir. 2008), where a contractor is prohibited under the FAR on a "settlement by determination." The contractor claimed that a termination for convenience settlement constituted a settlement by determination. The court disagreed that the contractor settled by determination, noting the distinction between a termination for convenience and a termination for default that is later converted to one of convenience—as was the case here. The contractor did not treat the termination as one for convenience and therefore waived its right to claim the prohibition of prejudgment interest under the FAR.

Page 1089, add to note 432:

; *see Takota Corp.,* 90 Fed. Cl. at 16 (a contracting officer's discretion to terminate a contract for default is "not boundless").

Page 1095, add after first full paragraph:

Case Study: *United Partition Systems, Inc.*
In *United Partition Systems, Inc.*, the Court of Federal Claims held that the government improperly terminated the contract for default and, therefore, the termination was converted to a termination for the government's convenience.[450.1] The Department of Air Force contracted with United Partition Systems, Inc. ("United") to provide prefabricated modular buildings to federal agencies. Well into the project, the Air Force issued a cure notice to United, identifying defects in the installation and asserting that the prefabricated buildings did not meet the Class A fire rating as required by the contract. Although United asserted that the supplied materials met the contract's specifications, the Air Force and the contracting officer terminated the contract for default. Even though it had substantially completed construction, United was asked to leave the project and never had the opportunity to complete the project. United then filed a claim with the Air Force, asserting an excusability defense. The matter, however, was not referred to the GSA for a decision until two years after the government had terminated United's contract. United never had a chance to cure the defects.
The Court of Federal Claims emphasized that United was prejudiced by the government's errors: "To reiterate the key legal point in this case, at the time the Air Force and United were addressing United's performance, where a contracting officer sought to terminate a contract for default and a contractor raised an excusability defense, the contracting officer had an obligation promptly to refer the matter to the pertinent GSA contracting officer who was responsible for making the determination as to whether the failure was excusable."
Because the Air Force failed to promptly refer the matter to the GSA and United was unable to complete the contract because the Air Force failed to take appropriate action, the court held that the default termination should be converted to a termination for convenience. The court awarded United the contract price minus costs for removal of two buildings and nonconforming wall panels.

[450.1] United Partition Systems, Inc. v. United States, 90 Fed. Cl. 74 (2009).

§ 28.04   OTHER GOVERNMENT CONDUCT LIMITING THE RIGHT TO TERMINATE

[A]   Terminations for Convenience and the Traditional Standard

[1]   Bad Faith

Page 1097, add to end of second full paragraph:

The Federal Circuit determined that the contractor must make this showing by clear and convincing evidence. *Am-Pro Protective Agency, Inc. v. United States*, 281 F.3d 1234 (Fed. Cir. 2002) ("we believe the clear and convincing standard most closely approximates the language traditionally used to describe the burden for negating the good faith presumption; namely, the 'well-nigh, irrefragable' proof standard"); *see also Galen Medical Associates, Inc. v. United States*, 369 F.3d 1324, 1330 (Fed. Cir. 2004).

Page 1097, add to note 459:

; Oregon Woods Inc. v. Dep't of Interior, CBCA No. 1072, 09-1 B.C.A. ¶ 34,014 (bad faith toward the contracting community in general is insufficient to show bad faith sufficient to overturn a termination for convenience).

[D]   Challenges Based on Abuse of Discretion

[2]   Role of Improper Motive

Page 1116, add to note 530:

; *See* Precision Pine & Timber, Inc. v. United States, 596 F.3d 817, 829 (Fed. Cir. 2010) (citations omitted) ("Cases in which the government has been found to violate the implied duty of good faith and fair dealing typically involve some variation of the old bait-and-switch. . . . The government may be liable for damages when the subsequent government action is specifically designed to reappropriate the benefits the other party expected to obtain from the transaction. . . ."); *but see* IMS Engr's-Architects, P.C. v. United States, 92 Fed. Cl. 52 (2010) (holding that contractor could not sue government for breach of implied duty of good faith and fair dealing stemming from termination of contracts when contractor had previously settled with government, releasing government from all claims arising under the contract).

CHAPTER 29

CONSTRUCTION FAILURES
Bruce W. Ficken

§ 29.02   LIABILITY OF PARTIES FOR CONSTRUCTION
FAILURES

[B]   Contractor Liability

[1]   Compliance with Plans and Specifications

Page 1126, in the second sentence of the second paragraph replace "Spearin Doctrine" with:

Spearin Doctrine

Page 1126, add to end of third full paragraph:

However, some jurisdictions that have adopted the *Spearin* Doctrine have limited its application to government entities and have refused to apply it in cases where the specifications are provided by a private, non-government entity.[4.1]

Page 1129, add to note 13:

; Dugan & Meyers Constr. Co., Inc. v. Ohio Dept. of Admin. Serv., 864 N.E.2d 68, 73 (Ohio 2007) (declining to extend the *Spearin* Doctrine to cases involving delays due to specification errors or changes).

[2]   Performance Specifications

Page 1130, replace text of note 16 with:

See, e.g., Stuyvesant Dredging Co. v. United States, 834 F.2d 1576, 1582 (Fed. Cir. 1987) ("Design specifications explicitly state how the contract

---

[4.1] *See, e.g.,* Thomas & Marker Constr., Co. v. Wal-Mart Stores, Inc., No. 3:06-cv-406, 2008 U.S. Dist. LEXIS 79072, *53–54 (S.D. Ohio Sept. 15, 2008) (stating that the Supreme Court of Ohio has only applied the *Spearin* Doctrine to cases involving contract specifications prepared by government entities and refusing to extend its application to cases involving only private entities).

is to be performed and permit no deviations. Performance specifications, on the other hand, specify the results to be obtained, and leave it to the contractor to determine how to achieve those results." (citing J.L. Simmons Co. v. United States, 412 F.2d 1360, 1362 (Cl. Ct. 1969))). *But see* Complete Gen. Constr. Co. v. Ohio Dept. of Transp., 593 N.E.2d 487, 490 (Ohio Ct. Cl. 1990) (stating that contractor was obligated to supply specified quality of concrete based on performance specifications even when there was "no chance in hell" that the approved concrete mix design would meet specifications).

Page 1131, add to end of subsection:

Furthermore, although design specifications are meant to give a contractor a very detailed guide on how to complete a project, they need not be perfect so long as they are reasonably accurate.[16.1] The specifications must be "substantially deficient or unworkable" so that the "cumulative effect or extent of the errors was either unreasonable or abnormal taking into account the scope and complexity of the project" in order to be considered a breach of contract.[16.2]

[C] Designer Liability

[4] Architect's Duty to "Observe"

Page 1140, replace text of note 54 with:

See Watson, Watson, Rutland Architects, Inc. v. Montgomery County Bd. of Educ., 559 So. 2d 168, 173 (Ala. 1990) (stating that claim generally exists against architect for failure to inspect compliance with plans and specifications); Eastover Corp. v. Martin Builders, 543 So. 2d 1358, 1361 (La. Ct. App. 1989) (holding that architect knew or should have known of improper spacing of sewer pipe hangers discoverable through reasonable inspection although owner subsequently waived warranty rights upon accepting building without complaint); 13 A.L.R.5th 289, 437–40, §§ 45–47 (1993).

Page 1141, replace text of note 57 with:

See Houma v. Municipal & Indus. Pipe Serv., 884 F.2d 886 (5th Cir. 1989) (finding engineer liable for failing to verify and inspect the work); Day v. Nat'l U.S. Radiator Corp., 128 So. 2d 660, 666 (La. 1961) (noting that

---

[16.1] Caddell Constr. Co., Inc. v. United States, 78 Fed. Cl. 406, 413 (2007) (citing Wunderlich v. United States, 351 F.2d 956, 964 (Ct. Cl. 1965)).

[16.2] Caddell Constr. Co., Inc. v. United States, 78 Fed. Cl. 406, 413 (2007) (citing Wunderlich v. United States, 351 F.2d 956, 964 (Ct. Cl. 1965)).

architects could have been liable for actual personal failure to observe lack of proper safety device on boiler, although architects exculpated in instant case); Bd. of Educ. v. Sargent, Webster, Crenshaw & Folley, 146 A.D.2d 190 (N.Y. App. Div. 3d Dept. 1989); South Union, Ltd. v. George Parker & Assoc., 504 N.E.2d 1131 (Ohio Ct. App. 1985) (finding architect had a duty to inform the owner of non-conforming electrical work); Alantic Mut. Ins. Co. v. Continental Nat'l Am. Ins. Co., 302 A.2d 177, 178–79 (N.J. Super. Ct. App. Div. 1973) (holding engineer's contract required it to supervise construction and assist in interpretation of plans and specifications).

[5] Standing to Sue the Architect

Page 1143, replace text of note 61 with:

See Town of Alma v. Azco Constr., Inc., 10 P.3d 1256 (Colo. 2000) (adopting economic loss doctrine but distinguishing between duties arising from contract as opposed to independent duties owed by professionals); City Express, Inc. v. Express Partners, 959 P.2d 836, 839–40 (Haw. 1998) (denying negligent misrepresentation claim against design professional for economic loss even where parties were in privity of contract); Floor Craft Floor Covering, Inc. v. Parma Community Gen. Hosp. Assoc., 560 N.E.2d 206, 207 (Ohio 1990) ("In the absence of privity of contract, no cause of action exists in tort to recover economic damages against design professionals involved in drafting plans and specifications."); Terracon Consultants Western, Inc. v. Mandalay Resort Group, 206 P.3d 81, 89 (Nev. 2009) (holding that the economic loss doctrine bars professional negligence claims for purely economic losses against architects and engineers). *See also,* Fireman's Fund Ins. v. SEC Donohue, Inc., 679 N.E.2d 1197 (Ill. 1997); Prendiville v. Contemporary Homes, Inc., 83 P.3d 1257 (Kan. Ct. App. 2004); Lempke v. Dagenais, 547 A.2d 290 (N.H. 1988); Floor Craft v. Parma Com. Gen. Hosp., 54 Ohio St. 3d 1, 560 N.E.2d 206 (Ohio 1990); Goose Creek Sch. Dist. v. Jarrar's Plumbing, 74 S.W.3d 486 (Tex. App. 2002); Carlson v. Sharp, 994 P.2d 851 (Wash. Ct. App. 1999); 1325 North Van Buren v. T-3 Group, 716 N.W.2d 822 (Wis. 2006) (all forbidding negligence claims against design professionals when only economic loss was at stake). *But see* Insurance Co. of. N. Am. v. Town of Manchester, 1998 WL 514711 (D. Conn. 1998) (holding contractor could recover purely economic losses against design professional in absence of contractual privity and personal injury or property damage); Owen v. Dodd, 431 F. Supp. 1239, 1241–42 (N.D. Miss. 1977) (architect has duty to use reasonable care in preparation of plans and can be liable in tort to general contractor if faulty plans cause economic loss even in absence of privity); Bilt-Rite Contractors, Inc. v.

Architectural Studio, 866 A.2d 270 (Pa. 2005) (holding that Pennsylvania's economic loss doctrine did not preclude a negligent misrepresentation claim against a design professional pursuant to section 552 of the Restatement (Second) of Torts absent contractual privity); Turner v. Kerin & Assoc., 938 P.2d 1368, 1374 (Mont. 1997) ("Thus, we hold that a third party contractor may successfully recover for purely economic loss against a project engineer or architect when the design professional knew or should have foreseen that the particular plaintiff for an identifiable class of plaintiffs were at risk in relying on the information supplied."); Tommy L. Griffin Plumbing & Heating Co. v. Jordon, Jones & Goulding, Inc., 463 S.E.2d 85 (S.C. 1995) (allowing contractor to sue engineer for breach of warranty and malpractice); Conforti & Eisele, Inc. v. John C. Morris Assoc., 418 A.2d 1290 (N.J. Super. Ct. App. Div. 1980) (holding design professional liable to contractor who sustains economic damages even in absence of privity of contract).

Page 1145, add to note 72:

But see In the Matter of Gosnell Dev. Corp. of Arizona, No. CV-04-998-PHX-RGS, 2007 U.S. Dist. LEXIS 31440, *11–12 (D. Ariz. Apr. 27, 2007). The District Court for the District of Arizona interpreted the holding of *Moransais* narrowly, finding that it required more than the existence of a special relationship between the parties from which fiduciary duties flowed. According to *Gosnell, Moransais* only applies in limited cases where the negligent acts which form the basis of the tort claim are independent from acts that breached the contract.

Page 1145, add to end of subsection:

In *Flagstaff Affordable Housing Limited Partnership v. Design Alliance, Inc.,* the Supreme Court of Arizona drew a distinction between contracting and non-contracting parties for purposes of determining whether the economic loss doctrine bars a tort claim against a design professional for purely economic damages.[72.1] The owner in Flagstaff contracted with an architect to design apartment buildings that were supposed to comply with the federal Fair Housing Act's accessibility guidelines, so that they would in turn qualify as a low-income housing project. After construction, the U.S. Department of Housing and Urban Development (HUD) filed a complaint against the owner alleging that the apartments violated the guidelines. The owner settled with HUD and asserted a negligence claim against the architect.[72.2] The court found that when a construction defect causes damage only to the building itself or other economic loss, common law contract remedies provide an adequate

---

[72.1] 223 P.3d 664 (Ariz. 2010).
[72.2] 223 P.3d 664, 665 (Ariz. 2010).

remedy; therefore, the economic loss doctrine applies and a "contracting party is limited to its contractual remedies for purely economic loss."[72.3] The court noted, however, that "the principal function of the economic loss doctrine . . . is to encourage private ordering of economic relationships and to uphold the expectations of the parties."[72.4] Because these concerns are not implicated where no contract exists between the parties, "whether a non-contracting party may recover economic losses for a defendant's negligent misrepresentation should depend on whether the elements of that tort are satisfied, including whether the plaintiff is within the limited class of persons to whom the defendant owes a duty."[72.5] Thus, in this case, the owner's claims were barred as a result of its contract with the architect.

§ 29.04   SPECIAL CONSIDERATIONS FOR CONSTRUCTION FAILURE CASES

[E]   Joint and Several Liability

Page 1159, in the last sentence of the carryover paragraph, replace "build" with:

"built."

[F]   Similar Incident Evidence

[2]   Prejudicial Effect

Page 1160, in the last sentence of the second paragraph of this section, delete:

"such."

[72.3] 223 P.3d 664, 669–70 (Ariz. 2010).

[72.4] 223 P.3d 664, 671 (Ariz. 2010).

[72.5] 223 P.3d 664, 671–72 (Ariz. 2010) (citing Donnelly Constr. Co. v. Oberg/Hunt/Gilleland, 677 P.2d 1292 (Ariz. 1984), which held that a contractor's negligence claims against an architect for increased costs were not barred due to the lack of privity between the parties).

CHAPTER **30**

COMPENSATORY DAMAGES

Louis R. Pepe
Joseph B. Schwartz[*]

§ 30.02 COMPENSATORY DAMAGES AVAILABLE
TO THE OWNER

[A] Defective Work/Breach of Warranty

[1] Cost of Repair

Page 1176, add to note 10:

; Kunkel v. P.K. Dependable Constr., LLC, 387 Ill. App. 3d 1153,
1158–59 (Ill. App. Ct. 5th Dist. 2009) (The measure of damages for the
breach of a contract when a contractor has provided defective performance is generally the cost of correcting the defective condition.
Diminution of value is not the correct measure of damages unless the
defects can only be corrected at a cost unreasonably disproportionate to
the benefit of the purchaser or if correcting the defects would entail an
unreasonable destruction of the builder's work.).

Page 1176, add to note 13:

; BP Amoco Chem. Co. v. Flint Hills Res., LLC, 2010 U.S. Dist. LEXIS
28477 (N.D. Ill. Mar. 25, 2010) (it is well-settled under Illinois law that
the measure of damages for breach of warranty involving injury to real
property, even in a commercial dispute, is generally the "cost of repair."
An exception applies, "[i]f, however, the defects could be corrected only
at a cost unreasonably disproportionate to the benefit to the purchaser, or
if correcting them would entail unreasonable destruction of the builder's
work." In such cases, "the amount by which the defects have reduced the
value of the property should be the measure of damages."); Naples v.
Keystone Bldg. & Dev. Corp., 295 Conn. 214 (2010) (owner was entitled
to damages in the amount of the labor necessary to repair and replace the
defective construction of his roof, as well as to repair and repaint
damaged portions of the home's interior. However, in doing so, the court

[*] Louis R. Pepe is a partner and Joseph B. Schwartz is an associate in the Hartford,
Connecticut office of the law firm of McElroy, Deutsch, Mulvaney & Carpenter/PH, LLP.

reiterated the fundamental rule of damages in construction cases—that the damage award should put the non-breaching party in the position it would have been in had the contract been performed correctly. It also explained that in defective or incomplete construction cases, the owner's damages are measured by computing either the reasonable costs of construction and completion in accordance with the contract, if that is possible and does not involve unreasonable economic waste; or, the difference between the value of the property if the contract had been performed and the value the property actually has given the breach—the diminution in value measure).

[2]   Diminution in Value

Page 1179, add to note 25:

; Cashman Equip. Corp. v. United States Fire Ins. Co., 2010 U.S. App. LEXIS 4675 (3d Cir. Mar. 5, 2010) ("the burden of proving that the cost of curing a construction defect is disproportionate to the probable loss in value rests with the contract breaker").

Page 1180, add to note 26:

But see Cashman Equip. Corp. v. United States Fire Ins. Co, 2008 U.S. Dist. LEXIS 80860 (E.D. Pa. Sept. 17, 2008) (distinguishing *Andrulis* and other similar cases from various jurisdictions with regard to the burden a contractor bears in proving economic waste, concluding that the offering of "some evidence" to show that the repair cost is not "clearly disproportionate to the probable loss in value to him" is enough).

[B]   Owner's Damages for Contractor Delay

Page 1181, note 32, add before Chestnut Hill Dev. Corp. citation:

; RMA Lumber, Inc. v. Pioneer Mach., LLC, 2008 U.S. Dist. LEXIS 86293 (W.D Va. Oct. 24, 2008) (following *Roanoke Hospital* in recognizing financing cost as direct damages).

Page 1181, add to note 33:

; Connecticut Dep't of Transp. v. White Oak Corp., 287 Conn. 1, 28 n.12 (2008) (reaffirming the remedies available to a wrongfully terminated party under a construction contract as: (a) rescission of the contract and recovery in quantum meruit for the value of the work performed; or (b) breach of contract seeking recovery of the profits that would have been earned by performance, and citing Valente v. Weisberg, 80 Conn. 134, 135 (1907)).

§ 30.03 CONTRACTOR'S COMPENSATORY DAMAGES

[B] Compensatory Damages for Extra and Additional Work

[1] Change Orders and Constructive Change

Page 1183, add to note 40:

; Info. Sys. & Networks, Corp. v. United States, 81 Fed. Cl. 740, 747 (2008) (discussing whether the constructive change doctrine can apply in the face of contract provisions that not only indicate that all changes are to be approved in writing by the contracting officer, but also repeatedly warn that the contractor should not perform additional work without such a written order and that it proceeds at financial risk, if it does so).

[C] Damage for Delay

[3] Calculating Field Office Damages and Home Office Damages

Page 1190, note 73 add after Triple R Paving, Inc. citation:

; Martin County v. Polivka Paving, Inc., 2010 Fla. App. LEXIS 6566 (Fla. Dist. Ct. App. 4th Dist. May 12, 2010) (maintaining the previous holding in *Triple R. Paving, Inc.*, the court held that "a contractor seeking entitlement to recover home office overhead damages from the government must prove that a government-imposed delay required the contractor to indefinitely stand by to the point that the contractor was effectively suspended and unable to take on additional work").

[D] Damages for Disruption (Lost Efficiency/Productivity)

[1] Total Cost/Modified Total Cost Method

Page 1196, add to note 103:

; Wayne Knorr, Inc. v. DOT, 973 A.2d 1061, 1097 (Pa. Commw. Ct. 2009) ("although the total cost method must be used with caution . . . the method may be applied where the nature of the particular loss renders it impossible or highly impracticable to determine damages with a reasonable degree of accuracy and where the loss is substantiated by reliable evidence").

Page 1197, add to note 105

; Elec. Mach. Enters. v. Hunt Constr. Group, Inc. (In re Elec. Mach. Enters.), 416 B.R. 801, 893 (Bankr. M.D. Fla. 2009) ("Use of either the total cost approach or the modified total cost approach requires establishing several specific elements." "The total cost approach is appropriate only 'when the nature of the excess costs is such that there is no other practicable means of measuring damages, the original bid was realistic, the actual costs were reasonable, and the plaintiff is not responsible for any of the additional expense.' ")

Page 1198, add to note 108:

; Kenneth Hantman, Inc. v. Whiting-Turner Contracting Co., 2008 U.S. Dist. LEXIS 67071 (E.D. Pa. Sept. 2, 2008) (Schiller, J.) (citing *John F. Harkins,* noting that the total cost method "is imprecise . . . fraught with danger" and finding that the plaintiff failed to prove that all of its actual costs, over the amount estimated in its bid for the project, were caused by the defendant's conduct. Therefore, to utilize the Total Cost Method in this instance would be inappropriate.).

[4]   Measured Mile Method

Page 1201, note 125, replace Net Constr., Inc. v. C&C Rehab. & Constr., Inc. citation with:

Net Constr., Inc. v. C&C Rehab. & Constr., Inc., 256 F. Supp. 2d 350 (E.D. Pa. 2003).

§ 30.04   DAMAGES RECOVERABLE WHEN THE CONTRACT IS TERMINATED

[A]   Termination for Convenience

Page 1204, add to note 139:

; Questar Builders, Inc. v. CB Flooring, LLC, 410 Md. 241, 270–72 (2009) (in a breach of contract action against the federal government, the party challenging the government's exercise of its right to terminate for convenience must show "well-nigh irrefragable proof that the Government acted in bad faith, in light of the strong presumption recognized in the federal cases that the government acted in good faith." However, in this case, the court declined to recognize for private parties "the near *carte-blanche* power to terminate that courts have given the federal government under convenience termination clauses.).

[B] Termination for Default

Page 1204, add to note 143:

; Bearingpoint, Inc. v. United States, 82 Fed. Cl. 181 (2008) (default termination "is a drastic sanction," and the government is held strictly accountable for its actions in enforcing this sanction).

[1] Damages Available for Proper Termination

Page 1204, note 145, replace Johnson v. Flammia citation with:

Johnson v. Flammia, 169 Conn. 491, 499–501 (Conn. 1975).

[2] Damages Available for Wrongful Termination

Page 1206, add to note 155:

; Denny Constr., Inc. v. City & County of Denver, 199 P.3d 742, 748 (Colo. 2009) (a plaintiff contractor may establish a reasonable basis for computing the amount of lost profits by presenting evidence of prior profitability).

Page 1206, add to note 157:

But see Denny Constr., Inc. v. City & County of Denver, 199 P.3d 742, 751 (Colo. 2009) (criticizing *Lewis Jorge* court for utilizing a subjective test to determine if lost profits were foreseeable. According to the Colorado Supreme Court, the requirement is objective, focusing on whether "at the time the parties entered into the contract . . . the defendant knew or should have known that these [lost profit] damages would probably be incurred by the plaintiff if [the defendant] breached the contract.").

CHAPTER **31**

CONSEQUENTIAL AND PUNITIVE DAMAGES

Carl E. Switzer
David K. Ismay

§ 31.07   PUNITIVE DAMAGES: WHAT ARE THE CHANCES?

[A]   General Principles

Page 1234, replace Philip Morris USA citation with:

549 U.S. 346, 352, 127 S. Ct. 1057, 1062 (2007).

CHAPTER 32

LIQUIDATED DAMAGES

Guy Randles
Stephen Kelly

---

§ 32.03   LIQUIDATED DAMAGES AS A REASONABLE ASSESSMENT OF ANTICIPATED OR ACTUAL DAMAGES

Page 1243, add to note 4:

For a discussion of a contractor's unsuccessful challenge of a liquidated damages provision as unconscionable, *see* Highway Specialties, Inc. v. Montana, 215 P.3d 667 (Mont. 2009).

[A]   Reasonableness to Be Determined as of the Time of Contracting

Page 1243, note 6, change "Assoc." to "Assocs."

§ 32.04   REQUIREMENT THAT PROOF OF ACTUAL DAMAGES BE DIFFICULT OR IMPOSSIBLE

Page 1245, add new footnote referent 11.1 at end of first sentence of opening paragraph of § 32.04 and add note 11.1:

[11.1] For a discussion of a contractor's unsuccessful challenge to a liquidated damages provision that the government's actual damages were not uncertain, that the government failed to demonstrate that it had analyzed before bidding whether delay damages were computable and measurable, that the provision was latently ambiguous, and that the government had a formula for measuring actual damages, *see* Appeal of Weis Builders, Inc., 2010-1 B.C.A. (CCH) ¶ 34,369 (A.S.B.C.A. 2010).

Page 1248, add to note 17:

; Highway Specialties, Inc., *supra* note 4.

Page 1248, note 18, change "Assoc." to "Assocs."

§ 32.05 ENFORCEMENT

Page 1249, add new footnote referent 22.1 to end of last sentence in third full paragraph and add note 22.1:

[22.1] *See, e.g.*, Carrothers Constr. Co. v. S. Hutchinson, 207 P.3d 231 (Kan. 2009) (in reviewing liquidated damages clause, court assessed definitions of "substantial completion" and "work" used in contract); The Weitz Co. v. Mackenzie House, No. 07-0103-CV-W-ODS 2008 WL 2980093 (W.D. Mo. Aug. 1, 2008) (court assessed meaning of "building" as used in liquidated damages clause).

§ 32.06 LIQUIDATED DAMAGES FOR DELAY AND OTHER BREACHES

Page 1250, add new footnote referent 22.2 at end of first sentence of first full paragraph and add note 22.2:

[22.2] *See, e.g.*, Repair Masters Constr., Inc. v. Gary, 277 S.W.3d 854 (Mo. Ct. App. 2009) (court ruled that liquidated damages clause for owner's cancellation of construction contract was unconscionable).

Page 1252, add to note 30:

But see Roberts Contracting Co. v. Valentine-Wooten Rd. Pub. Facility Bd., No CA 08-751, 2009 WL 1471809 (Ark. Ct. App. May 27, 2009) (court found that, in absence of end date in contract for liquidated damages, and with no replacement contractor engaged to complete work, liquidated damages accrued until case was filed).

§ 32.08 LIQUIDATED DAMAGES AS A LIMITATION OF LIABILITY

Page 1255, note 36, change "Joseph M. Perillo & Helen Hadjiyannakis Bender" to "Joseph M. Perillo."

§ 32.09 DEVELOPMENT OF LIQUIDATED DAMAGES CLAUSES

Page 1256, add new footnote referent 41.1 at end of third full paragraph and add note 41.1:

[41.1] *See, e.g.*, S. Elec. Corp. v. Util. Bd. of the City of Foley, No. 07-0575-CG-C, 2009 WL 307990 (S.D. Ala. Feb. 5, 2009) (court ruled that liquidated damages clause was unenforceable penalty meant to motivate contractor to complete work on time, and not enforceable estimate of damages owner would suffer from delay).

[B] Developing the Liquidated Damages Language

Page 1258, in list item 2, replace "this paragraph" with "_____ [note: insert reference appropriate to contract]."

CHAPTER 33

RECOVERY OF INTEREST AND ATTORNEYS' FEES

Michael I. Less
John Willet

§ 33.01   RECOVERY OF INTEREST

[A]   Introduction

Page 1261, replace text of note 6 with:

Bernard A. Reinert, *Limitations on Recoverable Damages*, 18 Constr. Law., No. 2, at 11 (Apr. 1998) (citing Denton Constr. Co. v. Mo. State Highway Comm'n, 454 S.W.2d 44, 49 (Mo. 1970)).

[B]   Interest Awards for Liquidated and Unliquidated Damages

Page 1262, replace text of note 10 with:

In re Estate of Miraglia, 658 S.E.2d 777 (Ga. App. Ct. 2008) (quotation omitted).

Page 1262, replace text of note 13 with:

Trus Joist Corp. v. Safeco Ins. Co. of Am., 735 P.2d 125, 139 (Ariz. Ct. App. 1986).

Page 1262, replace text of note 15 with:

See the following cases for references to decisions where courts have refused to allow prejudgment interest on a builder's unliquidated claim: Rite-Way Plumbing & Heating, Inc. v. Wil-Fred's Inc., 380 N.E.2d 992 (Ill. App. Ct. 1978); Church of the Holy Spirit v. Bevco, Inc., 338 N.W.2d 601 (Neb. 1983); Lange Indus., Inc. v. Hallam Grain Co., 507 N.W.2d 465 (Neb. 1993).

Page 1263, replace text of note 17 with:

ABI, Inc. v. City of Los Angeles, 153 Cal. App. 3d 669, 685, 200 Cal. Rptr. 563, 573 (Cal. Ct. App. 1984).

Page 1263, replace text of note 19 with:

 See Ladco Properties XVII, L.L.C. v. Jefferson-Pilot Life Ins. Co., 523 F. Supp. 2d 940, 950–52 (S.D. Iowa 2007); Melwood Constr. Corp. v. State, 481 N.Y.S.2d 289, 290 (N.Y. Ct. Cl. 1984); 22 Am. Jur. 2d *Damages*, §§ 683, 684 (1988).

[C] Interest as a Business Cost and on Capital

Page 1263, replace text of note 20 with:

Neb. Pub. Power Dist. v. Austin Power, Inc., 773 F.2d 960, 973 (8th Cir. 1985).

[1] Interest as a Business Cost

Page 1263, replace text of note 23 with:

558 A.2d 1155 (D.C. 1989).

Page 1264, replace text of note 29 with:

347 N.W.2d 728 (Mich. Ct. App. 1984).

[D] Recovery of Prejudgment Interest

Page 1265, replace text of note 40 with:

Monessen S.W. Ry. Co. v. Morgan, 486 U.S. 330, 335 (1988).

[E] Prejudgment Interest Authorized by State Statute

Page 1266, replace text of note 43 with:

Paradise Homes, Inc. v. Cent. Sur. & Ins. Corp., 437 P.2d 78, 80 (Nev. 1968).

Page 1266, replace text of note 45 with:

N.Y. C.P.L.R. § 5001(a) (McKinney 2007).

Page 1267, replace text of note 46 with:

N.Y. C.P.L.R. § 5001(b) (McKinney 2007).

Page 1267, replace text of note 49 with:

Tenn. Code Ann. § 47-14-123 (2007).

Page 1268, replace text of note 53 with:

Urbanational Developers, Inc. v. Shamrock Eng'g, Inc., 372 N.E.2d 742 (Ind. Ct. App. 1978).

Page 1268, replace text of note 56 with:

See, e.g., Tenn. Code Ann. § 66-34-104 (2008); Utah Code Ann. § 13-8-5 (2007).

Page 1268, replace text of note 58 with:

Portage Ind. Sch. Constr. Corp. v. A.V. Stackhouse, Co., 287 N.E.2d 564, 568 (Ind. Ct. App. 1972).

Page 1269, replace text of note 66 with:

See Blake Constr. Co., Inc. v. C.J. Coakley Co., Inc., 431 A.2d 569, 580 (D.C. 1981).

Page 1269, replace text of note 67 with:

Burlington Ins. Co. v. Okie Dokie Inc., 398 F. Supp. 2d 147, 159 (D.C. 2005) (quoting Fed. Mktg. Co. v. Impression Prods., Inc., 823 A.2d 513, 532 (D.C. 2003)).

Page 1270, replace text of note 70 with:

E.C. Ernst, Inc. v. Manhattan Constr. Co., 551 F.2d 1026, 1042 (5th Cir. 1977), *cert. denied*, 434 U.S. 1067 (1978); Kern Oil & Ref. Co. v. Tenneco Oil Co., 868 F.2d 1279 (Temp. Emer. Ct. App. 1989); Iron Head Constr., Inc. v. Gurney, 176 P.3d 453, 457 (Utah Ct. App. 2008). Also see the following cases, which demonstrated the award of prejudgment interest, even on unliquidated claims when the amount is capable of ascertainment by calculation: E.C. Ernst Co. v. Koppers Co., 520 F. Supp. 830 (W.D. Pa. 1981); E. Paul Kovacs & R.W. Dunteman Co. v. Village of Lombard, 666 N.E.2d 762 (Ill. App. Ct. 1996); Dave Kolb Grading, Inc. v. Lieberman Corp., 837 S.W.2d 924 (Mo. Ct. App. 1992); Laughlin

Recreational Enters., Inc. v. Zab Dev. Co., 646 P.2d 555 (Nev. 1982); Parsons v. Henry, 672 P.2d 717 (Or. 1983); Deal Dev. Co. v. Amarillo Concrete Contractors, Inc., 554 S.W.2d 294 (Tex. Civ. App. 1977); Silverdale Hotel Assocs. v. Lomas & Nettleton Co., 677 P.2d 773, 780 (Wash. Ct. App. 1984) (defining "liquidated claims" as those that are ascertainable by calculation).

[F] Prejudgment Interest Authorized by Case Law

Page 1270, note 70, replace citation to Iron Head Constr., Inc. v. Gurney with:

Iron Head Constr., Inc. v. Gurney, 207 P.3d 1231 (Utah 2009).

[G] Prejudgment Interest for Denied Use of Funds in Delay Claims

Page 1271, replace text of note 77 with:

  See, e.g., Tenn. Code Ann. § 66-34-104(2008) (requiring that all retained funds be placed in an interest bearing account the accumulation of which must be paid to the contractor entitled to the funds upon entitlement of the retainage amount).

Page 1271, replace text of note 79 with:

See Havens Steel Co. v. Randolph Eng'g Co., 613 F. Supp. 514, 541 (W.D. Mo. 1985); Portage Ind. Sch. Constr. Corp. v. A.V. Stackhouse, Co., 287 N.E.2d 564, 568 (Ind. Ct. App. 1972); City of Mound Bayou v. Roy Collins Constr. Co., 499 So. 2d 1354, 1361 (Miss. 1986).

Page 1271, replace text of note 80 with:

See, e.g., S.D. Codified Laws § 21-1-11 (2007). *But see* Cal. Civ. Code § 3287 (West 2008) (granting discretion to the trial court to assign prejudgment interest on an unliquidated claim from the date not earlier than the date the action was filed).

[H] Computing Prejudgment Interest

Page 1272, replace text of note 82 with:

Economic Dev. & Indus. Corp. v. United States, 13 Cl. Ct. 590 (Cl. Ct. 1987); Brookfield Constr. Co. v. United States, 661 F.2d 159 (Cl. Ct. 1981).

Page 1272, replace text of note 84 with:

See Bramble & Callahan, *supra* note 22, § 12:10; *see also* Macri v. United States, 353 F.2d 804 (9th Cir. 1965); Socony Mobil Oil Co. v. Klapal, 205 F. Supp. 388 (D. Neb. 1962).

[I]   Post Judgment Interest Authorized by Statute

Page 1273, replace text of note 85 with:

See TDS Painting & Restoration, Inc. v. Copper Beech Farm, Inc., 808 A.2d 726, 739 (Conn. App. Ct. 2002) (defining post judgment interest under a statute as beginning "to run from the date of judgment."); Mid-America Fed. Sav. & Loan v. Shearson/Am. Express, Inc., 962 F.2d 1470 (10th Cir. 1992), for a discussion of the award of post judgment interest on attorney's fee awards. The *Mid-America* court held that post judgment interest on attorney's fee awards "is a question of federal law, controlled by 28 U.S.C. § 1961, regardless of whether the fees were awarded under a federal statute or pendent state statute." *Id.* at 475. *But see* La. Power & Light Co. v. Kellstrom, 50 F.3d 319 (5th Cir. 1995).

Page 1273, replace text of note 89 with:

See RPR & Assocs., Inc. v. Univ. of N.C.-Chapel Hill, 570 S.E.2d 510, 515 (N.C. Ct. App. 2002). The court in *RPR* noted that the rule that states are not liable for interests absent a statute is "well-established." Additionally, states may be liable for interest when an agency enters into a contract that specifically allows recovery. *See* Faulkenbury v. Teachers' & State Employees' Ret. Sys. of N.C., 510 S.E.2d 675, 673 (N.C. Ct. App. 1999).

Page 1273, replace text of note 90 with:

See Kramer v. Mt. Carmel Shelter Care Facility, Inc., 750 N.E.2d 757 (Ill. App. Ct. 2001).

[K]   Prompt Payment Act

Page 1274, replace text of note 94 with:

31 U.S.C. §§ 3901–3905 (1982).

Page 1275, replace text of note 101 with:

Id. § 3907(c); Southern Comfort Builders, Inc. v. United States, 67 Fed. Cl. 124, 156 (Fed. Cl. 2005).

Page 1275, replace text of note 102 with:

31 U.S.C. § 3907(c); Sarang Corp. v. United States, 76 Fed. Cl. 560, 563 (Fed. Cl. 2007); *see Comfort Builders,* 67 Fed. Cl. at 156.

Page 1275, replace the last sentence of the first full paragraph, retaining note 103, with:

A party seeking to take advantage of remedies available under the Contract Disputes Act "must exhaust available administrative remedies by first submitting a 'claim' to and obtaining a 'final decision' from the contracting officer."[103]

Page 1275, replace text of note 103 with:

Sarang, 76 Fed. Cl. at 564 (citing 41 U.S.C. § 605(a)). The court in *Sarang* described in fair detail the process required under the Contract Disputes Act for obtaining relief. *See id.* 564–67; *see also* 41 U.S.C. §§ 601 *et seq.*

Page 1275, replace text of note 105 with:

Mo. Stat. § 34.057 (2007).

Page 1276, replace text of note 107 with:

United States *ex rel.* C.J.C., Inc. v. W. States Mech. Contractors, Inc., 834 F.2d 1533 (10th Cir. 1987).

Page 1276, replace the sentence following callout to note 110, retaining note 111, with:

All late payments subject to the Florida Prompt Payment Act are subject to an interest rate "of 1 percent per month, or the rate specified by contract, whichever is greater."[111]

Page 1276, replace the last sentence in the last paragraph with the following and retain note 112:

Finally, a contract between the local government and a construction provider may not prohibit the collection of late payment interest charges allowed by the Florida Prompt Payment Act.[112]

§ 33.02   RECOVERY OF ATTORNEYS' FEES

[A]   Introduction

Page 1277, replace text of note 119 with:

See, e.g., Rockwork, Inc. v. Pulaski Constr. Co., Inc., 933 A.2d 988, 991 (N.J. Super. Ct. App. Div. 2007).

Page 1277, replace text of note 120 with:

See, e.g., Colorado Structures, Inc. v. Ins. Co. of the West, 167 P.3d 1125, 1141 n.17 (Wash. 2007).

Page 1278, replace text of note 122 with:

See Shimman v. Int'l Union of Operating Eng'rs, 744 F.2d 1226, 1229–30 (6th Cir. 1984); see also 1 Attorneys' Fees § 6:5 (3d ed. 2007).

Page 1278, replace text of note 123 with:

See Rock Work, Inc., 933 A.2d at 991. A "prevailing party" is generally the one that obtains a net recovery when compared with the other party. Charles M. Sink, *Negotiating Dispute Clauses that Effect Damage Recovery*, 18 Constr. Law 22 (Apr. 1998).

Page 1278, replace text of note 124 with:

Daniel E. Toomey & Gregory Brown, *The Incredible Shrinking "American Rule": Navigating the Changing Rules Governing Attorneys' Fee Awards in Today's Construction Litigation*, 27 Constr. Law. 34, 34 (Spring 2007).

[C]   Attorneys' Fees Awarded as Authorized by Contract

Page 1279, replace text of note 130 with:

Ariz. Rev. Stat. Ann. § 12-341.01; Ark. Code Ann. § 16-22-308 (2007); Okla. Stat. tit. 12, § 936, (2007); Or. Rev. Stat. § 20.082 (2007) (providing for attorney fees to the prevailing party when the principal and interest of the contract underlying the suit is less than or equal to $10,000.00); Tex. Civ. Prac. & Rem. Code Ann. § 38.001 (Vernon 2007).

Page 1279, replace text of note 132 with:

Stewart v. Bennett, 727 N.W.2d 424, 429 (Neb. 2007) ("This court, however, has repeatedly held that in the absence of an uniform course of procedure or authorization by statute, contractual agreements for attorney's fees are against public policy and will not be judicially enforced." (citations omitted)).

[D]   Bad-Faith Exception to American Rule

Page 1281, replace text of note 137 with:

See, e.g., Ariz. Rev. Stat. § 12-341.01(C) (2007); Ga. Code § 13-6-11 (2007); Ind. Code § 34-52-1-1 (2007); Kan. Stat. Ann. § 60-211(c) (2007); Md. Rule 1-341 (2007); Minn. Stat. § 549.211 (2007); Neb. Rev. Stat. § 25-824 (2007); N.D. Cent. Code § 28-26-31 (2007); Or. Rev. Stat. 20.105(a) (2007); 42 Pa. CSA § 2503 (2007); Utah Code Ann. § 78B-5-825 (2008). *See also* Clark v. Optical Coding Laboratory, Inc., 80 Cal. Rptr. 3d 812, 165 Cal. App. 4th 150 (Cal. Ct. App. 2008) (in *Clark* the court held that the California legislature impliedly repealed Cal. Code Civ. Proc. § 128.5 by the enactment of Cal. Code Civ. Proc. § 128.7 which provides a more limited authorization for the imposition of attorney's fees as sanctions for the filing of improperly signed pleadings).

Page 1281, replace text of note 139 with:

Double Oak Constr., L.L.C. v. Cornerstone Dev. Int'l, L.L.C., 97 P.3d 140, 151 (Colo. App. 2003).

Page 1282, replace text of note 146 with:

Id. (citing Clark v. Aenchbacher, 238 S.E.2d 442 (Ga. Ct. App. 1977)); *see also* Double Oak Constr., L.L.C. v. Cornerstone Dev. Int'l, L.L.C., 97 P.3d 140, 151 (Colo. App. 2003) (holding that attorneys' fees may properly be characterized as an element of costs).

[G] Attorneys' Fees in Prompt Payment Statutes

Page 1284, replace text of note 161 with:

See, e.g., Ala. Code § 8-29-6 (2007); Ariz. Rev. Stat. Ann. § 32-1129.01 (2007); Conn. Gen. Stat. § 42-158j (2007); Ga. Code Ann. § 13-11-8 (West 2007); Me. Rev. Stat. Ann. tit. 10 § 1118 (2007); Md. Code Ann., Real Prop. § 9-303 (West 2007); Minn. Stat. § § 471.425, 137.36, 16a.1245, 337.10 (West 2007); Mo. Ann. Stat. § 34.057 (West 2007); Mont. Code Ann. § 28-2-2105 (2007); Ohio Rev. Code Ann. § 4113.61 (West 2007); 62 Pa. Cons. Stat. Ann. § 3935 (West 2007); Vt. Stat. Ann. tit. 9, § 4007 (2007).

Page 1285, replace the second sentence of the first full paragraph, retaining note 168, with:

For example, the Missouri prompt payment statute that governs public works projects provides that if a party asserts a claim, defense, or motion that is "frivolous and in bad faith," attorneys' fees and costs shall be awarded to the prevailing party.[168]

[H] Attorneys' Fees in Mechanic's/Construction Lien Cases

Page 1285, replace text of note 175 with:

Frank Hughes & Debera Massahos, *Statutes Permitting Recovery of Attorneys' Fees in Construction Cases*, 17 Constr. Law. 33 (Oct. 1997).

Page 1285, replace text of note 176 with:

See, e.g., Del. Code Ann. tit. 10, § 3912 (2007); Fla. Stat. Ann. § 713.28 (2007); Idaho Code Ann. § 45-513 (2007); Ind. Code § 32-28-3-14 (2007); Iowa Code § 572.32 (2007); Mich. Comp. Laws § 570.1118 (2007); Mont. Code Ann. § 71-3-124 (2007); N.M. Stat. § 48-2-14 (2007); Or. Rev. Stat. § 87.060 (2007); R.I. Gen. Laws § 34-28-19 (2007); S.C. Code Ann. § 29-5-10 (2007); S.D. Codified Laws § 44-9-42 (2007); Utah Code Ann. § 38-1-18 (2007); Wash. Rev. Code § 60.04.181 (2007); *see also* Toomey & Brown, *supra* note 124, at 35.

[J] Attorneys' Fees in Statutory Payment and Performance Bonds

Page 1286, replace text of note 185 with:

> *See* Ala. Code § 39-1-1 (2007); Fla. Stat. Ann. § 337.18 (2007); Idaho Code Ann. § 54-1929 (2007); Iowa Code § 573.21 (2007); Mont. Code Ann. § 18-2-207 (2007).

Page 1287, replace text of note 189 with:

Fla. Stat. Ann. § 255.05 (1996).

Page 1287, replace text of note 190 with:

Conn. Gen. Stat. Ann. § 49-42 (West 2007).

[K] Statutes Making Attorneys' Fees Reciprocal

Page 1287, replace footnote 194 with:

Fla. Stat. Ann. § 57.105 (2007).

Page 1288, replace the sentence following callout to note 196, retaining note 197, with:

In Oregon, if more than several parties prevail on separate claims that provide for attorneys' fees then the court, or arbitrator, must take steps to ensure that each party receives the share of fees to which it is entitled.[197]

[L] General Attorneys' Fees Statutes

Page 1288, replace text of note 201 with:

Idaho Code Ann. § 12-121 (2007).

[M] Award of Attorneys' Fees in Arbitration Proceedings

[1] California

Page 1289, in first sentence of carryover paragraph, replace Olivera v. Modiano/Schneider, Inc. with:

Olivera v. Modiano-Schneider, Inc.

Page 1290, replace text of note 207 with:

151 Cal. Rptr. 554 (Cal. Ct. App. 1978).

Page 1290, replace text of note 209 with:

118 Cal. Rptr. 309 (Cal. Ct. App. 1975).

Page 1290, replace text of note 211 with:

Taranow v. Brokstein, 185 Cal. Rptr. 532 (Cal. Ct. App. 1982).

Page 1290, replace text of note 213 with:

Downer Corp. v. Union Paving Co., 304 P.2d 756 (Cal. 1956), *cert. denied*, 354 U.S. 914 (1957). *See also* Kauffman v. Shearson, Hayden, Stone, Inc., 128 Cal. App. 3d 809 (Cal. Ct. App. 1982).

Page 1290, replace text of note 215 with:

Cal. Civ. Proc. Code § 998 (West 2007).

[4]   Michigan

Page 1291, replace text of note 223 with:

226 N.W.2d 276 (Mich. Ct. App. 1975).

[5]   New York

Page 1292, replace text of note 225 with:

361 N.Y. S.2d 47 (N.Y. App. Div. 1974).

Page 1292, replace text of note 226 with:

223 N.Y. S.2d 533 (N.Y. Sup. Ct. 1961), *aff'd*, 245 N.Y. S.2d 985 (N.Y. App. Div., *appeal dismissed*, 198 N.E.2d 602 (N.Y. 1964).

[6]   Oregon

Page 1292, replace text of note 228 with:

Harris, 637 P.2d at 919-920 (citing Or. Rev. Stat. § 87.060(4)). The statute has since been modified. The relevant language now provides the following: *In a suit to enforce a lien perfected under ORS 87.035 the court shall allow a reasonable amount as attorney fees at trial and on appeal to the party who prevails on the issues of the validity and foreclosure of the lien.* (Or. Rev. Stat. § 87.060(5) (2007)).

[N] Attorneys' Fees Provision in Indemnity Agreements

Page 1293, replace text of note 234 with:

96 N.W. 782 (Iowa 1903).

Page 1296, replace the first sentence of the last paragraph with:

In *Glen Johnson, Inc. v. Howdeshell, Inc.*, a Florida court considered a claim filed by a subcontractor against a contractor and its surety for labor and materials which included a claim for attorneys' fees under a provision in the payment bond.[254]

Page 1296, replace text of note 254 with:

520 So. 2d 297 (Fla. Dist. Ct. App. 1988). *But see* Fewox v. McMerit Constr. Co., 556 So. 2d 419 (Fla. Dist. Ct. App. 1989); Park Shore Dev. Co. v. Higley S., Inc., 556 So. 2d 439 (Fla. Dist. Ct. App. 1990).

Page 1297, replace text of note 259 with:

493 N.E.2d 146 (Ill. App. Ct. 1986).

[O] Attorneys' Fees in Miller Act Claims

Page 1297, replace text of note 262 with:

F.D. Rich Co. v. United States *ex rel.* Indus. Lumber Co., 417 U.S. 116 (1974).

Page 1297, replace text of note 263 with:

Id. at 129; *see also* 40 U.S.C. §§ 3131 *et seq. But see* United States *ex rel.* Cal's A/C & Elec. v. Famous Constr. Corp., 34 F. Supp. 2d 1042 (W.D. La. 1999) (legislatively overrules *F.D. Rich* decision).

---

[254] 520 So. 2d 297 (Fla. Dist. Ct. App. 1988). *But see* Fewox v. McMerit Constr. Co., 556 So. 2d 419 (Fla. Dist. Ct. App. 1989); Park Shore Dev. Co. v. Higley South, Inc., 556 So. 2d 439 (Fla. Dist. Ct. App. 1990).

Page 1298, replace text of note 264 with:

F.D. Rich Co. v. United States *ex rel.* Indus. Lumber Co., 417 U.S. 116, 129 (1974). *But see* United States *ex rel.* Cal's A/C & Elec. v. Famous Constr. Corp., 34 F. Supp. 2d 1042 (W.D. La. 1999) (legislatively overrules *F.D. Rich* decision).

Page 1298, replace text of note 266 with:

Id. at 128-129; United States *ex rel.* C.J.C. Inc. v. W. States Mech. Contractors, Inc., 834 F.2d 1533 (10th Cir. 1987).

Page 1298, replace text of note 267 with:

See Transamerica Ins. Co. v. Red Top Metal, Inc., 384 F.2d 752 (5th Cir. 1967); United States *ex rel.* Dixie Plumbing Supply Co. v. Taylor, 293 F.2d 717 (5th Cir. 1961); The Travelers Indem. Co. v. United States *ex rel.* W. Steel Co., 362 F.2d 896 (9th Cir. 1966). *But see* J.C. Snavely & Sons, Inc. v. Web M&E, Inc., 594 A.2d 333 (Pa. Super. Ct. 1991).

Page 1298, replace fourth sentence of first full paragraph, retaining note 268, with:

The Supreme Court explained as follows: "We think it better to extricate the Federal courts from the morass of trying to divine a 'state policy' as to the award of attorneys fees in suits on construction bonds."[268]

Page 1299, replace the first sentence of the last paragraph in this section with:

In *United States ex rel. Yonker Construction Co. v. Western Contracting Corp.,*[273] the federal court applied federal law and awarded attorneys' fees for a claim made in bad faith, which is an exception to the American Rule that was outlined in *F.D. Rich.*

---

[273] 935 F.2d 936 (8th Cir. 1991).

CHAPTER 34

PERFORMANCE BONDS

Roger P. Sauer
Kevin J. Russell
Philip W. Allogramento III

Please replace Philip W. Allogramento III with Gregory S. Arnold, LL.M and insert the following biography to About the Contributors:

Gregory S. Arnold, LL.M, is a Senior Bond Claims Representative II with The Hanover Insurance Group, Inc., Home Office, Worcester, Massachusetts, where he responds to contract surety, commercial surety and fidelity claims, plus assists with product development and training.

Mr. Arnold was a Non-Commissioned Officer, serving as a Military Courts-Martial Reporter in the United State Marine Corps, with duty stations in Japan and the Philippines. He then graduated from Union College and University with a Bachelor of Science in Political Science, *cum laude* and with Departmental Honors. He received a Juris Doctorate from Western State University College of Law and an LL.M (Insurance Law) from The University of Connecticut School of Law.

Mr. Arnold started his surety claims career as Bond Claims Trainee and then Bond Claims Manager for the West, with Great American Insurance Company in Orange, California, and then Bond Claims Manager for the Mid-West, at Great American's Home Office in Cincinnati, Ohio. He then accepted a position as Bond Claims Superintendent/ Assistant Secretary with Highlands Insurance Company at its Home Office in Houston, Texas, with his last position there being Assistant Vice President of Claims. Mr. Arnold then formed Claims Management Associates, Inc. in Houston, Texas, primarily providing surety claim run-off services for Highlands, plus performing desk relief and run-off assistance to other, smaller sureties and those in transition. After a brief period working for Mid-State Surety Corporation/Guarantee Company of North America USA, he accepted his current position in the Bond Claims Department at Hanover.

His recent contributions to international insurance scholarship include his law journal publications, *The Doubtful Impact of an Optional Federal Charter on the Reinsurance Collateral Debate*, 43 Tort Trial & Ins. Prac. L.J. 79 (2008), American Bar Association, and *Recent Developments in the Financial Products and Services Industry*, 43 The International Lawyer (2008), American Bar Association. His domestic surety and insurance scholarship include a writing contribution to the

CGL/Builder's Risk Monograph, 2004, Tort Trial & Insurance Practice Section, American Bar Association. His papers and panel participations include: "The Surety's Good Faith Investigation," CMA Group, Inc., National Claims Conference, Chicago, IL, April 1989; "The Good, Bad and Ugly: Lawyers, Consultants and Company People Traveling Down The Same Road Together," panel presentation, National Bond Claims Conference, Pinehurst, NC, Oct. 1994; "Treatment of Pay-When-Paid Clauses Under Federal Law on Bonded Projects in Virginia," Surety Association of South Texas, San Antonio, May 17, 2000; and *Issues and Practical Considerations for the Surety in Using Subcontractor Ratification Agreements*, 17th Annual Northeast Surety and Fidelity Claims Conference, Atlantic City, NJ, Sept. 2006.

Mr. Arnold has been a guest lecturer on surety law topics at Roger Williams University and is licensed and certified as an insurance and surety claims adjuster in several states.

CHAPTER 36

INDEMNITY OF THE CONTRACT SURETY

Joseph T. Getz
John Willet

§ 36.01   INTRODUCTION

Page 1410, replace text of note 6 with:

See, e.g., Ark. Code Ann. §§ 16-107-303, -304, -305 (West 2007); Cal. Civ. Code §§ 2847-2848 (West 2007); Ga. Code Ann. §§ 10-7-40, -41 (West 2007); Ind. Code §§ 34-22-1-1, *et seq.* (2007); La. Civ. Code Ann. art. 3052 (2007); Mont. Code Ann. §§ 28-11-413, -420 (2007); N.D. Cent. Code §§ 22-03-10, -11 (2007); Ohio Rev. Code Ann. §§ 1341.18 - 1341.21 (West 2007); Okla. Stat. Ann. Tit. 15 §§ 9-380, 9-381, 9-382 (2007); S.D. Codified Laws §§ 56-2-13, -14 (2007).

§ 36.02   COMMON-LAW RIGHTS OF INDEMNITY

[B]   Right to Demand Exoneration

Page 1412, replace text of note 11 with:

Nw. Nat'l Ins. Co. v. Alberts, 741 F. Supp. 424, 429 (S.D.N.Y. 1990).

[C]   Right of Subrogation

Page 1413, line 4 of note 18, insert space between ";" and "The."

Page 1413, replace text of note 20 with:

Nat'l Shawmut Bank v. New Amsterdam Cas. Co., 411 F.2d 843 (1st Cir. 1969).

[D]   Constraints

Page 1414, replace text of note 24 with:

Liberty Mut. Ins. Co. v. Aventura Engineering & Constr. Corp., 534 F. Supp. 2d 1290, 1309–1310 (S.D. Fla. 2008).

§ 36.03   CONSTRUCTION AND OPERATION OF THE WRITTEN AGREEMENT OF INDEMNITY

[A]   General Overview

Page 1415, replace text of note 28 with:

See Ulico Cas. Co. v. Atl. Contracting & Material Co., 822 A.2d 1257, 1266 (Md. Ct. Spec. App. 2003), *aff'd*, 844 A.2d 460 (Md. 2004).

Page 1415, replace text of note 31 with:

17 F.2d 38 (3d Cir. 1927).

[B]   Basic Indemnification Clause

Page 1417, replace text of note 36 with:

Pearlman v. Reliance Ins. Co., 371 U.S. 132, 136 (1962); Fid. & Deposit Co. v. Bristol Steel & Iron Works, Inc., 722 F.2d 1160, 1163 (4th Cir. 1983).

Page 1418, replace text of note 39 with:

Gen. Accident Ins. Co. of Am. v. Merritt-Meridian Constr. Corp., 975 F. Supp. 511 (S.D.N.Y. 1997).

Page 1419, replace text of note 45 with:

See Liberty Mut. Ins. Co. v. Aventura Engineering & Constr. Corp., 534 F. Supp. 2d 1290, 1316 (S.D. Fla. 2008); Continental Cas. Co. v. Gutterman, 708 F. Supp. 953, 954 (N.D. Ill. 1989).

Page 1419, replace text of note 46 with:

See Gen. Accident Ins. Co. of Am. v. Merritt-Meridian Constr. Corp., 975 F. Supp. 511, 516 (S.D.N.Y. 1997) (*citing* Fid. & Cas. Co. v. Finch, 3 A.D.2d 141 (N.Y. App. Div. 1957)); Ulico Cas. Co. v. Atl. Contracting &

Material Co., 822 A.2d 1257, 1266 (Md. Ct. Spec. App. 2003), *aff'd*, 844 A.2d 460 (Md. 2004).

Page 1420, replace text of note 54 with:

Arntz Contracting Co. v. St. Paul Fire & Marine Ins. Co., 54 Cal. Rptr. 2d 888 (Cal. Ct. App. 1996); *see also* PSE Consulting, Inc. v. Frank Mercede and Sons, Inc., 838 A.2d 135, 152 & n.12 (Conn. 2004).

[C]   Attorney's Fee Recovery Clause

Page 1423, replace text of note 69 with:

See T.P.K. Constr. Corp. v. So. Am. Ins. Co., 752 F. Supp. 105 (S.D.N.Y. 1990).

§ 36.04   COLLATERAL DEPOSIT CLAUSE

Page 1425, replace text of note 75 with:

See Abish v. Nw. Nat'l Ins. Co., 924 F.2d 448 (2d Cir. 1991); Borey v. Nat'l Union Fire Ins. Co., 934 F.2d 30 (2d Cir. 1991); Nw. Nat'l Ins. Co. v. Alberts, 937 F.2d 77 (2d Cir. 1991).

Page 1425, replace text of note 76 with:

See Safeco Ins. Co. of Am. v. Schwab, 739 F.2d 431, 434 (9th Cir. 1984).

Page 1426, replace text of note 80 with:

Charles A. Meeker, *Surety's Right to Specific Performance of Indemnity Agreements*, 3 Constr. Law. 2, at 1 (1982).

Page 1426, replace text of note 85 with:

26 N.Y.S.2d 227, 231 (N.Y. Sup. Ct. 1940).

§ 36.05   RIGHT OF SETTLEMENT CLAUSE

Page 1428, replace text of note 92 with:

See PSE Consulting, Inc. v. Frank Mercede & Sons, Inc., 838 A.2d 135, 146 (Conn. 2004) ("Right-to-settle clauses . . . generally are enforced according to their terms."); Fid. & Deposit Co. of Md. v. Fleischer, 772 S.W.2d 809 (Mo. Ct. App. 1989).

Page 1429, replace text of note 93 with:

Hess v. Am. States Ins., 589 S.W.2d 548, 552 (Tex. Civ. App. 1979).

Page 1429, replace text of note 94 with:

See Fid. & Deposit Co. v. Wu, 552 A.2d 1196 (Vt. 1988).

Page 1429, replace text of note 96 with:

See Fid. & Deposit Co. v. Bristol Steel & Ironworks, Inc., 722 F.2d 1160, 1164 (4th Cir. 1983).

§ 36.06   ASSIGNMENT CLAUSES

Page 1432, replace text of note 112 with:

See W. Cas. & Sur. Co. v. United States, 109 F. Supp. 422 (Ct. Cl. 1953); Petrossi Bros. Contracting Corp. v. Town of Greece, 29 N.Y.S.2d 305 (N.Y. Sup. Ct. 1941).

Page 1433, in first full paragraph, replace all instances of "Esperence" with "Esperance"

Compania de Remorque y Salvamento, S.A. v. Esperance, Inc.,

§ 36.07   *PRIMA FACIE* EVIDENCE CLAUSE

Page 1435, replace text of note 127 with:

See Curtis T. Bedwell & Sons, Inc. v. Int'l Fid. Ins. Co., 1989 WL 55388 (E.D. Pa. May 23, 1989). *See also* Cont'l Cas. Co. v. Am. Sec. Corp., 443 F.2d 649 (D.C. Cir. 1970).

Page 1435, replace text of note 131 with:

See Fid. & Deposit Co. v. Wu, 552 A.2d 1196, (Vt. 1988).

Page 1435, replace text of note 132 with:

See Int'l Fid. Ins. Co. v. Jones, 682 A.2d 263 (N.J. Super. Ct. App. Div. 1996).

Page 1435, replace text of note 134 with:

See Home Indem. Co. v. Wachter, 496 N.Y.S.2d 252 (N.Y. App. Div. 1985). *See also* Transamerica Ins. Co. v. Bloomfield, 401 F.2d 357, 362 (6th Cir. 1968) (citing Engbrock v. Fed. Ins. Co., 370 F.2d 784 (5th Cir. 1967), and United States Fid. & Guar. Co. v. Jones, 87 F.2d 346 (5th Cir. 1937)).

§ 36.08   UNIFORM COMMERCIAL CODE FILING CLAUSE

Page 1437, replace text of note 138 with:

See Nat'l Shawmut Bank v. New Amsterdam Cas., 411 F.2d 843 (1st Cir. 1969).

Page 1437, replace text of note 139 with:

See In re Jones Constr. & Renovation, Inc., 337 B.R. 579, 583 (Bankr. E.D. Va. 2006).

§ 36.09   DEFENSES TO INDEMNIFICATION

[A]   General Overview

Page 1441, replace text of note 163 with:

See Ulico Cas. Co. v. Atl. Contracting & Material Co., Inc., 822 A.2d 1257, 1265–66 (Md. Ct. Spec. App. 2003), *aff'd*, 844 A.2d 460 (Md. 2004); *see also* 74 Am. Jur. 2d *Suretyship* § 186.

[B]   Lack of Consideration

Page 1442, replace text of note 168 with:

See Engbrock v. Fed. Ins. Co., 370 F.2d 784, 789 (5th Cir. 1967).

Page 1442, replace text of note 169 with:

Am. Druggists' Ins. Co. v. Shoppe, 448 N.W.2d 103 (Minn. Ct. App. 1989).

[C]   Indemnitor's Failure to Sign or Understand Indemnity Agreement

Page 1443, replace text of note 173 with:

Jacobson v. Am. Fid. Fire Ins. Co., 541 P.2d 2, 3 (Nev. 1975).

Page 1443, replace text of note 174 with:

See Universal Sur. Co. v. Jed Constr. Co., 265 N.W.2d 219 (Neb. 1978); United States *ex rel.* Bussen Quarries, Inc. v. Thomas, 938 F.2d 831 (8th Cir. 1991); Ins. Co. of N. Am. v. Bath, 726 F. Supp. 1247 (D. Wyo. 1989).

[D]   Failure to Mitigate Damages

Page 1444, replace text of note 179 with:

Fid. & Deposit Co. v. Bristol Steel & Iron Works, Inc., 722 F.2d 1160 (4th Cir. 1983).

Page 1444, replace text of note 180 with:

See Engbrock v. Fed. Ins. Co., 370 F.2d 784, 789 (5th Cir. 1967).

Page 1444, replace text of note 182 with:

See Transamerica Ins. Co. v. Bloomfield, 401 F.2d 357 (6th Cir. 1968); Ward v. City of Portland, 857 F.2d 1373 (9th Cir. 1988); Fid. & Deposit Co. v. Bristol Steel & Iron Works, Inc., 722 F.2d 1160 (4th Cir. 1983).

[E]   Lack of Notice/Waiver Defenses

Page 1446, replace text of note 185 with:

Safeco Ins. Co. of Am. v. Gaubert, 829 S.W.2d 274 (Tex. App. 1992).

[F]   Nontypical Indemnification Defenses

Page 1446, replace text of note 189 with:

Lambert v. Md. Cas. Co., 418 So. 2d 553 (La. 1982). *See also* Gerstner Elec., Inc. v. Am. Ins. Co., 520 F.2d 790 (8th Cir. 1975).

Page 1447, replace text of note 192 with:

Nat'l Shawmut Bank v. New Amsterdam Cas. Co., 411 F.2d 843 (1st Cir. 1969).

Page 1447, replace text of note 194 with:

See Premier Elec. Constr. Co. v. Am. Nat'l Bank & Trust Co., 603 N.E.2d 733, 735 (Ill. 1992).

CHAPTER 37

NEW AND UNIQUE ASPECTS OF FEDERAL CONTRACTING

James F. Nagle

§ 37.01   INTRODUCTION

Page 1453, add new subsections to end of section:

[A]   The Stimulus Act

The American Recovery and Reinvestment Act of 2009, Pub. L. No. 111-5, 123 Stat. 115 (2009) (ARRA or the Recovery Act) changed the landscape, both financially and legally.

Besides appropriating huge sums, the Act demands accountability and transparency. Under Subtitle A, companies receiving contracts funded in whole or in part by ARRA monies will be required to report on a quarterly basis:

- the amount of ARRA funds invoiced for the reporting period;

- a list of all significant services performed or supplies delivered for which the contractor invoiced in the quarter;

- an assessment of the contractor's progress towards completion and expected outcomes or results;

- a description of the employment impact of the work (i.e., jobs created and jobs retained);

- information about subcontracts over a certain dollar threshold awarded under the contract; and

- in certain circumstances, the names and total compensation of each of the five most highly compensated officers of the contractor.

Similarly, Federal Acquisition Regulation (FAR) Part 4 requires the contracting officer to enter data in the Federal Procurement Data System on any action funded in whole or in part by the Recovery Act. FAR Subpart 5.7 is added to direct the contracting officer to use the Government-wide Point of Entry (https://www.fedbizopps.gov) to (1) identify the action as funded by the Recovery Act; (2) post pre-award notices for orders exceeding $25,000 for "informational purposes only";

(3) describe supplies and services (including construction) in a narrative that is clear and unambiguous to the general public; and (4) provide a rationale for awarding any action, including modifications and orders, that is not both fixed-price and competitive, and include the rationale for using other than a fixed-price and/or competitive approach.

Also, the FAR requires contractors to report on their use of Recovery Act funds under a new subpart 4.15, and a new clause, 52.204-11. Contracting officers must include the new clause in solicitations and contracts funded in whole or in part with Recovery Act funds, except classified solicitations and contracts.

Reports from contractors for all work funded, in whole or in part, by the Recovery Act, and for which an invoice is submitted prior to June 30, 2009, are due no later than July 10, 2009. Thereafter, reports shall be submitted no later than the 10th day after the end of each calendar quarter.

The Recovery Act authorizes the Comptroller General to conduct bimonthly audits and reviews and report on the use of the funds by select States and localities, with the results to be posted on the Internet for full public review.[01] The Comptroller General is authorized to examine all records of any transaction that would "directly pertain to" any contract let under the Stimulus Bill, whether that record be of a private contractor or subcontractor, or of a State or local agency.[02] For ARRA-funded contracts, the Government Accountability Office (GAO) and its agents will have expanded audit authority, which includes the authority to conduct interviews of contractor and subcontractor personnel and to audit commercial item contracts and contracts under the simplified acquisition threshold (two categories of contract not normally audited by the GAO). Agency inspectors general may access records of contractors and grantees, and interview their employees. These Recovery Act requirements are implemented in new alternate clauses to 52.212-5, "Contract Terms and Conditions Required to Implement Statutes or Executive Orders-Commercial Items," 52.214-26, "Audit and Records-Sealed Bidding," and 52.215-2, "Audit and Records-Negotiation." For the Comptroller General these alternate clauses provide specific authority to audit contracts and subcontracts and to interview contractor and subcontractor employees under contracts using Recovery Act funds. Agency inspector generals receive the same authorities, with the exception of interviewing subcontractor employees.

Subtitle B of the Recovery Act established the "Recovery Accountability and Transparency Board" (not surprisingly nicknamed the "RAT Board") and requires the Board to prepare quarterly and annual reports and maintain a public website, www.recovery.gov.

The Board is a separate body that is charged by § 1521 with the responsibility "to coordinate and conduct oversight of covered funds."

---

[01] Tit. IX, § 901(a).
[02] Tit. IX, § 902.

The statute allows the Chairperson of the Board to be either the Deputy Director of the Office of Management and Budget, or any other person who is appointed by the President and receives the advice and consent of the Senate. The members of the Board are the Inspector Generals for the Departments of Agriculture, Commerce, Education, Energy, Health and Human Services, Homeland Security, Justice, Transportation, Treasury, and the Treasury Inspector General for Tax Administration, and any other Inspector General as designated by the President from an agency using stimulus money.[03]

The Board has audit and review power that parallels that of the agency Inspector Generals (IGs); including the powers granted to the IGs by § 6 of the Inspector General Act of 1978, and can issue and enforce subpoenas with the same powers that are granted under that statute. The Board may conduct public hearings and enter into contracts in support of its investigative work.

Title XVI includes Section 1605 which adds a Buy American Act division and bans use of Recovery Act funds for a project for the construction, alteration, maintenance or repair of public building or public work unless all of the iron, steel and manufactured goods used are produced in the United States. A new FAR Subpart 25.6 implements the Act's Buy American Act Rules and adds new clauses. It prohibits the use of funds appropriated for the Recovery Act for any project for the construction, alteration, maintenance, or repair of a public building or public work unless all of the iron, steel, and manufactured goods used in the project are produced in the United States. However, section 1605 requires that the Buy American requirement be applied in a manner consistent with U.S. obligations under international agreements. Moreover, because Congress intended that least developed countries be excepted from section 1605, least developed countries can continue to be treated as designated countries.

[B]   The New E-Verify Rules

On June 6, 2008, President Bush had issued Executive Order 12989 to require all companies who contract with federal agencies to use the Department of Homeland Securities E-Verify System. The order was designed to insure that the federal government only contracts with providers who "do not knowingly employ unauthorized alien workers." The order also directed amendments to the FAR to insure that contractors who employ illegal aliens shall be considered for debarment or suspension. Implementation of the order is to be carried out in a manner that minimizes "the burden on participants in the Federal Procurement Process."

---

[03] Tit. XV, § 1522(b)(1),(2).

Six days later at 73 Fed. Reg. 33374, on June 12, 2008, a new FAR rule was proposed to require certain contractors and subcontractors to use the US Citizenship and Immigration Services Electronic Employment Eligibility Verification (E-Verify) System to insure that their employees are eligible to work in the United States. This implements EO 12989 and applies to both prime and subcontracts over $3,000. It does not apply to contracts for Commercially Off-The-Shelf (COTS) items or items that would be considered as COTS but for minor modifications. The rule would apply to solicitations issued and contracts awarded after the effective date of the final rule, but would only cover employment in the United States. Contractors would have to use the E-Verify System for all newly hired employees and all employees directly engaged in performance of work under federal contracts. That rule became final in FAC 2005-29, but was substantially delayed by court challenges.

Finally, on September 8, 2009, the Homeland Security Department implemented the long delayed rule requiring most federal contractors and subcontractors to use its E-Verify system to prove employees working on government projects are legally in the country.

The new E-Verify requirements are imposed in a new subpart 22.18-Employment Eligibility Verification and in a new clause, 52.222-54, which will be required in all solicitations and contracts that exceed the simplified acquisition threshold except those that: (1) are only for work that will be performed outside the United States; (2) are for a period of performance of less than 120 days; or (3) are only for (a) commercially available off-the-shelf items; items that would be COTS items but for minor modifications; or items that would be COTS items if they were not bulk cargo or commercial services that are part of the purchase of a COTS item performed by the COTS provider and are normally provided for that COTS item.

[C] Labor Rules

President Obama has issued rules decidedly more pro-labor than those of the Bush administration. For example, President Bush's Executive Order 13201 required contractors to post a notice informing employees of their rights concerning payment of union dues or fees and detailed that employees could not be required to join unions or maintain membership in unions to retain their jobs. President Obama's Executive Order 13496, of January 10, 2009, Notification of Employee Rights under Federal Labor Laws, revoked Executive Order 13201.

Issued Feb. 6, 2009, by President Obama, EO 13502, "Use of Project Labor Agreements for Federal Construction Projects," became effective April 13 (*see* 75 Fed. Reg. 19168 (Apr. 13, 2010)) and promotes the use of Project Labor Agreements (PLAs) in federal construction projects worth at least $25 million and revokes earlier executive orders prohibiting agencies from requiring such agreements. Project Labor

Agreements (PLAs) are collective bargaining agreements that establish the terms and conditions of employment for a specific construction project. The new rule encourages agency heads to consider requiring, on a project-by-project basis, the use of PLAs when awarding large-scale construction contracts. The rule creates a new FAR subpart 22.5.

§ 37.02 PROCUREMENT REGULATIONS

Page 1463, add new subsection [5] after [4]:

[H] Socioeconomic Rules

[5] Registry of Disaster Response Contractors

FAC 2005-37, 74 Fed. Reg. 52846 (Oct. 14, 2009) implements the Registry of Disaster Response Contractors provision, section 697 of the Department of Homeland Security (DHS) Appropriations Act, 2007 (6 U.S.C. § 796). The Act requires that the Federal Emergency Management Agency (FEMA) establish and maintain this registry. It also requires that the registry include business information consistent with the data that is currently required in the Central Contractor Registration (CCR) with two additional categories added to reflect the area served by the business, and the bonding level of the business concern. The CCR has been updated to include these changes. In addition, the FEMA website has been updated with a link to the CCR search feature which provides access to the disaster response registry. Contracting officers will be required to consult this registry during market research and acquisition planning.

CHAPTER **39**

WHEN AND HOW TO FILE A FEDERAL CONTRACT CLAIM

Joseph A. McManus, Jr.
Amanda K. Morken

§ 39.02 WHAT IS A CLAIM?

[A] Contract Disputes Act of 1978 (CDA)

Page 1534, add to note 3:

The False Claims Act, 31 U.S.C. § 3729 *et seq.*, also provides a civil penalty for anyone that presents or causes to be presented to the government, a false or fraudulent claim for payment or approval.

The False Claims Act was amended for the first time in more than 20 years by the Fraud Enforcement and Recovery Act ("FERA") of 2009. Pub. L. No. 111-21, 123 Stat. 1617 (2009). FERA substantially expands the scope of the False Claims Act and narrows some of the exceptions. *See* **Chapter 38**.

[C] FAR Definition of "Claim"

Page 1536, delete the third sentence of the block quote.

Page 1536, replace fourth sentence of the block quote with:

A voucher, invoice, or other routine request for payment that is not in dispute when submitted is not a claim.

Page 1536, replace third sentence of second full paragraph with:

Unless it is a proper CDA "claim" as defined above however, neither the contracting officer to whom the claim is submitted, the boards of contract appeals, nor the United States Court of Federal Claims will have jurisdiction to rule on the claim or entertain appeals from a purported contracting officer's final decision denying it.

Page 1536, add to note 9:

; Made in the USA Found. v. United States, 51 Fed. Cl. 252, 254–55 (2001).

§ 39.03   CLAIM CONTENTS

[A]   Basic Elements of a Claim

Page 1537, add footnote referent 11.1 to the end of the last sentence of the second full paragraph and add note 11.1:

   [11.1] Bell BCI Co. v. United States, No. 2008-5087, 2009 WL 1796783 (Fed. Cir. June 25, 2009.

Page 1538, replace sixth sentence of first full paragraph with:

Good claims drafters more often than not claim *more* than what was actually lost on the job site in the claim.

Page 1539, add to note 15:

; Jackson Constr. Co., Inc. v. United States, 62 Fed. Cl. 84 (2004).

Page 1539, add to note 17:

; *Jackson Constr. Co., Inc.*, 62 Fed Cl. at 98.

Page 1539, replace text of note 18 with:

Interstate Gen. Gov't Contractors, Inc. v. West, 12 F.3d at 1058–59.

Page 1539, add footnote referent 20.1 at the end of the last sentence of second full paragraph and add note 20.1:

   [20.1] FAR 31.205-33.

[B]   Claim Requirements

Page 1540, add to end of the second block quote, before the callout to note 23:

A voucher, invoice, or other routine request for payment that is not in dispute when submitted is not a claim. The submission may be converted to a claim, by written notice to the contracting officer as provided in

33.206(a), if it is disputed either as to liability or amount or is not acted upon in a reasonable time.

Page 1540, note 24, add after RSH cite:

; M. Maropakis Carpentry, Inc. v. United States, 84 Fed. Cl. 182, 196 (2008); Total Procurement Serv., Inc., ASBCA No. 54163, 08-1 B.C.A. ¶ 33,843 (holding that contractor's claim for damages in an amount in excess of $66 million did not state a sum certain as required by the CDA).

[1]   Written Demand to the Contracting Officer

[b]   *Submission of the Claim by the Contractor*

Page 1543, add to end of subsection:

A similar problem could arise for a contractor that is a joint venture. All claims must be in the name of the joint venture, not just one of the partners.

§ 39.04   CLAIM CERTIFICATION

[D]   Defective Certifications

Page 1561, add to note 137:

The failure to sign a certification, however, is not a defect which can be cured. *See* Appeal of Teknocraft, ASBCA No. 55438 (2009) (stating that a certification, marked with the typed designation "//signed//" above the name of the contractor's president, was not properly executed as it was not signed and that failure to sign is a fatal defect which can not be cured).

Page 1561, add to note 138:

; MedTek, Inc. v. Department of Veterans Affairs, CBCA No. 1153 (2008).

[E]   Consequences of False Certifications

Page 1562, replace text of note 142 with:

73 Fed. Cl. 547, 581 (2006), *aff'd* by 557 F.3d 1332 (Fed. Cir. 2009), *petition for cert. denied* 130 S. Ct. 490 (2009).

Page 1562, replace text of note 143 with:

73 Fed. Cl. 547 at 585.

Page 1562, add to end of the first full paragraph:

The issues of the government's burden of proof and the resulting new 2009 statute regarding false claims show that this area of the law is dynamic and should be monitored.[146.1] Issues of false claims have undergone some important changes in the past year. Most notably, the Fraud Enforcement and Recovery Act of 2009 ("FERA") brought about the first amendment to the False Claims Act ("FCA") in more than 20 years. FERA adds a new definition of "claim" and broadens FCA liability by only requiring some nexus to the government. *See* **Chapter 38.**

§ 39.06 CONTRACTING OFFICER'S AUTHORITY/TIMING OF CLAIM SUBMISSIONS AND FINAL DECISION

[D] Form and Content of the Final Decision

Page 1572, replace list item (3) in block quote and replace with:

(3) Coordinate with contract administration officer or contracting office, as appropriate; and

Page 1573, replace last sentence of the first full paragraph with:

The regulations require that the contracting officer's final decision contain paragraphs that are substantially as follows:

Page 1573, replace the block quote with:

> This is the final decision of the Contracting Officer. You may appeal this decision to the agency board of contract appeals. If you decide to appeal, you must, within 90 days from the date you receive this decision, mail or otherwise furnish written notice to the agency board of contract appeals and provide a copy to the Contracting Officer from whose decision the appeal is taken. The notice shall indicate that an appeal is intended, reference this decision, and identify the contract by number.
>
> With regard to appeals to the agency board of contract appeals, you may, solely at your election, proceed under the board's—

[146.1] Allison Engine Co. v. United States *ex rel.* Sanders, 12 S. Ct. 2123 (2008); 31 U.S.C. § 3729 *et seq.*

Small claim procedure for claims of $50,000 or less, or in the case of a small business concern (as defined in the Small Business Act and regulations under that Act), $150,000 or less; or

Accelerated procedure for claims of $100,000 or less.

Instead of appealing to the agency board of contract appeals, you may bring an action directly in the United States Court of Federal Claims (except as provided in the Contract Disputes Act of 1978, 41 U.S.C. § 603, regarding Maritime Contracts) within 12 months of the date you receive this decision.

§ 39.07   APPEALING THE CONTRACTING OFFICER'S FINAL DECISION

[A]   Contractor's Appeal to the Board of Contract Appeals

Page 1575, delete second sentence of note 180.

Page 1575, replace the first sentence of the third paragraph of the block quote with:

. . . Each other agency board shall have jurisdiction to decide any appeal from a decision of a contracting office relative to a contract made by its agency.

Page 1576, replace the last sentence of the second full paragraph with:

Unfortunately, this two-year period is often exceeded.

[B]   Contractor's Appeal Before the Court of Federal Claims

Page 1577, add to end of the first full paragraph:

Note also that when the case is filed in the court, the agency contracting office loses all authority to act.[183.1]

[183.1] *See* Sharman Co. v. United States, 2 F.3d 1564, 1571 (Fed. Cir. 1993) (stating that once a claim is in litigation, the Department of Justice has the exclusive authority to act in the pending litigation and the contracting office is divested of his authority to issue a final decision on a claim); Roxco, Ltd. v. United States, 77 Fed. Cl. 138, 149 (2007); Witherington Constr. Corp. v. United States, 45 Fed. Cl. 208, 211–12 (1999).

[C]   Appeal of Board and Court of Federal Claims Decisions

   [3]   Summary of Appeals Process

Page 1578, delete paragraph and heading.

**§ 39.08   TYPES OF CLAIMS EXCLUDED FROM THE COVERAGE
             OF THE CDA**

Page 1579, delete:

Figure 46-1. Summary of Appeals Process[190]

Page 1569, replace text of note 190 with:

[Reserved.]

CHAPTER 39A

TRANSPORTATION INVESTMENT AS PART OF ECONOMIC RECOVERY—IS THIS A NEW DAY FOR U.S. INFRASTRUCTURE?

Jeff Morales
Mortimer L. Downey

Page 1583, add new chapter 39A after Chapter 39:

§ 39A.01   Executive Summary

§ 39A.02   The Context for Stimulus Funding—Economic Situation

§ 39A.03   The Need for Greater Investment

§ 39A.04   The Economic Recovery and Reinvestment Act of 2009

§ 39A.05   Significance of Including Transportation in ARRA

§ 39A.06   Details of ARRA's Transportation Components

§ 39A.07   Tracking the Impacts on the Economy and Transportation Construction Industry

§ 39A.08   Early Progress in Delivery of Benefits

§ 39A.09   Implications for Future Policies and Programs, and Commitments to Transportation Investment

§ 39A.10   Conclusion

§ 39A.01   EXECUTIVE SUMMARY

Whether in terms of meeting absolute needs, or in comparison with other countries, the United States for decades has lagged in its investment in infrastructure, including transportation. The American Recovery and Reinvestment Act of 2009 (ARRA) made an unprecedented investment in transportation, the largest single federal focus on transportation systems in half a century, dating back to the 1956 creation of the National System of Interstate and Defense Highways. The $48 billion is a welcome and

221

long-overdue investment in aging and deteriorating transportation systems. But, does it represent a significant shift in U.S. policy toward
infrastructure investment? And, does it point to new policy directions
likely to be pursued by the Obama Administration and Congress?

In assessing these questions, it is important to recognize the
environment in which the ARRA's transportation funding was enacted.
First and foremost, the ARRA was economic recovery legislation, aimed
at economic stimulus and creating and/or preserving jobs. Transportation
investment was included to tap its job-creating capability. But the ARRA
was not a transportation bill—with a few exceptions, such as the urban
focus noted in this article, there was virtually no debate over programmatic changes or long-term plans. However, there are several reasons to
believe that the ARRA could be the first step in a more aggressive
approach to transportation investment in the United States. This chapter
assesses the significance of the transportation component of the ARRA,
and what it might portend for the future.

§ 39A.02   THE CONTEXT FOR STIMULUS
FUNDING—ECONOMIC SITUATION

The ongoing economic recession is the worst in decades. Although
there is some debate about when it started—and when it will end—the
National Bureau of Economic Research[1] points to December 2007 as the
beginning, already making it the longest downturn since the Great
Depression. Department of Labor statistics for May 2009 show that there
are 14.5 million unemployed Americans, an unemployment rate of 9.4%,
the highest in 25 years. When adding in the 11.3 million underemployed,
that grows to 25.8 million people, and a rate of 16.4%.

Although the recession has had broad impacts, the construction
sector has been hit particularly hard. Over 1.2 million construction jobs
have been lost, and the unemployment rate is over 19%. Given the
magnitude of these losses, early discussions about economic recovery
programs focused on programs that could produce benefits in the
construction sector. Transportation programs, such as highway and bridge
construction, transit and rail line expansions, and airport construction
offer significant opportunities for job preservation and/or creation. Traditional figures estimate approximately 24,000 jobs supported by every
billion dollars of transportation investment. Illustrating the significance of
transportation as an employer in the construction sector, the American

---

[1] Founded in 1920, the National Bureau of Economic Research is a private, nonprofit,
nonpartisan research organization dedicated to promoting a greater understanding of how
the economy works. The NBER is committed to undertaking and disseminating unbiased
economic research among public policymakers, business professionals, and the academic
community.

Road and Transportation Builders Association's Transportation Construction Employment Report shows that there were 242,300 workers directly employed by highway and bridge contractors in January 2009, *prior* to enactment of the ARRA. This does not include indirect and induced employment.

§ 39A.03   THE NEED FOR GREATER INVESTMENT

In addition to its job-creating impacts, transportation investment can also spur economic competitiveness. Industry advocates and many economists have long argued that the United States is paying a competitive price for its relative disinvestment in infrastructure, including transportation. Although there are differences of opinion over how to address the problem, there can be little debate that U.S. investments have not kept pace with needs. Over a third of all lane miles, some 61,000 miles, in the National Highway System are in fair or poor condition. According to USDOT statistics, one of every four bridges—more than 150,000—is structurally deficient or functionally obsolete. Over 32,000 public transit vehicles have exceeded their useful lives, and the largest public transit agencies face an $80 billion maintenance backlog to bring their rail systems to a state of good repair. Numerous studies and reports show that annual investment from all sources is far short of meeting needs, with significant near and long-term consequences that can range from safety problems to the inability to move goods to market.

Annual Disinvestment in U.S. Transportation
(Capital investments, federal and non-federal)[2]

Transportation Mode	Annual Investment Needs	Actual Annual Investments	Shortfall	Grade
Roads and Bridges	$930 billion	$380.5 billion	$549.5 billion	D
Transit	$265 billion	$74.9 billion	$190.1 billion	D
Aviation	$87 billion	$46.3 billion	$40.7 billion	D
Rail (passenger, freight)	$63 billion	$51.3 billion	$11.7 billion	D
Inland Waterways	$50 billion	$29.5 billion	$20.5 billion	D

U.S. investment in infrastructure not only is short of meeting needs, but is lagging the level of investment of other nations, raising concerns

---

[2] 2009 Report Card for America's Infrastructure. American Society of Civil Engineers.

about future competitiveness. The U.S. construction market remains the world's largest, at approximately $950 billion in 2007. However, the future outlook is questionable: the U.S. is not among the top ten construction markets in terms of growth rates.[3] Although the $800 billion ARRA was viewed by some critics as excessive, Moody's Economy.com calculates that, as a percentage of 2008 gross domestic product (GDP), the U.S. stimulus program was only about half of China, and significantly less than those of Russia, Japan, and Saudi Arabia. A recent report by the International Transport Forum showed the U.S. under-investing in transportation relative to major economic competitors. As a percentage of GDP, U.S. investment in transportation infrastructure between 1995 and 2007 was approximately three-quarters of the level in made in a group of Western European countries, and less than half that of Central European countries and the Russian Federation.

§ 39A.04   THE ECONOMIC RECOVERY AND REINVESTMENT ACT OF 2009

To help reverse the significant economic downturn that began with collapse of U.S. financial markets and spread throughout the American economy, President Barack Obama and the Congress collaborated on the ARRA. Development of the package began prior to President Obama's inauguration, and moved quickly, being signed into law on February 17, 2009, less than a month after the President's term began. As noted on the federal government website, www.recovery.gov, the goals of the ARRA are to:

• Save and create more than 3.5 million jobs over the next two years;

• Take a big step toward computerizing Americans' health records, reducing medical errors, and saving billions in health care costs;

• Revive the renewable energy industry and provide the capital over the next three years to eventually double domestic renewable energy capacity;

• Undertake the largest weatherization program in history by modernizing 75% of federal building space and more than one million homes;

• Increase college affordability for 7 million students by funding the shortfall in Pell Grants, increasing the maximum award level by $500, and providing a new higher education tax cut to nearly four million students;

---

[3] IHS Global Insight, April 2009.

- As part of the $150 billion investment in new infrastructure, enact the largest increase in funding of our nation's roads, bridges, and mass transit systems since the creation of the national highway system in the 1950s;

- Provide an $800 Making Work Pay tax credit for 129 million working households, and cut taxes for the families of millions of children through an expansion of the Child Tax Credit;

- Require unprecedented levels of transparency, oversight, and account-ability.

§ 39A.05   SIGNIFICANCE OF INCLUDING TRANSPORTATION IN ARRA

While the ARRA provides direct assistance to individuals through tax cuts and increased unemployment benefits, direct assistance to state and local governments, and interventions in particular sectors such as the development of electronic medical records, it also calls for a stepped up program of infrastructure investment. This represents an important shift in, or addition to, federal economic policy. In considerations of economic stimulus packages in prior years, transportation investment was often reduced or even eliminated, with prevailing policy downplaying the economic benefits. This negative bias was based on various factors, including: concerns about public agencies being able to deliver in a timely and effective basis; questions over the reported levels of need; questions over the capacity of the engineering and construction industry to respond; and, effective campaigns by opponents to classify transportation invest-ment as wasteful "pork barrel" spending.

The ARRA recognizes that investment in infrastructure can provide dual economic benefits: the short-term boost through job creation and preservation, and the longer-term benefit to growth and competitiveness brought about by improvements to transportation and energy systems, schools and other public buildings, and other similar investments.

Within the ARRA, infrastructure initiatives total upwards of $125 billion. The transportation investments—nearly $50 billion for transpor-tation projects over and above previously-approved spending—have been singled out as a prime means toward economic recovery and have drawn a great deal of public attention. While the primary focus of recovery has been on rapid job creation through activities that could be quickly mobilized—the so called "shovel-ready" projects—the longer term and secondary benefits of the program are very much worth noting. In addition to the benefits provided through direct investment in projects, the ARRA also is providing indirect benefits, acting as a stabilizing force for transportation agencies and the transportation market overall. Over the previous year, the combination of higher gas prices, reduced travel, and the economic slowdown led to significant declines in traditional revenues, forcing many state and local agencies to delay or cancel projects. The infusion of the ARRA funding, especially without the usual required non-federal match, is helping make the dip in programs shallower, and keeping high priority projects moving forward.

The infusion of new funding for a variety of transportation invest-ments is welcome. Starved for funding over many years, state and local capital programs are seeing the equivalent of an additional year of normal funding from the ARRA. Consistent with the primary focus on economic recovery, the ARRA emphasizes projects that have quick impacts, with many state and local agencies in a position to leverage new, 100% federal money that will quickly reduce the backlog of needed work to repave roads, fix intersections, order new buses, and the like.

§ 39A.06 DETAILS OF ARRA'S TRANSPORTATION COMPONENTS

The largest sum of money, $27.5 billion, is being distributed on a formula basis to state and local agencies using a current highway-based program as a framework. But within this category, steps were taken to assure a wide distribution of funds among both state and local govern-ments, and the funding recipients were given unprecedented flexibility to choose among potential uses—highways, bridges, transit, passenger rail, and even port and goods movement investments.

The transit allocation, totaling $8.3 billion, is going out largely on traditional formulas to transit agencies, but with a few discretionary opportunities, including the ability to accelerate already approved "new start" projects and to choose among local proposals for a special allocation of $100 million designated for transit investments that can best save energy and reduce greenhouse gases.

As with transit, the funding allocation to the airports program was flowed through the traditional Airport Improvement Program (AIP) channel, but with full discretion for the (Federal Aviation Administration) FAA to put the money to work in a way that meets national objectives for safety and capacity. In addition to the AIP funds, the recovery program also includes an allocation direct to FAA for upgrade of its aging physical infrastructure (e.g., air traffic control towers and centers) as well as money for NASA to speed up the development of a new generation of air traffic control technology—looking to the future when a growing economy will be generating record volumes of air travel.

At the President's urging, the program makes an important and unprecedented investment in intercity and high-speed rail. Clearly laying down a marker for a major policy shift, this forward looking element of the transportation program provides $9.3 billion in passenger rail invest-ment, with the largest share—$8 billion—going to stimulate intercity rail passenger service both through the development of new truly high speed corridors and through the upgrade of existing routes. Here is a place where the "reinvestment" part of the bill came to the fore—a conscious effort to put funds into the needs of the future beyond the needs of immediate job creation. The latter goal also will be met through an allocation of $1.3 billion to Amtrak's critical capital needs.

One of the smallest, but potentially most significant, programs allocated $1.5 billion to the Secretary of Transportation for discretionary investments across the board, going beyond the traditional modal "silos." The Secretary can allocate up to $200 million of this fund to leverage projects under the Transportation Infrastructure Finance and Innovation Act (TIFIA) program, which is an in-house equivalent of an infrastructure bank, leveraging funds to advance major complex projects. The balance of $1.3 billion can be used for a wide variety of projects unconstrained by traditional categorical restrictions but allocated on a competitive basis to projects that will have a significant impact on the Nation, a metropolitan area, or a region. A senior Department of Transportation official recently stated the Administration's intent to invest in so-called "last mile" projects that fill gaps and create intermodal connections. In past cases, such as the Alameda Corridor project at the Ports of Los Angeles and Long Beach, such flexible federal funds have proven to be the catalyst in unlocking substantial public and private contributions to projects that meet important needs.

§ 39A.07   TRACKING THE IMPACTS ON THE ECONOMY AND TRANSPORTATION CONSTRUCTION INDUSTRY

In a July 2, 2009 interview on National Public Radio's "All Things Considered," Mark Zandi, chief economist at Moody's Economy.com, noted that the U.S. has lost 6.5 million jobs since the onset of the recession in December 2007; but, that it would have been worse without the stimulus, with closer to 7 million jobs lost. "It's still bad . . . but better than the case without the stimulus," Zandi told NPR. Zandi believes that the stimulus package should start to show real results in the third and fourth quarters of this year. Increase in consumer spending—and confidence—should have a broader impact on the economy, including a reduction in job cuts. Zandi stated that, "I do think that by this time next year, the economy will be on much sounder ground."[4]

This timing is also coincidental with the heavy summer construction season for transportation. Under the ARRA's strict deadlines (meant in part to address the previous criticisms of transportation investment noted earlier), state departments of transportation and metropolitan transit agencies have moved quickly to get funds under contract. This should produce significant construction activity and jobs in the second half of the year.

---

[4] National Public Radio, "All Things Considered," July 2, 2009.

The ARRA contains significant and specific reporting requirements for transportation funding. These requirements apply both to the U.S. Department of Transportation, as administrator of the overall program, and to the recipients of funding. Much of this reporting, in terms of scope, frequency and content, are unprecedented, and are part of an overall focus on "transparency" in the ARRA. This is a new level of rigor and administrative burden that many agencies are only now facing up to, determining how to track the required information for reporting. It is a virtual certainty that such "transparency" reporting requirements will extend beyond the ARRA and will be built into long-term transportation programs.

Section 1201 of the ARRA requires USDOT to estimate the direct, indirect, and total (including induced) jobs created by the transportation projects funded under the ARRA. Recipients of funding must report job creation statistics to USDOT on May 18, 2009, August 17, 2009, February 17, 2010, February 17, 2011, and February 17, 2012. Separate from the statutory requirements, the Secretary of Transportation has indicated that the Department also plans to report on the number of jobs created every month. Following is a detailed description of the Department's reporting requirements and plans. Again, one significant aspect of this is the burden it will place on funding recipients, and how they will choose to meet their new federal requirements.

"Jobs will be reported in three categories: direct, indirect, and total employment. Direct jobs are those jobs represented by the number of people whose work is directly billed to the project. Indirect jobs represent employees working for producers of materials, equipment, and services that are used on the project, such as steel producers, producers of accounting services. Total employment will include direct, indirect and induced jobs, which are those jobs created when employees go out and spend their increased incomes on consumer goods and services.

"For the section 1201 reports, the Department has directed its grant recipients to report the number of direct job-hours (i.e., the number of people whose work is directly billed to DOT ARRA projects multiplied by the number of hours each person worked) generated by projects funded under the DOT ARRA programs from the enactment of the Act on February 17, 2009, to the reporting dates listed above. DOT staff will review those data for possible errors and make corrections after consultation with the grant recipients. DOT will then divide these job-hours by 173 (the average number of working hours in a month—40 hours per week times 52 weeks per year divided by 12 months per year) to estimate the total number of job-months worked since the enactment of the Act. Job-months can be divided by 12 to estimate job-years, but we believe that job-months are a more meaningful measure during the first months that the program is underway. We will therefore report job-months for the first two reports under section 1201, and begin reporting job-years for our report in February 2010.

"Indirect jobs will be estimated for our section 1201 reports using an input-output model that estimates the amount of input materials and services, and the number of jobs created in producing those materials and services, based on the level of expenditures. We will also use this input-output model to estimate direct employment in the production of vehicles, (e.g., buses, vans, and rail cars), which are an important part of the overall Recovery Act program for transit. Each section 1201 jobs report received from grant recipients will also include a report on federal expenditures on the project over the reporting period.

"Estimates of total employment will also be based on expenditure data, consistent with guidance from the Council of Economic Advisers (CEA). Total employment includes not only direct and indirect jobs, but also induced jobs. CEA estimates that total employment is increased by one job-year for every $92,000 in direct government spending. We will therefore take the expenditure data and divide by $92,000 to estimate the total job-years of employment created. To estimate job-months of total employment, we will divide expenditures by $7,667 (i.e., $92,000/12).

"For our monthly reports, we will generally use the same procedure, with each month's report showing the change in job-months since the last monthly report. The increase in job-months for the most recent month shows the average number of full-time employees at work over the past month. We will get monthly reports of direct job-hours and expenditures from all our grant recipients except for recipients of Federal Transit Authority (FTA) grants. So for the Federal Highway Administration, Federal Aviation Administration, Federal Railroad Administration, Maritime Administration, and the TIGER Discretionary Grants program administered by the Office of the Secretary of Transportation, we will use the same procedure to report monthly employment as we use to report employment for the periodic reports required by section 1201. For recipients of FTA grants, we will estimate monthly expenditures based on outlays from the U.S. Treasury for the previous month. We will then use those estimated expenditure levels in conjunction with the input-output model used to estimate indirect employment to estimate monthly direct employment for transit projects."[5]

§ 39A.08   EARLY PROGRESS IN DELIVERY OF BENEFITS

The future of the U.S. transportation program is in the hands of those involved in designing and executing the transportation recovery program. Public and legislative support for sustained increased funding will happen only if the capability and the willingness to get things done

---

[5] Estimates of Jobs Created by Department of Transportation Programs under the American Recovery and Reinvestment Act of 2009. www.dot.gov/recovery/docs/090609jobestimates.htm.

are clearly demonstrated throughout the implementation of the ARRA. Early returns bode well.

Funds from the Federal Highway Administration (FHWA), for example, were released on March 2, 2009. By June 29, 2009 (a deadline in ARRA), all 55 states and territories had met or exceeded the requirement to obligate half of their funds. As of the end of June, $19 billion had been obligated, funding over 5,300 projects; 2,000 of them are already underway. A recent McGraw-Hill economic forecast notes the effectiveness of this and similar measures in predicting that activity in the field of public works construction will be up more than 10% in 2009, while private and other construction (e.g., housing) is down as much as 20%. And, despite some inflationary concerns over "flooding the market" with the new funding, the overall state of the economy has led to strong competition. Construction bids for early recovery projects have come in well below engineers' estimates, suggesting that the program will exceed expectations both in terms of jobs created and legacy projects produced.

Other transportation agencies are expected to match the FHWA's record. The FAA has tentatively allocated all of its discretionary funding for airport improvements, and the Federal Transit Administration (FTA) is moving projects through its somewhat longer approval process, with $3.15 billion in grants awarded and another $4.18 billion in projects in the review pipeline as of mid-July.

§ 39A.09   IMPLICATIONS FOR FUTURE POLICIES AND PROGRAMS, AND COMMITMENTS TO TRANSPORTATION INVESTMENT

The inclusion of significant funding for transportation in the ARRA and the early signs of success provide reason for cautious optimism about greater longer-term focus on infrastructure. Three factors have come together simultaneously to create a more positive environment for a lasting policy shift:

Economic Crisis. The compelling need for economic stimulus, and consensus among policy makers on the value of transportation investments;

Climate Change. The growing recognition of the need to act on global climate change, and the realization that transportation needs to become part of the solution—meaning sound investments in ways that reduce congestion and produce reductions in greenhouse gases; and,

Political Change. The new Obama Administration and Congress demonstrated through the swift enactment of the ARRA that leadership is critical to changing long-standing policies toward transportation investment. Obama is the first president since Eisenhower to put such a heavy emphasis on transportation and his high speed rail program is unprecedented.

How successful will these factors be in affecting long-term, lasting changes? What might those changes be? Obviously, only time will tell, and it has only been a few months since enactment of the ARRA. However, the development and passage of the ARRA portend some interesting policy shifts and new directions—changes that will be debated, considered and perhaps enacted in upcoming legislative debates in the Congress. Below are some of the more notable areas for consideration.

High speed rail. The most notable element of ARRA transportation program, in terms of policy direction, is the inclusion of $8 billion for the development of high-speed rail corridors. The President coupled that $8 billion with the intent to request another $5 billion over five years for the program, along with potential changes in other programs to allow other transportation funds to be used toward high speed rail. There is probably no other mode of transportation where the U.S. has lagged other leading countries so dramatically. The world's first high speed rail line was opened between Tokyo and Osaka before the 1964 Olympics in Japan. Since then, Japan has continued to grow and improve its system, with *shinkansen*, or bullet trains, covering a network of 1,500 miles at speeds of 185 miles per hour. Systems have been developed and have been operating for decades in Italy, France, Spain, Germany, Belgium and the UK. Taiwan and China have recently built systems, with China's new lines introduced for the 2008 Olympics reaching speeds in excess of 200 mph. The US, in the meantime, has struggled to keep passenger rail systems afloat, and the closest thing to world-class high speed rail is a stretch of a few miles in the Northeast Corridor where Acela trains approach 150 mph, while averaging only 85 mph for their entire route. Citing economic and air quality benefits (one of the links to climate change noted earlier), Obama's program has identified ten corridors across the country as candidates for high speed rail. Furthest along is the California system, for which state voters approved a $10 billion bond program in November 2008.

Urban focus and control. Consistent with the Obama Administration's expected focus on urban areas, greater consideration and decision-making authority is given to metropolitan and cities. The U.S. Conference of Mayors has made it clear that greater authority and control for cities is going to be a major issue in the upcoming surface transportation authorization. While legislative debate will focus on which responsibilities and authorities should be shifted, local agencies will need to confront the realities of implementing their new powers—including the "transparency" reporting requirements.

Transparency—accountability and reporting. Being able to point to quantifiable benefits should reaffirm political and legislative support for ongoing increased investment. However, the hurdles of being able to collect, assess and report this information are major issues for agencies.

Issues of consistency, accuracy and timeliness are among the key areas of concern and legislative focus.

Expedited delivery. A significant, if not always vocalized, concern during the development of the ARRA was the question of whether state departments of transportation, metropolitan transit agencies, and other recipients could mobilize quickly enough to meet the very aggressive deadlines. Success could validate not only the stated needs in transportation, but also the economic value of investment. Failure would give credence to critics, and could doom prospects for sustained increased investment. It is likely that pressure to deliver the actual improvements—not just the up-front obligation of funds through contracts—will intensify, translating into regulatory and statutory changes.

Private participation. The USDOT under the Bush Administration placed high priority on greater private financing of transportation, through public-private partnerships and other means. Because the ARRA focused largely on construction-ready projects, rather than the early development of major projects, it is difficult to determine what direction the Obama Administration might take on this issue. However, the inclusion of funding for the TIFIA program, potentially as a step toward a larger national infrastructure bank concept, could signal interest in leveraging public money with private, especially for large, complex projects.

Climate change. The focus on energy efficiency, green buildings, and other means of helping reduce greenhouse gas emissions was a clear and strong policy statement in other parts of the ARRA. Working within the existing structure of transportation programs, the ARRA did provide direction toward and focus on funding projects that contributed positively to reduced emissions. It is a certainty that future legislative debate will focus on how to make transportation investments part of the climate change solution.

Financing. The question of how to fund increased investment in the future will be the single largest issue facing Congress and the Administration. The most significant change in the ARRA was that the $48 billion for transportation—almost all of which would normally come from dedicated trust funds and sources—was provided from the general fund. It is highly unlikely that the tradition of using dedicated sources, such as the gas tax, for transportation is going to be replaced wholesale with general funds, but the ARRA did suggest receptivity—based on general economic benefits, to be more expansive. One very important new financing tool was provided through ARRA: Build America Bonds, issued by states and municipalities at a taxable borrowing rate with a 35% federal reimbursement. This new tool was put to use quickly and has attracted important new sources of investment funds for transportation. In April, the New Jersey Turnpike Authority became the first to issue Build America Bonds, with $1.375 billion to support its $7 billion capital program. That was quickly followed by other transportation programs in

California—with the cash-strapped state issuing over $5.2 billion in Build America Bonds, and in New York City.

Earmarks. In significant contrast to recent transportation bills, the ARRA contained no Congressional earmarks. The choice of projects to be implemented rests with funding recipients, or will be the product of merit-based and competitive processes to allocate discretionary funds. With the growth in earmarks in previous transportation bills reaching epidemic status, the question of whether they should be allowed, or at least contained, may become a "line in the sand" issue in upcoming legislation.

Issues relating to policies and structure within transportation programs take on a greater significance in light of what the overall commitment to transportation will be. By providing the equivalent of well over a year's worth of funding, the ARRA has raised the bar, and expectations, for future investments. Discussions in the development and legislative consideration of the ARRA certainly suggested that this was not meant to be a one-time shot in the arm, but, rather, the first step in more serious commitment to investment. Ultimately, history will tell if this plays out. We see several positive and complementary signs that give some hope for a shift in U.S. policies toward greater transportation investment:

Link with economic recovery and development. There has been a notable shift in thinking among key economists and policy makers, with broad consensus that investments in transportation infrastructure are good for the economy. There have even been comments from Congressional leadership in recent days that a major long-term authorization of transportation programs could act, in effect, as a second stimulus package.

Level of investment in ARRA. Although some advocates called for more, the size of the transportation component in the ARRA was notable, in several respects. First, it was the single largest infusion of transportation funding in history. Second, during all of the debate in Congress, and the reduction in the overall size of ARRA, the transportation component was not the subject of debate, and was not targeted for reduction, suggesting broad bipartisan support.

Links with environmental goals. The pending emphasis on tackling climate change should have positive overall impact on transportation investment. Among key policy makers and advocates, there is a growing recognition that transportation needs to be seen as part of the solution, rather than just a major part of the problem. Investment in programs that reduce congestion, make public transportation more attractive, and promote cleaner technologies will be important elements of a comprehensive climate change program.

Forward-looking approach. As noted, the inclusion of the high speed rail funding signals a long-term and expanded federal commitment to transportation. This was intended as a major down payment on a new era of transportation development in the U.S. A recent bipartisan legislative proposal from the House Transportation and Infrastructure Committee shows interest in following through, with a proposed $50 billion high speed rail program, funded through a national infrastructure bank.

§ 39A.10   CONCLUSION

The first test for the transportation component of the American Recovery and Reinvestment Act will be how well it performs in supporting the turnaround of the American economy. Beyond that, its principles of targeted investment, transparency and accountability suggest that future transportation legislation can put into place a sustained, increased investment of federal funds to contribute to a sound, balanced transportation system that can be a foundation for future growth and prosperity.

CHAPTER **41**

CONTRACTING FOR INTERNATIONAL CONSTRUCTION WORKS

Carl E. Switzer
David K Ismay

§ 41.08 U.S. STATUTES PROHIBITING CERTAIN CONTRACTOR CONDUCT

[A] Liability Under the False Claims Act

Page 1685, add to end of subsection:

As originally reported in this chapter, a jury sitting in the Federal District Court for the Eastern District of Virginia in the case of *United States ex rel. DRC, Inc. v. Custer Battles, LLC* awarded damages against Custer Battles LLC to a number of relators seeking damages under the False Claims Act, 31 U.S.C.A. § 3729 et seq. Subsequently, the U.S. District Judge granted Custer Battles' motion for judgment as a matter of law, thus overturning the jury's verdict, on the ground that the evidence was insufficient to demonstrate that Custer Battles had "presented" fraudulent invoices to "an officer or employee of the United States Government or a member of the Armed Forces of the United States," as required by the False Claims Act. The U.S. Court of Appeals for the Fourth Circuit reversed the district court's limitation of damages and vacated the district court's judgment for Custer Battles.[28]

Among other things, the court of appeals held that the False Claims Act applied because the American employees working for the Coalition Provisional Authority were employees of the U.S. Government detailed to the CPA as part of their official duties, thus meeting the requirement of the False Claims Act that fraudulent invoices were presented to an employee of the U.S. Government. The court of appeals also overturned the district court's decision because U.S. funds were provided to the CPA, and that fact was a sufficient basis for a False Claims Act case. The plaintiffs were not required to prove that the defendant received U.S. funds.

---

[28] 562 F.3d 295 (4th Cir. 2009).

The importance of this decision is not limited to companies doing business with the CPA, which ceased to operate in 2004. Rather, the importance of this case is that contractors doing business with international or multinational governmental organizations, where U.S. Government employees have been seconded to the organization as part of their official duties, and where the U.S. Government has provided some funds to that organization, may be liable under the False Claims Act for any fraudulent conduct committed by the contractor in the performance of that contract.

CHAPTER 42

THE FOREIGN CORRUPT PRACTICES ACT AND MULTINATIONAL ANTI-BRIBERY INITIATIVES

Geoffrey T. Keating
Dennis Ehlers

§ 42.02 THE U.S. ANTI-FOREIGN CORRUPTION STATUTE: THE FCPA

[E] The FCPA Opinion Release Request Procedure

Page 1714, replace last paragraph of subsection with:

Although these release procedures are not used often, many companies have requested Opinions since the procedure was created. Twenty-two Opinions were issued from 1993 through 2006 by the DOJ under these established procedures. The Opinions themselves are not released, but "Opinion Releases," which describe the Opinion without naming the requestor are issued for every Opinion and are on the Department's website at www.usdoj.gov/criminal/fraud/fcpa.html. Recipients of a favorable opinion are entitled to a presumption of compliance in any subsequent enforcement action under the FCPA. Examples of such releases are seen in the several 2001 and 2002 matters on which the Department issued Opinions as follows:

• In Opinion Release 01-01, the DOJ opined that a U.S. company could form a joint venture with a French company to which each company contributed existing contracts where certain precautions, including termination of existing agency contracts and the institution of a rigorous compliance program, had been taken to ensure that neither company nor the joint venture made any payments to foreign agents that could have been in furtherance of any preexisting agreement to pay a bribe. The Opinion was expressly conditioned on the Department of Justice's understanding that the French company had represented that none of the contracts it was contributing to the joint venture had been obtained by payments that would have been in violation of either the new French foreign anti-bribery law, or any applicable foreign or domestic anti-bribery law.

- In Opinion Release 01-02, the DOJ opined that a U.S. company could retain as a consultant a company owned by a foreign official, provided that the official was not responsible for awarding any business to the company and undertook to recuse himself/herself from any discussion or decision in which such award of business was contemplated.

- In Opinion Release 01-03, the DOJ opined that a U.S. company could proceed with a transaction after investigating an employee's report that a dealer had made statements that the employee had understood to mean that payments to a public official had been or would be made. The company's investigation uncovered no evidence to corroborate this statement, the dealer had affirmatively represented that no payments had been or would be made and had repeated the same in a statement directed to the DOJ. Moreover, the proposed agreement with the dealer gave the U.S. company the right to audit the dealer and to terminate the agreement if it determined that an illegal payment had been made.

In none of the Opinions contained in the FCPA releases, have the DOJ and the Securities and Exchange Commission (SEC) pursued enforcement actions. Some suggest that this is because all of the requests made to the DOJ are easily identified as not involving bribery or other violations, inasmuch as companies would be reluctant to seek review of a transaction that might involve illegal payments. Note that requests for advisory Opinions must be made before taking action, not afterward.

[F] Enforcement Actions

Page 1714, replace first paragraph with:

Since the enactment of the Foreign Corrupt Practices Act in 1977, relatively few companies have been prosecuted for violations of the Act's requirements. In fact, in the 30 years since its passage, the U.S. Department of Justice brought approximately 35 criminal prosecutions and seven civil enforcement actions under the anti-bribery provisions of the FCPA. A summary of the most recent cases brought under the Act can be found at www.usdoj.gov/criminal/fraud/fcpa. The SEC has separate authority to bring charges under the FCPA and does so frequently when it determines that a company's actions relate to the accounting and financial records provisions of the Act.

Page 1714, add after second full paragraph:

The Sarbanes-Oxley Act of 2002 has clear implications for the FCPA even though it was aimed at U.S. domestic corporate operations.

For example, certification of the accuracy of a company's financial statements, by CEOs and CFOs and the added requirements for internal control procedures may identify FCPA violations relating to financial disclosure.

A company's voluntary disclosure of FCPA violations to the DOJ and the SEC can lead to avoidance of prosecution and reduced financial penalties in much the same way as in U.S. government contract fraud enforcement. This is so, even though the FCPA does not require voluntary disclosure. The SEC issued a report known as the "Seaboard Report," dated October 23, 2001. It describes various factors that may mitigate the initiation or outcome of enforcement actions, including voluntary disclosure. The DOJ issued its own report on January 20, 2003 setting forth factors which the DOJ may consider when deciding if it will prosecute a company for violating federal laws. This report is the "Principles of Federal Prosecution of Business Organizations," also known as the "Thompson Memorandum."

Note, as well, that FCPA violations may be significant factors in mergers and acquisitions of and among U.S. companies as will be seen in two recent cases enumerated herein.

Of the cases prosecuted, more have been brought for violations of the Act's accounting provisions than for violations of the anti-bribery provisions. Some recent cases enforcing the FCPA are discussed below to offer insight into the complexity and consequences of violations.

§ 42.03   BEYOND THE FCPA: MULTILATERAL ANTI-CORRUPTION INITIATIVES

[A]   The OECD Convention on Combating Bribery

Page 1729, add at end of subsection:

As reported in the "Sixth Annual Report on Enforcement and Monitoring of the OECD Convention," all 35 signatories ratified the Anti-bribery Convention and each party had adopted implementing regulation that is currently in force. (*See* U.S. Dept. of State, Bur. of Economic. and Bus. Affairs report, "Battling International Bribery," 2004.)

[B]   U.N. Convention Against Corruption

Page 1729, add before first paragraph:

The United Nation's Convention Against Corruption (UNCAC), entered into force on December 14, 2005 reflecting a global consensus that the international legal system must focus on fighting corruption. The

United States Senate approved the U.N. Convention Against Corruption in September 2006. The Convention includes provisions relating to the prevention and criminalization of corruption and the facilitation of asset recovery. As of spring 2006, 140 countries have signed the Convention. 55 countries, including China and Russia have ratified it. The U.N. Convention's represents universal prohibition against transnational bribery as it applies to countries which are not a party to the OECD Convention. The UNCAC goes beyond bribery of public officials. Private sector bribery is covered, as well as, money laundering, corporate record keeping, and law enforcement cooperation, including extradition and obstruction of justice. Thus it is more in line with the FCPA than the OECD Convention. It is believed that the U.N. Convention will reduce the competitive disadvantage suffered by U.S. companies which have been subject to the FCPA, while many of their overseas counterparts have not been so restrained. As with the OECD Convention, the UNCAC is not self-executing. Each signatory to the UNCAC must adopt its own legislation to implement the UNCAC's requirements.

The text of the UN Convention may be found at http://www .unodc.org/pdf/crime/convention/corruption/signing/Convention-e.pdf.

[C] The World Bank Policy Guidelines

Page 1731, add to end of subsection:

The World Bank now has introduced its Voluntary Disclosure Program to enhance its fight against corruption in Bank funded and supported contracts and projects. Among other factors, the Bank's Voluntary Disclosure Program seeks to incentivize companies to disclose the results of internal investigations into past or existing fraudulent or collusive, coercive or other corrupt acts in Bank financed and supported contracts and last to implement their own strong internal compliance programs with monitoring by Bank-approved individuals. Through its Voluntary Disclosure Program, the Bank expects to reduce companies' future misconduct and constantly limit company debarments for disclosed past misconduct so as to be able to continue to participate in bidding for Bank-supported projects, in return for full cooperation. *See* www.WorldBank.org.

Page 1734, add new subsections after [F]:

[G] Other International Anti-Corruption Initiatives

Although the FCPA and the multinational initiatives discussed above are the primary methods used to combat international corruption, many countries have used other non-legislative methods for combating corrupt business practices. As a result, the consequences of obtaining international contracts through corrupt methods may far outweigh any benefits that may result from the contract award.

[1] Executive Order 13116

On March 31, 1999, President William J. Clinton signed Executive Order 13116, "to ensure that the trade policies of the United States advance, to the greatest extent possible, the export of the products and services of the United States and that trade policy resources are used efficiently." Exec. Order No. 13,116, 64 Fed. Reg. 16,333 (1999). As part of this Order, the President required the United States Trade Representative (USTR) to submit to Congress by April 30 of each year, a report identifying foreign countries that have failed to apply transparent and competitive procedures or to maintain and enforce effective prohibitions on bribery and other corrupt practices in connection with government procurement. The USTR then is required to investigate discriminatory procurement practices and to initiate formal dispute settlement proceedings under the WTO Agreement on Government Procurement or the North American Free Trade Agreement.

[2] Jakarta, Indonesia

In February 1994, the Indonesian state electric company, PT Perusahaan Listrik Negara (PLN), entered into a power purchase contract for the Paiton I power plant in East Java. *P. T. Perusahaan Listrik Negara v. P. T. Paiton Energy,* Civil Case: 517/PDTG/1999/PN.JKT.PST (D. Central Jakarta, 1999). PLN later sued Paiton to nullify the contract, alleging that the agreement was made at a time when the former President Suharto controlled the State, and thus also controlled PLN. PLN then alleged corruption in the award of the State contract to construct an electric power plant. The plaintiff also alleged that the defendant excessively marked up the costs of the project. As such, the plaintiff further alleged that the agreement was "full of elements of corruption, collusion and nepotism."

The plaintiffs brought suit in the hopes that Paiton would be forced to change its contractual terms, including reducing its power price, over the period of the contract. *Id.* The court provisionally granted PLN's request and enjoined enforcement of portions of the contract, finding that the contract was in contradiction with the Law of Morality and Public Order. The case later was settled.

[3] Lesotho Highland Water Project

In 1987, work began in the Lesotho Highlands to dam Lesotho's abundant water resources and tunnel them north to the industrial heart-land around Johannesburg, South Africa. Victor Mallet, *World News: Western Contractors Face Bribery Charge over Lesotho Dam,* Financial Times, Nov. 19, 1999, at 14. In November 1999, Lesotho prosecutors charged several European, Canadian, and South African contractors working on the project with paying bribes, either directly or through intermediaries, to the Lesotho Highlands Development Authority. Representatives of the World Bank and European Union assured Lesotho officials that they would help to "bankroll" the anticipated lengthy and costly court case to show its commitment to fighting corruption.

[H] U.S. Implementing Legislation

The United States implementing legislation, amending the Foreign Corrupt Practices Act took effect on November 10, 1998. The ratification instrument was deposited with the OECD Secretary-General on December 8, 1998. The United States also has ratified the Inter-American Convention Against Corruption and signed the Council of Europe Criminal Law Convention Against Corruption.

Since the enactment of this 1998 legislation, the United States has taken the following steps to implement the Convention:

• The Civil Asset Forfeiture Reform Act (CAFRA) made it possible to seek civil and criminal forfeiture of the proceeds of foreign bribery.

• The President signed Executive Order 13259 on March 19, 2002, designating the European Union's organizations and Europol as public international organizations, making bribery of officials from these organizations a violation of the FCPA.

• The U.S. Sentencing Commission has promulgated amendments, effective November 2002, making violations of the FCPA and violations of the domestic bribery law subject to the same sentencing guidelines.

CHAPTER 43

INTERNATIONAL DISPUTE RESOLUTION

Andrew Ness
Ronan McHugh
Laura Thomson

---

§ 43.02   THE NEW INTERNATIONAL CONSTRUCTION DISPUTE RESOLUTION MATRIX

[A]   It's Not Just Arbitration Versus Litigation Any More

Page 1749, add to end of subsection:

The interconnectivity now existing between arbitration and litigation and the impact one can have on the other was indicated in the decision of the Grand Chamber of the European Court of Justice (ECJ) in *Allianz SpA and Generali Assicurazioni Generali SpA v. West Tankers, Inc.*, Case C-185/07, 2009 WL 303723 (Feb. 10, 2009). The ECJ ruled that anti-suit injunctions issued by courts of one Member State to restrain proceedings in courts of another Member State on the ground that such proceedings are in breach of an arbitration agreement are incompatible with Council Regulation No. 44/2001 On Jurisdiction and the Recognition and Enforcement of Judgments in Civil and Commercial Matters, (OJ 2001 L 12) (which regulates the interaction between courts in the European Union) ("the Regulation").

Under the Regulation, "a court second seised in an civil or commercial matter must of 'its own motion stay its proceedings until such times as the jurisdiction of the court first seised is established," and "where the jurisdiction of the court first seised is established, any [other] court . . . shall decline jurisdiction." *Id.* at Article 27 quoted in Spencer Wolff, *Tanking Arbitration or Breaking the System to Fix It? A Sink or Swim Approach to Unifying European Judicial Systems: The ECJ in Gasser, Turner, and West Tankers,* 15 Columbia Journal of European Law

---

* Mr. Ness is a Partner in Howrey LLP's Global Litigation—Construction practice based in Washington, D.C. Mr. McHugh is Counsel at Pillsbury Winthrop Shaw Pittman, LLP in Washington, D.C. They both practice international and domestic construction dispute resolution. Ms. Thomson is an associate in Howrey's Washington, D.C. Global Litigation—Construction practice. Full biographical details are available at www.howrey.com and www.pillsburylaw.com respectively.

65, 66 and n.8, *available at* http://www.cjel.net/online/15_2-wolff-2/, discussing the use of the Regulation by potential defendants in commercial litigation to "torpedo" lawsuits for years by pre-emptively seising in courts "infamous for their overloaded dockets and lethargic deliberations." The ECJ had previously ruled that anti-suit injunctions violated the doctrine of "mutual trust" and were incompatible with the Regulation. *See Erich Gasser GmbH v. MISAT Srl*, Case C-116/02, 2003 E.C.R. I-14693 (anti-suit injunction issued by Austria court to enjoin proceedings in an Italian court begun by a defendant in debt collection dispute where contract at issue conferred jurisdiction in Austria) and *Gregory Paul Turner v. Felix Fareed Ismail Grovit, Harada Ltd.,* Case C-159/02, 2004 E.C.R. I-3565 (anti-suit injunction issued by English court to restrain Spanish proceedings commenced "in bad faith.") Arbitration, however, is expressly excluded from the scope of the Regulation. *West Tankers*, at ¶ 5 citing Article 1(2)(d).

This case began in August 2000 when a vessel, the Front Comor, owned by West Tankers and chartered by Erg Petroli SpA ("Erg") collided with a jetty in the port of Syrascuse, Italy. Erg sought coverage from its insurers and commenced arbitration proceedings in London against West Tankers for its uncovered losses, as mandated by the charter party between Erg and West Tankers. Erg's insurers, Allianz and Generali, compensated Erg and then filed an action against West Tankers in the Tribunale di Siracusa based on the insurers' statutory right of subrogation under the Italian Civil Code. The Tribunale based its jurisdiction on Article 5(3) of the Regulation which provides that "A person domiciled in a Member State may, in another Member State be sued . . . in matters relating to tort, delict or quasi-delict, in the courts for the place where the harmful event occurred or may occur." West Tankers objected to the Tribunale's jurisdiction on the basis of the arbitration agreement. In parallel, West Tankers brought proceedings in the High Court in England, seeking a declaration that Allianz and Generali must pursue any claims against West Tanker in arbitration and seeking to enjoin the action before the Tribunale. The English court granted the anti-suit injunction and the insurers appealed to the House of Lords. The House of Lords referred the matter to the ECJ, acknowledging the principle of mutual trust set out in *Gasser* and *Turner*, and submitting that the doctrine does not extend to arbitration. The ECJ agreed that arbitration proceedings do not fall within the scope of the Regulation; however, whether a court has jurisdiction over a particular proceeding does fall within the scope of the Regulation and is a matter for that court to decide. Allowing a court from another Member State to prevent the forum court from deciding its own jurisdiction "runs counter to the trust which the Member States accord to one another's legal systems and judicial institutions and on which the system of jurisdiction under [the Regulation] is based." *Id.* at ¶ 30. This decision, therefore, raises the question of whether courts will grant anti-suit injunctions in the face of arbitration provisions, a matter which is potentially important to ensuring arbitration agreements are recognized and enforced and to avoiding multiple proceedings (both arbitral and court) in multiple jurisdictions.

§ 43.06   THE STRUCTURE OF THE PROJECT

[A]   Investor/State Projects

Page 1765, add to note 69.

A number of recent ICSID cases have further confirmed that construction projects are "investments" for the purposes of bilateral and multilateral investment treaties. *See, e.g., Toto Construzioni Generali S.P.A. v. The Republic of Lebanon*, ICSID Case ARB/07/12, Sep. 11, 2009, *available at* http://icsid.worldbank.org/ICSID/FrontServlet ("Toto"); *Pantechniki S.A. Contractors & Engineers v. Republic of Albania*, ICSID Case ARB/07/21, Jul. 30, 2009, *available at* http:// icsid.worldbank.org/ICSID/FrontServlet ("Pantechniki") and *Bayindir Insaat Turizm Ticaret ve Sanayi A.S. v. Islamic Republic of Pakistan*, ICSID Case ARB/03/29 ("Bayindir"), *available at* http://ita.law.uvic.ca/ documents/Bayindiraward.pdf. More importantly perhaps, however, as seen in these cases and others, there appears to be a recent trend in ICSID arbitration to reject contractor claims on the ground that the claim was a contract claim rather than a treaty claim. *See Bayindir v. Pakistan and the Decline and Fall of Investment Treaty Claims on International Construction Projects*, Akin Alcitepe and Ronan McHugh, 6 Ankara L. Rev. __ (2009) (forthcoming). As such, construction contractor investors need to seriously consider whether the pursuit of an investor-state claim is the best forum strategically in which to proceed.

For instance, the *Bayindir* case rejected the contractor's claim for USD $496.6 million, arising out of Bayindir's termination on a road building construction project against the Government of Pakistan. The Tribunal held that Bayindir had not produced sufficient evidence to show that Pakistan's National Highway Authority did not terminate and expel Bayindir for any reason other than a good faith belief that Bayindir did not adequately perform under the Contract. The Tribunal concluded that these were contract issues and not Treaty violations. A similar result occurred in the *Toto* case, albeit a decision on jurisdiction.

Toto, an Italian construction company, executed a contract with the Lebanese Republic-Conseil Executif des Grands Projets for the construction of the "Hadath Highway-Syrian Border Saoufar-Mdeirej Section" portion of the Arab Highway linking, inter alia, Beirut and Damascus. Contract completion was originally intended for October 24, 1999 with a following 12-month maintenance period until October 24, 2000. Actual completion occurred in December 2003, with the maintenance period ending in December 2004. Toto brought a number of investment treaty claims arising out of the delays and additional costs on the project. Though acknowledging that construction was an investment, the Tribunal rejected a large number of Toto's claims on the basis that they were contract claims. For example, Toto's claims for costs due to misleading information and design errors and changes were excluded from jurisdiction, because the Tribunal considered those "relate to the standard duties in a construction contract." Toto's claims of USD $15 Million for the additional costs incurred by Toto to perform the project were also rejected. The Tribunal noted that indirect expropriation involves, "government measures needed to 'effectively neutralize' the enjoyment of property." There must be a "radical deprivation." Toto failed to offer prima facie evidence for its assertion that it incurred increased costs of 37% of the project's initial value and Lebanon's failure to pay such was rejected as not being a treaty claim, but a contract claim.

Perhaps the more lucid example of a bad strategic choice between proceeding under the contract's dispute mechanism or choosing BIT arbitration is the *Pantechniki* case, where, again, the ICSID Tribunal rejected a claim, albeit one which prima face had been accepted in large part by the owner.

Pantechniki involved a road and bridge project in Albania. Pantechniki, a Greek contractor, entered into two contracts which were on FIDIC equivalent forms. The contracts contained an arbitration clause regarding disputes. The contracts also contained a provision that placed risk of loss due to civil disturbances on Albania's General Road Directorate. In 1997 there was severe civil unrest in Albania. Work was interrupted at site by several days of rioting and Pantechniki had to abandon site. Pantechniki claimed $4,893,623.93 in compensation. The Resident Engineer evaluated Claimant's damages at $3,123,199. A Special Commission created by the Albanian General Road Directorate further evaluated Claimant's loss at $1,821,796. The Albanian Ministry of Public Works informed the Albanian Minister of Finance of the evaluation, so that this sum could be paid to Pantechniki, which accepted it, but the Finance Ministry did not have funds to pay. The Minister of Finance stated it was not its obligation to make payment and that payment could only be made from a special fund of the Ministers' Council. Rather than invoking arbitration under the contract, Pantechniki sued in Albanian Court, allegedly after having been informed that payment would be made if there was an enforceable court judgment requiring the government to pay. The Albanian Court, however, dismissed the case on the basis that the risk of loss provision in the contract created liability without fault. Pantechniki decided not to pursue the claim to the Albanian Supreme Court and filed for ICSID arbitration.

The ICSID Tribunal ruled against Pantechniki. It did so, even though the Tribunal noted:

> The Claimant suffered losses which it appeared contractually entitled to recover. The Government negotiated a reduced amount. It then

refused to pay on grounds that are difficult to understand. Subsequently, Albanian courts denied the very validity of the underlying contract on equally obscure grounds. The claim does not fail for lack of inherent validity. It rather falters because the Treaty is unavailable to the Claimant in the circumstances.

Pantechniki, para 104.

These three cases highlight the care needed when giving up contract dispute remedies in favor of pursuing investor/state redress on construction projects.

§ 43.07   ENSURING AN EFFECTIVE ARBITRATION AGREEMENT

[B]   Scope of Arbitration

Page 1775, add after carryover paragraph:

In *Stolt-Nielsen S.A. v. AnimalFeeds Int'l Corp.*, No. 08-1198, 2010 U.S. LEXIS 3672 (Apr. 27, 2010), the U.S. Supreme Court again addressed the grounds for vacatur under the FAA, albeit obliquely, in a case principally addressing whether class arbitration could be imposed under an agreement silent on the issue. In doing so, the Court set down a prominent marker, however, regarding the effect of the parties' arbitration agreement's silence on an issue concerning the scope of the arbitration agreement and courts, not arbitrators', powers to decide such issues.

In a 5:3 decision (Justice Sotomayor taking no part), the court held that a party could not be compelled under the FAA to submit to class arbitration absent a contractual basis, and where the parties had stipulated that their arbitration agreement was silent on this issue—silent in this case meaning "there's been no agreement that has been reached on that issue"—there was no contractual basis. *Id.* at *46. Nor may an arbitrator infer that an agreement authorizes class-action solely on the basis that the parties' agreed to arbitrate their disputes. *Id.* at *42. According to the majority, the "differences between bilateral and class arbitration [are] too great to allow the arbitrators to presume that the parties' silence on the issue of class arbitration constituted consent." *Id.*

Stolt-Nielsen concerned antitrust claims brought by a class of customers for being allegedly charged supracompetitve prices over a period of several years by shipping companies that serve a large share of the world market for parcel tankers. The contracts at issue (Vegoilvoy charter parties—a particular form of a standard maritime contract) contained an arbitration clause which provided in part that "[A]ny dispute arising from the making, performance or termination of this Charter Party shall be settled in New York, Owner and Charterer each appointing an arbitrator, who shall be a merchant, broker or individual experience in the shipping business." *Id.* at *10. Following precedent from the US Court of Appeals for the Second Circuit, the parties submitted the question of whether the agreement provided for class arbitration to an AAA arbitration panel, which panel, in turn, concluded that it did having been largely persuaded by arbitral decisions decided after *Green Tree Financial Corp. v. Bazzle*, 539 U.S. 444 (2003) (a plurality opinion vacating and remanding a South Carolina State Supreme Court decision affirming an arbitration award in order to allow the arbitrators to decide whether an arbitration agreement was silent on the issue of class arbitration).

On the shipping companies' petition, the District Court for the Southern District of New York vacated the arbitration award concluding that the arbitrators "manifest disregard[ed]" the law by failing to conduct a choice of law analysis which would have led them to apply federal maritime law to interpret the agreement. *Id.* at *14-15. The Second Circuit reversed, holding that the "manifest disregard" standard survived the Supreme Court's *Hall Street Associates* decision "as a "judicial gloss" on the enumerated grounds for vacatur under the FAA, and that the arbitrators had not manifestly disregarded either federal maritime law or New York as neither of which precluded class arbitration." *Id.* at *15. Notably, the Supreme Court declined to decide whether "manifest disregard" survives *Hall Street*, but nonetheless found the standard satisfied (as characterized by the petitioner/customers, the standard "require[s] a showing that the arbitrators 'knew of the relevant legal principle, appreciated that this principle controlled the outcome of the disputed issue, and nonetheless willfully flouted the governing law by refusing to apply it') *Id.* at *19 n.3.

The majority reasoned that there was no room for an inquiry as to the parties' intent because the parties agreed that their agreement was "silent" (i.e., that they had not reached any agreement on the issue of class arbitration) *See id.* at * 27. The arbitrators' proper task was to identify what rule of law governs that situation and whether a default rule would allow class arbitration in the absence of express consent. *Id.* at *20. Instead, the court ruled, the panel "proceeded as if it had the authority of a common-law court to develop what it viewed as the best rule to be applied in such a situation," "impose[d] its own view of sound policy regarding class arbitration" and in doing so exceeded its powers. *Id.* at *22, 23. The court further determined that because there was only one proper outcome, derived from the FAA, there was no need to direct a rehearing by the arbitrators. *See id.* at *28.

Significantly, the dissent would have not reached the merits as it determined that the matter was not ripe, being an appeal of a partial final award. *Id.* at *47-55. Even if ripe, the dissent would have upheld the reversal because the sole ground raised by the shipping companies for vacatur was that the arbitrators had exceeded their powers under § 10(a)(4). *Id.* at * 57 According to the dissent, the question under this provision is "whether the arbitrators had the power, based on the parties' submissions or the arbitration agreement, to reach a certain issue, not whether the arbitrators correctly decided that issue." *Id.* (quoting *DiRussa v. Dean Witter Reynolds Inc.*, 121 F.3d 818, 824 (2d Cir. 1997); *Comprehensive Accounting Corp. v. Rudell*, 760 F.2d 138, 140 (7th Cir. 1985)). Because the parties expressly agreed to the issue decided by the panel, the dissent would have ruled that the parties empowered the panel to act as it did. *Id.*

The Supreme Court further considered the scope of an arbitration clause, and the doctrine of severability, in *Rent-A-Center West, Inc. v. Jackson*, 130 S. Ct. 1133 (2010). The case involved an employment discrimination suit by Jackson against his former employer. Rent-A-Center sought arbitration pursuant to the parties' arbitration agreement. Jackson opposed arbitration on the ground that the arbitration agreement was unenforceable as unconscionable under Nevada law. The issue in the case was who decided this question. The arbitration provision provided that the arbitrator had "exclusive authority to resolve any dispute relating the [arbitration agreement's] enforceability . . . including . . . any claim that all or any part of the [arbitration agreement] is void or voidable."

The Court held that there are two instances of validity challenges under Section 2 of the FAA: (1) where the agreement to arbitrate is challenged and (2) where the contract as a whole is challenged. But of these only the first is relevant to a Court's determination of an arbitration agreement's enforceability. The Court held that if the contract as a whole is being challenged, it must enforce the delegation provisions under the agreed upon arbitration clause unless the clause itself is unenforceable. As such, it held that the scope of the arbitration clause required the issue of unconscionability to be resolved by the arbitrators.

[C] Avoiding the Pathological Clause

Page 1776, add to end of subsection:

Not all hybrid clauses providing for the arbitration in accordance with more than one institution are considered unworkable. In a landmark decision in June 2009, the Singapore Court of Appeal, in a case of first impression, upheld a hybrid clause which provided for one arbitral institution to administer an arbitration under the rules of another under the principle of party autonomy. In *Insigma Technology Co. Ltd v. Alstom Technology Ltd*, SGCA 24 (June 2, 2009), the parties' arbitration agreement provided that

> Any and all such disputes shall be finally resolved by arbitration before the Singapore International Arbitration Centre in accordance with the Rules of Arbitration of the International Chamber of Commerce then in effect and the proceedings shall take place in Singapore . . .

Id., ¶ 4.

When a dispute over royalties could not be resolved by the parties, Alstom filed a request for arbitration with the ICC in August 2006, requested that the proceedings be conducted in Singapore at SIAC's premises. Insigma answered, disputing the ICC's jurisdiction and contending that the parties had agreed to submit the dispute to SIAC and to have SIAC administer the arbitration under the ICC's Rules. In response to a written request by Alstom, SIAC confirmed that it would accept jurisdiction and indicated that "the arbitration will be administered under the SIAC Rules with the ICC Rules to be applied as a guide to the essential features the parties would like to see in the conduct of arbitration, e.g., use of the Terms of Reference procedures, the scrutiny of awards. Accordingly, the SIAC is prepared and intends to undertake the Terms of Reference Procedure and scrutiny of awards as contemplated under the ICC Rules." *Id.* at ¶ 9. Alstom then commenced arbitration at the SIAC and withdrew the ICC arbitration. Insigma objected to the SIAC-administered arbitration, ultimately arguing that the clause was pathological and fatally defective.

Each party had by that time nominated one arbitrator and agreed that these two arbitrators would nominate a third to preside at the hearing, which tribunal was later confirmed by the SIAC. *See id.* at ¶¶ 8, 17. Once constituted, the Tribunal held a preliminary hearing on jurisdiction in September 2007 at which time Insigma argued that the clause was void for uncertainty and that the Tribunal had not been validly constituted. The Tribunal then wrote to the SIAC to ask if it "would be prepared to administer the arbitration in accordance with the ICC Rules to the exclusion of the SIAC Rules" and if so to confirm which bodies within the SIAC would perform certain key functions under the ICC Rules. *Id.* at ¶ 18. SIAC confirmed that it would so administer the arbitration and indicated that the SIAC Secretariat would undertake the role of the ICC Secretariat, the SIAC Registrar that of the ICC Secretary-General, and the SIAC Board of Directors that of the ICC Court. *Id.* at 19. The Tribunal rendered its decision on these preliminary matters in December 2007, determining that the agreement was valid, enforceable and capable of being performed and that the tribunal had been properly constituted under either the ICC or SIAC Rules. Insigma appealed to the Singapore High Court to set aside the Tribunal's decision. The High Court upheld the decision as did the Singapore Court of Appeal. The court of appeal also awarded Alstom its costs in large part for Insigma's conduct in first objecting to ICC's jurisdiction because the parties agreed that SIAC would administer the arbitration, and then later arguing that the clause was void for uncertainty and unworkable. *Id.* at ¶ 29, 44.

The court of appeal set forth a number of general principles in its decision: 1.) an arbitration agreement is construed like any other commercial agreement; and, 2.) where parties clearly and undisputedly intended to resolve their disputes by arbitration, the court should give all reasonable effort to give effect to that intention (further recognizing that arbitration agreements are not to be interpreted strictly and should be interpreted in an manner that prevents the clause from being rendered ineffective or useless).

The Court rejected Insigma's argument that the clause was pathological, first reporting that a defective clause is not void *ab initio*, and concluding in this case that the clause was rendered workable and certain by the SIAC agreeing to administer the arbitration. Insigma, the Court explained, "could not convince the court where the uncertainty lay or why the agreement could not or did not work." *Id.* at ¶ 35. On this point, the Court quoted from the High Court's decision explaining,

> The arrangement provided for in [the Arbitration Agreement] would be unworkable if the SIAC was unable to provide similarly equipped actors to fulfill the roles that the ICC Rules gave to the institutional bodies of the ICC. However, while it might not be advisable to use the ICC Rules for most *ad hoc* arbitrations because of the need for an administering body, if the *ad hoc* arbitration nominates a substitute institution to administer the arbitration and such substitute can arrange organs to carry out similar functions to those carried out by the different parts of the ICC apparatus, there should be no practical problem, as well as no objection in principle, to providing for such a hybrid *ad hoc* arbitration administer by one institution but governed by the rules (as adapted where necessary) of another. This freedom is inherent in the flexible nature of arbitration, especially *ad hoc* arbitration. In any case, inefficiency alone cannot render a clause invalid so long as the parties had agreed and intended for the arbitration to be conducted in this manner.

Id.

Ultimately, the court concluded that "[t]he choice of a hybrid form of arbitration is a matter of agreement between the parties and is wholly consistent with [Singapore law as well as UNCITAL Model Law on International Commercial Arbitration]." *Id*. at ¶ 43.

It remains to be seen if parties will seek to increasingly adopt hybrid institutional administration/applicable rules clauses and how courts and arbitral institutions will deal with such clauses. On this latter, the traditional institutional model that each cannot administer another's has become frayed by increased competition between institutions in recent years. In the U.S., for example, JAMS will administer AAA rules arbitrations. The decision in the *Insigma* case was assisted in large measure by the fact that SAIC modeled its 2007 rules on the ICC Rules, with a deliberate view to positioning itself as being able to provide such similar arbitral services. This development may allow parties to "cherry pick" rules and administrative institutions that provide them with the most efficient arbitration process from a cost and time and enforceability perspective.

[F]   Discovery Provisions: Providing for the IBA Rules on the Taking of Evidence

Page 1781, add at end of current section:

On May 29, 2010, the IBA adopted revised Rules on the Taking of Evidence in International Arbitration. The new Rules can be found on the IBA website: *www.ibanet.org.*[103.1]

Among the key updates is a new Article 2 that allows consultation between parties and the tribunal on "evidentiary issues." Consideration of the "scope, timing and manner" of the taking of evidence is encouraged from the parties at an early stage. Also, the tribunal is encouraged to identify relevant issues for which a preliminary determination may be appropriate. The new Rules also recognize that "expansive 'document discovery' is generally inappropriate in international arbitration." Article 3 deals with documents that the parties wish to introduce as evidence in the arbitration. It is recognized that documents are often the most reliable form of evidence for parties in arbitration. The Rules also give new guidance on the disclosure of electronic documents. These are to be submitted in a form "most convenient or economical . . . that is reasonably usable by the recipients," unless agreed otherwise. The Rules do not set out detailed procedures for dealing with electronic disclosure.

[2]   Discovery Under 28 U.S.C. § 1782 in International Arbitration from U.S. Parties

Page 1783, add to end of subsection:

Since *In re Roz Trading Ltd.,* 469 F. Supp. 2d 1221 (N.D. Ga. 2006), 28 U.S.C. § 1782 continues to be increasingly used as a vehicle for parties to seek U.S. style discovery in international arbitrations from U.S. entities. Though there remains a spit in U.S. Federal Courts regarding the applicability of 28 U.S.C. § 1782 to international arbitration, recent cases suggest that courts in undecided jurisdictions are deciding in favor of allowing such applications.

The recent case of *In re Application of Chevron Corp.,* S.D.N.Y, May 6, 2010, confirms further the application of 28 U.S.C. § 1782 to international treaty arbitrations, albeit the court mixed its decision by making by reference also to private commercial arbitration.The court granted Chevron's application for a subpoena for the production of outtakes of a documentary film entitled *Crude* from its U.S. based producer, pursuant to a bilateral investment treaty arbitration on-going between Chevron and Ecuador. The court noted that the application fell

---

[103.1] *See* http://www.ibanet.org/LPD/Dispute_Resolution_Section/Arbitration/Default. aspx.

within 28 U.S.C § 1782 because the arbitration was not an arbitration tribunal established by private parties, but instead "a tribunal established by an international treaty." (Memorandum Opinion at 14). The court also noted that in any event, the U.S. Supreme Court in *Intel Corp. v. Advanced Micro Devices, Inc.*, 542 U.S. 241 (2004) in construing the application of 28 U.S.C § 1782 had cited a law review article which noted that the term "tribunal" used in the statute "includes . . . administrative and arbitral tribunals . . . ." In this regard, the court stated that two district courts in the Second Circuit and one in the Third Circuit have followed this dictum and held that "international arbitral bodies operating under UNCITRAL rules constitute "foreign tribunals" for purposes of Section 1782." (Order at 15). Nevertheless the Chevron case has publicized widely, within the United States, 28 U.S.C § 1782 as a tool for obtaining information in an international arbitration proceeding.

28 U.S.C § 1782 can also be used to obtain discovery in advance of any international arbitration proceeding actually beginning. This is seen in, *In the Application of Winning (HK) Shipping Co. Ltd*, 2010 WL 1796579 (S.D. Fla. Apr. 30, 2010). Winning obtained a deposition and production under the statute of various documents purportedly in the possession of the manager of a ship, Ship Management Services ("SMS"), to assist it in an intended arbitration against the ship owner arising out of a time charter contract the performance of which was thwarted by a loss of power to the anchor windlass which caused the vessel ultimately to run aground. SMS was a Florida based company. The discovery sought and granted included discovery of documents and also the deposition of the SMS superintendent or such other persons knowledgeable about the management of the vessel.

The court, in what it noted was a close decision, noted that the arbitration was to be conducted in London under the London Maritime Arbitrators Association Rules and within the purview of the English Arbitration Act 1996. The court noted that this statute provides that "decisions of the arbitrators are reviewable by the English Courts." (at *9). As a consequence of this, the court determined using Intel Corp's functional analysis test regarding that the arbitral body was a "foreign tribunal" for the purposes of 28 U.S.C § 1782. It held that "to the extent that the arbitration forum at issue is subject to the Arbitration Act 1996 (of England) or the Parties have agreed to follow the rules of the London Maritime Arbitrator's Association, Winning is proceeding before a "foreign tribunal" and is therefore entitled to seek assistance from this court in pursuant to section 1782. (*10). The key to the application of 28 U.S.C § 1782, therefore, in the *Winning* case was the determination that the arbitral body "acts as a first instance decision maker whose decisions are subject to judicial review."

The continued and growing use of 28 U.S.C § 1782 perhaps to enable discovery that is otherwise not available from international arbitral tribunals, can create powerful leverage (particularly in the modern age of e-discovery and the burdens that go with that obligation) in the hands of parties to use against U.S. based entities on projects.

[G] Expedited Arbitrations and Split Process Arbitrations

Page 1783, add to end of subsection:

There is much continuing dialogue and discussion (particularly from large commercial users of international commercial arbitration) regarding the need to increase the speed of arbitral proceedings and reduce their costs and the mechanisms by which this might be done—ranging from "hottubbing" experts or other witnesses (i.e., having them testify together in a more dialogue approach to further restricting discovery). In this regard, the Corporate Counsel International Arbitration Group (CCIAG) continues to actively seek to promote more efficient and effective arbitral processes.[105.1] Arbitral institutions seem to be responding to these pressures. For example, the ICC now requires arbitrator nominees to confirm their availability to undertake the arbitration. The aim of this is to ensure that arbitrators complete their work and issue awards timely.[105.2]

One factor—aside from general current economic pressures—that may be exerting increasing pressure on the reducing the cost and time of arbitrations is the manner in which parties are funding international dispute resolution. In the last few years there has been an exponential growth in third party "investor" funders of international project disputes, whether they be investment banks, hedge fund type organizations or simply wealthy private investors. These entities, which are particularly active in investor-state matters, have a vested interest in seeing arbitrations conducted quickly and cost-effectively from the point of maximizing their financial investments. In this context, we have experienced personally investor favoritism for certain arbitral institutions and rules over others. The rise of the investor funded arbitration has a number of (at least theoretical) benefits. For the party the chief benefit is that it does not have to fund all of the legal fees out or costs of pocket. The party gets a contingency arrangement. The structure however, also benefits the law firm as they usually get paid some, but not a full, proportion of their fees on a monthly basis from the investor, perhaps with a "success" fee portion making up the delta. Finally, the investor benefits if the case is successful because it takes a contingency fee percentage of the recovery. It remains to be seen if this type of dispute resolution funding will remain popular or whether investors will retract from the "market." Nevertheless, in the current environment these funding structures are playing an important

---

[105.1] *See Group Works to Reform International Arbitration Process,* David Hechler, Feb. 3, 2010 Law.com at http://www.law.com/jsp/article.jsp?id=1202441909399.
[105.2] *See* http://www.iccwbo.org/court/arbitration/index.html?id=32208.

role in determining how, where, and with whom arbitrations of project disputes proceed.

[I]   Ad hoc or Institutional and Which Rules?

[5]   Other Arbitral Institutions

Page 1787, add to end of subsection:

There have been continued developments at arbitral institutions since our chapter was first published. The ICC, for example, has created a task force to review its rules.[122.1] The UNCITRAL Arbitration Rules have been revised.[122.2] There has also been much activity in regional centers to support arbitration dispute resolution. Some of these developments, of particular interest to the international construction community, include:

- **Dubai.** On December 14, 2009, the Ruler of Dubai issued Decree No. 57 of 2009 "Establishing a Tribunal to decide the Disputes Related to the Settlement of the Financial Position of Dubai World and its Subsidiaries." See http://www.dubaiworldtribunal.ae/index.html. This Decree established a tribunal exclusively applicable to Dubai World to address disputes raised by Dubai World's creditors. On March 30, 2010, the Special Tribunal issued Practice Direction No. 1 of 2010 stating that it has a policy "to respect and enforce arbitration agreements made between [Dubai World] and its creditors." The practice direction further states: "Where disputes have already arisen, the Tribunal expects the parties to continue with pending arbitration proceedings in accordance with their contractual obligations. Applications in relation to arbitration agreements or to pending arbitration references which would otherwise have been made to a Court may be made to the Tribunal." The first claim was filed in April 2010 by a former employee of a subsidiary, Limitless LCC. *See* Shaheen Pasha, Dubai World's Limitless first target of tribunal claim, Arabian Business.com, April 7, 2010, *available at* http://www.arabianbusiness-.com/585495-dubai-worlds-limitless-first-target-of-tribunal-claim.

- **Bahrain.** In June 2009, the Kingdom of Bahrain established the Bahrain Chamber for Dispute Resolution, to administer international arbitration and mediation "with particular emphasis on disputes in the construction, financial services, insurance, and energy sectors." The BCDR is an autonomous entity that operates in cooperation with

---

[122.1] *See* http://www.iccwbo.org/policy/arbitration/id28796/index.html.
[122.2] *See*   http://www.uncitral.org/pdf/english/texts/arbitration/arb-rules-revised/pre-arb-rules-revised.pdf.

the American Arbitration Association. The center-piece, and novel concept, of the BCDR is that it creates what has been described as the world's first "free arbitration zone" i.e., international arbitration matters brought to the BCDR are not subject to any intervention from the local courts in Bahrain. Like SAIC, BCDR also is seeking to position itself to perform arbitrations emanating from projects in other Gulf nations, such as Saudi Arabia. In this regard, it can provide arbitrations under Sharia law. See the Chamber's website at http://www.bcdr-aaa.org/ for rules.

- **LCIA India.** In keeping with the expansion of international arbitral institutions such as the AAA with the BCDR, in 2009, the LCIA established LCIA India, the "first independent subsidiary of the LCIA outside of London." LCIA India Rules for arbitration and mediation took effect as of April 17, 2010. See LCIA India's website for rules at http://www.lcia-india.org.

[R]   Appeals/Enforcement

[1]   Limited Role of Courts

Page 1807, add to end of subsection:

As noted above, the recent development of Bahrain Chamber for Dispute Resolution providing for a structure of international dispute resolution within a "free arbitration zone" entirely independent of the Bahrain courts is an extreme example of the willingness of some jurisdictions to entirely preclude courts from interfering in international arbitral matters. It remains open to see whether other jurisdictions will follow this lead and whether parties begin to use the BCDR because of this feature.

[3]   The New York Convention

Page 1807, add to end of subsection:

It should be mentioned that despite the provisions in the New York Convention for challenging an arbitral award, the right of a party to contest enforcement of an arbitration award is not automatic. Frequently parties prevailing in arbitration and courts require that a losing party post a bond in the amount of the arbitral award before entertaining an application to vacate an award. *See, e.g., Republic of Argentina v. National Grid, PLC*, Case No 09-248, (D. D.C. Mar 31, 2010) wherein the court ordered Argentina to post a bond of $54,126,388.46 and administratively closed the proceedings on Argentina's motion to vacate until posted.

CHAPTER **44**

CLAIMS AVOIDANCE AND DISPUTE MANAGEMENT

Victor C. Oblas, PE
Stephanie A. Kirby, PE

§ 44.02 PROJECT PLANS AND SPECIFICATIONS

Page 1815, replace third sentence of first paragraph with:

Owners select architects and engineers on the basis of their expertise and capability, but the cost of design and schedule soon become the primary concern of both parties: the owner resists paying more than what he or she considers "standard fees" (which translates into—as small a fee as possible) and the architect/engineer tries to complete the design as quickly as possible using canned plans and specifications. The architect/engineer seeks to avoid costly changes to those standard designs which may not provide most appropriate detail for the owner's project.

Page 1817, replace first full bullet point with:

• Do not hesitate to share your knowledge within the body of the specifications and drawings. The designer has spent months, maybe years with the design: a contractor gets six to eight weeks to bid it. If there are elements of the project that the engineer/architect believe the contractor may have problems with, that information should be shared. Many engineers and architects are reluctant to share their thoughts with contractors on potential pitfalls in the performance of specific tasks or means and methods of construction: that is, the sequence or technique that they, the designers, believe the contractor should consider during the execution of the work. They fear that by sharing their thoughts a contractor may come back and say that they followed the engineer's suggestions and failed, making the engineer partially or fully liable for the cost of such failure. The risk of being silent on matters that later prove to be problematic and costly to the owner when the designer had either superior knowledge of, or a viable technical solution is usually greater than offering that solution in the first instance. Keep in mind that a contractor's problem is always the owner's problem which frequently comes around to become a designer's problem. Sharing ideas reaps rewards that are never easy to quantify.

Page 1819, replace first full paragraph with:

This is all to say that in order to avoid disputes and potential clams resulting from changes in the field, a new paradigm is needed for Q/A reviews. By the time a design is complete to the point that there is enough information available for a thorough review to occur, the designer has become over-familiar with the design and the budget is nearly exhausted. What is needed is separation from the work and a review by an independent team that can clearly see the project design as a whole.

Page 1819, replace third full paragraph with:

Making changes to a design prior to it going out to bid is many times less costly than correcting problems in the field.

§ 44.03   SHARING THE RISK

Page 1820, replace seventh sentence of first full paragraph with:

Delineation of risk ownership from the outset with thorough and accurate contract documents is then key.

Page 1820, replace first sentence of third (carryover) paragraph with:

Basic risk allocation questions need be asked such as: do the terms and conditions dramatically skew this risk towards the contractor, or has the owner acknowledged and recognized that there are specific risks that they are willing to pay for, such as underground obstructions or un-documented utilities?

§ 44.04   INVOLVING NON-FIELD PEOPLE IN FIELD EXPERIENCES

Page 1821, replace first sentence of first paragraph with:

Involving non-field personnel in the field experiences is an important element of managing claims and disputes.

§ 44.08   CHANGE NEGOTIATIONS

Page 1825, replace first sentence of first paragraph with:

Volumes have been written about strategies and techniques for negotiating changes and it is not the intent of this chapter to provide an exhaustive review yet certain fundamentals remain.

CHAPTER **46**

ARBITRATION OF CONSTRUCTION DISPUTES AND ENFORCEABILITY OF AWARDS

Joe Canterbury
Kyle E. Hart

§ 46.07   SCOPE OF ARBITRATION AGREEMENT

Page 1861, add footnote referent 30.1 at end of second full paragraph and add note 30.1:

[30.1] In Buckeye Check Cashing, Inc. v. Cardegna, 546 U.S. 440, 126 S. Ct. 1204, 163 L. Ed. 2d 1038 (2006), the Court dealt with the issue of who decides whether a contract is invalid, the arbitrator or the court. The Court held that when the attack is on the contract's validity as a whole, as contrasted with the arbitration clause alone, they are "within the arbitrator's ken." *Accord* Preston v. Fener, 128 S. Ct. 978, 169 L. Ed. 2d 917 (2008) (Court relied on FAA to require arbitration).

Page 1861, add to end of section:

Another issue which arises is whether a court or the arbitrator has the power to determine if a contract that contains an arbitration agreement is enforceable. The United States Supreme Court in the case of *Granite Rock Co. v. International Brotherhood of Teamsters*,[32.1] determined that it is a court, not the arbitrator, that has the right to determine whether or not an agreement is arbitrable. In reaching this decision, the court re-affirmed its long-standing rule that whether parties have agreed to arbitrate is typically an issue for judicial determination.[32.2] Therefore, in order for a court to satisfy itself that an enforceable arbitration exists, it must also resolve any issues that call into question the specific arbitration clause

---

[32.1] ___ U.S. ___, No. 08-1214, 2010 WL 2518518 (June 24, 2010).
[32.2] *Id., citing* Howsam v. Dean Witter Reynoldsm, 573 U.S. 79, 83 (2002); First Options of Chicago, Inc. v. Kaplan, 514 U.S. 938, 944 (1995).

that the party seeks to enforce.[32.3] In *Granite Rock*, there was a question as to when the contract was formed. This was a material issue in the case since the ratification date determined the formation date of the contract, and whether the contract's provisions were enforceable during the period relevant to the parties' dispute. The court held that the determination of the formation date required judicial resolution, and was not arbitrable, since the question as to the formation of the contract is an issue that calls into question the enforceability of the arbitration agreement itself.

§ 46.14   WAIVER OF RIGHT TO ARBITRATION

Page 1863, add to note 43:

    See also Perry Hones v. Cull, 2008 WL 1922978 (Tex. May 2, 2008) (homeowner waived right to arbitrate by opposing developer's request to arbitrate and pursuing discovery for 14 months, until shortly before trial).

§ 46.15   APPEALABILITY OF ORDERS REGARDING COMPELLING OR STAYING ARBITRATION

Page 1864, note 48, change both instances of "applicable" to "appealable."

§ 46.18   PROCEDURE FOR VACATING AWARDS

Page 1866, add to end of section:

    However, a party can waive the right to appeal an arbitration award based upon the language in the contract. In the case of *MACTEC, Inc. v. Gorelick*, the Tenth Circuit Court of Appeals held that a clear and unequivocal agreement foreclosing judicial review of an arbitration award beyond the district court level was enforceable.[62.01] The clause in question stated that "any judgment upon the award rendered by the arbitrator would be final and non-appealable and may be entered in any court having jurisdiction thereof." Therefore, the court affirmed the trial court's judgment and held that it lacked the jurisdiction to disturb the award because the arbitration agreement provided that the losing party could not appeal beyond the district court.

[32.3] *Id., citing* Rent-A-Center West, Inc. v. Jackson, __U.S. __, No. 08-1457 (Mar. 23, 2010).

[62.01] 427 F.3d 821 (10th Cir. 2005).

§ 46.19   GROUNDS FOR VACATING AWARD—GENERALLY

Page 1866, add footnote referent 62.1 after section heading and add note 62.1:

[62.1] In Hall Street Associates, L.L.C. v. Mattel, Inc., 128 S. Ct. 1396, 170 L. Ed. 2d 254 (2008), the United States Supreme Court held that the grounds specified in the FAA to confirm, vacate or modify an arbitration award are exclusive and cannot be supplemented by contract to require review on the merits. Two dissents were filed, each arguing that parties seeking to arbitrate should be free to vary the scope of review, if desired.

Page 1868, add to end of section:

It is increasingly common for parties seeking to avoid arbitration to claim that the arbitration provision is unconscionable. In *Taylor Bldg. Corp. of Am. v. Benfield,*[70.01] the homeowner won this argument in the trial court, but lost in the appellate and Ohio Supreme Court. While the trial court focused on the overall one-sidedness of the construction contract in holding the arbitration agreement to be unconscionable, the appellate and Ohio Supreme Court held that when reviewing unconscionability, the focus must be on the arbitration clause as a stand-alone clause. When so viewed, it was not unconscionable.

Contrary to the decision in *Taylor Building Corp. of America v. Benfield,* a Texas court of appeals did find an arbitration agreement unenforceable because the arbitration fees were unconscionable. In *Olshan Foundation Repair Co. v. Ayala,*[70.1] a homeowner sued a contractor for the alleged breach of a $22,650 foundation repair contract. The contractor moved to compel arbitration, citing the contractual agreement to arbitrate under the American Arbitration Association ("AAA") rules, and the trial court granted the motion. The American Arbitration Association appointed a panel of three engineers to arbitrate the dispute and sent the parties an invoice for $63,670, of which $33,150 was immediately due from the homeowners (on top of the $4,130 filing fee they already had paid). The parties went back to court and the trial court ruled that the cost of the arbitration rendered the agreement unconscionable. The court of appeals upheld the trial court's decision and ruled that the trial court did not abuse its discretion when it refused to enforce the arbitration agreement.

[70.01] 2008 WL 696334 (Ohio Mar. 12, 2008).
[70.1] 180 S.W.3d 212 (Tex. App. 2005).

§ 46.22   FAILURE OF AN ARBITRATOR TO MAKE SUFFICIENT DISCLOSURE

Page 1870, add to end of section:

Some courts and commentators are starting to reign in the disclosure requirements. In *Agri-Systems, Inc. v. Foster Poultry Farms*,[84.1] the court held that an arbitrator had no duty to disclose his law firm's past representation of an adversary to one of the parties to the arbitration agreement. The court's holding would have been different if the law firm had previously represented one of the parties to the arbitration.

§ 46.24   ARBITRATORS EXCEEDED THEIR POWER

Page 1872, add after carryover paragraph:

Another example of an arbitrator exceeding the authority granted within the arbitration agreement is the case of *Stolt-Nielsen SA v. AnimalFeeds International Corp.,* wherein the United States Supreme Court decided whether imposing class arbitrations on parties whose arbitration clauses are "silent" on that issue is consistent with the Federal Arbitration Act.[104.1] The Court determined that class arbitrations may not be imposed unless specifically authorized by the terms of the agreement.

Although an arbitrator's authority is limited by the terms of the agreement, courts have held that an arbitrator does not exceed his powers by granting a motion for summary judgment during an arbitration proceeding. In *Sherrock Brothers, Inc. v. DaimlerChrysler Motors Co., LLC*,[104.2] the Third Circuit Court of Appeals rejected the argument that the arbitrators exceeded their powers by granting a summary judgment. The court stated as follows:

> [E]xcept where prohibited by the plain and express terms of the submission, an arbitrator is empowered to grant any relief reasonably fitting and necessary to a final determination of the matter submitted to him, including legal and equitable relief.' Granting summary judgment surely falls within this standard, and fundamental fairness is not implicated by an arbitration panel's decision to forego an evidentiary hearing because of its conclusion that there were no genuine issues of material fact in dispute.[104.3]

[84.1] 168 Cal. App. 4th 1128, 85 Cal. Rptr. 3d 917 (2008).

[104.1] 103 S. Ct. 1758 (2010).

[104.2] 260 Fed. Appx. 497 (3d Cir. 2008).

[104.3] 260 Fed. Appx. at 502, *citing* Bd. of Educ. of Dover Union Free Sch. Dist. v. Dover-Wingdale, 95 A.D.2d 497, 502 (N.Y.A.D. 2 Dept.1983) (emphasis in original); *see*

§ 46.26 MANIFEST DISREGARD OF LAW

Page 1873, add to end of section:

The United States Supreme Court ruled in *Hall Street Associates v. Mattel, Inc.* that agreements for expanded review of arbitration awards beyond the limited grounds for vacating or modifying agreements as allowed by Sections 10 and 11 of the Federal Arbitration Act are unenforceable.[116.1] While limiting its decision to actions under the Federal Arbitration Act, the opinion left open the question of whether expanded grounds of review may be enforceable in actions under state arbitration acts. As a result of the Supreme Court's decision, there is a split of authority as to whether or not manifest disregard of the law is a valid ground for vacatur or modification. Several jurisdictions have held that manifest disregard is no longer a valid basis for challenging arbitration awards,[116.2] while other jurisdictions have held that manifest disregard is still a valid basis for vacatur or modification of the award,[116.3] and other courts have held that manifest disregard of the law is encompassed within the grounds for vacatur or modification enumerated by the Federal Arbitration Act.[116.4] The Supreme Court was given an opportunity to clarify if it meant to eliminate manifest disregard of the law as a grounds for vacatur or modification of an award in the case of *Stolt-Nielsen SA v. AnimalFeeds International Corp.*[116.5] but declined to do so.

also College Hall Fashions, Inc. v. Philadelphia Joint Bd. Amalgamated Clothing Workers of Am., 408 F. Supp. 722, 728 (E.D.Pa.1976) (arbitrator has "wide latitude" in fashioning an appropriate remedy).

[116.1] 123 S. Ct. 1936 (2008).

[116.2] *See* Robert Lewis Rosen Assocs., Ltd. v. Webb, 2008 WL 2662015 (S.D.N.Y. 2008); ALS & Assocs., Inc. v. AGM Marine Constructors, Inc., 557 F. Supp. 2d (D. Mass. 2008); Prime Theraputics, LLC v. Omnicare, LLC., 555 F. Supp. 2d 993 (D. Minn. 2008); Hereford v. D.R. Horton, Inc., 2008 WL 4097594 (Ala. 2008); Millmaker v. Bruso, 2008 WL 4560624 (S.D. Tex. 2008); Citigroup Global Mkts., Inc. v. Bacon, 562 F.3d 349, 356 (5th Cir. 2009).

[116.3] Kashner Davidson Secs. Corp. v. Msciz, 531 F.3d 68 (1st Cir. 2008); Stolt-Nielsen Transp. Group Ltd. v. Animal Feeds Int'l Corp., 548 F.3d 84 (2d Cir. 2008); Parnell v. Tremont Capital Mgmt. Corp., 280 Fed. Appx. 76 (2d Cir. 2008); Reeves v. Chase Bank USA, NA, 2008 WL 2783231 (E.D. Mo. 2008); Fitzgerald v. H&R Block Fin. Advisors, Inc., 2008 WL 2397636 (E.D. Mich. 2008); LaPine v. Kyocera Corp., 2008 WL 216918 (N.D. Cal. 2008); Jimmy John's Franchise, LLC v. Kelsey, 549 F. Supp. 2d 1034, 1037 (C.D. Ill. 2008).

[116.4] Stevens & Co. v. Cikanek, 2008 WL 2705445 (N.D. Ill. 2008); Mastec N. Am., Inc. v. MSE Power Sys., Inc., 2008 WL 2704912 (N.D.N.Y. 2008).

[116.5] 103 S. Ct. 1758 (2010).

§ 46.29   CONCLUSION

Page 1875, add footnote referent 123.1 to end of last sentence in paragraph and add note 123.1:

[123.1] As this supplement goes to press, legislation is pending to amend the Federal Arbitration Act. The purported purpose of the amendment is to protect certain individuals with inferior bargaining power from being coerced into arbitration. Whether the legislation will be adopted and, if so, in what form, is unknown. However, if it is adopted, then it will certainly spawn a whole host of new disputes concerning whether various contracts or transactions are or are not between parties of unequal bargaining power.

TABLE OF CASES TO MAIN VOLUMES

References are to section numbers. Alphabetization is letter-by-letter.
This replaces the Table of Cases of the main volumes

A

A & M Petroleum, Inc., United States *ex rel.*, v. Santa Fe Eng'rs, Inc., 822 F.2d 547 (5th Cir. 1987), 35.05[A], 35.07[A][4]

A & W Concrete & Bldg. Materials, United States *ex rel.*, v. A.P. Johnson Contractor, 225 F. Supp. 727 (E.D. La. 1964), 35.08[B]

AAB Joint Venture v. United States, 75 Fed. Cl. 414 (2007), 23.04[B][1], 27.05[B][3][a]

A.A. Conte, Inc. v. Campbell-Lowrie-Lautermilch Corp., 477 N.E.2d 30 (Ill. App. Ct. 1985), 35.08[E][1]

ABB, 42.02[F]

Abbett Elec. Corp. v. United States, 142 Ct. Cl. 609, 162 F. Supp. 772 (1958), 24.02, 24.02[D]

ABB Ltd., 42.02[F][2]

Abbott v. Gatch, 13 Md. 314 (1859), 21.02

Abcon Assocs., Inc. v. United States, 44 Fed. Cl. 625 (1999), 28.03[D][1][a][i], 28.03[D][2]

Abcon Assocs., Inc. v. United States, 49 Fed. Cl. 678 (2001), 28.03[G]

Abel Homes at Naranja Villas, LLC. v. Hernandez, 960 So. 2d 891 (Fla. Dist. Ct. App. 3d Dist. 2007), 46.14

ABF Freight Syst., Inc. v. United States, 55 Fed. Cl. 392 (2003), 27.07[C]

ABI, Inc. v. City of L.A., 200 Cal. Rptr. 563 (Ct. App. 1984), 33.01[B]

Abish v. Northwestern Int'l Ins. Co., 924 F.2d 448 (2d Cir. 1991), 36.04

ABL Med. Transcription Serv., VACAB No. 3369, 92-1 B.C.A. ¶ 24,850 (1991), 28.03[G]

Abney Constr. Co., ASBCA No. 26358, 83-1 B.C.A. ¶ 16,426 (1982), 28.03[D][3]

Abramowitz v. Bank of America, 281 P.2d 380 (Cal. App. Dep't Super. Ct. 1955), 12.04[C][1][e]

ABS Baumaschinenvertrieb GmbH, ASBCA No.48207, 00-1 B.C.A. ¶ 31,090 (2000), 28.03[E][1][b], 28.04[D][3]

Absher Construction v. Kent School District No. 415, 77 Wn. App. 137, 890 P.2d 1071 (1995), 26.02[VV][4]

Ab-Tech Construction, Inc. v. United States, 31 Fed. Cl. 429 (1994), 38.02[C][1][c], 38.02[D]

ACE Constructors, Inc. v. United States, 70 Fed. Cl. 253 (2006), 22.06, 24.04, 24.04[B], 24.04[E], 27.05[D][4][b], 27.05[D][4][d]

Ace-Fed. Reporters, Inc. v. Barram, 226 F.3d 1329 (Fed. Cir. 2000), 28.02[B]

A/C Elec. Co. v. Aetna Inc. Co., 247 A.2d 708 (Md. 1968), 35.08[I]

Ace Stone, Inc. v. Township of Wayne, 47 N.J. 431, 221 A.2d 515 (1966), 26.02[EE][3]

ACMAT Corp. v. Greater N.Y. Mut. Ins. Co., 923 A.2d 697 (Conn. 2007), 33.02[D]

Acme Maintenance Eng'g Co., United States *ex rel.*, v. Wunderlich Contracting Co., 228 F.2d 66 (10th Cir. 1955), 35.08[B]

Acme Missiles & Constr. Corp., ASBCA No. 11,794, 68-1 BCA ¶ 6,734 (1967), 23.03[D]

Acme Process Equip. Co. v. United States, 171 Ct. Cl. 324 (1965), 23.03[D]

Acme Steak Co. v. Great Lakes Mech. Co., 2000 WL 1506199 (Ohio App. Sept. 29, 2000), 19.07[B]

Acme Transfer & Trucking Co., United States ex rel., v. H.S. Kaiser, Inc., 270 F. Supp. 215 (E.D. Wis. 1967), 35.05[A]

Acquest Gov't Holdings, OPP, LLC v. GSA, CBCA No. 413 (Nov. 7, 2007), 25.05[D]

ACS Constr. Co. of Mississippi v. CGU, 332 F.3d 885 (5th Cir. 2003), 19.07[B]

Action Support Servs. Corp., ASBCA Nos. 46524 et al., 2000 B.C.A. ¶ 30,701 (1999), 28.03[D][2]

Acudata Sys., Inc., DOT CAB Nos. 1198, 1233, 84-1 B.C.A. ¶ 17,046 (1983), 28.03[D][2]

ACUITY v. Burd & Smith Constr., Inc., 2006 N.D. 187, 721 N.W.2d 33 (N.D. 2006), 18.05[A][1], 19.07[B]

Acumen Constr. Inc. v. Nehr, 616 So. 2d 98 (Fla. Dist. Ct. App. 1993), 46.06

Adams v. United States, 358 F.2d 986 (Ct. Cl. 1966), 28.03[E][1][a]

Adams, ASBCA No. 34519, 89-2 B.C.A. ¶ 21,699 (1989), 28.04[C][1]

Adams Constr. Co., VACAB No. 4669, 97-1 B.C.A. ¶ 28,801 (1997), 28.03[B][2]

Adam Sommerrock Holzbau, GmbH v. United States, 866 F.2d 427 (Fed. Cir. 1989), 33.02[E]

Adel v. Greensprings of Vermont, Inc., 363 F. Supp. 2d 692 (D. Vt. 2005), 16.02[B]

Adler v. Federal Republic of Nigeria, 219 F.3d 869 (9th Cir. 1999), 42.02[F][1]

Adler & Neilson Co. v. Ins. Co. of N. Am., 56 N.Y.S.2d 540, 434 N.E.2d 1355 (1982), 18.05[A][2]

Adobe Masters, Inc. v. Downey, 883 P.2d 133 (N.M. 1994), 7.02[B][2][c]

Advanced Eng'g & Plumbing Corp., ASBCA Nos. 53366, 54044, 05-1 BCA ¶ 32,806 (2004), 23.06[A]

Advanced Materials, Inc. v. United States, 34 Fed. Cl. 480 (1995), 28.04[C][2][a]

Adventure Group, Inc., ASBCA No. 46683, 98-1 B.C.A. ¶ 29,386 (1997), 28.03[B][1]

Aerokits, Inc., ASBCA No. 12,324, 68-2 BCA ¶ 7088 (1968), 23.03[D]

Aerometals, Inc., ASBCA No. 53688, 03-2 B.C.A. ¶ 32,295 (2003), 28.03[D][1][a][i]

Aerosonic Corp., ASBCA No. 42696, 91-3 B.C.A. ¶ 24,214 (1991), 28.03[G]

Aesthetic Property Maintenance v. Capitol Indem. Corp., 900 P.2d 1210 (Ariz. 1995), 35.08[G]

Aetna v. Aluminum Co. of Am., 176 S.E.2d 654 (Ga. Ct. App. 1970), 35.06[B][3]

Aetna Cas. & Sur. Co. v. Buck, 594 So. 2d 280 (Fla. 1992), 35.08[J]

Aetna Cas. & Sur. Co. v. Butte-Meade Sanitary Water Dist., 500 F. Supp. 193 (D.S.D. 1980), 23.03[D]

Aetna Cas. & Sur. Co. v. Circle Equip. Co., 377 F.2d 160 (D.C. Cir. 1967), 35.07[B][1]

Aetna Cas. & Sur. Co. v. Commonwealth, 179 S.W.3d 830 (Ky. 2005), 18.05[B][1]

Aetna Cas. & Sur. Co. v. Consulting Environmental Engineers, Inc., 1989 WL 1110231 (R.I. Super. Ct. 1989), 19.07[B]

Aetna Cas. & Sur. Co. v. Continental Cas. Co., 413 Mass. 730, 604 N.E.2d 30 (1992), 18.04[B]

Aetna Cas. & Sur. Co. v. Doleac Elec. Co., 471 So. 2d 325 (Miss. 1985), 24.04[B]

Aetna Cas. & Sur. Co. v. George Hyman Constr. Co., 1998 U.S. Dist. LEXIS 22627 (E.D. Pa. May 13, 1998), 24.04

Aetna Cas. & Sur. Co. v. George Hyman Constr. Co., No. 93-CV-4750, 1998 U.S. Dist. LEXIS 22627 (E.D. Pa. May 13, 1998), 30.03[D][1], 30.03[D][2], 30.03[D][4]

Aetna Inc. v. Lexington Ins. Co., 2005 WL 2840327 (Pa. C.P. 2005), 45.04[F]

AFV Enters., Inc., PSBCA No. 2691 et al., 01-1 B.C.A. ¶ 31,338 (2001), 28.03[B][1], 28.03[D][2]

A.G. Cullen Construction, Inc. v. State System of Higher Education, 898 A.2d 1145 (Pa. Commw. Ct. 2006), 7.03[B][1][a], 27.04[A][1]

A.G. Gaston Constr. Co. v. Hicks, 674 So. 2d 545 (Ala. Civ. App. 1995), 35.04[B], 35.07[B][1]

AgGrow Oils, L.L.C. v. Nat'l Union Fire Ins. Co. of Pittsburg, Pa., 276 F. Supp. 2d 999 (D.N.D. 2003), 29.04[D][1], 34.04[F][2][a]

AgGrow Oils, L.L.C. v. Nat'l Union Fire Ins. Co. of Pittsburg, Pa., 420 F.3d 751 (8th Cir. 2005), 34.04[C]

A-Greater New Jersey Movers, Inc., ASBCA No. 54745, 2006 ASBCA LEXIS 3 (Jan. 24, 2006), 28.03[E][2]

Agritrack, Inc. v. DeJohn Housemoving, Inc., 25 P.3d 1187 (Colo. 2001), 27.05[B][5][d]

Air-A-Plane Corp. v. United States, 187 Ct. Cl. 269, 408 F.2d 1030 (1969), 27.05[B][4]

Air-A-Plane Corp. v. United States, 408 F.2d 1030 (Ct. Cl. 1969), 21.08, 28.03[E][3][b]

Air-Flo Cleaning Sys., ASBCA No. 39608, 90-3 B.C.A. ¶ 23,071 (1990), 28.04[C][2][a]

Airfreight Express Ltd v. Evergreen Air Ctr., Ind., 215 Ariz. 103, 158 P.3d 232 (Ariz. Ct. App. 2007), 26.02[C][1], 26.02[C][3], 26.02[C][4]

Airport Constr. & Materials, Inc. v. Bivens, 649 S.W.2d 830 (Ark. 1983), 35.06[A][2]

Airprep Tech, Inc. v. United States, 30 Fed. Cl. 488 (1994), 21.07, 27.05[B][4], 28.03[E][3][a], 28.03[E][3][b]

AIU Ins. Co. v. Superior Court, 51 Cal. 3d 807 (1990), 18.04[C][2], 18.05[B][1]

A.J. Wolfe Co. v. Baltimore Contractors, Inc., 244 N.E. 2d 717 (Mass. 1969), 25.02[C], 35.08[E][1]

Akassy v. William Penn Apartments Ltd. P'ship, 891 A.2d 291 (D.C. 2006), 27.03[B][2]

Ala. Dept. of Envtl. Mgmt. v. Wright Bros. Constr. Co., Inc., 604 So. 2d 429 (Ala. Civ. App. 1992), 11.03[A][1][a][iv]

Alamo Cmty. Coll. Dist. v. Browning Constr. Co., 131 S.W.3d 146 (Tx. App. 2004), 8A.08[D]

Alaska, Trustees for, v. E.P.A., 749 F.2d 549 (9th Cir. 1984), 11.03[A][1][b]

Albert Elia Bldg. Co. v. N.Y. State Urban Dev. Corp., 388 N.Y.S.2d 462 (N.Y. App. Div. 1976), 7.03[B][2][d]

Al-Cam Dev. Corp., In re, 99 B.R. 573 (Bank. S.D.N.Y. 1989), 46.13

Alcon Demolition, In re, 204 B.R. 440 (Bankr. D.N.J. 1997), 34.04[H], 36.02[C]

Aldridge, United States ex rel., v. Pickus Constr. & Equip. Co., 98-3261, 2000 WL 190574 (N.D. Ill. 2000), 35.06[A][1][b]

Aleutian Contractors v. United States, 24 Cl. Ct. 372 (Fed. Cl. 1991), 7.03[B][1][a]

Alexander Constr. Co. v. C & H Contracting, 354 N.W.2d 535 (Minn. Ct. App. 1984), 35.06[B][1]

Alfred Bronder, ASBCA, No. 29938, 86-3 B.C.A. (CCH) ¶ 19,102, 39.08[A]

Algernon Blair, Inc. v. Norfolk Redevelopment & Hous. Auth., 200 Va. 818, 108 S.E.2d 259 (1959), 26.02[UU][4]

Algernon Blair, Inc., ASBCA No. 23585, 81-2 B.C.A. ¶ 15,375 (1981), aff'd, 82-1 B.C.A. ¶ 15,491 (1981), 28.03[E][3][a]

Algernon-Blair, Inc., GSBCA No. 4072, 76-2 B.C.A. (CCH) ¶ 12,073 (1976), 27.05[D][6][b]

Algernon Blair, Inc., United States v., 479 F.2d 638 (4th Cir. 1973), 21.06

Al Johnson Constr. Co. v. United States, 854 F.2d 467 (Fed. Cir. 1988), 23.06[A], 28.03[E][1][b]

Allen Ballew Gen. Contractors, VABCA Nos. 6987 et al., 07-2 BCA ¶ 33,456 (2006), 23.06[D]

Allen Elec. Co. v. Fidelity & Deposit Co., No. 15, 1989 WL 54791 (Tenn. Ct. App. May 24, 1989), 35.08[A], 35.08[E][1]

Allen-Howe Specialties Corp. v. U.S. Construction, Inc., 611 P.2d 705 (Utah 1980), 26.02[SS][3], 26.02[SS][4]

Allen M. Campbell Co. v. General
Contractors, Inc., 708 F.2d 930 (4th
Cir. 1983), 16.04[E]
Alley-Cassetty Coal Co., ASBCA No.
33,315, 89 BCA ¶ 21,964 (1989),
23.03[B][1]
Allgood Elec. Co. v. Martin K. Eby
Constr. Co., 85 F.3d 1547 (11th Cir.
1996), 35.08[F][1]
Allied Bldg. Prods. Corp. v. United Pac.
Ins. Co., 549 A.2d 1163 (Md. Ct.
Spec. App. 1988), 35.07[B][1],
35.08[D][3]
Allied Bldg. Prods. Corp., United States
ex rel., v. Federal Ins. Co., 729 F.
Supp. 477 (D. Md. 1990), 35.04[A]
Allied Materials & Equip. Co. v. United
States, 569 F.2d 562 (Ct. Cl. 1978),
28.03[E][3][b]
Allied Materials & Equip. Co.,
B-293231, 2004 WL 228711 (Comp.
Gen. Feb. 5, 2004), 7.03[A]
Allied Roofers Supply Corp., City ex
rel., v. Joseph S. Smith Roofing, 599
A.2d 222 (Pa. Super. Ct. 1991),
35.08[D][3], 35.08[F][3]
All in One Maintenance Serv. v. Beech
Mountain Constr. Co., 318 S.E.2d
856 (N.C. Ct. App. 1984),
35.08[F][4]
Allison & Haney, Inc., IBCA No.
587-9-66, 69-2 B.C.A. (CCH) ¶ 9207
(1969), 27.05[E][2]
All Power, Inc. v. U.S., 60 Fed. Cl. 679
(2004), 27.05[C][2]
All Seasons Constr. & Roofing, Inc.,
ASBCA No. 45583, 98-2 B.C.A.
(CCH) ¶ 30,061 (1998), 24.04[C]
All Seasons Construction, Inc. v.
Mansfield Housing Auth., 920 So. 2d
413 (La. Ct. App. 2006), 32.06
All Seasons Water Users Assoc., Inc. v.
Northern Imp. Co., 339 N.W.2d 278
(N.D. 1987), 30.02[A][1]
All-State Constr., Inc., ASBCA No.
50586, 02-1 B.C.A. ¶ 31,794 (2002),
28.03[E][2]
All-State Constr., Inc., ASBCA No.
50586, 2006-2 BCA ¶ 33,344 (Jul.
12, 2006), 28.03[B][2]
All-State Constr., Inc., ASBCA No.
50586, 2007 ASBCA LEXIS 14 (Feb.
27, 2007), 28.03[B][2]

Allstate Ins. Co. v. Brown, 834 F. Supp.
854 (E.D. Pa. 1993), 20.05
Allstate Ins. Co. v. Langston, 358 So.
2d 1387 (Fla. App. 1978), 46.17
Alma, Town of, v. Azco Constr., Inc.,
10 P.3d 1256 (Colo. 2000),
29.02[C][5]
Alpha Elec. Supply v. F. Feaster, Inc.,
386 So. 2d 594 (Fla. Dist. Ct. App.
1980), 35.08[F][1]
Alrae Constr. Co., VACAB No. 970,
73-1 B.C.A. (CCH) ¶ 9872 (1973),
24.02[A]
Altman v. Young Lumber Co., 376 F.
Supp. 1290 (D.S.C. 1974),
35.06[A][1][b]
Altmayer v. Johsnon, 79 F.3d 1129
(Fed. Cir. 1996), 24.04[C]
Ambrogio v. Beaver Rd. Assocs., 267
Conn. 148 (2003), 30.02[B]
Am. Constr. Co., ENGBCA No. 5728,
91-2 B.C.A. ¶ 24,009 (1991),
28.03[F][2], 32.03[A]
Am. Eagle Indus., Inc. v. Secretary of
the Interior, 1999 U.S. App.
LEXIS 15680 (July 14, 1999),
28.02[A][2]
AMEC Civil, LLC v. Virginia, 74 Va.
Cir. 492 (2008), 23.04[B][1]
Amelco Elec. v. City of Thousand Oaks,
38 P.3d 1120 (2000), 30.03[D][1]
American Air Filter Co. v. Innamorati
Bros., Inc., 260 N.E. 718 (Mass.
1970), 35.07[B][1]
American Air Filter Co., 57 Comp. Gen.
285, 78-1 CPD ¶ 136 (1978),
28.03[E][3][b]
American Bank, United States ex rel., v.
CIT Constr. Inc. of Tex., 944 F.2d
253 (5th Cir. 1991), 35.06[A][2]
American Bldgs. Co. v. Wheelers
Stores, 585 P.2d 845 (Wyo. 1978),
35.03[B]
American Bonding Co. v. United States
ex rel. Francini, 233 F. 364 (3d Cir.),
error dismissed, 242 U.S. 661 (1916),
35.08[I]
Am. Bridge Co. v. State, 245 A.D. 535,
283 N.Y.S. 577 (1935),
26.02[MM][3]
American Bridge Co. v. State of New
York, 283 N.Y.S. 577 (N.Y. App. Div.
1935), 30.03[C][5]

American Cas. Co. v. Board of Educ., 228 F. Supp. 843 (W.D. Okla. 1964), 35.08[I]

American Cas. Co. v. Coastal Caisson Drill Co., 542 So. 2d 957 (Fla. 1989), 35.08[F][1]

American Cas. Co. v. Timmons, 352 F.2d 563 (6th Cir. 1965), 18.04[C][1]

American Druggists' Ins. Co. v. Shoppe, 448 N.W.2d 103 (Minn. Ct. App. 1989), 36.09[B]

American Druggists Ins. Co., United States v., 627 F. Supp. 315 (D. Md. 1985), 35.06[A][3]

Am. Family Mut. Ins. Co. v. Am. Girl, Inc., 268 Wisc. 2d 16, 673 N.W.2d 65 (2004), 18.05[A][1], 19.07[B]

American Gen. Fabrication, Inc., ASBCA No. 43518, 92-2 B.C.A. ¶ 24,955 (1992), 28.03[D][1][a][i]

American Home Assurance Co. v. Larkin Gen. Hosp. 593 So. 2d 195 (Fla. 1992), 34.04[F][3]

Am. Home Assur. Co. v. AGM Marine Contractors, Inc., 379 F. Supp. 2d 134 (D. Mass. 2005), 19.07[B]

American Ins. Co. v. Kinder, 640 S.W.2d 537 (Mo. Ct. App. 1982), 35.06[A][2]

American Int'l Constructors, EMGBCA Nos. 3633, 3667, 77-2 B.C.A. (CCH) ¶ 12,606 (1977), 27.05[D][5][c]

Am. Int'l Contractors, Inc./Capitol Indus. Constr. Groups, Inc., ASBCA Nos. 39,544 et al., 95-2 BCA ¶ 27,920 (1995), 23.03[B][1], 23.03[E][4], 28.03[B][2]

Am. Line Builders, Inc. v. United States, 26 Cl. Ct. 1155 (1992), 28.03[E][3][a]

American Mach. & Foundry Co., ASBCA No. 8862, 65-1 B.C.A. (CCH) ¶ 4654 (1965), 27.05[G][2][b]

American Masons' Supply Co. v. F.W. Brown Co., 384 A.2d 378 (Conn. 1978), 35.04[B], 35.07[B][1]

American Mfrs. Mut. Cas. Co., United States v., 901 F.2d 370 (4th Cir. 1990), 35.04[A]

American Mfrs. Mut. Ins. Co. v. Payton Lane Nursing Home, Inc., 2007 WL 674691 (E.D.N.Y. 2/28/07), 34.04[H]

American Motorists Ins. Co. v. Trane Co. (7th Cir. 1983) 718 F.2d 842, 18.04[C][2]

American Motorists Ins. Co. v. United Furnace Co., 876 F.2d 293 (2d Cir. 1989), 36.02[D]

American Nat'l Elec. Corp. v. Poythress Commercial, 604 S.E.2d 315 (N.C. App. 2004), 27.05[B][2]

American Oil Co. v. Brown Paving Co., 298 F. Supp. 528 (D.S.C. 1969), 35.08[D][2]

Am. Pipe & Constr. Co. v. Westchester County, 292 F. 941 (2d Cir. 1923), 26.02[KK][4]

American Radiator & Standard Sanitary Corp., v. Albany Mun. Hous. Comm'n, 441 S.W.2d 433 (Ky. 1969), 35.04[B]

Am. Renovation & Constr. Co., ASBCA No. 54039, 03-2 B.C.A. ¶ 32,296 (June 24, 2003), 28.03[D][1][a][ii]

Am. Sheet Metal Corp. v. GSA, GSBCA No. 14066 et al., 99-1 B.C.A. ¶ 30,329 (1999), 28.03[B][2], 28.03[D][1][a][ii], 28.03[D][2]

Am. Sheet Metal Corp., GSBCA No. 15165-C et al., 00-2 B.C.A. ¶ 31,126 (2000), 28.03[F][1], 28.03[F][4]

American States Ins. Co. v. Floyd I. Staub, Inc., 370 N.E.2d 989 (Ind. Ct. App. 1977), 35.08[F][1], 35.08[I]

American Sur. Co. v. United States, 317 F.2d 652 (8th Cir. 1963), 34.04[F][2]

American Sur. Co. v. Westinghouse Elec. Mfg. Co., 296 U.S. 133 (1935), 35.08[J]

American Sur. Co. of N.Y. v. Barrowagee Lab., Inc., 76 F.2d 67 (5th Cir. 1935), 35.03[A]

Am. Textile Mfrs. Inst., Inc. v. The Ltd., Inc., 190 F.3d 729 (6th Cir. 1999), 38.02[C][4]

Amerisure, Inc. v. Wurster Constr. Co., 818 N.E.2d 998 (Ind. App. 2004), 19.07[B]

Amerisure Mutual Ins. Co. v. Paric Corp., 2005 WL 2708873 (D. Mo. Oct. 21, 2005), 19.07[B]

Amertex Enters. v. United States, 108 F.3d 1392 (Fed. Cir. 1997), *cert. denied,* 118 S. Ct. 851 (1998), 28.03[E][3][b]

Ames v. Denning, Inc., ASBCA No. 6956, 62 B.C.A. (CCH) ¶ 3406 (1962), 27.05[C][3][a]

Amoco Oil Co. v. Capitol Indem. Corp., 291 N.W.2d 883 (Wis. Ct. App. 1980), 35.07[B][1]

AM/PM Franchise Ass'n v. Atlantic Richfield Co., 526 Pa. 110 (Pa. 1990), 30.01[A]

Anchorage, Municipality of, v. Frank Coluccio Constr. Co., 826 P.2d 316 (Alaska 1992), 30.03[D][1]

Anchor Concrete Co. v. Victor Sav. & Loan Ass'n, 664 P.2d 396 (Okla. 1983), 35.08[D][3]

Anderson v. Garafalo & Assocs., Inc., No. PC 1991-8501, 2003 R.I. Super. LEXIS 144 (Nov. 14, 2003), 7.02[B][2][c]

Anderson v. Golden, 569 F. Supp. 122 (S.D. Ga. 1982), 29.02[D][1]

Anderson v. Ichinose, 760 So. 2d 302 (La. 1999), 20.03

Anderson v. Whittzker Corp., 894 F.2d 804 (6th Cir. 1990), 29.04[F][1]

Anderson & Nafziger v. G.T. Newcomb, Inc., 100 Idaho 175, 595 P.2d 709 (1979), 26.02[M][3]

Andrews Constr. Co., GSBCA No. 4364, 75-2 BCA ¶ 11,598 (1975), 23.03[E][2]

Andrews, United States Dep't of Navy ex rel., v. Delta Contractors Corp., 893 F. Supp. 125 (D.P.R. 1995), 35.02[A], 35.04[A], 35.06[A][1][b], 35.08[H]

Andrulis v. Levin Constr. Corp., 331 Md. 354 (Md. 1993), 30.02[A][2]

Angelo Iafrate Constr. Co., Inc. v. Pennsylvania Tpk. Comm'n, Dkt. No. 3654, 2206 Pa. Bd. Cl LEXIS 4 (Pa. Bd. Cl. 2206), 30.03[D][4]

Animal Prot. Int. v. Martin, 511 F. Supp. 2d 196 (D. Me. 2007), 11.03[A][10]

Ann-Par Sanitation, Inc. v. Town of Brookhaven, 23 A.D.3d 380 (N.Y. App. Div. 2005), 16.09[B]

Anthem Elec., Inc. v. Pac. Employers Ins. Co., 302 F.3d 1049 (9th Cir. 2002), 19.07[B]

Anthony Dell'Aquilla, Enters. & Subsidiaries, U.S. v., 150 F.3d 329 (3d Cir. 1998), 11.03[A][6]

Anthony P. Miller, Inc. v. United States, 77 F. Supp. 209 (Ct. Cl. 1948), 30.03[C][3]

Anthony P. Miller, Inc. v. Wilmington Housing Authority, 165 F. Supp. 275 (D. Del. 1958), 26.02[H][3], 26.02[H][4]

Anzalone v. Doan, 540 So. 2d 385 (La. App. 1989), 46.25

APAC-Carolina, Inc. v. Greensboro-High Point Airport Auth., 431 S.E.2d 508 (N.C. App. 1993), 27.05[A][2], 27.05[D][3]

APAC-Ga., Inc. v. Dep't of Transp., 221 Ga. App. 604, 472 S.E.2d 97 (1996), 26.02[K][3]

Apex Contracting, Inc. v. City of Paris, 2004 WL 758276 (Ky. Ct. App. Apr. 9, 2004), 26.02[R][3]

Apex Int'l Mgmt. Serv., Inc., ASBCA Nos. 38087 et al., 94-2 B.C.A. ¶ 26,842 (1994), 28.04[C][1]

Apex Roofing, United States ex rel., v. Union Indem. Ins. Co., 865 F.2d 1226 (11th Cir. 1989), 35.06[A][3], 35.08[H]

Apple Corps. v. Apple Computer, Inc. [1191] [EWHC], 43.05[A]

Appley Bros. v. United States, 924 F. Supp. 935 (D.S.D. 1996), aff'd, 107 F.3d 876 (8th Cir. 1997), 35.08[J]

Applied Cos., ASBCA No. 43210, 94-2 BCA ¶ 26,837 (1994), 23.03[E][3]

Applied Industrial Materials Corp. (AIMCOR), v. Ovalar Makine Ticaret Ve Sanayi, A.S., 492 F.3d 132 (2d. Cir. 2007), 43.07[E]

Aptus Co. v. United States, 61 Fed. Cl. 638 (2004), 28.03[B][2]

Aragona Constr. Co., Inc. v. United States, 165 Ct. Cl. 382 (1964), 21.08, 28.03[E][3][b]

Arbor III Realty Co., HUD BCA No. 96-C-114-C5, 97-2 B.C.A. ¶ 29,344 (1997), 28.04[C][2]

Arch of Illinois, Inc. v. S.K. George Painting Contractors, Inc., 288 Ill. App. 3d 1080 (5th Dist. 1997), 30.02[A][1]

ARCO Eng'g Inc., ASBCA No. 52450, 01-1 B.C.A. ¶ 31,218 (2000), 28.03[F], 28.03[F][1]

Arctic Contractors, Inc. v. State, 564 P.2d 30 (Alaska 1977), 46.01

Arctic Corner, Inc., ASBCA No. 38075, 94-1 B.C.A. ¶ 26,317 (1993), 28.03[F][1]

Arctic Refrigeration & Air Conditioning, Inc., GSBCA No. 8073, 87-3 B.C.A. ¶ 20,078 (1987), 28.03[D][1][a][ii]

Ardsley, Inc. v. United Pac. Ins. Co., 332 P.2d 1000 (Nev. 1958), 35.08[I]

Arens Corp., ASBCA No. 50289, 02-1 B.C.A. ¶ 31,671 (2001), 28.03[D][2]

Arizona Gunite Builders, Inc. v. Continental Cas. Co., 459 P.2d 724 (Ariz. 1969), 35.04[B]

Arizona Laborers, Teamsters & Cement Masons Local 395 Health & Welfare Trust Fund v. New Pueblo Constructors, Inc., 640 P.2d 209 (Ariz. Ct. App. 1982), 35.04[B]

Arizona Prop. & Cas. Ins. Guar. Fund v. Helme, 735 P.2d 451 (Ariz. 1987), 20.04

Armco Steel Corp. v. Isaacson Structural Steel, 611 P.2d 507 (Alaska1980), 16.04[B]

Armstrong v. Royal Lakes Assoc., 502 S.E.2d 758 (Ga. Ct. App. 1998), 29.04[J]

Armstrong World Industries, Inc. v. Aetna Cas. & Sur. Co., 45 Cal. App. 4th 1, 52 Cal. Rptr. 2d 690, *review denied,* (1996), 18.04[C][2]

Army Athletic Ass'n., United States *ex rel.,* v. Reliance Ins. Co., 799 F.2d 1382 (9th Cir. 1986), 28.03[E][3][b]

Arnold M. Diamond, Inc., ASBCA, No. 45,072, 93-3 BCA ¶ 25,904 (1993), 23.03[E][2]

Arntz Contracting Co. v. St. Paul Fire & Marine Ins. Co., 54 Cal. Rptr. 2d 888 (Cal. App. Ct. 1996), 36.03[B]

Arrow Plumbing & Heating, Inc. v. North Am. Mechanical Servs. Corp., 810 F. Supp. 369 (D.R.I. 1993), 35.06[A][2]

A.R. Sales Co. v. United States, 51 Fed. Cl. 370 (2002), 28.03[D][2]

Arthur, United States v., 554 F.2d 730 (4th Cir. 1976), 42.02[B][3]

Arthur N. Olive Co. v. United States *ex rel.* Marino, 297 F.2d 70 (1st Cir. 1961), 25.03[B], 35.04[A]

Ascani Constr. & Realty Co., VACAB Nos. 1572 et al., 83-2 B.C.A. ¶ 16,635 (1983), 28.03[B][3][b], 28.03[E][1][a]

Asfaltos Panamenos, S.A., ASBCA No. 39425, 91-1 B.C.A. (CCH) ¶ 23,315, 39.08[A]

Asheville Contracting Co., DOT BCA No. 74-6, 76-2 B.C.A. ¶ 12,027 (1976), 28.03[E][1][a]

A.S. McGaughan Co., PSBCA [now Civilian BCA] Nos. 1752, 1754, 88-1 B.C.A. (CCH) ¶ 20,326 (1987), 27.05[B][3]

Associated Eng'rs & Contractors, Inc. v. Hawaii, 568 P.2d 512 (Haw. 1997), 28.03[E][4]

Associated Indem. Corp. v. CAT Contracting, Inc., 918 S.W.2d 580 (Tex. App. 1996), *rev'd in part* by Associated Indem. Corp. v CAT Contracting Firm, Inc., 964 S.W.2d 276 (Tex. 1998), 36.03[B]

Associated Indem. Corp. v. CAT Contracting Firm, Inc., 964 S.W.2d 276 (Tex. 1998), 34.04[D], 36.03[B]

AST Anlagen-Und Sanierungstechnik GmbH, ASBCA No. 39576, 04-1 B.C.A. ¶ 32,558 (2004), 28.03[D][2]

AST Anlagen-Und Sanierungstechnik GmbH, ASBCA No. 51,854, 04-2 B.C.A. ¶ 32,712, 39.07, 39.07[A]

Astro Cleaning & Packaging Corp., United States *ex rel.,* v. Jamison Co., 425 F.2d 1281 (6th Cir. 1970), 35.04[A]

Astro Dynamics, Inc., ASBCA No. 28,381, 88-3 BCA ¶ 20,832 (1988), 23.03[E][3]

Astro-Space Lab. v. United States, 470 F.2d 1003 (Ct. Cl. 1972), 28.03[F][1]

AT&T Communications, Inc. v. Wiltel, Inc., 1 F.3d 1201 (Fed. Cir. 1993), 28.03[E][3][b]

A. Teichert & Sons, Inc., United States *ex rel.,* v. Anchor Contractors, Inc., 257 F. Supp. 474 (N.D. Cal. 1966), 35.03[A]

Aten v. Scottsdale Ins. Co., 511 F.3d 818 (8th Cir. 2008), 18.05[A][2], 19.07[B]

Atherton Constr., ASBCA Nos. 44293 et al., 02-2 B.C.A. ¶ 31,918 (2002), 23.03[E][3], 24.04[C]

Atkins, United States *ex rel.*, v. McInteer, 470 F.3d 1350 (11th Cir. 2006), 38.02[B][1]

Atkinson v. Dist. Bond Co., 43 P.2d 867 (Cal. Ct. App. 1935), 28.03[B][3]

Atlanta Econ. Dev. Corp. v. Ruby-Collins, Inc., 206 Ga. App. 434, 425 S.E.2d 673 (1992), 26.02[K][3]

Atlantic Coast Mech. v. R.W. Allen Beers Constr., 264 Ga. App. 680, 592 S.E.2d 115 (2003), 26.02[K][3]

Atlantic Mut. Ins. Co. v. Continental Nat'l Am. Ins. Co., 302 A.2d 177 (N.J. Super. Ct. App. Div. 1973), 29.02[C][4]

Atlantic Sea-Con v. Dann Co., 582 A.2d 981 (Md. 1990), 35.03[B]

Atlas Contractors, Inc., 88-1 B.C.A. (CCH) ¶ 20,225 (1987), 24.02[A]

Atronix, Inc., ASBCA No. 16644, 72-2 B.C.A. ¶ 9763 (1972), 28.03[B][3][a]

Augusta Iron & Steel Works, Inc., v. USF&G, 790 F.2d 852 (11th Cir. 1986), 35.06[B][1]

Aulson Roofing, Inc., ASBCA No. 37677, 91-2 B.C.A. (CCH) ¶ 23,720, 39.08[A]

Aurora Painting, Inc., United States *ex rel.*, v. Fireman's Fund Ins. Co., 832 F.2d 1150 (9th Cir. 1987), 35.06[A][2]

Austin v. United States, 314 F.2d 518 (Fed. Cl. 1963), 5.03[C][8], 7.03[B][1][a], 28.03[E][4]

Austin v. Western Elec. Co., 337 F.2d 568 (9th Cir. 1964), 35.06[A][1][b]

Austin Elcon Corp. v. Avco Corp., 590 F. Supp. 507 (W.D. Tex. 1984), 35.08[E][4]

Austin-Griffith, Inc. v. Goldberg, 79 S.E. 2d 447 (S.C. 1953), 23.04[B][1]

Automated Servs., Inc., 81-2 B.C.A. ¶ 15303 (1981), 28.03[D][2]

Auto-Owners Ins. Co. v. Home Pride Cos., 684 N.W.2d 571 (Neb. 2004), 19.07[B]

Auto Owners Ins. Co. v. Virginia T. Newman and Trinity Construction, Opinion No. 26450, March 10, 2008, 19.07[B]

A.V. DeBlasio Constr., Inc., United States *ex rel.*, v. Mountain States Constr. Co., 588 F.2d 259 (9th Cir. 1978), 35.04[A]

Avedon Corp. v. United States, 15 Cl. Ct. 648 (1988), 24.02[C]

AXA Global Risks U.S. Ins. Co. v. Sweet Assocs., Inc., 302 A.2d 844, 755 N.Y.S.2d 759 (N.Y. App. Div. 2003), 28.03[C][1]

Axel Elec., Inc., ASBCA No. 18990, 74-1 B.C.A. ¶ 10,471 (1974), 28.03[E][3][b]

Aydin Corp. Microwave Div., ASBCA No. 34054, 89-1 B.C.A. ¶ 21,206 (1988), 28.04[C][2]

Aydin Corp. v. Widnall, 61 F.3d 1571 (Fed. Cir. 1995), 21.04

B

B&D Mechanical Contractors, Inc., United States *ex rel.*, v. St. Paul Mercury, Ins. Co., 70 F.3d 1115 (10th Cir. 1995), *cert. denied,* 116 S. Ct. 1568 (1996), 35.06[A][2]

B&M Constr., Inc., AGBCA No. 90-165-1, 93-1 B.C.A. ¶ 25,431 (1992), 28.03[F][1]

Bahrani, United States *ex rel.*, v. Conagra, Inc., 465 F.3d 1189 (10th Cir. 2006), 38.02[C][4]

Baifield Indus., Inc., ASBCA No. 14582, 72-2 B.C.A. ¶ 9676 (1972), 28.03[D][2]

Bailey v. Skipperliner Indus., Inc., 279 F. Supp. 2d 945 (N.D. Ind. 2003), 16.02[B]

Bailey-Lewis-Williams, Inc., United States *ex rel.*, v. Peter Kiewit Sons Co., 195 F. Supp. 752 (D.D.C. 1961), 25.02[A]

Baily v. Faux, 704 F. Supp. 1051 (D. Utah 1989), 35.06[A][1][b]

Bain, United States *ex rel.*, v. Georgia Gulf Corp., 2006 WL 3093637 (5th Cir. 2006), 38.02[B][3]

Bainbridge, Inc., ASBCA No. 15843, 71-1 B.C.A. ¶ 9351 (1972), 28.03[B][3][b]

Baisch v. Department of Revenue, 850 P.2d 1109 (Or. 1993), 17.07

Baker & Ford Co. v. United States *ex rel.* Urban Plumbing & Heating Co., 363 F.2d 605 (9th Cir. 1966), 35.04[A]

Balboa Ins. Co. v. Sippial Elec. Co., 379 So. 2d 579 (Ala. 1980), 35.06[A][2]

Balboa Ins. Co. v. United States, 775 F.2d 1158 (Fed. Cir. 1985), 36.02[C]

Balch Enters. Inc. v. Insurance Co. of Pennsylvania, Not Reported in F. Supp. 2d 2004 WL 556702 (N.D. Cal. 2004), 20.02

Baldi Bros. Constructors v. United States, 50 Fed. Cl. 74 (2001), 24.02[B]

Baldwin-Lima Hamilton Corp. v. United States, 434 F.2d 1371 (Ct. Cl. 1970), 29.04[A]

Balf Co., United States *ex rel.*, v. Casle Corp., 895 F. Supp. 420 (D. Conn. 1995), 35.04[A], 35.05[A], 35.07[A][4]

Balfour Beauttly Constr. v. Colonial Ornamental Iron, 986 F. Supp. 82 (D. Conn. 1997), 34.04[B]

Balimony Mfg. Co. of Venice, Inc., ASBCA No. 49730, 96-2 B.C.A. ¶ 28,605 (1996), 28.03[F][4], 28.03[G]

Ballard v. Buckley Powder Co., 60 F. Supp. 2d 1180 (D. Kan. 1999), 29.04[H]

Ballenger Corp., DOT CAB 74-32 et al., 84-1 B.C.A. (CCH) ¶ 16,973 (1983), 27.05[C][2], 27.05[C][3][b]

Ball v. Hahnischfeger Corp., 877 P.2d 45 (Okla. 1994), 19.07[A]

Baltimore Contractors, Inc. v. U.S., 12 Cl. Ct. 328 (1987), 11.04[B][4][a], 27.05[C][4]

Baltimore Cooperage Co., United States *ex rel.*, v. McCay, 28 F.2d 777 (D. Md. 1928), 35.08[B]

Baltimore, Mayor & City Council, v. Fidelity & Deposit Co., 386 A.2d 749 (Md. Ct. App. 1978), 34.03

Balzer Pac. Equip. Co., United States *ex rel.*, v. Fidelity & Deposit Co., 895 F.2d 546 (9th Cir. 1990), 35.08[J]

Bank of Auburn v. United States Fid. & Guar. Co., 295 F.2d 641 (5th Cir. 1961), 35.04[B]

Bank of Brewton, Inc. v. Int'l Fid. Ins. Co., 827 So. 2d 747 (Ala. 2002), 28.03[C][2]

Bank of California v. Opie, 663 F.2d 977 (9th Cir. 1981), 20.02

Bared & Co., The, ASBCA No. 47628, 95-2 B.C.A. (CCH) ¶ 27,710, 39.03[B][3]

Barret-Moore & Assoc. v. United States *ex rel.* Harwell, 367 F.2d 122 (10th Cir. 1966), 35.08[B]

Barnett v. Coppell North Texas Court, Ltd., 123 S.W. 3d 804 (Tex. App. Dallas 2003), 30.04[B]

Barnett v. Yonkers, 731 F. Supp. 594 (S.D.N.Y. 1990), 29.02[C][3]

Barrett Refining Corp. v. United States, 42 Fed. Cl. 128 (1998), 28.03[E][2]

Barr/Nelson, Inc. v. Tonto's Inc., 336 N.W.2d 46 (Minn. 1983), 36.09[F]

Bartec Indus., Inc., United States *ex rel.*, v. United Pac. Co., 976 F.2d 1274 (9th Cir. 1992), 35.04[A]

Barth, United States *ex rel.*, v. Ridgedale Electric, 44 F.3d 699 (8th Cir. 1995), 38.02[B][4][b]

Bartles Scott Oil Co. v. Western Sur. Co., 200 N.W. 937 (Minn. 1924), 35.06[B][3]

Barton & Sons Co., ASBCA 9477, 65-2 B.C.A. (CCH) ¶ 4874, 21.05

Barton & Sons Co., ASBCA No. 14097, 70-2 B.C.A. ¶ 8429 (1970), 28.03[D][3]

Barwise, IBCA No. 1690-6-83, 84-2 B.C.A. ¶ 17,347 (1984), 28.04[C][1]

Bash v. B.C. Constr. Co., 780 S.W.2d 697 (Mo. Ct. App. 1989); 380 F.3d 447 (8th Cir. 2004), 30.04[B][2]

Basic Asphalt & Constr. Corp. v. Parliament Ins. Co., 531 F.2d 702 (5th Cir. 1976), 35.08[I]

Basic Refractories v. Bright, 298 P.2d 810 (Nev. 1956), 35.08[J]

Basin Paving Co. v. Mike M. Johnson, Inc., 27 P.3d 609 (Wash. App. 2001), 27.05[A][2]

Bastianelli v. National Union Fire Ins. Co., 631 N.E.2d 566 (Mass. App. Ct. 1994), 35.05[B]

Bates & Assoc. v. Romei, 426 S.E.2d 919 (Ga. Ct. App. 1993), 35.08[B]

Bates & Rogers Construction Corp. v. Greeley & Hansen, 109 Ill. 2d 225, 486 N.E.2d 902 (1985), 26.02[N][3]

Bates & Rogers Constr. Corp. v. North Shore Sanitary Dist., 92 Ill. App. 3d 90 (2nd. Dist. 1980), 8A.08[G][3]

Bauer International Corp. v. Etablissements Souls & Cie, 25 N.Y. 2d 871, 303 N.Y.S.2d 884 (1969), 46.06

Bauhinia Corp. v. China Nat'l Mach. & Equip. Import & Export Corp., 819 F.2d 247 (9th Cir. 1987), 43.07[C]

Bay Cities Paving & Grading Inc. v. Lawyers' Mutual Ins. Co., 855 P.2d 1263 (Cal. 1993), 20.04

Bay Constr., VABCA No. 5594, 2002 WL 442118 (Mar. 19, 2002), 24.04[B]

Bayindir Insaat Turizm Ticaret Ve Sanayi A.S. v. Islamic Republic of Pakistan, 14 Nov. 2005 (ICSID Case. No. ARB/03/29), 43.06[A]

B.D. Collins Constr. Co., ASBCA No. 42,662, 92-1 BCA ¶ 24,659 (1991), 23.03[D]

Beach Resorts Int'l v. Clarmac Marine Constr. Co., 339 So. 2d 689 (Fla. Dist. Ct. App. 1976), 33.02[M][2]

Beachwalk Villas Condominium Ass'n v. Martin, 406 S.E.2d 372 (S.C. 1991), 29.02[C][3]

Beacon Constr. Co. v. U.S., 314 F.2d 501 (Ct. Cl. 1963), 8A.08[D]

Bean Stuyvesant LLC, ASBCA No. 53882, 06-2 B.C.A. (CCH) ¶ 33,420 (2006), 24.02[B]

Beard, ASBCA No. 42677, 42678, 93-3 B.C.A. ¶ 25,976 (1993), 28.03[B][3][b]

Beard, ASBCA No. 42677, 93-3 B.C.A. ¶ 25,976 (1993), 28.03[B][3]

Beard Family P'ship v. Commercial Indem. Ins. Co., 116 S.W.3d 839 (Tex. App. [Austin] 2003), 27.04[A][1]

Beard Plumbing & Heating v. Thompson Plastics, 152 P.3d 313 (4th Cir. 1998), 29.02[C][5]

Bear v. Tigerman, 140 Cal. App. 3d 979, 189 Cal. Rptr. 834 (1983), 46.25

Beauchamp Constr. Co. v. United States, 14 Cl. Ct. 430 (1988), 24.02[C], 24.02[D]

Beaumont-Gribin-von-Dyl Managment Co. v. California Union Ins. Co., 63 Cal. App. 3d 617 (Cal. Ct. App. 1976), 20.04

Beaver Excavating Co. v. Perry Township, 79 Ohio App. 3d 148, 606 N.E.2d 1067 (1992), 21.05

Beavers Constr. Co., AGBCA No. 83-125-1, 84-1 BCA ¶ 17,067 (AGBCA 1983), 30.03[C]

Beaves DOTCAB No. 1324, 83-1 B.C.A. (CCH) ¶ 16,232, 39.08[B]

Bechtel Envtl., Inc., ENGBCA Nos. 6137 et al., BCA ¶ 28,640; *reconsideration denied,* 97-1 BCA ¶ 28,851 (1997), 23.06[B][4]

Bechtel, United States, No. C-76-99, 1979 WL 1581 (N.D. Cal. Jan. 5, 1979), 17.08

Becker, United States *ex rel.,* v. Westinghouse Savannah River Co., 305 F.3d 284 (4th Cir. 2002), 38.02[B][2]

Beckman Constr. Co., ASBCA No. 24725, 83-1 BCA ¶ 16,326 at 81,159 (1983), 23.03[D]

Beeston, Inc., ASBCA No. 38969, 91-3 B.C.A. ¶ 24,241 (1991), 28.03[D][2]

Behan, United States v., 110 U.S. 338 (1884), 30.04[B][2]

Behlehem Steel Export Corp. v. Redondo Constr. Co., No. 92-1466 (DRD), 1997 WL 271485 (D.P.R. Feb. 20, 1997), *aff'd,* 140 F.3d 319 (1st Cir. 1998), 35.03[A]

Bell v. United States, 186 Ct. Cl. 189 (1968), 30.03[E]

Bell BCI Co. v. HRGM Corp., 276 F. Supp. 2d 462 (D. Md. 2003), 34.04[D]

Bell, Leola v. Commissioner, 219 F.2d 442 (5th Cir. 1955), 17.07[A]

Belmont, United States *ex rel.,* v. Mitty Bros. Constr. Co., 4 F. Supp. 216 (D. Idaho 1933), *aff'd,* 75 F.2d 79 (9th Cir. 1934), 35.04[A]

Bel Pre Med. Ctr., Inc. v. Frederick Contractors, Inc., 21 Md. App. 307, 320 A.2d 558, *rev'd on other grounds and remanded,* 274 Md. 307, 334 A.2d 526 (1974), 46.01

Belt Painting Corp. v. TIG Ins. Co., 100 N.Y.2d 377 (N.Y. 2003), 19.03[G][3][b]

Belz v. Clarendon America Ins. Co., 158 Cal. App. 4th 615 (2007), 18.04[A]

Ben C. Gerwick, Inc. v. United States, 152 Ct. Cl. 69, 285 F. 2d 432 (1961), 24.02, 24.02[D]

Bender GmgH v. Brownlee, 106 Fed. Appx. 728 (Fed. Cir. 2004), 28.03[B][2]

Bense v. Interstate Battery Sys. of Am., Inc., 683 F.2d 718 (2d Cir. 1982), 25.02[A]

Berkel & Co. Contractors v. Christman Co., 533 N.W.2d 838 (Mich. Ct. App. 1995), *appeal denied,* 549 N.W.2d 562 (Mich. 1996), 35.08[E][1]

Berkel & Co. Contractors v. Providence Hospital, 454 So. 2d 496 (Ala. 1984), 27.05[C][4]

Berkin Eng'g & Constr., Appeal of, ASBCA No. 8182, 63 BCA 3713 (1963), 30.03[C]

Berley Indus., Inc. v. New York, 45 N.Y.S.2d 683 (1978), 30.03[C][3]

Berlin Steel Constr. Co. v. Trataros Constr., Inc., 2007 WL 2482521 (Ct. Sup. 8/17/07), 34.02

Berman v. Schweiker, 531 F. Supp. 1149 (N.D. Ill. 1982), *aff'd,* 713 F.2d 1290 (7th Cir. 1983), 33.02[E]

Bernard Lumber Co. v. Lanier-Gervais Corp., 560 So. 2d 465 (La. Ct. App. 1st Cir. 1990), 35.06[A][2]

Bernhardt v. Polygraphic Co. of Am., Inc., 350 U.S. 198 (1955) ph, 46.04

Berry and Clay, Inc., PSBCA No. 4995, 2004 WL 1098320 (May 18, 2004), 24.02[B]

Bertot Indus., Inc., ASBCA No. 41262, 96-1 B.C.A. ¶ 28,230 (1996), 28.03[F][1]

Best Concrete Mix Corp. v. Lloyds of London Underwriters, 413 F. Supp. 2d 182 (E.D.N.Y. 2006), 43.07[A]

Beta Eng'g. Inc., ASBCA No. 53570, 02-2 B.C.A. ¶ 31,879 (2002), 28.03[D][2]

Bethesda Lutheran Church v. Twin City Constr. Co., 356 N.W.2d 344 (Minn. App. Ct. 1984), 30.02[A][1]

Bethlehem Corp. v. United States, 199 Ct. Cl. 247 (Fed. Cl.1972), 7.03[B][2][a]

Bethlehem Steel Co., United States v., 205 U.S. 105 (1907), 32.02

Bethlehem Steel Corp. v. United States Fid. & Guar. Co., 598 N.Y.S.2d 873 (App. Div. 1993), 35.08[H]

Betts, United States *ex rel.,* v. Continental Cas. Co., 230 F. Supp. 557 (W.D. Pa. 1964), 35.04[A]

Beverly Lee v. Phillips & Lomax Agency, Inc. 11 P.3d 632 (Okla. 2000), 29.04[J]

Bevis Constr. Co. v. Kittrell, 243 Miss. 549 (1962), 30.02[B]

B.F. Sturtevant Co. v. Fidelity & Deposit Co., 158 P.2d 740 (Wash. 1916), 35.08[D][2]

B.H.D. Inc. v. Nippon Ins. Inc., 46 Cal. App. 4th 1137 (Cal. Ct. App. 1996), 20.04

BIB Constr. Co. v. Fireman's Ins. Co., 625 N.Y.S.2d 550 (N.Y. App. Div. 1995), 36.04

B.I. Chipping Co. v. R.F. Scurlock Co., 2005 WL 3484306 (Ohio Ct. App. Dec. 20, 2005), 26.02[JJ][3], 26.02[JJ][4]

Biemann and Rowell Co. v. Donohoe Cos., Inc., 556 S.E.2d 1 (N.C. App. 2001), 27.05[B][2]

Big 3 Contracting Corp., ASBCA No. 20929, 79-1 B.C.A. ¶ 13,601 (1978), 28.03[B][3][a]

Big 4 Rents, Inc., United States *ex rel.,* v. Ogamba, 1997 WL 414193 (N.D. Cal. July 14, 1997), 35.04[A]

Big Chief Drilling Co. v. United States, 26 Ct. Cl. 1276 (1992), 21.04

Biggers Constr. Co., *In re,* 81-1 B.C.A. (CCH) ¶ 14,848 (1980), 22.08

Bill Curphy Co. v. Elliott, 207 F.2d 103 (5th Cir. 1953), 35.04[A]

Billows Elec. Supply Co., United States *ex rel.,* v. E.J.T. Constr. Co., 517 F. Supp. 1178 (E.D. Pa. 1981), *aff'd,* 688 F.2d 827 (3d. Cir. 1982), 35.04[A]

Bill Wright Painting & Decorating, ASBCA No. 33343, 87-1 B.C.A. (CCH) ¶ 19,666 (1987), 27.05[B][3][d]

Bilotta Constr. Corp. v. Village of Mamaroneck, 199 A.D.2d 230 (N.Y. 1993), 27.05[A][2]

Biltmore Constr. Co. v. National Union Fire, 572 So. 2d 532 (Fla. Dist. Ct. App. 1990), 35.06[B][3]

Bilt-Rite Contractors, Inc. v. Architectural Studio, 581 Pa. 454, 866 A.2d 270 (2008), 25.02[B]

Bilt-Rite Contractors, Inc. v. Architectural Studio, 886 A.2d 270 (Pa. 2005), 7.02[B][3], 29.02[C][5]

Bingham County Comm. v. Interstate Elec. Co., 665 P.2d 1046 (Idaho 1983), 33.02[M]

Binks Mfg. Co. v. Bedwell Co., 1997 U.S. Dist. LEXIS 1161 (E.D. Pa. 1997), 21.02

Birken Mfg. Co., ASBCA No. 32590, 90-2 B.C.A. ¶ 22,485 (1990), 28.03[F][1]

Bit-More Homes v. French, 130 N.W.2d 907 (Mich. 1964), 35.08[G]

Bituminous Cas. Corp. v. Altman Builders, Inc., 2006 WL 2137233 (D.S.C. 2006), 19.07[B]

Biwater Gauff (Tanzania) Ltd. v. United Republic of Tanzania, (ICSID Case No. ARB/05/22), 43.06[A]

B.J. Harland Electrical Co. v. Granger Bros., 24 Mass. App. Ct. 506, 510 N.E.2d 765 (1987), 26.02[V][3], 26.02[V][4]

Blackburn v. Columbia Med. Centre of Arlington Sub., L.P., 58 S.W.3d 263 (Tex. App. Ct. 2001), 17.01[A]

Blackhawk Corp. v. Gotham Ins. Co., 54 Cal. App. 4th 1090 (1997), 18.05[B][2]

Blackhawk Heating & Plumbing Co., GSBCA No. 2432, 75-1 B.C.A. (CCH) ¶ 11,261 (1975), *aff'd on reconsideration,* 76-1 B.C.A. (CCH) ¶ 11,649 (1975), 24.03

Blackhawk Heating & Plumbing v. Seaboard Sur. Co., 534 F. Supp. 309 (N.D. Ill. 1982), 34.04[C]

Blaine Econ. Dev. Auth. v. Royal Elec. Co., 520 N.W.2d 473 (Minn. Ct. App. 1994), 28.03[D][1][a][ii]

Blair, United States v., 321 U.S. 730 (1944), 30.03[C]

Blake Constr. Co., ASBCA No. 34480 et al., 88-2 B.C.A. (CCH) ¶ 20,552, 39.03[B][1]

Blake Constr. Co. v. C.J. Coakley, 431 A.2d 569 (D.C. 1981), 26.02[I][3], 28.03[E][1][a], 28.03[E][3][a], 33.01[E], 34.04[D]

Blake Constr. Co. v. United States, 987 F.2d 743 (Fed. Cir. 1993), 29.02[B][2]

Blake Constr. Co., Inc. v. U.S., 987 F.2d 743 (Fed. Cir. 1993), 27.05[B][3][b]

Blakeslee Arpaia Chapman, Inc. v. EI Constructors, Inc., 687 A.2d 506 (Conn. 1997), 35.02[B], 35.04[B]

Blanchard v. Terry & Wright, Inc., 331 F.2d 467 (6th Cir.), *cert. denied,* 379 U.S. 831 (1964), 35.06[A][2]

Blau Mech. Corp. v. City of N.Y., 158 A.2d 373, 551 N.Y.S.2d 228 (1990), 26.02[GG][4]

Blaunder Construction Co., ASBCA No. 9436, B.C.A. ¶ 4333 (1964), 37.02[I]

Bledsoe, United States ex rel., v. Community Health Systems, Inc., 342 F.3d 634 (6th Cir. 2003), 38.02[B][3]

Blinderman Constr. Co., ASBCA No. 24445, 84-3 BCA ¶ 17,527 (1984), 23.03[D]

Blinderman Constr. Co., Inc. v. United States, 39 Fed. Cl. 529 (1997), 23.06[B][2], 23.06[D]

Blinderman Constr. Co., Inc. v. United States, 695 F.2d (Fed. Cir. 1982), 24.02[D], 28.03[E][1][a]

Blinderman Constr. Co. v. U.S., 695 F.2d 552 (Fed. Cir. 1983), 23.03[D]

Blinne Contracting Co. v. Bobby Goins Enter., Inc., 715 F. Supp. 1044 (D. Kan. 1989), 35.04[B], 35.08[B]

Bloomsburg Mills, Inc. v. Sordini Construction Co., 164 A.2d 201 (Pa. 1963), 29.02[C][3]

Blount Bros. Construction Co. v. United States, 171 Ct. Cl. 478, 346 F.2d 962 (1965), 27.05[A][2]

Blount Bros. Construction Co. v. United States, 872 F.2d 1003 (Fed. Cir. 1989), 28.03[E][4]

Bluebonnet Sav. Bank FSB v. United States, 67 Fed. Cl. 231 (2005), 24.04

Blue Circle W., Inc., United States ex rel., v. Tucson Mech. Contracting Inc., 921 F.2d 911 (9th Cir. 1990), 35.05[A], 35.05[B]

Bluegrass Ctr., L.L.C. v. U.S. Intec, Inc., 49 Fed. Appx. 25, 2002 WL 31269650 (6th Cir. 2002), 29.03[D][1]

Bly-Magee, United States *ex rel.*, v. Premo, 470 F.3d 914 (9th Cir. 2006), 38.02[B][4][a]

Board of Educ. v. Sargent, Webster, Crenshaw & Folley, 146 A.D.2d 190 (N.Y. App. Div. 3d Dep't 1989), 29.02[C][4]

Board of Educ. v. Thompson Constr. Corp., 488 N.Y.S.2d 880 (N.Y. App. 3d Dep't 1985), 29.04[J]

Board of Educ. v. USF&G, 149 S.W. 46 (Mo. Ct. App. 1912), 35.06[B][3]

Board of Managers of the Riverview at Coll. Point Condominium III v. Schorr Bros. Dev. Corp., 182 A.D. 664 (N.Y. Ct. App. 1992), 20.02

Board of Pub. Instruction *ex rel.* Monmouth Plumbing Supply Co. v. Rood Constr. Co., 166 So. 2d 701 (Fla. Dist. Ct. App. 1964), 35.02[B]

Bob McGaughey Lumber Sales, Inc. v. Lemoine Co., 590 So. 2d 664 (La. Ct. App. 1991), 35.05[B]

Bodine Sewer, Inc. v. Eastern Ill. Precast, Inc., 493 N.E.2d 705 (Ill. App. Ct. 1986), 16.08[C]

Boeing Co. v. United States, 31 Fed. Cl. 289 (1994), 28.03[G]

Bogue Elec. Mfg. Co., ASBCA Nos. 25184 et al., 86-2 B.C.A. ¶ 18,925 (1986), 28.03[G]

Bogue Elec. Mfg. Co., ASBCA Nos. 25184 et al., 89-3 B.C.A. ¶ 21,951, 28.03[F][4]

Bolivar Insulation Co. v. R. Logsdon Builders, Inc., 929 S.W.2d 232 (Mo. Ct. App. 1996), 33.01[G]

Bolster Co. v. J.C. Boespflug Constr. Co., 330 P.2d 831 (Cal. Ct. App. 1958), 21.02

Bolt Co., The, v. Thomason Elec., Inc., No. 6:07-CV-00697 (S.C. 9/17/07), 34.02

Boomer v. Abbett, 263 P.2d 476 (Cal. 1953), 28.03[E][3][b]

Booth v. Mary Carter Paint Co., 202 So. 2d 8 (Fla. App. 1967), 25.05[B]

Bordallo Consol. Inc., United States *ex rel.*, v. Markowitz Bros., Inc., 249 F. Supp. 610 (D. Guam 1966), 35.04[A]

Borden, Inc. v. Florida E. Coast R.R. Co., 772 F.2d 750 (11th Cir. 1985), 29.04[F][1]

Boren v. Thompson & Assocs., 999 P.2d 438 (Okla. 2000), 20.02

Borey v. National Union Fire Ins. Co., 934 F.2d 30 (2d Cir. 1991), 36.04

Bornstein, United States, 423 U.S. 303 (1976), 38.02[D]

Borough of Nanty-Glo v. Fireman's Fund, 250 F. Supp. 329 (W.D. Pa. 1966), 35.06[A][3]

Boston Inv. Prop. #1 State v. E.W. Burman, Inc., 658 A.2d 515 (R.I. 1995), 29.02[B][3]

Boston Plate v. Window Glass Co. v. John Bowen Co., 141 N.E.2d 715 (Mass. 1957), 28.03[E][4]

Botzum Bros. Co. v. Brown Lumber Co., 150 N.E.2d 485 (Ohio 1957), 35.03[B]

Bower v. Tebbs, 314 P.2d 731 (Mont. 1957), 35.04[B]

Bowie v. Tucker, 204 N.C. 505, 168 S.E. 841 (1933), 46.27

Boyajian v. United States, 423 F. 2d 1231 (Ct. Cl. 1970), 30.03[D][1]

Boylston Hous. Corp. v. O'Toole, 321 Mass. 538 (1947), 30.02[B]

Boyte v. Dickson, 62 N.C. App. 682, 303 S.E.2d 418, *petition denied, appeal dismissed*, 309 N.C. 461, 307 S.E.2d 362 (1983), *reconsideration denied*, 313 S.E.2d 160 (N.c. 1984), 46.19

Bradford Builders, Inc. v. Sears, Roebuck & Co., 270 F.2d 649 (5th Cir. 1959), 29.02[B][1]

Bradford Dyeing Ass'n, Inc. v. J. Stog Tech GmbH, 765 A.2d 1226 (R.I. 2001), 27.04[A][2]

Bradley v. Bradley, 164 P.3d 537 (Wyo. 2007), 27.05[A][3]

Bradley, Terry L., Appeal of, PSBCA No. 5103 (June 27, 2005), 40.03[N]

Brady v. State, 965 P.2d 1 (Alaska 1998), 7.03[E]

Brand Inv. Co. v. United States, 58 F. Supp. 749 (Ct. Cl. 1944), 30.03[D][5]

Branham v. Miller Elec. Co., 118 S.E.2d 167 (S.C. 1961), 16.02[B]

Brannen v. Commissioner, 78 T.C. 417 *aff'd*, 722 F.2d 695 (11th Cir. 1984), 17.07

Brazier Lumber Co., ASBCA No. 18601, 76-2 B.C.A. ¶ 12,207 (1976), 28.03[E][4]

Breaux v. St. Paul Fire & Marine Ins. Co., 326 So. 2d 891 (La. Ct. App. 1976), 20.04, 20.05

Breland v. Shilling, 550 So. 2d 609 (La. 1998), 20.05

Brenner Metal Prods. Corp., ASBCA No. 25924, 82-1 B.C.A. ¶ 15,462 (1982), 28.03[B][3][b], 28.03[E][2]

Brent M. Davies, ASBCA No. 51938, 00-1 B.C.A. ¶ 30,678 (1999), 28.03[A]

Brett Fabrics, Inc. v. Gzran, Inc., 565 N.Y.2d 521 (1991), 46.06

Brewster, United States v., 506 F.2d 62 (D.C. Cir. 1974), 42.02[B][3]

Bricklayers & Allied Craftsmen Local No. 3 Health & Welfare Trust, Trustees of, v. Reynolds Elec. & Eng'g Co., 747 F. Supp. 606 (D. Nev. 1990), aff'd, 958 F.2d 378 (9th Cir. 1992), 35.03[A], 35.04[A]

Bridgewater Constr. Corp., Appeal of, 1990 WL 24908 (V.A.B.C.A.), 90-2 BCA P22, 764 VABCA No. 2866, VABCA No. 2919-2924 V.A.B.C.A., 39.03[B]

Briggs v. Travelers Indem. Co., 289 So. 2d 762 (Fla. Dist. Ct. App. 1974), 36.09[D]

Briggs, United States ex rel., v. Grubb, 358 F.2d 508 (9th Cir. 1966), 35.04[A], 35.08[D][2]

Bright, United States v., 517 F.2d 584 (2d Cir. 1975), 42.02[B][6]

Brinderson Newberg v. Pacific Erectors, 971 F.2d 272 (9th Cir. 1992), 34.04[D]

Brinich v. Jencka, 757 A.2d 388 (Pa. Super. Ct. 2000), 7.03[B][2][b]

Broadmoor Anderson v. Nat'l Union Fire Ins. Co., 912 So. 2d 400 (La. Ct. App. 2005), 18.05[A][1]

Broadmoor Anderson v. Nat'l Union Fire Ins. Co., 912 So. 2d 400 (La. Ct. App. 2005), cert. denied, 925 So. 2d 1239 (La. 2006), 19.07[B]

Broadmoor, LLC v. Ernest N. Morial New Orleans Exhibition Hall Auth., 867 So. 2d 651 (La. 2004), 17.01[A]

Brogran v. National Sur. Co., 246 U.S. 257 (1918), 35.04[A]

Bromion, Inc., ASBCA No. 12075, 67-2 BCA ¶ 6,543 (1967), aff'd, 411 F.2d 1020 (Ct. Cl. 1969), 23.03[B][1], 23.03[E][4]

Bromley Contracting Co., ASBCA Nos. 14884 et al., 72-1 B.C.A. ¶ 9252 (1971), 28.03[E][3][a]

Bromley Contracting Co. v. United States, 10 Cl. Ct. 668 (1986), 39.07

Bromley Contracting Co. v. United States, 14 Cl. Ct. 69 (1987), aff'd, 861 F.2d 729 (Fed. Cir. 1988), 28.03[E][1][b]

Bromley Contracting Co. v. United States, 15 Ct. Cl. 100 (1988), 21.07

Brookfield Constr. Co. v. United States, 661 F.2d 159 (Cl. Ct. 1981), 33.01[H]

Brookings Mun. Utils., Inc. v. Amoco Chem. Co., 103 F. Supp. 2d 1169 (D.S.D. 2000), 29.02[E]

Brooks Callaway Co., United States v., 318 U.S. 120 (1943), 28.03[B][1]

Brooks Lumber Co., ASBCA No. 40743, 91-2 B.C.A. ¶ 23,984 (1991), 28.03[D][3], 32.04

Brosnahan Builders, Inc. v. Harleysville Mut. Ins. Co., 137 F. Supp. 2d 517 (D. Del. 2001), 19.07[B]

Brotherhood of R.R. Trainmen v. Central of Ga. Ry., 415 F.2d 403 (5th Cir. 1969), 46.19

Bros. Builders Supply Co., United States ex rel., v. Old World Artisans, Inc., 702 F. Supp. 1561 (N.D. Ga. 1988), 35.05[A], 35.07[A][1]

Broward County v. Russell, Inc., 589 So. 2d 983 (Fla. Dist. Ct. App. 1991), 30.03[C][3]

Brower Co. Garrison, 468 P.2d 469 (Wash. Ct. App. 1970), 32.08

Brown & Kerr, Inc. v. St. Paul Fire & Marine Ins. Co., 940 F. Supp. 1245 (N.D. Ill. 1996), 35.08[A], 35.08[E][1]

Brown Bros. v. Metropolitan Government of Nashville & Davidson County, 877 S.W.2d 745 (Tenn. Ct. App. 1993), 26.02[QQ][3], 26.02[QQ][4]

Brown Construction Trades, Inc. v. United States, 23 Cl. Ct. 214 (1991), 38.03

Brown Mach. Div. of John Brown, Inc. v. Hercules, Inc., 770 S.W.2d 416 (Mo. Ct. App. 1989), 16.04[B]

Brown Mechanical Contractors v. Centennial Insurance Co., 431 So. 2d 932 (Ala. 1983), 27.05[E][3]

Brown, State ex rel. v. County of San Bernardino, No. CIVSS 07000329 (Cal. Super. Ct. Aug. 28, 2007), 11.03[A][10]

B.R. Servs., Inc., ASBCA No. 47673 et al., 99-2 B.C.A. ¶ 30,397 (1999), 28.03[B][1], 28.03[F][1]

Bruce-Anderson Co., ASBCA No. 35791, 89-2 B.C.A. ¶ 21,871 (1989), 28.03[E][3][b]

Bruce Construction Corp. v. United States, 324 F.2d 516 (Ct. Cl. 1963), 37.02[I]

Bruceton Bank v. United States Fid. & Guar. Ins. Co., 199 W. Va. 548, 486 S.E.2d 19 (1997), 18.05[A][1]

BRW, Inc. v. Dufficy & Sons, Inc., 99 P.3d 66 (Colo. 2004), 7.02[B][2][c]

Bryant Elec. Co. v. City of Fredericksburg, 762 F.2d 1192 (4th Cir. 1985), 29.02[C][5]

Bryant Elec. Co., United States ex rel., v. Aetna Cas. & Sur. Co., 297 F.2d 665 (2d Cir. 1962), 35.06[A][2]

Bryson v. Higdon, 222 N.C. 17, 21 S.E.2d 836 (1942), 46.26

B's Co., United States ex rel., v. Cleveland Elec. Co., 373 F.2d 585 (4th Cir. 1967), 35.08[F][1]

Buckley & Co. v. State, 140 N.J. Super. 289, 356 A.2d 56 (1975), 26.02[EE][3]

Buckner Constr. Co., State v., 704 S.W.2d 837 (Tex. Ct. App. 1985, writ ref'd n.r.e.), 28.03[E][1][a]

Buesing v. U.S., 47 Fed. Cl. 621 (2000), 27.05[E][4]

Bldg. Maint. Specialist, Inc., ENGBCA No. 4115, 83-2 B.C.A. ¶ 16,629 (1983), 28.03[E][2]

Bundy Tubing Co. v. Royal Indem. Co., 298 F.2d 151 (6th Cir. 1962), 18.04[C][1]

Burgess Constr. Co., GSBCA 2648, 68-2 B.C.A. ¶ 7201 (1968), 28.03[D][3]

Burke County Pub. Sch. Bd. of Educ. v. Juno Constr. Corp., 64 N.C. App. 158 (1983), 30.02[A][1]

Burlington Ins. Co. v. Oceanic Design & Constr., Inc., 383 F.3d 940 (9th Cir. 2004), 19.07[B]

Burlington Ins. Co. v. Okie Dokie, Inc., 398 F. Supp. 2d 147 (D.D.C. 2005), 33.01[E]

Burns v. Hanover Ins. Co., 454 A. 2d 325 (D.C. 1982), 30.03[C]

Burras v. Canal Constr. & Design Co., 470 N.E.2d 1362 (Ind. Ct. App. 1984), 28.03[E][2]

Burroughs Corp. v. United States, 223 Ct. Cl. 53, 617 F.2d 590 (1980), 28.04[A][2]

Business Men's Assurance Co. of Am. v. Graham, 891 S.W.2d 832 (Mo. Ct. App. 1993), 7.02[B][2][c]

Buss v. Superior Court, 16 Cal. 4th 35, 939 P.2d 766 (1997), 18.04[B]

Bussen Quarries, Inc., United States ex rel., v. Thomas, 938 F.2d 831 (8th Cir. 1991), 36.09[C]

Butler & Sidbury, Inc. v. Green Street Baptist Church, 90 N.C. App. 65 (1998), 30.02[A][1]

B.V. Constr., Inc., ASBCA No. 47766, 04-1 B.C.A. ¶ 32,604, 28.03[G]

Byrd Foods, Inc., VACAB No. 1679, 83-1 B.C.A. (CCH) ¶ 16,313, 39.06[D]

C

C&M Machine Prods., Inc., ASBCA No. 43348, 93-2 B.C.A. ¶ 25,748 (1993), 28.03[E][4]

C.A. Assocs. v. Dow Chem. Co., 918 F.2d 1485 (10th Cir. 1990), 29.04[F][2], 29.04[F][3]

Cable & Computer Tech, Inc., ASBCA No. 47420, 48846, 03-1 B.C.A. (CCH) ¶ 32,237 at 159,408 (2003), 24.02[C]

Caddell Constr., ASBCA 49333, 00-1 BCA ¶ 30,702, 27.05[D][6][c]

Calandro Dev., Inc. v. R.M. Butler Contractors, Inc., 249 So. 2d 254 (La. App. 1 Cir. 1971), 20.02

Caldwell & Santmyer, Inc. v. Glickman, 55 F.3d 1578 (Fed. Cir. 1995), 28.04[A], 28.04[A][1], 28.04[B][2]

Caldwell Foundry & Mach. Co., United States *ex rel.*, v. Texas Constr. Co., 237 F.2d 705 (5th Cir. 1955), 35.04[A]

Caldwell Tanks, Inc. v. Haley & Ward, Inc., 471 F.3d 210 (1st Cir. 2006), 33.02[C]

California Shipbuilding & Dry Dock Co., ASBCA No. 21394, 78-1 B.C.A. (CCH) ¶ 13,168 (1978), 24.04[B]

Callison Constr. Co., AGBCA No. 88-309-1, 92-3 BCA ¶ 25,071 at 124,952, 23.03[D]

Cal's A/C & Elec., United States *ex rel.*, v. Famous Constr. Corp., 34 F. Supp. 2d 1042, 33.02[O], 35.04[A]

Calvine Cotton Mills, Inc. v. Textile Workers Union of America, 238 N.C. 719, 79 S.E.2d 181 (1953), 46.19, 46.24

Camico Mut. Ins. Co. v. Rooney, Ida, Nolt and Ahern Accountancy Corp., 2006 WL 866321 (Cal. Ct. App. Apr. 5, 2006), 20.04

Camp v. Leonard, 515 S.E.2d 909 (N.C. App. 1999), 27.05[B][5][d]

Camrex Reliance Paint Co., GSBCA No. 6870, 85-3 B.C.A. ¶ 18,376 (1985), 28.03[F][1]

Canadian Commercial Corp., ASBCA No. 17187, 76-2 B.C.A. ¶ 12,145 (1976), *aff'd on reconsideration,* 77-2 B.C.A. ¶ 12,758 (1977), 28.03[E][4]

Canam Steel Corp. v. Bowdoin Constr. Corp., 613 N.E.2d 121 (Mass. App. Ct. 1993), 35.08[E][1]

Canion, United States *ex rel.*, v. Randall & Blake, 817 F.2d 1188 (5th Cir. 1987), 35.04[A]

Cannon Air Corp., United States *ex rel.*, v. National Homes Constr. Corp., 581 F.2d 157 (8th Cir. 1978), 35.08[B]

Canon Constr. Corp., ASBCA No. 16,142, 72-1 BCA ¶ 9,404 (1972), 23.06[B][4], 24.04[E]

Canter v. Koehring Co., 283 So. 2d 716 (La. 1973), *superseded by statue on other grounds,* 29.02[C][4]

Cantrell Dev. Corp., ASBCA Nos. 30160 et al., 89-2 B.C.A. ¶ 21,635 (1989), 28.03[B][1]

C.A. Oakes Constr. Co. v. Ajax Paving Indus., 652 So. 2d 914 (Fla. Dist. Ct. App. 1995), 35.08[B], 35.08[D][1]

Capital City Construction Co., DOT BCA 74-29, 75-1 B.C.A. ¶ 11,012 (1974), 28.03[D][3]

Capital Dev. Bd. *ex rel.* P.J. Gallas Elec. Contractors v. G.A. Rafel & Co., 493 N.E.2d 348 (Ill. App. Ct. 1986), 35.08[F][1]

Capital Elec. Co., 65 BCA No. 5316, 83-2 B.C.A. (CCH) ¶ 16,548 (1983), 24.04[B]

Capital Elec. Co. v. United States, 729 F.2d 743 (Fed. Cir. 1984), 24.04[C], 30.03[C][2], 30.03[C][3], 30.03[C][4]

Capital Indem. Corp., *In re,* 41 F.3d 320 (7th Cir. 1994), 34.04[H]

Capitol Elec. Supply Co., United States *ex rel.*, v. C.J. Elec. Contractors, Inc., 535 F.2d 1326 (1st Cir. 1976), 35.06[A][1][a]

Capitol Steel Fabricators, Inc. v. Mega Constr. Co., 58 Cal. App. 4th 1049 (1997), 21.05

Capolino Sons, Inc., United States *ex rel.*, v. Electronic & Missile Facilities, Inc., 364 F.2d 705 (2d. Cir. 1966), *cert. denied,* 385 U.S. 924 (1966), 25.02[A], 35.06[A][2]

Carabell v. U.S. Army Corps of Engineers, 391 F.3d 704 (6th Cir. 2004), 11.03[A][1][c]

Caranna v. Eades, 466 So. 2d 259 (Fla. App. 1985), 20.01

Carboline Co. v. Home Indem. Co., 522 F.2d 363 (7th Cir. 1975), 18.04[B]

Carlisle Constr. Co., United States *ex rel.*, v. Coastal Structures, Inc., 689 F. Supp. 1092 (M.D. Fla. 1988), 35.04[A], 35.06[A][1][b], 35.08[H]

Carlson, United States *ex rel.*, v. Continental Cas. Co., 414 F.2d 431 (5th Cir. 1969), 35.02[A], 35.04[A]

Carlson, William, United States *ex rel.*, v. Continental Cas. Co., 414 F.2d 431 (5th Cir. 1969), 35.07[A][3]

Carlton Hobbs Real Estate, LLC v. Sweeney & Conroy, Inc., 41 A.D.3d 214, 838 N.Y.S.2d 516 (1st Dep't 2007), 46.04

Carlyle Rubber Co., ASBCA No. 23070, 79-2 B.C.A. ¶ 14,117 (1979), 28.03[D][1][a][i]

Carney Gen. Contractors, Inc.,
NASABCA No. 375-4, 80-1 B.C.A.
(CCH) ¶ 14,243 (1980), 24.04[E]

Carolina Cas. Co. v. R.L. Brown &
Assocs., Inc., 2006 WL 2842733
(N.D. Ga. 9/29/06), 34.04[H]

Carolina Cas. Ins. Co. v. Ragan Mech.
Contractors, Inc., 548 S.E.2d 646
(Ga. App. 2003), 28.02[C],
28.03[C][2]

Carolina-Virginia Fashion Exhibitors,
Inc. v. Gunter, 230 S.E.2d 380 (N.C.),
46.23

Carolina-Virginia Fashion Exhibitors,
Inc. v. Gunter, 291 N.C. 208, 230
S.E.2d 380 (N.C. 1976), 46.23

Carousel Dev., Inc., ASBCA No. 50719,
01-1 B.C.A. (CCH) ¶ 31,262 (2001),
24.04[B]

Carpenter v. Susi, 121 A.2d 336 (Me.
1956), 35.07[B][1]

Carriage Square, Inc. v. Commissioner,
69 T.C. 119 (1977), 17.07

Carroll, United States ex rel., v. Beck,
151 F.2d 964 (6th Cir. 1945),
35.08[D][2]

Carrothers Constr. Co. v. City of Dallas,
1996 WL 625433 (5th Cir. Oct. 11,
1996), 26.02[RR][1], 26.02[RR][4]

Carter Equip. Co., United States ex rel.,
v. H.R. Morgan, Inc., 554 F.2d 164
(5th Cir. 1977), 33.02[O]

Carter Equip. Co., United States ex rel.,
v. H.R. Morgan, Inc., 554 F.2d 164
(5th Cir. 1977), reh'g granted, 554
F.2d 164 (5th Cir. 1977), 35.04[A]

Carter Industries, DOT BCA No. 4108,
02-1 B.C.A. ¶ 31,738 (2002),
28.04[B][2]

Carter-Schneider-Nelson, Inc., United
States ex rel., v. Campbell, 293 F.2d
816 (9th Cir. 1961), 35.04[A]

Carter v. Krueger, 916 S.W.2d 932,
(Tenn. Ct. App. 1995),
28.03[D][1][a][i], 28.03[E][1]

Carter v. Sherburne Corp., 132 Vt. 88,
315 A.2d 870 (1974), 26.02[TT][1]

Cascade Pac. Int'l v. United States, 773
F.2d 287 (Fed. Cir. 1985),
28.03[F][1], 30.04[B][1]

Case, Inc. v. United States, 88 F.3d
1004 (Fed. Cir. 1996), 39.06[C]

Case Prestressing Corp. v. Chicago
Coll. of Osteopathic Med., 455
N.E.2d 811 (Ill. App. 1983), 30.03[C]

Casey & Hurley v. MacFarlane Bros.
Mfg. Co., 83 Conn. 442, 76 A. 515
(1910), 21.02

Casson Constr. Co., GSBCA No. 4884,
83-1 B.C.A. (CCH) ¶ 16,523 (1983),
30.03[D][3]

Cass v. Smith, 240 S.W. 778 (Tenn.
1921), 35.07[B][1]

Castaldo v. Pittsburg-Des Moines Steel
Co., 376 A.2d 88 (Del. 1977),
29.02[C][1]

Cast-Crete Corp. v. West Baro Corp.,
339 So. 2d 413 (La. App. 1st Cir.
1976), writ denied, 341 So. 2d 900
(La. 1977), 35.08[C]

Castle Texas Prod. Ltd. P'ship v. Long
Trusts, 134 S.W.3d 267 (Tex. App.
Ct. 2003), 17.01[A]

Caswell Equip. Co., GSBCA No. 5645,
81-2 BCA ¶ 15,337 (1981),
23.03[B][1]

Cates Constr., Inc. v. Talbot Partners, 62
Cal. Rptr. 2d 548 (Ct. App. 1997),
34.04[D]

Cates Constr., Inc. v. Talbot Partners,
Inc., 980 P.2d 407 (Cal. 1999), 34.01,
34.02, 34.04[D], 34.04[F][3]

Catz Am. Co. v. Pearl Grange Fruit
Exch., Inc., 292
F. Supp. 549 (S.D.N.Y. 1968), 46.23

Cavalier Clothes, Inc. v. United States,
51 Fed. Cl. 339 (2001), 24.04

C.B.C. Enters., Inc. v. United States,
978 F.2d 669 (Fed. Cir. 1992),
24.04[C], 30.03[C][3]

C.C. & T. Constr. Co. v. Coleman Bros.
Corp., 391 N.E.2d 1256 (Mass. App.
Ct. 1979), 35.04[B]

CC&T Constr. Co. v. Coleman Bros.
Corp., 391 N.E.2d 1256 (Mass. App.
Ct. 1979), 35.07[B][1]

C.D. Murray Co., 89-1 B.C.A. (CCH)
¶ 21,275 (ENGBCA 1988), 32.06

Cecil I. Walker Mach. Co. v. Stauben,
Inc., 230 S.E.2d 818 (W.Va. 1976),
35.04[B]

Cedar Lumber, Inc. v. United States, 5
Cl. Ct. 539 (1984), 24.02[D],
28.03[E][1][a]

CEMS, Inc. v. United States, 59 Fed.
Cl. 168 (2003), 24.02[D],
27.05[B][3][d], 27.05[C][2]

Central Florida Plastering &
Development v. Sovran Construction
Co., 679 So. 2d 1226 (Fla. Dist. Ct.
App. 1996), 32.07

Central Ohio Joint Vocational Sch. Dist.
Bd. of Educ. v. Peterson Constr. Co.,
716 N.E.2d 1210 (Ohio Ct. App.
1998), 29.02[B][1], 29.02[D][1]

Central School Dist. No. 1 v. Double M
Construction Corp., 46 A.D.2d 800
(1974), 33.02[M][5]

Central Steel Erection Co. v. Will, 304
F.2d 548 (9th Cir. 1962), 21.06

Central Towers Apartment, Inc. v.
Martin, 453 S.W.2d 789 (Tenn. Ct.
App. 1969), 33.02[N], 36.03[C]

Centrotrade Minerals & Minerals, Inc.
v. Hindustan Copper Ltd., Civil
Appeal No. 2562 of 2006 (May 9,
2006), 43.07[B]

Century Constr. Co. v. United States, 22
Cl. Ct. 63 (1990), 39.04[F]

Century Marine, Inc. v. United States,
153 F.3d 225 (5th Cir. 1998),
28.03[F][3]

Certified Indus. v. Royal Indem. Co.,
252 N.Y.S.2d 345 (Sup. Ct. 1964),
35.08[B]

C.F.I. Constr. Co., DOTBCA No. 1782,
87-1 B.C.A. (CCH) ¶ 19,587 (1987),
24.04[C]

Champion Home Builders Co. v. ADT
Sec. Servs., Inc., 179 F. Supp. 2d 16
(N.D.N.Y. 2001), 29.02[E]

Champion Timberland Servs., Inc.,
IBCA No. 2061, 86-2 BCA ¶ 18,769
(1986), 23.03[B][1]

Chandler, United States ex rel., v. Cook
County, Illinois, Nos. 00-4110 &
01-1810, 2002 U.S. App. LEXIS
2587 (7th Cir. 2002), 38.02[C]

Chandler, United States ex rel., v.
Hektoen Inst. for Med. Research, 277
F.3d 969 (7th Cir. 2002), 38.02[C]

Chaney Bldg. Co. v. Tucson, 148 Ariz.
571, 716 P.2d 28 (1986), 20.01,
29.02[B][1]

Chapman v. EI Constructors, No. CV
0040938, 1995 WL 91391 (Conn.
Super. Ct. Feb. 21, 1995), aff'd, 687
A.2d 506 (Conn. 1997), 35.08[E][1]

Charles D. Weaver v. United States, 209
Ct. Cl. 714 (1976), 24.04[A]

Charles Equip. Co., City ex rel., v.
United States Fid. & Guar. Co., 491
N.E.2d 1269 (Ill. App. Ct. 1986),
35.08[D][1]

Charles G. Williams Constr. Inc. v.
White, 271 F.3d 1055 (Fed.
Cir. 2001), 30.03[B][2],
30.03[C][3]

Charles G. Williams Constr. Inc. v.
White, 326 F.3d 1376 (Fed. Cir.
2003), 24.04[C]

Chas. I. Cunningham, IBCA No.
242, 60-2 BCA ¶ 2816 (1960),
23.03[B]

Chas. I. Cunningham, IBCA No. 60,
57-2 BCA ¶ 1541 at 5483 (1957),
23.03[D]

Charles I. Hosmer, Inc. v.
Commonwealth, 302 Mass. 495, 19
N.E.2d 800 (1939), 26.02[V][4]

Charles L. Harney, Inc. v. Durkee, 237
P.2d 561 (Cal. Dist. Ct. App. 1951),
7.03[E]

Charles T. Parker Constr. Co. v. United
States, 193 Ct. Cl. 320, 433 F.2d 771
(1970), 24.02[B]

Charlotte v. Skidmore, Owings &
Merrill, 407 S.E.2d 571 (N.C. Ct.
App. 1991), 29.02[C][3]

C.H. Benton Inc., United States ex rel.,
v. Roelof Constr. Co., 418 F.2d 1328
(9th Cir. 1969), 35.07[A][2],
35.08[D][2]

CHE Consulting, Inc. v. U.S., 74 Fed.
Cl. 742 (2006), 27.03[B][1]

Chelios v. Kaye, 219 Cal. App. 3d 75
(1990), 31.06[D]

Chemetron Corp., United States ex rel.,
v. George A. Fuller Co., 250 F. Supp.
649 (D. Mont. 1965), 35.04[A],
35.07[A][1]

Chemithon Corp. v. United States, 1 Ct.
Cl. 747 (1983), 30.04[B][1]

Cherokee Tanning Extract Co. v.
Western Union Tel. Co., 55 S.E. 777
(N.C. 1906), 16.04[C]

Chestnut Hill Dev. Corp. v. Otis
Elevator Co., 739 F. Supp. 692 (D.
Mass. 1990), 30.02[B]

Chicago Bridge & Iron Gen. Elec. Co.,
1976 Trade Reg. Rep. (CCH)
¶ 50,194, 17.08

Chicago Coll. of Osteopathic Med. v. George A. Fuller Co., 776 F.2d 198 (7th Cir. 1985), 30.03[C][5]

Chicago, Milwaukee St. Paul & Pacific R. Co. v. U.S., 575 F.2d 839 (Ct. Cl. 1978), 11.03[A][2]

Chicago Rigging Co. v. Uniroyal Chem. Co., 718 F. Supp. 696 (N.D. Ill. 1989), 35.07[A][4]

Chouteau v. United States, 95 U.S. 61 (1877), 24.02[A]

Chris Berg, Inc. v. Dep't of Transp. & Pub. Facilities, 680 P.2d 93 (Alaska 1984), 7.03[C]

Chris Craft Indus. v. United States, 209 Ct. Cl. 700 (1976), 21.06

Christensen, AGBCA No. 95-188-R, 95-2 B.C.A. ¶ 27,724 (1995), 28.04[C][1]

Christie v. United States, 237 U.S. 234 (1915), 22.06

Christ Lutheran Church v. State Farm Fire and Casualty, 471 S.E.2d 124 (N.C. Ct. App. 1996), 20.04

Church ex rel. Smith v. Callanan Indus., 782 N.E.2d 50 (N.Y. 2002), 29.02[D][3]

Churchill & Closer, 61 Fed. Cont. Rep. at 756, 28.03[D][1][a][i]

Church of the Holy Spirit v. Bevco, Inc., 338 N.W.2d 601 (Neb. 1983), 33.01[B]

Cianbro Corp. v. Empresa Nacional de Ingeniera y Technologia, 697 F. Supp. 15 (D. Me. 1988), 25.03[B]

Cincinnati Elecs. Corp. v. United States, 32 Fed. Cl. 496 (1994), 28.03[G], 39.06[C]

Cincinnati Ins. Co. v. Gateway Constr. Co., 372 Ill. App. 3d 148 (App. Ct. 2007), 18.04[A]

Cincinnati Ins. Co. v. Putnam, 355 So. 2d 855 (Fla. Dist. Ct. App. 1976), 35.08[A]

CIT Group/Equip. Fin. Inc. v. Horizon Potash Corp., 884 P.2d 821 (N.M. Ct. App. 1994), 35.04[B]

Citibank v. Grupo Cupey, Inc., 382 F.3d 29 (1st Cir. 2004), 34.04[G][6]

Citizens Nat'l Bank v. L.L. Glascock, Inc., 243 So. 2d 67 (Miss. 1971), 21.05

City Elec. v. Industrial Indem. Co., 683 P.2d 1053 (Utah 1984), 35.07[B][1]

City Express, Inc. v. Express Partner, 959 P.2d 836 (Haw. 1998), 7.02[B][2][c], 29.02[C][5]

City Lumber Co. v. National Sur. Corp., 92 S.E.2d 128 (S.C. 1956), 35.08[D][3]

City of. See name of city.

Civic Associates v. Security Insurance Co., 749 F. Supp. 1076 (D. Kan. 1990), 20.04

C.J.C. Inc. v. Western States Mech. Contractors, Inc., 834 F.2d 1533 (10th Cir. 1987), 33.02[O], 35.04[A]

C.J.C., Inc., United States ex rel., v. Western States Mech. Contractors Inc., 834 F.2d 1533 (10th Cir. 1987), 33.01[K]

C.J. Longerfelder & Sons, Inc. v. Commonwealth, Dep't of Transp., 44 Pa. Commw. 585 (1979), 24.02[C]

C.J. Longerfelder & Sons, Inc. v. Pennsylvania Dep't of Transp., 404 A.2d 745 (Pa. 1970), 23.03[E][4]

C.J. Machine, Inc., ASBCA No. 54249, 04-1 B.C.A. ¶ 32,515, 39.06[C]

CJP Contractors, Inc. v. U.S. 45 Fed. Cl. 343 (1999), 27.05[B][3][c], 28.03[B][2], 28.03[D][1][b], 28.04[D][3]

Clafon Constr., Inc. v. United States, 18 Cl. Ct. 426 (1989), 23.04[B][1]

Clark v. Aenchbacher, 238 S.E.2d 442 (Ga. Ct. App. 1977), 33.02[D]

Clark v. Transcon, Ins. Co., 197 S.W.3d 449 (Ark. 2004), 29.02[C][3]

Clark Concrete Contr., Inc., GSBCA No. 14340 99-1 BCA 6 30,280 99-1 1999 WL 143977 (1999), 30.03[D][4]

Clark Constr. Group, Inc. v. Liberty Mut. Ins. Co., No. 00-1146-A et al. (E.D. Va. Apr. 16, 2001), 28.03[C][1]

Clark Eng'g Co., United States ex rel., v. Freeto Constr. Co., 547 F.2d 537 (10th Cir. 1977), 35.08[B]

Clark-Fontana Paint Co., United States ex rel., v. Glassman Constr. Co., 397 F.2d 8 (4th Cir. 1968), 35.08[D][3]

Clarkstown, Town of, v. North River Ins. Co., 803 F. Supp. 827 (S.D.N.Y. 1992), 34.04[C]

Clausen, United States ex rel., v. Laboratory Corp. of America, 290 F.3d 1301 (11th Cir. 2002), 38.02[C]

Claussen v. Aetna Casualty & Surety
Co., 754 F. Supp. 1576 (S.D. Ga.
1990), 18.05[B][1]

Clavier Corp., ASBCA No. 19144, 75-1
B.C.A. ¶ 11,241 (1975), 28.03[D][2]

Clay Bernard Sys. Int'l, Ltd., ASBCA
No. 25382, 88-3 B.C.A. ¶ 20,856
(1988), rev'd in part, 22 Cl. Ct. 804
(1991), 28.03[F][3]

Clearwater Constructors, Inc. v. United
States, 71 Fed. Cl. 25 (2006),
24.02[C]

Clemmer v. Hartford Ins. Co., 22 Cal.
3d 865 (1978), 18.04[A]

Clifford R. Gray Inc. v. City Sch. Dist.
of Albany, 227 A.D.2d 843, 716
N.Y.S.2d 795 (2000), 26.02[KK][4]

CMC Steel Fabricators Inc., U.S. ex
rel., 131 F. Supp. 2d 882 (S.D. Tex.
2000), 23.07[C][2]

Cmty. Heating & Plumbing v. Garrett, 2
F.3d 1143 (Fed. Cir. 1993),
28.03[F][4]

Cmty. Heating & Plumbing v. Garrett,
II, 2 F.3d 1143 (Fed. Cir. 1995),
33.02[E]

Coakley & Williams, Inc. v.
Shatterproof Glass Corp., 706 F.2d
456 (4th Cir. 1983), 29.02[E]

Coastline Fire Prot. Co. v. Peabody
Constr. Co., 18 Mass. L. Rep. 234,
_____ N.E.2d _____ (Mass. Super.
2004), 25.02[C]

Coatesville Contractors & Eng'rs, Inc.
v. Borough of Ridley Park, 506 A.2d
862 (Pa. 1986), 7.03[B][2][b]

Coatesville Contractors & Eng'rs, Inc.
v. Borough of Ridley Park, 509 Pa.
553, 506 A.2d 862 (Pa. 1986),
26.02[MM][4]

Coates v. United States Fid. & Guar.
Co., 525 S.W.2d 654 (Mo. Ct. App.
1975), 35.04[B]

Cobb-Strecker-Dunphy & Zimmerman,
Inc., United States ex rel., v. M.A.
Mortensen Co., 706 F. Supp. 685
(D. Minn. 1989), aff'd, 894 F.2d 311
(8th Cir. 1990), 35.04[A]

C.O. Falter Corp. v. City of
Binghamton, 684 N.Y.S.2d 86 (App.
Div.1999), 32.04

C.O. Falter, Inc. v. Crum & Forster Ins.
Cos., 361 N.Y.S.2d 968 (N.Y. Sup.
Ct. 1974), 19.07[B]

Coffee Bay Investors, LLC v. W.O.G.C.
Co., 878 So. 2d 665 (La. Ct. App.
2004), 17.01[A]

Coffey Constr. Co., VABCA Nos. 3361
et al., 93-2 BCA ¶ 25,788 at 128,328
(1993), 23.03[D], 23.06[B][2]

Coffey, United States ex rel., v. William
R. Austin Contr. Co., 436 F. Supp.
626 (W.D. Okla. 1977), 35.06[A][2]

Cogefar-Impresit U.S.A., Inc.,
DOTBCA No. 2721, 97-2 BCA
¶ 29,188 (1997), 23.06[B][2],
23.06[B][3]

Cohoon v. Ziman, 60 N.C. App. 226,
298 S.E.2d 279, petition denied, 307
N.C. 697, 301 S.E.2d 388 (1983),
46.26

Colard v. Am. Family Mut. Ins. Co.,
709 P.2d 11 (Colo. App. 1985),
19.07[B]

Colberg v. Rellinger, 770 P.2d 346
(Ariz. Ct. App. 1989), 29.02[C][5]

Colbert v. B.G. Garvin Constr. Co., 600
So. 2d 719 (La. App. 5 Cir. 1992),
20.01

Coleman Capital Corp. v. Fidelity &
Deposit Co., 43 F.R.D. 407 (S.D.N.Y.
1967), 35.08[A]

College Point Boat Corp. v. United
States, 267 U.S. 12 (1925),
28.02[A][3]

Collett v. Ins. Co. of the W., 64 Cal.
App. 4th 338 (1998), 18.05[A][2]

Colonial Gas Co. v. Aetna Cas. & Sur.
Co., 823 F. Supp. 975 (D. Mass.
1993), 18.04[C][2]

Colonial Metals Co. v. United States,
494 F.2d 1355 (Ct. Cl. 1974),
27.05[G][2][b]

Colo. Carpenters & Millwrights Health
Benefits Trust Fund, Trustees of, v.
Pinkard Constr. Co., 604 P.2d 683
(Colo. 1979), 35.04[A]

Colorado Structures, Inc. v. Ins. Co. of
the W., 106 P.3d 815 (Wash. App.),
cert. granted, 126 P.3d 1279 (2005),
34.04[B]

Colorado Structures, Inc. v. Insurance
Co. of the West, 167 P.3d
1125 (Wash. 2007), 33.02[A],
34.04[C]

Columbia, Mo., City of, v. Paul N.
Howard Co., 707 F.2d 338 (8th Cir.
1983), 22.06

Columbus v. Clark-Dietz & Assocs.-Eng'rs, Inc., 550 F. Supp. 610 (N.D. Miss. 1982), 29.02[C][2]

Comcraft, *In re*, 206 B.R. 551 (D. Or. 1997), 34.04[H]

Commerce & Indus. Ins. Co. v. Bank of Hawaii, 73 Haw. 322, 832 P.2d 733 (Haw. 1992), 20.02

Commerce & Indus. Ins. Co. v. Mahopac Assoc., 1998 U.S. Dist. LEXIS 18393 (S.D.N.Y. 1998), 29.02[E]

Commerce Int'l Co. v. United States, 167 Ct. Cl. 529-35, 338 F.2d 81 (1964), 24.02[D]

Commerce Int'l Co. v. United States, 338 F.2d 81 (Ct. Cl. 1964), 23.03[D]

Commercial Contractors v. Sumar Contractors, 302 So. 2d 88 (Ala. 1974), 27.05[C][1]

Commercial Contractors Equip., Inc., ABSCA No. 52,930, 52,931-52,935, 03-2 B.C.A. (CCH) ¶ 32,381 (2003), 24.02[B]

Commercial Contractors, Inc. v. USF&G, 524 F.2d 944 (5th Cir. 1975), 27.05[F]

Commercial Contractors, Inc. v. U.S., No. 97-5005, 1998 WL 559977 (1998), 38.02[B][2], 38.02[D]

Commercial Ins. Co. v. Pacific-Peru Constr. Co., 558 F.2d 948 (9th Cir. 1977), 36.04

Commercial Insurance Co. of Newark, New Jersey v. Pacific-Peru Construction Co., 558 F.2d 948 (9th Cir. 1977), 36.03[A]

Commercial Metals Co. v. BalFour, Guthrie & Co., Ltd., 577 F.2d 264 (5th Cir. 1978), 46.04

Commercial Standards Ins. Co. v. United States *ex rel.* Crane Co., 213 F.2d 106 (10th Cir. 1954), 35.04[A]

Commercial Union Ins. Co. v. Bert Thomas-Aitken Constr. Co., 253 A.2d 469 (N.J. 1969), 36.09[C]

Commercial Union Ins. Co. v. Gilbanc Bldg. Co., 992 F.2d 386 (1st Cir. 1993), 46.06

Commercial Union Ins. Co. v. Melikyan, 430 So. 2d 1217 (La. Ct. App. 1983), 36.03[A], 36.05

Commonwealth v. Musser Forests, Inc., 146 A.2d 714 (Pa. 1958), 7.03[B][2][b]

Commonwealth, Dep't of Highways v. S.J. Groves & Sons Co., 20 Pa. Commw. 526, 343 A.2d 72 (1975), 26.02[MM][4]

Commonwealth, Dep't of Highways v. S.J. Groves & Sons Co., 343 A.2d 72 (Pa. Commw. Ct. 1975), 7.03[B][2][b]

Commonwealth, State Highway & Bridge Auth., (Penn-DOT) v. Gen. Asphalt Paving Co., 46 Pa. Commw. 114, 405 A.2d 1138 (1979), 26.02[MM][4]

Commonwealth, State Highway and Bridge Auth. v. Gen. Asphalt Paving Co., 405 A.2d 1138 (Pa. Commw. Ct. 1979), 7.03[B][2][b]

Commonwealth Coatings Corp. v. Continental Cas. Co., 393 U.S. 145 (1968), 43.07[E]

Commonwealth Coatings Corp. v. Continental Cas. Co., 393 U.S. 145, 89 S. Ct. 337, 21 L. Ed. (1968), 46.21

Commonwealth Edison v. Federal Pac. Elec. Co., 1962 Trade Cas. (CCH) ¶ 70,488, 17.08[A]

Compania de Remorque y Salvamento, S.A. v. Esperence, Inc., 187 F.2d 114 (2d Cir. 1951), 36.06

Complete Gen. Constr. Co. v. Ohio Dept. of Transp., 593 N.E.2d 487 (Ohio Ct. Cl. 1990), 29.02[B][2]

Composite Int'l, Inc., ASBCA No. 43360, 92-1 B.C.A. ¶ 24,537 (1991), 28.03[G]

Composite Laminates, Inc. v. United States, 27 Fed. Cl. 310 (1992), 28.03[D][1][a][ii]

Compudyne Corp., *In re*, 255 F. Supp. 1004 (E.D. Pa. 1966), 46.23

Computer Management Sciences, Inc., GSBCA No. 10165, 90-3 B.C.A. (CCH) ¶ 22979, 37.02[I]

Comspace Corp., DOT BCA No. 4011, 02-1 B.C.A. ¶ 31,792 (2002), 28.03[D][1][a][i], 28.03[D][2]

Comtrol, Inc. v. United States, 294 F.3d 1357 (Fed. Cir. 2002), 22.06, 27.05[C][2]

Comtrol, Inc. v. U.S., 49 Fed. Cl. 294 (2001), *aff'd in part and vacated in part on other grounds,* Control, Inc. v. U.S. 294 F.3d 1357 (Fed. Cir. 2002), 27.05[C][2]

Conesco Indus. v. Conforti & Eisele, Inc., 627 F.2d 312 (D.C. Cir. 1980), 34.04[C]

Confederate Constr. Co., United States *ex rel.,* v. United States Fid. & Guar. Co., 644 F.2d 747 (8th Cir. 1981), 35.04[A]

Conforti & Eisele, Inc. v. John C. Morris Associates, 418 A.2d 1290 (N.J. Super. Ct. App. Div. 1980), 29.02[C][2], 29.02[C][5]

Congregation of the Passion, Holy Cross Province v. Touche Ross & Co., 636 N.E.2d 503 (Ill. 1994), 7.02[B][2][c]

Connell Rice & Sugar Co., AGBCA [new Civilian BCA] No. 85-483-1, 87-1 B.C.A. (CCH) ¶ 19,489 (1986), 27.05[B][5][b]

Conner Brothers Construction Co. v. United States, 65 Fed. Cl. 657 (2005), 22.08, 24.02[C], 27.03[B][2], 27.05[B][3][a]

Conner v. Quality Coach, Inc., 750 A.2d 823 (Pa. 2000), 29.02[B][1]

Consolidated Elec. & Mechanicals, Inc. v. Biggs General Contracting, Inc., 167 F.3d 432 (8th Cir. 1999), 35.04[A]

Consolidated Elec. Co., United States *ex rel.,* v. Gough Indus., 355 F.2d 437 (9th Cir. 1966), 35.08[D][1], 35.08[D][2]

Consolidated Elec. Distribs., Inc. v. Kirkham Chain & Kirkham, Inc., 95 Cal. Rptr. 673 (Ct. App. 1971), 35.07[B][1]

Consolidated Elec. Distribs., United States *ex rel.,* v. Altech, Inc., 929 F.2d 1089 (5th Cir. 1991), 35.05[A]

Construction Alternative, *In re,* 2 F.3d 670 (6th Cir. 1993), 34.04[H]

Construction Co. v. Commercial Dev. Corp., 392 F. Supp. 982 (D.V.I. 1975), 21.05

Construction Equip. Lease Co. v. United States, 26 Cl. Ct. 341 (1992), 39.02[C], 39.03[B][1][b]

Construction Materials v. American Fid. Fire Ins. Co., 383 So. 2d 1291 (La. Ct. App. 1st Cir. 1980), *rev'd,* 388 So. 2d 365 (La. 1980), 35.07[B][2]

Construct Tech Corp. v. City of Coeur d' Alene, No. 94-35666, 1995 U.S. App. LEXIS 28349 (9th Cir. 1995), 30.04[B][2]

Consumers Oil Co., ASBCA No. 24172, 86-1 B.C.A. (CCH) ¶ 18,647 (1985), 28.02[A][3], 28.03[E][2]

Contact Int'l, Inc. v. Widnall, 1997 U.S. App. LEXIS 548 (Fed. Cir. Jan. 15, 1997), 21.04

Container Sys. Corp., 92-1 B.C.A. ¶ 24,744 (1992), 28.03[F][4], 28.03[G]

Container Sys. Corp., ASBCA No. 43694, 92-1 B.C.A. ¶ 24,744 (1992), 28.03[G]

Conti Corp. v. Ohio Dep't of Admin. Servs., 629 N.E.2d 1073 (Ohio Ct. App. 1993), 30.03[C][3]

Continental Cas. Co. v. Allsop Lumber, 336 F.2d 445 (8th Cir. 1964), *cert. denied,* 379 U.S. 968, 85 S. Ct. 662, 13 L. Ed. 561 (1965), 35.07[A][3]

Continental Cas. Co. v. American Sec. Corp., 443 F.2d 649 (D.C. Cir. 1970), 36.07

Continental Cas. Co. v. Clarence L. Boyd Co., 140 F.2d 115 (10th Cir. 1944), 35.04[A]

Continental Cas. Co. v. Guterman, 708 F. Supp. 953 (N.D. Ill. 1989), 36.03[B]

Continental Cas. Co. v. McDowell & Colantoni, 668 N.E.2d 59 (Ill. Ct. App. 1996), 20.05

Continental Cas. Co. v. Schaefer, 173 F.2d 5 (9th Cir. 1949), 35.04[A]

Continental Collection & Disposal, Inc. v. United States, 29 Fed. Cl. 644 (1993), 28.04[A][1]

Continental Ill. Nat'l Bank v. United States, 121 Ct. Cl. 203, 101 F. Supp. 755, *cert. denied,* 343 U.S. 963 (1952), 24.02[A]

Continental Maritime of San Diego, ASBCA No. 37820, 89-2 B.C.A. ¶ 21,694 (1989), 28.03[F][4]

Continental Realty Corp. v. Andrew J. Crevolin Co., 380 F. Supp. 246 (S.D.W. Va. 1974), 34.04[E][5], 34.04[F][6]

Continental T.V., Inc. v. GTE-Sylvania, 433 U.S. 39, 97 S. Ct. 2549 (1977), *on remand,* 461 F. Supp. 1046 (N.D. Cal. 1978), *aff'd,* 694 F.2d 1132 (9th Cir. 1982), 17.08[B]

Contract Cleaning Maint., Inc. v. United States, 811 F.2d 586 (Fed. Cir. 1987), 39.03[A], 39.03[B], 39.03[B][1], 39.03[B][3]

Contract for Route 280 Section 7U Exit Project, *In re,* 431 A.2d 848 (N.J. Super. Ct. App. Div. 1981), 7.03[C]

Contractors Labor Pool, Inc. v. Westway Contractors, Inc., 53 Cal. App. 4th 152 (1997), 35.04[B]

Conveyor Rental & Sales Co., United States *ex rel.,* v. Aetna Cas. & Sur. Co., 981 F.2d 448 (9th Cir. 1992), 35.03[A]

Cook County v. United States *ex rel.* Chandler, 123 S. Ct. 1239, 2003 U.S. LEXIS 1957 (2003), 38.02[B][4][a]

Cook County v. United States *ex rel.* Chandler, 538 U.S. 119, 123 S. Ct. 1239, 2003 U.S. LEXIS 1957 (2003), 38.02[C]

Cook Indus., Inc. v. C. Itoh & Co., 449 F.2d 106 (2d Cir. 1971), *cert. denied,* 405 U.S. 921 (1972), 46.22

Cooper v. Computer Credit Sys., 40 A.D.2d 692, 336 N.Y.S.2d 380 (1972), 46.04

Cooper v. Firestone Tire and Rubber Co., 945 F.2d 1103 (9th Cir. 1991), 29.04[F][1]

Cooper v. Wal-Mart Stores, 959 F. Supp. 964 (C.D. Ill. 1997), 35.08[F][3]

Cooper Indus. v. Leatherman Tool Group, 532 U.S. 424 (2001), 31.07[A]

Corbetta Constr. Co. v. Michigan Mut. Liab. Co., 20 A.D.2d 375, 247 N.Y.S.2d 288 (1964), *aff'd,* 15 N.Y.S.2d 888, 206 N.E.2d 357, 258 N.Y.S.2d 423 (1965), 18.04[C][1]

Corbetta Constr. Co. v. United States, 461 F.2d 1130 (Ct. Cl. 1972), 27.05[B][3][c]

Corbetta Construction Co., PSBCA No. 299, 77-2 B.C.A. (CCH) ¶ 12,699 (1977), 24.04[E]

Corbetta Tech. Co., ASBCA No. 47742, 95-1 B.C.A. (CCH) ¶ 27,587, 39.03[B][2]

Corder v. Wm. W. Smith Excavating Co., 556 S.E.2d 77 (W. Va. 2001), 19.07[B]

Corinno Civetta Construction Corp. v. City of New York, 67 N.Y.2d 297, 493 N.E.2d 905, 502 N.Y.S.2d 681 (1986), 26.02[G][3], 26.02[G][4], 26.02[GG][3], 26.02[GG][4]

Corner Constr. Co. v. U.S. Fid. & Guar. Co., 638 N.W.2d 887 (S.D. 2002), 19.07[B]

Corsica Coop. Ass'n v. Behlen Mfg. Co., 967 F. Supp. 382 (D.S.D. 1997), 29.02[E]

Cortelyou & Cole, Inc., United States v., 581 F.2d 239 (9th Cir. 1976), 35.03[A]

Cortolano & Barone, Inc., United States *ex rel.,* v. Morano Constr. Corp., 724 F. Supp. 88 (S.D.N.Y. 1978), 28.03[D][1][a][i]

Corway, Inc., ASBCA Nos. 20683, 77-1 B.C.A. ¶ 12,357 (1977), 28.03[D][2]

Cosmo Constr. Co. v. United States, 194 Ct. Cl. 559, 439 F.2d 160 (1971), 24.02[A]

Costello Constr. of Md., Inc. v. J.D. Long Masonry, Inc., 236 Fed. App'x 877 (4th Cir. 2007), 32.07

Cottonwood, City of, v. James L. Fann Contracting, Inc., 179 Ariz. 185, 877 P.2d 284 (1994), 46.09

Couch Constr. Co. v. Dep't of Transp., 361 So. 2d 172 (Fla. Dist. Ct. App. 1978), 7.03[E]

Coulson v. Lake LBJ Mun. Util. Dist., 734 S.W. 2d 649 (Tex. 1987), *on remand,* 771 S.W.2d 145 (Tex. App.-Austin 1988), *rev'd,* 781 S.W. 2d 594 (Tex. 1989), 20.02

Council of Dorset Condominium Apartments v. Dorset Apartments, No. 90C-10-263, 1992 De. Super. LEXIS 373 (Del. Super. Ct. 1992), 7.02[B][2][c]

County Excavation, Inc. v. State, 44 Misc. 2d 1057 (N.Y. Ct. Cl. 1964), 30.03[C][5]

Cowen Constr., Inc., ASBCA No. 8165, 1963 B.C.A. ¶ 3882 (1963), 28.03[E][4]

Craig Johnson Constr. LLC v. Floyd Town Acrchitects, PA, 134 P.3d 648 (Idaho 2006), 27.04[A][1]

Crane Co., United States *ex rel.*, v. Johnson, Smathers & Rollins, 67 F.2d 121 (4th Cir. 1933), 35.08[D][2]

Crankshaw v. Stanley Homes, Inc., 131 Ga. App. 840 (Ga. App. 1974), 30.04[B][1]

C. Raymond Davis & Son, Inc. v. Liberty Mut. Ins. Co., 467 F. Supp. 17 (E.D. Pa. 1979), 18.04[C][1]

Cray Research, Inc. v. Department of Navy, 556 F.Supp. 201 (D.D.C. 1982), 34.04[G][1]

Cray Research, Inc. v. U.S. 41 Fed. Cl. 427 (1998), 27.05[G][2][b]

Creative Waste Mgmt., Inc. v. Capital Envtl. Servs., Inc., 495 F. Supp. 2d 353 (S.D.N.Y. 2007), 32.07, 33.01[B]

Crews, United States *ex rel.*, v. NCS Healthcare of Ill., Inc., 460 F.3d 853 (7th Cir. 2006), 38.02[B][1]

Crisp Co. v. S.J. Groves & Sons, 73 F.2d 327 (5th Cir. 1934), 21.02

Cross Constr. Co. v. United States, 225 Ct. Cl. 616 (1980), 39.03[F]

Crow Constr. Co., United States v., 826 F. Supp. 647 (E.D.N.Y. 1993), 35.03[A]

Crowder v. Fidelity & Deposit Co., 144 F. Supp. 322 (W.D. La. 1956), 21.06

Crown Plastering Corp. v. Elite Assoc., 560 N.Y.S.2d 694 (App. Div. 1990), 35.08[E][1]

Cruet v. Carroll, 2001 Conn. Super. LEXIS 3336 (Conn. Super. Ct. 2001), 29.02[C][3]

Crum & Foster Managers Corp. v. Resolution Trust Corp., 620 N.E.2d 1073 (Ill. 1991), 20.02

CS&T Gen. Contractors, Inc., ASBCA No. 43657, 93-1 BCA ¶ 25,438 at 126,683 (1992), 23.03[H]

CTA, Inc. v. United States, 44 Fed. cl. 684 (1999), 21.04

CTC Dev. Corp. v. State Farm Fire & Cas. Co., 704 So. 2d 579 (Fla. Dist. Ct. App. 1997), 18.04[C][1]

C3, Inc., ASBCA No. 38391, 91-2 B.C.A. ¶ 23,750 (1991), 28.03[D][1][a][ii]

C.T. Lewis Indus., Inc., ENGBCA No. 6255, *et al.*, 99-1 B.C.A ¶ 30,334 (1999), 28.03[F][3]

Cubic Corp. v. United States, 20 Cl. Ct. 610 (1990), 39.03[B]

Cuddy Mountain Concrete v. Citadel Constr., Inc., 520 N.W.2d 473 (Minn. Ct. App. 1994), 34.04[B]

Cuddy Mountain Concrete v. Citadel Constr., Inc., 824 P.2d 151 (Idaho Ct. App. 1992), 28.03[D][1][a][i]

Cullum Mech. Constr., Inc. v. South Carolina Baptist Hosp., 544 S.E.2d 838 (S.C. 2001), 29.02[C][5]

Cundy Asphalt Paving Constr., Inc. v. Angelo Materials Co., 915 P.2d 1181 (Wyo. 1996), 28.03[E][2]

Cunningham Bros., Inc. v. City of Waterloo, 254 Iowa 659, 117 N.W.2d 46 (1962), 26.02[P][3]

Curtis Elevator Co. v. Hampshire House, Inc., 142 N.J. Super. 537, 362 A.2d 73 (N.J. 1976), 23.03[E][2]

Curtis T. Bedwell & Sons, Inc. v. International Fid. Ins. Co., 1989 WL 55388 (E.D. Pa. May 23, 1989), 36.07

Custom Planning & Dev. Inc. v. Am. Nat'l Fire Ins. Co., 606 S.E.2d 39 (Ga. App. 2004), 19.07[B]

Custom Printing Co. v. United States, 51 Fed. Cl. 729 (2002), 28.04[B][2]

Cutler v. Cutler, 169 N.C. 482, 86 S.E. 301 (1915), 46.24

C v. D, [2007] EWHX 1541 (Comm.), 43.05[C][2]

CWC, Inc., ASBCA No. 26432, 82-2 BCA ¶ 15,907 at 78,838 (1982), 23.03[H]

CWC, Inc., ASBCA No. 28847, 84-2 B.C.A. ¶ 17,282 (1984), *aff'd on reconsideration,* 85-1 B.C.A. ¶ 17,876 (1995), 28.03[E][3][a]

CW Gov't Travel v. United States, 61 Fed. Cl. 559 (Fed. Cl. 2004), 7.03[B][2][d]

Cyrus Contracting, Inc., IBCA No. 3233, 98-2 B.C.A. (CCH) ¶ 30,036 (1998), 24.04[A]

Czeck v. Van Helslend, 241 N.E.2d 272 (Ind. Ct. App. 1968), 16.09[B]

D

D&L Constr. Co. v. Triangle Elec. Supply Co., 332 F.2d 1009 (8th Cir. 1964), 35.04[A]

D&P Corp., United States *ex rel.*, v. Transamerica Inc. Co., 881 F. Supp. 1505 (D. Kan. 1995), 35.04[A], 35.07[A][1]

Dadelin Depot, Inc. v. St. Paul Fire and Marine Ins. Co., 945 So. 2d 1216 (Fla. 2006), 34.02

Daewoo Eng'g & Constr. Co. v. United States, 73 Fed. Cl. 547 (2006), 24.02[C], 38.03, 39.04[E], 39.08[B]

Dakota Gasification Co. v. Pascoe Building Systems, 91 F.3d 1094 (8th Cir. 1996), 29.02[E]

Daly Constr., Inc. v. Garrett, 5 F.3d 520 (Fed. Cir. 1995), 24.04[C]

DANAC, Inc., ASBCA No. 33394, 97-2 BCA ¶ 29,184, *aff'd on recons.*, 98-1 BCA ¶ 29,454 (1997), 30.03[D][4]

Dangerfield v. Markel, 239 N.W.2d 373 (N.D. 1974), 16.04[E]

Daniel E. Terreri & Sons, Inc. v. Mahoning County Bd. of Comm'rs, 786 N.E.2d 921 (Ohio App. 2003), 27.05[B][2]

Danzig v. AEC Corp., 224 F.3d 1333 (Fed. Cir. 2000), *cert. denied*, 532 U.S. 995 (2001), 28.03[B][3][a]

Darger v. Nielsen, 605 P.2d 1223 (Utah 1979), 30.04[B][1]

Darin & Armstrong v. Monte Costella, 542 So. 2d 1052 (Fla. App. 1989), 46.25

Darwin Constr. Co. v. United States, 31 Fed. Cl. 453 (1994), 28.03[E][1][b]

Darwin Constr. Co. v. United States, 811 F.2d 593 (Fed. Cir. 1987), 28.04[A][2], 28.04[A][3], 28.04[D], 28.04[D][2], 28.04[D][4]

Daubert v. Merrell Dow Pharm., Inc., 509 U.S. 579 (1993), 23.07[C][2], 29.04[H]

Daugherty Co. v. Kimberly-Clark Corp., 14 Cal. App. 3d 151 (1971), 28.03[E][3][b]

Dave Kolb Grading, Inc. v. Lieberman Corp., 837 S.W.2d 924 (Mo. Ct. App. 1992), 33.01[F]

Davenport v. U.S. Fid. & Guar. Co., 56 Mass. App. Ct. 1109, 778 N.E.2d 1038 (2002), 19.07[B]

David Boland, Inc., VABCA No. 5858 et al., 01-2 B.C.A. ¶ 31,578 (2001), 28.03[E][1][c], 28.03[G]

David Boland, Inc. v. Trans Coastal Roofing, Co., 851 So. 2d 724 (Fla. 2003), 34.04[F][6]

David C. Olson v. Denver & Rio Grande W. R. R., 789 P.2d 492 (Colo. Ct. App. 1990), 35.08[E][1]

David Kay, United States v., 200 F. Supp. 2d 681 (S.D. Tex. 2002), 513 F.3d 432 (6th Cir. 2007), 42.02[F][1]

Davidson v. Smith, 530 S.W.2d 356 (Ark. 1975), 35.08[G]

Davidson & Jones, Inc. v. County of New Hanover, 255 S.E.2d 580 (N.C. Ct. App. 1979), 7.02[B][3]

Davies Precision Mach., Inc. v. United States, 35 Fed. Cl. 651 (1996), 28.03[E][4]

Davis/HRGM Joint Venture v. United States, 50 Fed. Cl. 539 (2001), 28.02, 28.04[C][2][a]

Davis v.McCall, 568 P.2d 956 (Alaska 1977), 30.04[B][1]

Dawco Constr., Inc. v. United States, 930 F.2d 872 (Fed. Cir. 1991), 39.03[C], 39.03[C][1], 39.03[C][2]

Dawco Constr., Inc. v. United States, 930 F.2d 872 (Fed. Cir. 1991), *overruled on other grounds* by Reflectone, Inc. v. Dalton, 60 F.3d 1572 (Fed. Cir. 1995), 39.03[B][1][a]

Dawson Constr. Co., VABCA No. 2322, 88-3 BCA ¶ 20,945 (1988), 23.03[E][5]

Dawson Constr. Co. v. GSBCA No. 4956, 79-2 B.C.A. (CCH) ¶ 13,989 (1979), 24.04[C]

Dawson Corp. v. National Union Fire Ins. Co., 666 A.2d 604 (N.J. Super. Ct. App. Div. 1995), 35.08[A], 35.08[E][2]

Day & Zimmerman-Madway, ASBCA No. 13367, 71-1 B.C.A. (CCH) ¶ 8622 (1970), 24.04[E]

D.C. McClain, Inc. v. Arlington County, 452 S.E.2d 659 (Va. 1995), 27.05[A][2]

DDC Interiors, Inc., United States *ex rel.*, v. Dawson Constr. Co., 895 F. Supp. 270 (D. Colo. 1995), *aff'd*, 82 F.3d 427 (10th Cir. 1996), 35.02[A], 35.08[E][1], 35.08[E][2], 35.08[F][1]

Deal Dev. Co. v. Amarillo Concrete Contractors, Inc., 554 S.W.2d 294 (Tex. Civ. App. 1977), 33.01[F]

Dean v. Seco Elec. Co., 519 N.E.2d 837 (Ohio 1988), 35.04[B]

De Armas v. United States, 108 Ct. Cl. 436, 70 F. Supp. 605 (1947), 27.05[E][3]

DEC Elec. v. Raphael Constr. Corp., 558 So. 2d 427 (Fla. 1990), 35.08[E][1]

Decker v. Gooley, 622 N.Y.S.2d 374 (N.Y. App. Div. 1995), 7.03

Decker & Co. v. West, 76 F.3d 1573 (Fed. Cir. 1996), 28.03[B][1]

Deer Creek Constr. Co., Inc. v. Peterson, 412 So. 2d 1169 (Miss. 1982), 27.05[D][2]

Dekalb County v. Lenowitz, 463 S.E.2d 539 (Ga. App. Ct. 1995), 17.01[A]

DeKonty Corp., ASBCA No. 32410 , 89-2 B.C.A. ¶ 21,586 (1989), *aff'd*, 90-2 B.C.A. ¶ 22,645 (1990), 28.03[E][2]

DeKonty Corp., United States v., 922 F.2d 826 (Fed. Cir. 1991), 28.03[B][3], 28.03[E][2]

Delco Elecs. Corp. v. United States, 17 Cl. Ct. 302 (Cl. Ct. 1989), 30.03[D][1]

Delcon Constr. Corp. v. United States, 27 Fed. Cl. 634 (1993), 28.03[E][1][b]

Delfor, Inc., VABCA Nos. 2049 et al., 89-1 BCA ¶ 21,394 (1988), 28.03[B][2]

Delfour, Inc., VACAB Nos. 3803 et al., 94-1 B.C.A. ¶ 26,385 (1993), 28.03[G]

Delicious Foods Co., Inc. v. Millard Warehouse, Inc., 507 N.W.2d 631 (Neb. 1993), 29.02[D][3]

Delmar Box Co, *In re*, 309 N.Y. 60, 127 N.E.2d 808 (1955), 46.23

Delta Constr. Co., ASBCA Nos. 42453 et al., 96-1 B.C.A. ¶ 28,106 (1995), *modified*, 96-1 B.C.A. ¶ 28,251 (1996), 28.03[F][1], 28.03[F][2]

Delta Constr. Int'l, Inc., ASBCA No. 52162, 01-1 B.C.A. ¶ 31,195 (2001), 28.02[B]

Delta Eng'g & Sales, Inc., ASBCA No. 16326, 72-1 B.C.A. ¶ 9373 (1972), 28.03[D][2]

Delta Metals, Inc., United States *ex rel.*, v. R. M. Wells Co., 497 F. Supp. 541 (S.D. Ga. 1980), 35.04[A]

DeMauro Constr. Co., ASBCA No. 17,029, 77-1 B.C.A. (CCH) ¶ 12,511 (1977), 24.02[B]

Demusz Mfg. Co., ASBCA No. 55310, 07-1 BCA ¶ 33,510 (2007), 23.03[B][1]

Demusz Mfg. Co., ASBCA No. 55311, 07-1 BCA ¶ 33,463 (2006), 23.03[B][2]

Denburg v. Parker Chapin Flattau & Klimpl, 82 N.Y.S.2d 375, 604 N.Y.S.2d 900, 624 N.E.2d 995 (1993), 45.01

Dennebaum v. Rotterdam Square, L.P., 776 N.Y.S.2d 136 (N.Y. App. Div. 2004), 29.02[D][3]

Denoth v. Carter, 85 N.J.L. 98, 88 A. 835 (1913), 21.05

Denton Constr. Co. v. Missouri State Highway Comm'n, 454 S.W.2d 44 (Mo. 1970), 33.01[A]

Denver, City and County of, v. District Court, 939 P.2d 1353 (Colo. 1997), 45.04[A]

Department of Army v. Blue Fox, 525 U.S. 225 (1995), 34.04[H]

Dep't of Transp. v. Anjo Constr. Co., 666 A.2d 753 (Pa. Commw. Ct. 1995), 30.03[C][6]

Dep't of Transp. v. APAC-Ga., Inc., 217 Ga. App. 103, 456 S.E.2d 668 (1995), 26.02[K][4]

Dep't of Transp. v. Arapaho Constr., Inc., 180 Ga. App. 341, 349 S.E.2d 196 (1986), *aff'd*, 257 Ga. 269, 357 S.E.2d 593 (1987) and quoting 357 S.E.2d at 594, 26.02[K][4]

Dep't of Transp. v. Fru-Con Constr. Corp., 206 Ga. App. 821, 426 S.E.2d 905 (1992), 26.02[K][3]

Dep't of Transp. v. Hawkins Bridge Co., 457 So. 2d 525 (Fla. Dist. Ct. App. 1984), 30.03[D][1]

Dep't of Transp. v. Herbert R. Imbt, Inc., 630 A.2d 550 (Pa. Commw. Ct. 1993), 30.03[C][3]

DePonte Invs., Inc. v. United States, 54 Fed. Cl. 112 (2002), 28.03[F][3]

DePue v. Sears, Roebuck & Co., 812 F. Supp. 750 (W.D. Mich. 1992), 29.04[F][2]

Design Prof'l Ins. Co. v. Chicago Ins. Co., 454 F.3d 906 (8th Cir. 2006), 20.03

Detweiler Bros., Minidoka County *ex rel.*, v. Krieger, 399 P.2d 962 (Idaho 1964), 35.08[F][1], 35.08[F][2], 35.08[I]

De Vito v. United States, 413 F.2d 1147 (Ct. Cl. 1969), 23.03[E][2], 28.03[A], 28.03[D][2], 28.03[F][2]

Dewey Jordon, Inc. v. Maryland Nat'l Park & Planning Comm'n, 258 Md. 490, 265 A.2d 892 (1970), 21.02, 30.03[C]

D.E.W. Inc., ASBCA No. 35173, 89-3 B.C.A. (CCH) ¶ 22,008, 39.04[C]

D.H. Blattner & Sons, Inc. v. Firemen's Ins. Co. of Newark, NJ, 535 N.W.2d 671 (Minn. App. 1995), 27.05[C][1]

D.H. Dave and Gerben Contracting Co., *In re,* A.S.B.C.A. No. 6257, 1962 B.C.A. (CCH) ¶ 3493 (1962), 27.05[C][3][b]

D.H. Dave, Inc. & Gerben Contracting Co., ASBCA No. 13,005, 73-2 B.C.A. (CCH) ¶ 10,191 (1973), 24.02[B]

Dial v. Freeto Constr. Co., 381 P.2d 363 (Kan. 1963), 35.04[B]

Diamond v. Dalton, 25 F.3d 1006 (Fed. Cir. 1994), 39.04

Diamond B Constr. Co., Inc. v. City of Plaquemine, 673 Co. 2d 636 (La. App. [1 Cir.] 1966), 27.05[E][4]

Diamos v. Hirsch, 372 P.2d 76 (Ariz. 1962), 28.03[B][3]

Dick, United States *ex rel.*, v. Long Island Lighting Co., 912 F.2d 13 (2d Cir. 1990), 38.02[B][4][b]

Dicon, Inc. v. Marben Corp., 618 F.2d 40 (8th Cir. 1980), 23.03[B][2]

Dietz v. Jackson, 291 S.E.2d 282 (N.C. Ct. App. 1982), 12.04[C][1][d][i]

DiGioia Bros. Excavating, Inc. v. Cleveland Department of Public Utilities, 135 Ohio app. 3d 436, 734 N.E.2d 438 (1999), 26.02[JJ][4]

Dillon Constr. Inc., ENGBCA No. PCC-36, 81-2 B.C.A. ¶ 15,416 (1981), 28.03[F][2]

Dillon County Sch. Dist. v. Lewis Sheet Metal Works, Inc., 332 S.E.2d 555, *cert. denied,* 337 S.E.2d 697 (S.C. 1985), *cert. dismissed,* 343 S.E.2d 613 (1986), 29.04[J]

DiMaria Construction, Inc. v. Interarch, 799 A.2d 555, 351 N.J. Super. 558 (N.J. Super. Ct. App. Div. 2001), *aff'd,* 797 A.2d 137, 172 N.J. 1823 (2002), 28.04[D][2]

Dingley v. Oler, 117 U.S. 490 (1986), 28.03[B][3]

Discount Co. v. United States, 554 F.2d 435 (Ct. Cl.), *cert. denied,* 434 U.S. 938 (1977), 28.03[B][2], 28.03[E][1][c]

District of Columbia v. C.J. Langenfelder & Sons., Inc., 558 A.2d 1155 (D.C. 1989), 33.01[C][1]

Diversacon Indus., Inc., ENGBCA No. 3284, 76-1 BCA ¶ 11,875 (1976), 23.03[E][2]

Dixie Plumbing Supply Co. v. Taylor, 293 F.2d 717 (5th Cir. 1961), 33.02[O]

Dixon Contracting, Inc., AGBCA No. 98-191-1, 00-1 B.C.A. ¶ 30,766 (2000), 28.03[D][3]

D.J. Talley & Son, Inc. v. New Orleans, 303 So. 2d 195 (La. Ct. App. 1974), 7.03[E]

D.K. Meyer Corp. v. Bevco, Inc., 292 N.W.2d 773 (Neb. 1980), 21.02, 21.05

DK's Precision Mach. & Mfg., ASBCA No. 39616, 90-2 B.C.A. ¶ 22,380 (1990), 28.03[E][2]

D.L. Braugher Co. v. West, 127 F.3d 1476 (Fed. Cir. 1997), 39.03[B][1][a]

Dockside Assoc., Inc. v. Detyens, Simmon & Carlisle, 337 S.E.2d 887 (S.C. 1985), 29.02[C][5]

DOD Contracts, Inc., ASBCA No. 47509, 95-2 B.C.A. (CCH) ¶ 27,641, 39.03[D]

Dodson v. St. Paul Ins. Co., 812 P.2d 372 (Okl. 1991), 19.07[B]

Doe v. Ill. St. Med. Inter-Insurance Exchange, 599 N.E.2d 983 (Ill. App. Ct. 1992), 20.04

Dominion Culvert & Metal Corp. v. United States Fid. & Guar. Co., 120 S.E.2d 518 (S.C. 1961), 35.08[D][1]

Donahoe Constr. Co., ASBCA Nos. 47310, 47311, 47312, 47315, 47535, 47538, 98-2 B.C.A. (CCH) ¶ 30,076 (1998), 24.03

Donald M. Drake Co. v. United States, 194 Ct. Cl. 549, 439 F.2d 169 (1971), 24.02[A], 24.02[D]

Donnelly Constr. Co. V. Oberg/Hunt/Gilleland, 677 P.2d 1292 (Ariz. 1984), 7.02[B][3]

Donovan v. General Motors Corp., 762 F. 2d 701 (8th Cir. 1985), 8A.08[A][1]

Don Siegel Constr. Co., United States ex rel., v. Atul Constr. Co., 85 F. Supp. 2d 414 (D.N.J. 2000), 34.04[D]

Dorfman, United States ex rel., v. Standard Sur. & Cas. Co., 37 F. Supp. 323 (S.D.N.Y. 1941), 35.04[A]

Dorman v. Carnes, 96 S.W.2d 869 (Ky. 1936), 35.06[B][3]

Double B Enters., Inc., ASBCA No. 52010 et al., 01-1 B.C.A. ¶ 31,396 (2001), 28.03[F][1]

Double Oak Const., L.L.C. v. Cornerstone Dev. Intern., L.L.C., 97 P.3d 140 (Colo. App. Ct. 2003), 33.02[D]

Doucet v. Huffine Roofing & Constr., 841 So. 2d 916 (La. Ct. App. 2003), 18.05[A][1], 20.02

Douglas Nw. Inc. v. Bill O'Brien & Sons Constr. Inc., 828 P.2d 565 (Wash. Ct. App. 1992), 28.03[E][1][a]

Do-Well Mach. Shop, Inc. v. United States, 870 F.2d 637 (Fed. Cir. 1989), 39.06[C]

Downer Corp. v. Union Paving Co., 304 P.2d 756 (Cal. 1956), cert. denied, 354 U.S. 914 (1957), 33.02[M][1]

Dow-Par Inc. v. Lee Corp., 664 N.E.2d 150 (Ind. Ct. App. 4th Cir. 1994), 35.07[B][2], 35.08[D][1]

Dox Planks v. Ohio Farmers Ins. Co., 621 A.2d 132 (Pa. Super. Ct. 1993), 35.08[H]

Doyle Shirt Mfg. Corp., ASBCA No. 13894, 71-1 B.C.A. ¶ 8621 (1970), 28.03[D][2]

DPC Gen Contractors, Inc. v. Cobo Co., 715 F. Supp. 367 (S.D. Fla. 1989), 35.04[A]

Dragon Constr., Inc. v. Parkway Bank & Trust, 287 Ill. App. 3d 29 (1997), 34.04[C]

Dragon Constr., Inc. v. Parkway Bank & Trust, 678 N.E.2d 55 (Ill. App. Ct. 1997), 28.03[D][1][a][i]

Dragone Bros., Inc., United States ex rel., v. Moniaros Constr. Corp., 882 F. Supp. 1267 (E.D.N.Y. 1995), 35.04[A], 35.07[A][3]

Drake & Piper, Inc., ASBCA Nos. 9824, 10199, 65-2 B.C.A.(CCH) ¶ 4868, 37.02[D]

Dravo Corp. v. United States, 219 Ct. Cl. 416, 594 F.2d 842 (1979), 30.03[E]

DRC, Inc., et al., United States ex rel., v. Custer Battles, LLC, 444 F. Supp. 2d 678 (E.D. Va. 2006), 38.02[C][1], 41.08[A]

Dresser Indus., Inc. v. Page Petroleum, Inc., 853 S.W.2d 505 (Tex. 1993), 26.02[RR][3]

Drexel Chem. Co. v. Bituminous Ins. Co., 933 S.W.2d 471 (Tenn. Ct. App. 1996), 18.04[B]

Droukas v. Dives Training Acad., Inc., 376 N.E.2d 548 (Mass. 1978), 16.08[C]

Duckworth v. Cameron, 244 S.E.2d (S.C. 1978), 35.08[G]

Dugan & Meyers Constr. Co. v. Ohio Dep't of Admin. Servs., 113 Ohio St. 3d 226, 864 N.E.2d 68 (2007), 26.02[JJ][1], 27.04[A][1]

Dugan & Meyers Constr. Co. v. Ohio Dep't of Admin. Servs., 864 N.E.2d 68 (2007), 27.05[C][1]

Dulles Networking Assocs., Inc., VABCA-6077 et al., 00-1 B.C.A. ¶ 30,775 (2000), 28.03[A]

Dunbar & Sullivan Dredging Co., ENGBCA No. 3165, 73-2 B.C.A. (CCH) ¶ 10,285 (1973), 24.02[B]

Dunleavy v. Paris Ceramics USA, Inc., No. CV020395709S, 2005 Conn. Super. LEXIS 970, (Conn. Super. Ct. Apr. 19, 2005), 16.02[B]

Dunleavy, United States *ex rel.*, v. County of Delaware, 123 F.3d 734 (3d Cir. 1997), *overruled in part, on other grounds,* by Cook County v. United States *ex rel.* Chandler, 123 S. Ct. 1239, 2003 U.S. LEXIS 1957 (2003), 38.02[B][4][a]

Dunleavy, United States *ex rel.*, v. County of Delaware, 279 F.3d 219 (3d Cir. 2002), 38.02[C]

Duquesne Light Co. v. Westinghouse Elec. Corp., 66 F.3d 604 (3d Cir. 1995), 7.02[B][2][c]

Durant v. Changing, 891 P.2d 628 (Okla. Ct. App. 1995), 35.06[B][3]

D.W.H. Painting Co., Inc. v. D.W. Ward Constr. Co., 620 S.E.2d 887 (N.C. App. 2005), 27.05[B][2], 27.05[B][3][a]

Dworshak Dam Constructors, ENGBCA No. 3240, 73-2 B.C.A. (CCH) ¶ 10,039 (1973), 24.02[A]

DWS, Inc. ASBCA No. 33245, 87-3 B.C.A ¶ 19,960, *aff'd on reconsideration,* 87-3 B.C.A. ¶ 20,133 (1987), 28.04[D][4]

Dynamic Drywell, Inc. v. Walton Constr. Co., _____ F. Supp. _____, 2007 U.S. Dist. LEXIS 5473 (D. Kan. 2007), 25.02[D]

E

E&R Constr. Co., United States *ex rel.*, v. Guy H. James Constr. Co., 390 F. Supp. 1193 (M.D. Tenn. 1972), 35.04[A]

Ealahan Elec. Co., Inc., DOTBCA No. 1959, 90-3 BCA ¶ 23,177 (1990), 23.07[B][6]

Eastern Airlines, Inc. v. Gulf Oil, 415 F. Supp. 429 (S.D. Fla. 1985), 23.03[B][2]

Eastern Heavy Constructors v. Fox, 188 A.2d 286 (Md. 1963), 35.08[E][1]

Eastern S.D. Painting Contractors, GSBCA No. 3316, 72-2 B.C.A. ¶ 9665 (1972), 28.03[F][2]

Eastern Steel Constructors, Inc. v. City of Salem, 549 S.E.2d 266 (W. Va. 2001), 29.02[C][3], 29.02[C][5]

Eastern Tunneling Corp. v. Southgate Sanitation District, Arapahoe County, 487 F. Supp. 109 (D. Colo. 1979), 22.02, 27.05[C][4]

Eastover Corp. v. Martin Builders, 543 So. 2d 1358 (La. Ct. App. 1989), 29.02[C][4]

East West Research, Inc., ASBCA No. 42166, 91-3 B.C.A. (CCH) ¶ 24,187 (1991), 24.02[D]

Eatherly Constr. Co. v. HTI Mem'l Hosp. (Tenn. Ct. App. Sept. 12, 2005), No. M2003-02313-COA-R3-CV, 2005 WL 2217078, 32.05

Ebasco Envtl., ASBCA No. 44547, 93-3 B.C.A. (CCH) ¶ 26,220, 39.03[B][1][b]

E.C. Ernst, Inc. v. Manhattan Constr. Co., 387 F. Supp. 1001 (S.D. Ala. 1974), *aff'd in part,* 551 F.2d 1026 (5th Cir. 1977), *cert. denied,* 434 U.S. 1067 (1978), 27.05[D][3]

E.C. Ernst, Inc. v. Manhattan Constr. Co., 551 F.2d 1026 (5th Cir. 1977), *cert. denied,* 434 U.S. 1067 (1978), 32.06, 33.01[F]

E.C. Ernst, Inc. v. Manhattan Constr. Co. of Texas, 551 F.2d 1026 (5th Cir. 1977), 23.03[D], 26.02[A][4], 26.02[I][4]

E.C. Ernst Co. v. Koppers Co., 520 F. Supp. 830 (W.D. Pa. 1981), 33.01[F]

Economic Dev. & Indus. Corp. v. United States, 13 Cl. Ct. 590 (1987), 33.01[H]

Eddies Sales & Leasing, Inc., United States *ex rel.*, v. Federal Ins. Co., 634 F.2d 1050 (10th Cir. 1980), 35.04[A]

Ed Goetz Painting Co., DOT CAB No. 1168, 83-1 B.C.A. (CCH) ¶ 16,144 (1982), 33.01[C][1]

EDO Corp. v. Beech Aircraft Corp., 1988 U.S. LEXIS 17058 (D. Kan. 1988), 28.02[C]

Edward E. Gillen Co. v. City of Lake Forest, 3 F.3d 192 (7th Cir. 1993), 29.02[B][1]

Edward R. Marden Corp. v. United States, 442 F.2d 364 (Ct. Cl. 1971), 21.07, 21.08, 28.03[E][3][b]

Edward R. Morgan Co. v. State Highway Comm'n, 212 Miss. 504, 54 So. 2d 742 (1951), 26.02[Y][3]

Edwards v. Hamill, 138 S.E.2d 151 (N.C. 1964), 12.04[C][1][d][i]

Edwards v. Hovensa, LLC, 497 F.3d 355 (3d Cir. 2007), 46.01

Edward S. Good, Jr. ASBCA No. 10514, 66-1 B.C.A. ¶ 5362 (1966), 28.03[D][3]

Edwin J. Dobson, Jr., Inc. v. State, 218 N.J. Super. 123, 526 A.2d 1150 (1987), 26.02[EE][3]

Edwin R. Marden Corp., 442 F.2d 364 (Ct. Cl. 1971), 28.02[A][3]

Edwin R. Marden Corp. v. United States, 803 F.2d 701 (Fed. Cir. 1996), 27.05[A][2]

EFG Assocs., Inc., ASBCA No. 50546 et al., 01-1 B.C.A. ¶ 31,324 (2001), 28.03[B][3][a]

Egan-Ryan Mechanical Co. v. Cardon Meadows Dev. Corp., 818 P.2d 146 (Ariz. Ct. App. 1990), 35.08[B]

Eger Block & Redi-Mix Co. v. Wheeler, 207 So. 2d 698 (Fla. Dist. Ct. App. 1968), 35.08[B]

E. H. Marhoefer, Jr., Co., DOTCAB No. 70-17, 71-1 B.C.A. (CCH) ¶ 8791 (1971), 24.03

Eichberger Enters., Inc., VABCA No. 3923, 95-2 B.C.A. (CCH) ¶ 27,693, 39.05[D]

Eichleay, 39.03[A], 45.04[B]

Eichleay Corp., Appeal of, 60-2 B.C.A. (CCH) ¶ 2688 at 13,568 (ASBCA July 29, 1960), 30.03[C][3]

Eichleay Corp., Appeal of, ASBCA No. 5183, 60-2 B.C.A. (CCH) ¶ 2688 (1960), 30.03[C][2]

Eichleay Corp., ASBCA No. 5183, 60-2 B.C.A. (CCH) ¶ 2688 (1960), aff'd on reconsideration, 61-1 B.C.A. (CCH) ¶ 2894, 24.04[C], 28.02[D], 30.03[C][3], 30.03[C][4], 47.02

Eichler Homes, Inc. v. Underwriters at Lloyd's, London, 238 Cal. App. 2d 532 (1965), 18.04[B]

Elec. & Missile Facilities, Inc., 69-2 B.C.A. (CCH) ¶ 7781 (1969), 22.09

Elec. & Missile Facility, Inc. v. United States, 416 F.2d 1345 (Ct. Cl. 1969), 28.03[E][1][a]

Elec. Enter., Inc., IBCA No. 972-9-72, 74-1 BCA ¶ 10,400 (1973), 23.03[B][2]

Elecs. Group, Inc. v. Central Roofing Co., 518 N.E.2d 369 (Ill. App. Ct. 1987), 28.03[E][1][b]

Elecs. of Austin, ASBCA No. 24912, 86-3 B.C.A. ¶ 19,307 (1986), 28.03[D][2]

Electric Constr. Co. v. Flickinger, 485 P.2d 547 (Ariz. 1971), 35.08[G]

Electric Mach. Enters., Inc., In re, 479 F.3d 791 (11th Cir. 2007), 46.13

Electric Supply Co. v. Eugene Freeman, Inc., 152 So. 510 (La. 1933), 35.08[I]

Electro Assocs., Inc. v. Harrop Constr. Co., 908 S.W.2d 21 (Tex. App.-Houston [1st Dist.] 1995), 26.02[RR][3]

Electronic & Missile Facilities, Inc., ASBCA No. 9325, 1964 BCA ¶ 4127 (1964), 23.03[E][2]

Electronic & Missile Facilities, Inc. v.United States, 416 F.2d 1345 (Ct. Cl. 1969), 30.03[D][5]

Electronic & Missile Facilities, Inc. v.United States Moseley, 306 F.2d 554 (5th Cir. 1962), rev'd on other grounds, 374 U.S. 167 (1963), 46.04

Elec. Workers Local Pension Fund, United States ex rel., Trustees of, v. D Bar D Enters., Inc., 772 F. Supp. 1167 (D. Nev. 1991), 36.02[D], 36.05

E.L. Hamm & Assocs., Inc. v. England, 379 F.3d 1334 (Fed. Cir. 2004), 24.02[C]

Eljer Mfg., Inc. v. Liberty Mut. Ins. Co., 972 F.2d 805 (7th Cir. 1992), 18.04[C][2]

Eljer Mfg., Inc. v. Liberty Mut. Ins. Co., 972 F.2d 805 (7th Cir. 1992), cert. denied, 507 U.S. 1005, 113 S. Ct. 1646 (1993), 18.04[C][2]

Ellis v. U.S., 711 F.2d 1571 (Fed. Cir. 1983), 33.02[E]

Elm Haven Constr. Ltd. P'ship v. Neri Constr. LLC, 281 F. Supp. 2d 406 (D. Conn. 2003), 28.03[D][1][a][ii]

Elm Haven Constr. Ltd. P'ship v. Neri Constr. LLC, 376 F.3d 96 (2d Cir. 2004), 15.15, 34.04[B]

Elrich Contracting, Inc., GSBCA No. 10936, 93-1 BCA ¶ 25,316 (1992), 23.03[H]

Elter S.A., ASBCA No. 52451, 01-1 B.C.A. (CCH) ¶ 31,373 (2001), 24.02[D]

Embrey v. United States, 17 Fed. Cl. 617 (1989), 28.02[A][2]

EMJ Corp. v. Laticrete Int'l, 934 F. Supp. 430 (M.D. Ga. 1996), 35.08[B]

Empire Constr. Co., ASBCA No. 27540, 84-3 B.C.A. ¶ 17,531 (1984), 28.03[E][1][c]

Empire Energy Mgmt. Sys., Inc., ASBCA No. 46741, 00-1 B.C.A. ¶ 30,636 (1999), 28.03[B][1]

Empire Energy Mgmt. Sys., Inc., ASBCA No. 46741, 00-1 B.C.A. ¶ 30,781 (2000), 28.03[D][2]

Empire State Sur. Co. v. City of Des Moines, 132 N.W. 837 (Iowa 1911), 35.04[B]

Employers Ins. Co. v. Rives, 264 Ala. 310, 87 So. 2d 653 (1955), *cert. denied,* 264 Ala. 696, 87 So. 2d 658 (1956), 18.04[C][1]

Employers Ins. of Wausau v. Able Green, Inc., 749 F. Supp. 1100 (S.D. Fla. 1990), 36.03[B]

Employers Ins. of Wausau v. Ehlco Liquidating Trust, 708 N.E.2d 1122 (Ill. 1999), 20.02, 20.05

Employers Mut. Cas. Co. v. United Fire & Cas. Co., 682 N.W.2d 452 (Iowa App. 2004), 34.04[F][6]

Employers Mut. Cas. Co. v. Walker, 811 S.W.2d 271 (Tex. App. 1991), 35.04[B]

Encore Constr. Corp. v. S.C. Bodner Constr., Inc., 756 N.E.2d 223 (Ind. Ct. App. 2002), 28.03[C][1]

Energy Masters Corp. v. Fulson, 839 S.W.2d 665 (Mo. Ct. App. 1992), 35.03[B]

Engbrock v. Federal Ins. Co., 370 F.2d 784 (5th Cir. 1967), 36.03[B], 36.07, 36.09[B], 36.09[D]

England v. Sherman R. Smoot Corp., 388 F.3d 844 (Fed. Cir. 2004), 27.05[D][4][b], 39.07[C]

Entech Sales & Serv., PSBCA No. 2061, 88-1 B.C.A. (CCH) ¶ 20,447 (1987), 27.05[C][3][b]

Envtl. Data Consultants, Inc. v. Gen. Serv. Admin., GSBCA No. 12951, 97-2 B.C.A. ¶ 29,208 (1997), 28.03[B][1]

Envtl. Data Consultants, Inc. v. GSA, GSBCA Nos. 13244 et al., 96-2 B.C.A. ¶ 28,614 (1996), 28.03[D][3]

Envtl. Safety Consultants, Inc., ASBCA No. 47498, 00-1 B.C.A. ¶ 30,826 (2000), 28.03[E][1][a]

Envtl. Tectonics, Corp., ASBCA No. 21204, 78-1 B.C.A. ¶ 12,986 (1978), 28.03[F][1]

E. Paul Kovas & Co. v. Alpert, 429 A.2d 829 (Conn. 1980), 33.01[F]

Episcopal Hous. Corp. v. Federal Ins. Co., 239 S.W.2d 647 (S.C. 1977), 46.04

ePlus Group, Inc. v. Travelers Prop. Cas. Co. of Am., 268 Fed. Appx. 117 (2d Cir. 2008), 18.05[A][3]

Eppco Metals Corp., ASCBA No. 38305, 90-1 BCA ¶ 22349 (1989), 23.03[B][2]

Equitable Cas. & Sur. Co. v. Helena Wholesale Grocery Co., 60 F.2d 380 (8th Cir. 1932), 35.04[A]

Equitable Sur. Co. v. United States *ex rel.* McMillan, 234 U.S. 448 (1914), 35.08[I]

Erb Lumber Co. v. Gregory Indus., Ltd., 769 F. Supp. 221 (E.D. Mich. 1991), 35.07[A][1]

Erickson Air Crane Co., EBCA Nos. 50-6-79, 52-7-79, 85-7-79, 83-1 B.C.A. (CCH) ¶ 16,145, 33.01[L]

Erickson Air Crane Co. of Wash., Inc. v. United States, 731 F.2d 810 (Fed. Cir. 1984), 39.03[F]

Erie Ins. Exch. v. Bledsoe, 141 N.C. App. 331 (Ct. App. 2000), 18.05[B][2]

Erie Ins. Exch. v. Colony Dev. Corp., 736 N.E.2d 941 (Ohio App. 1999), 19.07[B]

E.R. Mitchell Constr. Co. v. Danzig, 175 F. 3d 1369 (Fed. Cir. 1999), 30.03[C][3]

E.R. Mitchell Constr. Co. v. Secretary of the Navy, 175 F.3d 1369 (Fed. Cir. 1999), *rev'g* ASBCA No. 48745, 98-1 B.C.A. (CCH) ¶ 29,632 (1998), 24.04[C]

Essential Constr. Co., ASBCA Nos. 18491 et al., 78-2 B.C.A. (CCH) ¶ 13,314 (1978), 27.05[D][4][b]

Essential Constr. Co. & Himount Constructors, Ltd., ASBCA Nos. 18491 et al. 78-2 BCA ¶ 13,314 at 65,122 (1978), 23.03[E][1]

Essex Electro Engineers Inc., ASBCA No. 46202, 94-1 B.C.A. (CCH) ¶ 26,571, 39.03[B][1]

Essex Electro Engineers v. Danzig, 224 F.3d 1283 (Fed. Cir. 2000), 27.05[D][4][d]

Essex Electro Eng'rs Inc. v. United States, 960 F.2d 1576 (Fed. Cir. 1992), 39.03[B][2]

Essex Ins. Co. v. Holder, 2008 Ark. LEXIS 138 (Ark. 2008), 19.07[B]

E. Steel Constructors, Inc. v. City of Salem, 549 S.E.2d 266 (W. Va. 2001), 7.02[B][3]

ETS-Hokin Corp. v. United States, 420 F.2d 716 (Ct. Cl. 1970), 30.03[B][1]

Euclid-Mississippi v. Western Cas. & Sur. Co., 163 Wo. 904 (Miss. 1964), 35.07[B][1]

Eureka Stone Quarry, United States *ex rel.* v. Pennsylvania Nat'l Mut. Cas. Ins. Co., Civ. A. 92-6830, 1993 WL 483550 (E.D. Pa. Nov. 17, 1993), *aff'd,* 31 F.3d 1175 (3d Cir. 1994), 35.08[D][2]

Evansville, City of, v. Verplank Concrete, 400 N.E.2d 812 (Ind. Ct. App. 1980), 35.03[B]

Everett Painting Co. v. Padula & Wadsworth Constr., Inc., 856 So. 2d 1059 (2003), 25.02[C]

Everett Plywood Corp. v. United States, 512 F.2d 1082 (Ct. Cl. 1975), 28.04[A][2]

Evergreen Pipeline Constr. Co., United States *ex rel.* v. Merritt-Meridian Constr. Corp., 890 F. Supp. 1213 (S.D.N.Y. 1995), *judgement aff'd in part, vacated in part on other grounds,* 95 F.3d 153 (2d Cir. 1996), 26.02[KK][4]

Everman's Elec. Co. v. Evan Johnson & Sons Constr., Inc., 955 So. 2d 979 (Miss. Ct. App. 2007), 26.02[Y][3]

Excavation Constr., Inc., United States *ex rel.,* v. Glen-Stewart-Pinckney Builders & Developers., Inc., 388 F. Supp. 289 (D. Del. 1975), 35.05[A]

Executive Elevator Serv., Inc., VA BCA No. 2152, 87-3 B.C.A. ¶ 20,083, *aff'd,* B.C.A. ¶ 19,849 (1987), 28.04[D][4]

F

F&C Eng'g Co. v. Moore, 300 S.W.2d 323 (Tex. Civ. App. 1957), 35.08[D][3]

F&D Constr. Co., ASBCA Nos. 41441 et al., 91-2 B.C.A. ¶ 23,983 (1991), 28.03[B][3][b], 28.03[D][1][b], 28.03[D][3], 28.03[E][2]

F&L Packing Corp., ASBCA No. 42362, 93-1 B.C.A. ¶ 25,305 (1992), 28.03[D][2]

Faber v. City of N.Y., 118 N.E. 609 (N.Y. 1918), 22.08

Fab-Tech, Inc. v. E.I. Dupont de Nemours and Co., CIVIL No. 1:04CV275, 2006 U.S. Dist. LEXIS 92236 (D. Vt. Dec. 13, 2006), 16.02[B]

Fager & Friesen Ins. Agency, State *ex rel.,* v. Storms-Green Constr. Co., 382 S.W.2d 812 (Mo. Ct. App. 1964), 35.04[B]

Fairbanks Builders, Inc. v. Morton DeLima, Inc., 438 P.2d 194 (Alaska 1971), 33.01[E]

Fairchild & Co. v. Richmond, F. & P.R.R., 516 Supp. 1305 (D.D.C. 1981), 46.23

Fairfax Co. Redev & Hous. Auth. v. Worcester Bros. Co., 514 S.E.2d 147 (Va. 1999), 30.03[C][3]

Fairfield Scientific Corp., ASBCA No. 21151, 78-1 B.C.A. ¶ 13,082, *aff'd,* 655 F.2d 1062 (Ct. Cl. 1981), 28.03[B][3][a]

Fairfield Scientific Corp. v. United States, 611 F.2d 854 (Ct. Cl. 1979), 28.04[D], 28.04[D][1]

Falco Constr. Corp., United States *ex rel.,* v. Summit Gen. Contracting Corp., 760 F. Supp. 1004 (E.D.N.Y. 1991), 35.08[E][4]

Fallon Electric Co. v. Cincinnati Insurance Co., 121 F.3d 125 (3d Cir. 1997), 36.03[C], 36.07

Fanderlik-Locke Co. v. United States *ex rel.* Morgan, C.A., 10 (N.M.) 1960, 285 F.2d 939, *cert. denied,* 365 U.S. 860, 35.03[A]

Fanning, Phillips & Molnar, VABCA No. 3856R, 96-2 BCA ¶ 28,427 (1996), 23.03[E][3]

Fanning & Doorley Constr. Co. v. Geigy Chem. Corp., 305 F.Supp. 650 (D.R.I. 1969), 29.02[B][1]

Farell Constr. Co. v. Jefferson Parish, 693 F. Supp. 490 (E.D. La. 1988), 29.02[C][2]

Farley v. Clark Equip. Co., 484 S.W.2d 142 (Tex. Civ. App. 1972), 16.04[B]

Farm Credit Bank of Louisville v. United States Mineral Prod. Co., 864 F. Supp. 643 (W.D. Ky. 1994), 29.02[E]

Farmers Coop. Ass'n of Churchs Ferry v. Cole, 239 N.W.2d 808 (N.D. 1976), 16.04[E]

Farmers Union Cent. Exch., Inc. v. Reliance Ins. Co., 675 F. Supp. 1534 (D.N.D. 1987), 34.04[D], 35.07[B][1]

Farmer v. Town of Wilson, 202 N.C. 775, 164 S.E. 356 (1932), 46.27

Farnsworth & Chambero, Inc., Appeal of, ASBCA No. 5408, 59-2 BCA 2329 (1959), 30.03[C]

Farwest Steel Corp. v. Mainline Metal Works, 741 P.2d 58 (Wash. Ct. App. 1987), 35.03[B]

Fattore Co. v. Metro. Sewerage Comm'n, 454 F.2d 537 (7th Cir. 1971), 22.06, 22.08

Fattore Co. v. Metro. Sewerage Comm'n of County of Milwaukee, 505 F.2d 1 (7th Cir. 1974), 22.08

Faulkenbury v. Teachers' & State Employees' Retirement Sys. of N.C., 510 S.E.2d 675 (N.C. Ct. App. 1999), 33.01[I]

Faulkner Concrete Pipe Co. v. United States Fid. & Guar. Co., 218 So. 2d 1 (Miss. 1968), 35.04[B]

FCI Constructors v. Foothill/Eastern Transp. Corridor Agency, 2002 WL 31525388 (Cal. Ct. App. Nov. 14, 2002), 26.02[E][3]

F.D. Rich Co. v. United States *ex rel.* Industrial Lumber Co., 417 U.S. 116 (1974), 33.02[O]

F.D. Rich Co. v. United States *ex rel.* Industrial Lumber Co., 417 U.S. 116, 94 S. Ct. 2157, 40 L. Ed. 2d 703 (1974), 35.02[A], 35.03[A], 35.04[A], 35.06[A][2]

F.D. Rich Co. v. Wilmington Housing Authority, 392 F.2d 841 (3d Cir. 1968), 26.02[H][3], 26.02[H][4]

Fed. Data Corp., DOT BCA No. 2389, 91-3 B.C.A. ¶ 24,063 (1991), 28.04[C][2]

Federal Crop Ins. Corp. v. Merrill, 332 U.S. 380 (1947), 27.05[B][2]

Federal Crop Ins. Corp. v. Merrill, 332 U.S. 380, 68 S. Ct. 1, 92 L. Ed. 10 (1947), 27.05[B][5][b]

Fed. Identification Co., ASBCA No. 9117, 1964 B.C.A. ¶ 4191 (1964), 28.03[F][1]

Federal Ins. Co. v. Starr Elec. Co., 410 S.E.2d 684 (Va. 1991), 35.08[C]

Federal Ins. Co., United States v., 273 F. Supp. 758 (E.D. N.C. 1967), 21.06

Fed. Mktg. Co. v. Impression Prods., Inc., 823 A.2d 513 (D.C. 2003), 33.01[E]

Federal Mogul Corp. v. Universal Constr. Co., 376 So. 2d 716 (Ala. Civ. App. 1979), 29.02[C][3]

Federal Paving Co. v. Raschka, 141 N.E. 644 (Ind. Ct. App. 1923), 35.04[B]

Fejes v. Alaska Ins. Co., 984 P.2d 519 (Alaska 1999), 18.05[A][3], 19.07[B]

Felton Construction Co., AGBCA [now Civilian BCA] No. 406-9, 81-1 B.C.A. ¶ 14,932 (1981), 27.05[C][2]

Ferguson Mgmt. Co., AGBCA No. 83-207-3, 83-2 BCA ¶ 16,819 (1982), 23.03[B][1]

F.E. Robinson Co. v. Alpha-Continental, 273 F. Supp. 758 (E.D.N.C. 1967), *aff'd,* 404 F.2d 343 (4th Cir. 1968), 21.06

Ferris v. Haymore, 967 F.2d 946 (4th Cir. 1992), 35.04[B]

Ferris v. Mann, 99 R.I. 630 (R.I. 1965), 30.04[B][1]

Ferry v. Ohio Farmers Ins. Co., 27 Cal. Rptr. 471 (Ct. App. 1963), 35.08[F][1]

Fewox v. McMerit Constr. Co., 556 So. 2d 419 (Fla. Dist. Ct. App. 1989), 33.02[M][2], 33.02[N]

F. Garafalo Elec. Co., Inc. v. New York Univ., 300 A.2d 186, 754 N.Y.S.2d 227 (N.Y. App. Div. 2002), 28.03[D][3]

F.H. McGraw & Co. v. Milcor Steel Co., 149 F.2d 301 (2d Cir. 1945), 35.07[A][2], 35.08[D][2]

F.H. McGraw & Co. v. United States, 130 F. Supp. 394 (Ct. Cl. 1955), 30.03[C][3]

Fid. & Cas. Co. of N.Y. v. Envirodyne Eng'rs, Inc. 461 N.E.2d 471 (Ill. Ct. App. 1983), 20.02

Fidelity & Cas. Co. of N.Y. v. Mauney, 116 S.W.2d 960 (Ky. Ct. App. 1938), 33.02[N]

Fidelity & Deposit Co. of Maryland v. Rosenmutter, 614 F. Supp. 348 (N.D. Ill. 1985), 36.03[C]

Fid. & Deposit Co. of Md., ASBCA No. 32710, 87-1 B.C.A. ¶ 19,356 (1986), 28.03[F][2]

Fidelity & Deposit Co. of Md. v. Fleischer, 772 S.W.2d 809 (Mo. Ct. App. 1989), 36.05

Fidelity & Deposit Co. of Md. v. Harris, 360 F.2d 402 (9th Cir. 1966), 35.03[A]

Fid. & Dep. Co. of Md. v. Hartford Cas. Ins. Co., 189 F. Supp. 2d 1212 (D. Kan. 2002), 19.07[B]

Fidelity & Deposit Co. of Md. v. Stromberg Sheet Metal Works, Inc., 532 A.2d 676 (D.C. 1987), 35.06[A][2]

Fidelity & Deposit Co. v. Bristol Steel & Iron Works, Inc., 722 F.2d 1160 (4th Cir. 1983), 36.03[B], 36.05, 36.09[D]

Fidelity & Deposit Co. v. John Gill & Sons Co., 270 S.W. 700 (Mo. 1924), 35.08[I]

Fidelity & Deposit Co. v. McClintic-Marshall Corp., 171 A. 382 (N.J. Ch. 1934), aff'd, 176 A. 341 (N.J. 1935), 35.08[B]

Fidelity & Deposit Co. v. Wu, 552 A.2d 1196 (Vt. 1988), 36.05, 36.07

Fidelity and Guar. Ins. Underwriters, Inc. v. Wells Fargo Bank, N.A., 2006 WL 870683 (S.D. Tex. 3/31/06), 34.04[H]

Fidelity Casualty Co. v. Finch, 3 A.D.2d 141 (1957), 36.03[B]

Fidelity Construction Co., DOT CAB Nos. 1113, 1123, 80-2 BCA ¶ 14,819, 39.08[B]

Fidelity Homestead Ass'n v. Kennedy & Anderson, 105 So. 64 (La. 1925), 35.08[I]

Fiesta Leasing & Sales, Inc., ASBCA No. 29311, 86-3 B.C.A. ¶ 19,045 (1986), 28.04[C][2][a]

Fininen v. Barlow, 142 Cal. App. 185, 47 Cal. Rptr. 687 (2d Dist. 2006), 45.05[B]

Finn v. Krumroy Construction Co., 589 N.E.2d 58 (Ohio Ct. App. 1990), 33.01[F]

Fireman's Fund Ins. Co., United States ex rel., v. Frank Brisco Co., 462 F. Supp. 114 (E.D. La. 1978), 35.06[A][2], 35.08[A]

Fireman's Fund Ins. Co. v. Nizdil, 709 F. Supp. 975 (D. Or. 1989), 36.02[D], 36.09[A]

Fireman's Fund Ins. Co. v. Safeco Ins. Co. of Am., 2007 WL 4233317 (W.D.N.C. 9/28/2007), 34.04[E][2]

Fireman's Fund McGee Marine Underwriters v. A&B Welding & Mfg., Inc., No. 04-C-0576-C, 2005 U.S. Dist. LEXIS 4360 (W.D. Wis. Mar. 8, 2005), 16.02[B]

Firemen's Ins. Co. of Newark v. National Union Fire Ins. Co., 387 N.J. Super. 434, 904 A.2d 754 (2006), 19.07[B]

Fire Sec. Sys., Inc., VABCA No. 3086, 91-2 B.C.A. (CCH) ¶ 23,743 (1991), 24.04, 24.04[B]

Fire Security Sys., Inc., VABCA No. 5559-63, 02-2 B.C.A. ¶ 31,977 (2002), 24.04[C]

First Commercial Mortgage Co. v. Reece, 89 Cal. App. 4th 731, 108 Cal. Rptr. 2d 23 (2d Dist. 2001), 12.04[C][1][b]

First Cont'l Nat'l Bank & Trust Co., United States ex rel., v. Western Contracting Corp., 341 F.2d 383 (8th Cir. 1965), 35.04[A], 35.04[B]

First Financial Ins. Co. v. Jetco Contracting Corp., No. 99 Civ. 8664, 2000 U.S. Dist. LEXIS 10229 (S.D.N.Y. July 21, 2000), 18.04[A]

First Ins. Co. of Hawaii v. State, 66 Haw. 413, 665 P.2d 648 (Haw. 1983), 20.02, 20.05

First Nat'l Bank, United States ex rel., v. United States Fid. & Guar. Co., 240 F. Supp. 316 (N.D. Okla. 1965), 35.06[A][1][b]

First Nat'l Bank of Elkhart County v. Smoker, 286.E.2d 203 (Ind. Ct. App.), reh'g denied, 287 N.E.2d 788 (Ind. Ct. App. 1972), 16.08[B]

First Nat'l Bank v. William Can, 503 F. Supp. 419 (N. Dist. Ohio 1980), 8A.08[D]

Fischbach & Moore Int'l Corp., 987 F.2d 759 (Fed. Cir. 1993), 39.04[B]

Fischbach & Moore Int'l Corp., ASBCA No. 18,146, 77-1 B.C.A. (CCH) ¶ 12,300 at 59,224 (1976), aff'd, 617 F.2d 223 (Ct. Cl. 1980), 24.03

Fischback & Moore Int'l Corp., ASBCA No. 18146, 77-1 B.C.A. (CCH) ¶ 12,300 (1976), aff'd, 617 F.2d 233 (Ct. Cl. 1980), 24.02[A]

Fishbach-Natkin, Inc. v. Shimizu Amer. Corp., 854 F. Supp. 1294 (E.D. Mich. 1994), 29.04[D][1]

Fisher v. Am. Family Mut. Ins. Co., 579 N.W.2d 599, 1998 N.D. (1998), 18.05[A][1], 18.05[A][2], 19.07[B]

Fisher v. Klippstatter, 689 S.W.2d 870 (Tenn. Ct. App. 1985), 33.01[E]

Fite & Warmath Constr. Co. v. Mys Corp., 559 S.W.2d 729 (Ky. 1977), 46.04

532 Madison Ave. Gourmet Foods, Inc. v. Finlandia Ctr., Inc., 750 N.E.2d 1097 (N.Y. 2001), 29.02[D][5]

Fleischer Eng'g & Constr. Co. v. United States ex rel. Hallenbeck, 311 U.S. 15 (1940), 35.05[A]

Flexfab, L.L.C. v. U.S. 424 F.3d 1254 (Fed. Cir. 2005), 27.05[B][5][b]

Floor Craft Floor Covering, Inc. v. Parma Community Gen. Hosp. Assoc., 560 N.E.2d 206 (Ohio 1990), 29.02[C][5]

Florence Street Elec. and Mech., Inc., VABCA No. 1659, 82-1 BCA ¶ 15,742 (1982), 23.03[B][1], 23.03[E][4]

Florida Bd. of Regents v. Mycon Corp., 651 So.2d 149 (Fla. Dist. Ct. App. 1995), 7.03[B][1][a]

Florida Power & Light Co. v. Mid-Valley, Inc., 763 F.2d 1316 (11th Cir. 1985), 29.03[D][3]

Flynn's Camden Elec. Supply Co., United States ex rel., v. Home Indem. Ins. Co., 246 F. Supp. 27 (E.D. Pa. 1965), 35.06[A][1][b]

FMC Corp. v. Plaisted & Cos., 61 Cal. App. 4th 1132 (1998), 18.04[C][2]

FMI Contracting Corp. v. Federal Ins. Co., 829 S.W.2d 907 (Tex. App. 1992), 35.06[A][2]

Foley, United States v., 329 U.S. 64 (1946), 24.02[D]

Folk Constr. Co. v. United States, 2 Cl. Ct. 681 (1983), 24.04[A], 30.03[C][5], 39.03[F]

Fordham, United States ex rel., v. P.W. Parker, Inc., 504 F. Supp. 1066 (D. Md. 1980), 35.05[A], 35.08[D][3]

Foremost Mech. Sys., Inc. v. GSA, GSBCA Nos. 13250-C (12335) et al., 98-1 B.C.A. ¶ 29,652 (1998), 28.03[F][4]

Foremost Mech. Sys., Inc. v. GSA, GSBCA Nos. 14645-C (13584), 99-1 B.C.A. ¶ 30,352 (1999), 28.03[F][4], 28.03[G]

Forest Servs., Inc. v. Fidelity & Cas. Co. of N.Y., 171 S.E.2d 743 (Ga. Ct. App. 1969), 35.04[B]

Fortec Constructors, Forest Builders and Tectonics of Florida v. United States, 760 F.2d 1288 (Fed. Cir. 1985), 28.03[E][1][b]

Fortec Constructors v. United States, 8 Cl. Ct. 490 (1985), 23.06[A], 23.06[B][2]

Foshee v. Daoust Constr. Co., 185 F.2d 23 (7th Cir. 1950), 34.04[F][5]

Foster Constr. C.A. v. United States, 193 Ct. Cl. 587, 435 F.2d 873 (1970), 24.02[B]

Foster Constr. C.A. v. U.S., 435 F.2d 873 (Ct. Cl. 1970), 11.04[B][4]

Foster-Gardner, Inc. v. National Union
Fire Ins. Co., 18 Cal. 4th 857 (1998),
18.04[B]

Fountain Sand & Gravel v. Chilton
Constr. Co., 578 P.2d 664 (Colo. Ct.
App. 1978), 35.06[B][3]

Fournier Furniture, Inc. v. Waltz-Holst
Blow Pipe Co., 980 F. Supp. 187
(W.D. Va. 1997), 29.02[E]

Fourt v. United States *ex rel.*
Westinghouse Elec. Supply Co., 235
F.2d 433 (10th Cir. 1956),
35.07[A][2]

Foxgate Homeowners' Association v.
Bramalea California, Inc., 25 P.3d
1117 (2001), 45.05[A]

Fox v. The Giuseppe Mazzini, 110 F.
Supp. 212 (E.D.N.Y. 1953), 46.06

Framlau Corp. v. United States, 568
F.2d 687 (Ct. Cl. 1977), 30.03[E]

Frank v. L.L. Bean Inc., 377 F. Supp.
233 (D. Me. 2005), 45.04[E]

Frank Briscoe Co. v. Clark County, 857
F.2d 606 (9th Cir. 1988), 29.02[B][1]

Frankel v. J. Watson Co., Inc., 21 Mass.
App. Ct. 43, 484 N.E.2d 104 (1985),
18.05[A][2]

Frankfort Digital Servs. v. Kistler, 477
F.3d 1117 (9th Cir. 2007), 5.03[C][2]

Frank H. Conner Co. v. Spanish Inns
Charlotte, Ltd., 34 N.C. App. 341,
238 S.E.2d 525, *aff'd,* 294 N.C. 661,
242 S.E.2d 785 (1977), 46.18

Frank T. Hickey, Inc. v. L.A. Jewish
Cmty. Council, 128 Cal. App. 2d 676,
276 P.2d 52 (1954), 26.02[E][1]

Frantz v. Johnson, 116 Nev. 455, 465
n.4 (2004), 26.02[CC][4]

Franzen v. Southern Sur. Co., 246 P. 30
(Wyo. 1926), 35.07[B][1]

Fraser Constr. Co. v. United States, 384
F.3d 1354 (Fed. Cir. 2004), 23.03[G],
27.05[D][7], 30.03[C][6]

Frazier-Fleming Co., ASBCA No.
34537, 91-1 BCA ¶ 23,378 (1990),
23.03[H]

Fred A. Arnold, Inc., ASBCA No.
16,506, 72-2 BCA ¶ 9608 (1972),
23.03[E][2]

Fred A. Arnold, Inc. v. United States,
18 Cl. Ct. 1 (1989), 32.04

Fred Christensen, Inc. v. Hansen Constr.
Co., 21 P.2d 195 (Or. 1933),
35.08[D][1], 35.08[I]

Freedom, NY, Inc., ASBCA Nos. 35671,
43965, 96-2 B.C.A. ¶ 28,328,
modified in part, 96-2 B.C.A.
¶ 28,502 (1996), 28.03[D][2]

Freeman v. Dep't of Highways, 253 La.
105, 217 So. 2d 166 (1968),
26.02[S][1], 26.02[S][3], 26.02[S][4]

Freeman Contracting, Inc. v. Central
Sur. & Ins. Corp., 205 F.2d 607 (8th
Cir. 1953), 28.03[E][1][a]

Fremont Division Dynamics Corp. v.
America, ASBCA No. 15806, 75-1
B.C.A. (CCH) ¶ 11,139 (1975),
aff'd, 216 Ct. Cl. 448 (1978),
24.04[E]

Fremont Indem. Co. v. Special Earth
Equip. Corp., 131 Ill. App. 3d 1078,
474 N.E.2d 976, *appeal denied,*
(May, 1985), 18.04[C][1]

French v. Assurance Co. of America,
448 F.3d 693 (4th Cir. 2006),
19.07[B]

French v. York Int'l Corp., 72 Va. Cir.
538 (Va. Cir. Ct. 2007), 16.02[B]

Freuhauf Corp., PSBCA No. 477, 74-1
B.C.A. (CCH) ¶ 10,596 (1974),
24.04[B]

Friedrich Refrigerators, United States *ex
rel.,* v. Forrester, 441 F.2d 779 (5th
Cir. 1971), 35.08[D][3]

Friendship Heights Ass'n v. Vlastimil
Koubek, 573 F. Supp. 100 (D. Md.
1983), 29.02[C][3]

Frome, AGBCA No. 246, 71-1 B.C.A.
¶ 8611 (1970), 28.03[B][2]

Frontrange Solutions USA, Inc. v.
Newroad Software, Inc., 505 F. Supp.
2d 821 (D. Colo. 2007),
27.05[A][3]

Fru-Con Constr. Corp. v. United States,
44 Fed. Cl. 298 (1999), 23.03[E][1]

Fruehauf Corp. v. United States, 587
F.2d 486 (Ct. Cl. 1978), 24.02

Fukaya Trading Co. v. Eastern Marine
Corp., 322 F. Supp. 278 (E.D. La.
1971), 46.23

Fulford, 28.03[H]

Furia v. Helm, 111 Cal. App. 4th 945, 4
Cal. Rptr. 357 (1st Dist. 2003), *as
modified* Sept. 10, 2003,
45.05[B]

Fuschino v. Smith, No. 2000-CA-31,
2001 WL 9928 (Ohio Ct. App. Jan. 5,
2001), 32.03[B]

G

G&G Western Painting, Inc., ASBCA No. 50492, 01-2 B.C.A. ¶ 31,492 (2001), 28.03[E][3][b]

G&H Assoc. v. Hahn, Inc., 934 P.2d 229 (Nev. 1997), 29.04[J]

Gaddis Mining Co. v. Continental Materials Corp., 196 S. Supp. 860 (D. Wyo. 1961), 46.23

GAF Corp. v. United States, 19 Cl. Ct. 490 (Fed. Cl. 1990), 7.03[B][1]

GAIC v. Merritt-Meridian Constr. Co., 975 F. Supp. 511 (S.D.N.Y. 1997), 34.04[D]

Gallagher v. T.V. Sapno Bldg. Corp., 1995 WL 109082 (Del. Super. Ct. 1995), 11.03[A][3][a]

Gamm Constr. Co. v. Townsend, 336 N.E.2d 592 (Ill. App. Ct. 1975), 28.03[D][2]

Garaman, Inc. v. Williams, 912 P.2d 1121 (Wyo. 1996), 29.02[C][3]

Garden City Co. v. Bentrup, 228 F.2d 334 (10th Cir. 1955), 29.02[D][3]

Garden Sanctuary, Inc. v. Insurance Co. of N. Am., 292 So. 2d 75 (Fla. Dist. Ct. App. 1974), 18.04[B]

Gardner Displays Co. v. United States, 346 F.2d 585 (Ct. Cl. 1965), 23.03[H]

Garfield & Co. v. Wiest, 432 F.2d 849 (2d Cir. 1970), 46.22

Garibaldi, United States ex rel., v. Orleans Parish Sch. Bd., 244 F.3d 486 (5th Cir. 2001), 38.02[C]

Garikis, Wilson & Atkinson, Inc. v. Episcopal Fund of Jefferson County, Inc., 614 So. 2d 447 (Ala. 1993), 46.04

Garvey v. State Farm Fire & Cas. Co., 48 Cal. 3d 395 (1989), 18.05[B][2]

Gary G. Day Constr. Co. v. Clarendon America Ins. Co., 459 F. Supp. 2d 1039 (D. Nev. 2006), 19.07[B]

Gaskill v. Jennette, 554 S.E.2d 10 (N.C. App. 2001), 27.05[A][3]

Gasparini Excavating Co. v. Pa. Turnpike Comm'n, 187 A.2d 157 (Pa. 1963), 7.03[B][2][b]

Gasparini Excavating Co. v. Pa. Turnpike Comm'n, 409 Pa. 465, 187 A.2d 157 (Pa. 1963), 26.02[MM][3], 26.02[MM][4]

Gassman Corp., ASBCA Nos. 44975, 44976, 99-1 BCA ¶ 30,720 (1999), 23.06[A], 23.06[B][2]

Gateway Erectors v. Lutheran Gen. Hosp., 102 Ill. App. 3d 300 (1st Dist. 1981), 8A.08[F]

G.D. Searle & Co. v. Metric Contractors, 572 F. Supp. 836 (N.D. Ga. 1983), 46.04

Gear, United States ex rel., v. Emergency Med. Assocs. of Ill., Inc., 436 F.3d 726 (7th Cir. 2006), 38.02[B][4][b]

G.E. Boggs & Assocs., Inc. v. Roskens, 969 F.2d 1023 (Fed. Cir. 1992), 39.02[A], 39.08[F]

Geddes & Smith, Inc. v. St. Paul Mercury Indem. Co., 51 Cal. 2d 558 (1959), 18.04[C][1], 18.04[C][2]

Gemini Constr. Co. v. Childs, 355 S.E.2d 81 (Ga. Ct. App. 1987), 35.08[F][3]

General Accident Fire & Life Assurance Corp., United States ex rel., v. Maguire Homes, Inc., 186 F. Supp. 659 (D. Mass. 1959), 35.04[A]

General Accident Ins. Co. v. Manchester, 116 A.D.2d 790, 497 N.Y.S. 2d 180 (1986), 18.04[C][1]

General Accident Ins. Co. of Am. v. Merritt-Meridian Constr. Corp., 975 F. Supp. 511 (S.D.N.Y. 1997), 36.03[B]

General Crushed Stone Co. v. State, 225 N.E.2d 893 (N.Y. 1967), 35.08[D][1]

General Dynamics Corp. v. United States, 218 Ct. Cl. 40, 585 F.2d 457 (1978), 24.02[A]

General Dynamics Corp. v. United States, 585 F.2d 457 (Ct. Cl. 1978), 21.08, 28.03[E][3][b]

General Elec. Co. v. Southern Constr. Co., 383 F.2d 135 (5th Cir. 1967), cert. denied, 390 U.S. 955 (1968), 35.06[A][1][b]

General Elec. Corp., United States, 727 F.2d 1567 (Fed. Cir. 1984), 39.04[B]

General Elec. Supply Co., United States ex rel., v. Wiring, Inc., 646 F.2d 1037 (5th Cir. 1981), 35.07[A][2], 35.08[D][2]

General Equip., Inc. v. USF&G, 292 So. 2d 806 (La. Ct. App. 1st Cir. 1974), 35.06[A][2]

General Ins. Co. v. United States *ex rel.* Audley Moore & Son, 406 F.2d 442 (5th Cir.), *opinion on petition for reh'g*, 409 F.2d 1326 (5th Cir.), *cert. denied*, 396 U.S. 906 (1969), 35.06[A][1][b]

General Ins. Co. of Am. v. Hercules Constr. Co., 385 F.2d 13 (8th Cir. 1967), 24.02, 24.02[D], 24.04[B], 30.03[C][3], 30.03[C][4], 34.04[F][3]

General Rock & Sand Corp., United States *ex rel.*, v. Chuska Dev. Corp., 55 F.3d 1491 (10th Cir. 1995), 35.06[A][2]

Gen. Ship Corp. v. United States, 634 F. Supp. 868 (D. Mass. 1986), 23.03[B][1]

Geneva Pharm. Tech. Corp. v. Barr Lab, Inc., 386 F.3d 485 (2d Cir. 2004), 17.01[A]

Geneva Pipe Co. v. S & H Ins. Co., 714 P.2d 648 (Utah 1986), 35.08[D][2]

Geolar, Inc. v. Gilbert, 874 P.2d 937 (Alaska 1994), 27.05[D][6][b]

Geo-Marine, Inc. v. GSA, GSBCA No. 16247, 2005-2 BCA ¶ 33,048 (Aug. 17, 2005), 28.03[B][3]

George A. Fuller Co., ASBCA No. 8524, 1962 B.C.A. (CCH) ¶ 3619 (1962), 24.02[A]

George A. Fuller Co. v. United States, 108 Ct. Cl. 70, 69 F. Supp. 409 (1947), 24.02[D]

George A. Fuller Co. v. United States, 69 F. Supp. 409, 108 Ct. Cl. 70 (1947), 24.02[D]

George A. Fuller Co. v. United States, 69 F. Supp. 409 (Ct. Cl. 1947), 28.03[E][1][a]

George A. Fuller Co. v. U.S. F. & G., 200 A.D.2d 255 (App. Div.-1st Dept. 1994), 19.07[B]

George E. Jensen, Inc., ASBCA No. 20,234, 76-1 B.C.A. (CCH) ¶ 11,741 (1976), 24.02[B]

George F. Marshall & Gordon L. Blackwell, ENGBCA No. 6066, 01-1 B.C.A. ¶ 30,730 (2000), 28.03[F][1], 28.03[F][2]

George Hyman Constr. Co., The, v. The United States, 30 Fed. Cl. 170 (1993), 39.03[F]

George Hyman Constr. Co. v. Washington Metro. Area Transit Auth., 816 F.2d 753 (D.C. Cir. 1987), 24.04[C]

George J. Shaw Hauling Co., State *ex rel.*, v. Bob Eldridge Constr. Co., 397 S.W.2d 7 (Mo. Ct. App. 1965), 35.04[B]

George Sollitt Constr. Co. v. United States, 64 Fed. Cl. 229 (2005), 23.03[D], 23.06[B][2], 23.06[D], 27.05[D][4][a]

George T. Miller Constr. Co. v. Standard Oil Co., 185 N.E. 639 (Ind. 1933), 35.04[B]

Georgia Elec. Supply Co., United States *ex rel.*, v. United States Fid. & Guar. Co., 656 F.2d 993 (5th Cir. 1981), 35.04[A], 35.05[A], 35.06[A][1][b], 35.08[F][1]

Georgia Pac. Co., United States v., 421 F.2d 92 (9th Cir. 1970), 35.08[F][2]

Georgia Power Co. v. Georgia Pub. Serv. Comm'n, 396 S.E.2d 562 (Ga. Ct. App. 1990), 30.03[D][2]

Germaine, United States v., 99 U.S. 508 , 25 L. Ed. 482 (1878), 38.02[B][3]

Germantown Cent. School Dist. v. Clark, Clark, Millis & Gilson, AIA, 743 N.Y.S.2d 599 (3d Dep't 2002), *aff'd*, 761 N.Y.S.2d 141 (2003), 11.02

Gerstner Elec. Inc. v. American Ins. Co., 520 F.2d 790 (8th Cir. 1975), 34.04[A], 36.09[F]

Giant Powder Co. v. Fidelity & Deposit Co., 7 P.2d 1023 (Cal. 1932), 35.08[D][1]

Gibbons-Grable Co. v. Gilbane Bldg. Co., 34 Ohio App. 3d 170, 517 N.E.2d 559 (1986), 46.06

Gibbs v. Ernst, 647 A.2d 882 (Pa. 1994), 12.04[C][1][b]

Gibraltar Casualty Company v. A. Epstein and Sons, International, Inc., 562 N.E.2d 1039 (Ill. Ct. App. 1990), 20.04

Giddens v. Board of Educ. of City of Chicago, 398 Ill. 157, 75 N.E.2d 286 (1947), 46.22

Giesler v. U.S., 232 F.3d 864 (Fed. Cir. 2000), 27.03[B][2]

Gifford-Wood Co. v. Travelers Indem. Co., 249 N.Y.S.2d 317 (Sup. Ct. 1964), 35.06[A][2]

Gigliello, United States *ex rel.*, v. Sovereign Constr. Co., 311 F. Supp. 371 (D. Mass. 1970), 35.06[A][2]

Gilbane Bldg. Co. v. Brisk Waterproofing Co., 585 A.2d 248 (Md. App. 1991), 35.08[E][1]

Gilbert & Bennett Mfg. Co. v. Westinghouse Elec. Corp., 445 F. Supp. 537 (D. Mass. 1977), 16.04[B]

Gilbraltar Cas. Co. v. Sargent & Lundy, 574 N.E. 2d 664 (Ill. Ct. App. 1990), *appeal denied,* 580 N.E.2d 113 (Ill. 1991), 20.02

Gildersleeve Elec., Inc. v. Gen. Serv. Admin., GSBCA, No. 16404, 05-2 BCA ¶ 33011 (June 8, 2006), 28.02[C]

Giles, United States *ex rel.*, v. Sardie, No. CV-96-2002 (C.D. Cal. 2000), 38.02[C]

Gilliland v. Elmwood Props., 391 S.E.2d 577 (S.C. 1990), 12.04[C][1][b]

Gilmore v. Garrett, 582 So. 2d 387 (Miss. 1991), 29.02[B][4]

Giuliani Assocs., Inc., ASBCA No. 51672, 03-2 B.C.A. ¶ 32,368 (2003), 28.04[D][1]

Gjieli, United States v., 717 F.2d 968 (6th Cir. 1983), 42.02[B][3]

Glades County v. Detroit Fid. & Sur. Co., 57 F.2d 449 (5th Cir. 1932), 35.08[I]

Gladwynne Constr. Co. v. Mayor & City Council of Baltimore, 147 Md. App. 149 (2002), 30.03[C][3]

Glasgow v. Pennsylvania Dep't of Transp., 529 A.2d 576 (Pa. Commw. Ct. 1987), 30.03[D][1]

Glassell-Taylor Co. v. Magnolia Petroleum Co., 153 F.2d 527 (5th Cir. 1946), 35.04[A]

Glassman Constr. Co. v. Maryland City Plaza, Inc., 371 F. Supp. 1154 (D. Md. 1974), 21.02

Glazer Constr. Co. v. United States, 52 Fed. Cl. 513 (2003), 28.03[D][1][b]

G.L. Christian & Assoc. v. United States, 160 Ct. Cl. 1, 312 F.2d 418, *cert. denied,* 375 U.S. 954 (1963), 28.01

Glendenning's Limestone & Ready-Mix Co., Inc. v. Reimer, 721 N.W.2d 704 (Wis. App. 2006), 19.07[B]

Glickfield, United States *ex rel.*, v. Krendel, 136 F. Supp. 276 (D.N.J. 1955), 35.08[F][4]

Gloucester City Bd. of Educ. v. American Arbitration Ass'n, 333 N.J. Super. 511 (App. Div. 2000), 34.04[B]

Gloviak v. Tucci Constr. Co., Inc., 415 Pa. Super. 123 (1992), 30.02[A][1]

GMC Contractors, Inc., GSBCA No. 3730, 75-1 B.C.A. (CCH) ¶ 11,083, 39.05[D]

G.M. Shupe, Inc. v. United States, 5 Cl. Ct. 662 (1984), 23.06[A]

Gold v. Morrison-Knudson Co., 68 F.3d 1475 (2d Cir. 1995), 38.02[B][4][b]

Golden W. Constr. Co. v. United States *ex rel.* Bernadot, 304 F.2d 753 (10th Cir. 1962), 35.04[A]

Goldfarb v. Virginia State Bar, 421 U.S. 773 (1975), 8.02

Goldman v. Shapiro, 16 N.J. Super. 324 (App. Div. 1951), 30.04[B][1]

Golf Landscaping, Inc. v. Century Constr. Co., 39 Wash. App. 895, 696 P.2d 590 (1984), 24.04[C]

Golf Landscaping, Inc. v. Century Constr. Co., 696 P.2d 590 (Wash. Ct. App. 1984), 30.03[C][3]

Goodenow, United States *ex rel.*, v. Aetna, 5 F.2d 412 (6th Cir. 1925), 35.06[A][3]

Goodman's Office Furnishings, New Mexico *ex rel.*, v. Page & Wirtz Constr. Co., 690 P.2d 1016 (N.M. 1984), 35.07[B][1]

Goodmans Office Furnishings, State *ex rel.*, v. Page & Wirtz Constr. Co., 690 P.2d 1016 (N.M. 1984), 35.08[D][2]

Goose Creek Consol. Indep. Sch. Dist. v. Jarrar's Plumbing, Inc. 74 S.W.3d 486 (Tex. Crim. App. 2002), *review denied,* (Nov. 21, 2002), 7.02[B][2][c]

Gord Indus. Plastics, Inc. v. Aubrey Mfg., Inc., 469 N.E.2d 389 (Ill. App. Ct. 1984), 16.07[A]

Gorski Assoc., Inc., United States *ex rel.*, v. Chemical Waste Mgmt., Inc., 1994 WL 45145 (E.D. Pa. Feb. 14, 1994), 35.04[A]

Gov't Sys. Advisors, Inc. v. United States, 21 Cl. Ct. 400, *vacated,* 25 Cl. Ct. 554 (1990), 28.02

Grade-way Constr. v. United States, 7 Cl. Ct. 263 (Fed. Cl. 1985), 7.03[C]

Graham v. San Antonio Mach. & Supply Corp., 418 S.W.2d 303 (Tex. Civ. App. 1967), 35.08[B]

Graham Constr. Co. v. Earl, 208 S.W.3d 106 (Ark. 2005), 27.04[A][1]

Graham-Hall Sheet Metal Works, Ltd. v. Douglas, 164 P.2d 778 (Cal. App. 1946), 30.04[B][1]

Grain Dealers Mut. Ins. Co. v. Pat's Rentals, Inc., 228 Ga. App. 854 (1997), 18.05[B][2]

Grand Trunk W. R.R. v. H. W. Nelson Co., 116 F.2d 823 (6th Cir. 1941), 24.04[A]

Granite Broadway Dev. LLC v. 1711 LLC, 845 N.Y.S.2d 10 (App. Div. 2007), 32.07

Granite Computer Leasing Corp. v. Travelers Indem. Co., 894 F.2d 547 (2d Cir. 1989), 34.04[A]

Granite Constr. v. United States, 962 F.2d 998 (Fed. Cir.), *cert. denied,* 506 U.S. 1048 (1993), 28.03[E][1][a]

Granite Constr. Co. v. American Motorists Ins. Co., 29 Cal. App. 4th 658, 34 Cal. Rptr. 2d 835 (3d Cir. 1994), 35.02[B]

Grant Construction v. Burns, 92 Idaho 408, 443 P.2d 1005 (1968), 26.02[M][3]

Graves-Black, Appeal of, ENGBCA No. 4557, 85-3 B.C.A. (CCH) ¶ 18,398 (1985), 30.03[D][2]

Graybar Elec. Co. v. John A. Volpe Constr. Co., 387 F.2d 55 (5th Cir. 1967), 35.07[A][2], 35.08[D][2], 35.08[D][3]

Graybar Elec. Co. v. Stratton of Fla., 509 So. 2d 1133 (Fla. Dist. Ct. App. 1987), 35.08[H]

Gray v. Travelers Indem. Co., 280 F.2d 549 (9th Cir. 1960), 36.06

Greaig v. Park W. Constr. Co., 637 P.2d 1079 (Ariz. Ct. App. 1981), 35.04[B]

Great Am. Ins. Co. v. Gaspard, 608 So. 2d 981 (La. 1992), 20.05

Great Am. Ins. Co. v. North Austin Mun. Util. Dist. No. 1, 908 S.W.2d 415 (Tex. 1995), 34.02

Great Am. Ins. Co. v. Woodside Homes Corp., 448 F. Supp. 2d 1275 (D. Utah 2006), 19.07[B]

Great Lakes Dredge & Dock Co. v. United States, 119 Ct. Cl. 504, 96 F. Supp. 923 (Ct. Cl. 1951), 30.03[D][1]

Green Construction Company v. Kansas Power & Light Co., 1 F.3d 1005 (10th Cir. 1993), 22.02, 22.08, 29.02[B][1]

Greenhaven Corp. v. Hutchcraft & Assocs., 463 N.E. 2d 283 (Ind. Ct. App. 1984), 20.01

Green International, Inc. v. Solis, 951 S.W.2d 384 (Tex. 1997), 35.08[E][3], 26.02[RR][3]

Grendell v. Ohio EPA, 764 N.E.2d 1067 (Ohio Ct. App. 2001), 17.01[A]

Greulich, Inc., ENGBCA No. 3832, 78-2 B.C.A. (CCH) ¶ 13,417 (1978), 27.05[D][7]

Grimco Pneumatic Corp., ASBCA 50977, 00-1 B.C.A. ¶ 30,727 (2000), 28.03[F]

Grimes v. Home Ins. Co., 217 N.C. 259, 7 S.E.2d 557 (1940), 46.23

Grinnell Fire Prot. Sys. Co. v. Hartford Fire. Ins. Co., 1996 WL 651636 (Conn. Super. Ct. 1996), 35.05[B]

Grinnell Mut. Reinsurance Co. v. Employers Mut. Cas. Co., 494 N.W.2d 690 (Iowa 1993), 18.05[B][2]

Griswold, United States v., 24 F. 361 (D. Or. 1885), 38.02[A]

Grochal v. Ocean Tech. Servs., Corp., 476 F.3d 238 (4th Cir. 2007), 34.04[H]

Groisser & Shlager Iron Works, Inc, United States *ex rel.,* v. Walsh, 240 F. Supp. 1019 (N.D.N.Y. 1965), 35.04[A]

Gropper v. STO Corp., 552 S.E.2d 118 (Ga. Ct. App. 2001), 29.04[J]

Gross v. Sussex, 630 A.2d 1156 (Md. 1993), 12.04[C][1][b]

Grotnes Mach. Works, Inc., United States *ex rel.,* v. Henry B. Byors & Son, Inc., 454 F. Supp. 203 (D.N.H. 1978), 35.06[A][1][b]

Ground Improvement Techniques, Inc. v. Merchants Bonding Co., 63 F. Supp. 2d 1272 (D. Colo. 1999), 34.04[G][5]

Groves v. Erie Ins. Co., 333 F. Supp. 2d 568 (D.W. Va. 2004), 19.07[B]

Grudem Bros. Co. v. Great W. Piping Corp., 297 Minn. 313, 213 N.W.2d 920 (1973), 46.23

Grumman Aerospace Corp., United States v., 927 F.2d 575 (Fed. Cir. 1991), 39.04[D]

Grynberg v. Citation Oil & Gas Corp., 573 N.W.2d 493 (S.D. 1997), 31.07[A]

Grynberg ex rel. v. Praxair, Inc., 183 Fed. Appx. 724, 2006 WL 1531413 (10th Cir. 2006), 38.02[B][3]

GTE Sylvania, Inc., DOT BCA No. 78-57, 79-2 B.C.A. ¶ 14,069 (1979), 28.03[E][4]

Guardian Constr. Co. v. Tetra Tech Richardson, Inc., 583 A.2d 1378 (Del. 1990), 7.02[B][3]

Guidry, et al. v. Lee Consulting Eng'g, Inc., et al., 945 So. 2d 785 (La. Ct. App. 2006), 20.02, 20.03

Gulf, Mobile & Ohio R.R. Co. v. Illinois Cent. R.R. Co., 128 F. Supp. 311 (N.D. Ala. 1954), 27.04[A][2]

Gulf Constr. Co. v. Self, 676 S.W.2d 624 (Tex. Ct. App. 1984), 35.08[E][1]

Gulf Contracting v. Bibb County, 795 F.2d 980 (11th Cir. 1986), 7.02[B][3]

Gulf Contracting, Inc., ASBCA Nos. 30,195 et al., 89-2 BCA ¶ 21,812 (1989), 23.06[B][1], 23.07[B][6]

Gulf Ins. Co. v. Construx, Inc., 2001 WL 840240 (Tenn. Ct. App. Jul. 26, 2001), 36.05

Gulf Ins. Co. v. Dolan Fertig & Curtis, 433 So. 2d 512 (Fla. 1983), 20.04

Gulf States Creosoting Co. v. Loving, 120 F.2d 195 (4th Cir. 1941), 24.02

Guthrie v. Louisiana Med. Mut. Ins. Co., 975 So. 2d 804 (La. Ct. App. 2008), 20.03, 20.04

Gutman, United States ex rel., v. P.J. Carlin Constr. Co., 254 F. Supp. 1001 (E.D.N.Y. 1965), 35.08[A]

Guy James Construction Company v. Trinity Industries, Inc., 644 F.2d 525 (5th Cir. 1981), 30.03[C][4]

Guy M. Cooper, Inc. v. East Penn Sch. Dist., 903 A.2d 608 (Pa. Commw. Ct. 2006), 26.02[MM][4]

H

Hadley v. Baxendale, 156 Eng. Rep. 145 (1854), 27.06, 30.02[B], 31.02[A], 31.02[B], 31.04[B]

Haghighi v. Russian Am. Broad. Co., 173 F.3d 1086 (8th Cir. 1999), 45.04[F]

Hagood v. Sonoma County Water Agency, 81 F.3d 1465 (9th Cir. 1996), 38.02[C][3]

Hagood, United States ex rel., v. Sonoma County Water Agency, 929 F.2d 1416 (9th Cir. 1991), 38.02[B][2]

Hagstrom Constr. Co., ASBCA No. 6598, 61-1 B.C.A. (CCH) ¶ 3090 (1961), 24.04[E]

Hagy, AGBCA No. 92-189-1 et al., 94-2 B.C.A. (CCH) ¶ 26,634, 39.03[E]

Haight, United States ex rel., v. Catholic Healthcare West, 445 F.3d 1147 (9th Cir. 2006), 38.02[B][4][a]

Hall v. Simmons, 407 S.E.2d 816 (N.C. 1991), 35.08[G]

Hall Constr. Co. v. Beynon, 507 So. 2d 1225 (Fla. Dist. Ct. App. 1987), 32.07

Halliburton, United States, No. 73-1806, 1976 WL 1278 (S.D.N.Y. June 30, 1976), 17.08

Hall St. Assocs., LLC v. Mattel, Inc., No. 06-989, slip. op., 552 U.S. 128 S. Ct. 1396 (2008) (U.S. Mar. 25, 2008), 43.07[B]

Halvorson v. United States, 126 F. Supp. 898 (D. Wash. 1954), 21.02

Hamza v. United States, 31 Fed. Cl. 315 (1994), 39.03[B][2], 39.04[D]

Hanberry Corp. v. State Bldg. Comm'n, 390 So. 2d 277 (Miss. 1980), 27.05[D][5][b]

Hancock Elec. Corp. v. Washington Metro. Area Transit Auth., 81 F.3d 451 (4th Cir.), cert. denied, 117 S. Ct. 299 (1966), 28.03[E][3][b], 34.04[G][1]

Haney v. United States, 676 F.2d 584 (Cl. Ct. 1982), 23.06[A]

Hannon Elec. Co. v. United States, 31 Fed. Cl. 135 (1994), aff'd, 52 F.3d 343 (Fed. Cir. 1995), 28.03[D][1][a][ii], 28.03[D][2]

Hanrahan v. Audubon Builders, 614 A.2d 748 (Pa. Super. Ct. 1992), 7.03[B][2][b]

Harbor Court Associates v. Kiewit Constr. Co., 6 F. Supp. 2d 449 (D. Md. 1998), 18.05[A][2]

Hardeman-Monier-Hutcherson, ASBCA No. 11785, 67-1 B.C.A. (CCH) ¶ 6210 (1967), 24.04[A]

Hardeman-Monier-Hutcherson v. United States, 458 F.2d 1364 (Ct. Cl. 1972), 28.03[E][1][a]

Harder Indus. Contractors, Inc., United States v., 225 F. Supp. 699 (D. Or. 1963), 35.03[A]

Hardie-Tynes Mfg. Co., ASBCA No. 20582, 76-2 B.C.A. ¶ 11,972 (1976), 28.03[E][1][a]

Hardrives, Inc., IBCA No. 2319 et al., 91-2 B.C.A. (CCH) ¶ 23,769, 39.08[B]

Hardwick Bros. Co., II v. U.S., 36 Fed. Cl. 347 (1996), 27.05[C][2]

Hare Construction Co. v. Metropolitan Government of Nashville & Davidson County, 2003 WL 21537623 (Tenn. Ct. App. July 9, 2003), 26.02[QQ][3]

Hargis, United States ex rel., v. Maryland Cas. Co., 64 F. Supp. 522 (S.D. Cal. 1946), 35.05[A]

Harman v. American Cas. Co., 155 F. Supp. 612 (S.D. Cal. 1957), 18.04[C][2]

Harman Elec. Constr. Co. v. Consolidated Eng'r Co., 347 F. Supp. 392 (D. Del. 1972), 46.04

Harper Builders, Inc. v. Edens, 318 S.E.2d 363 (S.C. 1984), 46.27

Harper/Nielsen-Dillingham Builders, Inc. v. United States, 81 Fed. Cl. 667, 669 n.2 (2008), 25.05[C], 39.03[F]

Harpeth Valley Utils. Dist. of Davidson and Williamson Counties v. Due, 465 S.W.2d 353 (Tenn. 1971), 33.02[C]

Harrelson v. Hensley, 891 So. 2d 635 (Fla. Dist. Ct. App. 5th Dist. 2005), 45.04[E]

Harrington v. McCarthy, 420 P.2d 790 (Idaho 1966), 21.02

Harrington, United States ex rel., v. Trione, 97 F. Supp. 522 (D. Colo. 1951), 35.04[A], 35.08[A]

Harris v. Dyer, 637 P.2d 918 (Or. 1981), 33.02[M][6]

Harrison, United States ex rel., v. Westinghouse Savannah River Co., 352 F.3d 908 (4th Cir. 2003), 38.02[B][2]

Harrison Western Corp., Inc., ENGBCA Nos. 5556, 5576, 93-1 BCA ¶ 25,382 (1992), 23.06[B][4], 23.06[C], 23.07[B][3]

Harris Sys. Int'l, ASBCA No. 33280, 88-2 B.C.A. (CCH) ¶ 20,641 (1988), 27.05[B][3][a]

Harry & Keith Mertz Constr., AGBCA No. 94-165-1, 97-1 B.C.A. ¶ 2-8,802, 28.02[A][3]

Hartbridge, The, 57 F.2d 672 (2d Cir. 1932), cert. denied, 288 U.S. 601 (1933), 46.18

Hartford Accident & Indem. Co. v. Millis Roofing & Sheet Metal, Inc., 418 N.E.2d 645 (Mass. App. Ct. 1981), 36.03[B]

Hartford Fire Ins. Co. v. Associated Constr. and Mgmt. Corp., 2000 U.S. Dist. LEXIS 4959 (E.D. Pa. 2000), 29.04[J]

Hartford Fire Ins. Co. v. Lawrence, Dykes, Goodenberger, Bower & Clancy, 740 F.2d 1362 (6th Cir. 1984), 27.05[E][3]

Hartford Ins. Co. v. American Automatic Sprinkler Sys. Inc., 201 F.3d 538 (4th Cir. 2000), 29.04[J]

Hartigan, People ex rel., v. Kerr-McGee Chem. Corp., 568 N.E.2d 921 (Ill. 2d Dist. 1991), 11.03[A][1][a][iv]

Harvey Gulf Int'l Marine, Inc., United States ex rel., v. Maryland Cas. Co., 573 F.2d 245 (5th Cir. 1978), 35.06[A][1][b], 35.06[A][2]

Haselrig Constr. Co., Inc., PSBCA No. 4148, 00-1 B.C.A. ¶ 30,674 (1999), 28.03[B][2]

Hatzel & Buehler, Inc. v. Lovisa Constr. Co., No. CV-92-384, 1993 WL 276971 (E.D.N.Y. July 20, 1993), 35.08[E][1]

Hauenstein v. St. Paul-Mercury Indem. Co., 242 Minn. 354, 65 N.W.2d 122 (1964), 18.04[C][1], 18.04[C][2]

Havens Steel Co. v. Randolph Eng'g Co., 613 F. Supp. 514 (W.D. Mo. 1985), 33.01[G]

Havens Steel Co. v. Randolph Eng'g Co., 613 F. Supp. 514 (W.D. Mo. 1985), aff'd, 813 F.2d 186 (8th Cir. 1987), 30.03[C][5], 30.03[D][2], 30.03[D][3]

Hawaiian Holiday Macadamia Nut Co. v. Indust. Indent. Co., 76 Haw. 166, 872 P.2d 230 (Haw. 1994), 20.02

Hawaiian Rock Prods. Corp., United States ex rel., v. A.E. Lopez Enters., Ltd., 74 F.3d 972 (9th Cir. 1996), 35.02[A], 35.05[A]

Hawkeye-Sec. Ins. Co. v. Vector Constr. Co., 460 N.W.2d 329 (Mich. App. 1990), 19.07[B]

Hawley v. Orange County Flood Control Dist., 211 Cal. App. 2d 708, 27 Cal. Rptr. 478 (1963), 26.02[E][1], 26.02[E][3], 26.02[E][4]

Hayden v. City of Astoria, 74 Or. 525, 145 P. 1072 (1915), 26.02[LL][3]

Hayes Int'l Corp., ASBCA No. 9750, 65-1 B.C.A. (CCH) ¶ 4767 (1965), 37.02[I]

H.B. Mac, Inc. v. United States, 153 F.3d 1338 (Fed. Cir. 1998), 7.03[B][2][a]

H.B. Zachary Co. v. United States, 28 Fed. Cl. 77 (1993), aff'd, 17 F.3d 1443 (Fed. Cir. 1994), 28.03[E][1][b]

H.E. & C.F. Blinne Contracting Co., ENGBCA No. 4174, 83-1 B.C.A. ¶ 16,388 (1983), 28.03[E][2]

Health Possibilities, P.S.C., United States v., 207 F.3d 335 (6th Cir. 2000), 38.02[B][3]

Heath v. Huth Eng'rs, Inc., 420 A.2d 758 (Pa. Super. Ct. 1980), 13 A.L.R.5th 289 (1993), 29.02[C][4]

Heath v. Palmer, No. 05-142, 2006 WL 3456636 (Vt. Nov. 20, 2006), 16.10[B]

H.E. Davis & Sons, Inc. v. North Pacific Ins. Co., 248 F. Supp. 2d 1079 (D. Utah 2002), 19.07[B]

Heile v. Herrmann, 136 Ohio App. 3d 351, 736 N.E.2d 566 (Ct. App. 1999), 18.04[C][1], 19.07[B]

Heller Elec. Co., United States ex rel., v. William F. Klingensmith, Inc., 670 F.2d 1227 (D.C. Cir. 1982), 35.04[A], 35.07[A][1]

Henderson v. Evans, 232 S.E.2d 331 (S.C. 1977), 35.08[G]

Henderson, United States ex rel., v. Nucon Constr. Corp., 49 F.3d 1421 (9th Cir. 1995), 35.06[A][3]

Hendow, United States ex rel., v. Univ. of Phoenix, 461 F.3d 1166 (9th Cir. 2006), 38.02[C][2]

Hendrix, Mohr & Yardley, Inc. v. City of Daphne, 359 So. 2d 792 (Ala. 1978), 27.05[D][2]

Hendry Corp. v. Metro. Dade County, 648 So. 2d 140 (Fla. Dist. Ct. App. 1994), 22.08

Henry Shenk Co. v. Erie County, 319 Pa. 100, 178 A. 662 (1935), 26.02[MM][4]

Henry Spen & Co., ASBCA No. 16,296, 74-2 BCA ¶ 10,651 (1974), 23.03[E][3]

Hensel Phelps Constr. Co. v. King County, 57 Wn. App. 170, 787 P.2d 58 (1990), 26.02[VV][4]

Hensel-Phleps Construction Co., 2001-1 B.C.A. (CCH) ¶ 31,249; 2001 GSBCA LEXIS 10 (2001), 30.03[D][2]

Hensel-Phleps Construction Co. v. United States, 886 F.2d 1296 (Fed. Cir. 1989), 27.05[A][2]

Hensel Phleps Construction Co. v. United States ex rel. Reynolds Elec. & Eng'g Co., 413 F.2d 701 (10th Cir. 1969), 35.04[A]

Herbert & Brooner Constr. Co. v. Golden, 499 S.W.2d 541 (Mo. Ct. App. 1973), 23.04[B][1], 30.02[B]

Herbert A. Sullivan, Inc. v. Utica Mut. Ins. Co., 788 N.E.2d 522 (Mass. 2003), 12.04[C][1][d][iii]

Herbert M. Baruch Corp., Ltd. v. United States 93 Ct. Cl. 107 (1941), 30.03[C][3]

Hercules Construction Co., VABCA No. 2508, 88-2 B.C.A. (CCH) ¶ 20,527 (1988), 27.05[C][2]

Hercules Inc. v. United States, 116 S. Ct. 981 (U.S. 1996), 27.04[A][1]

Hercules Inc. v. United States, 24 F.3d 188 (Fed. Cir. 1994), 5.03[C][8]

Hertz Equip. Rental Corp. v. Homer Knost Const. Co., 273 So. 2d 685 (La. App. 1 Cir. 1973), 20.02

Herzog Contracting Corp. v. A&S Constr. Co., 751 P.2d 690 (N.M. 1988), 35.04[B]

Hess v. American States Ins., 589 S.W.2d 548 (Tex. Civ. App. 1979), 36.05

Heuerman v. B&M Construction, Inc., 833 N.E.2d 382 (Ill. Ct. App. 2005), 16.02[B]

Hewett-Kier Constr., Inc., v. Lemuel Ramos & Assoc., Inc., 775 So. 2d 373 (Fla. 2000), 7.02[B][3]

Hewlett v. Hewlett, 845 S.W.2d 717 (Mo. Ct. App. 1993), 12.04[C][1][a]

Heyl & Patterson, Inc. v. O'Keefe, 986 F.2d 480 (Fed. Cir. 1993), *rev'd on other grounds*, 39.04[B]

High Country Assoc. v. New Hampshire Ins. Co., 648 A.2d 474 (N.H. 1994), 19.07[B]

Hill Constr. Corp., ASBCA No. 43615, 93-3 B.C.A. ¶ 25,973 (1993), 28.03[D][3], 32.06

Hillebrand Constr., Inc., ASBCA No. 54853, 95-1 B.C.A. ¶ 27,464 (1995), 28.03[B][2]

Hilton v. Universal Constr. Co., 216 S.W. 1034 (Mo. Ct. App. 1919), 35.07[B][2]

Hilyer v. Morrison-Knudsen Constr. Co., 670 F.2d 208 (D.C. Cir. 1981), *rev'd on other grounds,* 461 U.S. 624 (1983), 35.04[A]

HIM Portland LLC v. DeVito Builders, Inc., 317 F.3d 41 (1st Cir. 2003), 45.04[A]

Hirsch Elec. Co., Inc. v. Community Servs., Inc., 145 A.D.2d 603 (N.Y. App. Div. 1988), 31.04[A]

Hirsch Elec. Co., Inc. v. Community Servs., Inc., 536 N.Y.S.2d 141 (1988), 30.04[B][2]

HiValley Constructors, Inc. v. Heyser, 428 P.2d 354 (Colo. 1967), 21.02

H.L. Fuller Constr. Co. v. Industrial Dev. Bd., 590 So. 2d 18 (Ala. 1991), 46.04

H.M. Ford v. Aetna Insurance Co., 394 S.W.2d 693 (Tex. Civ. App. 1965), 36.07

Hoang v. Assurance Co. of Am., 149 P.3d 798 (Colo. Jan. 8, 2007), 19.07[B]

Hochevar v. Maryland Cas. Co., 114 F.2d 948 (6th Cir. 1940), 35.08[I]

Hoel-Steffen Constr. Co. v. U.S., 456 F.2d 760 (Ct. Cl. 1972), 23.04[B][1], 39.05[D]

Hoffman Construction Co. v. United States, 7 Cl. Ct. 518 (1985), 39.03[B][2]

Hogan v. Midland Nat'l Ins. Co., 476 P.2d 825 (Cal. 1970), 19.07[B]

Hogan v. Walsh & Wells, 177 S.W.2d 835 (Tenn. 1944), 35.07[B][2]

Hol-Gar Mfg. Corp. v. United States, 360 F.2d 634 (Ct. Cl. 1966), 28.03[E][1][b]

Holland, U.S.v., 874 F.2d 1470 (11th Cir. 1989), 11.03[A][1][d]

Hollerbach v. United States, 233 U.S. 165 (1914), 22.06, 22.08

Hollerbach v. United States, 233 U.S. 165, 34 C. Ct. 533, 58 L. Ed. 933 (1915), 27.05[F]

Holloway Constr. Co. v. United States, 18 Cl. Ct. 326 (1989), 24.04[A]

Holt v. United States, 391-76, 1980 U.S. Cl. Ct. LEXIS 1151 (Ct. Cl. Aug. 20, 1980), 28.04[D][2]

Home Elec. Co. of Lenoir, Inc. v. Hall & Underdown Heating & Air Conditioning, Co., 358 S.E.2d 539 (N.C. Ct. App. 1987), 16.04[E]

Home Indem. Co. v. Wachter, 496 N.Y.S.2d 252 (N.Y. App. Div. 1985), 36.07

Home Ins. Co. v. Southport Terminals, 240 So. 2d 525 (Fla. Dist. Ct. App. 1970), 18.05[A][1]

Home Ins. Co. v. Zurich Ins. Co., 116 Cal. Rptr. 583 (Cal. Ct. App. 2002), 45.05[A]

Homes Ins. Co. v. Law Offices of Jonathan DeYoung, et al., 32 F. Supp. 2d 219 (E.D. Pa. 1998), 20.04

Honeywell, Inc., United States *ex rel.*, v. A & L Mech. Contractors, Inc., 677 F.2d 383 (4th Cir. 1982), 35.05[A]

Honig Indus. Diamond Wheel, Inc., ASBCA Nos. 46711 et al., 94-2 B.C.A. ¶ 26,955 (1994), 28.03[G]

Hoon v. Pate Constr. Co., 607 So. 2d 423 (Fla. Dist. Ct. App. 1992), 7.03[C]

Hopes Architectural Prods., Inc. v. Lundy's Constr., Inc., 762 F. Supp. 1430 (D. Kan. 1991), 35.07[B][1]

Hopkins Heating & Cooling, Inc., VACAB No. 4905E, 98-1 B.C.A. ¶ 29,449 (1997), 28.02[A][3]

Horstman, AGBCA No. 87-388-1, 89-2 B.C.A. ¶ 21,752 (1989), 28.03[F][1]

Horton v. United States, 58 Ct. Cl. 148 (1923), 21.05

Hospital Computer Sys., Inc. v. Staten Island Hosp., 788 F. Supp. 1351 (D.N.J. 1992), 7.02[B][2][c]

Hotel Des Artistes, Inc. v. General Accident Ins. Co. of America, 775 N.Y.S.2d 262 (N.Y. App. Div. 1st Dept. 2004), 19.03[G][1]

Hotel Roanoke Conference Center Comm'n. v. Cincinnati Ins. Co., 303 F. Supp. 2d 784 (W.D. Va. 2004), 19.07[B]

Houma v. Municipal & Indus. Pipe Serv., 884 F.2d 886 (5th Cir. 1989), 29.02[C][4]

Houma, City of, v. Municipal & Indus. Pipe Serv., 884 F.2d 886 (5th Cir. 1989), 34.04[G][3]

Hous. Auth. of Dallas v. Hubbell, 325 S.W.2d 880 (Tex. Civ. App. Dallas 1959, writ ref'd n.r.e.), 26.02[I][3]

Housing Auth. of Dallas v. Hubble, 325 S.W.2d 880 (Tex. Civ. App. Dallas 1959), 26.02[RR][1], 26.02[RR][4]

Housing Auth. of Texarkana v. E. W. Johnson Constr. Co., 264 Ark. 523 (1978), 30.03[B][1], 30.03[B][2]

Houston, City of, v. R.F. Ball Constr. Co., 570 S.W.2d 75 (Tex. Civ. App.-Houston [14th Dist.] 1978), 26.02[RR][1], 26.02[RR][3], 26.02[RR][4]

Houston Gen. Ins. Co. v. Maples, 375 So. 2d 1012 (Miss. 1979), 35.04[B]

Howard v. Usiak, 172 Vt. 227, 775 A.2d 909 (Vt. 2001), 20.01

Howard Contracting, Inc. v. G.A. MacDonald Construction Co., 71 Cal. App. 4th 38, 83 Cal. Rptr. 2d 509 (1998), 26.02[E][2]

Howard Mgmt. Group v. City of Kansas City, Kansas, 794 P.2d 1177 (Kan. Ct. App. 1990), 26.02[Q][3]

Howard P. Foley Co. v. J. L. Williams & Co., 622 F.2d 402 (8th Cir. 1980), 27.05[D][5][b]

H.R. Hayes Lumber Co. v. McConnell, 146 So. 14 (La. 1932), 35.04[B]

HSQ Tech., ASBCA No. 32272, 86-3 B.C.A. ¶ 19,221, 28.03[G]

H.T. Sweeney & Son, Inc., United States ex rel., v. E.J.T. Constr. Co., 415 F. Supp. 1328 (D. Del. 1976), 35.06[A][1][b]

Huang Int'l, Inc. v. Foose Constr. Co., 734 P.2d 975 (Wy. 1987), 21.02

Hubbard Constr. Co. v. Jacobs Civil, Inc., 969 So. 2d 1069 (Fla. Dist. Ct. App. 5th Dist. 2007), 46.14

Huber Lathing v. Aetna, 517 N.Y.S.2d 758 (App. Div. 1987), 35.06[B][3]

Hudson, County of, v. Terminal Constr. Co., 154 N.J. Super. 264, 381 A.2d 355 (App. Div. 1977), 34.04[G][4]

Hudson, United States ex rel., v. Peerless, 374 F.2d 942 (4th Cir. 1967), 35.06[A][3]

Hulett, AGBCA Nos. 91-230-3 et al., B.C.A. ¶ 25,389 (1992), 28.04[D][4]

Hunters Pointe Partners Ltd. P'ship v. USF&G, 442 N.W. 2d 778 (Mich. Ct. App. 1989), 34.04[G][6]

Huntington Constr., Inc., ASBCA Nos. 33525 et al., 87-2 B.C.A. ¶ 19,741 (1987), 28.03[F][4]

Hunt v. Bankers & Shippers Inc. Co., 423 N.Y.S.2d 718 (App. Div. 4th Dep't 1979), 34.04[F][4]

Hunt v. Owen Bldg. & Inv. Co., 219 S.W. 138 (Mo. Ct. App. 1920), 21.02, 21.05

Hutchison v. Tompkins, 259 So. 2d 129 (Fla. 1972), 32.04

Hutton Construction Co. v. County of Rockland, 52 F.3d 1191 (2d Cir. 1995), 36.05

Hutton Contracting Co. v. City of Coffeyville, 487 F.3d 772 (10th Cir. 2007), 32.06

H.W. Caldwell & Son v. United States ex rel. John H. Moon & Sons, 407 F.2d 21 (5th Cir. 1969), 35.08[E][2]

H.W. Detwiller Contracting, Inc., ASBCA No. 35,327, 89-2 BCA ¶ 21,612 (1989), 23.06[A]

Hyland Elec. Supply Co., United States ex rel., v. Franchi Bros. Constr. Corp., 378 F.2d 134 (2d Cir. 1967), 35.07[A][2], 35.08[D][2], 35.08[D][3]

I

I.B.E.W., AFL-CIO, Local Union No. 217, United States *ex. rel.*, v. G.E. Chem. Constr., Inc., 954 F. Supp. 195 (N.D. Cal. 1997), 38.02[C][1][a][ii]

Idaho State University v. Mitchell, 97 Idaho 724, 552 P.2d 776 (1976), 26.02[M][3]

Ideal Basic Indus. v. Juniata Farmers, 289 N.W.2d 192 (Neb. 1980), 35.03[B]

Ideal Elec. Sec. Co., Inc. v. Int'l Fid. Ins. Co., 129 F.3d 143 (D.C. Cir. 1997), 33.02[C]

Idela Constr. co., 01-2 B.C.A. (CCH) ¶ 31,437 (ASBCA 2001), 32.05

I.J.W. Mfg. Co., ASBCA No. 27484, 83-2 B.C.A. ¶ 16,557 (1983), 28.04[C][2][b]

Ilana Realty, Inc., *In re,* 154 B.R. 21 (S.D.N.Y. 1993), 33.01[B]

Illinois State Toll Highway Comm'n v. Boyle, 186 N.E.2d 390 (Ill. App. Ct. 1962), 35.03[B]

Illinois Sur. Co. v. John Davis Co., 244 U.S. 376 (1917), 25.03[B], 35.04[A]

Imagine Constr., Inc. v. Centex Landis Constr. Co., Inc., 707 So. 2d 500 (La. App. 4th Cir. 1998), 35.08[E][1]

Incorporated Village of Island Park, United States v., 888 F. Supp. 419 (E.D.N.Y. 1995), 38.02[C][1][b][i]

Indemnity Ins. Co. v. United States, 14 Cl. Ct. 219 (1988), 28.03[D][2]

Indemnity Ins. Co. of N. Am. v. Am. Aviation, Inc., 891 So. 2d 532 (Fla. 2004), 7.02[B][2][c]

Indemnity Ins. Co. of N. Am. v. Portsmouth Ice, Coal & Bldg. Material Co., 172 N.E. 152 (Ohio 1930), 35.04[B]

Independence, City of, v. Kerr Construction Paving Co., 957 S.W.2d 315 (Mo. Ct. App. 1997), 33.01[K]

Independence Sch. Dist. No. 74 v. Shurtleff-Gahareh, Inc., 2007 WL 2248159 (E.D. Okla. 8/2/2007), 34.04[F][2]

Indiana Carpenters Cen. & W. Ind. Pension Fund v. Seaboard Sur. Co., 601 N.E.2d 352 (Ind. Ct. App. 1992), 35.04[B]

Indiana Department of Transportation v. Shelly & Sands, Inc., 756 N.E.2d 1063 (Ind. Ct. App. 2001), 26.02[O][3], 26.02[O][4]

Indiana Farmers Mutual Insurance Co. v. Graham, 537 N.E.2d 510 (Ind. 1989), 19.03[G][3][a]

Indiana Funeral Directors Ins. Trust v. Trustmark Ins. Corp., 347 F.3d 652 (7th Cir. 2003), 20.05

Indiana Ins. Co. v. DeZutti, 408 N.W.2d 1275 (1980), 19.07[B]

Indianapolis v. Twin Lakes Enters., Inc., 568 N.E.2d 1073 (Ind. Ct. App. 1991), 28.03[E][1][a], 28.03[E][1][c]

Indiana Univ. Aetna Cas. & Sur. Co., 920 F.2d 429 (7th Cir. 1990), *overruled in part by* 29 F.3d 274 (7th Cir. 1994), 28.03[E][1][b]

Ind. Univ., Trustees of, v. Aetna Cas. & Sur. Co., 920 F.2d 429 (7th Cir. 1990), *overruled on other grounds by* Watson v. Amdeco Steel, Inc., 29 F.3d 274 (7th Cir. 1994), 16.10[A]

Indus. Constructors Corp., ASBCA No. 84-348-1, 90-2 BCA ¶ 22,767 (1990), 23.04[B][1]

Industrial Coatings Co. v. Fidelity & Deposit Co. of Md., 817 P.2d 393 (Wash. 1991), 35.06[B][1]

Industrial Indemnity Co. v. Wick Construction Co., 680 P.2d 1100 (Alaska 1984), 32.07

Industrial Research Associates, DOT BCA [now Civilian BCA] No. WB-5, 68-1 B.C.A. (CCH) ¶ 7069 (1968), 27.05[B][3]

Industrial Tectonics Bearings Corp. v. United States, 44 Fed. Cl. 115 (1999), 28.02[A][2]

Information Intern. Assocs., Inc. v. U.S., 74 Fed. Cl. 192 (2006), 27.03[B][2]

Info. Sys. & Network Corp., ASBCA Nos. 41514 et al., 92-1 B.C.A. ¶ 24,607 (1991), 28.03[G]

Information Systems and Networks Corp. v. U.S., 34 Fed. Cl. 457 (1995), 27.05[G][2][a], 28.03[E][1][a]

Ingalls Shipbuilding Div., Litton Sys., Inc., ASBCA No. 17,579, 78-1 B.C.A. (CCH) ¶ 13,038 (1978), 24.02[A]

Inland Real Estate Corp. v. Tower Constr. Co., 528 N.E.2d 421 (Ill. App. Ct. 1988), 29.02[C][5]

Insulation Specialties, Inc., ABSCA No. 52,090, 03-2 B.C.A. (CCH) ¶ 32,361 (2003), 24.02[D]

Insurance Co. v. Federal Kemper Ins. Co., 683 N.E. 2d 947 (Ill. Ct. App. 1997), 20.02

Insurance Co. of N. Am. v. Atlas Supply Co., 172 S.E2d 632 (Ga. Ct. App. 1970), 35.08[D][3]

Insurance Co. of N. Am. v. Bath, 726 F. Supp. 1247 (D. Wyo. 1989), 36.09[C]

Ins. Co. of N. Am. v. Forty-Eight Insulations, 633 F.2d 1212 (6th Cir. 1980), 18.04[C][2]

Insurance Co. of N. Am. v. Genstar Stone Prods. Co., 656 A.2d 1232 (Md. 1995), 35.08[D][2]

Ins. Co. of N. Am. v. Metro. Dade County, 705 So. 2d 33 (Fla. Dist. Ct. App. 1997), 28.03[D][1][a][i]

Insurance Co. of N. Am. v. Town of Manchester, 1998 WL 514711 (D. Conn. 1998), 29.02[C][5]

Insurance Co. of N. Am. v. United States, 951 F.2d 1244 (Fed. Cir. 1991), 35.08[J]

Insurance Company of the West v. United States, 55 Fed. Cl. 529 (2003), 34.04[H]

Integon Indem.Corp. v. Bull, 842 S.W.2d 1 (Ark. 1992), 35.04[B]

Intel Corp. v. Hartford Accident & Indem. Co., 952 F.2d 1551 (9th Cir. 1991), 18.04[C][2], 18.05[B][1]

Intercargo Ins. Co. v. United States, 41 Fed. Cl. 449 (1998), 28.03[A]

Intercontinental Mfg. Co., ASBCA No. 48,506, 2003 WL 40661 (Jan. 3, 2003), 24.02[D]

Int'l Builders of Fla., Inc., FAACAP No. 67-5, 69-1 B.C.A. (CCH) ¶ 7706 (1969), 24.04[A], 24.04[D]

International Data Prods. Corp. v. U.S., 492 F.3d 1317 (Fed. Cir. 2007), 27.05[B][4]

Int'l Elec. Corp. v. United States, 646 F.2d 496 (Ct. Cl. 1981), 28.03[E][4]

International Fidelity & Ins. Co. v. Jones, 682 A.2d 263 (N.J. Super. App. Div. 1996), 36.07

Int'l Fid. Ins. Co. v. County of Rockland, 98 F. Supp. 2d 400 (S.D.N.Y. 2000), 31.01, 31.02[B], 31.03, 31.03[A], 31.03[B]

International Fid. Ins. Co. v. DelMaura Sys. Corp., 2001 WL 541469 (Del. Super. 2001), appeal denied, 782 A.2d 264, 34.04[D]

International Fid. Ins. Co. v. U.S., 25 Cl. Ct. 469 (Cl. Ct. 1992), 27.05[G][2][a]

International Harvester Co. v. L. G. DeFelice & Son, Inc., 197 A.2d 638 (Conn. 1964), 35.07[B][1]

Interstate Gen. Gov't Contractors, Inc. v. United States, 40 Fed. Cl. 585 (1998), 29.03[D][2]

Interstate Gen. Gov't Contractors, Inc. v. West, 12 F.3d 1053 (Fed. Cir. 1993), 23.03[H], 24.04[C], 30.03[C][3], 30.03[C][4], 39.03[A]

Interstate Indus., Inc. v. Barclay Indus., Inc., 540 F.2d 868 (7th Cir. 1976), 16.04[B]

Interstate Power v. Kansas City Power & Light Co., 909 F. Supp. 1284 (N.D. Iowa 1994), 11.03[A][4][a]

Interstate Reforesters, AGBCA No. 87-374-3, 89-1 B.C.A. ¶ 21,375 (1988), 28.03[B][3][b], 28.03[E][1], 28.03[E][3][a], 28.03[E][4]

Interstate Reforesters, AGBCA No. 89-114-1, 91-1 B.C.A. ¶ 23,660 (1990), 28.03[F][1]

Inter-Tribal Council, IBCA No. 1234-12-78, 83-1 B.C.A. ¶ 16,433 (1983), 27.05[E][4]

InVision, 42.02[D], 42.02[F]

Iowa Supply Co. v. Grooms & Co. Constr., 428 N.W.2d 662 (Iowa 1988), 35.08[D][3]

Iron Head Const., Inc. v. Gurney, 176 P.3d 453 (Utah Ct. App. 2008), 33.01[F]

Irving Materials, Inc. v. Zurich American Insurance Company, et al., 2007 WL 1035098 (S.D. Ind. 2007), 20.02

Island House Developers v. Amac Constr., 686 So. 2d 1377 (Fla. Dist. Ct. App. 1997), 35.08[G]

Island Lathing & Plastering, Inc. v. Travelers Indem. Co., 161 F. Supp. 2d 278 (S.D.N.Y. 2001), 18.04[C][2]

Isles Eng'g & Constr. Inc. v. United States, 26 Cl. Ct. 240 (1992), 39.03[A], 39.03[B]

ITG Corp., ASBCA No. 27285, 85-1 B.C.A. ¶ 17,935 (1985), 28.04[C][2][a]

ITXC Corp., 42.02[F][2]

Ivanov v. Process Design Access, 267 Ill. App. 3d 440 (Ill. App. Ct. 1993), 8A.08[A][1]

J

J & B Steel Constractors, Inc. v. C. Iber & Sons, Inc., 162 Ill. 2d 265, 642 N.E.2d 1215 (1994), 26.02[N][3], 26.02[N][4]

J & D Enter. of Duluth, U.S. v., 955 F. Supp. 1153 (D. Minn. 1997), 11.03[A][6]

J & S Constr. Co. v. Travelers Indem. Co., 520 F.2d 809 (1st Cir. 1975), 25.03[B]

Jack B. Anglin Co. v. Tipps, 842 S.W.2d 266 (Tex. 1992), 46.04

Jack Cooper Constr. Co., 84-3 B.C.A. (CCH) ¶ 17,703 (1984), 21.08

Jack L. Olsen, Inc., AGBCA No. 87-345-1, 93-2 B.C.A. (CCH) ¶ 25,767 (1993), 22.02

Jackson Constr. Co. v. United States, 62 Fed. Cl. 84 (2004), 23.03[H], 24.04[C]

Jacob v. Russo Builders, 224 2d 436, 592 N.W. 2d 271 (Wis. 1999), 20.02

Jacob & Youngs, Inc. v. Kent, 230 N.Y. 239 (1921), 30.02[A][2]

Jacobs, United States v., 475 F.2d 270 (2d Cir. 1973), 42.02[B][6]

Jacobs, United States ex rel., v. Patrol Servs., Inc., 202 Fed. Appx. 357, 2006 WL 2990211 (11th Cir. 2006), 38.02[B][3]

Jacobs Eng'g Group, Inc. v. United States, 434 F.3d 1378 (Fed. Cir. 2006), 28.03[G]

Jacobson v. American Fid. Fire Ins. Co., 541 P.2d 2 (Nev. 1975), 36.09[C]

J.A. Jones Constr., ENGBA Nos. 3035, 3226, 72-1 BCA ¶ 9261 (1972), 23.06[A]

J.A. Jones Constr., ENGBCA Nos. 6348 et al., 00-2 BCA ¶ 31,000 (2000), 23.03[H]

J.A. Jones Constr. Co., ENGBCA No. 6252, 97-1 BCA ¶ 28,918 (1997), 23.06[B][2]

J.A. Jones Constr. Co., ENGBCA No. 6258, 97-1 B.C.A. ¶ 29,918 (1997), 28.03[C][1]

J.A. Jones Constr. v. U.S., 390 F.2d 886 (Ct. Cl. 1968), 27.05[C][3][a]

J.A. Jones Construction Co. v. Lehrer McGovern Bovis, Inc., 120 Nev. 277, 89 P.3d 1009 (2004), 26.02[CC][3]

Jalaprathan Cement Co., ASBCA No. 21248, 79-2 B.C.A. ¶ 13,927 (1979), 28.03[E][4]

Jamco Constructors, Inc., VACAB Nos. 3271 et al., 94-1 B.C.A. ¶ 26,405 (1993), 28.03[G], 28.04[D][1]

James A. Cummings, Inc. v. Young, 589 So. 2d 950 (Fla. Dist. Ct. App. 1992), 35.08[B]

James Constr. Group, L.L.C. v. State of Louisiana, No. 2007 CA 0225, 2007 WL 3246740 (La. Ct. App. Nov. 2, 2007), 32.04

James D. Shea Co. v. Perini Corp., 321 N.E.2d 831 (Mass. App. Ct. 1975), 35.03[B]

James E. McFadden v. Baltimore Contractors, Inc., 609 F. Supp. 1102 (E.D.Pa. 1985), 34.04[E][2]

James Graham Brown Foundation, Inc. v. St. Paul Fire & Marine Ins. Co., 814 S.W.2d 273 (Ky. 1991), 19.07[B]

James Julian, Inc. v. President & Comm'r of Elkton, 341 F. Supp. 205 (D. Md. 1965), 21.02, 22.04

James McKinney & Son v. Lake Placid 1980 Olympic Games, Inc., 462 N.E.2d 137 (N.Y. 1984), 36.06

James M. Ellett Constr. Co. v. United States, 93 F.3d 1537 (Fed. Cir. 1996), 28.02[A][3], 28.03[G], 39.03[B][1][a], 39.03[C][1]

James Reeves Contractor, Inc. v. United States, 31 Fed. Cl. 712 (1994), 39.03[F]

James Reilly Repair & Supply Co. v. Smith, 177 F. 168 (2d Cir. 1910), 21.02

James Talcott Constr. v. P&D Land
Enters., 333 Mont. 107 (2006),
28.03[E][2]

James W. Miller v. The City of Broken
Arrow, 660 F.2d 450 (10th Cir.
1981), *cert. denied,* 455 U.S. 1020
(1982), 28.03[E][1][a],
28.03[E][1][b], 28.03[E][4]

J.A. Thompson & Son, Inc. v. State,
465 P.2d 148 (Haw. 1970), 22.02,
22.08

Javeler Constr. Co. v. Federal Ins. Co.,
472 So. 2d 258 (La. Ct. App. 1st
Cir.), *writ denied,* 476 So. 2d 354
(La. 1985), 35.07[B][1]

J.C. Co., AGBCA No. 80-154-9, 82-1
B.C.A. (CCH) ¶ 15,542 (1982),
27.05[G][3][c]

J.C. Snavely & Sons, Inc. v. Web M&E,
Inc., 594 A.2d 333 (Pa. Super. Ct.
1991), 33.02[O]

JDC Corp. v. Amerifirst Fla. Trust Co.,
736 F. Supp. 1121 (S.D. Fla. 1990),
46.04

J.D. Hedin Constr. Co. v. United States,
171 Ct. Cl. 70 (1965), 21.04

J.D. Hedin Constr. Co. v. United States,
171 Ct. Cl. 70, 347 F.2d 235 (1965),
overruled on other grounds by Wilner
v. United States, 24 F.3d 1397, 39
Cont. Cas. Fed. (CCH) ¶ 76665 (Fed.
Cir. 1994) (en banc), 24.02, 24.04[C]

J.D. Hedin Constr. Co. v. United States,
347 F.2d 235 (Ct. Cl. 1965),
overruled on other grounds, by
Wilner v. United States, 24 F.3d 1397
(Fed Cir. 1994), 30.03[C]

J.D. Hedin Constr. Co. v. United States,
408 F.2d 424 (Ct. Cl. 1969),
23.03[B][2], 28.03[A], 28.03[E][1][a],
30.04[B]

J.E. Brenneman Co. v. Commonwealth
of Pennsylvania, Department of
Transportation, 424 A.2d 592 (Pa.
Commw. Ct. 1981), 22.08

J.E. Hathaway & Co. v. United States,
249 U.S. 460 (1919), 32.07

Jennie-O Foods v. United States, 580
F.2d 400 (Ct. Cl. 1978),
27.05[D][4][b], 28.03[E][4]

Jeremiah Sullivan & Sons v.
Kay-Locks, Inc., 459 N.E.2d 837
(Mass. App. Ct. 1984), 35.08[E][1]

J.E. Sadler & Co., United States *ex rel.,*
v. W.H. French Dredging & Wrecking
Co., 52 F.2d 235 (D. Del. 1931),
35.04[A]

J.E. Salvage Co. v. United States, 37
Fed. Cl. 256 (1997), 39.04[A],
39.04[D]

Jessop, Melba Elaine, v. City of
Alexandria, 871 So. 2d 1140 (La. Ct.
App. 2004), 18.04[A]

Jewell, United States v., 532 F.2d 697
(9th Cir. 1976), 42.02[B][6]

J.F. Shea & Co. v. United States, 4 Cl.
Ct. 46 (1983), 39.04[C]

J.F. White Eng'g Corp. v. United States
ex rel. Pittsburg Plate Glass Co., 311
F.2d 410 (10th Cir. 1962), 35.04[A]

J.G. Watts Constr. Co., ASBCA No.
9454, 1964 B.C.A. (CCH) ¶ 4325,
37.02[I]

J.H. Strain & Sons, Inc., 90-2 B.C.A.
(CCH) ¶ 22,770 (ASBCA 1990),
32.04

Jimenez, Inc. VABCA Nos. 6351 et al.,
02-2 B.C.A ¶ 32,019 (2002),
28.04[C][2][a]

Jim's Excavating Serv., Inc. v. HKM
Assoc., 878 P.2d 248 (Mont. 1994),
7.02[B][3]

J.J. Barnes Constr. Co., ASBCA No.
27876, 85-3 B.C.A. (CCH) ¶ 18,503
(1985), 27.05[B][3][d]

J.J. Seifert Mach. Co., ASBCA No.
41398, 91-2 B.C.A. ¶ 23,075 (1991),
28.03[D][2]

J.L. Manta, Inc. v. Braun, 393 N.W.2d
490 (Minn. 1986), 7.03[E]

J.L. Simmons Co. v. United States, 158
Ct. Cl. 393 (1962), 39.03[F]

J.L. Simmons Co. v. United States, 412
F.2d 1360, 188 Ct. Cl. 684 (Ct. Cl.
1969), 29.02[B][2]

J.L. Simmons Co. v. United States, 412
F.2d 1360 (Cl. Ct. 1969), 29.02[B][2]

J.M. Beeson Co. v. Sartori, 553 So. 2d
180 (Fla. Dist. Ct. App. 1989), *aff'd,*
584 So. 2d 572 (Fla. Dist. Ct. App.
1991), 28.03[D][3]

J.M.T. Mach. Co., Inc., ASBCA No.
29739, 86-1 B.C.A. (CCH) ¶ 18,684,
reconsideration denied, 86-2 B.C.A.
(CCH) ¶ 18,917, *aff'd,* 826 F.2d 1042
(Fed. Cir. 1987), 39.03[B][3]

J.M.T. Mach. Co. v. United States, 826 F.2d 1042 (Fed. Cir. 1987), 28.03[F][4], 28.03[G]

Johanson v. Huizenga Holdings, 963 F. Supp. 1175 (S.D. Fla. 1997), 29.02[C][5]

John A. Johnson & Sons v. United States, 180 Ct. Cl. 969 (1967), 24.02[D]

John Burns Constr. Co. v. City of Chicago, 234 Ill. App. 3d 1027, 601 N.E.2d 1024 (1992), 26.02[N][3], 26.02[N][4]

John Driggs Co., ENGBCA No. 4926, 87-2 BCA ¶ 19,833 (1987), 23.06[B][4]

John E. Green Plumbing & Heating Co. v. Turner Constr. Co., 500 F. Supp. 910 (E.D. Mich. 1984), 8A.08[G][3]

John E. Green Plumbing & Heating Co. v. Turner Constr. Co., 500 F. Supp. 910 (E.D. Mich. 1980), aff'd, 742 F.2d 965 (6th Cir. 1984), 26.02[KK][4]

John E. Green Plumbing & Heating Co. v. Turner Constr. Co., 742 F.2d 965 (6th Cir. 1984), 26.02[F][4], 26.02[W][3]

John E. Gregory & Son, Inc. v. Guenther & Sons Co., 147 Wis. 2d 298, 432 N.W.2d 584 (1988), 26.02[XX][3], 26.02[XX][4]

John F. Harkins Co., Inc. v. School Dist. of Philadelphia, 460 A.2d 260 (1983), 30.03[D][1]

John Martin Co. v. Morse/Diesel, Inc., 819 S.W.2d 428 (Tenn. 1991), 8A.08[D]

John McShain, Inc. v. Cessna Aircraft Co., 563 F.2d 632 (3d Cir. 1977), 29.04[F][2]

John McShain, Inc. v. United States, 412 F.2d 1281 (Ct. Cl. 1969), 28.03[E][1][b]

John Murphy Constr. Co., AGBCA No. 418, 79-1 BCA ¶ 13,836 (1979), 23.06[B][4]

John Reiner & Co., 163 Ct. Cl., 325 F.2d at 443, 28.02[A][3], 28.04[A]

John Reiner & Co. v. United States, 325 F.2d 438 (Ct. Cl. 1963), cert. denied, 377 U.S. 931 (1964), 28.02, 28.02[A][2], 28.02[A][3], 28.04[A]

Johnson v. Advanced Eng'g & Planning Corp., 292 F. Supp. 2d 846 (E.D. Va. 2003), 39.03[C][1]

Johnson v. All-State Constr., Inc., 329 F.3d 848 (Fed. Cir. 2003), 28.03[B][2], 28.03[E][2]

Johnson v. Flammia, 161 Conn. 491 (Conn. 1975), 30.04[B][1]

Johnson v. Howdeshell, 520 So. 2d 297 (Fla. Dist. Ct. App. 1988), 33.02[N]

Johnson v. Norcross Bros., 209 Mass. 445, 95 N.E. 833 (1911), 21.02

Johnson v. Salem Title Co., 425 P.2d 519 (Or. 1967), 29.02[C][2]

Johnson, United States v., 621 F.2d 1073 (10th Cir. 1980), 42.02[B][3]

Johnson, United States ex rel., v. Morely Constr. Co., 17 F. Supp. 378 (W.D.N.Y. 1936), aff'd in part and rev'd in part, 98 F.2d 781 (2d Cir. 1938), 35.07[A][2]

Johnson, United States ex rel., v. Morley, 98 F.2d 781 (2d Cir. 1938), 35.08[B]

Johnson & Son Erector Co., ASBCA No. 23,689, 86-2 BCA ¶ 18,931 (1986), 23.03[B][1], 23.03[E][4]

Johnson Contr. Corp. v. United States, 132 F. Supp. 698 (Ct. Cl. 1955), 28.04[D][1]

Johnson Controls, Inc., United States v., 713 F.2d 1541 (Fed. Cir. 1983), 39.03[F], 39.04[F]

Johnson Controls World Servs., Inc., ASBCA No. 49011, 96-1 BCA ¶ 28,163 (1996), 23.03[E][1]

Johnson Serv. Co. v. Transamerica Ins. Co., 485 F.2d 164 (5th Cir. 1973), 35.06[A][1][b]

Johnson-Voiland-Archuleta, Inc. v. Roark Assocs., 572 P.2d 1220 (Colo. Ct. 1977), 29.02[C][3]

John T. Jones Constr. Co., ASBCA Nos. 48303, 48593, 1997 ASBCA LEXIS 220 (Nov. 10, 1997), 28.03[C][1]

John W. Johnson, Inc. v. Basic Constr. Co., 429 F.2d 764 (D.C. Cir. 1970), 28.03[E][3][a]

Jones & Hardy Contractors, ASBCA Nos. 20853 et al., 78-2 B.C.A. (CCH) ¶ 13,353, 39.09

Jones Const. & Renovation, Inc., In re, 337 B.R. 579 (Bankr. E.D. Va. 2006), 36.08

Joseph J. Hock, Inc. v. Baltimore Contractors, Inc., 249 A.2d 135 (Md. 1969), 35.06[B][1]

Joseph Morton Co. v. United States, 757 F.2d 1273 (Fed. Cir. 1985), 28.03[D][1][b]

Joseph Pickard's Sons Co. v. United States, 209 Ct. Cl. 643, 532 F.2d 739 (1976), 24.04[B]

Joseph T. Richardson, United States ex rel., v. E.J.T. Constr. Co., 453 F. Supp. 435 (D. Del. 1978), 35.06[A][1][b]

Joshi, United States ex rel., v. St. Luke's Hosp., Inc., 441 F.3d 552 (8th Cir. 2006), 38.02[B][1]

Josun, Inc., AGBCA Nos. 80-113-4, 82-249-4, 88-2 B.C.A. (CCH) ¶ 20,590 (1988), 27.05[C][2]

Joyner v. Adams, 361 S.E. 2d 902 (N.C. App. 1987), 27.05[A][3]

Joy v. Bell Helicopter Textron, Inc., 999 F.2d 549 (D.C. Cir. 1993), 29.04[F][1]

J.P. Bryne & Co., United States ex rel., v. Fire Ass'n of Phila., 260 F.2d 541 (2d Cir. 1958), 35.04[A]

J.P. Greathouse Steel Erectors, Inc. v. Blount Brothers Construction Co., 374 F.2d 324 (D.C. Cir.), cert. denied, 389 U.S. 847 (1967), 46.24

JP Inc., ASBCA Nos. 38426 et al., 90-1 B.C.A. ¶ 22,348, aff'd, 90-1 B.C.A. ¶ 22,616 (1990), 28.03[E][2]

J.R. Snyder Co. v. Soble, 226 N.W.2d 276 (Mich. 1975), 33.02[M][4]

J.S. Alberici Construction Co. v. Mid-West Conveyor Co., Inc., 750 A.2d 518 (Del. 2000), 29.03[D][3]

J.S.U.B., Inc. v. U.S. Fire Ins. Co., 906 So.2d 303 (Fla. 2007), 19.07[B]

J.T. Moran Fin. Corp., In re, 124 B.R. 926 (Bankr. S.D.N.Y. 1991), 36.02[A]

J.W. Bateson Co. v. United States, 308 F.2d 510 (5th Cir. 1962), 27.05[G][3][e]

J.W. Bateson Co. v. United States ex rel. National Automatic Sprinkler Indus. Pension Fund, 1978, 434 U.S. 586, 98 S. Ct. 873. 55 L. Ed. 2d 50 (1978), 35.02[A]

J.W. Bibb, Inc., ASBCA No. 19589, 76-2 B.C.A. ¶ 12,135 (1976), 28.03[B][3][a]

J.W.D., Inc. v. Federal Ins. Co., 806 S.W.2d 327 (Tex. App. 1991), 35.04[B]

J.W. Smith & Co., United States ex rel., v. Aetna Cas. & Sur. Co., 480 F.2d 1095 (8th Cir. 1973), 35.08[F][4]

J.Z.G. Resources, Inc. v. King, 987 F.2d 98 (2nd Cir. 1993), cert. denied, 510 U.S. 993 (1993), 19.07[B]

K

Kadri Int'l Co., AGBCA No. 2000-170-1, 02-1 B.C.A. ¶ 31,791 (2002), 28.03[D][2]

Kaiser Aluminum & Chemical Corp. v. Catellus Development Corp., 976 F.2d 1338 (9th Cir. 1992), 11.03[A][4][a]

Kaiser Indus. Corp. v. United States, 340 F.2d 322 (Ct. Cl. 1965), 35.08[H]

Kajima/Ray Wilson v. Los Angeles County Metro. Transp. Auth., 96 Cal. Rptr. 2d 747, 1 P.3d 63 (2003), 27.03[A]

Kalchthaler v. Keller Constr. Co., 591 N.W.2d 169 (Wis. Ct. App. 1999), 19.07[B]

Kalell v. Mutual Fire & Auto. Ins. Co., 471 N.W.2d 865 (Iowa 1991), 18.05[B][2]

Kalisch-Jarcho, Inc. v. City of N.Y., 58 N.Y.S.2d 377, 448 N.E.2d 413, 461 N.Y.S.2d 746 (1983), 26.02[GG][4]

Kalisch-Jarcho, Inc. v. City of N.Y., 58 N.Y.S.2d 377 (N.Y. 1983), 30.03[C]

Kalvar Corp. v. United States, 543 F.2d 1298 (Ct. Cl. 1976), cert. denied, 434 U.S. 830 (1977), 28.04[A][1]

Kampendonk v. American Bonding Co., 107 P.2d 588 (Wash. 1940), 35.06[B][3]

Kanag'Iq Constr. Co. v. United States, 51 Fed. Cl. 38 (2001), 39.03[B][1], 39.04[A]

Kane Constr. Co., GSBCA No. 2005, 66-2 B.C.A. ¶ 5992 (1966), 28.03[D][3]

Kansas City Marble & Tile Co. v. Penker Constr. Co., 86 F.2d 287 (4th Cir. 1936), 35.08[F][1]

Kaplan v. Shure Bros., Inc., 266 F.3d 598 (7th Cir. 2001), 20.02

Kaplan, United States v., 832 F.2d 676 (1st Cir. 1987), 42.02[B][6]

Karppinen v. Karl Kiefer Mach. Co., 187 F.2d 32 (2d Cir. 1951), 46.20

Kasler Elec. Company, DOTCAB No. 1425, 84-2 BCA ¶ 17374 (May 21, 1984), 28.03[G]

Kato Corp., ASBCA No. 51462, 06-2 B.C.A. (CCH) ¶ 33,293 (2006), 24.03

Katz. v. Innovator of Am., 552 So. 2d 724 (La. Ct. App. 1st Cir. 1989), 35.06[B][3]

Kauffman v. Shearson, Hayden, Stone, Inc., 128 Cal. App.3d 809 (1982), 33.02[M][1]

K.B. Weygand & Assoc., P.C. v. Deerwood Lake Land Co., 2001 Ala. LEXIS 120 (Ala. 2001), 29.02[C][3]

Keco Indus. v. United States, 364 F.2d 838 (Ct. Cl. 1966), 21.08

Keco Indus., Inc., ASBCA No. 15,184, 15,547, 72-2 BCA ¶ 9576 (1972), 30.03[C][5]

Keco Indus., Inc., ASBCA No. 15,184, 72-2 B.C.A. (CCH) ¶ 9576 (1972), 24.04[D]

Keco Indus., Inc. v. United States, 492 F.2d 1200 (Ct. Cl. 1974), 28.04[D][1]

Keeter Trading Co., Inc. v. U.S., 79 Fed. Cl. 243 (2007), 27.05[G][2][b]

Kehm Corp. v. United States, 93 F. Supp. 620 (Ct. Cl. 1950), 28.03[E][1][a]

Kelly v. Heron Ridge, Inc., 16 Fed. Appx. 695, 2001 WL 873828 (9th Cir. 2001), 29.03[D][1]

Kelso v. Kirk Bros. Mech. Contractors, 16 F.3d 1173 (Fed. Cir. 1994), 28.03[D][1][b]

Kemmons-Wilson, Inc., ASBCA No. 16167, 72-2 B.C.A. (CCH) ¶ 9689 (1972), 24.04[C]

Ken Cucchi Constr., Inc. v. O'Keefe, 973 S.W.2d 520 (Mo. App.1998), 21.02

Keneke Roofing, Inc. v. Island Ins. Co., Ltd., 98 P.3d 246 (Haw. 2004), 19.07[B]

Ken Rogge Lumber Co., AGBCA No. 85-510-10, 87-1 B.C.A. (CCH) ¶ 19,341 (1987), 33.02[E]

Kern Oil & Ref. Co. v. Tenneco Oil Co., 868 F.2d 1279 (Temp. Emer. Ct. App. 1989), 33.01[F]

Kevin Wells, AGBCA No. 82-284-3, 83-1 BCA ¶ 16,507 (1982), 23.03[B][1]

Key Constructors, Inc. v. H&M Gas Co., 537 So. 2d 1318 (Miss. 1989), 35.04[B], 35.07[B][1]

Keys Community College v. Insurance Co. of N. Am., 456 So.2d 1250 (Fla. Dist. Ct. App. 1984), 35.07[B][2]

Kids Cloz, Inc. v. Officially for Kids, Inc., 320 F. Supp. 2d 164 (S.D.N.Y. 2004), 17.01[A]

Kilgallon Constr. Co., Inc., Appeals of, 03-2 BCA P 32380, ASBCA No. 52582 (Sept. 30, 2003), 27.05[A][2]

Killingsworth, United States ex rel., v. Northrop Corp., 25 F.3d 715 (9th Cir. 1994), 38.02[B][3]

Killough, United States v., 848 F.2d 1523 (11th Cir. 1988), 38.02[C][1][b][iii]

Kilsby, United States ex rel., v. George, 243 F.2d 83 (5th Cir. 1957), 35.08[B]

Kinetic Builders, ASBCA No. 32627, 88-2 B.C.A. (CCH) ¶ 20,657 (1988), 27.05[C][2]

King v. Alaska State Hous. Auth., 512 P.2d 887 (Alaska 1973), 7.03[C]

King Enters., Inc., In re, 678 F.2d 73 (8th Cir. 1982), 21.02

Kingston Constr., Inc., 97-1 B.C.A. (CCH) ¶ 28,646 (ENGBCA 1996), 32.05

Kingston Trust Co. v. State, 291 N.Y.S.2d 208 (N.Y. Sup. Ct. 1968), 35.03[B]

Kinoshita & Co., In re, 287 F.2d 951 (2d Cir. 1961), 46.07

Kinsey Contracting Co. v. City of Fayetteville, 416 S.E.2d 607 (N.C. Ct. App. 1992), 7.03[C]

Kirchdorfer v. M.J. Kelley Corp., 995 F.2d 656 (6th Cir. 1993), 35.06[A][2]

Kirkpatrick v. Temme, 98 Nev. 523 (1982), 30.04[B][1]

Kirk Reid Co. v. Louis B. Fine, 205 Va. 778, 139 S.E.2d 829 (1965), 21.05

Kirk Williams, Inc. v. Six Indus., 463 N.E.2d 1266 (Ohio Ct. App. 1983), 35.08[F][3]

Kisco Co. v. United States, 610 F.2d 742 (Ct. Cl. 1979), 28.03[D][1][a][ii]

Kiser v. Fisman, 590 N.Y.S.2d 230 (N.Y. App. Div. 1992), 30.03[E]

KiSKA Constr. Corp., U.S.A. v. Wash. Metro. Area Transit Auth., 321 F.3d 1151 (D.C. Cir. 2003), 29.02[B][1]

Kisle v. St. Paul Fire & Marine Ins. Co., 262 Or. 1, 495 P.2d 1198 (1972), 19.07[B]

Kit-San-Azusa, J.V. v. United States, 32 Fed. Cl. 647 (Ct. Cl. 1995), 30.03[D][4]

Klein v. Catalano, 437 N.E.2d 514 (Mass. 1982), 29.02[C][5]

Knik Construction Co., PSBCA [now Civilian BCA] No. 1423, 86-2 B.C.A. (CCH) ¶ 18,762 (1986), 27.05[B][5][b]

Knotts v. United States, 121 F. Supp. 630 (Ct. Cl. 1954), 28.04[A][2]

Knotts v. United States, 128 Ct. Cl. 489, 121 F. Supp. 630 (1954), 28.04[A][1]

Knoxville, City of, v. Melvin F. Burgess, Inc., 175 S.W.2d 548 (Tenn. 1943), 35.08[I]

Kobashigawa Shokai, ASBCA No. 13,741, 69-2 BCA ¶ 7973 (1969), 23.03[E][2]

Koch v. Construction Techs., 924 S.W.2d 68 (Tenn. 1996), 35.08[E][1]

Koch Eng'g Co., Inc. v. Gibralter Cas. Co., 78 F.3d 1291 (8th Cir. 1996), 18.04[C][1]

Koehler v. Donnelly, 838 P.2d 980 (N.M. 1992), 35.08[G]

Kolar, Inc., ASBCA No. 28482, 84-1 B.C.A. ¶ 17,044, 39.08[A]

Koppers Co., Inc. v. Inland Steel Co., 498 N.E. 2d 1247 (Ind. Ct. App. 3d Dist. 1986), 30.02[B]

Koppers Co., United States ex rel., v. Five Boro Constr. Corp., 310 F.2d 701 (4th Cir. 1962), 35.08[F][1]

Kraemer Bros., Inc. v. U.S. Fire. Ins. Co., 89 Wis. 2d 555 (1979), 18.05[B][2]

Kraft Constr. Co., ASBCA No. 4976, 59-2 B.C.A. (CCH) ¶ 2347 (1959), 24.02[D]

Kramer v. Mt. Carmel Shelter Care Facility, Inc., 750 N.E.2d 757 (Ill. Ct. App. 2001), 33.01[I]

Kreekside Partners v. Nord Bitumi U.S., Inc., 963 F. Supp. 968 (D. Kan. 1997), 12.04[C][1][d][i]

Kreindler, United States ex rel., v. United Techs. Corp., 985 F.2d 1148 (2d Cir. 1993), 38.02[B][2]

Krizek, United States v., 111 F.3d 934 (D.C. Cir. 1997), 38.02[B][2]

Kroeger v. Franchise Equities, Inc., 212 N.W.2d 348 (Neb. 1973), 30.03[C]

Kross Elec. Co., In re, 9 B.R. 408 (W.D. V.A. 1981), 46.13

Krupp Steel Prods., United States ex rel., v. Aetna Ins. Co., 831 F.2d 978 (11th Cir. 1987), rev'd on other grounds, 923 F.2d 1521 (1991), 35.04[A], 35.07[A][3], 35.08[F][2]

Krupp Steel Prods., United States ex rel., v. Aetna Ins. Co., 923 F.2d 1521 (11th Cir. 1991), 33.02[O]

Krygoski Construction Co. v. United States, 94 F.3d 1537 (Fed. Cir. 1996), 7.03[B][2][d], 27.05[B][4]

Krygoski Construction Co. v. United States, 94 F.3d 1537 (Fed. Cir. 1996), cert. denied, 137 L. Ed. 2d 819 (1997), 28.04[B][2]

Krygoski Construction Co. v. United States, 94 F.3d 1537 (Fed. Cir. 1996), cert. denied, 520 U.S. 1210 (1997), 28.02[A][1], 28.04[A], 28.04[A][1], 28.04[C], 30.04[A]

Krygoski Construction Co. v. United States, 94 F.3d 1537 (Fed. Cir.), reh'g and reh'g en banc denied, No. 95-5136, 1966 U.S. App. LEXIS 30308 (Fed. Cir. Nov. 7, 1996), cert. denied, 117 S. Ct. 1691 (1997), 27.05[G][2][b]

KSC-TRI Sys., USA, Inc., ASBCA No. 54638, 2006-1, BCA ¶ 33,145 (Dec. 8, 2005), 28.03[C][1]

Kukui Plaza, Association of Owner of, v. Swinerton & Walbey Co., 68 Haw. 99, 705 P.2d 28 (1985), 46.15

Kumho Tire Co. v. Carmichael, 526 US 137 (1999), 23.07[C][2], 29.04[H]

Kurz-Kasch, Inc., ASBCA No. 32486, 88-3 B.C.A. ¶ 21,053 (1988), 28.04[D][4]

Kvaerner Metals v. Commercial Union Ins. Co., 908 A.2d 888 (Pa. 2006), 19.07[B]

K-W Ind. v. Nat'l Sur. Corp., 855 F.2d 640 (9th Cir. 1988), 25.03[B]

Kyocera Corp. v. Prudential-Bache
Trade Servs., Inc., 341 F.3d 987
(2003), 43.07[B]

L

L&A Contracting Co. v. Southern
Concrete Servs., Inc., 17 F.3d 106
(5th Cir. 1994), 15.15, 34.04[B],
34.04[C]

L&H Constr. Co., ASBCA No. 23620,
81-1 B.C.A. (CCH) ¶ 14,823 (1980),
30.03[C][4]

L&H Constr. Co., ASBCA No. 43833,
97-1 B.C.A. ¶ 28,766 (1997),
28.03[E][1][a], 28.04[D][3]

L&M Construction Co., 28.04[D][3]

LaBelle Indus., Inc., ASBCA No.
49307, 96-1 B.C.A. ¶ 28,158 (1996),
28.03[G]

Laboratory Furniture Co., United States
ex rel., v. Reliance Ins. Co., 274 F.
Supp. 377 (D. Mass. 1967),
35.06[A][1][b]

Laborer's Pension Trust Fund, Detroit
& Vicinity, United States ex rel., v.
Safeco, Ins. Co. of Am., 707 F. Supp.
286 (E.D. Mich. 1988), 35.07[A][4]

Laburnum Constr. Corp. v. United
States, 163 Ct. Cl. 339, 325 F.2d 451
(1963), 24.02[C], 24.04[A], 24.04[C]

Lachkar v. Lachkar, 182 Cal. App. 3d
641, 227 Cal. R. Tr. 501 (1986),
46.15

LaCorte Elec. Constr. & Maint. Inc. v.
N.Y. State Dep't of Soc. Serv., 663
N.Y.S.2d 446 (N.Y. App. Div. 1997),
7.03[E]

Ladco Properties XVII, L.L.C. v.
Jefferson-Pilot Life Ins., 523 F. Supp.
2d 940 (S.D. Iowa 2007), 33.01[B]

Lafarge Corp. v. Hartford Cas. Ins. Co.,
61 F.3d 389 (5th Cir. 1995), rev'd on
other grounds, 241 F.3d 396 (5th Cir.
2001), 18.04[C][1]

Lafayette Coal Co., ASBCA No. 32174,
89-3 B.C.A. ¶ 21,963 (1989),
28.04[D][4]

LaGrand Steel Prods. Co. v. A.S.C.
Constructors, Inc., 702 P.2d 855
(Idaho Ct. App.), review denied, 766
P.2d 828 (Idaho 1985), 35.02[B],
35.03[B]

La Grow Corp., ASBCA No. 42386,
91-2 B.C.A. ¶ 23,945 (1991),
28.03[D][2]

Laka Tool & Stamping Co. v. United
States 226 Ct. Cl. 83, 639 F.2d 738
(1980), cert. denied, 454 U.S. 1086
(1981), 28.03[F][3]

Lake Union Drydock Co., Inc. v. United
States, 2007 U.S. Dist. LEXIS 78282,
(W.D. Wash. 2007), 29.02[B][2]

La Liberte, LLC v. Keating Bldg. Corp.,
2007 WL 4323687 (E.D. Pa.
12/11/2007), 34.04[G][4]

LA Ltd., LA Hizmet Isletmeleri,
ASBCA No. 53447, 04-1 BCA
32,478 (2004), 30.03[D][5]

Lamar Constr. Co., ASCBA No. 39,593,
92-2 BCA ¶ 24,813 (1992),
23.04[B][1]

Lamar Homes, Inc. v. Mid-Continent
Cas. Co., 242 S.W.3d 1 (Tex. 2007),
18.04[C][1], 19.07[B]

Lamb Eng'g & Constr. Co., ASBCA
Nos. 53304, 53356. 53357, 53358,
53359, 06-1 B.C.A. (CCH) ¶ 33,178
(2006), 24.02[C]

Lamb Eng'g & Constr. Co., ENGBCA
No. C-9304172, 97-2 BCA ¶ 29,207
(1997), 23.06[A]

Lambert v. Maryland Casualty Co., 418
So. 2d 553 (La. 1982), 34.04[E][2],
36.09[F]

Lambert Constr. Co. DOT BCA 77-9,
78-1 B.C.A. ¶ 13,221 (1978),
28.03[D][3]

Lamberton v. Travelers Indem. Co., 325
A.2d 104 (Del. Super. Ct. 1974),
20.04

Lamp, Inc. v. International Fidelity
Insurance Co., 493 N.E.2d 146 (Ill.
Ct. App. 1986), 33.02[N]

Lamparter Acoustical Prods. v.
Maryland Cas. Co., 407 N.Y.S.2d 579
(App. Div. 1978), 35.08[E][3]

Landis v. North Am. Co., 299 U.S. 248
(1936), 39.08[B]

Landlords Prof'l Servs., 215 Cal.
App.3d at 1609, 5.03[C][2]

Landmark Land Co. v. Jemison, 558 So.
2d 802 (La. Ct. App. 1990),
29.02[C][3]

Land Paving Co. v. D.A. Constr. Co.,
338 N.W.2d 779 (Neb. 1983),
33.01[E]

Lane Constr. Corp. v. Brown & Root, Inc., 29 F. Supp. 2d 707 (E.D. Va. 1998), 26.02[UU][4]

Lange Industries v. Hallam Grain Co., 507 N.W.2d 465 (Neb. 1993), 33.01[B]

Langevin v. United States, 100 Ct. Cl. 15 (1943), 30.03[C]

Lank Woodwork Co., United States *ex. rel.*, v. C.S.H. Contractors, Inc., 452 F. Supp. 922 (D.D.C. 1978), 35.06[A][1][b]

Lanzen Fabricating, Inc., ASBCA No. 40328, 93-3 B.C.A. ¶ 26,079 (1993), 28.03[D][1][a][i], 28.03[D][1][a][ii], 28.03[D][2]

L.A.P.D., Inc. v. General Elec. Corp., 132 F.3d 402 (7th Cir. 1997), 17.08[C]

La Pietra v. Freed, 151 Cal. Rptr. 554 (1978), 33.02[M][1]

Larry Armbruster & Sons v. State Pub. Bldg. Auth., 505 A.2d 395 (Pa. Commw. Ct. 1986), 30.03[D][1]

Larson Concrete Co. v. Stroschein, 353 N.W.2d 354 (S.D. 1984), 35.08[D][2]

Lathan Co. v. United States, 20 Cl. Ct. 122 (Fed. Cl. 1990), 7.03[B][2][a], 28.03[E][3][a]

Lattea v. City of Akron, 458 N.E.2d 868 (Ohio Ct. App. 1982), 29.04[D][2]

Laughlin Recreational Enters., Inc. v. Zab Dev. Co., 646 P.2d 555 (Nev. 1982), 33.01[F]

Law Bros. Contracting Corp. v. O'Shea, 435 N.Y.S.2d 812 (N.Y. App. Div. 1981), 7.03[E]

Law Co., The, v. Mohawk Constr. & Supply Co., 532 F. Supp. 2d 1276 (D. Kan. 2007), 26.02[Q][3]

Lawrence Tractor Co. v. Carlisle Ins. Co., 249 Cal. Rptr. 150 (Ct. App. 1988), 35.08[J]

Lawson v. Brown's Day Care Ctr., 776 A.2d 390 (Vt. 2001), 45.05[A]

L.A. Young Sons, Constr. Co. v. County of Toole, 575 P.2d 1034, (Okla. 1978), 22.02

Lea County Constr. Co., ASBCA No. 10,093, 67-1 B.C.A. (CCH) ¶ 6423 (1967), 24.02[D]

Lear Astronics Corp., ASBCA No. 37,228, 93-2 BCA ¶ 25,892 (1993), 23.03[E][3]

Lee Builders, Inc. v. Farm Bur. Mut. Ins. Co., 137 P.3d 486 (Kan. 2006), 19.07[B]

Leiden Corp., ASBCA No. 26136, 83-2 B.C.A. (CCH) ¶ 16,612 (1983), 27.05[C][2]

Leila Hosp. & Ctr. v. Xonics Med. Sys., 948 F.2d 271 (6th Cir. 1991), 34.04[G][6]

L'Enfant Plaza Properties, Inc. v. United States, 645 F.2d 886 (Ct. Cl. 1981), 39.08[A]

Lennar Corp. v. Auto-Owners Ins. Co., 151 P. 3d 538 (Ariz. App. 2007), 19.07[B]

Lennar Corp. v. Great Am. Ins. Co., 200 S.W.3d 651 (Tex. App. 2006), 18.05[A][2]

Lenning v. Commercial Union Ins. Co., 260 F.3d 574 (6th Cir. 2001), 19.07[B]

Lennox, City of, v. Mitek Indus., Inc., 519 N.W.2d 330 (S.D. 1994), 29.02[E]

Leno, United States *ex rel.*, v. Summitt Constr. Co., 892 F.2d 788 (9th Cir. 1989), 35.04[A]

Lenry, Inc. v. United States, 156 Ct. Cl. 46, 297 F.2d 550 (1962), 24.02[D]

Leo Michuda & Son Co. v. Metro. Sanitary Dist., 422 N.E.2d 1078 (Ill. App. Ct. 1981), 7.03[E]

Leonard B. Hebert, Jr. & Co. v. Kinler, 336 So.2d 922 (La. Ct. App. 1976), 35.03[B]

Leon Keyser, Inc., *In re*, 89 A.2d 917 (N.H. 1952), 35.07[B][2]

Leslie Miller, Inc. v. Arkansas, 352 U.S. 187 (1956), 35.08[G]

Les Schwab Tire Ctrs., Inc., City of Weippe *ex rel.*, v. Yarno, 528 P.2d 201 (Idaho 1974), 35.04[B]

Levesque v. D & M Builders, Inc., 170 Conn. 177 (1976), 30.02

Levin Metals Corp. v. Parr-Richmond Terminal Co., 781 F. Supp. 1454 (N.D. Cal. 1991), 11.03[A][4][a]

Levy v. Schnabel Found. Co., 584 A.2d 1251 (D.C. Ct. App. 1991), 29.02[D][5]

Lewis v. Anchorage Asphalt Paving Co., 535 P.2d 1188 (Alaska 1975), *appeal after remand,* 579 P.2d 532 (Alaska 1978), *appeal after remand,* 629 P.Ed 65 (Alaska 1981), 73 A.L.R.3d 1213 (1976 & 2007 Supp.), 29.02[B][4]

Lewis v. Hughes, 346 A.2d 231 (Md. 1975), 16.06[C]

Lewis Constr. Co., ASBCA No. 5509, 60-2 B.C.A. (CCH) ¶ 2732 (1960), 24.04[E]

Lewis Jorge Construction Mgmt., Inc. v. Pomona Unified Sch. Dist., 34 Cal. 4th 960 (2004), 30.04[B][2]

Lewis Jorge Construction Mgmt., Inc. v. Pomona Unified Sch. Dist., 102 P.3d 257 (Cal. 2004), 31.01, 31.02[B], 31.04[A]

Lewis-Nicholson, Inc. v. United States, 550 F.2d 26 (Ct. Cl. 1977), 28.03[E][1][a]

L. Harvey Concrete v. Agro Constr. & Supply Co., 939 P.2d 811 (Ariz. Ct. App. 1997), 35.08[E][1]

Libertatia v. United States, 46 Fed. Cl. 702 (2000), 28.03[G]

Libertatia Associates, Inc. v. United States, 46 Fed. Cl. 702 (2002), 28.04[D][2]

Liberty Ins. Corp. v. Ferguson Steel Co., Inc., 812 N.E.2d 228 (Ind. Ct. App. 2004), 18.04[A]

Liberty Mut. Ins. Co., LBCCA No. 1999-DBA-11, 00-1 B.C.A. ¶ 30,660 (1999), 28.03[A]

Liberty Mutual Insurance Co. v. Aventura Eng'g & Constr. Corp., F. Supp. 2d _____, 2008 WL 420031 (S.D. Fla. Jan. 8, 2008), 36.02[D], 36.03[B]

Liberty Mutual Insurance Co. v. Aventura Eng'g & Constr. Corp., 534 F. Supp. 2d 1290 (S.D. Fla. 2008), 34.04[H]

Liberty Mut. Ins. Co. v. Rawls, 404 F.2d 880, *reh'g denied,* (5th Cir. 1969), 20.04

Liberty Mut. Ins. Co. v. Vanderbush Sheet Metal Co., 512 F. Supp. 1159 (E.D. Mich. 1981), 29.04[E]

Libman v. Zuckerman, 33 Mass. App. Ct. 341 (1992), 30.02[A][1]

Librach v. United States, 147 Ct. Cl. 605 (1959), 28.04[A][1]

Lichter, United States *ex rel.,* v. Henke Constr. Co., 157 F.2d 13 (8th Cir. 1946), 35.08[B]

Liebo, United States v., 923 F.2d 1038 (8th Cir. 1991), 42.02[B][3]

Liles Constr. Co. v. United States, 455 F.2d 527 (Ct. Cl. 1972), 23.03[E][3], 28.03[E][1][a]

Limbach Co., LLC v. Zurich Am. Ins. Co., 396 F.3d 358 (4th Cir. 2005), 18.05[A][2]

Linan-Faye Constr. Co. v. Housing Auth., 847 F. Supp. 1191 (D.N.J. 1994), *aff'd in part, rev'd in part,* 49 F.3d 915 (3d Cir. 1995), 28.02[A][2]

Lincoln Elec. Prods. Co., United States *ex rel.,* v. Green Elec. Serv., 252 F. Supp. 324 (E.D.N.Y. 1996), *aff'd,* 379 F.2d 207 (2d Cir. 1967), 35.05[A]

Linden v. Cascade Stone Co., Inc., 699 N.W.2d 189 (Wi. 2005), 16.02[B]

Lindsay v. McEnearney Associates, Inc., 260 Va. 48, 531 S.E.2d 573 (Va. 2000), 27.05[B][5][d]

Lindsay Drilling & Contracting v. U.S. Fid. & Guar. Co., 676 P.2d 203 (Mont. 1984), 19.07[B]

Lindsey Masonry Co. v. Jenkins & Assoc., 897 S.W.2d 6 (Mo. Ct. App. 1995), 35.08[B]

Liquidation of Union Indem. Ins. Co. v. Superintendent of Ins., 632 N.Y.S.2d 788 (App. Div. 1st Dep't 1995), 34.04[G][1]

Lisbon Contractors, Inc. v. United States, 828 F.2d 759 (Fed. Cir. 1987), 28.03[B][2], 28.03[B][2][a], 28.03[B][3][a], 28.03[D], 30.03[D][5]

LISN, Inc. v. Commercial Union Ins. Cos., 83 Ohio App. 3d 625, 615 N.E.2d 650 (Ct. App. 1992), 18.05[A][2]

Litton Microwave Cooking Prods. v. Leviton Mfg. Co., 15 F.3d 790 (8th Cir. 1994), 16.04[B]

L.J. Casey Co., AGBCA No. 75–148, 76-2 B.C.A. ¶ 12,196 (1976), 28.03[E][4]

L-J Inc. v. Bituminous Fire and Marine Ins. Co., 366 S.C. 117, 621 S.E.2d 33 (2005), 18.04[C][1]

L.K. Comstock v. N.Y. Convention Ctr. Dev. Corp., 584 N.Y.S.2d 472 (N.Y. App. Div. 1992), 7.03[C]

L.K. Comstock & Co., Inc. v. United Eng'rs & Constructors, Inc., 880 F.2d 219 (9th Cir. 1989), 21.02

L.L. Hall Constr. Co. v. United States, 177 Ct. Cl. 870 (1966), 30.03[C][5]

L.L. Hall Constr. Co. v. United States, 177 Ct. Cl. 870, 379 F.2d 559 (1966), 24.02[D], 24.04[A]

L.L. Lewis Const. L.L.C v. Adrian, 142 S.W.3d 255 (Mo. Ct. App. W.D. 2004), 30.02[A][1]

Lloyd Moore Constr., AGBCA Nos. 87-151-3 et al., 89-2 BCA ¶ 21, 875 (1989), 23.04[B][1]

Lobak Partitions v. Atlas Constr. Co., 749 P.2d 716 (Wash. Ct. App. 1988), 35.08[G]

L.O. Brayton & Co., IBCA No. 641-5-67, 70-2 B.C.A. (CCH) ¶ 8510 (1970), 24.02[D], 24.04[E]

Local 771 v. RKO Gen., Inc., 419 F. Supp. 553 (S.D. N.Y. 1976), 46.26

Local Contractors, Inc., ASBCA No. 37, 108, 92-1 BCA ¶ 24,491 (1991), 23.03[B]

Lochridge-Priest, Inc., United States ex rel., v. Con-Real Support Group, Inc., 950 F.2d 284 (5th Cir. 1992), 35.04[A], 35.07[A][1]

Lockheed Corporation, 42.02[F][1]

Lockheed Martin Librascope Corporation, Appeal of, 00-1 BCA P 30635, ASBCA No. 50508 (Oct. 29, 1999), 27.05[B][3][c]

London, United States v., 66 F.3d 1227 (1st Cir. 1995), 42.02[B][6]

Louisiana Power & Light Co. v. Kellstrom, 50 F.3d 319 (5th Cir. 1995), 33.01[I]

Louisville Edible Oil Prods., Inc., U.S. v., 926 F.2d 584 (6th Cir. 1991), 11.03[A][6]

Lovell Clay Prods. Co. v. Statewide Supply Co., 580 P.2d 1278 (Colo. Ct. App. 1978), 35.03[B]

Lovett v. Union Pac. R.R. Co., 201 F.3d 1074 (8th Cir. 2001), 29.04[F][1]

Lowder v. N.C. State Hwy. Comm'n, 217 S.E.2d 682 (N.C. App. 1975), 27.05[C][4]

Loyal Order of Moose Lodge 1392 v. International Fid. Ins. Co., 767 P.2d 622 (Alaska 1990), 34.04[D]

L. Rosenman Corp. v. United States, 390 F.2d 711 (Ct. Cl. 1968), 27.05[A][2]

L.T.M. Builders Co. v. Village of Jefferson, 399 N.E.2d 1210 (Ohio 1980), 35.08[B]

Luis A. Cabrera, S.E., United States ex rel., v. Sun Eng'g Enters., Inc., 817 F. Supp. 1009 (D.P.R. 1993), 35.06[A][1][b]

Lundstrom Constr.Co. v. Dygert, 94 N.W.2d 527 (Minn. 1959), 21.02

Luria Bros. & Co. v. United States, 177 Ct. Cl. 676, 369 F.2d 701 (1966), 24.02, 24.04, 24.04[B], 24.04[C], 30.03[D]

Luria Bros. & Co. v. United States, 369 F.2d 701 (Ct. Cl. 1966), 21.08

Luther Benjamin Constr. Co., ASBCA Nos. 40401 et al., 93-1 B.C.A. ¶ 25,459 (1992), 28.03[D][2]

L.W. Foster Sportswear Co. v. United States, 186 Ct. Cl. 499, 405 F.2d 1285 (1969), 24.02[C]

L.W. Matteson, Inc. v. U.S. 61 Fed. Cl. 296 (2004), 27.05[C][3][a]

Lyle Signs, Inc. v. Evroks Corp., 562 A.2d 785 (N.H. 1989), 35.03[B]

Lynch v. United States, 292 U.S. 571 (1934), 28.02

Lyndon Property Inc. Co. v. Duke Levy & Assocs., LLC, 475 F.3d 268 (5th Cir. 2007), 29.02[C][4], 34.04[H]

M

Maccaferri Gabions, Inc. v. Dynateria, Inc., 91 F.3d 1431 (11th Cir. 1996), 35.05[A]

Mac Constr. Co. v. Thrasher Contracting Co., 162 S.E.2d 152 (N.C. App. 1968), 27.05[B][4]

MacEvoy Co. v. United States ex rel. Calvin Tomkins Co., 322 U.S. 102 (1944), 35.03[A]

MacIssac & Menke Co. v. Cardox Corp., 14 Cal. Rptr. 523 (Ct. App. 1961), 35.08[F][4]

Mackby, United States v., 339 F.3d 1013 (9th Cir. 2003), 38.02[D]

MacLean Townhomes, L.L.C. v.
America 1st Roofing & Builders,
Inc., 138 P.3d 155 (Wash. App.
2006), 27.05[A][3]

Macri v. United States, 353 F.2d 804
(9th Cir. 1965), 33.01[H]

Maddux Supply Co. v. St. Paul Fire &
Marine Ins. Co., 86 F.3d 332 (4th Cir.
1996), 35.02[A], 35.04[A]

Madge v. Rod O'Kelley, Inc., 855
N.E.2d 712 (Ind. Ct. App. 2006),
16.08[F]

Madison v. Frank Lloyd Wright Found.,
20 Wis. 2d 1361, 122 N.W.2d 409
(1963), 46.14

Madison, City of, v. Bailey-Laffey
Constr., 495 N.W.2d 95 (S.D. 1993),
36.06

Madsen v. Wyoming River Trips, Inc.,
31 F. Supp. 2d 1321 (D. Wyo. 1999),
29.03[D][3]

Magnum, Inc., ASBCA No. 53890, 04-1
B.C.A. ¶ 32,489, 39.06[C]

Mahana v. Alexander, 263 P. 260 (Cal.
Ct. App. 1927), 35.06[B][3]

Mahana v. Miller, 573 P.2d 1238 (Or.
1978), 35.08[G]

Maintenance Eng'rs, ASBCA No.
17474, 74-2 B.C.A. (CCH) ¶ 10,760
(1974), 24.02[D]

MAI Steel Serv., Inc. v. Blake Constr.
Co., 981 F.2d 414 (9th Cir. 1992),
35.04[A], 35.07[A][1]

Malone v. United States, 849 F.2d 1441
(Fed. Cir. 1988), 28.03[E][1][a],
28.03[F][4]

Malone v. United States, 849 F.2d 1441
(Fed. Cir. 1988), reh'g granted in
part, corrected, 857 F.2d 787 (Fed.
Cir. 1988), 28.03[E][1],
28.03[E][1][a]

Malone v. United States, 849 F.2d 1441
(Fed. Cir.), modified in part, 857 F.2d
787 (Fed. Cir. 1988), 28.03[B][3][b]

Malor Constr. Corp., 84-1 BCA
¶ 17,023 (IBCA 1984), 30.03[C]

Malpass Constr. Co., United States ex
rel., v. Scotland Concrete Co., 294 F.
Supp. 1299 (E.D.N.C. 1968),
35.04[A], 35.08[D][1]

Mamaroneck, Town of, v. Byron Elec.
Co., 148 A.D.2d 458, 538 N.Y.S.2d
612 (1989), 46.06

M.A. Mortenson Co., Appeals of, 05-1
BCA P 32846, ASBCA No. 53146
(Jan. 7, 2005), 27.05[E][2]

M.A. Mortenson Co., ASBCA 40750,
97-1 BCA ¶ 28623, 27.05[D][6][c]

M.A. Mortensen Co. v. United States,
40 Fed. Cl. 389 (1998), 29.02[B][1]

M.A. Mortenson Co. v. United States,
843 F.2d 1360 (Fed. Cir. 1988),
27.05[D][5][a]

Manart Textile Co. v. United States, 77
F. Supp. 924 (Ct. Cl. 1948),
28.03[F][2]

Manerud v. City of Eugene, 62 Or. 196,
124 P. 662 (1912), 26.02[LL][3]

Manganaro Corp. v. Hitt Contracting,
Inc., 193 F. Supp. 2d 88 (D.D.C.
2002), 25.02[E]

Manriquez Aribizo, United States v.,
883 F.2d 244 (10th Cir. 1987),
42.02[B][6]

Manuel Bros., Inc. v. United States, 55
Fed. Cl. 8 (2002), 27.05[C][2],
27.05[C][3][b]

Manuel Bros., Inc. v. United States, 55
Fed. Cl. 8 (2002), aff'd, 95 Fed.
Appx. 344 (Fed. Cir. 2004), 24.02[B],
24.02[D], 24.03

MaRae Grocery Co. v. Independence
Indem. Co., 33 F.2d 494 (4th Cir.
1929), 35.08[D][1]

Marathon Oil Co. v. Hollis, 305 S.E.2d
864 (Ga. Ct. App. 1983), 28.03[E][1]

Marcou Constr. Co. v. Tinkham Indus.
& Dev. Corp., 371 A.2d 1187 (N.H.
1977), 30.04[B][1]

Marcus, United States ex rel., v. Hess,
317 U.S. 537 (1943), 38.02[A],
38.02[C][1][b][i]

Mariana, United States ex rel., v. Piracci
Constr. Co., 405
F. Supp. 904 (D.D.C. 1975), 35.04[A]

Marina Road, LLC v. Zennett Props.,
LLC, 296 Wis. 2d 935, 724 N.W. 2d
273, 2006 WL 2670963 (Wis. Ct.
App. 2006), 20.02

Marine Constr. & Dredging, Inc.,
ASBCA Nos. 38412 et al., 98-1
B.C.A. ¶ 27,286 (1994),
28.04[C][2][a]

Marine Constr. & Dredging, Inc.,
ASBCA Nos. 39,913 et al., 95-1
BCA ¶ 27,286 (1995), 23.03[B][2]

Mark Bombara Interior Design v. Bowler, 446 Mass. 413 (2006), 28.03[E][2]

MarketXT Holdings Corp., *In re,* 376 B.R. 390 (Bankr. S.D.N.Y. 2007), 32.05

Mark Smith Constr. Co., ASBCA No. 25058, 81-2 B.C.A. ¶ 15,306 (1981), 28.03[D][3]

Marley v. United States, 423 F.2d 324 (Ct. Cl. 1970), 28.03[F][1]

Marriott Corp. v. Dasta Constr. Co., 26 F.3d 1057 (11th Cir. 1994), 26.02[J][4]

Mars, Inc. v. Heritage Builders of Effingham, Inc., 763 N.E.2d 428 (Ill. App. 2002), 29.02[E]

Marshall Contractors v. Incorporated Peerless Inc. Co., 827 F. Supp. 91 (D.R.I. 1993), 34.04[F][1]

Martin v. Hartford Accident & Indem. Co., 316 S.E.2d 126 (N.C. Ct. App. 1984), 35.04[B]

Martin J. Simko Constr. Co. v. United States, 11 Cl. Ct. 257 (1986), *vacated, remanded on other grounds,* 852 F.2d 540 (Fed. Cir. 1988), 27.05[G][2][a], 28.03[D][2]

Martin K. Eby Constr. Co., Inc. v. Jacksonville Transp. Auth., 178 Fed. Appx. 894 (11 Cir. 2006), 27.05[A][2]

Martin Steel Constructors, Inc., United States *ex rel.,* v. Avanti Constructors, Inc., 750 F.2d 759 (9th Cir. 1984), *cert. denied,* 474 U.S. 817 (1985), 35.02[A], 35.07[A][3], 35.08[B]

Martusciello v. JDS Homes, Inc., 838 N.E.2d 9 (Ill. App. Ct. 2005), 7.02[B][2][c]

Maryland Cas. v. Reeder, 221 Cal. App. 3d 961 (1990), 18.04[C][2]

Maryland Cas. Co. v. Portland Constr. Co., 71 F.2d 658 (2d Cir. 1934), 35.08[I]

Maryland Casualty Co. v. Straubinger, 240 N.Y.S.2d 228 (N.Y. App. Div. 1963), 36.04

Maryland Minerals & Cranesville Stone Co., United States *ex rel.* v. U.S. Fid. & Guar. Co., _____ F. Supp. _____, 2007 U.S. Dist. LEXIS 41893 (N.D. W. Va. 2007), 25.03[B]

Massachusetts v. EPA, 127 S. Ct. 1438 (2007), 11.03[A][5][a]

Massachusetts Bay Ins. Co. v. Ferraiolo Constr. Co., 584 A.2d 608 (Me. 1990), 19.07[B]

Mass. Bonding & Ins. Co. v. Orkin Exterminating Co., 416 S.W.2d 396 (Tex. 1967), 18.04[C][1]

Massachusetts Bonding & Ins. Co. v. United States *ex rel.* Clarksdale Mach. Co., 88 F.2d 388 (5th Cir. 1937), 35.04[A]

Mass. Constr. Group, Inc., ASBCA No. 55440, 2006 WL 3290971 (Oct. 30, 2006), 24.02[B]

Mass. Highway Dept. v. Perini Corp., 13 Mass. L. Rep. 564 (Mass. Super. 2001), 43.04[B][3][b]

Mass. Highway Dept. v. Perini Corp., 14 Mass. L. Rep. 452 (Mass. Super. 2002), 43.04[B][3][b]

Mass. Highway Dept. v. Perini Corp., 828 N.E.2d 34 (Mass. 2005), 43.04[B][3][b]

Masterclean Inc. v. Star Ins. Co., 556 S.E.2d 371 (S.C. 2001), 34.04[D]

Masterfile Sec. Corp., GSBCA No. 4451, 77-2 B.C.A. (CCH) ¶ 12,762 (1977), 27.05[G][2][b]

Mastrobuono v. Shearson Lehman Hutton, Inc., 514 U.S. 52 (1995), 46.04

Matanuska Valley Bank v. Arnold, 223 F.2d 778 (9th Cir. 1995), 17.01[A]

Material Serv. Co., United States *ex rel.,* v. Wolfson, 362 F. Supp. 454 (E.D. Mo. 1973), 35.08[F][1]

Matthew Andrew Kalosinakis, ASBCA No. 41337, 91-2 B.C.A. ¶ 23,744 (1991), 28.03[D][3]

Maxima Corp. v. United States, 847 F.2d 1549 (Fed. Cir. 1988), 28.02, 28.02[A][2], 28.02[A][3], 28.02[B], 28.04[B][2]

Maxon Corp. v. Tyler Pipe Indus., Inc., 497 N.E.2d 570 (Ind. Ct. App. 1986), 16.07[B]

Maxum Funds, Inc. v. Salus Corp., 779 F.2d 974 (4th Cir. 1985), 46.06

Mayer v. Alexander & Baldwin, Inc., 56 Haw. 195, 532 P.2d 1007 (1975), 26.02[L][3]

Mayfair Construction Co. v. United
States, [34 CCF ¶ 75,540], 841 F.2d
1576 (Fed. Cir.), *cert. denied,* 488
U.S. 980 (1988), 39.03[C][1]

McClain v. Kimbrough Constr. Co., 806
S.W.2d 194 (Tenn. Ct. App. 1990),
28.03[D][1][a][i]

McCloskey & Co. & C.H. Leavell &
Co., 74-1 B.C.A. (CCH) ¶ 10,479
(1974), 22.05

McDaniel v. Berhalter, 405 So. 2d 1027
(Fla. Dist. Ct. App. 1981),
33.02[M][2]

McDevitt & Street Co. v. Dep't of Gen.
Servs., 377 So. 2d 191 (Fla. Dist. Ct.
App. 1979), 30.03[D][1]

McDevitt & Street Co. v. Marriott
Corp., 713 F. Supp. 906 (E.D. Va.
1989), 23.04[B][1], 26.02[UU][3]

McDonald, United States *ex rel.,* v.
Barney Wilkerson Constr. Co., 321 F.
Supp. 1294 (D.N.M. 1971), 21.02

McDonnell Douglas v. U.S., 50 Fed. Cl.
311 (2001), 28.03[B][2][a]

McDonnell Douglas v. U.S., 35 Fed. Cl.
358 (1996), 28.03[B][2][a]

McDonnell Douglas v. U.S., 182 F.3d
1319 (1999), 28.03[B][2][a]

McDonnell Douglas Corp. v. U.S., 35
Fed. Cl. 358
(1996), 28.04[D], 28.04[D][2]

McDonnell Douglas Corp. v. U.S., 35
Fed. Cl. at 374, 28.03[D][1][a][i],
28.03[D][1][b]

McDonnell Douglas Corp. v. United
States, 37 Fed. Cl. 285 (1997),
28.03[G]

McDonnell Douglas Corp. v. U.S., 323
F.3d 1006 (Fed. Cir. 2003),
27.04[A][2], 28.03[B][2][a]

McElhose v. Universal Sur. Co., 158
N.W.2d 228 (Neb. 1968), 35.04[B]

McGee Landscaping, Inc., Appeal of,
AGBCA No. 91-172-1, 93-3
B.C.A. (CCH) ¶ 25,946 (1993),
30.03[D][2]

McGee Steel Co. v. State *ex rel.*
McDonald Indus. Alaska, Inc., 723
P.2d 611 (Alaska 1986), 35.04[B],
35.07[B][1]

McGrath, United States *ex rel.,* v.
Travelers Indem. Co., 253 F. Supp.
330 (D. Ariz. 1966), 35.06[A][1][b]

McGregor Architectural Iron Co.,
United States *ex rel.,* v.
Merritt-Chapman & Scott Corp., 185
F. Supp. 381 (M.D. Pa. 1960),
35.05[A]

McGuire & Hester v. City & County of
San Francisco, 113 Cal. App. 2d 186,
247 P.2d 934 (1952), 26.02[E][4]

McIntire v. Green-Tree Cmtys., Inc.,
318 So. 2d 197 (Fla. Dist. Ct. App.
1975), 26.02[J][4]

McIntyre v. Farrell Corp., 97 F.3d 779
(5th Cir. 1996), 29.04[J]

McKeen Homeowner's Assoc., Inc. v.
Oliver, 586 So. 2d 679 (La. App. 2
Cir. 1991), 20.01

McKenzie v. Standard Accident Ins., 1
S.E.2d 502 (S.C. 1939), 35.06[B][3]

McMath Constr. Co. v. Dupuy, 897 So.
2d 677 (La. App. 2004), 19.07[B]

McMillan v. United States, 112
F. 3d 1040 (9th Cir. 1997),
8A.08[A][1]

McNairy v. Sugar Creek Resort, 576
So. 2d 185 (Ala. 1991), 35.08[G]

McNally Wellman Co. v. New York
State Elec. & Gas Corp., 63 F.3d
1188 (2d Cir. 1995), 26.02[GG][3]

McNulty v. Keyser Office Bldg. Co.,
112 Md. 638, 76 A. 1113 (1940),
21.05

McQueen Contracting, Inc. v. Fidelity
& Deposit Co. of Md., 871 F.2d 32
(5th Cir. 1989), 35.04[B]

McRae Grocery Co. v. Independence
Indem. Co., 33 F.2d 494 (4th Cir.
1929), 35.08[I]

M.D.R.-RIC, PSBCA No. 4472, 01-1
B.C.A. ¶ 31,302 (2001), 28.03[F][1]

M.E. Brown, ASBCA No. 40,043, 91-1
BCA ¶ 23,293 (1990), 23.03[E][3]

Mecanique C.N.C., Inc. v. Durr Envtl.
Inc., 304 F. Supp. 2d 971 (S.D. Ohio
2004), 29.02[E]

Mech-Con Corp. v. West, 61 F.3d 883
(Fed. Cir. 1995), 24.04[C],
30.03[C][4]

Medema Homes, Inc. v. Lynn, 647 P.2d
664 (Colo. 1982), 30.02[B]

Medford Sch. Dist. *ex rel.* North Coast
Elec. Co. v. Peterson & Jones
Commercial Constr., 708 P.2d 623
(Or. Ct. App. 1985), 35.08[D][3]

Medical Dev. Corp. v. Industrial Molding Corp., 479 F.2d 345 (10th Cir. 1973), 46.06

Mediterranean Enters., Inc. v. Ssangyong Corp., 708 F.2d 1458 (9th Cir. 1983), 46.07

Medlin Constr. Group, Ltd. v. Harvey, 449 F.3d 1195 (Fed. Cir. 2006), 27.05[A][2]

Med Plus Props. v. Colcock Constr. Group, Inc., 628 So. 370 (Ala. 1993), 27.06

Mega Constr. Co., Inc. v. U.S., 29 Fed. Cl. 396 (1993), 27.05[D][5][b], 27.06, 39.03[B][3]

Meinhard v. Salmon, 249 N.Y. 458, 164 N.E. 545 (1928), 17.06, 17.09[L]

Melka Marine, Inc. v. United States, 187 F.3d 1370 (Fed. Cir. 1999), 30.03[C][3], 39.03[A]

Melka Marine, Inc. v. United States, 187 F.3d 1370 (Fed. Cir. 1999), aff'd in part, vacating in part and remanding, 41 Fed. Cl. 122 (1998), 24.04[C]

Mellon Stewart Constr., Inc. v. Metropolitan Water Reclamation Dist., 1995 U.S. Dist. LEXIS 5376 (N.D. Ill. 1995), 21.07

Mellon Stuart Construction, Inc. v. Metropolitan Water Reclamation District of Greater Chicago, 1995 WL 239371 (N.D. Ill. Apr. 21, 1995), 26.02[N][4]

Melwood Constr. Corp. v. State of New York, 481 N.Y.S.2d 289 (Ct. Cl. 1984), 32.04, 33.01[B]

Memorex Corp.—Recon., B-200722.2, Apr. 16, 1982, 82-1 CPD ¶ 249, 28.03[E][3][b]

Mendrop v. Shelter Mut. Ins. Co., No. 2:05CV15-P-B, 2007 U.S. Dist. LEXIS 86902, (N.D. Miss. Nov. 26, 2007), 18.04[C][1]

Merando, Inc., GSBCA No. 3300, 71-1 BCA ¶ 8892 (1971), 23.04[B][1]

Meredith Relocation Corp., GSBCA No. 9124, 90-2 B.C.A. (CCH) ¶ 22,677, 39.08[B]

Mergentine Corp. v. WMATA, No. Civ. 89-1055, 2006 WL 416177 (D.D.C. Feb. 22, 2006), 28.03[B][3][b]

Merrillville Conservancy District v. Atlas Excavating, Inc. 764 N.E.2d 718 (Ind. Ct. App. 2002), 32.08

Merritt v. Peninsula Constr. Co., 91 Md. 453, 46 A. 1013 (1900), 21.02

Merritt-Chapman & Scott Corp. v. United States, 192 Ct. Cl. 848, 429 F.2d 431 (1970), 24.02

Merritt-Chapman & Scott Corp. v. United States, 194 Ct. Cl. 461, 439 F.2d 185 (1971), 24.02[D]

M.E.S., Inc., PSBCA No. 4462, 06-1 BCA ¶ 33,184 (Nov. 1, 2006), 28.03[B][1]

Messer Griesheim Indus. v. Cryotech of Kingsport, Inc., 131 S.W.3d 457 (Tenn. Ct. App. 2003), 17.01[A]

Messina & Briante, Inc. v. Blitman Construction Corp., 223 N.Y.S.2d 533 (Sup.Ct. 1961), aff'd, 19 A.D.2d 862 (1963), appeal dismissed, 198 N.E.2d 602 (N.Y. 1964), 33.02[M][5]

Mestek, Inc. v. United Pac. Ins. Co., 667 N.E.2d 292 (Mass. App. Ct.), review denied, 671 N.E.2d 952 (Mass. 1996), 35.08[A]

Metal Mfg., Inc., United States ex rel., v. Federal Ins. Co., 656 F. Supp. 1194 (D. Ariz. 1987), 35.05[A]

Metal Prods. Workers Union v. Torrington, 242 F. Supp. 813 (D. Conn.), aff'd, 358 F.2d 103 (2d Cir. 1965), 46.26

Metcalf & Eddy, Inc., United States v., No. 1:99CV12566 (D. Mass. Dec. 14, 1999), 42.02[F][1]

Methanex v. United States, 43.06[A]

Metric Constr. Co. v. United States, 1 Cl. Ct. 383 (1983), 39.04[A]

Metric Constr. Co. v. United States, 14 Cl. Ct. 177 (1988), 39.03[B][2]

Metric Constr. Co. v. United States, 80 Fed. Cl. 178 (2008), 24.02[C]

Metro Builders, ASBCA No. 30626, 86-2 B.C.A. (CCH) ¶ 18,782 (1986), 27.05[A][2]

Metropolitan Cas. Inc. Co. v. N.Y. v. Natural Rock Asphalt Corp., 6 N.E.2d 739 (Ind. Ct. App. 1937), 35.04[B]

Metropolitan Life Ins. Co. v. Olsen, 123 A. 576 (N.H. 1923), 16.02[B]

Metropolitan Paving Co. v. United States, 325 F.2d 241 (Ct. Cl. 1963), 23.03[H]

Metro. Sewerage Comm'n v. R.W. Constr., Inc., 241 N.W.2d 371 (Wis. 1976), 22.08

Metropolitan Steel Indus. v. Fidelity & Deposit Co., 414 N.Y.S.2d 588 (App. Div. 1979), 35.08[F][3]

Meyer Labs., Inc., ASBCA No. 19525, 87-2 B.C.A. ¶ 19,810 (1987), 28.03[F][1]

MGM Constr. v. Education Facilities Auth., 220 N.J. Super. 483, 532 A.2d 764 (Law Div. 1987), 34.04[F][5]

Miami Heart Inst., Inc. v. Heery Architects and Eng'rs, Inc., 765 F. Supp. 1083 (S.D. Fla. 1991), aff'd, 44 F.3d 1007 (11th Cir. 1994), 31.03

Mich. Joint Sealing, Inc., ASBCA No. 41477, 93-3 B.C.A. ¶ 26,011 (1993), aff'd, 22 F.3d 1104 (Fed. Cir. 1994), 28.03[B][2], 28.04[D][4]

Mich. Laborer's Health Care Fund, Trustees for, v. Warranty Builders, Inc., 921 F. Supp. 471 (E.D. Mich. 1996), 35.04[B]

Micro-King Co., United States ex rel., v. Community Science Tech., 574 F.2d 1292 (5th Cir. 1978), 33.02[C]

Mid-America Fed. Sav. & Loan v. Shearson/American Express, Inc., 962 F.2d 1470 (10th Cir. 1992), 33.01[I]

Mid-Am. Painters, Inc., ENGBCA No. 5703, 91-1 B.C.A. ¶ 23,367 (1990), 28.03[B][3][a]

Mid-Atlantic Sec. Servs., Inc., ENGBCA No. 6302, 97-2 B.C.A. ¶ 29,012 (1997), 28.04[C][2][a]

Mid-Continent Cas. Co. v. P&H Supply Co., 490 P.2d 1358 (Okla. 1971), 35.07[B][1]

Mid-Eastern Indus., Inc., ASBCA No. 53016, 01-2 B.C.A. ¶ 31,657 (2001), 28.02[B]

Midland Eng'g Co. v. John A. Hall Constr. Co., 398 F. Supp. 981 (N.D. Ind. 1975), 35.08[E][1]

Mid Seven Transp., United States ex rel., v. Blinderman Constr. Co., 735 F. Supp. 272 (N.D. Ill. 1990), 35.04[A]

Midsouth Land Co. v. A. E. Hughes, Jr., Inc., 434 So. 2d 239 (Ala. 1983), 27.05[E][4]

Mid-State Precast Systems Inc. v. Corbetta Constr. Co., Inc., 608 N.Y.S.2d 546 (App. Div.), leave to appeal dismissed, 645 N.E.2d 1220 (N.Y. 1994), 35.08[J]

Mid States Steel Products Co. v. University of Kentucky, 2006 WL 1195914 (Ky. Ct. App. May 5, 2006), 26.02[R][3]

Midwest Dredging Co. v. McAninch Corp., 424 N.W. 2d 216 (Iowa 1988), 28.03[E][1][b]

Midwest Properties, LLC v. GSA, GSBCA No. 15822, 03-2 B.C.A. ¶ 32,344 (Aug. 1, 2002), 28.03[D][1][a][ii]

Mike Bradford & Co. v. F. A. Chastain Constr., Inc., 387 F.d 942 (5th Cir. 1968), 35.06[A][1][b]

Milano Bros. v. Joseph Rugo, Inc., 233 N.E.2d 919 (Mass. 1968), 35.08[B]

Milau Assocs., Inc. v. North Ave. Dev. Corp., 368 N.E.2d 1247 (N.Y. 1977), 29.02[C][3]

Miley v. Johnson & Johnson Orthapedics, Inc., 668 N.E.2d 369 (Mass. App. Ct. 1996), 33.02[C]

Miller & Sons Co. v. Homeopathic Med. & Surgical Hosp. & Dispensary of Pittsburg, 243 Pa. 502, 90 A. 394 (1914), 21.02

Miller Elevator Co. v. United States, 30 Fed. Cl. 662 (1994), 21.04, 21.08, 28.03[E][3][a], 28.03[E][3][b]

Miller Farms Nursery, Inc. v. Nedegaard Constr. Co. Inc., 2003 WL 21500052 (9th Cir. 2003), 29.02[E]

Millers Mut. Ins. Co. of Tex., United States v., 942 F.2d 946 (5th Cir. 1991), 35.03[A]

Millgard Corp. v. McKee/Mays, 49 F.3d 1070 (5th Cir. 1995), 22.06, 22.08, 27.05[C][4]

Milltex Prop. v. Johnson, No. 565866, 2004 Conn. Super. LEXIS 653 (Conn. Super. Ct. Mar. 15, 2004), 16.02[B]

Milner Constr. Co., DOT CAB No. 2043, 91-3 B.C.A. ¶ 24,195 (2000), 28.03[D][3]

Milovich v. City of L.A., 42 Cal. App. 2d 364, 108 P.2d 960 (1941), 26.02[E][3]

Milo Werner Co., IBCA No.
1202-227-78, 82-1 B.C.A. ¶ 15,698
(1982), 28.03[B][3], 28.03[B][3][a],
28.03[D][2]

Mil-Pak Co., GSBCA No. 6222, 83-1
BCA ¶ 16,486 at 81,966 (1983),
23.03[D]

Milton J. Womack, Inc. v. House of
Representatives, 509 So. 2d 62 (La.
App. 1 Cir. 1987), 20.02

Milwaukee v. Illinois, 451 U.S. 304
(1981), 11.03[A][1][b]

Milwaukee Construction Co. v. Glens
Falls Insurance Co., 367 F.2d 964
(9th Cir. 1966), 36.04

Milwaukee, County of, v. Schmidt,
Garden & Erikson, 168 N.W.2d 559
(Wis. 1969), 29.04[J]

Minelli v. United States, 61 F.3d 920
(Fed. Cir. 1995), 28.04[D][4]

Ming C. Phua, PSBCA No. 4180,
00-1 B.C.A. ¶ 30,872 (2000),
28.03[D][2]

Minmar Builders, Inc., GSBCA No.
3430, 72-2 BCA ¶ 9599 (1972),
23.06[A]

Miracle Mile Shopping Ctr. v. National
Union Indem. Co., 299 F.2d 780 (7th
Cir. 1962), 34.04[F][2]

Miraglia, In re Estate of, _____ S.E.2d
_____, 2008 WL 565703 (Ga. App.
Ct. 2008), 33.01[B]

Miree Painting Co. v. Woodward
Constr. & Design, Inc., 627 So. 2d
389 (Ala. Civ. App. 1992), rev'd on
other grounds, 627 So. 2d 393 (Ala.
1993), 28.03[D][1][a][i]

Mishara Constr. Co. v. Transit-Mixed
Concrete Corp., 310 N.E.2d 363
(Mass. 1974), 28.03[E][4]

Mississippi Road Supply Co., United
States ex rel., v. H.R. Morgan, Inc.,
542 F.2d 262 (5th Cir. 1976),
35.04[A]

Mississippi Road Supply Co. v. Western
Cas. & Sur. Co., 150 So. 2d 847
(Miss. 1963), 35.04[B]

Mississippi Transportation Commission
v. Ronald Adams Contractor, Inc.,
753 So. 2d 1077 (Miss. 2000),
26.02[Y][3], 26.02[Y][4]

Mississippi Transportation Commission
v. SCI, Inc., 717 So. 2d 332 (Miss.
1998), 26.02[Y][3], 26.02[Y][4]

Missouri v. Jenkins, 491 U.S. 274
(1989), 33.02[B]

Mistry Prabhaudas Manji Eng. Pvt. Ltd.
v. Raytheon Eng'rs & Constructors,
213 F. Supp. 2d 20 (D. Mass. 2002),
31.05, 48.03[I]

Mitchell v. Flandro, 506 P.2d 455
(Idaho 1972), 33.01[F]

Mitchell Canneries v. United States, 111
Ct. Cl. 228, 77 F. Supp. 498 (1948),
27.05[D][4][b]

Mitchell Eng'g & Constr. Co., 89-2
B.C.A. (CCH) ¶ 21,753 (ENGBCA
1989), 32.03[A]

M.J. Lee Constr. Co. v. Oklahoma
Transp. Auth., 125 P.3d 1205 (Okla.
2005), 27.05[A][3]

M.M. Sundt Constr. Co., ASBCA No.
17475, 74-1 B.C.A. (CCH) ¶ 10,627
(1974), 27.05[C][2]

Mobil Chem. Co. v. Blount Bros. Corp.,
809 F.2d 1175 (5th Cir. 1987),
33.01[G]

Mobile Premix Concrete v. Santa Fe
Eng'rs, 515 F. Supp. 512 (D. Colo.
1981), 35.08[F][1]

Modern Sys. Tech. Corp., 24 Cl. Ct.
699 (1992), 28.04[C][2][a]

Mod-Form, United States ex rel., v.
Barton & Barton, 769
F. Supp. 235 (E.D. Mich. 1991),
35.06[A][1][b]

Mohawk Mountain Ski Are Inc. v.
American Home Assurance Co., 1994
WL 9986 (Conn. Super. Ct. Jan. 6,
1994), 20.04

Mojave Enters. v. United States, 3 Cl.
Ct. 353 (1983), 28.03[E][1][c]

Moline Consumers Co., State ex rel. v.
American Ins. Co., 557 N.E.2d 932
(Ill. App. Ct. 1990), 35.08[B],
35.08[F][1]

Molokai Chamber of Commerce v.
Kukui (Molokai), Inc., 891 F. Supp.
1389 (D. Haw. 1995), 11.02

Monahan Insulation Co., United States
ex. rel., v. Acme Missiles & Constr.
Corp., 221 F. Supp. 733 (W.D. Pa.
1963), 35.06[A][1][b]

Monessen S. Ry. Co. v. Morgan, 486
U.S. 330 (1988), 33.01[D]

Monmouth Lumber Co. v. Indemnity
Ins. Co., 122 A.2d 604 (N.J. 1956),
35.08[J]

Montgomery v. Southern Sur., 162 N.E. 31 (Ind. Ct. App. 1928), 35.04[B]

Montgomery Ross Fisher, Inc., ASBCA No. 16,843, 73-1 BCA ¶ 9799 (1972), 23.03[E][2]

Montgomery-Ross-Fisher, Inc., PSBCA Nos. 1033, 1096, 84-2 BCA ¶ 17,492 (1984), 23.06[B][4]

Montrose Chem. Corp. v. Admiral Ins. Co., 10 Cal. 4th 645 (1995), 18.04[C][2]

Moody, United States ex rel., v. American Ins. Co., 835 F.2d 745 (10th Cir. 1987), 35.05[A], 35.08[E][4]

Mooney's, Inc. v. South Dakota Dep't of Transp., 482 N.W.2d 43 (S.D. 1992), 27.04[A][1]

Moore v. Continental Cas. Co., 366 F. Supp. 954 (W.D. Okla. 1973), 35.08[E][1]

Moore v. First Bank of San Luis Obispo, 996 P.2d 706 (Cal. 2000), 33.02[M][1]

Moore Bros. Co. v. Brown & Root, Inc., 207 F.3d 717 (4th Cir. 2000), 25.02[C], 27.05[D][5][b]

Moore Bros. Constr. Co. v. Brown & Root, Inc., 962 F.Supp. 838 (E.D. Va. 1997), 35.08[E][1]

Moore Elec. Supply, Inc. v. Ward, 450 S.E.2d 96 (S.C. 1994), 35.03[B], 35.04[B]

Moorhead Constr. Co. v. City of Grand Forks, 508 F.2d 1008 (8th Cir. 1975), 24.02[B], 30.03[D][1]

Moransais v. Heathman, 744 So. 2d 973 (Fla. 1999), 29.02[C][5]

Mor-Ben Ins. Markets Corp., In re, 73 B.R. 644 (9th in 1987), 46.13

Moreno v. United States, 965 F. Supp. 521 (S.D.N.Y. 1997), 29.02[D][3]

Morgan Grenfell Ltd. v. Sutherland Borough Council, 8-CLD-09-01 (Q.B. 1990), 33.01[H]

Morganti Nat'l, Inc. v. U.S., 49 Fed. Cl. 110 (2001), 27.05[D][4][d], 27.05[G][3][c], 28.03[B][2], 28.03[F][2]

Morgen & Oswood Constr. Co. v. USF&G, 535 P.2d 170 (Mont. 1975), 35.06[B][3]

Morin Indus., Inc., ASBCA No. 33611, 87-2 B.C.A. (CCH) ¶ 19,586, 24.04[B]

Mork v. Eureka-Security Fire & Marine Insurance Co., 230 Minn. 382, 42 N.W.2d 33 (1950), 46.19

Morris, City of, v. Duininck Bros., 531 N.W.2d 208 (Minn. App. 1995), 46.09

Morris Constr., Inc., United States ex rel., v. Aetna Cas. Ins. Co., 908 F.2d 375 (8th Cir. 1990), 35.04[A]

Morrison-Kundson Co. v. Makahuena Corp., 690 P.2d 1310 (Haw. Ct. App. 1984), 33.02[M][6]

Morrison Knudsen Corp. v. Fireman's Fund Ins. Co., 175 F.3d 1221 (10th Cir. 1999), 28.02[C]

Morrison-Maierle, Inc. v. Selsco, 606 P.2d 1085 (Mont. 1980), 29.02[C][3]

Mortensen Christiansen Bros. v. State, 90 Wn. 2d 872, 586 P.2d 840 (1978), 26.02[VV][3], 26.02[VV][4]

Morton Elecs., Inc., ASBCA No. 14904, 72-1 B.C.A. ¶ 9185 (1971), 28.03[D][2]

Morton Mfg., Inc., ASBCA No. 30716, 89-1 B.C.A. ¶ 21,326 (1988), 28.03[F][1]

Moseley, United States ex rel., v. Mann, 197 F.2d 39 (10th Cir. 1952), 35.04[A]

Moses H. Cone Mem'l Hosp. v. Mercury Constr. Corp. 460 U.S. 1 (1983), 25.03[B], 46.04, 46.07

Moshonov v. Walsh, 996 P.2d 699 (Cal. 2000), 33.02[M][1]

Motorola Computer Sys., Inc., ASBCA No. 26794, 87-3 B.C.A. ¶ 20,032 (1987), 28.03[D][2]

Mound Bayou, City of, v. Roy Collins Constr. Co., 499 So.2d 1354 (Miss. 1986), 33.01[G]

Mounds View, City of, v. Walijarvi, 263 N.W. 2d 420 (Minn. 1978), 29.02[C][3]

Mountaineer Euclid, Inc. v. Western Cas. & Sur. Co., 250 N.E.2d 768 (Ohio Ct. App. 1969), 35.04[B]

M-Pax, Inc. v. Dependable Ins. Co., 335 S.E.2d 591 (Ga. Ct. App. 1985), 36.05

Mrozic Constr. v. Lovering Assoc., 461
  N.W.2d 49 (Minn. Ct. App. 1990),
  35.08[E][1]
Municipal Leasing Corp. v. United
  States, 1 Cl. Ct. 771 (1983),
  28.04[B][2]
Municipal Leasing Corp. v. United
  States, 7 Cl. Ct. 43 (1984),
  27.05[G][2][b], 28.04[C][1]
Murphy v. Campbell Inv. Co., 486 P.2d
  1080 (Wash. 1971), 35.08[G]
Murphy Oil USA, Inc., U.S. v., 155 F.
  Supp. 2d 1117 (W.D. Wis. 2001),
  11.03[A][2]
Murphy, United States v., 937 F.2d
  1032 (6th Cir. 1991), 38.02[C][2]
Murray v. Shatterproof Glass Co., 758
  F.2d 266 (8th Cir. 1985), 29.04[F][3]
Muskegon, County of, United States v.,
  33 F. Supp. 2d 614 (W.D. Mich.
  1998), 28.01
Mustang Pipeline Co., Inc. v. Driver
  Pipeline Co., Inc., 134 S.W.3d 195
  (Tex. 2004), 28.03[B][4]
M/V Bremen v. Zapata Off-Shore Co.,
  407 U.S. 1, 15, 32 L. Ed. 2d 513, 92
  S. Ct. 1907 (1972), 25.02[A]
M.V.I. Precision Mach, Ltd., ASBCA
  No. 37393, 91-2 B.C.A. ¶ 23,898
  (1991), 28.03[B][3], 28.03[B][3][a],
  28.03[D][2]
MW Builders v. VT Props., 435 S.E.2d
  145 (Va. 1993), 35.08[F][3]
Myers v. Alta Constr. Co., 235 P.2d 1
  (Cal. 1951), 35.04[B]
Myint v. Allstate Ins. Co., 970 S.W.2d
  920 (Tenn. 1998), 33.01[E]
Mystic Color Lab, Inc. v. Auctions
  Worldwide, LLC, 934 A.2d 227
  (Conn. 2007), 27.05[A][3]

N

Naberhaus-Burke, Inc., United States *ex
  rel.*, v. Butt & Head, Inc., 535 F.
  Supp. 1155 (S.D. Ohio 1982),
  35.03[A], 35.04[A]
Nachtsheim Beech Aircraft Corp., 847
  F.2d 1261 (7th Cir. 1988),
  29.04[F][1], 29.04[F][2]
Nagy Enters., ASBCA Nos. 48815 et
  al., 98-1 B.C.A. ¶ 29,695 (1998),
  28.03[F][2]

Narragansett Impl. Co. v. United States
  ex rel. Mello, 290 F.2d 577 (1st Cir.
  1961), 35.08[B]
NAS Sur. Group v. Precision Wood
  Products, Inc., 271
  F. Supp. 2d 776 (N.D. N.C. 2003),
  19.07[B]
Nat Harrison Assocs., Inc. v. Gulf States
  Util. Co., 491 F.2d 578 (5th Cir.
  1974), 24.04[E]
National Elec. Ass'n, United States v.,
  1956 Trade Cas. (CCH) ¶ 68,534,
  17.08[A]
National Glass, Inc. v. J. C. Penney
  Props., Inc., 336 Md. 606, 650 A.2d
  246 (1994), 25.03[A]
National Housing P'ship v. Municipal
  Capital Appreciation Partners I, L.P.,
  935 A.2d 300 (D.C. Cir. 2007),
  27.05[A][3]
Nat'l Med. Staffing, Inc., ASBCA No.
  40391, 92-2 B.C.A. ¶ 24,837 (1992),
  28.04[D][4]
National Resources Defense Council v.
  Costle, 568 F.2d 1369 (D.C. Cir.
  1977), 11.03[A][1][b]
National Shawmut Bank v. Amsterdam
  Cas. Co., 411 F.2d 843 (1st Cir.
  1969), 36.08, 36.09[F]
National Shawmut Bank v. New
  Amsterdam Cas. Co., 411 F.2d 843
  (1st Cir. 1969), 36.02[C]
National Society for Professional
  Engineers v. United States, 432 U.S.
  679 (1978), 8.02
Nat'l State Bank v. Am. Home Ins.,
  492 F. Supp. 393 (S.D.N.Y. 1980),
  20.04
National State Bank of Newark v.
  Terminal Constr. Co., 217 F. Supp.
  341 (D.N.J. 1963), *aff'd per curiam*,
  328 F.2d 315 (3d Cir. 1964),
  35.04[A]
National Sur. Co. v. United States, 228
  F. 577 (6th Cir. 1916), *rev'd on other
  grounds*, 246 U.S. 257, 38 S. Ct. 250,
  62 L. Ed. 703 (1918), 35.07[A][1]
National Surety Corp. v. Titan
  Construction Corp., 26 N.Y.S.2d 227
  (Sup. Ct. 1940), 36.04
National Union Fire Ins. Co. v.
  Structural Sys. Technology, Inc., 756
  F. Supp. 1232 (E.D. Mo. 1991),
  18.05[A][2]

National Union Fire Insurance Company v. David. A. Bramble, Inc., 879 A.2d 101 (Md. 2005), 15.15

Nat'l Union Fire Ins. Co. v. Terra Indus., Inc., 216 F. Supp 2d 899 (N.D. Iowa 2002), 18.04[C][2]

Nations Enter., Inc. v. Process Equip. Co., 579 P.2d 655 (Colo. Ct. App. 1978), 16.04[B]

Nationwide Roofing & Sheet Metal Co. v. United States, 14 Cl. Ct. 733 (1988), 28.04[A][1]

Natural Resources Defense Council v. Kempthorne, 506 F. Supp. 2d 322 (E.D. Cal. 2007), 11.03[A][10]

Natural Resources Defense Council et al v. EPA et al. (C.D. Cal. 2006, Case No. CV-04-8307 GHK), 11.03[A][1][a][i]

Natural Resources Defense Council, Inc. v. U.S. E.P.A., 966 F.2d 1292 (9th Cir. 1992), 11.03[A][1][d]

Natus Corp. v. United States, 371 F.2d 450 (Ct. Cl. 1967), 28.03[E][1][b], 28.03[E][4]

Naylor Pipe Co. v. Murray Walter, Inc., 421 A. 2d 1012 (N.H. 1980), 35.08[D][1]

Neal & Co., Inc. v. United States, 36 Fed. Cl. 600 (1996), aff'd, 121 F.3d 683 (Fed. Cir. 1997), 23.03[E][3]

Neal & Co., Inc. v. United States, 945 F.2d 385 (Fed. Cir. 1991), 39.03[B][1][a]

Neal & Son, Inc. v. United States, 36 Fed. Cl. 600 (1996), aff'd, 121 F.3d 683 (Fed. Cir. 1997), 23.03[E][3]

Ne. Constr. Co. v. Romney, 485 F.2d 752 (D.C. Cir. 1973), 7.03[C]

Ne. Eng'g Inc., ASBCA No. 6504, 61-2 B.C.A. ¶ 3108 (1961), 28.03[B][3][a]

Nebraska Pub. Power Dist. v. Austin Power, Inc., 773 F.2d 960 (8th Cir. 1985), 33.01[C]

Nebraska State Bar Ass'n v. Addison 412 N.W.2d 855 (Neb. 1987), 45.05[A]

Nello L. Teer, ENGBCA No. 4376, 86-3 BCA ¶ 19,326 (1983), 23.06[D]

Nelse Mortensen & Co. v. Group Health Cooperative of Puget Sound, 90 Wn. 2d 843, 586 P.2d 469 (1978), 26.02[VV][3]

Nelson v. Glascoe, 231 N.W.2d 766 (N.D. 1975), 16.04[E]

Nelson v. Hagen, 146 N.W.2d 873 (N.D. 1966), 35.04[B]

NE Plate Glass Corp. v. Murray Walter, Inc., 537 N.Y.S.2d 657 (App. Div. 1989), 28.03[E][1][b]

Nesbitt v. United States, 345 F.2d 583 (Ct. Cl. 1965), cert. denied, 383 U.S. 926 (1966), 28.03[D][1][b]

Net Constr., Inc. v. C&C Rehab. & Constr., Inc., 256 F. Supp. 350 (E.D. Pa. 2003), 30.03[D][4]

New Amsterdam Cas. Co. v. Allen Co., 446 S.W.2d 278 (Ky. 1969), 35.08[E][1]

New Amsterdam Cas. Co. v. Mitchell, 325 F.2d 474 (5th Cir. 1963), 30.02[B]

Newark Laborers' Pension-Welfare Funds v. Commercial Union Inc. Co. of N.Y., 312 A.2d 649 (N.J. Super. Ct. App. Div. 1973), 35.04[B]

Newberry Square Development Corp. v. Southern Landmark, Inc., 578 So. 2d 750 (Fla. Dist. Ct. 1991), cause dismissed, 584 So. 2d 999 (1991), 26.02[J][4]

Newbery Alaska, Inc., 225 Ct. Cl. 608 (1980), 21.06

New Era Constr. v. United States, 890 F.2d 1152 (Fed. Cir. 1989), 39.08[F]

Newhall Land & Farming Co. v. McCarthy Constr., 106 Cal. Rptr.2d 10 (Cal. Ct. App. 2d Dist. Div. 2, 2001), 29.04[E]

Newport, City of, v. Fact Concerts, Inc., 453 U.S. 247 (1981), 38.02[C]

Newport Trust Co. v. Susi, 134 A.2d 543 (Me. 1957), 35.04[B]

New Regency Productions, Inc. v. Nippon Herald Films, Inc., 501 F.3d 1101 (9th Cir. 2007), 43.07[E], 46.20

New Viasys Holdings, LLC v. Hanover Ins. Co., 2007 WL 783179 (E.D. Va. 2007), 34.04[C]

New York Cas. Co., United States ex rel., v. Standard Sur. & Cas. Co., 32 F. Supp. 836 (S.D.N.Y. 1940), 35.04[A]

New York Ship Bldg. Co., ASBCA No. 16164, 72-1 B.C.A. (CCH) ¶ 11,979 (1971), 30.03[E]

New York State Chapter, Inc. v. New York State Thruway Auth., 666 N.E.2d 185 (N.Y. 1996), 7.03

New York State Elec. & Gas Corp. v. Westinghouse Elec. Corp., 564 A.2d 919 (Pa. Super. Ct. 1989), 7.02[B][2][c]

Nexus Constr. Co., ASBCA No. 31070, 91-3 B.C.A. ¶ 24,203, aff'd, 92-1 B.C.A. ¶ 24,577 (1991), 28.03[D][2], 28.03[E][2]

Nichols v. R.R. Beaufort & Assocs., Inc., 727 A.2d 174 (R.I. 1999), 29.02[B][3]

Nichols, State ex rel., v. Safeco Ins. Co. of Am., 671 P.2d 1151 (N.M. Ct. App. 1983), 35.04[B]

Nickell v. United States ex rel. D.W. Falls, Inc., 355 F.2d 73 (10th Cir. 1966), 35.04[A]

Nick v. Morgan's Foods, Inc., 270 F.3d 590, 45.05[A]

Nicon, Inc. v. United States, 51 Fed. Cl. 324 (2001), 28.02[D]

Nicon, Inc. v. United States, 331 F.3d 878 (Fed. Cir. 2003), 24.02[D], 24.04[C], 28.02[D]

Nielson's Inc., 82-2 B.C.A. (CCH) ¶ 16,034 (1982), 24.02[D]

Nikiforos P. Kalfountzos v. Hartford Fire Insurance Company, 44 Cal. Rptr. 2d 714 (Ct. App. 1995), 35.08[A]

95 Lorimer LLC v. Insurance Co. of the State of Pennsylvania, 6 Misc. 3d 500 (N.Y. Sup. Ct. 2004), 34.04[G][6]

Nisei Constr. Co., ASBCA No. 51464 et al., 99-2 B.C.A. ¶ 30,448 (1999), 28.03[D][1][a][i], 28.03[D][2], 28.04[D][4]

Nissho-Iwai Co. v. Occidental Crude Sales, 729 F.2d 1530 (5th Cir. 1984), 27.05[D][2]

Nitro Distrib., Inc. v. Dunn, 194 S.W.3d 339 (Mo. 2006), 27.03[B][2]

N. Maltese & Sons, Inc., United States use of, v. Juno Constr. Corp., 759 F.2d 253 (2d Cir. 1985) (election of remedies), 30.04[B][1]

Nohcra Commc'ns, Inc. v. AM Commc'ns, Inc., 909 F.2d 1007 (7th Cir. 1990), 30.04[B][2]

Nohe v. Robyn Dev. Corp., 686 A.2d 382 (N.J. Super. Ct. App. Div. 1997), 16.09[B]

Nolan Bros., Inc. v. United States, 194 Ct. Cl. 1, 437 F.2d 1371 (1971), 24.04[A]

Noland Co. v. Allied Contractors, Inc., 273 P.2d 917 (4th Cir. 1959), 35.05[A]

Noland Co. v. West End Realty Corp., 147 S.E.2d 105 (Va. 1966), 35.08[A], 35.08[D][1], 35.08[J]

Norair Eng'g Corp. v. United States, 666 F.2d 546 (Ct. Cl. 1981), 21.02, 21.04, 27.05[D][7]

Norair Eng'g Corp. v. United States, 666 F.2d 546, 229 Ct. Cl. 160 (Ct. Cl. 1981), 30.03[C][6]

Norquip Rental Corp. v. Sky Steel Erectors, Inc., 854 P.2d 1185 (Ariz. Ct. App. 1993), 35.04[B]

N. Chicago Disposal Co., ASBCA No. 25535, 82-1 B.C.A. ¶ 15,488 (1981), 28.02[B]

Northeast Clackamas County Electric Co-operative v. Continental Casualty Co., 221 F.2d 329 (9th Cir. 1955), 26.02[LL][3]

Northern Clearing, Inc. v. Larson-Juhl, Inc., 2004 WL 2093311 (Wis. Ct. App. Sept. 21, 2004), 26.02[XX][3]

Northern Helex Co. v. United States, 197 Ct. Cl. 118, 455 F.2d 546 (1972), 27.05[G][3][c]

No. Ill. Gas. Co. v. Energy Co-op, Inc., 461 N.E.2d 1049 (Ill. App. Ct. 1984), 32.08

Northern Petrochemical Co. v. Thorsen & Thorshov, Inc., 211 N.W.2d 159 (Minn. 1983), 29.04[E]

North Harris County Jr. College Dist. v. Fleetwood Constr. Co., 604 S.W.2d 247 (Tex. Civ. App. 1980), 35.08[E][1]

North Miami v. Berger, 828 F. Supp. 401 (E.D. Va. 1993), 11.03[A][4][a]

Northrop Carolina, Inc., ASBCA No. 16052, 74-1 B.C.A. ¶ 10449 (1973), 28.03[D][2]

Northrop Grumman Corp. v. United States, 46 Fed. Cl. 622 (2000), 27.05[G][2][b], 28.04[B][2], 30.04[A]

North Star Alaska Hous. Corp. v. United States, 76 Fed. Cl. 158 (2007), 24.04, 23.03[E][3]

Northwestern Nat'l Ins. Co. v. Alberts, 741 F. Supp. 424 (S.D.N.Y. 1990), 36.02[B]

Northwestern Nat'l Ins. Co. v. Alberts, 937 F.2d 77 (2d Cir. 1991), 36.04

Northwest Mech., Inc. v. Public Util. Comm'n of City of Va., 283 N.W.2d 522 (Minn. 1979), 46.04

Norwood Co. v. RLI Ins. Co., 2002 WL 485694 (E.D. Pa. 2002), 34.04[D]

Norwood Mfg., Inc. v. United States, 21 Cl. Ct. 300 (1990), aff'd, 930 F.2d 38 (Fed. Cir. 1991), 28.04[A][1]

Nova Enters., United States ex rel., v. Reliance Ins. Co., 977 F.2d 575, 1992 WL 296346 (4th Cir. 1992), 35.08[F][1]

Novelty Prods. Co., ASBCA No. 21077, 78-1 B.C.A. ¶ 12,989 (1978), 28.03[D][2]

NTC Group, Inc., The, ASBCA Nos. 53720 et al., 04-2 BCA ¶ 32,706 (2004), 23.03[E][2]

N-Y Associates, Inc. v. Bd. of Comm'r of the Orleans Parish Levee Dist., 926 So. 2d 20 (La. App. 4th Cir. 2006), 28.04[A][1]

O

O & M Constr. v. Louisiana Div. of Admin., 576 So. 2d 1030 (La. Ct. App. 1991), 30.02[A]

Oak Crest Constr. Co. v. Austin Mut. Ins. Co., 329 Or. 620, 998 P.2d 1154 (2000), 18.04[C][1], 19.07[B]

Oakdale Park Ltd. v. Byrd, 346 So.2d 648 (Fla. 1977), 33.02[M][2]

Oak Environmental Consultants, Inc. v. United States, 77 Fed. Cl. 688 (Fed. Cl. 2007), 30.03[C][3], 39.03[A]

Oates v. JAG, Inc., 333 S.E.2d 222 (N.C. 1985), 12.04[C][1][d][i]

Oberer Constr. Co. v. Park Plaza, Inc., 179 N.E.2d 168 (Ohio 1961), 21.08

Obray v. Mitchell, 567 P.2d 1284 (Idaho 1977), 33.01[F]

O'Brien, United States v., 220 U.S. 321 (1911), 28.03[B][3][a]

Obrisco Elecs., Inc., ASBCA No. 18533, 76-2 B.C.A. ¶ 12,049, aff'd on reconsideration, 76-2 B.C.A. ¶ 12186 (1976), 28.03[D][2]

OBS Co. v. Pace Constr. Co., 558 So. 2d 404 (Fla. 1990), 35.08[E][1]

Ocean Ridge Dev. Corp. v. Quality Plastering, Inc., 247 So. 2d 72 (Fla. Dist. Ct. App. 1971), 28.03[D][3]

Ocean Salvage, Inc., ENGBCA Nos. 3485 et al., 76-1 B.C.A. ¶ 11,905 (1976), 28.03[E][4]

O'Dell v. Custom Builders Corp., 560 S.W.2d 862 (Mo. 1978), 27.04[A][1]

Oden Constr. Co. v. Helton, 65 So. 2d 442 (Miss. 1953), 28.04[D][4]

OFEGRO, HUDBCA No. 88-3410-C7, 91-3 B.C.A. ¶ 24,206 (1991), 28.03[D][2]

Ogden Foods, Inc. v. State Farm Prods. Show Comm'n, 315 A.2d 329 (Pa. Commw. Ct. 1974), 7.03[E]

Okatie Hotel Group v. Amerisure Ins. Co., 2006 WL 91577 (D.S.C. Jan. 13, 2006), 19.07[B]

Olam v. Congress Mortgage, 68 F. Supp. 1110 (N.D. Cal. 1999), 45.05[A]

Old Dominion Elec. Coop. v. Ragnar Benson, Inc., Civil Action No. 3:05CV34, 2006 U.S. Dist. LEXIS 56145 (E.D. Va., Aug. 6, 2006), 23.04[B][1]

Olin Jones Sand Co. v. United States (1980), 225 Ct. Cl. 741, 30.04[B][2]

Olivera v. Modiano/Schneider, Inc., 23 Cal. Rptr. 30 (Cal. Ct. App. 1962), 33.02[M][1]

Olmsted Elec. Inc., United States ex rel., v. Neosho Constr. Co., 599 F.2d 930 (10th Cir. 1979), 35.05[A]

Olsberg Excavating Corp., DOTCAB No. 1288, 84-1 BCA ¶ 16,931 at 84,236 (1983), 23.03[E][1]

Olsen v. Moore, 202 N.W.2d 236 (Wis. 1972), 20.04

Olsen Plumbing & Heating Co. v. United States, 602 F.2d 950 (Ct. Cl. 1979), 28.03[F][2]

Olson Plumbing & Heating Co., ASBCA Nos. 17965 et al., 75-1 B.C.A. ¶ 11,203 (1975), aff'd, 602 F.2d 950 (Ct. Cl. 1979), 28.03[D][2]

Olson, United States *ex rel.*, v. W.H. Cates Constr. Co., 972 F.2d 987 (8th Cir. 1992), 35.04[A]

Olympic Prods. Co. v. Roof Sys., Inc., 363 S.E.2d 367 (N.C. Ct. App.), *cert denied,* 366 S.E.2d 862 (N.C. 1988), 12.04[C][1][d][i]

Olympus Corp. v. U.S., 98 F.3d 1314 (Fed. Cir. 1996), 27.05[C][3][a]

Omni Dev. Corp., AGBCA No. 97-203-1 et al., 01-2 B.C.A. ¶ 31,487 (2001), 28.03[B][2], 28.03[B][3][a]

Omni Development Corp., AGBCA No. 97-203-1, 05-2 BCA ¶ 32,982 (May 25, 2005), 28.03[B][3][a]

120 Greenwich Dev. Assoc., LLC v. Reliance Co., 2004 WL 1277998 (S.D.N.Y. June 8, 2004), 34.04[C]

1199 Housing Corp. v. International Fid. Ins. Co., 788 N.Y.S.2d 88 (N.Y.A.D. 2005), 34.04[C]

Oni Constr., Inc., ASBCA No. 45394, 93-3 B.C.A. (CCH) ¶ 26,063, 39.03[B][3]

Operational Services Corp., ASBCA Nos. 27059 et al., 93-3 B.C.A. ¶ 26,190 (1993), 28.04[C][1]

Orbas & Assocs. v. United States, 34 Fed. Cl. 68 (1995), 39.04[C]

Ore-Ida Potato Prods. v. United Pac. Ins. Co., 392 P.2d 191 (Idaho 1964), 35.08[I]

Oriental Commercial & Shipping Co. v. Rosseel, N.V., 609 F. Supp. 75 (S.D.N.Y. 1985), 46.06

Orlosky, Inc. v. United States, 68 Fed. Cl. 296 (2005), 24.04[B], 24.04[C]

O'Rourke v. New Amsterdam Cas. Co., 362 P.2d 790 (N.M. 1961), 19.07[B]

Ortec Sys., Inc., ASBCA No. 43467, 92-2 B.C.A. ¶ 24,859 (1992), 28.03[B][3][a]

O'Shaughnessy v. Smuckler Corp., 543 N.W. 2d 99 (Minn. Ct. App. 1996), 19.07[B]

Otis Elevator Co. v. George A. Fuller Co., 569 N.Y.S.2d 118 (App. Div. 1991), 35.08[E][1]

Otis Elevator Co., United States *ex rel.*, v. Piracci Constr. Co., 405 F. Supp. 908 (D.D.C. 1975), 35.04[A]

Overhead Elec. Co., ASBCA No. 25656, 85-2 B.C.A. ¶ 18,026 (1985), 28.03[D][2]

Overton v. Consolidated Ins. Co., 145 Wash.2d 417, 38 P.3d 322 (Wash. 2002), 19.07[B]

Owen v. Dodd, 431 F. Supp. 1239 (N.D. Miss. 1977), 29.02[C][5]

Owen Constr. Co. v. Iowa State Dep't fo Transp., 274 N.W.2d 304 (Iowa 1979), 26.02[P][3], 26.02[P][4]

Owens-Corning Fiberglass Corp., United States *ex rel.*, v. Brandt Constr. Co., 826 F.2d 643 (7th Cir. 1987), *cert. denied,* 484 U.S. 1026 (1988), 35.06[A][2]

Owsley v. Henderson, 45 S.E.2d 263 (N.C. 1947), 35.04[B]

P

Paccon, Inc. v. United States, 185 Ct. Cl. 24, 339 F.2d 162 (1968), 24.02[D]

Paccon, Inc., ASBCA No. 7890, 1963 B.C.A. (CCH) ¶ 3659 (1963), 24.04[B]

Paccon, Inc., ASBCA No. 7890, 65-2 B.C.A. (CCH) ¶ 4996 (1963), 24.04[C]

Pacific Architects & Eng'rs, Inc. v. United States, 491 F.2d 734, 203 Ct. Cl. 499 (1974), 39.03[C][2]

Pacific Architects Collaborative v. State, 166 Cal. Rptr. 184 (Cal. Ct. App. 1979), 7.03[E]

Pac. Gas and Elec. Co., *In re,* No. C 02-3464 SI, 2004 U.S. Dist. LEXIS 22023 (N.D. Cal. Sept. 30, 2004), 16.02[B]

Pacific Lining Co. v. Algernon-Blair Constr. Co., 812 F.2d 237 (5th Cir. 1987), 35.08[E][1]

Pacific Marine Dredging & Construction, *In re,* 79 B.R. 924 (Bankr. D. Or. 1987), 36.08

Pacocha, *In re,* 9 B.R. 531, 1980 Bankr. LEXIS 4178 (Bankr. W.D. Wis. 1980), 25.04[A]

Page v. Structural Wood Components, 102 S.W.3d 720 (Tex. 2003), 28.02[C]

Paine v. Spottiswoode, 612 A.2d 235 (Me. 1992), 29.02[B][3]

Painters Local Union No. 171 v.
Williams & Kelly, Inc., 605 F.2d 535
(10th Cir. 1979), 35.08[A]
PAJ, Inc. v. Hanover Ins. Co., 243
S.W.3d 630 (Tex. 2008), 18.04[A]
Palco Linings, Inc. v. Pavex, Inc., 755
F. Supp. 1269 (M.D. Pa. 1990),
7.02[B][2][c]
Palmer Asphalt Co., United States *ex
rel.*, v. Debardelaben, 278 F. Supp.
722 (D.S.C.), *aff'd,* 388 F.2d 309 (4th
Cir. 1967), 35.06[A][1][b]
Palmer Constr. Co. v. Wichita Bank
Instrument Co., 7 Kan. App. 363, 642
P.2d 127 (1982), 46.04
Palmer Supply Co., State *ex rel.*, v.
Walsh & Co., 575 P.2d 1213 (Alaska
1978), 35.08[D][2]
Pangori & Sons, Inc., *In re,* 53 B.R.
711 (Bankr. E.D. Mich. 1985), 36.08
Paradise Homes, Inc. v. Central Sur. &
Ins. Corp., 437 P.2d 78 (Nev. 1968),
33.01[E]
Paragon Energy Corp. v. United States,
227 Ct. Cl. 176 (1981), *aff'd,* 230 Ct.
Cl. 884 (1982), 39.06[C]
Paragon Energy Corp. v. United States,
229 Ct. Cl. 524 (1981), 21.08,
27.05[B][4]
Paragon Energy Corp. v. United States,
645 F.2d 971, 39.03[B]
Paragon Energy Corp. v. United States,
945 F.2d 966, 229 Ct. Cl. 524
(1981), 227 Ct. Cl. 176 (1981),
39.02[C]
Paragon General Contractors, Inc. v.
Larco Constr., Inc., 227 S.W.3d
876 (Tex. App. [Dallas] 2007),
27.06
Paranzino v. Barnett Bank of S. Florida,
690 So. 2d 725 (Fla. Dist. Ct. App.
4th Dist.), 45.05[A]
Parker Excavating, Inc., *In re,* 06-1
BCA p 33217, ASBCA No. 54637
(February 28, 2006), 27.05[C][2],
27.05[C][4]
Park Shore Dev. Co. v. Higley Smith,
Inc., 556 So. 2d 439 (Fla. App.
1990), 33.02[N]
Parsons v. Henry, 672 P.2d 717 (Or.
1983), 33.01[F]
Parsons Constr. Co., *In re* Appeal of,
180 Neb. 839, 146 N.W.2d 211
(1966), 26.02[BB][3]

Partridge v. Presley, 189 F.2d 645 (D.C.
Cir.), *cert. denied,* 342 U.S. 850
(1951), 28.03[E][4]
Pastorelli v. Associated Eng'r Inc., 176
F. Supp. 159 (D.R.I. 1959),
29.02[C][1]
Pathman Constr. Co., ASBCA No.
14285, 71-1 B.C.A. (CCH) ¶ 8905
(1971), 24.04[E]
Pathman Constr. Co., ASBCA No.
23,392, 85-2 BCA ¶ 18,096 (1985),
23.07[B][6]
Pathman Constr. Co. v. Hi-Way Elec.
Co., 65 Ill. App. 3d 480, 383 N.W.2d
453 (1978), 24.03
Pathman Constr. Co. v. United States,
817 F.2d 1573 (Fed. Cir. 1987), 39.07
Patten & Davies Lumber Co. v.
McConville, 25 P.2d 429 (Cal. 1933),
35.08[I]
Paul E. Lehman, Inc. v. United States,
673 F.2d 352 (Ct. Cl. 1982), 39.04[A]
Paul Hardeman, Inc. v. United States,
186 Ct. Cl. 743, 406 F.2d 1357
(1969), 24.02[A]
Pavarini Construction Co. v. Continental
Ins. Co., 304 A.D. 2d 501 (App.
Div.-1st Dept. 2003), 19.07[B]
PCC Constr. Components, United States
ex rel., v. Harvey Harris Contractors,
120 F.3d 264 (4th Cir. 1997),
35.08[C]
PCL Constr. Servs. v. United States, 47
Fed. Cl. 745 (2000), 29.02[B][1]
PCL Constr. Servs. v. United States, 53
Fed. Cl. 479 (2002), 23.07[B][6],
27.05[D][4][d]
PDM Plumbing & Heating, Inc. v.
Findlen, 13 Mass. App. Ct. 950
(1982), 30.03[C][3]
Peacock Constr. Co. v. Modern Air
Conditioning, 353 So. 2d 840 (Fla.
1977), 35.08[E][1]
Peacock Constr. Co. v. Turner Concrete,
159 S.E.2d 114 (Ga. Ct. App. 1967),
35.08[B]
Pearce v. E.F. Hutton Group, Inc., 828
F.2d 826 (D.C. Cir. 1987), 46.10
Pearlman v. Reliance Insurance Co.,
371 U.S. 132 (1962), 34.04[H],
36.01, 36.02[A], 36.03[B], 36.08
Pebble Bldg. Co. v. G.J. Hopkins, Inc.,
288 S.E.2d 437 (Va. 1982),
30.03[D][2]

Peerless Ins. Co. v. Board of County Comm'rs for Prince George's County *ex rel.* Ben Dyer Assoc., Inc., 237 A.2d 15 (Md. 1968), 35.04[B]

Peerless Ins. Co. v. Brennon, 564 A.2d 383 (Me. 1989), 19.07[B]

Peil Constr. Co. v. Commonwealth *ex rel.* Hendricks, 35 F.2d 265 (3d Cir. 1929), 35.08[I]

Pellerin Constr., Inc. v. Witco Corp., 169 F. Supp. 2d 568 (E.D. La. 2001), 26.02[S][1], 26.02[S][3], 26.02[S][4]

Pelletier v. Sordoni/Skanska Constr. Co., 38 Conn. L. Rptr. 404 (Conn. Super. Dec.16, 2004), 8A.08[A], 8A.08[E]

Pembee Mfg. Corp. v. Cape Fear Constr. Co., 329 S.E.2d 350 (N.C. 1985), 29.04[J]

Pembroke Steel Co., United States *ex rel.*, v. Phoenix Gen. Constr. Co., 462 F.2d 1098 (4th Cir. 1972), 35.08[F][1]

Penalosa Co-op v. Farmland Mut. Ins., 789 P.2d 1196 (Kan. Ct. App. 1990), 20.04

Pennex Aluminum Co. v. International Fid. Ins. Co., 818 F. Supp. 772 (M.D. Pa. 1993), 35.07[B][1]

Pennington, Estate of, v. Wolfe, 262 F. Supp. 2d 1254 (D. Kan. 2003), 18.05[B][2]

Penn-Olin Chem. Co., United States v., 378 U.S. 158, 84 S. Ct. 1710 (1964), 17.08, 17.08[A]

Penn-Olin Chem. Co., United States v., 378 U.S. 158, 84 S. Ct. 1710 (1964), *on remand,* 246 F. Supp. 917 (D. Del. 1965), *aff'd per curiam,* 389 U.S. 308, 88 S. Ct. 502 (1967), 17.03[D]

Pa. Dep't of Transp. v. Anjo Constr. Co., 587 A.2d 455 (Pa. 1985), 28.03[E][1][b]

Pa. Exch. Bank v. United States, 170 F. Supp. 629 (Ct. Cl. 1959), 28.03[B][3][a]

Pennsylvania Fire Ins. Co. v. American Airlines, 180 F. Supp. 239 (E.D.N.Y. 1960), 35.08[J]

Penole Indus., ASBCA No. 42025, 91-2 B.C.A. (CCH) ¶ 23,857, 39.07

Pensacola Constr. Co., United States *ex rel.*, v. St. Paul Fire & Marine Ins. Co., 710 F. Supp. 638 (W.D. La. 1989), 35.04[A]

People v. *See name of party or opposing party.*

Pepper Burns Insulation, Inc. v. Artco Corp., 970 F.2d 1340 (4th Cir. 1992), 35.05[A]

Pepper-Reed Co. v. McBro Planning & Dev. Co., 564 F. Supp. 569 (D.V.I. 1983), 8A.08[C]

Perini, Horn, Morrison-Knudsen, 87-1 BCA 19545, ENGBCA No. 4821 (February 5, 1987), 27.05[D][5][c]

Perkins v. Thompson, 551 So. 2d 204 (Miss. 1989), 33.02[N], 36.03[C]

Perosi Elec. Corp., United States *ex rel.*, v. Manshul Constr. Corp., 940 F. Supp. 492 (E.D. N.Y. 1996), 35.04[A], 35.08[B]

Perry v. Thomas, 482 U.S. 483 (1987), 46.04

Perry v. United States, 294 U.S. 330 (1935), 28.02

Pertun Construction Co., United States *ex rel.* v. Harvesters Group, Inc., 918 F.2d 915 (11th Cir. 1990), 26.02[J][3], 27.05[D][3], 35.04[A], 35.07[A][1], 35.08[E][3]

Peter Gross GmbH & Co. KG, ASBCA No. 49437, 96-2 B.C.A. ¶ 28,290 (1996), 28.03[G]

Peter Gross GmbH & Co. KG, ASBCA No. 49437, 96-2 B.C.A. ¶ 28,529 (1996), 28.03[G]

Peter Kiewit & Sons' Co. v. State Highway Comission, 184 Kan. 737, 339 P.2d 267 (1959), 26.02[Q][3]

Peter Kiewit & Sons' Co. v. United States, 151 F. Supp. 726 (Ct. Cl. 1957), 28.03[E][1][a]

Peter Kiewit Sons' Co. v. Iowa Southern Utilities Co., 355 F. Supp. 376 (S.D. Iowa 1973), 26.02[P][3], 26.02[P][4], 26.02[QQ][4]

Peter Kiewit Sons' Co. v. Summit Constr. Co., 422 F.2d 242 (8th Cir. 1969), 21.08, 27.06, 28.03[E][3][b]

Peter Kiewit Sons' Co. v. United States, 138 Ct. Cl. 668, 151 F. Supp. 726 (1957), 24.02[D]

Peter Salvucci & Sons, Inc. v. State, 110 N.H. 136, 268 A.2d 899 (1970), *aff'd*, 111 N.H. 259, 281 A.2d 164 (1971), 24.02[D], 24.04[A]

Peter Scalamandre & Sons, Inc. v. Village Dock, Inc., 187 A.D.2d 496, 589 N.Y.S.2d 191 (1992), 26.02[GG][3]

Petrossi Bros. Contracting Corp. v. Town of Greece, 29 N.Y.S.2d 305 (Sup. Ct. 1941), 36.06

Pettinaro Constr. Co. v. Harry C. Partridge, Jr. & Sons, Inc., 408 A.2d 957 (Del. Ch. 1979), 46.01

Pevar Co. v. United States, 32 Fed. Cl. 822 (1995), 39.04[D]

Phelps v. Lengyel, 237 F. Supp. 2d 829 (N.D. Ohio 2002), 29.02[E]

Philip Morris USA v. Williams, 549 U.S. 349, 127 S. Ct. 1057 (2007), 31.07[A]

Phillips Constr. Co. v. United States, 184 Ct. Cl. 249, 394 F.2d 834 (1968), 27.05[C][3][b]

Phoenix Contractors, Inc. v. Gen. Motors Corp., 135 Mich. App. 787, 355 N.W.2d 673 (1984), 26.02[W][3], 26.02[W][4]

Phoenix Indem. Co. v. Board of Pub. Instruction of Alachua County, 114 So. 2d 478 (Fla. Dist. Ct. App. 1959), 35.04[B]

PHT Supply Corp. v. U.S. 71 Fed. Cl. 1 (2006), 27.03[B][2], 27.05[G][2][b]

Picciandra, United States v., 788 F.2d 36 (1st Cir. 1986), 42.02[B][6]

Piccirillo v. Beltrone-Turner, 284 A.D.2d 854 (N.Y. App. Div. 2001), 8A.08[A][1]

Pickens v. Kanawha River Towing, 916 F. Supp. 702 (S.D. Ohio 1996), 38.02[C][4]

Pi-Con, Inc. v. A.J. Anderson Constr. Co., 458 N.W.2d 639 (Mich. 1990), 35.05[B]

Pierce v. J.W. Charles-Bush Secs., Inc., 603 So.2d 625 (Fla. Dist. Ct. App. 1992), 33.02[M][2]

Pierce v. Underwood, 487 U.S. 552 (1988), 33.02[E]

Pierce Assoc., Inc. v. Nemours Found., 865 F.2d 530 (3d Cir. 1988), *cert. denied*, 492 U.S. 907 (1989), 32.03[A], 32.04

Pierce Contractors, Inc. v. Peerless Cas. Co., 81 So. 2d 747 (Fla. 1955), 35.06[A][2]

Pike v. Howell Building Supply Co., Inc., 748 So. 2d 710 (Miss. 1999), 29.02[B][4]

Pima County by City of Tuscon v. Maya Constr. Co., 761 P.2d 1055 (Ariz. 1988), 33.02[M]

Pinkerton Laws Inc. v. Marco Constr., Inc., 485 S.E.2d 797 (Ga. Ct. App. 1997), 34.04[G][5]

Pipeline Constr. Inc., ASBCA No. 50744, 98-2 B.C.A. ¶ 29,991 (1998), 28.03[B][1]

Pittman Construction Co., Appeals of, GSBCA—4897 and 4923, 81-1 B.C.A. ¶ 14,847 (GSBCA 1980), 30.03[B][4]

Pittsburg Constr. Co. v. Griffith, 834 A.2d 572 (Pa. Super. Ct. 2003), 7.02[B][2][c]

Pittsburgh Steel Co. v. Standard Accident & Ins. Co., 55 F. Supp. 36 (E.D.S.C. 1944), 35.08[F][1]

Pittsburg Plate Glass Co. v. American Surety Co., 19 S.E.2d 357 (Ga. Ct. App. 1942), 35.08[C]

Pittsburg Tank & Tower, Inc., United States *ex rel.*, v. G&C Enters., Inc., 62 F.3d 35 (1st Cir. 1995), 35.06[A][2]

P.J. Dick, Inc., VABCA Nos. 5597 at al., 01-2 BCA ¶ 31,647 (2001), 23.06[B][2]

P.J. Dick, Inc. v. Department of Veterans Affairs, 324 F.3d 1364 (Fed. Cir. 2003), 30.03[C][4]

P.J. Dick, Inc. v. GSA, GSBCA No. 11783, 94-3 B.C.A. (CCH) ¶ 27,172, 39.03[A], 39.03[B][2]

P.J. Dick, Inc. v. Principi, 324 F.3d 1364 (Fed. Cir. 2003), 24.04[C]

P.J. Maffei Bldg. Wrecking Corp. v. United States, 732 F.2d 913 (Fed. Cir. 1984), 28.03[E][1][c]

Planning Research Corp. v. Department of Commerce, GSBCA Nos. 11286-COM et al, 94-1 B.C.A. (CCH) ¶ 26,566, 39.03[F]

Plaquemine, City of, v. North American Constructors, Inc., 683 So. 2d 386 (La. Ct. App. 1996), 18.05[A][2]

Platt, State v., 845 P.2d 815 (N.M. Ct. App. 1992), 35.08[G]

Plum Run, Inc., ASBCA Nos. 46091 et al., 2005-1 BCA ¶ 32,977 (May 23, 2005), 28.03[D][3]

Podell v. Commissioner, 55 T.C. 429 (1970), 17.07

Pollard v. Saxe & Yolles Dev. Co., 525 P.2d 88 (Cal. 1974), 28.03[D][1][a][i]

Pollin Constr. Co., GSBCA No. 2780, 70-2 B.C.A. ¶ 8562 (1970), 28.03[D][3]

Poly Design, Inc. ASBCA No. 50862, 98-1 B.C.A. ¶ 29,458 (1997), 28.03[G]

Poly-Flex, Inc. Cape Max County Mun. Utils. Auth., 832 F. Supp. 889 (D.N.J. 1993), 35.07[B][1]

Poly Software Int'l v. Su, 880 F. Supp. 1487 (D. Utah 1995), 45.04[G]

Pomona Tile Mfg. Co, United States ex rel., v. Kelley, 456 F.2d 148 (9th Cir. 1972), 35.08[D][3]

Portage Indiana School Constr. Corp. v. A.V. Stackhouse Co., 287 N.E.2d 564 (Ind. Ct. App. 1972), 33.01[E], 33.01[G]

Portal Pipe Line Co. v. Stonewall Ins. Co., 845 P.2d 746 (Mont. 1993), 19.07[B]

Port Blakely Mill Co., United States ex rel., v. Massachusetts Bonding & Ins. Co., 198 F. 923 (W.D. Wash. 1912), 35.04[A]

Port Chester Elec. Constr. Corp. v. HBE Corp., 894 F.2d 47 (2d Cir. 1990), 26.02[GG][3]

Port Chester Elec. Constr. Corp. v. HBE Corp., 978 F.2d 820 (2d Cir. 1992), 30.03[C]

Porter Coatings v. Stein Steel & Supply Co., 277 S.E.2d 272 (Ga. App.), review denied, 278 S.E.2d 377 (Ga. 1981), 35.03[B]

Porter-Lite Corp. v. Warren Scott Contracting, Co., 191 S.E.2d 95 (Ga. Ct. App. 1972), 35.08[D][1]

Portland, City of, v. George D. Ward & Associates, Inc., 750 P.2d 171 (Or. Ct. App. 1988), 36.05

Portland Constr. Co., United States ex rel., v. Weiss Pollution Control Corp., 532 F.2d 1009 (5th Cir. 1976), 35.06[A][1][b]

Positive Software Solutions, Inc. v. New Century Mortgage. Corp., 476 F.3d 278 (5th Cir. 2007), 43.02[A], 43.07[E]

Post Bros. Constr. Co. v. Yoder, 569 P.2d 133 (Cal. 1977), 35.08[D][3]

Poston Logging, AGBCA Nos. 99-143-R, 99-145-R, 00-1 B.C.A. ¶ 30,829 (2000), 28.02[A][3]

Potomac Iron Works, Inc., ENGBCA No. 5428, 88-1 BCA ¶ 20,511 (1988), 23.03[E][1]

Pots Unlimited, Ltd. v. United States, 600 F.2d 790 (Ct. Cl. 1979), 28.03[D][1][b]

Power & Pollution Servs. v. Suburban Power Piping Corp., 598 N.E.2d 69 (Ohio Ct. App. 1991), 35.08[E][1]

Powerline Oil Co., EBCA No. 278, 89-3 B.C.A. (CCH) ¶ 22,143, 39.05[D]

Power Regulator Co., United States ex rel., v. Hartford Accident & Indem. Co., 376 F.2d 811 (1st Cir. 1967), 35.03[A]

Powers Regulator Co. v. Joseph Rugo, Inc., 202 N.E.2d 799 (Mass. 1964), 35.06[B][3]

Pozsgai, U.S. v., 999 F.2d 719 (3d Cir. 1993), 11.03[A][1][d]

Praecomm, Inc. v. U.S. 78 Fed. Cl. 5 (2007), 27.05[G][2][b]

Prairie State Nat'l Bank of Chicago v. United States, 164 U.S. 227 (1896), 34.04[H]

Prairie Wood Prods., Inc., AGBCA No. 91-197-1, 94-1 B.C.A. (CCH) ¶ 26,424, 39.03[F]

Praught Constr. Co., ASBCA No. 39,670, 93-2 BCA ¶ 25,896 (1993), 23.03[B][2]

Precision Pine & Timber, Inc. v. United States, 50 Fed. Cl. 35 (2001), 24.02[D]

Precision Pine & Timber, Inc. v. United States, 62 Fed. Cl. 635 (2004), 28.03[B][4]

Preferred Accident Ins. Co. of N.Y., State v., 149 So. 2d 632 (La. 1963), 21.07

Premier Bldg. Servs., Inc., ASBCA No. 51804, 01-2 B.C.A. ¶ 31,626 (2001), 28.03[F][1]

Premier Elec. Constr. Co. v. American Nat'l Bank & Trust Co., 603 N.E. 2d 733 (Ill. 1992), 36.09[F]

Premix-Marblette Mfg. Co. v. SKW, 145 F. Supp. 2d 1348 (S.D. Fla. 2001), 16.06[E]

Preventive Main. Servs., Inc., ASBCA No. 44,661, 94-3 BCA ¶ 27,115 (1994), 23.03[H], 39.03[E]

Price v. Phila. Parking Auth., 221 A.2d 138 (Pa. 1966), 7.03

Prier v. Refrigeration Eng'g Co., 442 P.2d 621 (Wash. 1968), 29.02[C][3]

Prima Paint Corp. v. Flood & Conklin Manufacturing Co., 388 U.S. 395 (1967), 46.07

Prima Print Corp. v. Flood & Conklin Mfg. Co., 388 U.S. 395 (1967), 46.04

Prime Ins. Syndicate, Inc. v. Damaso, 471 F. Supp. 2d 1087 (D. Nev. 2007), 20.03

Prince George's County, Md. v. Local Gov't Ins. Trust, 388 Md. 162, 183 n.9, A.2d 81 94 n.9 (2005), 18.04[A]

Princeton Disposal Serv., Inc. v. North Brunswick, 381 A.2d 1220 (N.J. Super. Ct. App. Div. 1977), 7.03[E]

Process & Storage Vessels, Inc. v. Tank Serv., 541 F. Supp. 725 (D. Del. 1982), aff'd, 760 F.2d 260 (3d Cir. 1985), 35.06[B][2]

Prod. Corp., ASBCA No. 45600, 97-2 B.C.A. ¶ 29,164 (1997), 28.03[B][1]

Production Corp., DOTBCA No. 2424, 92-2 B.C.A. (CCH) ¶ 24,796, 39.03[A], 39.03[B][2]

Prof'l Bldg. Servs. & Maint., ASBCA No. 42480, 91-3 B.C.A. ¶ 24,360 (1991), 28.03[B][3], 28.03[B][3][a]

Prof'l Servs. Supplier, Inc. v. United States, 45 Fed. Cl. 808 (2000), 28.03[D][1][a][i]

Pronto Aire Panama, S.A. 96-2 B.C.A. (CCH) ¶ 28,538 (ENGBCA 1996), 32.03[A]

Propellex Corp. v. Brownlee, 342 F.3d 1335 (2003), 24.04

Propulsion Tech., Inc. v. Attwood Corp., 396 F.3d 896 (5th Cir. 2004), 16.02[B]

Protective Coatings Co., ENGBCA No. 3205, 72-1 B.C.A. ¶ 9431 (1972), 28.03[B][3][a]

Protective Roofing Co., ENGBCA No. PCC-37, 82-1 BCA ¶ 15,647 (1982), 23.03[B][2]

Prudential Ins. Co. of Am. v. United States, 801 F.2d 1295 (Fed. Cir. 1986), cert. denied, 479 U.S. 1086 (1987), 23.03[B][2]

Prudential Ins. Co. v. Stratton, 685 S.W.2d 818 (Ark. Ct. App. 1985), 28.03[D][3]

Prudential-Lmi Com. Ins. v. Superior Court, 51 Cal. 3d 674, 798 P.2d 1230 (1990), 18.04[C][2]

Pryde v. Pryde, (2007 Wash. App. LEXIS 3039), 45.04[F]

Psaty & Fuhrman v. Hous. Auth. of Providence, 76 R.I. 87, 68 A.2d 32 (1949), 26.02[BB][4]

PSE Consulting, Inc. v. Frank Mercede and Sons, Inc., 838 A.2d 135 (Conn. 2004), 36.03[B], 36.05

P.T. & L. Constr. Co. v. State, Dep't of Transp., 531 A.2d 1330 (N.J. 1987), 29.02[B][1]

Public Water Supply Dist. No. 3 ex rel. Victor L. Phillips Co. v. Reliance Ins. Co., 708 S.W.2d 190 (Mo. Ct. App. 1986), 35.04[B]

Puroflow Corp., ASBCA No. 36058, 93-3 B.C.A. ¶ 26,191 (1993), 28.03[F][1]

Pursell Constr., Inc. v. Hawkeye-Security Ins. Co., 596 N.W.2d 67 (Iowa 1999), 19.07[B]

P.W. Constr., Inc. v. United States, 53 Fed. Appx. 555 (Fed. Cir. 2002), 30.03[D][4]

PYCA Industries, Inc. v. Harrison County Waste Water Mgmt. Dist., 177 F.3d 351 (5th Cir. 1999), 27.05[B][2]

Q

Q Int'l Courier, United States v., 131 F.3d 770 (8th Cir. 1997), 38.02[C][4]

Quality Elec. Serv., In re, ASBCA 25811, 81-2 B.C.A. (CCH) ¶ 15380 (1981), 27.03[B][2]

Quality Env't Sys., ASBCA No. 22178, 87-3 B.C.A. ¶ 20,060 at 101,568 (1987), 28.04[A][2]

Quality Equip. Co. v. Transamerica Ins. Co., 502 N.W.2d 488 (Neb. 1993), 35.07[B][1]

Quality Granite Constr. Co., ASBCA No. 43846 , 93-3 B.C.A. ¶ 26,073 (1993), aff'd, 26 F.3d 138 (Fed. Cir. 1994), 28.03[D][1][b]

Quality Landscaping & Tree Serv. v. Armond Cassil Co., No. 94-CV-439, 1995 WL 434550 (E.D. Pa. July 21, 1995), 35.08[H]

Quality Trust, Inc., U.S. ex rel., v. Cajun Contractors, Inc., 486 F. Supp. 2d 1255 (D. Kan. 2007), 28.03[G]

Quest Diagnostics, Inc. v. MCI WorldCom, Inc., 656 N.W.2d 858 (Mich. Ct. App. 2002), appeal denied, 671 N.W.2d 886 (Mich. 2003), 7.02[B][2][c]

Quin Blair Enter., Inc. v. Julien Constr. Co., 597 P.2d 945 (Wy. 1979), 23.04[B][1]

Quincy Mut. Fire Ins. Co. v. Borough of Bellmawr, 172 N.J. 409, 799 A.2d 499 (2002), 18.04[C][2]

R

R & R, Inc. of Louisville v. Commonwealth, 2005 Wl 626391, (Ky. Ct. App. Mar. 18, 2005), 26.02[R][3]

Rachman Bag Co. v. Liberty Mut. Ins. Co., 46 F.3d 230 (2d Cir. 1995), 34.04[G][5]

RaCON, Inc. v. Tuscaloosa County, 953 So. 2d 321 (Ala. 2006), 26.02[A][3], 27.05[D][3]

Racon Elec. Co., ASBCA No. 8020, 1962 ASBCA LEXIS 1270 (1962), 28.03[F][1]

Radenbaugh v. Farm Bureau Gen. Ins. Co., 240 Mich. App. 134, 610 N.W.2d 272 (Ct. App. 2000), 18.05[A][2], 19.07[B]

Radichel v. Federal Sur. Co., 212 N.W. 171 (Minn. 1927), 35.08[D][2]

Ragan v. Tri-County Excavating, 62 F.3d 501 (3d Cir. 1995), 35.08[A]

Ragan Enters., Inc. v. L & B Constr. Co., 228 Ga. App. 852, 492 S.E.2d 671 (1997), 26.02[K][3]

Ralbo, Inc., ASBCA No. 49541 et al., 99-2 B.C.A. ¶ 30,438 (1999), 28.03[D][2]

Ramada Dev. Co. v. USF&G, 626 F.2d 517 (6th Cir. 1980), 34.04[G][2]

Ran-Paige Co. v. United States, 1994 U.S. Claims LEXIS 244 (Fed. Cl. 1994), 28.04[B][2], 28.04[C][1]

Rapanos v. U.S., 376 F.3d 629 (6th Cir. 2004), 11.03[A][1][c], 11.03[A][1][d]

Rapanos v. U.S., 547 U.S. 715 (2006), 11.03[A][1][c]

Rapidigm, Inc. v. ATM Mgmt. Serv., LLC, 63 Pa. D & C 4th 234 (Allegheny County July 10, 2003), 7.02[B][2][c]

Rapp v. United States, 2 Cl. Ct. 694 (1983), 27.05[B][5][e]

Ray Gains, Inc., United States ex rel., v. Essential Constr. Co., 261 F. Supp. 715 (D. Md. 1966), 35.06[A][2]

Raymond A. Bergen, Inc., United States ex rel., v. DeMatteo Constr. Co., 467 F. Supp. 22 (D. Conn. 1979), 35.08[D][1]

Reading Steel Casting Co. v. United States, 268 U.S. 186 (1925), 24.02[D]

R.E. Bean Constr. Co. v. Middlebury Assocs., 428 A.2d 306 (Vt. 1980), 33.01[F], 33.01[I]

Record Steel and Construction, Inc. v. United States, COFC No. 03-2274C (Oct. 19, 2004), 37.03[B]

R-E Corp., ASBCA No. 18692, 1974 ASBCA LEXIS 378 (Jan. 31, 1974), 23.03[E][3]

Redland Soccer Club, Inc. v. Department of the Army, 801 F. Supp. 1432 (M.D. Pa. 1992), 11.03[A][4][a]

Reed, United States ex rel., v. Callahan, 884 F.2d 1180 (9th Cir. 1989), 35.04[A]

Reflectone, Inc. v. Dalton, 60 F.3d 1572 (Fed. Cir. 1995), 39.03[B][1][a], 39.03[C], 39.03[C][2], 39.06[C]

Reflectone, Inc. v. Kelso, 34 F.3d 1031 (Fed. Cir. 1994), 39.03[C][1]

Reflectone, Inc. v. Kelso, ASBCA No. 43081, 93-1 B.C.A. (CCH) ¶ 25,512, *rev'd in part on reconsideration,* 93-3 B.C.A. (CCH) ¶ 25,966, *rev'd in part,* 34 F.3d 1031, 39.03[C][1]

Reliance Ins. v. Treasure Coast Travel, 660 So. 2d 1136 (Fla. Dist. Ct. App. 1995), 20.04

Reliance Ins. Co. v. Colbert, 365 F.2d 530 (D.C. Cir. 1966), 28.03[E][3][b]

Reliance Ins. Co. v. First Miss. Nat'l Bank, 263 Co. 2d 555 (Miss. 1972), 36.08

Renda Marine, Inc. v. United States, 71 Fed. Cl. 789 (2006), 39.07[B]

Rent It Co., United States *ex rel.,* v. Aetna Cas. & Sur. Co., 988 F.2d 88 (10th Cir. 1993), 35.04[A]

Rex Sys., Inc., ASBCA No. 31177, 91-1 B.C.A. ¶ 23,301 (1990), 28.03[B][2]

Rex Systems, Inc., 52247, 00-1 B.C.A. ¶ 30,671 (1999), 28.03[G]

Reynolds, People *ex rel.,* v. Banhagel, 114 N.W. 669 (Mich. 1908), 35.08[B], 35.08[I]

Reynolds Bros. v. Commonwealth, 412 Mass. 1, 586 N.E.2d 977 (1992), 26.02[V][3]

Reynolds' Estate, *In re,* 221 N.C. 449, 20 S.E.2d 348 (1942), 46.26

Reynolds Sec., Inc. v. Macquown, 459 F. Supp. 943 (W.D. Pa. 1978), 46.26

Rhea v. Marko Constr. Co., 652 S.W.2d 332 (Tenn. 1983), 35.08[C], 35.08[F][4]

Rhode Island Hosp. Trust Nat'l Bank v. Ohio Cas. Ins. Co., 789 F.2d 74 (1st Cir. 1986), 35.08[A]

Rhode Island Turnpike & Bridge Authority v. Bethlehem Steel Corp., 119 R.I. 141, 379 A.2d 344 (1977), 26.02[NN][3], 26.02[NN][4]

Rhone Poulenc Rorer Pharms. Inc. v. Newman Glass Works, 112 F.3d 695 (3d Cir. 1997), 29.02[B][2]

Rice, United States v., 317 U.S. 61 (1942), 24.02[A]

Richard Am. Homes of Colo., Inc. v. United States, 80 Fed. Cl. 656 (2008), 30.03[C][3]

Richard, Estate of, v. Am. Wrecking Corp., 134 F. Supp. 2d 252 (D. Conn. 2001), 17.01[A]

Richards & Conover Steel Co. v. Nielsons, Inc., 755 P.2d 644 (Okla. 1988), 35.03[B]

Richlin Sec. Serv. Co. v. Chertoff, 128 S. Ct. 2007 (2008), 28.03[F][4]

Richmond Am. Homes of Colo., Inc. v. United States, 80 Fed. Cl. 656 (2008), 24.03, 24.04[C]

Richmond, City of, v. Madison Mgmt. Group, Inc., 918 F.2d 438 (4th Cir. 1990), 12.04[C][1][a]

Rifenburg Const. Inc. v. Brier Creek Assoc. Ltd. P'ship, 586 S.E.2d 813 (N.C. Ct. App. 2003), 17.01[A]

RII, *Matter of,* No. B-251436, 1993 WL 76588 (Comp. Gen. Mar. 10, 1993), 7.03[A]

Riko Enters. v. Seattle Supersonics Corp., 357 F. Supp. 521 (S.D.N.Y. 1973), 46.18, 46.23

Riley Bros. Constr., Inc. v. Shuck, 704 N.W.2d 197 (Minn. App. 2005), 27.03[B][2]

Riley Constr. Co. v. Schillmoeller & Kroft Co., 236 N.W.2d 195 (Wis. 1975), 35.08[A], 35.08[E][1]

Riley-Stabler Constr. Co. v. Westinghouse Elec. Corp., 396 F.2d 276 (5th Cir.), *reh'g denied,* 401 F.2d 526 (5th Cir. 1968), 35.07[B][1]

Riley Stoker Corp., Appeal of, 92-3 BCA P 25143, ASBCA No. 37019 (June 9, 1992), 27.05[E][2]

Rite-Way Plumbing & Heating, Inc. v. Wil-Fred's Inc., 380 N.E.2d 992 (Ill. App. Ct. 1978), 33.01[B]

River Constr. Corp. v. United States, 159 Ct. Cl. 254 (1962), 30.03[D][5]

Riverfront Lofts Condo. Owners Ass'n v. Milwaukee/Riverfront Props. L.P., 236 F. Supp. 2d 918 (E.D. Wis. 2002), 29.02[B][3]

Rivers v. Richard Schwartz-Neil Weber, Inc., 459 N.W.2d 166 (Minn. Ct. App. 1990), 8A.05

Riverside Iron Works v. Insurance Co. of Am., 549 N.Y.S.2d 877 (App. Div. 1989), 35.08[E][1]

R.J. Longo Constr. Co. v. Transit Am. Inc., 921 F. Supp. 1295 (D.N.J. 1996), 29.02[C][3]

R.J. Russo Trucking & Excavating, Inc. v. Pennsylvania Resource Sys., Inc., 573 N.Y.S.2d 95 (App. Div. 1991), 35.04[B]

RLI Ins. Co. v. Indian River Sch. Dist., CIV. A. No. 05-858-JJF, 2007 U.S. Dist. LEXIS 89519 (D. Del., Dec. 4, 2007), 23.07[C][2]

RMS Tech, Inc. v. TDY Indus., Inc., 64 Fed. Appx. 853 (5th Cir. 2003), 16.02[B]

R.M. Taylor, Inc. v. General Motors Corp., 187 F.3d 809 (8th Cir. 1999), 21.02

R.N. Thompson & Assoc., Inc. v. Monroe Guar. Ins. Co., 686 N.E.2d 160 (Ind. App. 1997), 19.07[B]

Roanoke Hosp. Ass'n v. Doyle & Russell, Inc., 214 S.E.2d 155 (Va. 1975), 31.03[B]

Roanoke Hosp. Ass'n v. Doyle & Russell, Inc., 215 Va. 796, 214 S.E.2d 155 (1975), 30.02[B]

Robberson Steel, Inc. v. J.D. Abrams, Inc., 582 S.W.2d 558 (Tex. Civ. App. 1979), 35.08[B]

Robert DeFilippis Crane Servs., Inc., United States ex rel., v. William L. Crow Constr. Co., 826 F. Supp. 647 (E.D.N.Y. 1993), 35.05[A], 35.07[A][3]

Robert E. Tardiff, Inc. v. Twin Oaks Realty Trust, 130 N.H. 673 (1988), 30.02[B]

Robert McMullan & Sons, Inc., ASBCA No. 19,023, 76-1 B.C.A. (CCH) ¶ 11,728 (1976), 24.02[A]

Robert P. Jones Co., AGBCA No. 391, 76-1 BCA ¶ 11,824 (1976), 23.03[D]

Roberts v. United States Great Am. Co., 357 F.2d 938 (Ct. Cl. 1966), 29.04[A]

Roberts Constr. Co., ASBCA No. 35156, 89-1 B.C.A. ¶ 21,420 (1988), 28.03[E][2]

Roberts Constr. Co., In re, 172 Neb. 819, 111 N.W.2d 767 (1961), 26.02[BB][3]

Roberts Schaefer Co. v. Hardaway Co., 152 F.3d 1283 (11th Cir. 1998), 28.01

Robillard v. Asahi Chem., 1999 Conn. Super, LEXIS 2555 (1999), 29.04[H]

Robinson v. United States, (1923), 23.03[D]

Robson v. United Pac. Ins. Co., 391 S.W.2d 855 (Mo. 1965), 35.08[A]

Rochester City Sch. Dist. v. Rochester Teachers Ass'n, 41 N.Y.2d 578, 362 N.E.2d 977, 394 N.Y.S.2d 179 (1977), 46.19

Rochester Optical Manufacturing Co., B-292247, B-292247.2, (Aug. 6, 2003), 37.02[H][2]

Rockwell Int'l Corp. v. United States, 127 S. Ct. 1397 (2007), 38.02[A], 38.02[B][3], 38.02[B][4], 38.02[B][4][b]

Rockwork, Inc. v. Pulaski Constr. Co., Inc., 933 A.2d 988 (N.J. Super. Ct. App. Div. 2007), 33.02[A]

Rodriguez De Quijas v. Shearson/American Express, Inc., 490 U.S. 477, 109 S. Ct. 1917, 104 L. Ed. 2d 526 (1989), 46.21, 46.26

Roe v. State, 560 So. 2d 474 (La. Ct. App. 1990), 7.03[E]

Roethke v. Sanger, 68 S.W.3d 352 (Ky. 2001), 17.01[A]

Roger J. Au & Sons, IBCA No. 1303-9-79, 84-1 B.C.A. (CCH) ¶ 17,094 (1983), 27.05[C][2]

Rogers v. Speros Constr. Co., 580 P.2d 750 (Ariz. Ct. App. 1978), 35.04[B]

Rogers & Rogers, United States v., 161 F. Supp. 132 (S.D. Cal. 1958), 29.02[C][2]

Rogers & Willard, Inc. v. Harwood, No. 2060134, 2007 WL 2684542 (Ala. Civ. App. Sept. 14, 2007), 32.06

Rohauer v. Little, 736 P.2d 403 (Colo. 1987), 32.05

Rojas v. Superior Court, 33 Cal. 4th 407, 15 Cal. Rptr. 3d 643, 93 P.3d 260 (2004), 45.05[A]

Rojas v. Superior Court, 126 Cal. Rptr. 2d 97 (App. 2d Dist. 2002), review granted and opinion superseded, 130 Cal. Rptr. 653, 63 P.3d 212 (Cal. 2003), 45.05[A]

Rollinson, United States, 866 F.2d 1463 (D.C. Cir.), cert. denied, 493 U.S. 818 (1989), 28.03[E][3][b]

Romanac, In re, 245 F. Supp. 882 (W.D. Va. 1965), aff'd, 386 F.2d 225 (4th Cir. 1967), 25.03[A]

Ronald A. Coco, Inc. v. St. Paul's Methodist Church, 428 P.2d 636 (N.M. 1967), 35.03[B]

Rosales, United States *ex rel.*, v. San Francisco Housing Authority, 2001 WL 370176 (N.D. Cal. 2001), 38.02[C]

Rose v. Davis, 474 So. 2d 1058 (Ala. 1985), 27.05[G][3][c]

Ross Eng'g Co. v. United States, 92 Ct. Cl. 253 (1940), 24.02[D]

Rowan Cos. v. Southwest Tenant Constr., Inc., No. 01-95-01514-CV, 199 Tex. App. LEXIS 1067 (1st Dist. App. Tex. 1999), 30.03[C][3]

Rowan County Bd. of Ed. v. United States Gypsum Co., 418 S.E.2d 648 (N.C. 1992), 12.04[C][1][a]

Roxco, Ltd. v. United States, 60 Fed. Cl. 39 (2004), 28.03[H], 39.07[C]

Roy A. Elam Masonry, Inc.v. Fru-Con Construction, Inc., 922 S.W.2d 783 (Mo. Ct. App. 1996), 26.02[Z][2], 26.02[Z][3], 26.02[Z][4]

Roy Frischhertz Constr. Co., *In re,* No. 05-21605, 2007 WL 3253143 (Bankr. E.D. La. Aug. 22, 2007), 32.03[A], 32.06

Roylex, Inc. v. S & B Eng'rs, 592 S.W.2d 59 (Tex. Civ. App. 1979), 35.08[F][4]

Roy McGinnis & Co., ASBCA No. 40004, 91-1 B.C.A. (CCH) ¶ 23,395, 39.03[B][1][a]

Roy Strom Excavating & Grading Co. v. Miller-Davis Co., 509 N.E.2d 105 (Ill. App. Ct. 1986), 33.01[B]

Roz Trading Ltd., *In re,* 469 F. Supp. 2d 1221 (N.D. Ga. 2006), 43.07[F][2]

R.P. Farnsworth & Co. v. Elec. Supply Co., 112 F.2d 150 (5th Cir. 1940), 35.08[D][2]

R.P. Farnsworth & Co. v. Electrical Supply Co., 112 F.2d 150, 130 A.L.R. 192 (5th Cir.), *reh'g denied,* 113 F.2d 111, 130 A.L.R. 197 (5th Cir. 1940), *cert. denied,* 311 U.S. 700, 61 S. Ct. 139, 85 L. Ed. 454 (1941), 35.07[A][2]

RPR & Assocs. v. O'Brien/Atkins Assocs., 921 F. Supp. 1457 (M.D.N.C. 1995), 29.02[C][2]

RPR & Assocs. Inc. v. Univ. of N.Carolina-Chapel Hill, 570 S.E.2d 510 (N.C. Ct. App. 2002), 33.01[I]

R.P. Richards Constr. Co. v. United States, 51 Fed. Cl. 116 (2001), 24.06

R.P. Wallace, Inc. v. United States, 63 Fed. Cl. 402 (2004), 23.03[B][1], 23.03[D], 27.05[D][4][b], 27.05[D][4][d]

RSH Constructors, Inc. v. United States, 14 Cl. Ct. 655 (1988), 39.03[B]

R.S. Noonan, Inc. v. Morrison-Knudsen Co., 522 F. Supp. 1186 (E.D. La. 1981), 8A.08[F], 30.03[C]

R.T. Woodfield, Inc. v. Montgomery County Bd. of Educ., *ex rel.* International Tel. & Tel. Corp., 248 A.2d 895 (Md. 1969), 35.04[B]

Ruby Collins, Inc. v. Charlotte, 740 F. Supp. 1159 (W.D.N.C. 1990), 29.02[B][1]

Rueter, United States *ex rel.*, v. Sparks, 939 F. Supp. 636 (C.D. Ill. 1996), *aff'd without opinion,* 111 F.3d 133 (7th Cir. 1997), 38.02[B][2]

Rumley v. United States, 285 F.2d 773 (Ct. Cl. 1961), 28.03[F][1]

Rumsfeld v. Freedom NY, Inc., 329 F.3d 1320 (Fed. Cir. 2003), 27.05[B][4]

Rural High Sch. Dist. No. 3 v. Ican Sur. Co., 84 S.W.2d 648 (Mo. Ct. App. 1935), 35.06[B][1]

Rush Presbyterian St. Luke's Medical Center v. Safeco Insurance Co. of America, 712 F. Supp. 1344 (N.D. Ill. 1989), 36.03[B]

Rush Presbyterian St. Luke's Medical Center v. Safeco Insurance Co. of America, 722 F. Supp. 485 (N.D. Ill. 1989), 36.09[D]

Russell Cty. Health Facilities, Inc. v. American Hosp. Bldg. Corp., No. 78-0163-A (W.D. Va. 1980), *aff'd per curiam,* No. 80-1200 (4th Cir. Dec. 26, 1981), 46.19

R.W. Dunteman Co. v. Village of Lombard, 666 N.E.2d 762 (Ill.2d Dist. 1996), 33.01[F]

R.W. Granger & Sons, Inc. v. City School Dist. of Albany, 744 N.Y.S.2d 567 (N.Y. App. Div. 2002), 28.03[D][2]

Ryan v. Thurmond, 481 S.W.2d 199 (Tex. Ct. App. 1972), 31.03

Ryan Co., ASBCA No. 48151, 00-2 B.C.A. ¶ 31,094 (2000), 28.04[D][3]

S

S&M Plumbing Co. v. Commissioner, 55 T.C. 702 (1971), 17.07

Saddler v. United States, 287 F.2d 411 (Ct. Cl. 1961), 21.08

SAE/Am.-Mid Atlantic, Inc. v. GSA, GSBCA Nos. 12294 et al., 98-2 B.C.A ¶ 30,084 (1998), 28.03[B][2]

Safeco Ins. Co. of Am. v. Criterion Inv. Co., 732 F. Supp. 834 (E.D. Tenn. 1989), 36.03[B]

Safeco Ins. Co. of Am. v. Gaubert, 829 S.W.2d 274 (Tex. Ct. App. 1992), 36.02[D], 36.09[E]

Safeco Ins. Co. of Am. v. Schwab, 739 F.2d 431 (9th Cir. 1984), 36.04

Safeco Ins. Co. of Am. v. W.B. Browning Constr., 886 F.2d 807 (6th Cir. 1989), 35.03[B]

Safeway Stores, Inc. v. Certainteed Corp., 687 S.W.2d 22 (Tex. App. 1984), 34.04[G][4]

St. Paul Fire & Marine Ins. v. Commodity Credit Corp., 646 F.2d 1064 (5th Cir. 1981), 34.04[G][5]

St. Paul Fire & Marine Insurance Company v. City of Green River Wyoming, 93 F. Supp. 2d 1170 (D. Wyo. 2000), 34.04[B]

St. Paul Fire & Marine Ins. Co. v. Georgia Interstate Elec. Co., 370 S.E.2d 829 (Ga. Ct. App. 1988), 35.08[E][1]

St. Paul Fire & Marine Ins. Co. v. Pepsico, Inc., 160 F.R.D. 464 (S.D.N.Y. 1995), 34.04[D]

St. Paul Fire & Marine Ins. Co. v. Travelers Indem. Co., 401 F. Supp. 927 (D. Mass. 1975), 35.06[B][2]

St. Paul Fire & Marine Ins. Co. v. United States ex rel. Dakota Elec. Supply Co., 309 F.2d 22 (8th Cir. 1962), 35.08[D][2]

St. Paul Mercury Indem. Co. v. United States, 238 F.2d 917 (10th Cir. 1956), 35.07[A][1]

Saks v. Nicosia Contracting Corp., 215 A.D.2d 832, 625 N.Y.S.2d 758 (1995), 18.04[C][1]

Salesin v. State Farm Fire & Cas. Co., 581 N.W.2d 781 (Mich. Ct. App. 1998), 33.02[A]

Salsbury Indus. v. United States, 905 F.2d 1518 (Fed. Cir. 1990), cert. denied, 498 U.S. 1024 (1991), 28.04[A], 28.04[A][1], 28.04[B][2], 28.04[C][2][a]

S.A. Mineraco D. Trinidade-Samitri v. Utah Int'l, Inc., 745 F.2d 190 (2d Cir. 1984), 46.07

Sam Macri & Sons, Inc. v. United States, 313 F.2d 119 (9th Cir. 1963), 21.06

Sammons-Robertson Co. v. Massman Constr. Co., 156 F.2d 53 (10th Cir. 1946), 26.02[KK][1], 26.02[KK][3]

Samuel T. Isaac & Assocs., Inc. v. United States, 7 Cl. Ct. 225 (1985), 28.03[D][1][b]

San Antonio v. Forgy, 769 S.W.2d 293 (Tex. Ct. App. 1989, writ denied), 28.03[E][1][b]

SanColMar Indus., Inc., ASBCA No. 16478, 74-1 B.C.A. ¶ 10,391 (1973), 28.03[B][3][b]

Sandel & Lastrapes v. City of Shreveport, 129 So. 2d 620 (La. Ct. App. 1961), 26.02[S][3]

Sanderson v. HCA-The Healthcare Corp., 447 F.3d 873 (6th Cir. 2006), 38.02[B][1]

San Joaquin Blocklite, United States ex rel., v. Lloyd E. Tull, Inc., 770 F.2d 862 (9th Cir. 1985), 35.08[D][3]

San Martine Compania De Navegacion v. Saguenay Terms., Ltd., 293 F.2d 796 (9th Cir. 1961), 46.26

Santa Fe, Inc., VABCA No. 2168, 87-3 BCA ¶ 20,104 (1987), 23.06[B][2]

Santee Dock Builders, AGBCA No. 96-161-1, 99-1 B.C.A. ¶ 30,190 (1998), 28.03[B][2]

Sarang Corp. v. U.S., 76 Fed. Co. 560 (Fed. Co. 2007), 33.01[K]

Sarhank Group v. Oracle Corp., 404 F.3d 657 (2d Cir. 2005), 43.07[A]

Satellite Elec. Co. v. Dalton, 105 F.3d 1418 (Fed. Cir. 1997), 24.04[C]

Satterfield v. Edenton-Chowan Bd. of Educ., 530 F.2d 567 (4th Cir. 1975), 46.21

Sauer, Inc. v. Danzig, 224 F.3d 1340 (Fed. Cir. 2000), 24.03, 27.05[D][5][a], 30.03[C][3], 39.03[A]

Savery & Cook, Inc., State *ex rel.*, v. Fidelity & Deposit Co., 194 A.2d 858 (Del. 1963), 35.08[I]

Savoy Constr. Co., ASBCA No. 21218, 22300, 22330, 22696, 22763, 22915, 80-1 B.C.A. (CCH) ¶ 14,392 (1980), 30.03[C][4]

Sawhorse, Inc. v. Southern Guar. Ins. Co. of Ga., 604 S.E.2d 541 (Ga. App. 2004), 19.07[B]

SCA Constr. Supply v. Aetna, 754 P.2d 1339 (Ariz. 1987) (en banc), 35.06[B][3]

Scandale Associated Builders & Engr's, Ltd. v. Bell Justice Facilities Corp., 455 F. Supp. 271 (M.D. Pa. 2007), 25.03[B]

Scarborough, United States *ex rel.*, v. C&M Contractors, Inc., 444 F. Supp. 23 (D. Miss. 1977), 35.06[A][1][a]

Schenectady Air Sys., Inc. v. Campito Plumbing & Heating, Inc., 84 A.D.2d 863 (N.Y. App. Div. 1981), 31.07[A]

Scherer Constr., LLC v. Hedquist Constr., Inc., 18 P.3d 645 (Wyo. 2001), 27.05[D][2]

Schlesinger, 28.03[B][2][a]

Schlesinger v. United States, 390 F.2d 702 (Ct. Cl. 1968), 28.04[A][2], 28.04[D], 28.04[D][1], 28.04[D][2]

Schneider v. J.W. Metz Lumber Co., 715 P.2d 329 (Colo. 1986), 35.03[B]

Schnitzer Steel, 42.02[F][1]

School Bd. of Broward County v. Great Am. Ins. Co., 807 So. 2d 750 (Fla. Dist. Ct. App. 2002), 28.03[C][2]

School Dist. *ex rel.* Koken Iron Works v. Livers, 49 S.W. 507 (Mo. 1899), 35.08[I]

School Dist. *ex rel.* Midland Paving Co. v. Transamerica Ins. Co., 633 S.W.2d 238 (Mo. Ct. App. 1982), 35.08[D][2]

Scoccolo Construction, Inc. *ex rel.* Curb One, Inc. v. City of Renton, 158 Wn. 2d 506, 145 P.3d 371 (2006), 26.02[VV][4]

Scope Elecs., ASBCA No. 20359, 77-1 B.C.A. (CCH) ¶ 12,404 (1977), 27.05[G][2][b]

Scottsdale Ins. Co. v. Van Nguyen, 158 Ariz. 476 (Ariz. Ct. App. 1988), 18.05[B][2]

Seaboard Surety Co. v. Town of Greenfield, 370 F.3d 215 (1st Cir. 2004), 34.04[B], 34.04[C]

Seaboard Sur. Co., United States v., 817 F.2d 956 (2d Cir. 1987), 34.04[F][6]

Sea Crest Constr. Corp. v. United States, 59 Fed. Cl. 615 (2004), 2004 WL 51835, 24.02[C]

Sealey v. Boulevard Constrution Co., 437 N.E.2d 305 (Ohio Ct. App. 1980), 33.01[E]

Seal Tite Corp. v. Ehret, Inc., 589 F. Supp. 701 (D.N.J. 1984), 35.08[E][1]

Searcy v. Phillips Electronics of North America Corp., 117 F.3d 154 (5th Cir. 1997), 38.02[B][3]

Seattle, City of, v. Kuney, 311 P.2d 420 (Wash. 1957), 7.03[B][1][a]

Seaview Elec. Co., ASBCA No. 7189, 1962 BCA ¶ 3331 (1962), *rev'd on other grounds*, 23.03[E][2]

Secretary of Labor v. Summit Contractors, Inc., OSHRC Docket No. 03-1622, 8A.08[A][3]

Secretary of the Army v. Edsall Constr. Co., Inc., 296 F.3d 1081 (Fed. Cir. 2002), 29.02[B][1]

SEC v. Montedison, S.p.A., No. 1:96CV02631 (D.D.C. Nov. 21, 1996), 42.02[F][1]

SEC v. Triton Energy Corp., No. 1:97CV00401 (D.D.C.) (Litigation release No. 15266, Feb. 27, 1997), 42.02[F][1]

Security Fence Group, Inc. v. City of Cincinnati, No. C-020827, 2003 WL 22270179 (Ohio Ct. App. Oct. 3, 2003) (unpublished), 32.04

Security Ins. Co. v. United States *ex rel.* Haydis, 338 F.2d 444 (9th Cir. 1964), 35.06[A][1][a]

Seiler v. Ostarly, 525 So. 2d 1207 (La. App. 5 Cir. 1988), 20.01

Seldeon v. S&S Aggregates Co., 441 S.W.2d 950 (Tex. Civ. App. 1969), 35.04[B]

Seldner Corp. v. W.R. Grace & Co., 22 F. Supp. 388 (D. Md. 1938), 46.23

Select Ins. Co. v. Superior Court, 226 Cal. App. 3d 631 (1990), 18.04[A]

Sellick, ASBCA No. 21869, 78-2 B.C.A. ¶ 13,510 (1978), 28.03[D][2], 28.03[F][2]

Seminole Sheet Metal Co., United States *ex rel.* v. SCI, Inc., 828 F.2d 671 (11th Cir. 1987), 26.02[J][4], 35.08[E][3]

Sentinel Industrial Contracting Corp. v. Kimmins Industrial Service Corp., 743 So. 2d 954 (Miss. 1999), 27.05[B][3]

Sentinel Ins. Co. v. First Ins. Co. of Hawaii, 76 Haw. 277, 875 P.2d 894 (Haw. 1994), 20.02

Serafini, U.S. v., 750 F. Supp. 168 (M.D. Pa. 1990), 11.03[A][3][a]

Sergent Mech. Sys., Inc. v. United States, 34 Fed. Cl. 505 (1995), 28.03[E][1][a], 28.03[E][1][c]

Servidone Constr. Co. v. United States, 19 Cl. Ct. 346 (Cl. Ct. 1990), 27.04[A][2]

Servidone Constr. Co. v. United States, 19 Cl. Ct. 346 (Fed. Cl. 1990), 7.03[B][2][a], 27.05[C][2]

Servidone Constr. Co. v. United States, 19 Cl. Ct. 346 (Fed. Cl. 1990), *aff'd,* 931 F.2d 860 (Fed. Cir. 1991), 24.04

Servidone Constr. Co. v. United States, 931 F.2d 860 (Fed. Cir. 1991), 24.04, 28.03[E][3][a], 30.03[D][1]

Severin v. United States, 99 Ct. Cl. 435 (1943), *cert. denied,* 322 U.S. 733, 64 S. Ct. 1045, 88 L. Ed. 1567, 101 Ct. Cl. 872 (1944), 25.05[C], 39.03[F]

Seybold v. Magnolia Land Co., 376 So. 2d 1083 (Ala. 1979), 27.05[G][2][c]

SGB Universal Builders Supply, United States *ex. rel.,* v. Fidelity & Deposit Co., 475 F. Supp. 672 (E.D.N.Y. 1979), 35.08[H]

Shade Foods v. Innovative Prods. Sales & Mktg., 78 Cal. App. 4th 847 (2000), 18.04[C][2]

Shamman v. Int'l Union of Operating Eng'rs, 744 F.2d 1226 (6th Cir. 1984), 33.02[A]

Shank/Balfour Beatty v. Metro. Water Dist. of S. Cal., 2007 WL 2052133 (Cal. Ct. App. July 19, 2007), 26.02[E][3]

Shankle-Clairday, Inc., United States *ex rel.,* v. Crow, 414 F. Supp. 160 (M.D. Tenn. 1976), 36.02[A]

Shannon H. Holloway Const. Co. v. Louisville & Jefferson County Metro Sewer Dist., 674 S.W.2d 523(Ky. Ct. App. 1983), 7.03[C]

Shannon R. Ginn Constr. Co. v. Reliance Ins. Co., 51 F.Supp.2d 1347 (S.D. Fla. 1999), 34.04[D]

Sharjon, Inc., ASBCA No. 22954, 79-1 B.C.A. ¶ 13,585 (1978), 28.03[B][3][a]

Sharman Co., The, v. United States, 2 F.3d 1564 (Fed. Cir. 1993), 28.03[G]

Shaw v. AAA Eng'g & Drafting, Inc., 213 F.3d 519 (10th Cir. 2000), 38.02[B][2]

Shaw v. Aetna Cas. & Sur. Co., 407 F.2d 813 (7th Cir. 1969), 20.02

Shaw v. Kuhnel & Assoc., 102 N.M. 607, 698 P. 880 (1985), 46.11

Shawn K. Christensen, AGBCA No. 95-188-R, 95-2 B.C.A. ¶ 27,724 (1995), 28.04[D][2]

Shearman & Assoc. v. Continental Cas. Co., 901 F. Supp. 199 (D.V.I. 1995), 35.08[E][1]

Shelby Mut. Ins. Co. v. Ferber Sheet Metal Works, Inc., 156 So. 2d 748 (Fla. Dist. Ct. App. 1963), 18.04[C][1]

Shell Oil Co. v. Winterthur Swiss Ins. Co., 12 Cal. App. 4th 715 (1993), 18.04[A], 18.05[B][1]

Shepard Div., ASBCA No. 15571, 74-1 BCA ¶ 10,498 (1974), 28.03[D][2]

Shepard Div./Vogue Instrument Corp., ASBCA No. 15,571, 74-1 BCA ¶ 10,498 (1974), 23.03[E][3]

Sherman, United States *ex rel.,* v. Carter, 353 U.S. 210 (1957), 35.04[A]

Sherman R. Smoot Corp., ASBCA No. 52261, 03-1 B.C.A. (CCH) ¶ 32197 (2003), 24.04[C]

Sherman R. Smoot Corp., ASBCA No. 52,261 (2001), 27.05[D][6][c]

Sherman R. Smoot Co. v. Ohio Dep't of Admin. Servs., 136 Ohio App. 3d 166, 736 N.E.2d 69 (Ohio Ct. App. 2000), 30.03[C][6]

Sheyer v. Lowell, 66 P. 307 (Cal. 1904), 12.04[C][1][d][ii]

Shields, Inc. v. Metric Constructors, Inc., 416 S.E.2d 597 (N.C. App. 1992), 27.05[B][3]

Shinrone, Inc. v. Insurance Co. of North
America, 570 F.2d 715 (9th Cir.
1978), 18.05[B][2]
Shively v. Bellevue Twp. High Sch.
Dist. No. 201, 329 Ill. App. 3d 1156,
(5th Dist. 2002), 8A.04
Short Bros/Constr. Inc. v. Korte &
Kuthohan Contractors, Inc., 356 Ill.
App. 3d 958, 293 Ill. Dec. 444, 828
N.E.2d 754 (5th Cir. 2005), 45.04[A]
Shreck, People v., 22 P.3d 68 (Colo.
2001), 29.04[H]
Siam Humhong Prods. Co. v.
Eastimpex, 866 F. Supp. 445 (N.D.
Cal. 1994), 16.04[E]
Siebert, et al. v. Bayport Beach and
Tennis Club Ass'n, Inc., 573 So. 2d
889 (Fla. Ct. App. 1991), 20.01
Siefford v. Hous. Auth. of Humbolt, 192
Neb. 643, 223 N.W.2d 816 (1974),
26.02[BB][3], 26.02[BB][4]
Sierra Rock v. Regents of Univ. of
California, ASBCA No. 9705223,
99-2 B.C.A. ¶ 30,507 (1999),
28.04[A][1]
Signal Contracting, Inc., DOTCAB No.
1279, 83-1 BCA ¶ 16,424 (1982),
23.03[B][1], 23.03[E][4]
Sikorsky Aircraft Div. v. United States,
27 Fed. Cl. 393 (1992),
28.03[E][1][a]
Silk v. Flat Top Constr., Inc., 192 W.
Va. 522, 453 S.E.2d 356 (1994),
18.05[A][1]
Silliman Co. v. S. Ippolito & Sons, 467
A.2d 1249 (Conn. App. Ct. 1983),
35.08[B], 35.08[C]
Silverdale Hotel Assocs. v. Lomas &
Nettleton Co., 677 P.2d 773 (Wash.
Ct. App. 1984), 33.01[F]
Silver Enters., CBCA 63-C, 07-1 B.C.A.
¶ 33,496 (2007), 28.03[F][4]
Silver Hill Concrete Corp. v. Thomason
Indus. Corp., 556
F. Supp. 291 (D.D.C. 1982),
35.07[A][2]
Silver Hill Concrete Corp. v. Thomason
Indus. Corp., 556
F. Supp. 291 (D.D.C. 1982), aff'd,
704 F.2d 1294 (D.C. Cir. 1983),
35.08[D][2]
Simmons v. Bank of Miss., 593 So. 2d
40 (Miss. 1992), 26.02[Y][3]

Simplex Mfg. Corp., ASBCA No.
13897, 71-1 B.C.A. ¶ 8814 (1971),
28.03[B][3][a]
Simpson v. United States, 172 U.S. 372
(1899), 24.02[B]
Simpson Timber Co. v. Palmberg
Constr. Co., 377 F.2d 380 (9th Cir.
1967), 24.02[B]
Sims Brothers Constr., Inc., U.S. v., 277
F.3d 734 (5th Cir. 2001),
11.03[A][3][e]
Sims' Crane Serv., Inc. v. Reliance Ins.
Co., 514 F. Supp. 1033 (S.D. Ga.
1981), 35.04[B]
Sims Paving Corp., DOT BCA No.
1822, 90-3 B.C.A. ¶ 22,942 (1990),
28.03[E][1][c]
Singer Co. v. United States, 568 F.2d
695 (Ct. Cl. 1977), 30.03[E]
Singleton Contr. Corp., GSBCA No.
7429, 85-2 B.C.A. (CCH) ¶ 18,124,
37.04[A]
Singleton Contr. Corp. v. Harvey, 395
F.3d 1353 (Fed. Cir. 2005), 24.04[C]
Sipco Servs. & Marine, Inc. v. United
States, 41 Fed. Cl. 196 (1998),
27.05[B][3][d], 28.03[E][1][a],
28.03[E][1][b], 28.03[G]
Skip Kirchdorfer, Inc., United States ex
rel., v. Aegis/Zublin Joint Venture,
869 F. Supp. 387 (E.D. Va. 1994),
35.04[A], 35.07[A][1]
Sklar v. Clough, 2007 WL 3407533
(N.D. Ga. 2007), 45.05[B]
Slagle-Johnson Lumber Co. v. Landis
Constr. Co., 379 So. 2d 479 (La.
1979), 35.04[B]
Slater v. U.S. Fidelity and Guaranty
Co., 400 N.E.2d 1256 (Mass. 1980),
20.04
Sligh, United States ex rel., v. Fullerton
Constr. Co., 296
F. Supp. 518 (D.S.C. 1968), aff'd,
407 F.2d 1339
(4th Cir. 1969), 35.06[A][2]
SME Industries v. Thompson, Ventulett,
Stainback and Assocs., Inc., 28 P.3d
669 (Utah 2001), 29.02[C][3],
29.02[C][5]
SMI Owen Steel Co., Inc. v. Marsh USA,
Inc., No. 06-41387, 2008 U.S. App.
LEXIS 5024 (5th Cir. Mar. 7, 2008),
7.02[B][2][c]

Smith v. Arbaugh's Rest., Inc., 496 F.2d 97 (D.C. Cir. 1973), 29.02[D][3]

Smith v. Goff, 325 P.2d 1061 (Okla. 1958), 20.01

Smith v. Smith, 154 F.R.D. 661 (N.D. Tex. 1999), 45.05[A]

Smith v. Smith, 278 N.W.2d 155 (S.D. 1979), 29.02[D][2]

Smith v. United States, 34 Fed. Cl. 313 (1995), 24.02[A]

Smith, H.L., v. Dalton, 49 F.3d 1563 (Fed. Cir. 1995), 39.03[B][1]

Smith, State ex rel., v. Tyonek Timber, 680 P.2d 1148 (Alaska 1984), 35.08[G]

Smith Plumbing Co. v. Aetna Cas. & Sur. Co., 720 P.2d 499 (Ariz. 1986), 35.08[A]

Smith Truck & Dragline Service, Inc. v. United States, 49 Fed. Cl. 443 (2001), 24.02[D]

SMS Data Prods. Group, Inc. v. United States, 19 Cl. Ct. 612 (1990), 28.04[A][1]

Snapping Shoals Elec. Membership Corp. v. RLI Ins. Co., 2005 WL 3434803 (N.D. Ga.), 34.04[G][4]

Snapp v. State Farm Fire & Cas. Co., 206 Cal. App. 2d 827 (1962), 18.04[C][2]

Snowberger v. Young, 24 Ariz. App. 177, 536 P.2d 1069 (1975), 46.01

Sobel v. Hertz, Warner & Co., 469 F.2d 1211 (2d Cir. 1972), 46.26

Sobel v. Jones, 394 P.2d 415 (Ariz. 1964), 35.08[G]

Socony Mobil Oil Co. v. Klapal, 205 F. Supp. 338 (Neb. 1962), 33.01[H]

Sofarelli Associates, Inc. v. United States, 716 F.2d 1395 (Fed. Cir. 1983), 39.07[C][2]

Software Testing Solutions, Inc. v. U.S., 58 Fed. Cl. 533 (Fed. Cl. 2003), 27.03[B][1]

Solai Cameron, Inc. v. Plainfield Community Consolidated School District No. 202, 871 N.E.2d 944 (Ill. App. 2007), 34.04[C]

Solar Form Insulation, ASBCA No. 46278, 94-1 B.C.A. (CCH) ¶ 26,288 (1993), 24.04[E]

Solite Masonry Units Corp. v. Piland Constr. Co., 232 S.E.2d 759 (Va. 1977), 35.02[B], 35.04[B], 35.07[B][1]

Solomon v. Dep't of State Highways & Transp., 345 N.W. 2d 717 (Mich. 1984), 23.03[E][4]

Son-Shine Grading, Inc. v. ADC Constr. Co., 68 N.C. App. 417, 315 S.E.2d 346 (1984), 21.02

Sons of Thunder Inc. v. Borden, Inc., 148 N.J. 396 (1997), 34.04[D]

Sork v. United Benefit Fire Ins. Co., 161 So. 2d 54 (Fla. Dist. Ct. App. 1964), 36.07

Sornsin Constr. Co. v. State, 590 P.2d 125 (Mont. 1978), 22.08

Source AV, B-241155, Jan. 25, 1991, 91-1 CPD ¶ 75, 28.03[E][3][b]

S. Brooke Purll, Inc. v. Vailes, 850 A.2d 1135 (D.C. 2004), 32.05

S. Comfort Builders, Inc. v. U.S. 67 Fed. Cl. 124 (Fed. Co. 2005), 33.01[K]

S. Gulf Utils., Inc. v. Boca Ciega Sanitary Dist., 238 So. 2d 458 (Fla. Dist. Ct. App. 1970), 26.02[J][4]

S. Leo Harmonay, Inc. v. Binks Mfg., 597 F. Supp. 1014 (S.D.N.Y. 1984), 27.05[D][6][b]

S. Leo Harmonay, Inc. v. Binks Mfg., 597 F. Supp. 1014 (S.D.N.Y. 1984), aff'd, 762 F.2d 990 (2d Cir. 1985), 24.04, 30.03[C], 30.03[C][6], 30.03[D][4]

S. New England Constr. Co. v. Connecticut, 165 Conn. 644 (1974), 30.03[C][3]

S. Patti Constr. Co., ASBCA No. 8423, 1964 B.C.A. (CCH) ¶ 4225 (1964), 24.02[D]

Southeastern Mun. Supply Co., United States ex rel., v. National Union Fire Ins. Co., 876 F.2d 92 (11th Cir. 1989), 33.02[O], 35.04[A]

Southern Comfort Builders, Inc. v. United States, 67 Fed. Cl. 124 (2005), 23.06[A], 27.05[D][5][a]

Southern Constr. Co. v. United States, 364 F.2d 439 (Ct. Cl. 1966), 39.03[F]

Southern New Eng. Contracting Co. v. State, 165 Conn. 644, 345 A. 2d 550 (1979), 24.04[C]

Southern Painting Co. of Tenn. v.
    United States, 222 F.2d 431 (10th Cir.
    1955), 21.06
Southern Roofing & Petroleum Co. v.
    Aetna Ins. Co., 293
    F. Supp. 725 (E.D. Tenn. 1968),
    34.04[F][3]
Southern States Masonry v. J.A. Jones
    Constr. Co., 507 So. 2d 198 (La.
    1987), 35.08[E][1]
Southern Steel Co. v. United Pac. Ins.
    Co., 935 F.2d 1201 (11th Cir. 1991),
    35.06[A][1][b]
Southland Corp. v. Keating, 465 U.S. 1
    (1984), 46.04
South Union, Ltd. v. George Parker &
    Assoc., 504 N.E.2d 1131 (Ohio Ct.
    App. 1985), 29.02[C][4]
Southwest Engineering Co. v. United
    States, 341 F.2d 998 (8th Cir. 1965),
    32.03[A]
Southwestern Sash & Door Co. v.
    American Employers, Ins. Co., 20
    P.2d 928 (N.M. 1933), 35.08[I]
Southwestern Sheet Metal Work, Inc.,
    ASBCA 22748, 79-2 B.C.A. (CCH)
    ¶ 13,949, 21.04
Southwest Marine, Inc., ASBCA No.
    39472, 93-2 B.C.A. (CCH) ¶ 25,682
    (1992) (denying recovery),
    24.04[B]
Southwood Builders, Inc. v. Peerless
    Ins. Co., 366 S.E.2d 104 (Va. 1998),
    34.04[G][2]
Sovereign Constr. Co., GSBCA No.
    910, 1964 B.C.A. (CCH) ¶ 4037
    (1964), 24.04[E]
Space Corp. v. United States, 470 F.2d
    536, 200 Ct. Cl. 1 (1972), 24.02[C]
Spadafora Ironworks, Inc. v. Morse Co.,
    Inc., 1998 WL 283206 (Mass. App.
    Div. 1998), 21.02
Spang Indus. v. The Aetna Cas. & Sur.
    Co., 512 F.2d 365 (2d Cir. 1975),
    35.08[H]
Sparks v. St. Paul Ins. Co., 100 N.J.
    325, 495 A.2d 406 (N.J. 1985),
    20.03
Spearin, United States v., 248 U.S. 132
    (1918), 5.03[C][8], 5.05[C],
    7.02[B][1], 7.03[B][1][a], 21.04,
    22.02, 22.06, 22.08, 24.02[C],
    28.03[E][1][b], 29.02[B][1],
    29.02[D][4]
Spearin, United States v., 248 U.S. 132,
    39 S. Ct. 59, 63 L. Ed. 166 (1918),
    27.04[A][1], 27.05[F]
Spears v. Smith, 117 Ohio App. 3d 262,
    690 N.E.2d 557 (1996), 18.05[A][2]
Specialty Assembling & Packing Co. v.
    United States, 174 Ct. Cl. 153, 355
    F.2d 554 (1966), 24.02[A],
    30.03[D][5]
Spector Indus. v. Mitchell, 63 N.C. App.
    391, 305 S.E.2d 738 (1983), 46.19
Sphere Drake Ins. Co. v. Tremco, Inc.,
    513 N.W.2d 473 (Minn. App. 1994),
    18.05[A][1], 18.05[A][2]
Sphere Drake Ins. Co. v. Y.L. Realty
    Co., 900 F. Supp. 240 (S.D.N.Y.
    1997), 19.03[G][3][b]
Spight, United States ex rel., v.
    Dominique, No. 95-3683, 1996 WL
    696267 (E.D. La. Nov. 25, 1996),
    35.04[A]
Spight, United States ex rel., v.
    Marshall, CA 92-1193, 1993 WL
    390115 (E.D. La. Sept. 29, 1993),
    35.08[H]
Spivack v. Berks Ridge Corp., 586 A.2d
    402 (Pa. Super. Ct. 1991),
    7.02[B][2][c]
SP No. 54 Limited P'ship v. Fidelity
    and Deposit Co. of Maryland, 2005
    WL 3555836 (Fla. App.), 34.04[F][4]
Spotless Janitorial Servs., ASBCA Nos.
    44365 et al., 93-2 B.C.A. ¶ 25,873
    (1993), 28.03[G]
Springfield Terminal Ry., United States
    ex rel., v. Quinn, 14 F.3d 645 (D.C.
    Cir. 1994), 38.02[B][3]
SPS Mech. Co., ASBCA No. 48643,
    01-1 B.C.A. ¶ 31,318 (Feb. 9, 2001),
    28.03[E][1][b]
Staff Indus., Inc. v. Hallmark
    Contracting, Inc., 846 S.W.2d 542
    (Tex. Ct. App. 1993), 35.07[B][1]
Stagl v. Delta Airlines, Inc., 52 F.3d 463
    (2d Cir. 1995), 29.02[D][3]
Standard Accident Inc. Co. v. United
    States ex rel. Powell, 302 U.S. 442
    (1938), 35.04[A]
Standard Coating Service, Inc., ASBCA
    No. 48611 et al., 00-1 B.C.A.
    ¶ 30,725 (2000), 28.03[F][2]
Standard Oil Co. v. Detroit Fid. & Sur.
    Co., 157 N.E. 418 (Ohio 1927),
    35.07[B][1]

Standard Oil Corp. v. Marvill, 206 N.W. 37 (Iowa 1925), 35.07[B][1]

Standard Surety & Casualty Co. v. Caravel Industries Corp., 15 A.2d 258 (N.J. Ch. 1940), 36.04

Standard Tankers (Bahamas) Co. v. Motor Tank Vessel, Akti, 438 F. Supp. 153 (E.D.N.C. 1977), 46.19, 46.23, 46.24

Stangl v. Todd, 554 P.2d 1316 (Utah 1976), 30.02[A][2]

Stanley J. How & Assocs., Inc. v. Boss, 222 F. Supp. 936 (S.D. Iowa 1963), 21.05

Star Contracting Corp. v. Manway Constr. Co., 337 A.2d 669 (Conn. Super. Ct. 1973), 35.08[A], 35.08[E][1]

Starry Constr. Co. v. Murphy Oil USA, Inc., 785 F. Supp. 1356 (D. Minn. 1992), 16.04[E]

Star Sprinkler Corp. of Fla. v. Mead & Mount Constr. Co., 508 P.2d 801 (Colo. Ct. App. 1973), 35.07[B][1]

State Dep't of Natural Res. v. Transamerica Premier Insur. Co., 856 P.2d 766 (Alaska 1993), 7.02[B][2][c]

State Elec. Supply Co., United States ex. rel., v. Hesselden Constr. Co., 404 F.2d 774 (10th Cir. 1968), 35.05[A]

State Farm Auto. Ins. Co. v. Roberts, 166 Vt. 452 (1997), 18.05[B][2]

State Farm Fire & Cas. Co. v. Hatherly, 621 N.E.2d 39 (Ill. App. Ct. 1993), 20.02

State Farm Fire & Cas. Co. v. Tillerson, 777 N.E.2d 986 (Ill. App. 2002), 19.07[B]

State Farm Mutual Auto Insurance v. Campbell, 538 U.S. 408, 123 S. Ct. 1513 (2003), 31.07[B]

State Farm Mut. Auto Ins. Co. v. Partridge, 10 Cal. 3d 94 (1973), 18.05[B][2]

State Highway Administration v. Greiner Engineering Sciences, Inc., 83 Md. App. 621, 511 A.2d 363 (1990), 26.02[U][3], 26.02[U][4]

State Highway Comm'n v. Brasel & Sims Constr. Co., 688 P.2d 871 (Wyo. 1984), 30.03[D][1]

State v. See name of defendant.

Statoil, 42.02[F][1]

Stebner, United States ex rel., v. Stewart & Stephenson Servs., Inc., 144 Fed. Appx. 389 (5th Cir. 2005), 38.02[C][2]

Steele & Sons, Inc., ASBCA No. 49077, 00-1 B.C.A. (CCH) ¶ 30,837 (2000), 24.02[D]

Steenberg Constr. Co. v. Prepakt Concrete Co., 381 F.2d 768 (10th Cir. 1967), 28.03[E][1][a], 35.06[A][1][b]

Steffen v. United States, 213 F.2d 266 (6th Cir. 1954), 32.04

Steffes v. Lemke, 41 N.W. 302 (Minn. 1889), 35.08[I]

Steigerwald v. Bradley, 136 F. Supp. 2d 460 (D. Md. 2001), 12.04[C][1][a]

Stelko Elec., Inc. v. Taylor Cmty. Sch. Bldg. Corp., 826 N.E.2d 152 (Ind. Ct. App. 2005), 26.02[O][3]

Stella Mfg. Co. v. Tennessee Valley Auth., 707 F. Supp. 782 (E.D. Pa. 1989), 21.02

Stephan v. Rocky Mountain Chocolate Factory, Inc., 129 F.3d 414 (7th Cir. 1997), 30.03[C][6]

Stephen J. Yarlin, 75-2 BCA ¶ 11,450 (AGBCA 1975), 30.03[C]

Stephenson v. Frazier, 399 N.E.2d 794 (Ind. Ct. App. 1980), trans. denied, 425 N.E.2d 73 (Ind. 1981), 16.08[D]

Stephenson Associates, GSBCA Nos. 6573, 6815, 86-3 B.C.A. (CCH) ¶ 19,071 (1986), 27.05[D][5][b]

Sterling Millwrights, Inc. v. United States, 26 Cl. Ct. 49 (1992), 28.03[E][1][a], 28.03[E][3][a], 38.02[C][1][b][ii]

Sterling Tool, Inc., ASBCA No. 19790, 75-2 B.C.A. ¶ 11,577 (1975), 28.03[F][1]

Stermer v. Modiano Construction Co., 118 Cal. Rptr. 309 (1975), 33.02[M][1]

Stevens Van Lines, Inc. v. U.S., 89 Fed. Cl. 163, 2008 WL 215820 (2008), 27.05[B][5][b]

Stewart v. Hammond, 471 P.2d 90 (Wash. 1970), 35.08[G]

Stiefel v. Illinois Union Ins. Co., 452 N.E.2d 73 (Ill. 1993), 20.04

Stiley v. Block, 925 P.2d 194 (Wash. 1996), 12.04[C][1][a]

Stoeckert v. United States, 391 F.2d 639 (Ct. Cl. 1968), 28.03[B][3][b]

Stone, United States *ex rel.*, v. Rockwell Int'l Corp., Nos. 99-1351, 99-1352, 99-1353, 2002 U.S. LEXIS 3409 (2002), 38.02[B][3]

Stone & Webster, Inc., *In re,* 279 B.R. 748 (D. Del. 2002), 28.03[B][2]

Stonewall Ins. Co. v. City of Palos Verdes Estates, 46 Cal. App. 4th 1810, *review denied,* 1996 Cal. LEXIS 6040 (Oct. 23, 1996), 18.04[C][2]

Stoney Run Co. v. Prudential-LMI Commercial Ins. Co., 47 F.3d 34 (2d Cir. 1995), 19.03[G][3][b]

Straus Sys., Inc., United States *ex rel.* v. Associated Indem. Co., 969 F.2d 83 (5th Cir. 1992), 26.02[RR][1]

S-Tron, ASBCA No. 45890, 94-3 B.C.A. (CCH) ¶ 26,957, 39.03[D]

Strong v. C.I.R., Inc., 516 N.W.2d 719 (Wis. 1994), 35.04[B]

Structural Painting Corp., ASBCA No. 36813, 89-2 B.C.A. ¶ 21605 (1989), 28.03[D][2]

Structural Sales v. Vavrus, 477 N.E.2d 745 (Ill. App. Ct. 1985), 35.08[B]

Structural Sys. Tech., Inc., ASBCA No. 36950 (Feb. 1989), 7.03[B][2][a]

Structures, Inc., *In re,* 27 F.3d 73 (3d Cir. 1994), 34.04[H]

Stuart v. Bennett, 727 N.W.2d 424 (Neb. 2007), 33.02[C]

Sturdy Concrete Corp. v. Nab Constr. Corp., 65 A.D.2d 262 (N.Y. 1978), 28.03[D][1][a][i]

Stuyvesant v. United States, 834 F.2d 1576 (Fed. Cir. 1987), 7.03[B][1], 7.03[B][2][a], 24.02[C], 29.02[B][1]

Stuyvesant Dredging Co. v. United States, 11 Cl. Ct. 853 (1987), 29.02[B][2]

Stuyvesant Dredging Co. v. United States, 834 F.2d 1576 (Fed. Cir. 1987), 5.03[C][8], 29.02[B][2]

Subsurfco, Inc. v. B-Y Water Dist., 337 N.W.2d 448 (S.D. 1983), 21.02

Suez and Others v. The Argentine Republic (ICSID Case No ARB/03/19), 43.06[A]

Suffolk Sports Ctr., Inc. v. Belli Constr. Corp., 212 A.D.2d 241 (N.Y. 1995), 31.07[A]

Sugar Top Resort Condominium Ass'n v. Batson-Cook of Atlanta, 87 F.3d 1309 (4th Cir. 1996), 29.04[J]

Summit Contractors v. U.S., 21 Cl. Ct. 767, 777 Cl. Ct. 1990, 27.03[B][2]

Sumner Dev. Corp. v. Shivers, 517 P.2d 757 (Alaska 1974), 35.08[G]

Sunbelt Pipe Corp., United States *ex rel.*, v. United States Fid. & Guar. Co., 785 F.2d 468 (4th Cir. 1986), 35.04[A]

Sun Cal, Inc. v. United States, 21 Cl. Ct. 31 (1990), 28.03[D][2]

Sun-Lite Glazing Contractors, Inc. v. J.E. Berkowitz, L.P., 37 Fed. Appx. 677, 2002 WL 1343235 (4th Cir. 2002), 29.03[D][1]

Sun Oil Co. v. United States, 572 F.2d 786 (Ct. Cl. 1978), 28.03[E][1][a]

Sunshine Birds & Supplies v. United States Fid. & Guar. Co., 696 So. 2d 907 (Fla. Dist. Ct. App. 1997), 18.04[B]

Sunshine Const. & Engineering, Inc. v. United States, 64 Fed. Cl. 346 (2005), 24.04[C], 39.03[A]

Sunstate Elecs., ASBCA No. 32468, 87-2 B.C.A. ¶ 19,750 (1987), 28.03[F][2]

Superior Abatement Serv., Inc., Appeal of, ASBCA No. 47118 (Oct. 1994), 7.03[B][2][a]

Superior Gunite v. Mitzel, 117 Cal. App. 4th 301, 12 Cal. Rptr. 3d 423 (2004), 26.02[E][3]

Superior Insulation Co., United States *ex rel.*, v. Robert E. McKee, 702 F. Supp. 1298 (N.D. Tex. 1988), 35.04[A]

Supermex, Inc. v. United States, 35 Fed. Cl. 29 (1996), 38.03

Suprema Specialties, Inc., 370 B.R. 517 (Bankr. S.D.N.Y. 2007), 36.08

Sutton Corp. v. Commonwealth, 412 Mass. 1003, 586 N.E.2d 975 (1992), 26.02[V][3]

S.W. Elecs. & Mfg. Corp. v. United States, 665 F.2d 1078 (Ct. Cl. 1981), 30.03[D][5]

SW Eng'g Co. v. United States, 341 F.2d 998 (8th Cir.), *cert. denied,* 382 U.S. 819 (1965), 28.03[F][2]

S.W. Heischman, Inc. v. Reliance Ins. Co., 30 Va. Cir. 235 (Cir. Ct. 1993), 18.04[C][2]

Sydney Constr. Co., ASBCA No. 21377, 77-2 BCA ¶ 12,719 (1977), 23.03[H], 24.04[D], 27.05[D][6][c]

Symons Corp. v. Ins. Co. of N. Am., 380 S.E.2d 550 (N.C. Ct. App. 1989), 35.04[B]

Syro Steel Co. v. Eagle Constr. Co., 460 S.E.2d 371 (S.C. 1995), 35.04[B], 35.07[B][1]

Syro Steel Co. v. Hubbell Highway Signs, Inc., 424 S.E.2d 208 (N.C. 1993), 35.07[B][1], 35.08[F][2]

Systems Architects, Inc., ASBCA Nos. 28861, 29456, 90-2 B.C.A ¶ 22,860 (1990), 28.04[C][2][b]

Szarkowski v. Reliance Inc. Co., 404 N.W.2d 502 (N.D. 1987), 36.09[F]

T

T&B Builders, Inc., ENGBCA No. 3664, 77-2 B.C.A. (CCH) ¶ 12,663 (1977), 24.02[B]

T&M Distribs., Inc. v. United States, 42 Cont. Cas. Fed. ¶ 77,313, 1998 U.S. Claims LEXIS 50 (Fed. Cl. 1998), 28.04[B][2]

T&M Distribs., Inc. v. United States, 185 F.3d 1279 (Fed. Cir. 1999), 28.04[B][2]

T&R Painting Constr. v. St. Paul Fire & Marine Ins. Co., 29 Cal. Rptr. 2d 199 (Ct. App. 1994), 35.08[J]

T&R Painting Constr., Inc. v. St. Paul Fire & Marine Ins. Co., 29 Cal. Rptr. 2d 199 (Ct. App. 1994), 35.04[B]

Tabb Lakes, Inc. v. U.S., 26 Cl. Ct. 1334 (Ct. Cl. 1992), 11.03[A][1][b]

Tacoma Athletic Club, Inc. v. Indoor Comfort Sys., Inc., 902 P.2d 175 (Wash. Ct. App. 1995), 29.02[E]

Tacon Mech. Contractors v. Grant Sheet Metal, 889 S.W.2d 666 (Tex. Ct. App. 1994), 35.08[C]

Tamarac Dev. Co. v. Delamater Freund & Assoc., 675 P.2d 361 (Kan. 1984), 29.02[C][3]

Tamp Corp., ASBCA No. 25692, 84-2 B.C.A. ¶ 17,460 (1984), 28.04[C][1]

Taranow v. Brokstein, 185 Cal. Rptr. 532 (1982), 33.02[M][1]

Tarzan Constr., Inc., IBCA No. 1840, 85-2 BCA ¶ 18,052 (1985), 23.03[D]

Tassinari v. Loyer, 189 So.2d 651 (Fla. Dist. Ct. App. 1996), 33.02[M][2]

Tate v. Colony House Builders, Inc., 508 S.E.2d 567 (Va. 1999), 12.04[C][1][a]

Taxpayers Against Fraud, United States ex rel., v. General Electric Co., 41 F.3d 1032 (6th Cir. 1994), 38.02[B][3]

Taykinswell, Inc., United States ex rel., v. Bencon Constr. Co., 248 F. Supp. 502 (D. Md. 1965), aff'd, 369 F.2d 405 (4th Cir. 1966), 35.06[A][1][b]

Taylor & Polk Constr. Co., United States ex rel., v. Mill Valley Constr., Inc., 29 F.3d 154 (4th Cir. 1994), 35.04[A]

Taylor-Morley-Simon, Inc. v. Michigan Mut. Ins. Co., 645 F. Supp. 596 (E.D. Mo. 1986), aff'd, 822 F.2d 1093 (8th Cir. 1987), 19.07[B]

Taylor, United States ex rel., v. Fidelity Deposit Co. of Md., 4 F. Supp. 211 (D. Idaho 1930), 35.04[A]

Tayor & City Council of Baltimore v. Clark, 128 Md. 291, 97 A. 911 (1916), 21.02

T.C. Bateson Constr. Co., ASBCA No. 5985, 60-2 B.C.A. (CCH) ¶ 2767, ASBCA No. 6028, 1963 B.C.A. (CCH) ¶ 3692 (1960) (same), 24.02[D]

T.C. Bateson Constr. Co., ASBCA No. 6028, 1963 B.C.A. (CCH) ¶ 3692, 24.04[B]

TDC Managment Corp., DOTCAB 1802, 90-1 B.C.A. ¶ 23,880, 39.08[B]

TDS Constr. Co. v. Burke Co., 425 S.E.2d 359 (Ga. App. 1992), 35.07[B][1]

TD S Painting & Restoration, Inc. v. Copper Beech Farm, Inc., 808 A.2d 726 (Conn. App. Ct. 2002), 33.01[I]

Teacher's Ret. System of La. v. La. State Emp. Ret., 444 So. 2d 193 (La. App. 1 Cir. 1983), 20.02

TEC Constr., Inc., DOT BCA No. 2725, 94-2 B.C.A. ¶ 26,924 (1994), 28.03[E][1][c]

Techdyne Sys. Corp. v. Whittaker Corp., 427 S.E.2d 334 (Sup. Ct. Va. 1993), 27.05[D][6][c]

Technical Communications Elec. Consultants, Ltd., ASBCA Nos. 29143, 39395, 93-1 B.C.A. ¶ 25,311 (1992), 28.03[F][4]

Technocratica, ASBCA No. 46,006, 94-2 BCA ¶ 26,606 (1993), 23.03[E][3]

Technocratica, ASBCA Nos. 48060, 48061, 48054, 47992, 47993, 06-2 B.C.A. (CCH) ¶ 33,316 (2006), 24.03

Tecom v. United States, 732 F.2d 935 (Fed. Cir. 1984), 39.04[C]

Tectron Corp., ASBCA No. 12901, 73-1 B.C.A. ¶ 9786 (1972), 28.03[D][2]

Teerlink Ranch, Ltd., In re, 886 F.2d 1233 (9th Cir. 1989), 34.01

Tele-Sentry Sec., Inc., GSBCA No. 10945, 91-2 B.C.A. (CCH) ¶ 23,880, 39.08[C]

Tele-Sentry Sec., Inc., GSBCA No. 10945, 93-2 B.C.A. (CCH) ¶ 25,815, 39.03[E]

Tempo, Inc. v. Rapid Electric Sales & Services, 347 N.W.2d 728 (Mich. App. 1984), 33.01[C][1]

Tenaska Washington Partners II, L.P. v. United States, 34 Fed. Cl. 434 (1995), 40.02[B]

Tennant v. United States Fidelity & Guaranty Co., 17 F.3d 38 (3d Cir. 1927), 36.03[A]

Tennessee Elec. Power Co. v. White County, 52 F.2d 1065 (6th Cir. 1931), 30.03[C]

Tesco Controls, Inc. v. Monterey Mechanical Co., 21 Cal. Rptr. 3d 751 (Cal. Ct. App. 2004), 33.02[G]

Texas Bitulithic Co., United States ex rel., v. Fidelity & Deposit Co., 813 F.2d 697 (5th Cir. 1987), 35.06[A][1][b], 35.06[A][2]

Thacker, United States ex. rel., v. Allison Engine Co., Inc., 471 F.3d 610 (6th Cir. 2006) (cert. granted October 29, 2007), 38.02[C][1]

Thayer, Charles H., United States ex rel., v. Metro Constr. Co., 330 F. Supp. 386 (E.D. Va. 1971), 35.03[A]

Thayer, United States ex rel., v. Metro. Constr. Corp., 330 F. Supp. 386 (E.D. Va. 1971), 35.04[A]

Theisen v. County of L.A., 54 Cal. 2d 170 (1960), 35.03[B]

Therm-Air Mfg. Co., ASBCA No. 11047, 66-1 B.C.A. ¶ 5672 (1966), 28.03[D][2]

Therm-Air Mfg. Co., NASA BCA Nos. 180-2 et al., 82-2 B.C.A. ¶ 15,881 (1982), 28.03[B][3], 28.03[B][3][a]

Thermodyn Contractors, Inc. v. GSA, GSBCA No. 12510, 94-3 B.C.A. ¶ 27,071 (1994), 28.03[D][3]

Thomas v. Howard, 51 N.C. App. 350, 276 S.E.2d 743 (1981), 46.19

Thomas & Associates, Inc. v. Metropolitan Government of Nashville & Davidson County, 2003 WL 21302974 (Tenn. Ct. App. June 6, 2003), 26.02[QQ][3], 26.02[QQ][4]

Thomas & Sons Bldg. Contractors, Inc., ASBCA No. 51,950, 02-1 B.C.A. (CCH) ¶ 31,837 (2002), 24.02[B]

Thomas & Sons Bldg. Contractors, Inc., DOT B.C.A. No. 3013 01-1 B.C.A. (CCH) ¶ 31,386 (2001), 1174

Thomas & Sons, Inc., ASBCA No. 51874, 01-1 B.C.A. ¶ 31,166 (2000), 28.03[C][1], 28.03[E][1][c]

Thomas Indus., Inc.v. C&L Elec., Inc., 550 N.W2d 558 (Mich. Ct. App. 1996), 35.05[B]

Thomas J. Dyer Co. v. Bishop Int'l Eng'g Co., 303 F.2d 655 (6th Cir. 1962), 25.02[C], 35.08[E][1]

Thomas M. Durkin & Sons, Inc. v. Dep't of Transp. 742 A.2d 233 (Pa. Commw. Ct. 1999), 7.03[B][2][a]

Thomas Somerville Co. v. Broyhill, 200 Va. 358, 105 S.E.2d 824 (1958), 25.03[B]

Thompson v. Budd Co., 199 F.3d 799 (6h Cir. 1999), 29.03[D][3]

Thompson v. McCarthy, 289 A.D.2d 663 (3d Dep't 2001), 30.02[A][1]

Thompson-Starrett Int'l, Inc. v. Tropic Plumbing, Inc., 457 F.2d 1349 (3d Cir. 1972), 21.05

Thompson Transport Co. v. Middlestates Constr. Co., 397 P.2d 368 (Kan. 1964), rev'd on other grounds, 403 P.2d 999 (Kan. 1965), 35.04[B]

Thornton Constr. Co., People *ex rel.*, v. United States Fid. & Guar. Co., 154 N.W.2d 532 (Mich. Ct. App. 1967), 35.08[B]

Thorton v. E.I. Du Pont de Nemours & Co., 22 F.3d 284 (11th Cir. 1994), 29.02[D][2]

3D Enters. Contracting Corp. v. Louisville & Jefferson Cty. Metro. Sewer Dist., 174 S.W.3d 440 (Ky. 2005), 33.01[B]

3550 Stevens Creek Assocs. v. Barclays Bank of Cal., 915 F.2d 1355 (9th Cir. 1990), 11.03[A][6]

T.H.S. Northstar Assocs. v. W.R. Grace & Co., 767 F. Supp. 969 (D. Minn. 1991), 29.02[E]

Thurman v. Star Elec. Supply, 307 So. 2d 283 (La. 1975), 35.03[B]

T.I. Constr. Co. v. Kiewit E. Co., 1992 U.S. Dist. LEXIS 19213 (E.D. Pa. 1992), 28.02[C]

Tilbury, Inc., ASBCA No. 25792, 82-1 B.C.A. ¶ 15,644 (1982), 28.03[G]

Time Contractors, DOTCAB No. 1669, 86-2 B.C.A. (CCH) ¶ 19,003, 39.08[B]

Time Contractors, J.V., DOTBCA No. 1669, 87-1 BCA (CCH) ¶ 19,582 (1987), 23.03[C], 24.02, 24.04[B]

Times Fiber Communications v. Travelers Indemnity Co. of Illinois, 2005 Conn. Super. LEXIS 335, 19.07[B]

Timmons, Butt & Head, Inc., ASBCA No. 15,948, 72-1 B.C.A. (CCH) ¶ 9247 (1971), 24.02[A]

Tioga County, County Comm'rs of, v. C. Davis, Inc., 266 A.2d 749 (Pa. 1970), 35.07[B][1]

Titan Corporation, 42.02[B][6], 42.02[F]

Titan Mountain States, 85-1 BCA ¶ 17,931 (1985), 23.06[D]

Titan Pacific Constr. Corp. v. United States, 17 Cl. Ct. 630 (1989), 23.06[B][1]

Titan Stone, Tile & Masonry, Inc. v. Hunt Constr. Group, Inc., No. 90-345, slip op. 2007 WL 3232588 (D.N.J. Oct. 31, 2007), 28.03[B][4]

Title Guar. & Trust Co. v. Crane Co., 219 U.S. 24 (1910), 35.04[A]

T.J. Stevenson & Co. v. 81,193 Bags of Flour, 629 F.2d 338 (5th Cir. 1980), *reh'g denied,* 651 F.2d 779 (5th Cir. 1981), 16.08[C]

TK Power, Inc. v. Textron, Inc., 433 F. Supp. 2d 1058 (N.D. Cal. 2006), 16.02[B]

T.L. James & Co. V. Traylor Bros., Inc., No. 97-0342 Sec. "B" (5), 2000 U.S. Dist. LEXIS 4378 (E.D. La. Mar. 23, 2000), *aff'd,* 294 F.3d 743 (5th Cir. 2002), 24.02

TLT Constr. Corp., ASBCA NO. 40501, 92-1 B.C.A. ¶ 24,458 (1991), 28.04[C][1]

T.L. Wallace Constr. Co., United States *ex rel.*, v. Fireman's Fund Ins. Co., 790 F. Supp. 680 (S.D. Miss. 1992), 35.06[A][1][b]

T.M.S. Mech. Constructors, Inc., United States *ex rel.*, v. Millers Mut. Fire Ins. Co. of Tex., 942 F.2d 946 (5th Cir. 1991), 35.04[A], 35.07[A][1], 35.08[E][1]

T/N Plumbing & Heating Co., United States *ex rel.*, v. Fryd Corp., 423 F.2d 980 (5th Cir. 1970), 35.08[E][2]

Toll, Inc. v. Elias/Avion Adver., Inc., 811 A.2d 10 (Pa. Super. Ct. 2002), 7.02[B][2][c]

Tombigbee Constructors v. United States, 420 F.2d 1037 (Ct. Cl. 1970), 28.03[E][4]

Tom Growney Equip., United States *ex rel.*, v. Fisher, 457 F.2d 1298 (10th Cir. 1972), 35.08[H]

Tommy L. Griffin Plumbing & Heating Co. v. Jordan, Jones & Goulding, Inc., 320 S.C. 49, 463 S.E.2d 85 (1995), 20.02

Tommy L. Griffin Plumbing & Heating Co. v. Jordan, Jones & Goulding, Inc., 463 S.E.2d 85 (S.C. 1995), 29.02[C][3], 29.02[C][5]

Tompkins v. Commissioner, 97 F.2d 396 (4th Cir. 1938), 17.07

Tompkins, Inc. v. City of Bridgeport, 94 Conn. 659 (1920), 30.04[B][2]

Tom P. McDermott, Inc., United States *ex rel.*, v. Woods Constr. Co., 224 F. Supp. 406 (N.D. Okla. 1963), 35.04[A]

Toombs & Co. v. United States, 4 Cl. Ct. 535 (1984), *aff'd,* 770 F.2d 183 (Fed. Cir. 1985), 28.03[E][1][b]

Toombs & Co., Inc., ASBCA Nos. 35085, 35086, 89-3 B.C.A. (CCH) ¶ 21,997, 39.04[C]

Topro Servs. v. McCarthy W. Constructors, 856 F. Supp. 1461 (D. Colo. 1994), 35.08[G]

Torncello v. United States, 231 Ct. Cl. 20, 681 F.2d 756 (1982), 27.05[G][2][b], 28.02, 28.04[A][1], 28.04[B], 28.04[B][1], 28.04[B][2], 28.04[C], 28.04[C][1], 28.04[C][2][a], 28.04[D]

Total Prop. Serv. of New England, Inc. v. Q.S.C.V., Inc., 30 Conn. App. 580, 621 A.2d 316 (1993), 46.06

Totten, United States *ex rel.,* v. Bombardier Corp., 380 F.3d 488 (2004), 38.02[C][1]

Towerridge, Inc. v. TAO, Inc., 111 F.3d 758 (10th Cir. 1997), 35.04[A], 35.08[B]

T.P.K. Constr. Corp. v. Southern Am. Ins. Co., 752 F. Supp. 105 (S.D.N.Y. 1990), 36.03[C]

Tracer Research v. National Envtl. Servs., Inc., 42 F. 3d 1292 (9th Cir. 1994), 46.07

Trafalgar House Construction, Inc. v. United States, 73 Fed. Cl. 675 (2006), 22.06, 22.09, 24.05

Trainor v. Aetna Cas. & Sur. Co., 290 U.S. 47 (1933), 34.04[F][1]

Trane Co. v. Whitehurst-Lassen Constr. Co., 881 F.2d 996 (11th Cir. 1989), 35.08[F][1], 35.08[F][2]

Transamerica Insurance Co. v. Barnett Bank of Marion County, 524 So. 2d 439 (Fla. Dist. Ct. App. 1988), 36.08

Transamerica Ins. Co. v. Bloomfield, 401 F.2d 357 (6th Cir. 1968), 36.03[A], 36.07, 36.09[D]

Transamerica Ins. Co. v. City of Kennewick, 785 F.2d 660 (9th Cir. 1986), 34.04[G][2]

Transamerica Ins. Co. v. Housing Auth., 669 S.W.2d 818 (Tex. App. 1984), 34.04[G][3]

Transamerica Ins. Co. v. Red Top Metal, Inc., 384 F.2d 752 (5th Cir. 1967), 33.02[O]

Transamerica Ins. Co. v. United States, 973 F.2d 1572 (Fed. Cir. 1992), *rev'd on other grounds,* 39.03[B][3], 39.04[A]

Transamerica Ins. Corp. v. United States, 973 F.2d 1572 (Fed. Cir. 1992), *rev'd on other grounds,* 39.03[B][1]

Trans-American Steel Corp. v. J. Rich Steers, Inc., 670 F.2d 558 (5th Cir. 1982), 35.08[D][2]

Transamerica Premier Ins. Co. v. Brighton Sch. Dist., 940 P.2d 348 (Colo. 1997), 34.04[D]

Transamerica Premier Ins. Co. v. Collins & Co., General Contractors, Inc., 735 F. Supp. 1050 (N.D. Ga. 1990), 46.06

Transamerica Premier Ins. Co. v. Ober, 894 F. Supp. 471 (D. Me. 1995), 35.04[A], 35.08[J]

Transamerica Premium Ins. Co. v. Cavalry Constr. Inc., 552 So. 2d 225 (Fla. Dist. Ct. App. 1989), 36.02[B]

Transatlantic Fin. Corp. v. United States, 259 F.Supp. 725 (D.D.C. 1965), 7.03[B][2][a]

Transatlantic Fin. Corp. v. United States, 363 F.2d 312 (D.C. Cir. 1966), 28.03[E][4]

Trans Coastal Roofing Co., United States *ex rel.,* v. David Boland, Inc., 922 F. Supp. 597 (S.D. Fla. 1996), 35.08[E][2]

Transco Contracting Co., ASBCA No. 25315, 82-1 B.C.A. (CCH) ¶ 15,516 (1981), 27.05[E][2]

Trans World Airlines, Inc. v. Travelers Indemnity Co., 262 F.2d 321 (8th Cir. 1959), 32.07, 33.01[B]

Trataros Construction, Inc. v. General Services Administration, 01-1 BCA 31310, GSBCA No. 15081 (February 21, 2001), 27.05[E][3]

Travel Centre v. GSA, GSBCA No. 14057, 98-1 B.C.A. ¶ 29,536 (1997), 28.04[C][1]

Travelers Cas. & Sur. Co. v. White Plains Pub. Sch., 2007 WL 935612 (S.D.N.Y. 2007), 34.04[E][3]

Travelers Cas. and Sur. Co of Am. v. United States, 74 Fed. Cl. 75 (2006), 29.02[B][2]

Travelers Cas. and Sur. Co of Am. v. U.S., 75 Fed. Cl. 696 (2007), 27.05[A][2], 27.05[C][2]

Travelers Indem. Co. v. Ballantine, 436 F. Supp. 2d 707 (M.D. Pa. 2006), 36.03[A]

Travelers Indem. Co. v. Clark, 254 So. 2d 741 (Miss. 1971), 36.09[E]

Travelers Indem. Co. v. Housing Auth. of Miami, 256 So. 2d 230 (Fla. Dist. Ct. App. 1972), 35.04[B]

Travelers Indem. Co. v. Miller Bldg. Corp., 142 F. Appx. 147 (4th Cir. 2004), 19.07[B]

Travelers Indem. Co. v. United States *ex rel.* Western Steel Co., 362 F.2d 896 (9th Cir. 1996), 35.04[A]

Travelers Indem. Co. of Am. v. Moore & Assocs., Inc., 216 S.W.3d 302 (Tenn. 2007), 18.04[C][1], 19.07[B]

Travelers Indem. Co. of Am. v. Moore & Assocs., No. M2004-01233-COA-R3-CV, 2005 Tenn. App. LEXIS 596 (Ct. App. Sept. 20, 2005), *aff'd,* 216 S.W.3d 302 (Tenn. 2007), 18.05[A][2]

Travelers Indem. Co., The, v. United States *ex rel.* Western Steel Co., 362 F.2d 896 (9th Cir. 1966), 33.02[O]

Traylor v. Henkels & McCoy, Inc., 585 P.2d 970 (Idaho 1978), 30.04[B][2]

Tretting Printing, Inc. v. Fitzpatrick & Assocs., Inc., 640 A.2d 788 (N.J. 1994), 46.16

Triangle, United States v., 277 F.3d 1251 (10th Cir. 2002), 17.01[A]

Triax Co., ASBCA No. 33899, 88-3 B.C.A. (CCH) ¶ 20,830, 39.08[B]

Tribble & Stephens Co. v. Consolidated Servs., 744 S.W.2d 945 (Tex. Ct. App. 1987, writ denied), 28.03[E][1][a]

Tri-City P'ship, 206 Ga. App. 506, 426 S.E.2d 57 (1992), 46.04

Tricon Kent Co. v. Lafarge North America, Inc. et al, 186 P.3d 155 (Colo. App. 2008), 26.02[F][3], 26.02[F][4]

Trident Indus. Prods. Corp., DOT BCA No. 2807 et al., 98-1 B.C.A. ¶ 26,619 (1998), 28.03[D][3]

Trinity Installers, Inc., AGBCA No. 2004-139-1, 05-1 BCA ¶ 32,868 (2005), 28.03[G]

Trinity Universal Ins. Co. v. Girdner, 379 F.2d 317 (5th Cir. 1967), 35.06[A][1][b]

Triple R Paving, Inc. v. Broward County, 774 So. 2d 50 (Fla. Dist. Ct. App. 2000), 26.02[J][3], 26.02[J][4], 30.03[C][3]

Tri-State Aggregates Corp. v. Metro. Transp. Auth., 485 N.Y.S.2d 754 (N.Y. App. Div. 1985), 7.03[E]

Tri-State Constr. Co., 79-1 B.C.A. (CCH) ¶ 13,644 (ASBCA 1979), 32.06

Tri-State Ins. Co. v. United States, 340 F.2d 542 (8th Cir. 1965), 34.04[F][5]

Tropical Supply Co. v. Verchio, 402 So. 2d 1284 (Fla. Dist. Ct. App. 1981), 35.08[D][3]

Tropic Plumbing, Inc. v. Thompson-Starrett Int'l, Inc., 325 F. Supp. 449 (D.V.I. 1971), *rev'd,* 457 F.2d 1349 (3d Cir. 1972), 21.05

TRU & Assocs., Inc., ASBCA No. 45263, 96-2 B.C.A. ¶ 28,389 (1996), 28.03[F][1]

Trus Joist Corp. v. Safeco Ins. Co. of Am., 735 P.2d 125 (Ariz. App. Ct. 1986), 33.01[B]

T Square Equip. Co., United States *ex rel.*, v. Gregor J. Schaefer Sons, Inc., 272 F. Supp. 962 (E.D.N.Y. 1967), 35.06[A][1][b]

Tull v. Gundersons, Inc., 709 P.2d 940 (Colo. 1985), 30.04[B][2]

Tupelo Redevelopment Agency v. Gray Corp., 972 So. 2d 495 (Miss. 2007), 26.02[Y][3], 26.02[Y][4]

Turkcell Consortium, Comp. Gen. Dec. B-293048.2, 2003 CPD ¶ 196, 45 GC ¶ 478, 41.07[A], 41.07[B]

Turner v. Kerin & Assoc., 938 P.2d 1368 (Mont. 1997), 29.02[C][5]

Turner v. Nicholson Props., Inc., 341 S.E.2d 42 (N.C. App. 1986), 46.21

Turner Constr. Co., United States v., 827 F.2d 1554 (Fed. Cir. 1987), 39.04[F]

Turnkey Enters. v. United States, 597 F.2d 750 (Ct. Cl. 1979), 27.05[C][3][b]

TVA v. Hill, 437 U.S. 153 (1978), 11.03[A][10]

Twigg Corp. v. GSA, GSBCA Nos. 14386 et al., 00-1 B.C.A. ¶ 30,772 (2000), 28.03[F]

Two State Constr. Co., DOT BCA No. 78-31, 81-1 B.C.A. ¶ 15,149 (1981), 28.03[D][3]

2314 Lincoln Park West Condo, Ass'n v. Mann, Gin, Ebel & Frazier, Ltd., 555 N.E.2d 346 (Ill. 1990), 29.02[C][5]

T.W. Poe & Sons v. University of N.C., 248 N.C. 617, 104 S.E.2d 189 (1958), 46.25

Tyco, 42.02[G]

Tyger Constr. Co. v. United States, 28 Fed. Cl. 35 (1993), 38.02[C][1][a][i]

Tyger Constr. Co. v. United States, 31 Fed. Cl. 177 (1994), 28.03[E][1][b], 38.02[C][1][a][i]

Tyree Org. v. Cashin Assocs., No. 12361-05, 2007 WL 171906 (N.Y. Gen. Term Jan. 22, 2007), 16.07[A]

U

Udis v. United States, 7 Cl. Ct. 379 (1985), 28.04[A][2]

Uhl Constr. v. Fidelity & Deposit Co., 538 A.2d 562 (Pa. Super. 1988), 35.08[D][2]

Ulico Cas. Co. v. Atlantic Contracting & Material Co., Inc., 822 A.2d 1257 (Md. Ct. App. 2003), aff'd, 844 A.2d 460 (Md. 2004), 36.03[A], 36.03[B], 36.09[A]

Umpqua River Navigation Co. v. Crescent City Harbor Dist., 618 F.2d 588 (9th Cir. 1980), 22.04, 22.08

Unadilla Silco Co. v. Hess Bros., Inc., 586 A.2d 226 (N.J. 1991), 35.03[B]

UNC/Lear Services, Inc., United States v., Plea Agreement (W.D. Ky. 1999), 42.02[F][1]

Underground Festival v. McAfee Eng'g Co., 447 S.E.2d 683 (Ga. Ct. App. 1994), 35.08[G]

Underwriters at Interest v. SCI Steelcon, 905 F. Supp. 441 (W.D. Mich. 1995), 18.05[A][2], 18.05[A][3]

Unicon Mgmt. Corp., ASBCA No. 10,196, 65-1 BCA ¶ 4778 at 22,860 (1965), 23.03[B][1]

Union Asphalt, Inc. v. Planet Ins. Co., 21 Cal. App. 4th 1762 (1994), 35.03[B]

Union Indem. Co. v. Ricks, 140 So. 597 (Ala. 1932), 35.08[B]

Union Ins. Co. v. Hottenstein, 83 P.3d 1196 (Colo. App. 2003), 19.07[B]

Union Pac. R.R. v. Bridal Veil Lumber Co., 219 F.2d 825 (9th Cir. 1955), 36.09[A]

Union Plate Glass Co. v. Metal Trims Indus., 525 A.2d 468 (Pa. Commw. Ct. 1987), 35.08[E][1]

Uniroyal, Inc. v. A. Epstein & Sons, Inc., 428 F.2d 523 (7th Cir. 1970), 46.06

United Ass'n of Journeymen & Apprentices v. Stine, 351 P.2d 965 (Nev. 1976), 46.14

United Bonding Ins. Co. v. Atlantic Roofing & Sheet Metal Co., 221 So. 2d 461 (Fla. Dist. Ct. App. 1969), 35.08[I]

United Bonding Ins. Co. v. M.D. Moody & Sons, Inc., 213 So. 2d 263 (Fla. Dist. Ct. App. 1968), 35.04[B]

United Bonding Ins. Co. v. Stein, 273 F. Supp. 929 (E.D. Pa. 1967), 36.04

United Bonding Ins. Co. v. W. S. Newell, Inc., 232 So. 2d 616 (Ala. 1969), 35.08[I]

United Nuclear Corp. v. Combustion Eng'g Inc., 302 F. Supp. 539 (E.D. Pa. 1969), 17.08[A]

United Pac. Ins. Co., ASBCA No. 53051, 01-2 B.C.A. ¶ 31,527 (2001), 28.03[C][2]

United Riggers & Erectors v. Marathon Steel Co., 725 F.2d 87 (10th Cir. 1984), 33.02[N], 36.03[C]

United States v. See name of opposing party

United States Cas. Co. v. Noland Co., 286 F. Supp. 333 (M.D.N.C. 1968), 35.08[D][2]

United States Fid. & Guar., 676 F.2d 630, 28.04[A][2]

United States Fidelity & Guaranty v. Hittle, 96 N.W. 782 (Iowa 1903), 36.03[C]

United States Fid. & Guar. v. Tafel
Elec. Co., 91 S.W.2d 42 (Ky. Ct.
App. 1936), 35.06[B][1]

United States Fid. & Guar. Co. v.
American Blower Co., 84 N.E. 555
(Ind. Ct. App. 1908), 35.08[I]

United States Fid. & Guar. Co. v.
Armstrong, 479 So. 2d 1164 (Ala.
1985), 18.04[C][1]

United States Fid. & Guar. Co. v.
Blankenship Plumbing Co., 265
S.E.2d 66 (Ga. Ct. App. 1980),
36.09[B]

United States Fid. & Guar. Co. v.
Borden Metal Prods. Co., 539 S.W.2d
170 (Tex. Civ. App. 1976), 35.08[I]

United States Fid. & Guar. Co. v.
Briscoe, 239 P.2d 754 (Okl. 1951),
19.07[B]

United States Fid. & Guar. Co. v.
Feenaughty Mach. Co., 85 P.2d 1085
(Wash. 1939), 35.04[B], 35.08[D][2]

United States Fid. & Guar. Co. v. Jones,
87 F.2d 346 (5th Cir. 1937), 36.07

United States Fid. & Guar. Co. v.
Miami Sheet Metal Prods., 516 So.
2d 29 (Fla. Dist. Ct. App. 1987),
35.08[C]

United States Fid. & Guar. Co. v.
Miller, 549 S.W.2d 316 (Ky. Ct. App.
1977), 35.04[B]

United States Fid. & Guar. Co. v.
United Penn Bank, 524 A.2d 958 (Pa.
Super. Ct. 1987), 36.06

United States Fid. & Guar. Co. v.
United States, 231 U.S. 237, 34 S.
Ct. 88, 58 L. Ed. 200 (1913),
35.07[A][1]

United States Fid. & Guar. Co. v.
United States ex rel. Bartlett, 231
U.S. 237 (1913), 35.04[A]

United States Fid. & Guar. Co. v.
United States ex rel. Golden Pressed
& Fire Brick, So., 191 U.S. 416
(1903), 35.08[I]

United States Fid. & Guar. Co. v. West
Point Constr. Co., 837 F.2d 1507 (4th
Cir. 1988), 25.03[B], 46.06

United States Fid. & Guar. Co. v.
Wilkin Insulation, 578 N.E.2d 926
(Ill. 1991), 20.02, 20.05

United States Fid. & Guar. Co., United
States v., 601 F. 2d 1136 (10th Cir.
1979), 20.02

United States Fid. & Guar. Ins. Co. v.
Andalusia Ready Mix, Inc., 436 So.
2d 868 (Ala. 1983), 19.07[B]

United States Fid. & Guar. Ins. Co. v.
Bonitz Insulation Co., 424 So. 2d 569
(Ala.1982), 19.07[B]

United States Fid. & Guar. Ins. Co. v.
Wilkin Insulation Co., 578 N.E.2d
926 (Ill.1991), 19.07[B]

United States Indus., Inc. v. Blake
Constr. Co., 671 F.2d 539 (D.C. Cir.
1982), 24.04[B], 30.03[D][4]

United States Lighting Serv., Inc. v.
Llerrad Corp., 800
F. Supp. 1513 (N.D. Ohio 1992),
vacated on other grounds,
29.02[C][5]

United States Lines lnc., In re
Arbitration, v. Liverpool & London
Steamship Prot. & Indem. Ass'n.
Ltd., 833 F. Supp. 350 (S.D.N.Y.
1993), 43.07[C]

United States Pollution Control v.
National Am. Ins. Co., 663 So. 2d
119 (La. Ct. App. 3d Cir. 1995),
35.08[J]

United States Rubber Co., United States
ex rel., v. Ambursen Dam Co., 3
F. Supp. 548 (N.D. Cal. 1933),
35.04[A]

United States Surety Co. v. KeyCorp.,
2007 WL 2331942 (N.D. Ohio
8/13/07), 34.04[H]

United Structures of Am. v. G.R.G.
Eng'g, 927 F. Supp. 556 (D.P.R.
1996), 35.08[B]

United Structures of Am. v. G.R.G.
Eng'g, 9 F.3d 966 (1st Cir. 1993),
35.08[B]

United Techs. Corp., Pratt & Whitney
Group, Gov't Engines & Space
Propulsion, ASBCA Nos. 41766 et
al., 96-1 B.C.A. (CCH) ¶ 28,226,
39.03[B][2]

United Telecomm., Inc. v. Am.
Television & Commc'n Corp.,
536 F.2d 1310 (10th Cir. 1976),
31.03[B]

Universal Bonding v. Gittens &
Sprinkle Enters., 960 F.3d 73 (3d Cir.
1994), 34.04[H]

Universal Bonding Ins. Co. v. Gittens &
Sprinkle Enters., Inc., 960 F.2d 366
(3d Cir. 1992), 25.04[A]

Universal Builders, Inc. v. Moon Motor Lodge, Inc., 430 Pa. 550, 224 A.2d 10 (1968), 21.02

Universal Builders, Inc., *In re*, 53 B.R. 183 (Bankr. M.D. Tenn. 1985), 36.08

Universal Contracting & Brick Pointing Co. v. U.S., 19 Cl. Ct. 785 (1990), 11.04[B][4][a]

Universal Fiberglass Corp. v. United States, 537 F.2d (Ct. Cl. 1976), 28.03[D][2]

Universal Sur. Co. v. Jed Constr. Co., 265 N.W.2d 219 (Neb. 1974), 36.09[C]

Univ. of Cal., Regents of the, v. Hartford Accident & Indem. Co., 147 Cal. Rptr. 486, 581 P.2d 197 (1978), 34.04[G][4]

Urbanational Developers, Inc. v. Shamrock Eng'g. Inc., 372 N.E.2d 742 (1978), 33.01[E]

Urban Masonry Corp. v. N & N Contractors, 676 A.2d 26 (D.C. 1996), 35.08[E][1]

USA Info. Sys., Inc., B-291488, 2002 WL 31689243 (Comp. Gen. Dec. 2, 2002), 7.03[A]

U.S. Eng'g Co. v. United Excel Corp., F. Supp. _____, 2007 U.S. Dist. LEXIS 9361 (D. Kan. 2007), 25.02[D]

U.S. Fidelity & Guaranty Co. v. Hittle, 96 N.W. 782 (1903), 33.02[N]

US Fire Ins. co. v. J.S.U.B., Inc., 979 So. 2d 871 (Fla. 2007), 18.04[C][1]

U.S. Floors, Inc., 94-2 B.C.A. (CCH) ¶ 26,636 (ASBCA 1994), 32.09[A]

U.S. Home Corp., *In re*, 236 S.W.3d 761 (Texas 2007), 45.04[A]

U.S. Indus., Inc. v. Blake Constr. Co., 671 F.2d 539 (D.C. Cir. 1982), 24.04

U.S. Servs. Corp., ASBCA No. 8291, 1963 B.C.A. ¶ 3703 (1963), 28.03[E][2]

U.S. Steel Corp. v. Missouri Pacific Railroad, 668 F.2d 435 (8th Cir. 1982), 26.02[D][3], 26.02[D][4], 26.02[KK][4]

V

V&W Constr. & Servs. Co., AGBCA No. 2003-147, 04-2 BCA ¶ 32,692 (2004), 23.03[B][1]

Valley Bancorporation v. Auto Owners Ins. Co., 212 Wis. 2d 609 (1997), 18.05[B][2]

Valley Forge Ind. v. Armand Constr., 394 A.2d 677 (Pa. Commw. Ct. 1978), 35.06[B][1]

Valley Landscape Co. v. Rolland, 237 S.E.2d 120 (Va. 1977), 29.02[C][5]

Valley Metal Works v. A.O. Smith-Inland, Inc., 572 S.W.2d 138 (Ark. 1978), 35.03[B]

Valloric v. Dravo Corp., 357 S.E.2d 207 (W. Va. 1987), 33.02[C]

Vandenberg v. Centennial Ins. Co., 21 Cal. 4th 815, 982 P.2d 229 (1999), 19.07[B]

Vandenberg v. Superior Court, 21 Cal. 4th 815, 982 P.2d 229, 88 Cal. Rptr. 2d 366 (Cal. 1999), 19.03[G][1]

Van Elk, Ltd., ASBCA No. 45311, 93-3 B.C.A. (CCH) ¶ 25,995, 39.03[B][2]

Van Engers. v. Perini Corp., 1993 U.S. Dist. LEXIS 8736 (E.D. Pa. 1993), 28.02[C]

Vanguard Prods. v. American States Ins., 863 P.2d 991 (Kan. Ct. App. 1993), 35.03[B]

Van Huff v. Sohio Alaska Petro. Co., 835 P.2d 1181 (Alaska 1992), 33.02[L]

Vankirk v. Green Construction Co., 466 S.E.2d 782 (W. Va. 1995), 32.07

Vann v. Travelers Cos., 39 Cal. App. 4th 1610 (1995), 18.04[C][2], 18.05[B][1]

Vann v. United States, 420 F.2d 968 (Ct. Cl. 1970), 28.02[A][3], 28.03[E][1][c], 28.03[E][4]

Vaugh Elec. Co., DOT BCA No. 1638, 87-1 B.C.A. ¶ 19,588 (1987), 28.03[B][3][b]

Vermont Agency of Natural Resources v. United States *ex rel.* Stevens, 529 U.S. 765, 120 S. Ct. 1858 (2000), 38.02[B][3], 38.02[C]

Vicari v. United States, 53 Fed. Cl. 357 (2002), 24.04[C]

Viktoria Transp. GmbH & Co., ASBCA No. 30371, 88-3 B.C.A. ¶ 20,921 (1988), 28.04[A][2]

Village of Fox Lake v. Aetna Cas. & Sur. Co., 534 N.E.2d 133 (Ill. App. Ct. 1989), 34.04[F][6]

Vincent Builders, Inc. v. American Application Sys., 547 A.2d 1381 (Conn. App. 1988), 46.23

Vogt Bros. Mfg. Co. v. United States, 160 Ct. Cl. 687 (1963), 28.03[E][1][a]

Volt Information Sciences, Inc. v. Board of Trustees of Leland Stanford Junior Univ., 489 U.S. 468 (1989), 46.04

Volume Servs., Inc. v. C.F. Murphy & Asscos., Inc., S.W.2d 785 (Mo. App. 1983), 20.02

W

Waldinger Corp. v. Ashbrook-Simon-Hartley, Inc., 564 F. Supp. 970 (C.D. Ill. 1983), 8A.08[G][1]

Walker & Co. v. Harrison, 81 N.W. 2d 352 (Mich. 1957), 30.04[B]

Walker Bank & Trust Co. v. Smith, 501 P.2d 639 (Nev. 1972), 35.08[G]

Wallace, United States *ex rel.* v. Flintco, Inc., 143 F.3d 955 (5th Cir. 1998), 26.02[RR][3], 26.02[RR][4]

Walnut Grove Partners LP v. Am. Family Mut. Ins. Co., No. 4:04-CV-10168, 2004 U.S. Dist. LEXIS 30518 (S.D. Iowa Oct. 4, 2004), 18.05[B][1]

Walser v. United States, 23 Cl. Ct. 591 (1991), 27.05[C][3][b]

Walsky Constr. Co., ASBCA No. 41541, 94-1 B.C.A. ¶ 26,264, *aff'd on reconsideration,* 94-2 B.C.A. ¶ 26,698 (1994), 28.04[D][2], 28.04[D][4]

Walsky Constr. Co., ASBCA No. 41541, 94-2 B.C.A. ¶ 26,698 (1994), 28.03[D], 28.04[D]

Walsky Constr. Co., ASBCA No. 52772, 01-2 B.C.A. ¶ 31,557 (2001), 28.03[G]

Walter Concrete Constr. Corp. v. Lederle Labs., 99 N.Y. 2d 603 (Ct. App. 2003), 34.04[B]

Walters Tire Serv., Inc., Commonwealth *ex rel.*, v. National Union Fire Ins. Co., 252 A.2d 593 (Pa. 1969), 35.04[B]

Wang, PSBCA No. 504, 72-1 B.C.A. ¶ 9473 (1972), 28.03[B][2]

Wanzek Constr., Inc. v. Emplrs. Ins., 667 N.W.2d 473 (Minn. Ct. App. 2003), 18.05[A][2]

Ward v. City of Portland, 857 F.2d 1373 (9th Cir. 1988), 36.09[D]

Warner Indus., Inc., ASBCA No. 13461, 70-1 B.C.A. ¶ 8151 (1970), 28.03[D][2]

Warren Bros. Co. v. Sentry Ins., 433 N.E.2d 1253 (Mass. App. Ct. 1982), 35.08[D][2]

Warrior Constructors v. Harders, Inc., 387 F.2d 727 (5th Cir. 1967), 35.08[F][1]

Warstler v. Cibrian, 859 S.W.2d 162 (Mo. Ct. App. 1993), 33.01[B]

Warwick Constr., Inc., GSBCA Nos. 5070, 5387, 5388, 5457, 5543, 82-2 B.C.A. (CCH) ¶ 16,091 (1982), 24.02, 24.03

Wasatch Bank of Pleasant Grove v. Surety Ins. Co. of Cal., 703 P.2d 298 (Utah 1985), 35.04[B]

Washington-Baltimore Newspaper Guild, Local 35 v. Washington Post, 959 F.2d 288 (D.C. Cir. 1992), 46.09

Wasserman's Inc. v. Township of Middletown, 645 A.2d 100 (N.J. 1994), 16.09[B]

Wasyl v. First Boston Corp., 813 F.2d 1579 (9th Cir. 1987), 46.01

Watson v. Amdeco Steel, Inc., 29 F.3d 274 (7th Cir. 1994), 16.10[A]

Watson Elec. Construction Co. v. City of Winston-Salem, 109 N.C. App. 194, 426 S.E.2d 420 (1993), 26.02[HH][3]

Watson, Watson, Rutland Architects, Inc. v. Montgomery County Bd. of Educ., 559 So. 2d 168 (Ala. 1990), 29.02[C][4]

Waukesha Concrete Prods. Co. v. Capitol Indem. Corp., 379 N.W.2d 333 (Wis. Ct. App. 1985), 35.08[D][2]

Wausau v. Constr. Mgmt. Eng'rs Inc., 377 S.E.2d 119 (S.C. Ct. App. 1989), 28.03[E][3][b]

Wayne Rosa Constr. v. Hugo Key & Son, 153 F.R.D. 481 (D. Me. 1994), 35.08[J]

Weatherguard Roofing Co., Inc. v. D.R. Ward Const. Co., Inc., 214 Ariz. 344, 152 P.3d 1227 (Ct. App. Div. 2007), 46.06

Weaver-Bailey Contractors, Inc. v. United States, 19 Cl. Ct. 474 (1990), 23.03[H], 23.07[B][2]

Weaver Constr. Co., ASBCA No. 12,577, 69-1 B.C.A. (CCH) ¶ 7455 (1969), 24.04[A]

Webb Elec. Co. of Fla., Inc., ASBCA No. 54293, 07-2 BCA ¶ 33,717 (2007), 23.06[D]

Webb Elec. Co. of Fla., Inc. v. New Thought Finishing, Inc., No. 92-2563, 1995 U.S. Dist. LEXIS 6633 (E.D. La. May 4, 1995), 35.04[B]

Webcraft Packaging, B-194087, Aug. 14, 1979, 79-2 CPD ¶ 120, 28.03[E][3][b]

Webster County Solid Waste Auth. v. Brackenrich & Assocs., Inc., 217 W. Va. 304, 617 S.E.2d 851 (W. Va. Ct. App. 2005), 20.02

Weddington Prods. Inc. v. Flick, 60 Cal. App. 4th 793, 71 Cal. Rptr. 265 (2d Cir. 1998), 45.04[F]

Weedo v. Stone-E-Brick, Inc., 81 N.J. 233, 405 A.2d 788 (N.J. 1979), 18.04[C][1], 19.07[B]

Weekley Homes, Inc. v. Jennings, 936 S.W.2d 16 (Tex. App. San Antonio 1996), *reh'g overruled,* (Nov. 27, 1996), and *writ denied* (Apr. 18, 1997) and *reh'g of writ of error overruled* (June 12, 1997) and *subsequent mandamus proceeding,* 985 S.W.2d 211 (Tex. App–San Antonio 1998), 45.04[A]

Weeks Dredging & Contracting, Inc. v. U.S., 13 Cl. Ct. 193 (1987), *aff'd,* 861 F.2d 728 (Fed. Cir. 1988), 27.05[C][2]

Weeshoff Constr. Co. v. Los Angeles County Flood Control District, 88 Cal. App. 3d 579 (1979), 28.03[E][3][a]

W.E. Foley & Bros., Inc., United States *ex rel.,* v. United States Fid. & Guar. Co., 113 F.2d 888 (2d Cir. 1940), 35.05[A]

W.E. Garrison Grading Co. v. Piracci Constr. Co., 27 N.C. App. 725, 221 S.E.2d 512 (1976), 21.02

Wehr Constructors, Inc. v. Steel Fabricators, Inc., 769 S.W.2d 51 (Ky. Ct. App. 1988), 32.03[A], 32.03[B]

Weill Construction Co. v. Thibodeaux, 491 So. 2d 166 (La. App. 3 Cir. 1986), 20.01

Weinberger v. Romero-Barcelo, 456 U.S. 305 (1982), 11.03[A][1][b]

Weldfab, Inc., IBCA No. 268, 61-2 B.C.A. (CCH) ¶ 3121 (1961), 24.02[A]

Wellington Power Corp. v. CNA Sur. Corp., 614 S.E.2d 680 (W. Va. 2005), 25.02[C]

Wells Benz, Inc. v. United States, 333 F.2d 89 (9th Cir. 1964), 28.03[B][1]

Wells Benz, Inc. v. United States *ex rel.* Mercury Elec. Co., 333 F.2d 89 (9th Cir. 1964), 35.08[B]

Wells Bros. Co. v. United States, 254 U.S. 83 (1920), 24.02[D]

Welsbach Elec. Corp. v. MasTec N. Am., Inc., 859 N.E.2d 498 (N.Y. App. 2006), 25.02[D]

Wertheimer Constr. Corp. v. United States, 406 F.2d 1071 (Ct. Cl. 1969), 28.03[F][2]

Werwinski v. Ford Motor Co., 286 F.3d 661 (3d Cir. 2002), 7.02[B][2][c]

West v. All State Boiler, Inc., 146 F.3d 1368 (Fed. Cir. 1998), 24.04[C]

West v. Roberts, 143 P.3d 1037 (Colo. 2006), 16.02[D]

West, United States *ex rel.,* v. Peter Kiewit & Sons' Co., 235 F. Supp. 500 (D. Alaska 1964), 35.04[A]

West American Ins. Co. v. J.R. Constr. Co., 334 Ill. App. 3d 75 (App. Ct. 2002), 18.04[A]

Westates Construction Co. v. City of Cheyenne, 775 P.2d 502 (Wyo. 1989), 26.02[YY][3]

West Chester Elec. & Elec. Co., United States *ex rel.,* v. Sentry Ins., 774 F.2d 80 (4th Cir. 1985), 35.08[D][2]

W. Contracting Corp. v. United States, 144 Ct. Cl. 318 (1958), 30.03[D][5]

Westclox Military Prods., ASBCA No. 25592, 81-2 B.C.A (CCH) ¶ 15,270, 39.03[B][1], 39.04[C]

Westerhold v. United States, 28 Fed. Cl. 172 (1993), 24.02[C]

Western & Southern Indem. Co. v. Carmer, 10 N.E.2d 440 (Ind. Ct. App. 1937), 35.08[D][2]

Western Cas. & Sur. Co. v. Stribling Bros. Mach. Co., 139 So. 2d 838 (Miss. 1962), 35.04[B]

Western Cas. & Sur. Co. v. United States, 109 F. Supp. 422 (Ct. Cl. 1953), 36.06

Western Contracting Corp., ENGBCA Nos. 3835 et al., 82-1 B.C.A. (CCH) ¶ 15,486 (1981), 27.05[G][2][a]

Western Contracting Corporation v. United States v., 13 F.3d 489 (1st Cir. 1994), 38.04

Western Engineers, Inc. v. State ex rel. Road Commission, 20 Utah 2d 294, 437 P.2d 216 (1968), 26.02[SS][3], 26.02[SS][4]

Western Exterminating Co. v. Hartford Accident & Indemnity Co., 479 A.2d 872 (D.C. App. 1984), 19.07[B]

Western Insulation Servs. v. Central Nat'l Ins. Co., 460 N.W.2d 335 (Minn. Ct. App. 1990), 35.08[D][2]

West-Fair Elec. Contrs. v. Aetna Cas. & Sur. Co., 638 N.Y.S.2d 394 (N.Y. 1995), 35.08[E][1]

West-Fair Elec. Contrs. v. Aetna Cas. & Sur. Co., 661 N.E.2d 967 (N.Y. 1995), 25.02[C]

Westinghouse Elec. Corp., ASBCA No. 20306, 76-1 B.C.A. ¶ 11,883 (1976), 28.03[D][2]

Westinghouse Elec. Corp. Uranium Contracts Litig., In re, 517 F. Supp. 440 (E.D. Va. 1981), 27.05[D][4][b]

Westinghouse Elec. Supply Co., Florida ex rel., v. Marvin, 280 F. Supp. 1019 (S.D. Fla. 1967), 35.07[B][1]

Westinghouse Elec. Supply Co., United States ex rel., v. Endebrock-White Co., 275 F.2d 57 (4th Cir. 1960), 35.04[A]

Westinghouse Elec. Supply Co., United States ex rel., v. Robbins, 125 F. Supp. 25 (D. Mass. 1954), 35.04[A]

Westinghouse Elec., United States ex rel., v. James Stewart Co., 336 F.2d 777 (9th Cir. 1964), 35.08[A]

Westminster, City of, v. Centric-Jones Constructors, 100 P.3d 472 (Colo. Ct. App. 2003), 30.02[A][1]

West Point Research, Inc., ASBCA No. 25511, 83-1 B.C.A. ¶ 16,443 (1983), 28.03[F][3]

Weyerhaeuser Co. v. Twin City Millwork Co., 191 N.W.2d 401 (Minn. 1971), 35.03[B]

W.G. Cornell Co. v. Ceramic Coating Co., 626 F.2d 990 (D.C. Cir. 1980), 24.04[C], 30.03[C][4], 30.03[C][5]

W.G. Cornell Co. v. United States, 376 F.2d 299 (Ct. Cl.1967), 28.03[E][1][a]

W.G. Yates & Sons Constr. Co., ASBCA No. 49398, 01-02 B.C.A. (CCH) ¶ 31,428 (2001), 24.04[D], 30.03[D][4]

W.G. Yates & Sons Constr. Co. v. United States, 53 Fed. Cl.83 (2002), 7.03[B][1][a]

W.H. Barber Co. v. McNamara-Vivant Construction Co., 293 N.W.2d 351 (Minn. 1979), 16.04[E]

Wheeler v. John Deere Co., 862 F.2d 1404 (10th Cir. 1988), 29.04[F][1]

White v. Edsall Const. Co. Inc., 296 F.3d 1081 (Fed. Cir. 2002), 5.03[C][8], 27.05[A][2], 29.02[B][1], 29.02[B][2], 29.03[D][1]

White Buffalo Constr., Inc., AGBCA No. 90-133-1-1, 93-3 B.C.A. ¶ 26,236 (1993), 28.03[D][2]

White Oak Corp. v. Department of Transportation, 217 Conn. 281, 585 A.2d 1199 (1991), 26.02[G][3], 30.03[C][5]

White River Dev. Co. v. Meco Sys., Inc., 806 S.W.2d 735 (Mo. Ct. App. 1991), 28.03[E][2]

Whiting-Turner/A.L. Johnson Joint Venture v. GSA, GSBCA No. 15,401, 2001 WL 1552412 (Dec. 5, 2001), 27.05[C][4]

W.H. Lyman Constr. Co. v. The Village of Gurnee, 403 N.E.2d 1325 (Ill. App. Ct. 1980), 22.02

W.H. Mosely Co., United States v., 730 F.2d 1472 (Fed. Cir. 1984), 39.06[C]

Wichita Sheet Metal Supply, Inc. v. Dahstrom & Ferrell Constr. Co., 792 P.2d 1043 (Kan. 1990), 34.04[G][4], 35.03[B]

Wickes Lumber v. Coleman Village, Inc., 314 N.W.2d 541 (Mich. Ct. App. 1981), 35.03[B]

Wickham Contracting Co. v. Fischer, 12 F.3d 1574 (Fed. Cir. 1994), 23.03[H], 24.04[C], 30.03[C][2], 30.03[C][3]

Wiechmann Eng'rs v. State, 107 Cal. Rptr. 529 (Cal. Ct. App. 1973), 7.03[B][2][a]

Wieman v. United States, 230 Ct. Cl. 563 (1982), 21.04

Wiener v. Anderson, 370 So. 2d 665 (La. Ct. App. 1979), 33.02[M][3]

Wiggins Constr. Co. v. Joint Sch. Dist. No. 3, 35 Wis. 632, 151 N.W.2d 642 (1967), 21.05

Wilderness Bldg. Sys. v. Chapman, 699 P.2d 766 (Utah 1985), 35.08[G]

Wildwoods of Lake Johnson Assocs. v. L.P. Cox Co., 362 S.E.2d 615 (N.C. App. 1987), 46.23

Wilhelm Lubrication Co. v. Brattrud, 268 N.W. 634 (Minn. 1936), 16.04[C]

Wilko v. Swan, 346 U.S. 427, 74 S. Ct. 182, 98 L. Ed. 168 (1953), *overruled on other grounds*, 46.21, 46.26

Wilks v. American Bakeries Co., 563 F. Supp. 560 (W.D.N.C. 1983), 46.19

WillBros Group Inc., 42.02[F][2]

Willets Ponit Contracting Corp. v. Hartford Ins. Group, 429 N.Y.S. 2d 230 (N.Y. App. Div. 1980) *aff'd*, 423 N.E.2d 42 (N.Y. 1981), 19.07[B]

William Aupperle & Sons v. American Indem. Co., 394 N.E.2d 725 (Ill. App. Ct. 1979), 35.08[F][1]

Wm. C. Vick Constr. Co. v. Pa. Nat'l Mut. Cas. Ins. Co., 52 F. Supp. 2d 569 (E.D. N.C. 1999), *aff'd,* 213 F.3d 634 (4th Cir. 2000), 19.07[B]

Williamette Crushing Co. v. State by and Through DOT, 932 P.2d 1350 (Ariz. Ct. App. 1997), 29.02[B][1]

William F. Klingensmith, Inc., Appeal of, 03-1 B.C.A. (CCH) ¶ 32,072 (ASBCA 2002), 32.06

William Green Construction Co., Inc. v. United States, 477 F.2d 930 (Ct. Cl. 1973) *accord*, 30.04[B][2]

William M. Hendrickson, Inc. v. Nat'l Railroad Passenger Corp., 47 U.C.C. Rep. Serv. 2d 1284, 2002 WL 398641 (E.D. Pa. 2002), 28.03[B][1]

William P. Clarke Corp. v. Safeco Ins. Co. of Am., 938 P.2d 372 (Cal. 1997), 25.02[C]

Wm. R. Clarke Corp. v. Safeco Inc. Co., 938 P.2d 372 (Cal. 1997), 35.08[E][1]

Williams v. Ashland Eng'g Co., 863 F. Supp. 46 (D. Mass. 1994), *aff'd,* 45 F.3d 588 (1st Cir. 1995), 35.04[B]

Williams v. Obstfeld, 314 F.3d 1270 (11th Cir. 2002), 17.01[A]

Williams Electric Co., United States *ex rel.* v. Metric Constructors, Inc., 325 S.C. 129, 480 S.E.2d 447 (1997), 26.02[OO][3], 35.08[E][3]

Willow Spring Condominium Assoc., Inc. v. Seventh BRT Dev. Corp., 245 Conn. 1 (1998), 30.02[A][1]

Wilner v. United States, 24 F.3d 1397, 39 Cont. Cas. Fed. (CCH) ¶ 76665 (Fed. Cir. 1994) (en banc), 24.02, 24.04[C]

Wilner v. United States, 24 F.3d 1397, (Fed. Cir. 1994), 30.03[C]

Wilson v. Bicycle South, Inc., 915 F.2d 1503 (11th Cir. 1990), 29.04[F][3]

Wilson v. Wilson, 2007 WL 4124349 (Ga. Nov. 2007), 45.05[A]

Wilson, PSBCA No. 3469, 98-1 B.C.A. ¶ 29,499 (1998), 28.04[C][2]

Wilson & Co. v. Walsenburg Sand & Gravel Co., 779 P.2d 1386 (Colo. Ct. App. 1989), 35.08[B], 35.08[C]

Windowmaster Corp., *Contra,* v. B.G. Danis Co., 511 F. Supp. 157 (S.D. Ohio 1981), 25.03[B]

Windowmaster Corp. v. Morse/Diesel, Inc., 722 F. Supp. 1532 (N.D. Ill. 1988), 34.04[D]

Windsor, United States *ex rel.*, v. Dyncorp., Inc., 895 F. Supp. 844 (E.D. Va. 1995), 38.02[C][1][a][ii]

Winfrey v. Simmons Foods, Inc., 495 F.3d 549 (8th Cir. 2007), 46.21

Winter v. Cath-dr/Balti Joint Venture, 497 F.3d 1339 (Fed. Cir. 2007), 27.05[B][2], 27.05[B][5][b], 27.05[B][5][e], 48.02[D]

Wiss v. Royal Indem. Co., 282 S.W. 164 (Mo. 1926), 35.07[B][1]

Witherington Constr. Corp. v. United States, 45 Fed. Cl. 208 (1999), 28.03[A]

W.L. Hailey & Co. v. County of Niagara, 388 F.2d 746 (2d Cir. 1967), 24.02[C]

W.M. Schlosser, Inc. v. U.S., 50 Fed. Cl. 147 (2001), 27.05[D][6][c]

Woessner v. Air Liquide, Inc., 242 F.3d 469 (3d Cir. 2001), 29.04[J]

Wolff v. Munier, Inc. v. Whiting-Turner Contracting Co., 946 F.2d 1003 (2d Cir. 1991), 30.01[B]

Wolf, Phyllis, AGBCA No. 96-102-1, 96-2 BCA ¶ 28,504 at 142,334 (1996), 23.04[B][1]

Wolther, United States *ex rel.*, v. New Hampshire Fire Ins. Co., 173 F. Supp. 529 (E.D.N.Y. 1959), 35.04[A]

Wolther, United States *ex rel.*, v. Seacoast Repair Co., 147 F. Supp. 686 (E.D.N.Y. 1957), 35.07[A][2]

Worthington Corp. v. Consol. Aluminum Corp., 544 F.2d 227 (5th Cir. 1976), 32.08

WRB Corp. v. U.S., 183 Ct. Cl. 409 (1968), 23.03[E][3], 24.04

Wrecking Corp., United States *ex rel.*, v. Edward M. Marden Corp., 406 F.2d 525 (1st Cir. 1969), 35.06[A][1][b]

Wu & Assocs., Inc., DOL Nos. 2003-BCA-1, 2004-BCA-2, 2007 DOL BCA LEXIS 1 (Jan. 5, 2007), 23.03[D]

Wunderlich Contracting Co. v. United States, 173 Ct. Cl. 180, 351 F.2d 956 (1965), 24.03, 28.03[E][3][a]

Wunderlich Contracting Co. v. United States, 240 F.2d 201 (10th Cir.), *cert. denied,* 353 U.S. 950 (1957), 21.06

Wunderlich Contracting Co. v. United States, 351 F.2d 956 (Ct. Cl. 1965), 21.07, 21.08, 28.03[E][1][b], 28.03[E][3][b]

Wunderlich Contracting Co. v. United States, 423 P.2d 545, 22.08

Wunderlich Contracting Co. v. United States *ex rel.* Reischel & Cottrell, 240 F.2d 201 (10th Cir. 1957), 35.04[A]

Wunderlich v. State, 423 P.2d 545 (Cal. 1967), 73 Fed. Cl. at 703, 22.06

Wyatt & Kipper Eng'rs, Inc., United States *ex rel.*, v. Ramstad Constr. Co., 194 F. Supp. 379 (D. Alaska 1961), 35.07[A][1]

Wyczaleck v. Rowe Constr. Servs. Co., 148 Ohio App. 3d 328 (Ohio Ct. App. 2001), 8A.08[A][1]

Wynne v. United States *ex rel.* Mid-States Waterproofing Co., 382 F.2d 669 (10th Cir. 1967), 35.04[A]

Wyskiver, Lee Ann, PSBCA No. 3621, 94-3 B.C.A. (CCH) ¶ 27,118, 39.03[A]

Wyskiver, PSBCA No. 3621, 94-3 B.C.A. (CCH) ¶ 27,118, 39.03[B][1], 39.04[C]

X

Xplo Corp., DOT BCA No. 1289, 86-3 B.C.A. ¶ 19,125 (1986), 28.03[E][4]

XTRA Lease, Inc. v. United States, 50 Fed. Cl. 612 (2001), 27.07[C]

Y

Yakima Cement Prods. Co. v. Great Am. Ins. Co., 22 Wash. App. 536, 590 P.2d 371 (1979), *rev'd on other grounds,* 93 Wash. 2d 210, 608 P.2d 254 (1980), 18.04[C][1], 19.07[B]

Yates Paving & Grading Co. v. Bryan Co., 549 S.E.2d 756 (Ga. Ct. App. 2004), 33.02[G]

Yeshiva Univ. v. Fidelity & Deposit Co. of Md., 116 A.D.2d 49, 500 N.Y.S.2d 24 (1st Dep't 1986), 34.04[G][4]

Yohe v. Lower Burrel Twp., 208 A.2d 847 (Pa. 1965), 7.03

Yokel v. Hite, 809 N.E.2d 721 (Ill. App. Ct. 2004), 17.01[A]

Yonkers Contracting Co. v. New York State Thruway Authority, 250 N.E.2d 27 (N.Y. 1969), *amended by* 259 N.E.2d 483 (N.Y. 1970), 33.01[E]

Yonkers Construction Co., United States *ex rel.*, v. Western Contracting Corp., 935 F.2d 936 (8th Cir. 1991), 33.02[O], 35.04[A]

York Engineering Co. v. City of Montgomery, 374 So. 2d 884 (Ala. 1979), 27.05[B][5][d]

Young v. City of Plaquemine, 818 So. 2d 892 (La. Ct. App. 2002), 7.02[B][2][c]

Young v. Johnston, 475 So. 2d 1309 (Fla. Dist. Ct. App. 1985), 31.03[B]

Young Assoc., Inc. v. United States, 471 F.2d 618 (Ct. Cl. 1973), 32.04

Youngdale & Sons Constr. Co. v. United States, 27 Fed. Cl. 516 (Fed. Cl. 1993), 7.03[B][2][a], 23.07[B][2], 27.05[D][6][c]

Youngdale & Sons Constr. Co. v. United States, 27 Fed. Cl. 516 (Fed. Cl. 1993), *aff'd,* 499 F.3d 1357 (Fed. Cir. 2007), 24.04[B]

Youngstown Welding & Eng'g Co., United States *ex rel.,* v. Travelers Indem. Co., 802 F.2d 1164 (9th Cir. 1986), 35.08[D][3], 35.08[F][2]

Z

Zapata v. Burns, 542 A.2d 700 (Conn. 1988), 27.05[E][3]

Zara King Co., United States v., 146 F.2d 606 (2d Cir. 1944), 21.06

Zaretsky, United States *ex rel.,* v. Johnson Controls, Inc., 44 F.3d 699 (8th Cir. 1995), 38.02[B][4][b]

Zen Mach. Co., ASBCA No. 39462, 91-3 B.C.A. ¶ 24,085 (1991), 28.03[F][1]

Zimmerman v. Continental Airlines, Inc., 712 F.2d 55 (3d Cir. 1983), 46.13

Zinger Construction Co. v. United States, 807 F.2d 979 (Fed. Cir. 1986), 27.05[B][3][b]

Zolman Constr. & Dev. Inc., 96-2 B.C.A. (CCH) ¶ 28,463 (ASBCA 1996), 32.06

Zulla Steel, Inc. v. A & M Gregos, Inc., 174 N.J. Super. 124 (App. Div. 1980), 30.04[B][1]

TABLE OF CASES

[References are to section numbers. Alphabetization is letter-by-letter (e.g., "Allison" precedes "All Season Constr.").]

A

ABI, Inc. v. City of Los Angeles, 153 Cal. App. 3d 669, 200 Cal. Rptr. 563, (Cal. Ct. App. 1984) 33.01[B]

Abish v. Nw. Nat'l Ins. Co., 924 F.2d 448 (2d Cir. 1991) 36.04

Ace Constructors, Inc. v. U.S., 70 Fed. Cl. 253 (2006) 22.05

Agri-Systems, Inc. v. Foster Poultry Farms, 168 Cal. App. 4th 1128, 85 Cal.Rptr.3d 917 (2008) 46.22

Alcan Aluminum Corp., United States v., 964 F.2d 252 (C.A.3 1992) 11.03[A][4][a]

Allianz SpA and Generali Assicurazioni Generali SpA v. West Tankers, Inc., Case C-185/07, 2009 WL 303723 (Feb. 10, 2009) 43.02[A]

Allison Engine Co. v. United States *ex rel.* Sanders, 12 S. Ct. 2123 (2008) 39.04[E]

ALS & Assocs., Inc. v. AGM Marine Constructors, Inc., 557 F. Supp. 2d (D. Mass. 2008) 46.26

Am. Druggists' Ins. Co. v. Shoppe, 448 N.W.2d 103 (Minn. Ct. App. 1989) 36.09[B]

American Petroleum Institute (API) v. Johnson, 541 F. Supp. 2d 165 (D.D.C. 2008) 11.03[A][1][c]

American Protection Ins. Co. v. Acadia Ins. Co., 814 A.2d 989 (2003) 19.03[B]

Am-Pro Protective Agency, Inc. v. United States, 281 F.3d 1234 (Fed. Cir. 2002) 28.04[A][1]

Andrulis v. Levin Constr. Corp., 331 Md. 354 (Md. 1993) 30.02[A][2]

APAC-Carolina, Inc. v. Greensboro-High Point Airport Auth., 110 N.C. App. 664, 431 S.E.2d 508 (1993) 26.02[HH][1]

Arntz Contracting Co. v. St. Paul Fire & Marine Ins. Co., 54 Cal. Rptr. 2d 888 (Cal. Ct. App. 1996) 36.03[B]

Atlantic Mut. Ins. Co. v. Continental Nat'l Am. Ins. Co., 302 A.2d 177, 178-79 (N.J. Super. Ct. App. Div. 1973) 29.02[C][4]

Atlas Contractors, Inc., ASCBA No. 34,545, 88-1 B.C.A. (CCH) ¶ 20,225 (1987) 24.02[A]

Austin Co. v. United States, 314 F.2d 518 (Ct. Cl. 1963) 5.03[C][8]

B

Bailey v. Skipperliner Indus., 278 F. Supp. 2d 945 (N.D. Ind. 2003) 16.02[B]

Bayindir v. Pakistan and the Decline and Fall of Investment Treaty Claims on International Construction Projects, Akin Alcitepe and Ronan McHugh, 6 Ankara L. Rev. __ (2009) 43.06

Bayindir Insaat Turizm Ticaret ve Sanayi A.S. v. Islamic Republic of Pakistan, International Centre for Settlement of Investment Disputes ("ICSID") Case ARB/03/29 43.06

Bearingpoint, Inc. v. United States, 82 Fed. Cl. 181 (2008) 30.04[B]

Bell BCI Co. v. United States, No. 2008-5087, 2009 WL 1796783 (Fed. Cir. June 25, 2009) 39.03[A]

Bell BCI v. United States, 570 F.3d 1337 (2009) 24.03

Bell Petroleum Services, Inc., *In re*, 3 F.3d 889 (C.A.5 1993) 11.03[A][4][a]

Bilt-Rite Contractors, Inc. v. Architectural Studio, 866 A.2d 270 (Pa. 2005) 29.02[C][5]

Bily v. Arthur Young & Co., 3 Cal.4th 370 (1992) 5.05[C][4]

Blake Constr. Co., Inc. v. C.J. Coakley Co., Inc., 431 A.2d 569 (D.C. 1981) 33.01[E]

Blake Constr. Co., Inc./Poole & Kent v. Upper Occoquah Sewage Auth., 266 Va. 564, 571, 587 S.E.2d 711 (2003) 26.02[UU][1]

Board of Educ. v. Sargent, Webster, Crenshaw & Folley, 146 A.D.2d 190 (N.Y. App. Div. 3d Dep't 1989) 29.02[C][4]

Bd. of Educ. of Dover Union Free Sch. Dist. v. Dover-Wingdale, 95 A.D.2d 497 (N.Y.A.D. 2 Dept.1983) 46.24

Board of Managers of the Riverview at Coll. Point Condominium III v. Schorr Bros. Dev. Corp., 182 A.D.2d 664 (N.Y. Ct App. 1992) 20.02

Borey v. Nat'l Union Fire Ins. Co., 934 F.2d 30 (2d Cir. 1991) 36.04

BP Amoco Chem. Co. v. Flint Hills Res., LLC, 2010 U.S. Dist. LEXIS 28477 (N.D. Ill. Mar. 25, 2010) 30.02[A][1]

Brookfield Constr. Co. v. United States, 661 F.2d 159 (Cl. Ct. 1981) 33.01[H]

Buckeye Check Cashing, Inc. v. Cardegna, 546 U.S. 440, 126 S.Ct. 1204, 163 L.Ed.2d 1038 (2006) 46.07

Burlington Ins. Co. v. Okie Dokie Inc., 398 F. Supp. 2d 147 (D.C. 2005) 33.01[E]

Burlington Northern and Santa Fe Railway Company, et al. v. United States Environmental Protection Agency, et. al., 129 S.Ct. 1870 (US. 2009) 11.03[A][4][a]

Bussen Quarries, Inc., United States ex rel. v. Thomas, 938 F.2d 831 (8th Cir. 1991) 36.09[C]

C

Caddell Constr. Co., Inc. v. U.S., 78 Fed. Cl. 406, 413 (2007) 29.02[B][2]

Cal's A/C & Elec., United States ex rel. v. Famous Constr. Corp., 34 F. Supp. 2d 1042 (W.D. La. 1999) 33.02[O]

Carlson v. Sharp, 994 P.2d 851 (Wash. Ct. App. 1999) 29.02[C][5]

Carrothers Constr. Co. v. S. Hutchinson, 207 P.3d 231 (Kan. 2009) 32.05

Cashman Equip. Corp. v. United States fire Ins. Co., 2008 U.S. Dist. LEXIS 80860 (E.D. Pa. Sept. 17, 2008) 30.02[A][2]

Cashman Equip. Corp. v. United States Fire Ins. Co., 2010 U.S. App. LEXIS 4675 (3d Cir. Mar. 5, 2010) 30.02[A][2]

Central School District No. 1 v. Double M Construction Corp., 361 N.Y. S.2d 47 (N.Y. App. Div. 1974) 33.02[M][5]

Chem-Dyne Corp., United States v., 572 F.Supp. 802 11.03[A][4][a]

Chem-Nuclear Systems, Inc. v. Bush, 292 F.3d 254 (C.A.D.C.2002) 11.03[A][4][a]

Chevron Corporation, S.D.N.Y, In re Application of, May 6, 2010 43.07[F][2]

Church of the Holy Spirit v. Bevco, Inc., 338 N.W.2d 601 (Neb. 1983) 33.01[B]

Citigroup Global Mkts., Inc. v. Bacon, 562 F.3d 349 (5th Cir. 2009) 46.26

City of. See name of city

City Express, Inc. v. Express Partners, 959 P.2d 836 (Haw. 1998) 29.02[C][5]

C.J.C., Inc., United States ex rel. v. W. States Mech. Contractors, Inc., 834 F.2d 1533 (10th Cir. 1987) 33.01[K], 33.02[O]

Clark v. Aenchbacher, 238 S.E.2d 442 (Ga. Ct. App. 1977) 33.02[D]

Clark v. Optical Coding Laboratory, Inc., 80 Cal. Rptr. 3d 812, 165 Cal. App. 4th 150 (Cal. Ct. App. 2008) 33.02[D]

College Hall Fashions, Inc. v. Philadelphia Joint Bd. Amalgamated Clothing Workers of Am., 408 F.Supp. 722 (E.D.Pa.1976) 46.24

Colorado Structures, Inc. v. Ins. Co. of the West, 167 P.3d 1125 (Wash. 2007) 33.02[A]

Columbia, Mo., City of, v. Paul N. Howard Co., 707 F.2d 338 (8th Cir. 1983) 22.06

Commonwealth v. AMEC Civil, LLC, 677 S.E.2d 633, 650 (Va. App. 2009) 24.04[C]

Complete Gen. Constr. Co. v. Ohio
Dept. of Transp., 593 N.E.2d 487
(Ohio Ct. Cl. 1990) 29.02[B][2]

Comprehensive Accounting Corp. v.
Rudell, 760 F.2d 138 (7th Cir. 1985)
43.07[B]

Conforti & Eisele, Inc. v. John C.
Morris Assoc., 418 A.2d 1290 (N.J.
Super. Ct. App. Div. 1980)
29.02[C][5]

Connecticut Department of
Transportation v. White Oak Corp.,
287 Conn. 1, 28 n. 12 (2008)
30.02[B]

Cont'l Cas. Co. v. Am. Sec. Corp.,
443 F.2d 649 (D.C. Cir. 1970)
36.07

Continental Cas. Co. v. Gutterman, 708
F.Supp. 95, 954 (N.D. Ill. 1989)
36.03[B]

Cumberland Cas. & Sur. Co. v. United
States, 2008 WL 4725449 (Fed. Cl.
July 3, 2008) 24.03

Curtis T. Bedwell & Sons, Inc. v. Int'l
Fid. Ins. Co., 1989 WL 55388 (E.D.
Pa. May 23, 1989) 36.07

Cyrus Contracting, Inc., IBCA No.
3233, 98-2 B.C.A. (CCH) ¶ 30,063
(1998) 24.04[A]

D

Daewoo Engineering and Construction
Co., Ltd. v. United States, 73 Fed. Cl.
547 (2006), *aff'd* by 557 F.3d 1332
(Fed. Cir. 2009), *petition for cert.
filed,* (U.S. June 26, 2009) (No. 09-3)
39.04[E]

Dave Kolb Grading, Inc. v. Lieberman
Corp., 837 S.W.2d (Mo. Ct. App.
1992) 33.01[E]

Day v. Nat'l U.S. Radiator Corp., 128 So.
2d 660 (La. 1961) 29.02[C][4]

DCX-CHOL Enterprises, Inc., ASBCA
No. 54707, 08-2 BCA ¶ 33,889
28.03[D][1][a], 28.03[D][2]

Deal Dev. Co. v. Amarillo Concrete
Contractors, Inc., 554 S.W.2d
294 (Tex. Civ. App. 1977)
33.01[E]

Denny Const., Inc. v. City & County of
Denver, 199 P.3d 742 (Colo. 2009)
30.04[B][2]

Denton Constr. Co. v. Mo. State
Highway Comm'n, 454 S.W.2d 44
(Mo. 1970) 33.01[A]

D.F.K. Enterprises, Inc. v. U.S., 45 Fed.
Cl. 280 (1999) 22.08

DiRussa v. Dean Witter Reynolds Inc.,
121 F.3d 818 (2d Cir. 1997) 43.07[B]

Dixie Plumbing Supply Co., United
States *ex rel.* v. Taylor, 293 F.2d 717
(5th Cir. 1961) 33.02[O]

Dobson Bros. Constr. v. Ratliff, Inc.,
2008 U.S. Dist. LEXIS 97283 (D.
Neb. November 6, 2008) 25.02[D]

Donnelly Constr. Co. v.
Oberg/Hunt/Gilleland, 677 P.2d 1292
(Ariz. 1984) 29.02[C][5]

Double Oak Constr., L.L.C. v.
Cornerstone Dev. Int'l, L.L.C., 97
P.3d 140 (Colo. App. 2003) 33.02[D]

Downer Corp. v. Union Paving Co., 304
P.2d 756 (Cal. 1956), *cert. denied,*
354 U.S. 914 (1957) 33.02[M][1]

DRC, Inc. et al., United States *ex rel.* v.
Custer Battles, LLC et al., 562 F.3d
295 (4th Cir. 2009) 41.08[A]

Dugan & Meyers Constr. Co., Inc. v.
Ohio Dept. of Admin. Serv., et al.,
864 N.E.2d 68 (Ohio 2007)
29.02[B][1]

E

Eastern Tunneling Corp. v. Southgate
Sanitation District, 487 F. Supp. 109
(D. Colo. 1979), rev'd on other
grounds, 26 F.3d 141 (Fed. Cir. 1994)
22.02

Eastover Corp. v. Martin Builders, 543
So. 2d 1358 (La. Ct. App. 1989)
29.02[C][4]

E.C. Ernst, Inc. v. Manhattan Constr.
Co., 551 F.2d 1026 (5th Cir. 1977),
cert. denied, 434 U.S. 1067 (1978)
33.01[E]

E.C. Ernst Co. v. Koppers Co., 520
F.Supp. 830 (W.D. Pa. 1981)
33.01[E]

Economic Dev. & Indus. Corp. v.
United States, 13 Cl. Ct. 590 (Cl. Ct.
1987) 33.01[H]

Elec. & Missile Facilities, Inc. v. U.S.,
189 Ct.Cl. 237, 416 F.2d 1345 (1969)
22.09

Elec. Mach. Enters. v. Hunt Constr.
Group, Inc. (*In re* Elec. Mach.
Enters.), 416 B.R. 801 (Bankr. M.D.
Fla. 2009) 30.03[D][1]

E. Paul Kovacs & R.W. Dunteman Co.
v. Village of Lombard, 666
N.E.2d 762 (Ill. App. Ct. 1996)
33.01[E]

Engbrock v. Fed. Ins. Co., 370 F.2d 784
(5th Cir. 1967) 36.07, 36.09[B],
36.09[D]

Erich Gasser GmbH v. MISAT Srl, Case
C-116/02, 2003 E.C.R. I-14693
43.02[A]

Essex Electro Eng'rs v. Danzig, 224
F.3d 1283 (Fed. Cir. 2000) 24.02[C],
24.03

F

Fab-Tech, Inc. v. E.I. Du Pont de
Nemours & Co., 311 Fed. Appx. 443
(2d Cir. 2009) 16.02[B]

Fattore Co. v. Metro. Sewerage
Comm'n, 454 F.2d 537 (7th Cir.
1971) 22.06

Faulkenbury v. Teachers' & State
Employees' Retirement Sys. of N.C.,
510 S.E.2d 675, 673 (N.C. Ct. App.
1999) 33.01[I]

F.D. Rich Co. v. United States *ex rel.*
Industrial Lumber Co., 417 U.S. 116
(1974) 33.02[O]

Fed. Mktg. Co. v. Impression Prods.,
Inc., 823 A.2d 513 (D.C. 2003)
33.01[E]

Fewox v. McMerit Constr. Co., 556
So.2d 419 (Fla. Dist. Ct. App. 1989)
33.02[N]

Fid. & Cas. Co. v. Finch, 3 A.D.2d 141
(N.Y. App. Div. 1957) 36.03[B]

Fid. & Deposit Co. v. Bristol Steel &
Iron Works, Inc., 722 F.2d 1160
(4th Cir. 1983) 36.03[B], 36.05,
36.09[D]

Fid. & Deposit Co. v. Wu, 552 A.2d
1196 (Vt. 1988) 36.05, 36.07

Fid. & Deposit Co. of Md. v. Fleischer,
772 S.W.2d 809 (Mo. Ct. App. 1989)
36.05

Fireman's Fund Ins. v. SEC Donohue,
Inc., 679 N.E.2d 1197 (Ill. 1997)
29.02[C][5]

First Nat'l Bank of Elkhart County v.
Smoker, 286 N.E.2d 203 (Ind. Ct.
App. 1972), *reh'g denied*, 287 N.E.3d
788 (Ind. Ct. App. 1972) 16.08[B]

First Options of Chicago, Inc. v.
Kaplan, 514 U.S. 938 (1995) 46.07

Fitzgerald v. H&R Block Fin. Advisors,
Inc., 2008 WL 2397636 (E.D. Mich.
2008) 46.26

Flagstaff Affordable Housing Limited.
Partnership v. Design Alliance, Inc.,
223 P.3d 664 (Ariz. 2010)
29.02[C][5]

Floor Craft v. Parma Com. Gen. Hosp.,
54 Ohio St. 3d 1, 560 N.E.2d 206
(Ohio 1990) 29.02[C][5]

Frankfort Digital Servs. v. Kistler, 477
F.3d 1117 (9th Cir. 2007) 5.03[C][2]

Freeman v. Dep't of Highways, 253 La.
105, 217 So. 2d 166 (1968)
26.02[S][1], 26.02[S][4]

G

Galen Medical Associates, Inc. v.
United States, 369 F.3d 1324 (Fed.
Cir. 2004) 28.04[A][1]

Gen. Accident Ins. Co. of Am. v.
Merritt-Meridian Constr. Corp., 975
F. Supp. 511 (S.D.N.Y. 1997)
36.03[B]

George Sollitt Constr. Co. v. U.S., 64
Fed. Cl. 229 (2005) 22.05

Gerstner Elec., Inc. v. Am. Ins. Co., 520
F.2d 790 (8th Cir. 1975) 36.09[F]

Gillette, City of v. Hladky Construction,
Inc., 196 P.3d 184 (2008)
26.02[YY][3], 26.02[YY][4]

Glen Johnson, Inc. v. Howdeshell, Inc.,
520 So.2d 297 (Fla. Dist. Ct. App.
1988) 33.02[N]

Goose Creek Sch. Dist. v. Jarrar's
Plumbing, 74 S.W.3d 486 (Tex. App.
2002) 29.02[C][5]

Gosnell Development Corporation of
Arizona, In the Matter of, No.
CV-04-998-PHX-RGS, 2007 U.S.
Dist. LEXIS 31440, *11-12 (D. Ariz.
Apr. 27, 2007) 29.02[C][5]

Granite Rock Co. v. International
Brotherhood of Teamsters, ___ U.S.
___, No. 08-1214, 2010 WL 2518518
(June 24, 2010) 46.07

Green Tree Financial Corp. v. Bazzle, 539 U.S. 444 (2003) 43.07[B]

Gregory Paul Turner v. Felix Fareed Ismail Grovit, Harada Ltd., Case C-159/02, 2004 E.C.R. I-3565 43.02[A]

Guthrie v. Louisiana Med. Mut. Ins. Co., 975 So.2d 804 (La. Ct. App. 2008) 20.03

H

Hall Street Associates v. Mattel, Inc., 123 S.Ct. 1936 (2008) 46.26

Hall Street Associates, L.L.C. v. Mattel, Inc., 128 S.Ct. 1396, 170 L.Ed.2d 254 (2008) 46.19

Harper/Nielsen-Dillingham, Builders, Inc. v. United States, 81 Fed. Cl. 667 (2008) 24.04[C]

Harris v. Dyer, 637 P.2d at 919-920 33.02[M][6]

Havens Steel Co. v. Randolph Eng'g Co., 613 F. Supp. 514 (W.D. Mo. 1985) 33.01[G]

Henriquez v. Parsippany Const. Co., Inc., 62 A.D.3d 749, 879 N.Y.S.2d 512, (N.Y. 2009) 8A.08[D]

Hercules, Inc., United States v., 247 F.3d 706 (C.A.8 2001) 11.03[A][4][a]

Hercules Inc. v. United States, 24 F.3d 188 (1994) 5.03[C][8]

Hereford v. D.R. Horton, Inc., 2008 WL 4097594 (Ala. 2008) 46.26

Hess v. Am. States Ins., 589 S.W.2d 548 (Tex. Civ. App. 1979) 36.05

Highway Specialties, Inc. v. Montana, 215 P.3d 667 (Mont. 2009) 32.03

Home Indem. Co. v. Wachter, 496 N.Y.S.2d 252 (N.Y. App. Div. 1985) 36.07

Houma v. Municipal & Indus. Pipe Serv., 884 F.2d 886 (5th Cir. 1989) 29.02[C][4]

Howsam v. Dean Witter Reynolds, 573 U.S. 79 (2002) 46.07

Hunt Const. Group, Inc. v. U.S., 281 F.3d 1369 (C.A.Fed. 2002) 8A.08[D]

I

IMS Engineers-Architects, P.C. v. U.S., 92 Fed. Cl. 52 (2010) 28.04[D][2]

Info. Sys. & Networks, Corp. v. United States, 81 Fed. Cl. 740 (2008) 30.03[B][1]

In Roz Trading Ltd, 469 F. Supp. 2d 1221 (N.D. Ga 2006) 43.07[F][2]

Insigma Technology Co. Ltd v. Alstom Technology Ltd, SGCA 24 (June 2, 2009) 43.07[C]

Insurance Co. of N. Am. v. Bath, 726 F. Supp. 1247 (D. Wyo. 1989) 36.09[C]

Insurance Co. of. N. Am. v. Town of Manchester, 1998 WL 514711 (D. Conn. 1998) 29.02[C][5]

Intel Corp. v. Advanced Micro Devices, Inc., 542 U.S. 241 (2004) 43.07[F][2]

Interstate Gen. Gov't Contractors, Inc. v. West, 12 F.3d at 1058-59 39.03[A]

Int'l Fid. Ins. Co. v. Jones, 682 A.2d 263 (N.J. Super. Ct. App. Div. 1996) 36.07

Iron Head Const., Inc. v. Gurney, 176 P.3d 453 (Utah Ct. App. 2008) 33.01[E]

Iron Head Const., Inc. v. Gurney, 207 P.3d 1231 (Utah 2009) 33.01[F]

J

Jackson Construction Co., Inc. v. United States, 62 Fed. Cl. 84 (2004) 39.03[A]

Jacobson v. Am. Fid. Fire Ins. Co., 541 P.2d 2 (Nev. 1975) 36.09[C]

James Corp. v. N. Alleghany Sch. Dist., 938 A.2d 474 (Pa. Commw. Ct. 2007) 26.02[MM][4]

J.C. Snavely & Sons, Inc. v. Web M&E, Inc., 594 A.2d 333 (Pa. Super. Ct. 1991) 33.02[O]

Jimmy John's Franchise, LLC v. Kelsey, 549 F.Supp.2d 1034 (C.D. Ill. 2008) 46.26

J.L. Simmons Co. v. United States, 412 F.2d 1360 (Cl. Ct. 1969) 29.02[B][2]

John F. Harkins Co., Inc. v. School Dist. of Philadelphia, 460 A.2d 260 (1983) 30.03[D][1]

Johnson v. Flammia, 169 Conn. 491 (Conn. 1975) 30.04[B][1]

Jones Constr. & Renovation, Inc., *In re*, 337 B.R. 579 (Bankr. E.D. Va. 2006) 36.08

J.R. Snyder Co. v. Soble, 226 N.W.2d 276 (Mich. Ct. App. 1975) 33.02[M][4]

K

Kashner Davidson Secs. Corp. v. Msciz, 531 F.3d 68 (1st Cir. 2008) 46.26

Kauffman v. Shearson, Hayden, Stone, Inc., 128 Cal.App.3d 809 (Cal. Ct. App. 1982) 33.02[M][1]

Kenneth Hantman, Inc. v. Whiting-Turner Contr. Co., 2008 U.S. Dist. LEXIS 67071 (E.D. Pa. Sept. 2, 2008) 30.03[D][1]

Kern Oil & Ref. Co. v. Tenneco Oil Co., 868 F.2d 1279 (Temp. Emer. Ct. App. 1989) 33.01[E]

Kostmayer Construction, LLC, ASBCA No. 55053, 08-2 BCA ¶ 33,869 (2008) 28.03[B][2]

Kramer v. Mt. Carmel Shelter Care Facility, Inc., 750 N.E.2d 757 (Ill. App. Ct. 2001) 33.01[I]

Kunkel v. P.K. Dependable Constr., LLC, 387 Ill. App. 3d 1153 (Ill. App. Ct. 5th Dist. 2009) 30.02[A][1]

L

Labat-Anderson, Inc., ASBCA No. 54904, 08-1 BCA ¶ 33761 28.03[D][2]

Ladco Properties XVII, L.L.C. v. Jefferson-Pilot Life Ins. Co., 523 F.Supp. 2d 940 (S.D. Iowa 2007) 33.01[B]

Lambert v. Md. Cas. Co., 418 So. 2d 553 (La. 1982) 36.09[F]

Lange Indus., Inc. v. Hallam Grain Co., 507 N.W.2d 465 (Neb. 1993) 33.01[B]

LaPine v. Kyocera Corp., 2008 WL 216918 (N.D. Cal. 2008) 46.26

La. Power & Light Co. v. Kellstrom, 50 F.3d 319 (5th Cir. 1995) 33.01[I]

Laughlin Recreational Enters., Inc. v. Zab Dev. Co., 646 P.2d 555 (Nev. 1982) 33.01[E]

LB&B Associates Inc. v. U.S., 91 Fed. Cl. 142 (2010) 24.03[E][3][a]

Lempke v. Dagenais, 547 A.2d 290 (N.H. 1988) 29.02[C][5]

Lewis Jorge Construction Mgmt., Inc. v. Pomona Unified Sch. Dist., 34 Cal. 4th 960 (2004) 30.04[B][2]

Liberty Mut. Ins. Co. v. Aventura Engineering & Const. Corp., 534 F. Supp. 2d 1290 (S.D. Fla. 2008) 36.02[D], 36.03[B]

Liles Constr. Co. v. United States, 197 Ct.Cl. 164, 185, 455 F.2d 527, 538 (1972) 22.08

Linden v. Cascade Stone Co., Inc., 699 N.W.3d 189 (Wis. 2005) 16.02[B]

Lisbon Contractors, Inc. v. United States, 828 F.2d 759 (Fed. Cir. 1987) 28.03[B][2], 28.03[B][2][a]

Little Rock Wastewater Util. v. Larry Moyer Trucking, Inc., 321 Ark. 303, 311, 902 S.W.2d 760 (1995) 26.02[D][3]

L.K. Comstock & Co., Inc. v. Morse/UBM Joint Venture, 153 Ill.App.3d 475, 505 N.E.2d 1253 (Ill. App. 1st Dist. 1987) 8A.08[G][3]

M

Macri v. United States, 353 F.2d 804 (9th Cir. 1965) 33.01[H]

MACTEC, Inc. v. Gorelick, 427 F.3d 821 (10th Cir. 2005) 46.18

Made in the USA Found. v. United States, 51 Fed. Cl. 252 (2001) 39.02[C]

Malone, George Jerry, PSBCA No. 6129, 08-02 BCA ¶ 33958 (2008) 28.03[B][3]

Martin County v. Polivka Paving, Inc., 2010 Fla. App. LEXIS 6566 (Fla. Dist. Ct. App. 4th Dist. May 12, 2010) 30.03[C][3]

Mastec N. Am., Inc. v. MSE Power Sys., Inc., 2008 WL 2704912 (N.D.N.Y. 2008) 46.26

McDonnell Douglas, 323 F.3d at 1018 28.03[B][2][a]

McDonnell Douglas Corp. v. United States, 567 F.3d 1340 (Fed. Cir. 2009) 28.03[B][2], 28.03[B][2][a]

McDonnell Douglas Corp. v. United States, 76 Fed. Cl. 385 (2007) 28.03[B][2][a]

McWane Inc. v. United States, 505 F.3d 1208 (11th Cir. 2007) 11.03[A][1][c]

MedTek, Inc. v. Department of Veterans Affairs, CBCA No. 1153 (2008) 39.04[D]

Mega Constr. Co., Inc. v. United States, 29 Fed. Cl. 396 (1993) 24.02[D]

Melwood Constr. Corp. v. State, 481 N.Y.S.2d 289 (N.Y. Ct. Cl. 1984) 33.01[B]

Messina & Briante, Inc. v. Blitman Construction Corp., 223 N.Y. S.2d 533 (N.Y. Sup. Ct. 1961), aff'd, 245 N.Y. S.2d 985 (N.Y. App. Div., appeal dismissed, 198 N.E.2d 602 (N.Y. 1964) 33.02[M][5]

Millgard Corp. v. McKee/Mays, 49 F.3d 1070 (5th Cir. 1995) 22.06

Millmaker v. Bruso, 2008 WL 4560624 (S.D. Tex. 2008) 46.26

Miraglia, In re Estate of, 658 S.E.2d 777 (Ga. App. Ct. 2008) 33.01[B]

Missouri f/u/b MWE Services, Inc., State of, v. Sircal-Kozeny-Wagner, JV, 2009 U.S. Dist. LEXIS 13644 (W.D. MO., Feb. 23, 2009) 25.05[D]

M.L. Young Const. Corp., U.S. ex rel., 2005 WL 2396597 at *5 26.02[KK][3], 26.02[KK][4]

M.L. Young Const. Corp., U.S. ex rel., The Austin Co., NO. CIV-04-0078-T, 2005 WL 2396597, *5 (W.D. Okla. Sept. 28, 2005) 26.02[KK][1]

M. Maropakis Carpentry, Inc. v. United States, 84 Fed. Cl. 182 (2008) 39.03[B]

Mohegan Tribal Gaming Authority v. Kohn Pedersen Fox Associates, 36 Conn L. Rptr. 249 (2003) 19.03[C]

Monessen S.W. Ry. Co. v. Morgan, 486 U.S. 330 (1988) 33.01[D]

Monsanto Co., United States v., 858 F.2d 160 (C.A.4 1988) 11.03[A][4][a]

Morrison-Knudsen Corp. v. Fireman's Fund Ins. Co., 175 F3d 1221 (10th Cir. 1999) 28.03[G]

Morrison Knudsen Corp. v. Ground Improvement Techniques, Inc., 532 F.3d 1063 (10th Cir. 2008) 28.03[G]

Motiva Enterprises v. St. Paul Fire and Marina Ins. Co., 445 F.3d 381 (5th Cir. 2006) 19.03[F][2]

Mound Bayou, City of, v. Roy Collins Constr. Co., 499 So.2d 1354 (Miss. 1986) 33.01[G]

N

Naples v. Keystone Bldg. and Dev. Corp., 295 Conn. 214 (2010) 30.02[A][1]

Nat'l Shawmut Bank v. New Amsterdam Cas. Co., 411 F.2d 843 (1st Cir. 1969) 36.02[C], 36.08, 36.09[F]

Natural Resources Defense Council et al. v. EPA et al. (C.D. Cal. 2006, Case No. CV-04-8307 GHK) 11.03[A][1][a][i]

Neb. Pub. Power Dist. v. Austin Power, Inc., 773 F.2d 960 (8th Cir. 1985) 33.01[C]

Net Constr., Inc. v. C&C Rehab. & Constr., Inc., 256 F. Supp. 2d 350 (E.D. Pa. 2003) 30.03[D][4]

Northeast Clackamas County Electric Co-operative v. Continental Casualty Co., 221 F.2d 329 (9th Cir. 1955) 26.02[LL][3]

North Slope Technical Ltd., Inc. v. United States, 14 Cl.Ct. 242 (1988) 22.08

Nw. Nat'l Ins. Co. v. Alberts, 937 F.2d 77 (2d Cir. 1991) 36.04

Nw. Nat'l Ins. Co. v. Alberts, 741 F. Supp. 424 (S.D.N.Y. 1990) 36.02[B]

O

Olshan Foundation Repair Co. v. Ayala, 180 S.W.3d 212 (Tex. App. 2005) 46.19

O'Neil v. Picillo, 883 F.2d 176 (C.A.1 1989) 11.03[A][4][a]

1325 North Van Buren v. T-3 Group, 716 N.W.2d 822 (Wis. 2006) 29.02[C][5]

Oregon Woods Inc. v. Dept of Interior, CBCA No. 1072, 09-1 BCA ¶ 34,014 28.04[A][1]

Owen v. Dodd, 431 F. Supp. 1239
(N.D. Miss. 1977) 29.02[C][5]

P

Pantechniki S.A. Contractors &
Engineers v. Republic of Albania,
ICSID Case ARB/07/21, Jul. 30,
2009 43.06

Paradise Homes, Inc. v. Cent. Sur. &
Ins. Corp., 437 P.2d 78 (Nev. 1968)
33.01[E]

Park Shore Dev. Co. v. Higley South,
Inc., 556 So.2d 439 (Fla. Dist. Ct.
App. 1990) 33.02[N]

Parnell v. Tremont Capital Mgmt. Corp.,
280 Fed. Appx. 76 (2nd Cir. 2008)
46.26

Parsons v. Henry, 672 P.2d 717 (Or.
1983) 33.01[E]

Pearlman v. Reliance Ins. Co., 371 U.S.
132 (1962) 36.03[B]

Pellerin Constr., Inc. v. Witco Corp.,
169 F. Supp. 2d 568 (E.D. La. 2001)
26.02[S][1], 26.02[S][2], 26.02[S][4]

Perry Hones v. Cull, 2008 WL 1922978
(Tex. May 2, 2008) 46.14

Petrossi Bros. Contracting Corp. v.
Town of Greece, 29 N.Y.S.2d 305
(N.Y. Sup. Ct. 1941) 36.06

Pierce Assocs., Inc. v. Nemours Found.,
865 F.2d 530 (3d Cir. 1988), *cert.
denied,* 492 U.S. 907 (1989) 32.03[A]

Portage Ind. Sch. Constr. Corp. v. A.V.
Stackhouse, Co., 287 N.E.2d 564
(Ind. Ct. App. 1972) 33.01[E],
33.01[G]

Positive Software Solutions, Inc. v. New
Century Mortgage Corp., 436 F.3d
495 (5th Cir. 2006) 46.22

Precision Pine & Timber, Inc. v. United
States, 596 F.3d 817 (Fed.Cir.2010)
28.04[D][2]

Premier Elec. Constr. Co. v. Am. Nat'l
Bank & Trust Co., 603 N.E.2d 733
(Ill. 1992) 36.09[F]

Prendiville v. Contemporary Homes,
Inc., 83 P.3d 1257 (Kan. Ct. App.
2004) 29.02[C][5]

Presnell Const. Managers, Inc. v. EH
Const., LLC, 134 S.W.3d 575 (Ky.
2004) 8A.08[D]

Preston v. Fener, 128 S.Ct. 978, 169
L.Ed.2d 917 (1008) 46.07

Prime Theraputics, LLC v. Omnicare,
LLC., 555 F.Supp.2d 993 (D. Minn.
2008) 46.26

PSE Consulting, Inc. v. Frank Mercede
and Sons, Inc., 838 A.2d 135 (Conn.
2004) 36.03[B], 36.05

P. T. Perusahaan Listrik Negara v. P. T.
Paiton Energy, Civil Case:
517/PDTG/1999/PN.JKT.PST (D.
Central Jakarta, 1999) 42.03[G][2]

Q

Quality Trust, Inc., U.S. ex rel., v.
Cajun Contractors, Inc., 486 F. Supp.
2d 1255 (D. Kan. 2007) 28.03[G]

Questar Builders, Inc. v. CB Flooring,
LLC, 410 Md. 241 (2009) 30.04[A]

R

Rapanos v. United States, 547 U.S. 715
(2006) 11.03[A][1][c]

Reeves v. Chase Bank USA, NA,
2008 WL 2783231 (E.D. Mo. 2008)
46.26

Reno v. Concrete Coring, Inc., 2005
Ohio 3062, 2004 Ohio App. LEXIS
2856 (2005) 8A.08[A][1]

Rent-A-Center West, Inc. v. Jackson,
130 S.Ct. 1133 (2010) 43.07[B]

Rent-A-Center West, Inc. v. Jackson,
__U.S.__, No. 08-1457 (March 23,
2010) 46.07

Repair Masters Constr., Inc. v. Gary,
277 S.W.3d 854 (Mo. Ct. App. 2009)
32.06

Republic of Argentina v. National Grid,
PLC, Case No 09-248, (D. D.C.
March 31, 2010) 43.07[R][3]

Rite-Way Plumbing & Heating, Inc. v.
Wil-Fred's Inc., 380 N.E.2d 992 (Ill.
App. Ct. 1978) 33.01[B]

RMA Lumber, Inc. v. Pioneer Mach.,
LLC, 2008 U.S. Dist. LEXIS 86293
(W.D. Va. Oct. 24, 2008) 30.02[B]

Roanoke Hosp. Ass'n v. Doyle &
Russell, Inc., 215 Va. 796, 214
S.E.2d 155 (1975) 30.02[B]

Robert Lewis Rosen Assocs., Ltd. v. Webb, 2008 WL 2662015 (S.D.N.Y. 2008) 46.26

Robert McMullan & Sons, Inc., ASBCA No. 19,023, 76-1 B.C.A. (CCH) ¶ 11,728 (1976), *overruled on other grounds by* England v. Sherman R. Smoot Corp., 388 F.3d 844 (Fed. Cir. 2004) 24.02[A]

Roberts Contracting Co. v. Valentine-Wooten Rd. Pub. Facility Bd., No CA 08-751, 2009 WL 1471809 (Ark. Ct. App. May 27, 2009) 32.06

Rockwork, Inc. v. Pulaski Const. Co., Inc., 933 A.2d 988 (N.J. Super. Ct. App. Div. 2007) 33.02[A]

Roxco, Ltd. v. United States, 77 Fed. Cl. 138 (2007) 39.07[B]

RPR & Assocs., Inc. v. Univ. of N.C.-Chapel Hill, 570 S.E.2d 510 (N.C. Ct. App. 2002) 33.01[I]

R.W. Meyer, Inc., United States v., 889 F.2d 1497 (C.A.6 1989) 11.03[A][4][a]

Ryco Const., Inc. v. U.S., 55 Fed. Cl. 184 (2002) 22.08

S

Safeco Ins. Co. of Am. v. Gaubert, 829 S.W.2d 274 (Tex. App. 1992) 36.09[E]

Safeco Ins. Co. of Am. v. Schwab, 739 F.2d 431 (9th Cir. 1984) 36.04

Sarang Corp. v. U.S., 76 Fed. Co. 560 (Fed. Co. 2007) 33.01[K]

Sauer Inc. v. Danzig, 224 F.3d 1340 (C.A. Fed. 2000) 22.09

Schnip Bldg. Co. v. U.S., 227 Ct.Cl. 148, 645 F.2d 950 (1981) 22.05

S. Comfort Builders, Inc. v. U.S., 67 Fed.Cl. 124 (2005) 22.02

Seaboard Lumber Co. v. United States, 45 Fed.Cl. 404 (1999) 22.05

S. Elec. Corp. v. Util. Bd. of the City of Foley, No. 07-0575-CG-C, 2009 WL 307990 (S.D. Ala. Feb. 5, 2009) 32.09

Servidone Constr. Corp. v. United States, 931 F.2d 860 (Fed. Cir. 1991) 24.04

Shafer Redi-Mix, Inc. v. Craft, _____ F. Supp. _____, 2009 U.S. Dist. LEXIS 21144 (W.D. Mich. March 17, 2008) 25.04[A]

Sharman Co. v. United States, 2 F.3d 1564 (Fed. Cir. 1993) 39.07[B]

Shaw v. Aetna Casualty & Surety Co., 407 F.2d 813 (7th Cir. 1969) 20.02

Shepherd v. United States, 125 Ct.Cl. 724, 113 F.Supp. 648 (1953) 22.05

Sherrock Brothers, Inc. v. DaimlerChrysler Motors Co., LLC, 260 Fed. Appx. 497 (3d Cir. 2008) 46.24

Shimman v. Int'l Union of Operating Eng'rs, 744 F.2d 1226 (6th Cir. 1984) 33.02[A]

Silverdale Hotel Assocs. v. Lomas & Nettleton Co., 677 P.2d 773 (Wash. Ct. App. 1984) 33.01[E]

Slater v. U.S. Fidelity and Guaranty Co., 400 N.E.2d 1256 (Mass. 1980) 20.04

Socony Mobil Oil Co. v. Klapal, 205 F.Supp. 388 (D. Neb. 1962) 33.01[H]

Southern Comfort Builders, Inc. v. U.S., 67 Fed. Cl. 124 (Fed. Cl. 2005) 33.01[K]

South Union, Ltd. v. George Parker & Assoc., 504 N.E.2d 1131 (Ohio Ct. App. 1985) 29.02[C][4]

Spearing, United States v., 248 U.S. 132 (1918) 5.03[C][8]

State of. *See name of state*

Stevens & Co. v. Cikanek, 2008 WL 2705445 (N.D. Ill. 2008) 46.26

Stewart v. Bennett, 727 N.W.2d 424 (Neb. 2007) 33.02[C]

Stolt-Nielsen S.A. v. AnimalFeeds Int'l Corp., No. 08-1198, 2010 U.S. LEXIS 3672 (April 27, 2010) 43.07[B]

Stolt-Nielsen SA v. AnimalFeeds International Corp., 103 S.Ct. 1758 (2010) 46.24, 46.26

Stolt-Nielsen Transp. Group Ltd. v. Animal Feeds Int'l Corp., 548 F.3d 84 (2d Cir. 2008) 46.26

Stuyvesant Dredging Co. v. United States, 834 F.2d 1576 (Fed. Cir. 1987) 5.03[C][8], 29.02[B][2]

T

Takota Corp. v. U.S., 90 Fed. Cl. 11 (2009) 28.03[B][4][a]

Taranow v. Brokstein, 185 Cal. Rptr. 532 (Cal. Ct. App. 1982) 33.02[M][1]

Tarsitano v. Bd. of Educ., 385 Ill.App.3d 868, 324 Ill. Dec. 573, 896 N.E.2d 359 (1st Dist. 2008) 8A.04

Taylor Bldg. Corp. of Am. v. Benfield, 2008 WL 696334 (Ohio, March 12, 2008) 46.19

TDS Painting & Restoration, Inc. v. Copper Beech Farm, Inc., 808 A.2d 726 (Conn. App. Ct. 2002) 33.01[I]

Tecom Inc. v. United States, 86 Fed. Cl. 437 (2009) 24.04

Teknocraft, Appeal of, ASBCA No. 55438 (2009) 39.04[D]

Tempo, Inc. v. Rapid Electric Sales & Services, 347 N.W.2d 728 (Mich. Ct. App. 1984) 33.01[C][1]

Tennant v. United States Fidelity & Guaranty Co., 17 F.2d 38 (3d Cir. 1927) 36.03[A]

Terracon Consultants Western, Inc. v. Mandalay Resort Group, 206 P.3d 81 (Nev. 2009) 29.02[C][5]

Thomas & Marker Constr., Co. v. Wal-Mart Stores, Inc., No. 3:06-cv-406, 2008 U.S. Dist. LEXIS 79072, *53-54 (S.D. Ohio Sept. 15, 2008) 29.02[B][1]

TK Power v. Textron, Inc., 433 F. Supp. 2d 1058 (N.D. Cal. 2006) 16.02[B]

Tommy L. Griffin Plumbing & Heating Co. v. Jordon, Jones & Goulding, Inc., 463 S.E.2d 85 (S.C. 1995) 29.02[C][5]

Total Procurement Serv., Inc., ASBCA No. 54163, 08-1 BCA ¶ 33,843 39.03[B]

Toto Construzioni Generali S.P.A. v. The Republic of Lebanon, ICSID Case ARB/07/12, Sep. 11, 2009 43.06

Town of Alma v. Azco Constr., Inc., 10 P.3d 1256 (Colo. 2000) 29.02[C][5]

T.P.K. Constr. Corp. v. So. Am. Ins. Co., 752 F. Supp. 105 (S.D.N.Y. 1990) 36.03[C]

Trafalgar House Constr., 73 Fed. Cl. at 703 22.06

Transamerica Ins. Co. v. Bloomfield, 401 F.2d 357 (6th Cir. 1968) 36.09[D], 36.07

Transamerica Ins. Co. v. Red Top Metal, Inc., 384 F.2d 752 (5th Cir. 1967) 33.02[O]

The Travelers Indem. Co. v. United States ex rel. W. Steel Co., 362 F.2d 896 (9th Cir. 1966) 33.02[O]

Trocom Const. Corp. v. City of New York, 51 A.D.3d 533, 859 N.Y.S.2d 41 (N.Y.A.D. 2008) 8A.08[F]

Trus Joist Corp. v. Safeco Ins. Co. of Am., 735 P.2d 125 (Ariz. Ct. App. 1986) 33.01[B]

Turner v. Kerin & Assoc., 938 P.2d 1368 (Mont. 1997) 29.02[C][5]

U

Ulico Cas. Co. v. Atl. Contracting & Material Co., 822 A.2d 1257 (Md. Ct. Spec. App. 2003), aff'd, 844 A.2d 460 (Md. 2004) 36.03[A], 36.03[B], 36.09[A]

United Partition Systems, Inc. v. U.S., 90 Fed. Cl. 74 (2009) 23.03[G]

United States Fid. & Guar. Co. v. Jones, 87 F.2d 346 (5th Cir. 1937) 36.07

United States Supreme Court in Coeur Alaska, Inc. v. Southeast Alaska Conservation Council, 2009 WL 1738643 (US 2009) 11.03[A][1][b]

United States v. See name of defendant

Universal Sur. Co. v. Jed Constr. Co., 265 N.W.2d 219 (Neb. 1978) 36.09[C]

Urbanational Developers, Inc. v. Shamrock Eng'g, Inc., 372 N.E.2d 742 (Ind. Ct. App. 1978) 33.01[E]

U.S. Fidelity & Guaranty Co. v. Hittle, 96 N.W. 782 (Iowa 1903) 33.02[N]

U.S. Surety Co. v. U.S., 83 Fed. Cl. 306 (2008) 28.03[A]

V

Valente v. Weisberg, 80 Conn. 134 (1907) 30.02[B]

Volume Servs., Inc. v. C.F. Murphy, 656 S.W.2d 785 (Mo. App. 1983) 20.02

W

Ward v. City of Portland, 857 F.2d 1373 (9th Cir. 1988) 36.09[D]

Watson, Watson, Rutland Architects, Inc. v. Montgomery County Bd. of Educ., 559 So. 2d 168 (Ala. 1990) 29.02[C][4]

Wayne Knorr, Inc. v. Dept. of Transp., 2009 WL 1324068, at *16 (Pa. Commw. Ct. May 14, 2009) 24.02[D]

Wayne Knorr, Inc. v. DOT, 973 A.2d 1061 (Pa. Commw. Ct. 2009) 30.03[D][1]

W. Cas. & Sur. Co. v. United States, 109 F. Supp. 422 (Ct. Cl. 1953) 36.06

Weis Builders, Inc., Appeal of, 2010-1 B.C.A. (CCH), 34,369 (A.S.B.C.A. 2010) 32.04

Weitz Co., LLC v. Alberici Constructors, Inc., 2009 WL 115980, at *2-3 (D. Neb 2009) 26.02[BB][3]

Weitz Co., The v. Mackenzie House, No. 07-0103-CV-W-ODS 2008 WL 2980093 (W.D. Mo. Aug. 1, 2008) 32.05

Westates Construction Co. v. City of Cheyenne, 775 P.2d 502 (Wyo. 1989) 26.02[YY][3]

West v. Triple B Servs., LLP, 264 S.W.3d 440, 449 n.9 (Tex. Civ. App. - Houston [14th Dist.] 2008) (*distinguishing R.F. Ball Constr. Co.*) 26.02[RR][1]

W.G. Yates & Sons Constr. Co., ASBCA No. 49398, 01-2 B.C.A. (CCH) ¶ 31428 (2001) 24.04[D]

White v. Edsall Const.Co. Inc., 296 F.3d 1081 (Fed. Cir. 2002) 5.03[C][8]

Whyte v. Am. Bd. of Physical Medicine and Rehabilitation, 393 F.Supp.2d 880 (D.Minn. 2005) 22.08

Williams v. Martin Marietta Alumina, Inc., 817 F.2d 1030 (3rd Cir. 1987) 8A.08[A][1]

Winning (HK) Shipping Co. Ltd, In the Application of, 2010 WL 1796579 (S.D. Fla), April 30, 2010 43.07[F][2]

Witherington Const. Corp. v. United States, 45 Fed. Cl. 208 (1999) 39.07[B]

Worth Constr. Co., Inc. v. TRC Engineers, Inc., 55 A.D.3d 388, 865 N.Y.S.2d 95 (2008) 26.02[FF][3]

Wunderlich v. State, 423 P.2d 545 (Cal. 1967) 22.06

Wunderlich v. U.S., 351 F.2d 956 (Ct. Cl. 1965) 29.02[B][2]

Y

Yonker Construction Co., United States ex rel, v. Western Contracting Corp., 935 F.2d 936 (8th Cir. 1991) 33.02[N]

Young Assocs., Inc. v. United States, 471 F.2d 618 (Ct. Cl. 1973) 32.04

TABLE OF STATUTES AND REGULATIONS

References are to section numbers.

FEDERAL STATUTES

American Recovery and Reinvestment Act of 2009

§ 1201	39A.07

Clean Water Act

§ 404	11.03[A][1][c]
§ 404(a)	11.03[A][1][b]

Code of Federal Regulations

33 C.F.R.	
§ 328.3(c)	11.03[A][1][c]
40 C.F.R.	
§ 450	11.03[A][1][a]
§ 450.21(a)	11.03[A][1][a]
§ 450.21(b)	11.03[A][1][a]
§ 450.21(c)	11.03[A][1][a]
§ 450.21(d)	11.03[A][1][a]
§ 450.21(e)	11.03[A][1][a]
§ 450.22(a)	11.03[A][1][a]
73 C.F.R.	
§ 33374	37.01[B]
74 C.F.R.	
§ 52846	37.02[5]
75 C.F.R.	
§ 19168	37.01[C]

Energy Improvement and Extension Act of 2008

Div. A, Sec. 107	10.02[B][3][d][iii][a]

Energy Policy Act of 2005

§ 791	11.03[A][5][a]
§ 797	11.03[A][5][a]

Federal Acquisition Regulation

31.205-33	39.03[A]
52.203-6	15.16
52.203-7	15.16
52.203-12	15.16
52.203-13	15.16
52.203-14	15.16
52.204-2	15.16
52.209-6	15.16
52.212-5	15.16
52.215-2	15.16
52.215-12	15.16
52.215-13	15.16
52.219-8	15.16
52.219-9S	15.16
52.219-22	15.16
52.222-4	15.16
52.222-6	15.16
52.222-7	15.16
52.222-8	15.16
52.222-9	15.16
52.222-10	15.16
52.222-11	15.16
52.222-12	15.16
52.222-13	15.16
52.222-14	15.16
52.222-15	15.16
52.222-21	15.16
52.222-26	15.16
52.222-27	15.16
52.222-35	15.16
52.222-36	15.16
52.222-37	15.16
52.222-50	15.16
52.222-54	15.16
52.223-14	15.16
52.225-13	15.16
52.227-1	15.16
52.227-2	15.16
52.228-5	15.16
52.228-5	15.16

Federal Rules of Civil Procedure

12(b)(6)	26.02[BB][3]

Regulatory Guidance Letter

07-01	11.03[A][1][c]
08-02	11.03[A][1][c]

United States Code

6 U.S.C.	
§ 796	37.02[5]
28 U.S.C.	
§ 1782	43.07[F][2]
§ 1961	33.01[I]

31 U.S.C.

§§ 3729 *et seq.*	39.02[A], 39.04[E], 41.08[A]
§§ 3901-3905	33.01[K]
§ 3907(c)	33.01[K]

33 U.S.C.

§ 403	11.03[A][1][c]

40 U.S.C.

§ 31	10.02[B][3][d][iv]
§ 3131	33.02[O]

41 U.S.C.

§§ 601 *et seq.*	33.01[K]
§ 603	39.06[D]
§ 605(a)	33.01[K]

42 U.S.C.

§ 9607(a)(3)	11.03[A][4][a]

STATE STATUTES

Alabama Code

§ 8-29-6	33.02[G]
§ 39-1-1	33.02[J]

Arkansas Code Annotated

§ 16-22-308	33.02[C]
§ 16-107-303	36.01
§ 16-107-304	36.01
§ 16-107-305	36.01

Arizona Revised Statutes

§ 12-341.01	33.02[C]
§ 12-341.01(C)	33.02[D]
§ 32-1129.01	33.02[G]

California Business and Professions Code

§ 5535.1	5.03[C][2]
§ 6703	5.03[C][2]

California Civil Code

§ 2847	36.01
§ 2848	36.01
§ 3287	33.01[G]

California Code of Civil Procedure

§ 128.5	33.02[D]
§ 128.7	33.02[D]
§ 998	33.02[M][1]

California Rules of Court

8.1115	26.02[E][3]

Connecticut General Statute

§ 42-158j	33.02[G]
§ 49-42	33.02[J]

Delaware Code Annotated

Tit. 10

§ 3912	33.02[H]

Florida Statutes Annotated

§ 57.105	33.02[K]
§ 255.05	33.02[J]
§ 337.18	33.02[J]
§ 713.28	33.02[H]

Georgia Code Annotated

§ 10-7-40	36.01
§ 10-7-41	36.01
§ 13-6-11	33.02[D]
§ 13-11-8	33.02[G]

Idaho Code Annotated

§ 12-121	33.02[L]
§ 45-513	33.02[H]
§ 54-1929	33.02[J]

Indiana Code Annotated

§ 32-28-3-14	33.02[H]
§§ 34-22-1-1, *et seq.*	36.01
§ 34-52-1-1	33.02[D]

Iowa Code

§ 572.32	33.02[H]
§ 573.21	33.02[J]

Kansas Statutes Annotated

§ 60-211(c)	33.02[D]

Louisiana Civil Code

art. 3052	36.01

Louisiana Revised Statutes Annotated

§ 38:2216	26.02[S][1]
§ 38:2216(H)	26.02[S][2]

Maryland Rules

1-341	33.02[D]
9-303	33.02[G]

Michigan Comp. Laws

§ 570.1118	33.02[H]

Minnesota Statutes Annotated

§ 16a.1245	33.02[G]
§ 137.36	33.02[G]

§ 337.10	33.02[G]
§ 471.425	33.02[G]
§ 549.211	33.02[D]

Missouri Statutes

§ 34.057	33.01[K], 33.02[G]

Montana Code Annotated

§ 18-2-207	33.02[J]
§ 28-2-2105	33.02[G]
§ 28-11-413	36.01
§ 28-11-420	36.01
§ 71-3-124	33.02[H]

Nebraska Revised Statutes

§ 25-824	33.02[D]

New Jersey Statutes Annotated

§ 18A:18A-41	26.02[EE][2]

New Mexico Statutes Annotated

§ 13-1-170	26.02[FF][2]
§ 48-2-14	33.02[H]

North Dakota Century Code

§ 22-03-10	36.01
§ 22-03-11	36.01
§ 28-26-31	33.02[D]

Ohio Revised Code Annotated

§ 1341.18	36.01
§ 1341.19	36.01
§ 1341.20	36.01
§ 1341.21	36.01
§ 4113.61	33.02[G]

Oklahoma Statutes Annotated

Tit. 12
§ 936	33.02[C]

Tit. 15
§ 9-380	36.01
§ 9-381	36.01
§ 9-382	36.01
§ 2-105(1)	16.01[B]
§ 2-106(1)	16.01[B]
§ 2A-103(1)(h)	16.01[B]

Oregon Revised Statutes Annotated

§ 20.082	33.02[C]
§ 20.105(a)	33.02[D]
§ 87.035	33.02[M][6]
§ 87.060	33.02[H]
§ 87.060(4)	33.02[M][6]
§ 87.060(5)	33.02[M][6]
§ 279C.315	26.02[LL][2]

Pennsylvania Consolidated Statutes Annotated

42 Pa. CSA § 2503	33.02[D]
62 Pa. CSA § 3935	33.02[G]

Rhode Island General Laws

§ 34-28-19	33.02[H]

South Carolina Code Annotated

§ 29-5-10	33.02[H]

South Dakota Codified Laws

§ 44-9-42	33.02[H]
§ 56-2-13	36.01
§ 56-2-14	36.01

Tennessee Code Annotated

§ 21-1-11	33.01[G]
§ 47-14-123	33.01[E]
§ 66-34-104	33.01[E], 33.01[G]

Texas Civil Practice & Remedies

§ 38.001	33.02[C]

Utah Code Annotated

§ 13-8-5	33.01[E]
§ 38-1-18	33.02[H]
§ 78B-5-825	33.02[D]

Vermont Statutes Annotated

§ 4007	33.02[G]

Virginia Code Annotated

§ 2.2-4335(A)	26.02[UU]][2]

Washington Revised Code

§ 60.04.181	33.02[H]

TABLE OF AUTHORITIES

References are to section numbers.

DEPARTMENT OF JUSTICE

Opinion Release 01-01	42.02[e]
Opinion Release 01-02	42.02[E]
Opinion Release 01-03	42.02[E]

EXECUTIVE ORDERS

No. 13,116, 64 Fed.	
Reg. 16,333 (1999)	42.03[G][1]
No. 13259 (2002)	42.03[H]

RESTATEMENTS

Restatement (Second) of Torts

§ 433A	11.03[A][4][a]
§ 433A(1)(b)	11.03[A][4][a]
§ 552	5.03[C][7],
	5.05[C][4], 29.02[C][5]
§ 875	11.03[A][4][a]
§ 881	11.03[A][4][a]

UNIFORM COMMERCIAL CODE

Article 2	16.01[B]
Article 2A	16.01[B]

INDEX

References are to section numbers.

A

Abandonment, default termination, 28.03[B][3]

AIA contract documents
  construction management, 14.05[B]
  integrated project delivery, 14.05
    A295 documents, 14.05[A][2]
    guide, 14.05[A][1]
    multi-party agreement, 14.05[A][4]
    SPE documents, 14.05[A][3]
  owner-architect agreement forms, 14.03
    article-by-article-description of A201-2007, 14.03[C][2]

Air pollution, 11.03[A][5][a]

Airport Improvement Program (AIP), 39A.06

American Clean Energy & Security Act (ACES), 13.06A[D]

American Institute of Architects (AIA)
  Integrated Project Delivery: A Guide, 5.05[B]

American Institute of Architects California Counsel (AIACC), 5.05[B]

American Recovery and Reinvestment Act of 2009 (ARRA)
  benefit delivery, 39A.08
  goals of, 39A.04
  investment, need for greater, 39A.03
  purpose of, 10.02[B][3][d]
  tax credits, 10.02[B][3][d][i]
    cash grants, 10.02[B][3][d][ii]
    Clean Renewable Energy Bonds, 10.02[B][3][d][iii], 10.02[B][3][d][iii][a]
    investment tax credits, 10.02[B][3][d][i][b]
    loan guarantees, 10.02[B][3][d][iv]
    production tax credits, 10.02[B][3][d][i][a]
    Qualified Energy Conservation Bonds, 10.02[B][3][d][iii], 10.02[B][3][d][iii][b]
    tax credit bonds, 10.02[B][3][d][iii]
  testing, 39A.10
  tracking impacts on the economy, 39A.07
  transportation investment, 39A.01, 39A.05

American Rule, recovery of attorneys' fees, 33.02[M]
  bad faith exception to, 33.02[D]

Anticipatory repudiation, default termination, 28.03[B][3]

Arbitration
  agreements
    scope of, 46.07
  arbitrators
    disclosure requirements, 46.22
    exceed power, 46.24
  manifest disregard of law, 46.26
  vacating awards
    grounds for, 46.19
    procedure for, 46.18
  waiver of right to, 46.14

Arizona
  "no-damages-for-delay" clauses, exceptions, 26.02[C]

Arkansas
  "no-damages-for-delay" clauses, exceptions, 26.02[D]

ARRA, 39A.01. See American Recovery and Reinvestment Act of 2009 (ARRA)

Asia
  climate change mitigation, 13.06A[B]

Attorneys' fees
  contract, awarded as authorized by, 33.02[C]
  Miller Act claims, 33.02[O]
  recovery of
    American Rule, bad faith exception to, 33.02[D]

arbitration proceedings, 33.02[M]
California, 33.02[M][1]
indemnity agreements, 33.02[N]
Michigan, 33.02[M][4]
New York, 33.02[M][5]
Oregon, 33.02[M][6]
prompt payment statutes, 33.02[G]

B

Bad faith
American Rule, exception in recovery
of attorneys' fees, 33.02[D]
convenience terminations
government's right to terminate,
28.04[A][1]
Bonds
tax credit bonds, 10.02[B][3][d][iii]
Bribery
OECD Convention on Combating
Bribery, 42.03[A]
UN convention against, 42.03[B]
Brownfields, 11.03[A][4]
Building information modeling (BIM),
5.01–5.06
collaborative framework, as, 5.05
commercial issues, 5.03[B]
absence of standard contract
document, 5.03[B][1]
ConsensusDOCS contract
addendum, 5.03[B][3]
Contractor's Guide to BIM,
5.03[B][2]
ConsensusDOCS contract addendum,
5.03[B][3]
defined, 5.02[A]
growing use of, 5.01
how used, 5.02[B]
3D modeling and conflict
resolution, 5.02[B][4]
BIMStorm™, 5.02[B][14]
code compliance checking,
5.02[B][13]
conflict identification and
resolution, 5.02[B][4],
5.02[B][5]
consistent design bases, 5.02[B][3]
constructability reviews, 5.02[B][10]
design efficiency, 5.02[B][2]
energy optimization, 5.02[B][9]
estimating information, 5.02[B][6]
fabrication drawing, 5.02[B][7]
facilities management, 5.02[B][12]
4D simulations, 5.02[B][10]

functional simulations,
5.02[B][10][a]
reduced fabrication costs and errors,
5.02[B][11]
shop drawing, 5.02[B][7]
single data entry, multiple use,
5.02[B][1]
take-offs, 5.02[B][6]
visualization of alternatives,
5.02[B][8]
Worldwide Real-Time
Collaboration, 5.02[B][14]
implementation issues, 5.03
integrated project delivery, 5.05
comparison of, 5.05[E]
development of, 5.05[B]
implications of, 5.05[F]
minor elements of, 5.05[D]
need for, 5.05[A]
structural elements of, 5.05[C]
interoperability, 5.03[A][3], 5.03[C][5]
legal issues, 5.03[C]
adequacy of data, 5.03[C][6]
data translation, 5.03[C][6]
design delegation, 5.03[C][5]
insurability, 5.03[C][4]
intellectual property, 5.03[C][3]
privity, third party reliance and the
economic loss doctrine,
5.03[C][7]
professional responsibility,
5.03[C][2]
Spearin implied warranties,
5.03[C][8]
standard of care, 5.03[C][1]
licensing of models, 5.04[B]
models, use of, 5.04[A]
owner mandated standards,
5.03[A][2]
ownership of models, 5.04[B]
administration of model and,
5.04[B][6]
all parties own what they create,
5.04[B][3]
contractual status of model,
5.04[B][4]
designer owns, 5.04[B][2]
owner owns, 5.04[B][1]
specification of requirements and,
5.04[B][5]
standards, 5.03[A][1]
structural elements of integrated
project delivery, 5.05[C]
early involvement of key
participants, 5.05[C][1]

jointly developed and validated targets, 5.05[C][5]

joint project control, 5.05[C][3]

liability exposure, 5.05[C][4]

shared risk/reward, 5.05[C][2]

subcontractors, consultants and joining agreements, 5.05[C][6]

technical guidelines and standards, 5.03[A]

web sites and, 5.01

C

California
attorneys' fees, recovery of, 33.02[M][1]
"no-damages-for-delay" clauses, exceptions, 26.02[E]

Canada
climate change mitigation, 13.06A[C]

Cash grants, 10.02[B][3][d][ii]

CERCLA.
See Comprehensive Environmental Response, Compensation, and Liability Act (CERCLA)

Changes and extras
delays, causes of, 24.02
negotiation of, 44.08

Claims
avoidance strategies
change negotiations, 44.08
non-field people involved in field experiences, 44.04
plans and specifications, 44.02
risk, delineation of, 44.03
federal contracts
basic elements of claim, 39.03[A]
Board of Contract Appeals, contractor's appeal to, 39.07[A]
certification requirements, 39.04
contents of claim, 39.03
Contract Disputes Act of 1978, 39.02[A]
contracting officer's authority/timing of claim submissions and final decision, 39.06[D]
Court of Federal Claims, contractor's appeal to, 39.07[B]
defined, 39.02[C]
Federal Acquisition Regulation (FAR), 39.02[C]
requirements, 39.03[B]

written demand to contracting officer, 39.03[B][1]

Clean Air Act (CAA)
diesel engines, 11.03[A][5][a]

Clean Renewable Energy Bonds, 10.02[B][3][d][iii], 10.02[B][3][d][iii][a]

Clean Water Act (CWA), 11.03[A][1]

Climate change
investment in, 39A.09
mitigation efforts, 13.06A
ACES Act, 13.06A[D]
Asia, 13.06A[B]
EU-ETS, 13.06A
North America, 13.06A[C]

Colorado
"no-damages-for-delay" clauses, exceptions, 26.02[F]

Compensatory damages
additional work, contractor's recovery of, 30.03[B]
breach of warranty, 30.02[A]
change orders, contractor's recovery of, 30.03[B][1]
constructive changes, 30.03[B][1]
contractors, recovery of
change orders, 30.03[B][1]
constructive change, 30.03[B][1]
delay, 30.03[C]
disruptions, 30.03[D]
extra and additional work, 30.03[B]
field office damages, 30.03[C][3]
home office damages, 30.03[C][3]
lost efficiency or productivity, 30.03[D]
convenience terminations, 30.04[A]
cost of repair, 30.02[A][1]
default terminations, 30.04[B]
proper, 30.04[B][1]
wrongful, 30.04[B][2]
defective work, 30.02[A]
delay
by contractor, 30.02[B]
disruptions, contractor's recovery of, 30.03[D]
measured mile, 30.03[D][4]
total cost, 30.03[D][1]
extra work, contractor's recovery of, 30.03[B]
lost efficiency or productivity, contractor's recovery of, 30.03[D]
owner's recovery of, 30.02
breach of warranty, 30.02[A]
cost of repair, 30.02[A][1]

defective work, 30.02[A]
delay by contractor, 30.02[B]
terminations, 30.04
convenience, 30.04[A]
default, 30.04[B]
wrongful default terminations,
30.04[B][2]
value, diminution of, 30.02[A][2]
Comprehensive Environmental Response,
Compensation, and Liability
Act (CERCLA)
liability and brownfields, 11.03[A][4]
responsibility for meeting
requirements, 11.03[A][4][a]
ConsensusDOCS
design-build contracts, 8.08[B][11][a]
federal construction projects, 15.16
green building addendum, 15.20
current practice not best practice,
15.20[B]
elected green status and measure,
15.20[C]
Green Building Facilitator, 15.20[E]
neutral rating system, 15.20[D]
outlook, 15.20[G]
overview, 15.20[A]
risk allocation, 15.20[F]
procedures and revision cycle, 15.19
standard subsubcontract agreement,
15.17
Construction failure
contractor liability
performance specifications,
29.02[B][2]
plans and specifications, compliance
with, 29.02[B][1]
Spearin doctrine, 29.02[B][1]
Spearin doctrine, 29.02[B][1]
designer liability
duty to "observe," 29.02[C][4]
standing to sue architect,
29.02[C][5]
Construction management 14.05[B]
liability
bodily injury, 8A.08[A][1]
contract administration, 8A.08[G][3]
delayed site access, 8A.08[F]
design defects, 8A.08[D]
manager licensing, 8A.04
Construction Manager as Adviser (CMa),
14.05[B]
Construction Manager as Constructor
(CMc), 14.05[B]

Construction Users Roundtable (CURT),
integrated project delivery
policy report, 5.05[A]
Contractor liability
performance specifications,
29.02[B][2]
plans and specifications, compliance
with, 29.02[B][1]
Spearin doctrine, 29.02[B][1]
Contracts and agreements
arbitration agreements
scope of, 46.07
BIM
absence of standard contract
document, 5.03[B][1]
ConsensusDOCS addendum,
5.03[B][3]
contract performance
terminations, 28.03
Convenience terminations
bad faith, 28.04[A][1]
default terminations, conversion into,
28.03[G]
Corruption
international construction contracts
Anti-Foreign Corruption Statute,
42.02[F]
Executive Order 13116,
42.03[G][1]
Jakarta, Indonesia, 42.03[G][2]
Lesotho Highland Water Project,
42.03[G][3]
multilateral anti-corruption
initiatives, 42.03[3]
OECD Convention on Combating
Bribery, 42.03[A]
UN Convention Against Corruption,
42.03[B]
World Bank Policy Guidelines,
42.03[C]
U.S. implementing legislation,
42.03[H]
Cost of the work agreement,
ConsensusDOCS, 15.18

D

Damages
attorneys' fees, recovery of
American Rule, bad faith exception
to, 33.02[D]
contract, awarded as authorized by,
33.02[C]

interest, recovery of
liquidated and unliquidated
damages, interest awards for,
33.01[B]
Prompt Payment Act, 33.01[K]
statute, post judgment interest
authorized by, 33.01[I]
Miller Act claims, 33.02[O]
recovery of
indemnity agreements, 33.02[N]
Default terminations, 28.03[A]
abandonment, 28.03[B][3]
anticipatory repudiation, 28.03[B][3]
background, 28.03[A]
change orders, 28.03[E][3][a]
compensatory damages, 30.04[B]
constructive changes, 28.03[E][3][a]
convenience termination, conversion
into, 28.03[G]
conversion into termination for
convenience, 28.03[G]
grounds
abandonment, 28.03[B][3]
anticipatory repudiation, 28.03[B][3]
failure to make progress,
28.03[B][2]
material breach justifying default
Takota Corporation, 28.03[B][4][a]
progress, failure to make, 28.03[B][2]
wrongful, 28.03[D]
compensatory damages, 30.04[B][2]
effect of, 28.03[G]
notice, 28.03[D][1][a]
set forth in cure notice,
28.03[D][1][b]
waiver, 28.03[D][2]
Defective work
compensatory damages, 30.02[A]
Delays
causes of, 24.02, 24.02[D]
defective plans and specifications,
24.02[C]
claims for, 24.03
expenses of, 24.04
additional overhead, 24.04[C]
liquidated damages, 32.06
Department of Energy (DOE)
loan guarantees, 10.02[B][3][d][iv]
Department of Justice
FCPA violations, 42.02[F]
opinion release request procedure,
42.02[E]
Design build
AIA contract document forms, 8.08[A]
ConsensusDOCS, 8.08[B][11][a]

contractual arrangements, 8.07
private sector
contract document forms, 8.08
public sector
state statutes, 8.09[A]
risk allocation, 8.11[B]
Standard Form of Agreement Between
Architect and Consultant,
8.08[A][4][a]
Standard Form of Agreement Between
Contractor and Subcontractor,
8.08[A][2][a]
Design defects
management liability, 8A.08[D]
Diesel engines, 11.03[A][5][a]
Disclosure
arbitrators, disclosure of relationships,
46.22
Discovery
international arbitration, 43.07[F][2]
Dispute control
avoidance strategies
change negotiations, 44.08
non-field people involved in field
experiences, 44.04
plans and specifications, 44.02
risk, delineation of, 44.03
Dispute resolution
international construction contracts
beyond arbitration and litigation,
43.02[A]

E

Earmarks in transportation bills,
39A.09
Economic loss doctrine, BIM privity and
third party reliance, 5.03[C][7]
Economic Recovery and Reinvestment
Act of 2009, 39A.04
Economic recovery, transportation
investment as part of
benefit delivery, 39A.08
details of, 39A.06
disinvestment in US transportation,
39A.03
Economic Recovery and Reinvestment
Act of 2009, 39A.04
executive summary, 39A.01
future policies and programs, 39A.09
climate change, 39A.09
delivery, expedited, 39A.09
earmarks, 39A.09
economic crisis, 39A.09

economic recovery and
  development, 39A.09
environmental goals, 39A.09
financing, 39A.09
forward-looking approach, 39A.09
high speed rail, 39A.09
investment level, 39A.09
political change, 39A.09
private participation, 39A.09
transparency, accountability and
  reporting, 39A.09
urban focus and control, 39A.09
investment, need for greater, 39A.03
significance of including
  transportation, 39A.05
stimulus funding, context for, 39A.02
tracking impacts on the economy,
  39A.07
Efficiency, loss of, 24.04[B]
Energy Policy Act of 2005
diesel engines, 11.03[A][5][a]
loan guarantees, 10.02[B][3][d][iv]
Environmental issues
air pollution
  diesel engines, 11.03[A][5][a]
CERCLA
  liability and brownfields,
    11.03[A][4]
  responsibility for meeting
    requirements, 11.03[A][4][a]
Clean Air Act
  diesel engines, 11.03[A][5][a]
climate change.
See Climate change
dredge and fill, 11.03[A][1][b]
federal legislation, 11.03[A]
hazardous substances
  brownfields, 11.03[A][4]
oil spill prevention, 11.03[A][2]
polychlorinated biphenyl (PCB) waste
  requirements and risks,
    11.03[A][7]
stormwater
  overview, 11.03[A][1][a][i]
  responsibility for permit,
    11.03[A][1][a][ii]
transportation investment, 39A.09
wetlands
  defined, 11.03[A][1][c]
  dredge and fill, 11.03[A][1][b]
  significant nexus, 11.03[A][1][c]
Equipment, compensable delay expenses,
  24.04[A]
EU-ETS, 13.06A

E-Verify rule, 37.01[B]
Evidence
international arbitration
  28 U.S.C. § 1782, discovery under,
    43.07[F][2]
Excalation effects, compensable delay,
  24.04[D]
Executive Order 13116, 42.03[G][1]
Expenses
of delays, 24.04
  additional overhead, 24.04[C]
  escalation effects, 24.04[D]
  idle personnel and equipment,
    24.04[A]
  losses of efficiency, 24.04[B]

F

False Claims Act, liability under,
  41.08[A]
Federal Acquisition Regulation (FAR)
certification requirements
  defective certifications, 39.04[D]
clauses, 15.16. See also Government
  contracts
federal contracts, filing claims,
  39.02[C]
Federal Aviation Administration (FAA)
Airport Improvement Program (AIP),
  39A.06
economic benefit delivery, 39A.08
Federal contracts
claims
  basic elements of claim, 39.03[A]
  Board of Contract Appeals,
    contractor's appeal to,
    39.07[A]
  certification requirements, 39.04
  contents of claim, 39.03
  Contract Disputes Act of 1978,
    39.02[A]
  contracting officer's
    authority/timing of claim
    submissions and final decision,
    39.06[D]
  Court of Federal Claims,
    contractor's appeal to, 39.07[B]
  defined, 39.02[C]
  Federal Acquisition Regulation
    (FAR), 39.02[C]
  requirements, 39.03[B]
  written demand to contracting
    officer, 39.03[B][1]
E-Verify rule, 37.01[B]

Labor rules, 37.01[C]
socioeconomic rule
    Registry of Disaster Response
        Contractors, 37.02[H][5]
    Stimulus Act, 37.01[A]
Financing
    government agencies, 10.02[B][3][d]
    transportation investment, 39A.09
Foreign Corrupt Practices Act (FCPA)
    enforcement, 42.02[F]
    opinion release request procedure,
        42.02[E]

G

Government agencies
    project finance, 10.02[B][3][d]
Government contracts
    cost of the work agreement, 15.18
    Federal Acquisition Regulation, 15.16
    standard subcontract for work, 15.16
    standard subsubcontract agreement,
        15.17
Green building addendum,
    ConsensusDOCS, 15.20
    current practice not best practice,
        15.20[B]
    elected green status and measure,
        15.20[C]
    Green Building Facilitator, 15.20[E]
    neutral rating system, 15.20[D]
    outlook, 15.20[G]
    overview, 15.20[A]
    risk allocation, 15.20[F]
Green design and construction
    generally, 12.01
    negligence, 12.04[C][1][d][i]
    risks and rewards, 12.03
        insurance considerations, 12.03[I]
        LEED certified vs. certifiable and
            certification challenges,
            12.03[G]
        legal and insurance issues, 12.03[H]
        reference standards vs. contractual
            and legal requirements,
            12.03[F]

I

Implied warranties
    Spearin Doctrine
        BIM designs and, 5.03[C][8]
Indemnity
    attorneys' fees, recovery of, 33.02[N]

Insurance
    BIM models 5.03[C][4]
    green building project, 12.03[I]
    wrap-up coverage
        adequacy of limits, 19.03[D],
            19.03[D][3]
        deductibles, 19.03[C]
        excess endorsements, 19.03[D][3]
        self-insured retentions, 19.03[C]
        voluntary payments, 19.03[F][2]
        who is an insured, 19.03[B]
Integrated project delivery (IPD), 14.05
    A295 documents, 14.05[A][2]
    comparison of, 5.05[E]
    development of, 5.05[B]
    guide, 14.05[A][1]
    implications of, 5.05[F]
    minor elements of, 5.05[D]
    multi-party agreement, 14.05[A][4]
    need for, 5.05[A]
    SPE documents, 14.05[A][3]
    structural elements of, 5.05[C]
Intellectual property
    BIM designs, and, 5.03[C][3]
Interest
    recovery of damages
        liquidated and unliquidated
            damages, interest awards for,
            33.01[B]
        Prompt Payment Act, 33.01[K]
        statute, post judgment interest
            authorized by, 33.01[I]
International Alliance for
    Interoperability, BIM standards,
        5.03[C][5]
International arbitration
    discovery
        28 U.S.C. § 1782, discovery under,
            43.07[F][2]
    expedited arbitrations, 43.07[G]
    limited role of courts, 43.07[R][1]
    New York Convention, 43.07[R][3]
    pathological clause, avoiding,
        43.07[C]
    scope of arbitration, 43.07[B]
    split process arbitrations, 43.07[G]
International Centre for Settlement of
    Investment Disputes (ICSID),
        43.06[A]
International construction contracts
    corruption, prevention
        Anti-Foreign Corruption Statute,
            42.02[F]
        Executive Order 13116, 42.03[G][1]

Jakarta, Indonesia, 42.03[G][2]
Lesotho Highland Water Project,
   42.03[G][3]
multilateral anti-corruption
   initiatives, 42.03
OECD Convention on Combating
   Bribery, 42.03[A]
UN Convention Against Corruption,
   42.03[B]
World Bank Policy Guidelines,
   42.03[C]
dispute resolution
beyond arbitration and litigation,
   43.02[A]
Investment tax credits,
   10.02[B][3][d][i][b]

J

Jakarta, Indonesia, anti-corruption
   initiatives, 42.03[G][2]

K

Kyoto Protocol
   Asia, 13.06A[B]
   Canada, 13.06A[C]

L

Labor rules, 37.01[C]
Lesotho Highland Water Project,
   anti-corruption initiatives,
   42.03[G][3]
Liability
   construction management
      bodily injury, 8A.08[A][1]
      contract administration, 8A.08[G][3]
      delayed site access, 8A.08[F]
      design defects, 8A.08[D]
Licenses
   BIM models, 5.04[B]
Liquidated damages
   clauses, development of
      language, development of, 32.09[B]
   delay for, 32.06
   enforcement, 32.05
Loan guarantees
   for project financing,
      10.02[B][3][d][iv]
Louisiana
   "no-damages-for-delay" clauses,
      exceptions, 26.02[S]

M

Michigan
   attorneys' fees, recovery of,
      33.02[M][4]
Miller Act
   attorneys' fees, recovery of, 33.02[O]

N

Nebraska
   "no-damages-for-delay" clauses,
      exceptions, 26.02[BB]
New Jersey
   "no-damages-for-delay" clauses,
      exceptions, 26.02[EE]
New Mexico
   "no-damages-for-delay" clauses,
      exceptions, 26.02[FF]
New York
   attorneys' fees, recovery of,
      33.02[M][5]
   "no-damages-for-delay" clauses,
      exceptions, 26.02[GG]
New York Convention, 43.07[R][3]
"No-damages-for-delay" clauses,
   exceptions
   Arizona, 26.02[C]
   Arkansas, 26.02[D]
   California, 26.02[E]
   Colorado, 26.02[F]
   Louisiana, 26.02[S]
   Nebraska, 26.02[BB]
   New Jersey, 26.02[EE]
   New Mexico, 26.02[FF]
   New York, 26.02[GG]
   North Carolina, 26.02[HH]
   Oklahoma, 26.02[KK]
   Oregon, 26.02[LL]
   Pennsylvania, 26.02[MM]
   Texas, 26.02[RR]
   Virginia, 26.02[UU]
   Washington, 26.02[VV]
   Wyoming, 26.02[YY]
North America
   climate change mitigation, 13.06A[C]
North Carolina
   "no-damages-for-delay" clauses,
      exceptions, 26.02[HH]

O

Obama, President
   climate change action, 13.06A[D]

Oil spill prevention, 11.03[A][2]
Oklahoma
  "no-damages-for-delay" clauses,
    exceptions, 26.02[KK]
Oregon
  attorneys' fees, recovery of,
    33.02[M][6]
  "no-damages-for-delay" clauses,
    exceptions, 26.02[LL]
Organization for Economic Cooperation
    and Development (OECD)
  anti-corruption initiatives, 42.03[A]
Overhead, compensable delay expenses,
    24.04[C]
Owners
  compensatory damages available to,
    30.02
  defaults in payment, subcontractor's
    rights and remedies
    contract clauses, 25.02
    incorporation by reference, contract
      clause, 25.02[D]
    liquidating agreements, 25.05
    trust fund statues, 25.04[A]

P

Patents
  BIM, patent deficiency exception to
    Spearin, 5.03[C][8]
Pennsylvania
  "no-damages-for-delay" clauses,
    exceptions, 26.02[MM]
Personnel idle, compensable delay,
    24.04[A]
Plans and specifications
  avoidance of claims and disputes,
    44.02
Polychlorinated biphenyl (PCB) waste
    requirements and risks,
    11.03[A][7]
Procedures and Revision Cycle,
    ConsensusDOCS, 15.19
Production tax credits,
    10.02[B][3][d][i][a]
Prompt Payment Act, 33.01[K]

Q

Qualified Energy Conservation Bonds,
    10.02[B][3][d][iii],
    10.02[B][3][d][iii][b]

R

Rail, transportation investment in,
    39A.09
Recovery and Reinvestment Act,
    11.03[A][5][a]
Registry of Disaster Response
    Contractors, 37.02[H][5]
Risk management
  avoidance of claims and disputes, 44.03

S

Sales contracts
  performance of
    passing of title, 16.08[B]
  terms of contract
    generally, 16.06[A]
  UCC applicability, 16.02[B]
  UCC Article 2, 16.01[B]
Sarbanes-Oxley Act of 2002
  FCPA violations, 42.02[F]
Securities and Exchange Commission
    (SEC)
  Seaboard Report, 42.02[F]
Site access, delayed
  management liability, 8A.08[F]
Site conditions
  damages, 22.09
  disclaimer clauses, 22.08
  inspections, 22.08
  proving category I differing claim,
    22.06
Spearin doctrine
  BIM designs and, 5.03[C][8]
  contractor liability, 29.02[B][1]
Standard forms of agreement
  design-build project
    between architect and consultant,
      8.08[A][4][a]
    between contractor and
      subcontractor, 8.08[A][2][a]
Stimulus Act, 37.01[A]
Stimulus funding, 39A.02. See also
    Economic recovery,
    transportation investment as
    part of
Stormwater discharges at construction
    sites
  overview, 11.03[A][1][a][i]
  responsibility for permit,
    11.03[A][1][a][ii]

Subcontractors
  owner's failure to make payment to
    contract clauses and, 25.02
    incorporation by reference, 25.02[D]
    liquidating agreements, 25.05
    trust fund statues, 25.04[A]
Subsubcontract agreement,
    ConsensusDOCS, 15.17
Superfund liability, 11.03[A][4]
  responsibility for meeting
    requirements, 11.03[A][4][a]

T

Takota Corporation, 28.03[B][4][a]
Tax credits
  American Recovery and Reinvestment
    Act of 2009 (ARRA),
    10.02[B][3][d][i]
  cash grants, 10.02[B][3][d][ii]
  Clean Renewable Energy Bonds,
    10.02[B][3][d][iii],
    10.02[B][3][d][iii][a]
  investment tax credits,
    10.02[B][3][d][i][b]
  loan guarantees, 10.02[B][3][d][iv]
  production tax credits,
    10.02[B][3][d][i][a]
  Qualified Energy Conservation
    Bonds, 10.02[B][3][d][iii],
    10.02[B][3][d][iii][b]
  tax credit bonds, 10.02[B][3][d][iii]
Terminations
  abuse of discretion
    government's right to convenience
      terminations, 28.04[A]
    improper motive role, 28.04[D][2]
  default terminations.
  See Default terminations
  government's right to convenience
    terminations
    bad faith, 28.04[A][1]
  notice to cure
    inadequate notice, 28.03[D][1][a]
    set forth in cure notice,
      28.03[D][1][b]
    wrongful default terminations,
      28.03[D][1]
Texas
  "no-damages-for-delay" clauses,
    exceptions, 26.02[RR]
Transportation Infrastructure Finance and
    Innovation Act (TIFIA),
    39A.06

Transportation investment for economic
    recovery
  benefit delivery, 39A.08
  details of, 39A.06
  disinvestment in US transportation,
    39A.03
  Economic Recovery and Reinvestment
    Act of 2009, 39A.04
  executive summary, 39A.01
  future policies and programs,
    39A.09
    climate change, 39A.09
    delivery, expedited, 39A.09
    earmarks, 39A.09
    economic crisis, 39A.09
    economic recovery and
      development, 39A.09
    environmental goals, 39A.09
    financing, 39A.09
    forward-looking approach, 39A.09
    high speed rail, 39A.09
    investment level, 39A.09
    political change, 39A.09
    private participation, 39A.09
    transparency, accountability and
      reporting, 39A.09
    urban focus and control, 39A.09
  investment, need for greater, 39A.03
  significance of including
    transportation, 39A.05
  stimulus funding, context for, 39A.02
  Transportation Infrastructure Finance
    and Innovation Act, 39A.06
  tracking impacts on the economy,
    39A.07

U

UN Convention Against Corruption
  anti-corruption initiatives, 42.03[B]
Uniform Commercial Code (UCC)
  Article 2, Sales, 16.01
    applicability, 16.01[B]
United States
  implementing legislation,
    anti-corruption initiatives,
    42.03[H]

V

Virginia
  "no-damages-for-delay" clauses,
    exceptions, 26.02[UU]

W

Warranties
  Spearin Doctrine
    BIM designs and, 5.03[C][8]
Washington
  "no-damages-for-delay" clauses,
    exceptions, 26.02[VV]
Websites (projects)
  BIM and, 5.01
Wetlands
  defined, 11.03[A][1][c]
  dredge and fill, 11.03[A][1][b]
  significant nexus, 11.03[A][1][c]
Workforce
  shortages
    causes, 3.01

World Bank
  corruption, policy guidelines,
    42.03[C]
Wrap-up coverage
  adequacy of limits, 19.03[D]
    excess endorsements,
      19.03[D][3]
  deductibles, 19.03[C]
  self-insured retentions, 19.03[C]
  voluntary payments, 19.03[F][2]
  who is an insured, 19.03[B]
Wrongful default terminations
  defective notice to cure, 28.03[D][1]
  waiver, 28.03[D][2]
Wyoming
  "no-damages-for-delay" clauses,
    exceptions, 26.02[YY]